An Intellectual
and Cultural History
of the Western World

CONTRIBUTING AUTHORS FOR VOLUME ONE

Art

BERNARD MYERS
Editor-in-Chief, Art Book Department,
McGraw-Hill Book Company, Inc.

JOHN C. GALLOWAY
Oakland University

Anthropology

ALFONSO SOLIMENE
Hunter College

Literature (In Part)

WALTER B. SCOTT
Northwestern University

EDWARD HUBLER
Princeton University

WILLARD THORP
Princeton University

Music

MARTIN BERNSTEIN
New York University

An Intellectual
and Cultural History
of the Western World

by

HARRY ELMER BARNES

THIRD REVISED EDITION

IN THREE VOLUMES

VOLUME ONE

From Earliest Times through the Middle Ages

Dover Publications, Inc., New York

Published in Canada by General Publishing Company, Ltd., 30 Lesmill Road, Don Mills, Toronto,
Ontario.
Published in the United Kingdom by Constable
and Company, Ltd., 10 Orange Street, London WC 2.

This Dover edition, first published in 1965, is a
revised and enlarged republication of the second
edition published by Reynal and Hitchcock, Inc.
in 1941. The first edition of this work was published
by the Cordon Company, Inc., in 1937. The work,
originally in one volume, now appears in three
volumes.

Standard Book Number: 486-21275-0

Library of Congress Catalog Card Number: 63-21675

Manufactured in the United States of America
Dover Publications, Inc.
180 Varick Street
New York, N. Y. 10014

PREFACE TO DOVER EDITION

This book is a history of thought and culture in the Western World. It represents an approach to the history of civilization with a completely different emphasis from that manifested in my *History of Western Civilization*. There the main stress was laid upon institutional history, merely indicating the intellectual and cultural by-products of institutional developments. Here there has been no effort to present more institutional history than is necessary to understand the trends in thought and culture. So this book is in no sense an abridgment or condensation of the earlier and longer work. Such an abridgment and clarification was prepared in John Geise's *Man and the Western World,* and my *Survey of Western Civilization.*

In organizing this book there has been a resolute avoidance of any hard-and-fast schematic arrangement. The main periods and trends of intellectual and cultural development are portrayed as they have actually occurred, instead of being forced into some preordained framework. If one is familiar with the field he realizes that the intellectual and cultural history of the Western World very naturally and logically organizes itself. The proper combination of the chronological and topical presentation has been followed. No little aid in blocking out the field has been obtained from the syllabus on *The Outline of the History of the European Mind* by James Harvey Robinson, the last and enlarged edition of which I prepared under Professor Robinson's direction in 1920. Many suggestive details have also been derived from the syllabus prepared by Ferdinand Schevill and others for the "Humanities" course given at the University of Chicago.

My interest in the field of intellectual history was aroused by Professor James Harvey Robinson's famous course at Columbia University, the most stimulating and inspiring survey of the history of European thought ever presented in academic precincts. But the Robinsonian influence has been supplemented by many other contributions in the more than forty years since I was a student in his notable class on "The History of the Intellectual Class in Europe." From Paul Radin's account of primitive thinking to Jacques Barzun's strictures on contemporary intellectuals I have found plenty of grist for my mill. And I would especially acknowledge a heavy debt to the writings of J. H. Breasted, Gilbert Murray, H. O. Taylor, Lynn Thorndike, C. H. Haskins, Preserved Smith, Carl Becker, J. H. Randall, George Sarton, Arthur C. McGiffert, Bertrand Russell, and Harlow Shapley.

This history is a comprehensive introduction to the story of how we have come to think, live, and utilize our leisure moments as we do in the second half of the twentieth century. The history of the thought and culture of the past is reviewed mainly in order to throw light upon our present age. Only such a view of history and its services can raise the subject above the level of a literary antique shop. This does not imply that one may be careless or arbitrary about dealing with the past; it does mean that his care in reconstructing the past is justified mainly by the value of such efforts in helping us the better to understand our own age and, incidentally, to have a somewhat more intelligent attitude towards the future. It is high time that the fundamental distinction between the historian and the antiquarian compiler should be brought into high relief.

While principally concerned with the development of European thought and culture I have made a sincere effort to trace the main intellectual and cultural influences which have come to Europe from other areas or have been transmitted to extra-European regions from Europe itself. In other words, an attempt has been made to write a history of the thought and culture of the whole Western World, into which scene the United States has entered in ever more prominent fashion since 1800.

The story begins with our animal heritage, from which we pass to the thought and culture of primitive man who ranged over the planet during at least ninety-nine percent of the total duration of human life to date. Then we recount the rise of historic, or literary, civilizations in the ancient Near Orient where impressive material cultures first put in their appearance, not to be markedly improved upon until the industrial revolution of the eighteenth century of our era. Next we describe how in Greece intellectual freedom and a scientific spirit arose for the first time in human history and led to the creation of an unrivaled philosophy of civilized existence. The Hellenization of the world by Alexander and the Romans is then described in connection with a survey of Hellenistic thought and culture and the civilization of the Romans.

After this follows an account of the decline of classical thought and culture and of the process whereby it was supplanted by a civilization founded on the otherworldly Christian religion of the Middle Ages. In connection with the latter we trace the rise and integration of the remarkable synthesis of Christianity and pagan thought known as scholasticism. Then comes the story of the dissolution of the medieval synthesis as a result of new scientific interests, the increased zeal for the classics, the individualistic aestheticism of the humanists, and, above all, the expansion of European civilization overseas and the reaction of this process on Europe itself. Adequate attention is paid to the Muslim contributions to the advances in European thought and culture.

The remarkable developments in science, philosophy, religious thought, tolerance, political liberty, and historical optimism in the seventeenth and eighteenth centuries form an important chapter in the intellectual and cultural life of man. We treat these in detail, as well as the strong reaction against this type of intellectual interest and outlook in the Romanticist and Idealist philosophies. The latter, whatever the intellectual fog they may have spread over the European intellectual landscape, were not without certain positive contributions to European culture, especially in the fields of history, social science, literature, art, and music.

Finally, by the latter part of the eighteenth century we come to an age when economic factors become of transcendent importance in determining man's re-actions to the world and human problems. The empire of machines launches a movement of secularization more pervasive and irresistible than any skeptical phi-losophy had ever been able to produce. Materialism becomes ascendent and standardization advances beyond previous bounds. Modes of living change more in a few generations than in previous millenniums. But social institutions and social thinking are far outdistanced by material progress, thus creating the dan-gerous discrepancy between machines and institutions that, in the form of nuclear and other appalling types of warfare, threatens in our day to obliterate civilization and wipe out most of the advances made by man since the Stone Age. This threat to civilization, due to cultural lag, together with the new and staggering cosmic spectacle presented to man by contemporary astrophysics, con-stitute the two chief novelties in twentieth-century thought and culture.

For the first time in human history, mankind is directly confronted with a com-pulsory and relatively expeditious choice between utopia and barbarism, and it is impossible at this time to be sure which road will be chosen. If the paralyzing burden of the "dead hand" of antique ideas and institutions can be lifted from the back of man, he may enter utopia. Otherwise, chaos and barbarism are all but inevitable. It is hoped that this book will contribute very directly to undermining the influence of the "dead hand," and making it possible for man to claim the rich heritage which awaits intelligent choice in human affairs. But care has been taken not to distort historical facts in order to promote social well-being. A straightforward account of human intellectual development is sufficient to ex-pose and challenge the "dead hand." So far as I am capable of doing so, I have told the story of human intellectual development without either fear or favor. The book is neither a polemic nor an apology.

I was criticized by some for devoting too much attention to the nineteenth and twentieth centuries in my *History of Western Civilization*. While not personally conceding the validity of this criticism, I have felt it expedient to be guided by it to some degree in planning the present work.

Since the allotment of space to literature, art, and music has been very generous, it has been deemed wise to rely upon experts in each of these fields rather than for me to attempt a necessarily amateurish exposition. This innovation has made it possible for the aesthetic sections of the book to possess as much authority as those devoted to intellectual history. This is, I believe, something without prece-dent in any previous historical work of such a general character.

The book has been designed to meet the needs of both the intelligent general reader of history and the college student. It is believed that the style and organiza-tion are equally well suited to both audiences. The bibliographic aids and quo-tations in the book are limited mainly to works in English. Those able to use the foreign literature do not require elementary assistance or guidance of this sort. Commendation of John Herman Randall Jr.'s *The Career of Philosophy,* and briefer general works on the same subject, such as Crane Brinton's *Ideas and Men* and Bertrand Russell's *Wisdom of the West,* is made herewith.

Because so much of the pictorial matter originally included has become so readily available, it was not thought necessary to reproduce it in this edition. In the text, considerable new material has been added, particularly on the thought and public problems of the mid-twentieth century, and the complete edition has been thoroughly revised from beginning to end. In this revision I have been able to profit by many reviews and critical comments by readers. These have enabled me to eliminate such errors of fact and interpretation as existed in earlier editions.

June 15, 1964   HARRY ELMER BARNES

NOTE OF ACKNOWLEDGMENT

I have received valuable aid in the preparation and revision of this book. The readers of the intellectual and cultural sections of my *History of Western Civilization* made many suggestions which have been of much assistance in preparing the more complete treatment of such subjects in the present work. In this connection, I would mention especially Professor John Herman Randall of Columbia University and Professor Max Otto of the University of Wisconsin. Professor Howard Robinson of Oberlin College, Ohio, read over very carefully a preliminary draft of the manuscript, and his criticisms have been of great assistance in the complete rewriting of the material. Professor George S. Counts of Teachers College, Columbia University, has made important observations relative to the history of modern education. Professor Salvatore Russo of Auburn, N. Y., gave me a constructive criticism of the sections on modern philosophy. Professor Leslie A. White of the University of Michigan read and criticized the material on early man and on primitive life and culture. Professor William R. P. Davey of Syracuse University read and criticized the chapter on Greek thought and culture, and Professor Harold L. Cleasby rendered the same service with respect to the material dealing with Roman thought and culture. Particularly helpful has been the meticulous reading of the galley proofs by Professor David S. Muzzey of Columbia University, and Professor Lowell J. Ragatz of George Washington University. Mr. John H. Collins of New York City prepared the Index and Glossary of historical terms. I have received extensive aid in stylistic emendations and in rewriting some sections of the book from Mr. Anthony Netboy. He has done much to clarify the expression. He also helped to prepare the first draft of the material on ancient and early medieval literature and art.

The able and indispensable work of Professors Edward Hubler and Willard Thorp of Princeton University, of Professor Walter B. Scott of Northwestern University, of Professor Martin Bernstein of New York University, and of Dr. Bernard Myers of the McGraw-Hill Book Company, Inc., in preparing the material on the history of literature, art, and music has been indicated and credited elsewhere. Professor Justus Buchler of Columbia University and Professor Gerald Gruman of Harvard University have made helpful suggestions for corrections in the preparation of the Dover edition.

I am similarly indebted to the following contributors of material to Chapters XXVI and XXVII, Volume III, in which have been summarized current developments in specific fields: Professors Banesh Hoffmann and Saul Novack of Queens College of the City University of New York, Mr. Jagjit Singh, Professor O. Theodor Benfey of Earlham College, Dr. Howard A. Schneider of the Rockefeller Institute, Professor Richard D. Walk of George Washington

University, Mr. Thomas E. Keys of the Mayo Clinic, Dr. Carroll Lane Fenton, Professor John Fred Bell of the University of Illinois, Professor George Dennis O'Brien of Princeton University, Professor Donald W. Treadgold of the University of Washington, Professor Anthony Netboy of Portland State College, and Professor John C. Galloway of Oakland University. Professor Galloway also made many valuable suggestions for other art sections throughout the book. Each of these contributors should be held responsible only for that portion of the book bearing his name; elsewhere the final responsibility is mine. Similarly, Mr. Alfonso Solimene of Hunter College kindly consented to bring up to date certain sections of Chapters I and II in Volume I. He should in no way, however, be held accountable for the ideas or opinions expressed there, which remain completely my own.

The publishers of books and magazines quoted have given their permission for the use of the material, and thanks are hereby extended to them for their courtesy.

TABLE OF CONTENTS

VOLUME ONE

Part One: The Reign of Supernaturalism

I. OUR ANIMAL HERITAGE   3

    i. The New Perspective of Human Development   3
    ii. The Rise of the Evolutionary Theory   7
    iii. Implications of Evolution   8
    iv. Man as an Animal   10
    v. Man as a Primate   11
    vi. Man Dominates the Primate World   14
    vii. Man's Emergence from the Animal Kingdom   15
    viii. Nature and Nurture   17
    ix. A Dynamic Conception of the Human Mind   19
    x. Race and Culture   20

II. PRIMITIVE THOUGHT AND CULTURE   27

    i. Our Knowledge of Early Man   27
    ii. Early Types of Man   28
    iii. Preliterary Material Culture   31
    iv. The Evolution of the Human Mind   39
    v. Some Traits of Primitive Mentality   41
    vi. Religion in Primitive Life   43
    vii. The Origins of Spoken Language   53
    viii. The Art of Preliterate Man   55
    ix. Summary of Human Progress in the Preliterary Period   59

III. ORIENTAL FOUNDATIONS OF CLASSICAL THOUGHT AND CULTURE   63

    i. Bringing to Light a Great Civilization   63
    ii. The Military-Religious Civilization of the Ancient World   66
    iii. Political and Legal Evolution   66
    iv. The Material Culture of the Ancient Orient   69
    v. Social Differentiation and the Rise of a Leisure Class   73
    vi. The Origins of Natural Science in Egypt and Babylonia   74
    vii. The Profusion of Oriental Religions   76
    viii. Moral Progress in the Ancient Orient   82
    ix. The Alphabet and the Origins of Writing   89
    x. Literary Achievements of the Ancient Orient   91
    xi. The Achievements in Art   102

Part Two: Classical Thought and Culture: The Beginnings of Skepticism

IV. HELLENIC THOUGHT AND CULTURE   117

    I. The Greek Heritage from the Orient   117
    II. The Origins of the Liberal-Legal Stage of Civilization   119
    III. The City-State Perspective of Greek Culture   120
    IV. The Birth of Free Thought   122
    V. Early Greek Thought   124
    VI. The Sophists, Socrates, Plato, and Aristotle   131
    VII. Greek Thought after Aristotle   145
    VIII. Scientific Achievements of the Greeks   151
    IX. The Religion of the Greeks   160
    X. Greek Literature   165
    XI. Hellenic Art   178
    XII. Greek Music   190
    XIII. The Debt of Western Civilization to Hellenic Culture   192

V. ROMAN CULTURE AND INTELLECTUAL LIFE   195

    I. The Roman Episode in History   195
    II. The Influence of Roman Politics and Imperialism on Roman Culture   197
    III. The Importation of Hellenic Thought and Culture   203
    IV. Roman Science   206
    V. Types of Roman Philosophy   214
    VI. Religious Beliefs and Practices of Ancient Rome   224
    VII. Roman Law   228
    VIII. Latin Literature   232
    IX. Roman Engineering and Architecture   248
    X. Roman Sculpture and Painting   252
    XI. The Legacy of Rome   254

VI. THE DECLINE OF CLASSICAL THOUGHT AND CULTURE   257

    I. The Material Basis of the Decline   257
    II. Political Anarchy and Military Dictatorship   259
    III. Intellectual Decadence under Paganism   259
    IV. Weakness of Hellenic Science   260
    V. The Popularity of Hellenic Metaphysics and Neoplatonism   262
    VI. The Substitution of Rhetoric for Thought   265
    VII. Martianus Capella and the Rise of the Seven Liberal Arts   266
    VIII. Compilations of Pseudoscientific Knowledge and Superstition   267
    IX. The Rise of Mystery Cults   267
    X. Persian Dualism and Shifting Intellectual Interests   269
    XI. The Gradual Transition to Medievalism   270

Part Three: The Medieval Synthesis

VII. THE CHRISTIAN WORLD VIEW   275

    I. The Cultural Background of the Triumph of Christianity   275
    II. The Evolution of the Christian Religion   278
    III. The Victory of Christianity over Roman Paganism   281
    IV. The Elaboration of Worship and Churchly Organization   282
    V. The Sacramental System of the Catholic Church   285
    VI. The Repression of Heresy   287
    VII. The Monastic Movement   291
    VIII. Christian Otherworldliness, the Devil, Hell, and the Last Judgment 295
    IX. The Augustinian Synthesis and the Christian Epic   300
    X. The Intellectual Patterns of Early Christianity   306
    XI. The Patristic Attitude towards Secular Learning   312
    XII. Art and Architecture   315
    XIII. Early Christian Literature   319

VIII. THE THOUGHT AND CULTURE OF THE DARK AGES   326

    I. The Nature of the Dark Ages   326
    II. The Fusion of Pagan and Christian Learning   329
    III. Aspects of the Thought and Culture of the Dark Ages   336
    IV. Early Medieval Education   348
    V. Natural Science in the Dark Ages   352
    VI. Political Philosophy: Church versus the State   357
    VII. Literature in the Dark Ages   359
    VIII. Art in the Dark Ages   372
    IX. Music   383

IX. MEDIEVAL THOUGHT FROM ABELARD TO DANTE: THE
    MEDIEVAL SYNTHESIS   387

    I. The Material Background   387
    II. The Cultural Heritage from West and East   395
    III. Abelard and the Enthronement of Logic   407
    IV. The Rise of Universities in the Middle Ages   409
    V. The Ascendancy of Aristotle in Medieval Thought: Scholasticism 417
    VI. Medieval Mysticism   425
    VII. Medieval Natural Science to Roger Bacon   426
    VIII. Political, Social, and Economic Theory in the Middle Ages 435

X. LITERATURE, ART, AND MUSIC: 1100-1300   442

    I. Literature of Religion and Romance   442
    II. Romanesque and Gothic Art   456
    III. The Beginnings of Multivoiced Music   476

XI. THE DECLINE OF MEDIEVALISM FROM ROGER BACON TO
PETRARCH   480
   I. The Historical Background   480
   II. Developments in Thought and Philosophy during the Later Middle
      Ages   485
   III. Education in the Later Middle Ages   490
   IV. Medieval Science from Roger Bacon to Copernicus   493
   V. Political and Social Theory during the Decline of the Medieval
      System   509
   VI. A New Age Arrives   513

XII. LITERATURE, ART, AND MUSIC: 1300-1450   516
   I. The Triumph of the Vernacular in Literature   516
   II. Art in Italy and Northern Europe   529
   III. The First Schools of Composition   540

Part One

THE REIGN OF SUPERNATURALISM

I

Our Animal Heritage

I. THE NEW PERSPECTIVE ON HUMAN DEVELOPMENT

No discovery of modern science has more sharply challenged and upset pre-conceived ideas than the revelation of the vast time element involved in the origins and development of the physical cosmos by cosmogonists and geologists. The results of these researches, chiefly during the present century, have been so revolutionary as veritably to outrun the resources of the human imagination. The age of the total cosmos—the universe of universes—which may run into the hundreds or thousands of trillions of years is quite beyond human understanding. Indeed, the very notion that the total cosmos had *any* beginning at all may well be the product of our limited human concepts and perspectives. Astronomical calculations, geological formations, and fossil remains provide convincing evidence that the age of the earth itself, after its separation from the parent sun, which was a newcomer in terms of cosmic time, is around 4.5 billion years, a mere flash when compared to the endless expanse of time that preceded the origins of the earth. This vast and complex process of cosmic and terrestrial development seems to have been accomplished in part through slow and orderly growth and then at times as a result of violent and abrupt changes.

Historians need not pause too long in speculation over the drama or dates of origins. It suffices to recognize that in a still hypothetically remote past and in a manner as yet only conjectured, the cosmos and earth came into existence. Against this background, historians can follow the process of evolution in an ever more clear and precise manner. We shall attempt by a series of diagrams[1] to indicate in a rough manner the brevity of the earth's history in terms of astronomical time, and the slight span of human life when compared to the age of the earth and the origins of other forms of life on our planet.

1 The clock diagrams on the following pages can give only a rough schematic representation of the temporal progression of events. These diagrams should on no account be taken as literal representations of the actual sequence of events.

3

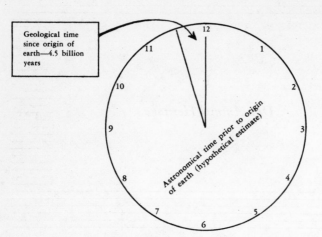

1 *hour* = *infinite period of time, c.* 10 *billion years*

FIG. 1. ASTRONOMICAL AND GEOLOGICAL TIME

This is merely a rough estimate of an indeterminate problem.
The object is to illustrate the brevity of geological as compared
to astronomical time. Estimating geological time as about 4.5
billion years, it is probable that astronomical time is grotesquely
minimized and reduced on this diagram.

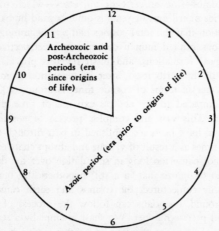

1 *hour* = 450 *million years*

FIG. 2. GEOLOGICAL TIME BEFORE AND AFTER ORIGINS OF LIFE

Geologists estimate that the time prior to the origins of life
on the earth was over three times as long as that which has
elapsed since life first appeared in the Archeozoic period.

In Figure 1 we assume that if "astronomical time"—that is, the total duration of the cosmos—is twelve hours, then "geological time," or the age of the earth, is a little less than a half hour. Even so, astronomical time is fantastically underestimated. One leading astronomer of our day has estimated the origins of the cosmos as taking place 200 trillion years ago, but most astronomers now believe that ordinary human conceptions of time cannot be applied to the age of the cosmos. Figure 2 shows that if the earth parted from the sun at 12:00, it was nearly ten o'clock before any life appeared on the earth. Figure 3 provides a rough time scheme for the successive periods of the origins of the main types of organic life. Mammals appeared about eleven o'clock, and man came on the scene between 1 and 2 minutes to twelve.

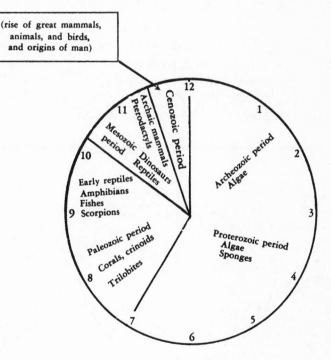

1 *hour* = 90 *million years*

FIG. 3. EVOLUTION OF LIFE

This diagram will indicate the recency of the period in which mammals appeared as compared with the whole span of life on the planet. On this clock early man would have appeared between 1 and 2 minutes to twelve.

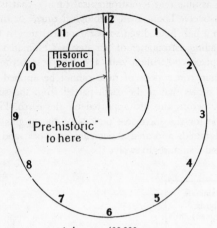

1 *hour* = 400,000 *years*

FIG. 4. "PREHISTORIC" AND HISTORIC TIME

This diagram is designed to indicate the utter chronological insignificance of the period of recorded history when compared with the whole period of human existence on the earth.

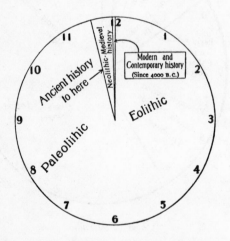

1 *hour* = 50,000 *years*

FIG. 5. THE NEW HISTORICAL CHRONOLOGY

This diagram attempts to indicate the nature of historical chronology when applied to the whole period of recorded human culture as established by prehistoric archæology.

Looking at the matter in another way, we note that if mammals were in existence at the start of the clock at twelve, a distinctive type of being called man appeared about eleven hours later in the Tertiary period. In other words, if mammals have been on the earth for some 60 million years, man has been here only somewhere between one and three million.

Finally, Figures 4 and 5 show the utter chronological insignificance of recorded history when compared with the whole period of human existence on earth, and suggest the need of a more comprehensive historical chronology. What we know of man since he was able to leave any written record behind him comprises less than one percent of his total experience on the planet.

This newer time-perspective renders the conventional historical labels hopelessly inadequate. Ancient history is supposed to cover the period from 4000 B.C. to A.D. 325, the date of the establishment of the Eastern Empire by Constantine. Medieval history comprises the period from 325 to 1453, the time of the fall of Constantinople. Modern history falls within the period since 1453.

If we were to apply the new and realistic chronological concepts to history, we should have to push ancient history back to the beginning of the Eolithic age well over 700,000 years ago. Medieval history would begin at the dawn of the Neolithic or New Stone Age, about 15,000 years ago. Modern history might extend from the age of metals and the beginning of written records about 4000 B.C. to the coming of the industrial revolution in the middle of the eighteenth century. The period since the industrial revolution, so different from anything which has gone before in human history, might be properly designated as the contemporary period.

II. THE RISE OF THE EVOLUTIONARY THEORY

The new time-perspective is an outgrowth of what we call the doctrine of evolution, which is probably the chief contribution of the nineteenth century to man's intellectual equipment. Every historian now has to take into account the meaning and implications of evolution. Evolution is, in fact, the new lens of history which refocuses the material content of the story. The evolutionary doctrine stands out in marked contrast to the older theory of a special creation a few thousand years ago. According to this older view, man and all the species of animals were created perfect and unchangeable within the space of a couple of days in the original creative week. The evolutionary view, on the contrary, emphasizes the fact that all living organisms, including man, have gradually evolved by natural processes extending over millions of years.

The doctrine of evolution itself falls into two main divisions. One is the general philosophical conception of evolution as the master key to our understanding of the development of the cosmos, our universe, the earth, organic life, man, social institutions, and human culture. The other aspect of evolution is the specific interpretation of the biological laws of heredity—explaining how organic matter has developed on the planet, especially how species have appeared and multiplied.

The philosophical doctrine of evolution was, in a rough way, enunciated by the

Greek philosophers Heracleitus, Empedocles, and Anaxagoras. The best surviving text of the ancient point of view is Lucretius' great cosmological poem, *De Rerum Natura,* where we find a sweeping conception of evolution, covering the development of the universe, organic life, man, society, and culture. There was little improvement upon Lucretius' broad conceptions of cosmic evolution until Herbert Spencer rephrased the idea on the basis of modern astronomy, physics, and biology in the middle of the nineteenth century.

The biological aspects of evolution, including the origin of life and species and the laws of heredity, began to be discussed in Greek days. Anaximander stressed the longer period of human infancy. Aristotle believed in an ascending series of species, proceeding from the simple to the complex. He also had some elementary grasp of the processes of reproduction. The students of biology in the later Middle Ages added much to our knowledge of plants and animals. Linnaeus (1707-1778) worked out the first practicable scheme for the classification of organic life. This suggested that there might be a common parentage for existing species, though Linnaeus himself rejected the idea of evolution. The great French naturalist, Buffon (1707-1788), clearly understood some of the broader implications of evolution, especially the relation between the environment and the slow differentiation of species. Erasmus Darwin (1731-1802), grandfather of Charles, elaborated the concept of adaptation to environment. Malthus (1766-1834), a social economist, emphasized the importance of the struggle for existence. Sir Charles Lyell, in his *Principles of Geology* (1830-1833), brought together the impressive geological evidence to support the notion of evolution.

Jean Lamarck (1744-1829) had already enunciated a doctrine of organic evolution in which the theory of the mutability of species was based on the assumed inheritance of acquired characteristics. Lamarck's classic example was the giraffe, which, he thought, developed its long neck by stretching to reach high leaves and branches. Each generation stretched its neck a little more—and passed the extra "stretch" on to its progeny.

Charles Darwin (1809-1882) tied together all previous concepts of evolution, and, with the support of a mass of original evidence, formulated the general theory which is now basically accepted by all scholars, though many of its details have been modified or abandoned. The chief tenets of the Darwinian doctrine of evolution are: (1) existing species of plants and animals are descended from earlier, and in most cases, more rudimentary types; (2) all organic life is interlinked in an ascending scale, from the simplest organisms to the most complex; and (3) man comes in direct line of descent from the lower primates.

III. IMPLICATIONS OF EVOLUTION

The first major lesson of evolution is the vast new time-perspective which is forced upon us. We learn from the astrophysical perspective of evolution that the sun had already passed its maximum radiance before the earth originated. Jeans estimated the age of the cosmos at 200 trillion years—a stretch of time which the ordinary human mind simply cannot comprehend. Indeed, we may have to admit that, in the new views of the universe, the very notion of time, as we understand it in earthly uses, is nothing more than a convenient working hypothesis.

The second important implication of evolution is that change is the universal principle of cosmic development. Everything is in a state of flux. Everything is moving towards a different state, be it better or worse.

A third vital corollary of the evolutionary view is that man is neither a worm nor an angel, but the master primate—king of the animal kingdom. The new outlook which science and evolution have thus created for man is admirably summed up by Professor Kirtley F. Mather:

Joshua's world was made expressly for man. Everything in it was designed especially to contribute to his welfare or to punish him when he incurred the displeasure of his god. He occupied the summit of the tall pinnacle of superiority, not because he had won his way to that proud eminence, but because he had been placed there by the Creator. The locality where he lived was the center of the universe; sun, moon and stars revolved around him and it. Joshua's concept of man's place in nature has lingered long in the minds of his descendants; echoes of that concept are still with us. Did not Linnaeus give the name "Primates" to that order of mammals which he defined as including man?

But Our World is not so flattering. "What is man that thou art mindful of him?" has a new meaning since Betelgeuse was measured. In geologic time, man has lived for but a moment in the earthly day. In astronomic space, he is a speck of foam on the crest of a single wave in the midst of a Pacific Ocean. The earth is neither the smallest nor the biggest, the hottest nor the coldest, the most central nor the most remote among the planets of the solar system. Presumably there are many other similar bodies in the heavens. Except for the fact that you and I are on its surface, there is nothing especially distinguished about it. The sun is just an ordinary star. There are many larger, many smaller; many hotter, many colder; many brighter, many duller. Presumably many of its neighbors in the heavens have fully comparable planetary dependents in their train. The stellar galaxy is but one of the many far-flung aggregates of stars. So far as we are aware, it may be duplicated many times in space. Only our presence for a brief span of years upon this insignificant earth gives importance to one particular star in one of the many galaxies of stars.

There is no reason for assuming that human life is the most superior expression of the vital impulse which the universe has yet achieved. It is scarcely likely that the Administration of the Universe has staked all on this one type of life in this one locality. Perhaps on some distant planet the achievements of the Universal Spirit far outstrip anything that man has yet attained. But for us, Our World in this particular geologic epoch gives the Opportunity. It is Man's hour; the prize is almost in his grasp. Dominion over his fellow-creatures is for all practical purposes his; mastery over the forces of inanimate nature is well-nigh assured; only Self, individual and aggregate, remains to be subdued. Our world is not a furnished stage on which the puppet man enacts a rôle; it is a challenge to the best in man to overcome all handicaps and emerge successful in the attempt to achieve a truly satisfactory life.[2]

2 *World Unity*, October, 1927, pp. 35-36.

Evolution in its social implications means that every human institution—religious, economic, political, legal, educational, or moral—has been the product of naturalistic influences operating from a very remote period in the human past. Every phase of our culture, as Sumner has suggested, is the result of broad evolutionary processes—trial, error, accident, and adaptation.[3]

Man has faced nature under a great diversity of circumstances. His efforts to perpetuate life have compelled him to attack the problems of existence in a variety of ways. The result has been an extensive diversity of human institutions. Some of them perished in due time. Others have survived. Hence, all civilizations harbor, along with a valuable heritage from the past, a vast baggage of archaic institutions and conventions which clutter up the social scene, retard progress, and lessen human well-being.

Another important implication of evolution is the emphasis we must now place, for all practical purposes, on the axiom that "man is the measure of all things." This has proven to be far truer than even the humanists of the sixteenth century or the eighteenth-century deists and reformers had believed. Modern natural science and social science not only stress the importance of man in relation to nature and the organic kingdom, but also tell us just what man is, what will make him happiest, and how his well-being can best be promoted. Human well-being on this earth has now become the frame of reference of all informed and civilized social philosophy.

IV. MAN AS AN ANIMAL

Man seems to many to be so very different from all the common animal forms that they cannot believe him to be related to the animals at all. When we begin to study man's body, however, and compare it, organ by organ, with that of other animals, his seeming biological uniqueness disappears. It is only the thin veneer of culture which so deceptively obscures our intrinsic animalism.

Men, fish, frogs, snakes, birds, and horses are all related. These diverse organisms are all members of a group labeled Vertebrata. As vertebrates these forms share certain physical characteristics. These characteristics are:

Bilateral symmetry (the left side being the mirror image of the right side at some time during ontogenic development).

Respiration by means of gills or gill modifications (i.e., lungs).

A dorsal, tubal spinal cord.

An enlarged end brain.

A protective brain case of bone and/or cartilage.

Sense organs closely associated with the brain and in the same general spatial relationship.

The presence of an endoskeleton of bone or cartilage.

The presence of a notochord sometime during ontogenetic development.

A single digestive system.

A single excretory system.

3 W. G. Sumner, *Folkways*, Dover Publications, Inc., 1959.

All living organisms which possess these traits are vertebrates and therefore are distinguishable from forms such as spiders, clams, flies, crabs, worms, sea urchins, and indeed plants, to mention a few.

The basic similarity of the vertebrates reflects their common evolutionary relationship. In other words, although all life ultimately descends from a common source, the vertebrates represent a group more closely related genetically to one another than to other forms of life. Indeed, the eight commonly recognized vertebrate classes, with the exception of the cartilaginous fish (sharks and rays) and the birds, represent an evolutionary progression from the fishes through the amphibians and reptiles to the mammals. Within the mammalian group the progression continues from the insectivorous tree shrews through the early lemurs and tarsiers to present-day human populations. The cartilaginous fish have evolved from the primitive armored fish (placoderms) in the Silurian period, and the birds from the reptiles in the Jurassic period.

Man is not only a vertebrate but also a member of a more restricted, specialized class of vertebrates, the ·mammals. Man and other mammals such as horses, dogs, seals, cows, whales, lions, and mice share many characteristics. These characteristics are:

Placental reproduction.
The presence of hair instead of scales.
The presence of sweat glands.
Lactating glands (breasts).
A stable internal body temperature (warm-bloodedness).
A four-chambered heart.
A single dentary bone articulating directly with the skull.
Three inner ear bones (incus, stapes, malleus).

In a general sense the mammals show a more efficient adaptation to their environment than do reptiles sharing the same environment. This specifically mammalian adaptation creates the necessary background for the development and emergence of the primates and man.

As a final word of caution against any feeling of exclusiveness and arrogance on the part of man, it may be well to point out that in many respects man is quite inferior to certain other animals. He is far weaker physically than the elephant, rhinoceros, lion, gorilla, or bull. He is slow-moving compared to the fleet-footed antelope or gazelle. His eyesight is poor compared to the hawk's. His sense of smell in no way approaches that of the bloodhound. As an individual, without tools or machines, he is helpless in conquering nature when contrasted with the lion or tiger. Finally, his life epoch is shorter than the crocodile's, the elephant's, and some other quadrupeds.

V. MAN AS A PRIMATE

Man's closest living kin are the monkeys and apes. There is hardly need to stress our general external likeness to the higher apes, chimpanzees, gorillas, and orangutans. The likeness is, however, more than a mere physical resemblance. We have only to watch a mother orang with her child, or a young chimpanzee at play, to realize how close is the similarity of behavior. The simian mother handles her baby in her arms, kisses it, strokes its head; her gesture and the expression on her face often have a likeness to the reaction of a human mother. Her grief at the death of her child appears even more intense physically than that of a human mother.

Let us look a little closer, now, at the resemblances between man and the lower primates. In the first place, man shares with the other primates all those common characteristics which arise from the fact that both are vertebrates and placental mammals. Man and the other primates alike have front limbs, or arms, which are free for grasping and climbing. The hand has an opposable thumb to improve the grasping powers. Instead of claws, both man and lower primates possess flat nails. The hands of both are well suited for manipulative operations. The sensitivity of the hands—tactile sense—is extreme in both. There is a correspondence, almost bone for bone, between man and the primates. The grinding teeth are also closely similar. Moreover, their blood reactions are alike. Both have a relatively long period of embryonic development, or gestation period, and a protracted infancy or period of postnatal growth.

Man and the other primates are alike in having a relatively deeply furrowed and convoluted forebrain which overhangs the back or lower brain to some extent. The specialized functions of the two brains are roughly the same in both. The visual apparatus in man and the primates is similar. Both have bony eye sockets and bony back walls for the eye. The eyes in both have a frontal position, which makes possible stereoscopic vision and permits optical discrimination as to form, size, and distance. The females in both have monthly periods and a single pair of axillary positioned breasts.

In the case of the larger anthropoid apes the resemblances to man are even greater. To the above similarities is added that of greater bodily size in the gorilla. Man and the apes share considerable biochemical similarities and all are tailless forms. Other similarities are in their social patterns.

The freeing of the human hand for prehensile and manipulating purposes was one of the major turning points in the history of man. Hence it is worthwhile to inquire into its causes.

Most anthropologists presently subscribe to Sir Arthur Keith's theory of an early arboreal stage in the evolution of man. The fore extremities were not used primarily for weight support in the trees. When man or his immediate ancestors returned to a terrestrial habitat and assumed an erect, bipedal posture, the hands were freed completely from their locomotive and supportive function and, still being anatomically unspecialized, could be used for manipulation. The importance of postulating an arboreal stage lies in the nonspecialization of the fore extremities for weight support and their availability for grasping. Franz Müller-Lyer has admirably summarized this important matter of arboreal life and its relation to man's upright stature and the development of the hand and human "handiness":

The enormous usefulness of the hand could only be apparent after tools, no matter how primitive, were invented.

What did man do with his hand before the invention of tools? Wherein lay its function, its use?

It is well known that all mammals belonged originally to the quadrupeds, thus the early ancestors of man were four-footed. This we must conclude from the history of his evolution and also from various characteristics which he still bears today; for example, the rudimentary intercostal vein valves which could only have had a function so long as the body was carried horizontally, not upright. The upper extremities of man were thus, like the lower ones, originally organs of motion. How then did hands originate from them?

As the simplest solution of the riddle it is suggested that the forefeet were changed into hands through adaptation to life on trees. In conformity with this suggestion is the striking affinity of man with the tree-climbing ape, which is distinguished from other animals by the possession of the hand, and stands nearest to man of all kinds of mammals. . . . If we arrange a series with all the transitions from the lowest of the apes up to man, we find a gap in the continuity of the line of development. This gap does not come, as we should have expected, between the anthropoid ape and man, but between very low and the lowest apes, between the apes of the Old and New World and the lemurs. According to Huxley, the difference between man and the chimpanzee is almost unimportant in comparison with the difference between a chimpanzee and a lemur.

Further, the adaptation to tree life explains in the most natural way not only the genealogy of the hand, but the later upright walk of man. Through this, adaptation of the body was directed from the horizontal to the upright position and was prepared for the later differentiation of the upper extremities into prehensile organs and the lower exclusively into organs of locomotion. On these and many other grounds which it is not necessary to discuss here, we have come to the conclusion that the hand became prehensile before the invention of tools in order to serve as an organ for climbing, that it was a corollary of the tree life, and that the primitive ancestors of man were tree climbers.[4]

Man's ancestors were fortunate to stay in trees just long enough to get the maximum advantages from arboreal life, without sharing to any great degree the disadvantages of permanent brachiation. One such disadvantage would have been to distract the use of the hand from exclusively manipulating functions while adapting it better to clutch branches. Man's ancestors fortunately did not remain in the trees long enough to have their forearms take on an exaggerated length or their hands lose complete manipulative dexterity.

The most important consideration growing out of the fact that man is a member of the ape or primate group still awaits scientific study. We have a vast body of scientific literature devoted to demonstrating man's physical affinity with the primates. But this affinity is of little significance if left hanging in the air as a mere matter of physical resemblance. The really important question is whether this physical resemblance implies mental similarities and, if so, what the fundamental facts of primate nature really are.

In short, the comparative anatomists and physical anthropologists have shown that we are primates. But the comparative psychologists and cultural anthropolo-

4 Franz Müller-Lyer, *The History of Social Development*, Knopf, 1921, pp. 44-45.

gists have shirked their duty in failing to make clear the significance of all this labor which has been devoted to proving our primate physical heritage. If human nature is a glorified primate nature, what is this glorified primate nature and what is its significance for the understanding of human behavior and the history of mankind? Even the elaborate books on primate intelligence and behavior are mainly descriptive and give little or no inkling as to what primate nature is, as distinguished from bovine nature, feline nature, canine nature, and the like. The only book which has attempted to perform this task is the admittedly semihumorous work of a clever journalist—Clarence Day's *This Simian World*. The clarification of our simian nature is a challenge which awaits a man who combines the biological knowledge and constructive imagination of an H. G. Wells.

Until the task is executed, we shall only "see through a glass darkly" in dealing with human history and human behavior. It is not going too far to say that all the energy and learning thus far expended in tracing the physical heritage of man will remain largely wasted effort until the problems of our fundamentally simian nature are thoroughly threshed out and their implications for a better understanding of the human race are clearly set forth. Whoever performs this task will have made an even greater contribution than Charles Darwin.

VI. MAN DOMINATES THE PRIMATE WORLD

One question that is often and logically asked is the anthropocentric question as to how man arose to the top rank in the animal kingdom.

In the first place, while we must remember that physically man is not necessarily the most advanced and promising of the primates, certain physical differences from the other primates were advantageous in helping man to exploit his ecological niche. Professor Earnest A. Hooton admirably summarized some of these differences:

> Man differs physically from the anthropoid apes and the lower primates in the great absolute and relative size of his brain; his supporting, non-prehensile foot with its massive, non-opposable great toe; the reduced size and lessened protrusion of his jaws; the development of a positive chin eminence and the absence of projecting, interlocking canine teeth; the possession of a lumbar curve and a basin-shaped, tilted pelvis modified for the functions of balancing and supporting the body in the erect posture; greatly hypertrophied and elongated lower limbs adapted for biped gait; shortened and refined upper limbs with broad hands provided with long and perfectly opposable thumbs and short fingers; a prominent nose with well developed tip and wings; complete absence of tactile hair or feelers together with a marked sparsity of secondary body hair except on the head, in the pubic and axillary regions and on the face of adult males; and the presence of full, everted membranous lips. [5]

One of the most decisive of the differences between man and the other primates was man's gradual adoption of a permanently vertical posture which was made possible by the structural advantages listed above. This vertical position freed the hands from all tasks save those involved in grasping and manipulating. The

5 Article "Man" in *Encyclopedia of the Social Sciences*, X, 71. See also his *Up from the Ape*, Macmillan, 1946, p. 39.

jaws were rarely used any longer for tearing and biting and entirely ceased to be used for seizing. From now on they could be used for the mastication of food. Because of this less arduous work mutations reducing the size of the snout had a selective advantage.

Man's head is so balanced on the vertebral column that it projects to an equal extent before and behind. It likewise develops in height, a fact which had important consequences. As the skull grows in height, it dominates the ears, already immobile in monkeys, and since it widens at the same time, it brings the eyes, more or less laterally placed on most mammals, to a frontal position.

The characteristic features of the human face thus followed the development of the brain, itself stimulated by the development of the hand.[6] Once past the stage of the lemur, it would appear, the simple erection of the body into a vertical position opened the way that was to lead slowly but surely to the human form by the uninterrupted and almost exclusive progress of the organs of intelligence.

The evolutionary trend in the primates has been towards greater adaptability. This evolutionary trend of the nervous system and cerebral apparatus resulted in man's brain completely outdistancing that of any other primate in absolute size and in powers of cognition. Man's brain is more than twice as large as that of a gorilla. As Professor Hooton sums up the whole matter: "By the adoption of a terrestrial life and the assumption of an erect posture and biped gait proto-human primates emancipated their hands from locomotor functions and brought to full fruition the powers engendered by their bodily inheritance and fostered by the arboreal habitat of their ancestors." We may now turn briefly to a consideration of how man's physical advantages made possible not only dominion over the animal kingdom but also the creation of a complex material culture—something which man alone has achieved.

VII. MAN'S EMERGENCE FROM THE ANIMAL KINGDOM

One of the most interesting of all human and historical problems is the question of how man passed beyond a purely animal state and created a material culture, a literary civilization, and formal social institutions.

No answer can be given with assurance. The usual appeal to brain size both in absolute and relative terms is no longer completely tenable. Whales have larger brains than man. The ratio of brain weight to body weight in man ranges from 1:42 to 1:48, and in some New World monkeys the ratio is 1:17. Further, Neanderthal man, who may or may not have been ancestral to Homo sapiens, had a larger brain than present-day populations.

It is contended, nevertheless, that the human brain is "handmade." By this is meant that the activities man carried on with his hands had an advantageous selective value upon his mentality and tended to mold and increase his intelligence. Nature favored those species of apes which could best use their forelegs in a handlike fashion. This manual dexterity in turn increased "mental ingenuity" and "brain power." It was certainly a cumulative process after the larger brain had been developed.

6 Cf. W. K. Gregory, *Our Face from Fish to Man*, Putnam, 1929.

There has been a very marked development of the brain—particularly in the cerebrum, where the thought centers are located—since man separated from the apes and became a definitely human being. The skulls of very primitive human types prove that their brain case was relatively smaller than that of Homo sapiens. The frontal lobes, or cerebrum, were less developed among the ancestors of Homo sapiens. There is no evidence, however, that our innate capacity for intelligence has at all increased since we reached the Homo sapiens stage or the stage of our immediate ancestors.

Man's greater brain power provided him with important assets—increased curiosity and a fertile imagination, involving him in a far wider range of interests than his animal competitors. Hence he made headway along infinitely more avenues of achievement, and was held down less rigorously to a few well-worn reactions.

Accompanying man's larger brain was that other distinctively human attribute —a better memory. Animal memory is not to be despised. An elephant, for instance, can perform astonishing memory feats. But man's excellent memory, working hand in glove with his manipulating ability, enabled him to explore countless situations closed to other animals; and, at the same time, it permitted him to profit more directly from his past experiences. This use of accumulated experience has been an invaluable asset to him.

Further, man is the only animal who has a very striking imitative capacity. It was believed, down to the rise of modern comparative psychology, that the ape, for example, possessed unusual powers of imitation. But effective psychological tests have disproved this belief. As one writer humorously observed, "the ape will monkey but will not ape." Through man's superior imitative ability, every advantageous discovery made by an individual could be imitated by the group. In this way, individual inventiveness was thoroughly socialized. Moreover, man's ingenuity caused him to vary and extend his imitations—thus, often improving upon the original and producing inventions.

His superior imitative capacity and his remarkable memory permitted him to accumulate and consolidate his cultural achievements, and to hand them on to his progeny. This enabled mankind to produce the beginnings of human culture, and to improve on that culture until it reached the status of a civilization. Such a gift was denied other members of the animal kingdom.

While recognizing the more highly developed curiosity, better memory, and superior capacity for imitation possessed by man, it is also desirable to stress the importance of the rôle played by articulate speech in the achievement of human dominion over the animal world and in the creation of a culture. Speech helped to stimulate the operation of those very faculties and qualities in which man could claim superiority over the other primates. Curiosity and fertility of imagination were abetted by the use of speech and the development of communication. His better memory was greatly enhanced by linguistic habits and verbal retentiveness. And imitativeness is, in part, a sharing of experience by means of articulate speech.

One of the sweeping differences between man and his fellow primates is man's ability to use language and symbols. Apes can use tools. With man, however, who has articulate speech at his command, tool-using becomes continuous and, hence, cumulative in nature. Human culture may be regarded as derived, in the last analysis, from the use of tools and symbols. Since tool-using became culturally effective only after articulate speech had been mastered, we may fairly say that the essence of human culture is the spoken word and symbolic communication.

Though man is weak compared to many animals, man's social sense, more intelligently developed than that of any other species, compensated for his physical frailty. Social life, division of labor, and cooperative activities offset the weakness of the individual. Besides, through his cleverness and cunning, he devised weapons which overcame the superior physical strength of other animals.

In this process of establishing human supremacy, the prolongation of human infancy—the longer period of dependency of the human progeny—may have played an important part. It permitted a slower and more complete mental and nervous development. It also made it possible for the human youth to absorb more perfectly the mental and cultural achievements of his elders. He was able to start adult life with the previous achievements of the race at his personal disposal.

VIII. NATURE AND NURTURE

The preceding material gives us the proper background for dealing with the important and interesting question of the rôle of "human nature" in history. No term or concept is more misunderstood or more abused. We are often told, when some modest social reform is suggested, that it simply can't be done, for "you can't change human nature." It is implied that any considerable alteration of our customary ways of thinking or acting involves a change in human nature. Such an attitude is a complete misunderstanding of human nature and its place in history.

First, let us be clear as to just what human nature really is. It is our physical make-up, including body and mind, if one wishes to preserve the older artificial distinction between body and mind. It is that physical and mental equipment whose origins and nature we have been dealing with thus far in this chapter. It is our animal nature, which in this case, is a specific primate nature. So far as human thinking is concerned, human nature is made up of the brain, the central nervous system, the autonomic nervous system, and the bodily surroundings and processes that affect them.

Now, so far as it relates to the history of human civilization, one may regard this physical or human nature as relatively static and changeless. It doubtless changed in some details between about 1,000,000 and 30,000 B.C., during which time man advanced from a very early form of cultural attainment to the stage of present-day man. It is possible, too, that human nature will change in the future, as a result of natural causes, artificial breeding, or both.

But between about 30,000 and 50,000 years ago, when Homo sapiens became the sole human inhabitant in Europe, and our own day, there have been no essential changes in human nature. Man, thirty or more thousand years ago, was physically just what he is today. He had just as good a brain—in fact, the same brain—as we possess today. He would have been just as easily and extensively educable as we are, if the appropriate fund of information and teaching methods had then been available. All that separates us from the Homo sapiens of 50,000 B.C. are the cultural changes which have occurred since.

These considerations should serve to make clear that what we regard as human civilization has developed without any change in human nature. Our institutions, literature, art, and religion have grown from the most rudimentary beginnings to their present forms without involving the slightest changes in the physical equipment which we designate as human nature. We have passed from cave dwellings to the Empire State building and Rockefeller Center, from small clans and tribes to great national states and colonial empires, from the possession of a few skins and bone implements to billionaires, and from illiteracy to the wisdom of a John Dewey or the erudition of a Joseph McCabe. And all of these advances have been accomplished with our same old human nature, persisting unchanged.

A consideration of these facts, of course, entirely obliterates the conventional notion that we cannot improve conditions without a change in human nature— that we cannot have consumer's coöperation, economic planning, or conservation, for example, because such things are opposed to human nature. Any reforms likely to be proposed today are trifling changes compared to the totality of insti- tutional and cultural changes which have occurred in the last thirty thousand years.

Russia, today, affords the best proof of the fallacy of the older "human nature complex." Nearly all aspects of Russian life, and most social attitudes, have been diametrically transformed since 1917, but no informed person would imagine that the physical and mental equipment of the Russian people has altered an iota in so short a space of time.

Yet, if the physical basis of human nature has not changed for thirty thousand years, this should not lead us to take too rigid and static a view of the character and workings of human nature. Behavior is the product of two forces: (1) the physical and social environment, and (2) the responses of our physical organism to the environment. Though the organism may not change, its responses are bound to alter as new stimuli arise from radical changes in the environment. Hence, there is no reason to doubt that human nature responds quite differently in a metropolitan center today from the way it did in the simple environment of the cave dwellers.

Over against our relatively changeless human nature we have the very fluid and changeable human nurture. By human nurture we mean the sum total of in- stitutional and cultural surroundings within which human nature operates. It is the totality of civilization and resulting mental patterns at any given time. Human nurture, unlike human nature, is subject to the most radical alterations. Indeed, it is the aim of this book to sketch some of the more notable aspects of nurtural modifications. Everything that set us off from the Cro-Magnon days of 30,000 to 50,000 years ago represents, exclusively, changes in human nurture.

It will be evident that human nurture rather than human nature is the province of the historian. Human nature was fixed in its present mold many thousands of years before the conventional dawn of history. The history of civilization is primarily the history of human nurture. The mutations and progressions of the latter constitute the data and raw material of history. The historian takes his view of human nature from biologists, psychologists, and anthropologists, and then tries to find out what cultural transformations have been effected through the course of the ages—in other words, tries to trace the development of human nurture.

Though the historian is not able to trace changes in human nature, he cannot be a really competent student of history unless he is acquainted with the character of human nature. If his task is to study the creations of human nature, namely, human nurture, he must first acquaint himself with human nature itself. A nurture is bound to be determined by the kind of nature that produced it. If this chapter has fulfilled its function, readers should have a good working knowledge of human nature and be in command of the facts and perspective which will enable them intelligently to explore its achievements in nurture.

IX. A DYNAMIC CONCEPTION OF THE HUMAN MIND

Man's glory, as James Harvey Robinson suggests, is his mind, the instrument which enabled him to build the edifice called civilization, including religions, arts, social and economic and political institutions, and material inventions. But what is mind? Is it a separate entity, existing apart from the body, as the old dichotomy between body and mind assumed? Is mind a thing, a force, or a being within a being? Is it, as John Stuart Mill expressed it, "that mysterious something which thinks and feels"?

The indisputable fact about mind is that it manifests itself by thinking. Thinking, however, depends upon words. And here lies a tremendous pitfall; words are used which have little relation to things. Philosophers have a stock of words like "beauty," "truth," "virtue," and "good" which they seem to use as if they were things. Medieval thinkers erected dizzy edifices of philosophy on the slender basis of words. They seemed, as Francis Bacon pointed out, to confuse words with things, to accept words as things.[7]

Modern thinking has not been free from this error. The words "reason," "will," "soul," and "mind," for instance, have been used as if they were palpable things you could actually lay your hands on. The reaction against this kind of thinking has gone to that extreme where the existence of mind itself is denied. In other words, we find in contemporary thinking the paradox of mind refusing to believe in its own existence.

Another traditional conception of mind is that it is a kind of invisible and immaterial puppetmaster, controlling the action of the body. Such a concept, however, involves us in another paradox. How can immaterial mind cause such material actions as walking, talking, lifting, moving, and the like? We know that a stone thrown into the water causes movement of water. This is matter acting

7 See Stuart Chase, *The Tyranny of Words*, Harvest Books, 1959.

upon matter. But can nonmatter act upon matter? Clearly it cannot. Thus the distinction between mind and body must be abandoned.

Somehow or other, in ways that are not yet very clear, body and mind are intertwined, like a knife and cutting. In fact, the question of how (apparently) immaterial mind can cause material actions seems on the way to being answered. We know that matter is galvanic and never at rest. Matter is composed of electrons and other "-ons" which are always in a state of motion. This mobility and changeableness has been taken advantage of by chemists to the extent of manufacturing useful and beautiful articles out of ugly and apparently useless stuffs.

This new conception of matter has given us an exalted notion of the human body. Far from being the vulgar vessel of clay which medieval theologians imagined, the body is an extraordinary and wonderful mechanism of many parts functioning harmoniously. Furthermore, the existence of body preceded any extended mental accumulations. Man reached the highest level in the animal kingdom because his body became more dextrous than that of other animals, and as his body became more dextrous his brain improved. In other words, his body and brain seem to have developed first and his mental equipment later. Mind was gradually acquired, and as it was acquired the texture of civilization was erected, like a web spun by a spider.

Hence mind is not, as Mill thought, a mysterious something, but a condition of gradually becoming aware of the environment, and utilizing that growing awareness (i.e., knowledge) for civilized ends. The increase of "mind" means an extension of knowledge, and an expansion of our control over the environment. This is the new conception of mind, and it is not as Mill thought, a mysterious entity. In fact, it is not an entity but a *function,* in Robinson's apt phrase, a "trick":

> *There can be indefinitely more "mind" accumulated as time goes on, now that we have the trick.* Never was the "mind" in general so good as it now is; it has been vastly improved during the past fifty years, and there seems nothing to prevent it from being vastly better fifty years hence. Evidently the mind and body are not separate things. The body antedated the human mind by hundreds of millions of years and we may expect a great increase of wisdom when we get over the older notions of the mind being an independent entity aspiring to go its way regardless of the shrewd old organism which has proved its ability to manage living so long before the mind came into action.[8]

X. RACE AND CULTURE

One of the most misleading of the notions that have distorted the vision of the writers and readers of historical materials has been the idea that race has played a dominating rôle in determining the course of human development. It will be best to examine this illusion very early in this book—in the sections dealing with physical factors and human culture.

Before dealing with racial misinterpretations of history it will be well to have

8 James Harvey Robinson, *The Human Comedy,* Harper, 1936, pp. 58-59.

clearly in mind the elementary facts about race. The term race is a matter of physical anthropology which refers to a certain set of physical traits that characterize the different groups of mankind on the planet. Further, these traits are generally limited to populations which habitually interbreed. These populations differ from other populations in the statistical frequency of these traits. All breeding populations, e.g. "races," have the same traits; however, the frequency of each trait differs from population to population. These traits are physical adaptations to specific environments and have no relation to cultural attainment or intelligence.[9]

Race is thus a physical matter. It has nothing directly to do with cultural traits. That certain races may have peculiar mental traits may be true, but it is virtually impossible to determine how much they are a matter of the physical fact of race and how much a product of cultural factors independent of race. All efforts to prove any comprehensive superiority of one or another of the races or subraces of man have turned out to be unsuccessful. The tests have been unable to exclude cultural factors which upset all possibility of isolating the purely racial elements.

The origins of the race myth, or the "chosen people" complex, go back to the aversion of primitive tribes to strangers. The Jews called all strangers gentiles; the Greeks called them barbarians.

In its modern form, the idea is part of the nationalistic complex propagated by the romanticists at the close of the eighteenth century. It was forcefully enunciated by Johann Gottlieb Fichte in his famous *Lectures to the German People* in 1807, in which he said that perhaps the most precious element in the German heritage was the unique German language. This emphasis on language had one beneficial effect, since it stimulated the remarkable nineteenth-century discoveries in philology.

The upshot of these discoveries was that certain European languages were found to be linked with the Sanskrit and a few other languages of ancient India and Iran. The two branches, European and Asiatic, were believed to stem directly from a hypothetical common tongue, which was called Aryan. It was further maintained that back of this Aryan language was a race, also Aryan, from whom the best stocks in Europe have sprung.

This false inference of the identity between race and language would not by itself have furnished the basis for a racial obsession. What was needed was a vigorous exposition of the cultural and historic superiority of the Aryan race. This was supplied by Count Joseph Arthur de Gobineau in his famous *Essay on the Inequality of the Human Races,* published in 1854. Gobineau contended that nearly all the worthwhile achievements of man had been the product of the white race generally, and of the Aryan race in particular. He also propounded the corollary of this doctrine—so vigorously taken up by Adolf Hitler—that race mixture is a distinctly degenerating process.

9 For a further discussion of this point, see Carleton S. Coon, S. M. Garn, and Joseph B. Birdsell, *Race,* C. C. Thomas, 1950; S. M. Garn, *Human Races.* C. C. Thomas, 1961, and *Readings on Race,* C. C. Thomas, 1961; and Theodosius Dobzhansky, *Genetics and the Origin of Species,* Columbia University Press, 1951.

From Gobineau's time onward, it came to be regarded as a matter of great importance to prove that one's nation was predominantly Aryan. At first this brewed relatively little chauvinism, since it was assumed that the broad similarities of European languages—with the exception of Basque and certain Turanian dialects—meant that the overwhelming majority of Europeans were Aryans.

This happy illusion was demolished in the 1870's by a number of German scholars, especially Theodor Pösche and Carl Penka, who proved convincingly that the identification of race and language was false. The same race may have many different languages, while several different races may speak the same language. Hence, it was apparent that not all Europeans were necessarily Aryans. Therefore, from the 1880's on, there was a feverish effort on the part of nationalistic writers to prove that their nation was the only true Aryan stock, while their neighbors were of adulterated Aryan clay or non-Aryans altogether.

It is frequently believed that the Teutonic writers were the only ones who succumbed to this fanaticism. As a matter of fact, every state had its propagandists who interpreted national culture on the basis of their alleged superior Aryan heritage. The racialists in England and France easily matched the Teutons for assurance and arrogance.

While the racial obsession was becoming more widespread, scientists were patiently assembling data which were to reveal the fundamental inaccuracy of the whole race myth. An American scholar, W. Z. Ripley, two generations ago combined the researches of European scholars into a comprehensive work, *The Races of Europe* (1898), which thoroughly demolished the theory that there ever was such a thing as an Aryan race.

The term Aryan was shown to apply technically, if at all, only to certain languages common to particular peoples in Europe and Asia. It was proved to be highly dubious whether the term could be accurately used to describe even the social and cultural institutions of the peoples who spoke the so-called Aryan languages. Least of all could the term Aryan be legitimately employed to describe the purely physical fact of race. As the eminent anthropologist, Sir G. Elliot Smith, has well put the matter: "An ethnologist who speaks of Aryan race, Aryan blood, Aryan eyes and hair, is as great a sinner as the linguist who speaks of a dolichocephalic [longheaded] dictionary or a brachycephalic [roundheaded] grammar."

Professor Ripley and an Italian anthropologist, Giuseppe Sergi, sought to demonstrate that the Teutonic peoples were not of Asiatic origin and could not have been the original bearers of the Aryan language and culture. It is the consensus of the best anthropological opinion that if there is any such thing as Aryan culture, it must have been brought into Europe by the roundheaded Alpine or Eurasian race. Hence, the term "Indo-Germanic," used to describe a unified race or culture, is a scientific monstrosity, even though it is still commonly employed by many historians, especially English and German medievalists.

It is more accurate to use "Indo-European" when describing the roundheaded Alpine race—but the longheaded Mediterranean and Nordic groups do not belong to the Indo-European family.

When one examines the thesis that all worthwhile civilizations have been a Nordic (Germanic) product, the whole racial myth becomes transparent nonsense. For instance, the great civilizations of oriental antiquity were almost 100 percent non-Nordic. This is especially apparent as soon as we accept the modern scientific view that the Nordics were in no physical sense related to the peoples of ancient India, or to the Eurasian Alpines who probably migrated from central Asia to Europe late in the Paleolithic age and in Neolithic times.

The great European cultural heritage which came in from Egypt and Mesopotamia was absolutely devoid of Nordic elements. Furthermore, we must by no means assume that human civilization was limited to the area between the Tigris and the Thames. In many respects the civilizations of China and India were more advanced and mature than those of the Occident. That they were non-Nordic scarcely needs to be pointed out to even Lothrop Stoddard and Madison Grant, the chief American exponents of the racial myth.

The high civilizations of the ancient Aegean age were likewise mainly Mediterranean, and free from any significant Nordic admixture. To pass on to classical times, there was only a sprinkling of Nordics among the Hellenes and Romans. In the Middle Ages cultural leadership passed from western Europe to the Eastern or Greek Empire, and to the Muslims of northern Africa and Spain. The Muslims were, of course, entirely non-Nordic, while among the peoples who maintained Byzantine culture until the final conquest by the Turks in the middle of the fifteenth century, there was only a minor Nordic element.

Even in a political and military sense, no convincing case can be made for Nordic supremacy during the medieval period. We now know that medieval France was predominantly non-Nordic. In medieval England the non-Nordic group was certainly as important as the Nordic element.

Indeed, if one were to accept for a minute the thesis of racial causation in politics, European history since the fall of the Roman Empire would overwhelmingly indicate the relative political incapacity of these very Nordics who are so hysterically eulogized by Teutonic and other writers. Germanic states were the least united and the least well disciplined in a political sense in the Middle Ages and were the last to achieve unification in modern times.

In conclusion, we may say that it should hardly be necessary any longer to seek to disprove the racial interpretation of national culture. Everyone knows that Europe is a conglomeration of races. No special racial strain can be discerned which has held up pure and undefiled until the present day.

Even if we were to assume, for example, that the civilization of Germany or of France is the product of a definite and unique race—shall we assign it, in the case of France, to the Nordics of the northeast, the Celts of the central portion, or the Mediterraneans of the south? Or, in the case of Germany, is her culture primarily a product of the so-called Nordics in the north, or of the Alpines in the south?

Even if we could feel sure—which we certainly cannot—that there is an important relationship between race and culture, the increasingly complex mixture of

European races since the Neolithic period would certainly rule out any attempt at a racial interpretation of European history. This fact can best be driven home through a concrete illustration, such as Karl Pearson's summary of the racial heritage of Charles Darwin, long considered to be, physically and mentally, a typical Englishman of pure Nordic blood:

> He is descended in four different lines from Irish kinglets; he is descended in as many lines from Scottish and Pictish kings. He has Manx blood. He claims descent in at least three lines from Alfred the Great, and so links up with Anglo-Saxon blood, but he links up also in several lines with Charlemagne and the Carlovingians. He sprang also from the Saxon Emperors of Germany, as well as from Barbarossa and the Hohenstaufens. He had Norwegian blood and much Norman blood. He had descent from the Duke of Bavaria, of Saxony, of Flanders, the Princes of Savoy, and the Kings of Italy. He had the blood in his veins of Franks, Alamans, Merovingians, Burgundians, and Longobards. He sprang in direct descent from the Hun rulers of Hungary and the Greek Emperors of Constantinople. If I recollect rightly, Ivan the Terrible provides a Russian link. There is probably not one of the races of Europe concerned in folk-wanderings which has not had a share in the ancestry of Charles Darwin. If it has been possible in the case of one Englishman of this kind to show in a considerable number of lines how impure is his race, can we venture to assert that if the like knowledge were possible of attainment, we could expect greater purity of blood in any of his countrymen? [10]

Now that we have shown how man rose to the top in the animal kingdom, and have traced the development of his physical equipment, we may turn to the record of cultural origins and describe human achievements in that long period—some ninety-nine percent of human history—before man could set down his doings in the written word.

SELECTED READINGS

Baldwin, Ernest, *An Introduction to Comparative Biochemistry,* Cambridge University Press, 1949.

Barnett, S. A., ed., *A Century of Darwin,* Harvard University Press, 1958.

Berrill, N. J., *The Origin of Vertebrates,* Oxford University Press, 1955.

Blum, H. F., "On the Origin and Evolution of Living Machines," *American Scientist,* 49: 474-501 (1961).

———— "Perspectives in Evolution," *American Scientist,* 43: 595-610 (1955).

———— *Time's Arrow and Evolution,* Princeton University Press, 1962.

Bondi, Hermann, *Cosmology,* Cambridge University Press, 1961.

Brooks, C. E. P., *Climate Through the Ages,* Ernest Benn, 1949.

Brown, H., "The Age of the Solar System," *Scientific American, 196:* 80-95, (1957).

Cain, A. J., *Animal Species and Their Evolution,* Harper, 1960.

Carter, G. S., *A Hundred Years of Evolution,* Macmillan, 1958.

———— *Animal Evolution: A Study of Recent Views of Its Causes,* Sidwick & Jackson, 1951.

Childe, V. G., *Man Makes Himself,* Mentor, 1952.

10 *Scientific Monthly,* November, 1920, p. 455.

Clark, W. E. Le Gros, *History of Primates*, Phoenix, 1957.
———*The Antecedents of Man*, Quadrangle Books, 1959.
Colbert, E. H., *The Dinosaur Book*, McGraw-Hill, 1951.
———*Evolution of the Vertebrates*, Wiley, 1955.
Coon, C. S., *The Origin of Races*, Knopf, 1962.
———*The Races of Europe*, Macmillan, 1939.
Darwin, C. W., *The Descent of Man*, Modern Library.
———*On the Origin of Species*, Mentor.
———*The Voyage of the Beagle*, Bantam.
———*The Autobiography of Charles Darwin and Selected Letters*, ed. Francis Darwin, Dover Publications, Inc., 1958.
Darwin, C. W., and Wallace, A. R., *Evolution by Natural Selection*, Cambridge University Press, 1958.
De Beer, G. R., *Embryos and Ancestors*, Oxford University Press, 1958.
Dice, L. R., *Man's Nature and Nature's Man*, University of Michigan Press, 1955.
Dixon, R. B., *The Racial History of Man*, Scribner, 1939.
Dobzhansky, Theodosius, *Genetics and the Origin of Species*, Columbia University Press, 1951.
———*Mankind Evolving*, Yale University Press, 1962.
Dowdeswell, W. H., *The Mechanism of Evolution*, Beacon, 1960.
Dunbar, C. O., *Historical Geology*, Wiley, 1960.
———*Principles of Stratigraphy*, Wiley, 1957.
Eiseley, Loren, *Darwin's Century*, Doubleday, 1958.
Flint, R. T., *Glacial and Pleistocene Geology*, Wiley, 1957.
Florkin, Marcel, *Biochemical Evolution*, Academic Press, 1949.
Gaffron, H., "The Origin of Life," in *Evolution After Darwin*, ed. Sol Tax, University of Chicago Press, 1960.
Gamow, George, *Biography of the Earth*, Compass, 1959.
———*The Creation of the Universe*, Viking, 1952.
———"The Origin and Evolution of the Universe," *American Scientist, 39:* 393-406 (1951).
Garn, S. M., *Human Races*, C. C. Thomas, 1961.
Garn, S. M., ed., *Readings on Race*, C. C. Thomas, 1961.
Glass, B., Temkin, O., and Straus, W., eds., *Forerunners of Darwin, 1745–1859*, Johns Hopkins Press, 1959.
Goodrich, E. S., *Studies on the Structure and Development of Vertebrates*, 2 Vols., Dover Publications, Inc., 1958.
Greene, J. C., *The Death of Adam*, Mentor, 1959.
Gregory, W. K., *Evolution Emerging*, 2 Vols., Macmillan, 1951.
Hays, H. R., *From Ape to Angel*, Knopf, 1958.
Henderson, L. J., *The Fitness of the Environment*, Beacon, 1958.
Himmelfarb, Gertrude, *Darwin and the Darwinian Revolution*, Doubleday, 1959.
Hooton, E. A., *Up from the Ape*, Macmillan, 1946.
———*Why Men Behave like Apes and Vice Versa*, Princeton University Press, 1940.
Hurley, P. M., *How Old Is the Earth?*, Doubleday, 1959.
Huxley, J. S., *Evolution in Action*, Mentor, 1957.
———*Evolution: The Modern Synthesis*, Harper, 1942.
———*The Living Thoughts of Darwin*, Premier, 1959.
Hyman, L. H., *Comparative Vertebrate Anatomy*, University of Chicago Press, 1942.
Irvine, William, *Apes, Angels and Victorians*, McGraw-Hill, 1955.

Keith, Arthur, *Man,* Holt, 1912.

Klinberg, Otto, *Race Differences,* Harper, 1935.

Köhler, Wolfgang, *The Mentality of Apes,* Vintage, 1959.

La Barre, Weston, *The Human Animal,* University of Chicago Press, 1960.

McElroy, W. D., and Glass, B., eds., *The Chemical Basis for Heredity,* Johns Hopkins Press, 1957.

Martin, C. P., *Psychology, Evolution and Sex,* C. C. Thomas, 1956.

Mason, Frances, ed., *Creation by Evolution,* Macmillan, 1928.

Merrell, D. J., *Evolution and Genetics,* Holt, 1962.

Miller, S. L., "A Production of Amino Acids Under Possible Primitive Earth Conditions," *Science, 117:* 528-529 (1953).

Moody, P. A., *Introduction to Evolution,* Harper, 1962.

Montagu, M. F. Ashley, *Man: His First Million Years,* Signet, 1959.

Muller, H. J., *The Uses of the Past,* Oxford University Press, 1952.

Nelsen, O. E., *Comparative Embryology of the Vertebrates,* McGraw-Hill, 1953.

Newman, H. H., ed., *The Nature of the World and of Man,* University of Chicago Press, 1926.

Noble, G. K., *The Biology of Amphibia,* Dover Publications, Inc., 1954.

Oparin, A. I., *The Origin of Life,* Dover Publications, Inc., 1953.

Proceedings of the First International Congress on the Origin of Life on Earth (Moscow, 1957), Pergamon, 1959.

Rensch, Bernard, *Evolution Above the Species Level,* Columbia University Press, 1960.

Rhodes, F. H. T., *The Evolution of Life,* Pelican, 1962.

Robinson, J. H., *Mind in the Making,* Harper, 1921.

Roe, Anne, and Simpson, G. G., eds., *Behavior and Evolution,* Yale University Press, 1958.

Romer, A. S., *Man and the Vertebrates,* 2 Vols., Pelican.

—————*The Vertebrate Body,* Saunders, 1955.

—————*Vertebrate Paleontology,* University of Chicago Press, 1945.

—————*The Vertebrate Story,* University of Chicago Press, 1959.

Ross, H. H., *Synthesis of Evolutionary Theory,* Prentice-Hall, 1962.

Rutten, M. G., *The Geological Aspects of the Origin of Life on Earth,* American Elsevier, 1962.

Scientific American, eds., *The Universe,* Simon & Schuster, 1957.

Segan, C., "On the Origin and Planetary Distribution of Life," *Radiation Research, 15:* 174-192 (1961).

Shapley, H., "On the Evidence of Inorganic Evolution," in *Evolution After Darwin,* ed. Sol Tax, University of Chicago Press, 1960.

Simpson, G. G., *Life of the Past,* Yale University Press, 1953.

—————*The Major Features of Evolution,* Columbia University Press, 1953.

—————*The Meaning of Evolution,* Yale University Press, 1960.

Smith, H. W., *From Fish to Philosopher,* Little, Brown, 1953.

—————*Kamongo,* Compass, 1956.

Smith, J. M., *The Theory of Evolution,* Pelican, 1958.

Tax, Sol, ed., *Evolution After Darwin,* 3 Vols., University of Chicago Press, 1960.

Von Koenigswald, G. H. R., *The Evolution of Man,* Ann Arbor Books, 1962.

Wallace, Bruce, and Srb, A. M., *Adaptation,* Prentice-Hall, 1961.

Wendt, Herbert, *The Road to Man,* Pyramid, 1962.

Yerkes, R. M., *Almost Human,* Century, 1925.

Young, J. Z., *The Life of Vertebrates,* Oxford University Press, 1950.

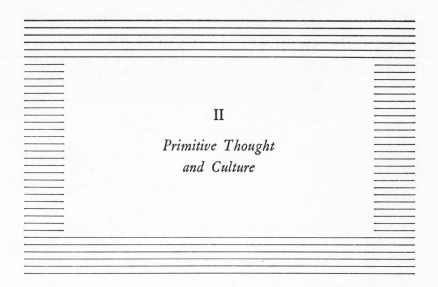

II

Primitive Thought
and Culture

I. OUR KNOWLEDGE OF EARLY MAN

How have we come to learn about early man? The anthropologists and archaeologists of the nineteenth century discovered skeletal remains of men who were neither like living human beings nor identical with existing primates. These skeletons clearly proved that there must have been a long period of human life and culture before the proverbial 4004 B.C., from which creation date the orthodox chronology begins.

This fact of a long human past was demonstrated not only by the skeletons of early man, but also by a large accumulation of stone implements going back tens of thousands of years. The existence of stone tools was known even in classical times. But such objects were then believed to be "thunderstones" hurled by the gods, though some writers, like Lucretius, seem partly to have recognized their true significance.

A French archaeologist, Jacques Boucher de Perthes, was the first to publish (in 1846) a systematic description of Stone Age remains. He recovered large numbers of so-called "river-drift" stone implements in ancient geological deposits in the Somme Valley. He argued that these "artifacts" (archaeological remains) must obviously have been man-made. If this hypothesis was true, it meant that man had existed on earth long before Adam, since the strata in which the stone implements were found are of great antiquity. At first, Boucher de Perthes was ridiculed, but within a couple of decades his arguments were accepted.

The next problem was to work out a time scheme into which these remains could be fitted. Lucretius, who lived in the first century B.C., had divided the cultural history of man into three stages: Stone, Bronze, and Iron ages. This classification was revived in 1834 by C. J. Thomsen of the Copenhagen Museum.

Since that time, anthropologists and archæologists have been able, with the aid of materials uncovered, to subdivide these broad periods. The Stone Age, as thus classified, consists of three periods: (1) Eolithic, or early Stone Age; (2) Paleolithic, or Old Stone Age; and (3) Neolithic, or New Stone Age. Each of these has been subdivided, along with transitional stages.

These periods and subdivisions represent the sequence of cultural evolution, and at the same time reflect the growth of technical perfection in producing stone weapons and implements. Since there was no calendar or yearly chronology for the history of preliterary man, these artifacts and the age of the strata in which they are found, as well as of the animal and human remains usually existing along with them, are all we have to guide us. These give us roughly the age of the old stone implements and of the human beings who used them. More recently sensational chemical techniques, notably the Carbon-14 method discovered by Walter Libby, have been developed to determine the actual age of the bones which have been exhumed back as far as 50,000 years. The still controversial potassium-argon process may be able to push our dating back fairly accurately to several million years. Such data and information enable us to place the types of early man accurately enough in time to serve the purpose of tracing and explaining the evolution of the human race and its ancestors.

II. EARLY TYPES OF MAN

Over a century of investigation by geologists, paleontologists, archaeologists and anthropologists has provided impressive and convincing information that reveals the physical origins and development of mankind over an enormous period of time, compared to the traditional biblical chronology which assigns mankind an antiquity of less than 6,000 years.

The fact that anthropologists have agreed that mankind did not descend from any existing types of apes or monkeys has led many to adopt the attractive but misleading notion that man does not have any ape or monkey ancestry, however remote. This misconception has been exploded by Professor George Gaylord Simpson of Harvard: "Apologists emphasize that man cannot be a descendant of any living ape and go on to state that man is not descended from an ape or a monkey at all but from an earlier common ancestor. In fact, however, that common ancestor would certainly be called an ape or monkey in popular speech by anybody who saw it. Since the terms 'ape' and 'monkey' are defined by popular usage, man's ancestors were apes or monkeys (or successively both)."

Whether man made the transition from a remote simian or hominoid ancestry, common to both apes and mankind, at one crucial time and place—known as the monogenist theory—or whether the transformation was accomplished in several widely separated areas at different times, as the polygenist position maintains, has been long and widely debated. A half century ago the monogenist theory was upheld by the great majority of physical anthropologists. Discoveries of the extremely wide distribution of early human types, along with knowledge that man has developed diversified physical characteristics in different parts of the world, have led to further confusion and conflicting theories.

Although human remains dating back at least 100,000[1] years were found in western Germany a little over a century ago, the first dramatic discovery of a very early type of man was made by a Dutch doctor, Eugene Dubois, at Trinil in central Java in 1891-1892. This primordial human type was designated as *Pithecanthropus erectus*. It is thought to have lived about 500,000 years ago. Later discoveries in Java revealed the further evolution of man in this area. The next impressive find was the uncovering of a very ancient human jaw near Heidelberg, Germany, by an anatomist, Otto Schoetensack, in 1907. This specimen has come to be known as the Heidelberg man, from the site of the discovery, and is thought to have lived about 450,000 years ago.

Next in order in revealing early types of man were the investigations carried on in the Peking area in China after 1927 under the direction of Davidson Black, an English anatomist, aided by the Swedish geologist Birger Bohlin, the Chinese paleontologist Weng Chung Pei, and the German anthropologist Franz Weidenreich. The first well-preserved skull of an early human type in this region was discovered late in 1929, and within the next decade about fifty such skulls were recovered. This so-called Peking man (*Sinanthropus pekinensis*) is thought to have lived 450,000 years ago, being coeval with Heidelberg man.

The existence of early man in South Africa was demonstrated in 1921 when what has come to be known as Rhodesian man was exhumed and seems likely to have been an African example of the widely distributed Neanderthal race. Far more sensational and productive was the work carried on after 1936 by Robert Broom, curator of the National History Museum in Pretoria, aided by the paleontologist John Talbot Robinson and conferring occasionally with the great French authority, Henri Breuil. They carried on their work mainly at Sterkfontein, Swartkrans, and Krugersdorp near Johannesburg.

In 1936, Broom obtained from a construction worker at Sterkfontein most of the skull of what was then described as "the first of all human beings hitherto known to have lived on this earth." Several specimens were later recovered. Broom gave it the name *Plesianthropus* and it is estimated to have lived over 1,750,000 years ago. Two years later, in the Krugersdorp Valley, he obtained most of the skull, teeth, and other bones of what he called the Kromdraai man, or *Paranthropus*, estimated to have an age of one million years. In 1948 and 1949, Broom and Robinson (Broom died in 1951) discovered at Swartkrans what they called *Telanthropus capensis*, or the Swartkrans man. It was the earliest form of a truly proto-human type to be exhumed to that time, and it lived somewhere between 250,000 and 500,000 years before the early men of Java, Peking, and Heidelberg. As Herbert Wendt observes: "There is every indication that with his appearance toward the close of the Tertiary period a great stretch of the road leading to true humanity had been left behind."

No earlier researches into the physical origins of the human race have been as controversial as those carried on in Tuscany since 1956. Parts of more than fifty

---

1 All dates in this chapter are at best approximations. New fossil discoveries and the development of new dating techniques, especially in the field of radioactivity, have led to many conflicting interpretations.

skeletons, and some perfect ones, have been found in coal mines at the village of Baccinello. The subhuman type exhumed here has been studied in detail by Dr. Johannes Hurzeler of Basel, Switzerland, and Dr. William L. Strauss, Jr., of Johns Hopkins University. It has been called *Oreopithecus bambolii gervais* by Hurzeler.

The skeletal remains have been found in strata believed to be at least 12 million years old, thus being from six to ten times as old as any in which even semihuman types have previously been discovered. *Oreopithecus* exhibits more definitely human traits than any other type thus far exhumed. Dr. Strauss thus states the situation: "No matter how it is precisely classified, the most important thing about this creature is that it shows us that human characters had begun to make their appearance at least 12 million years ago. This is more than 11 million years earlier than any we have been able to find up to this time."

These recent Italian discoveries may push back the origins of man further than any previous estimates; their implications may also reveal the vast antiquity of the common ancestors of both present-day apes and man. As Dr. Hurzeler puts the matter: "Men and apes have a common ancestor ten times older than we thought, perhaps 60 to 70 million years back. At least 10 million years ago, manlike characteristics were in full swing." If we accept these interpretations, an estimate of 5 million years ago as a probable date of the appearance of definitely human types[2] is a restrained figure. This is ten times the antiquity of *Pithecanthropus,* long regarded as the oldest human type.

As controversial in its way as these Italian discoveries was the recent excavation of the oldest known man who had attained the tool-making stage—the earliest Paleolithic man—in East Africa. Christened *Zinjanthropus boisei*, he was discovered in July, 1959, near Nairobi in Tanganyika by the veteran British archaeologist, Louis S. B. Leakey, and assigned an age of 1,750,000 years.

We have now dealt with the discoveries related to establishing the simian or hominoid heritage of man and his evolution down to what are, in terms of evolution and physical anthropology, relatively recent times. The best-known and most widely distributed of later types of prehistoric man is what is known as Neanderthal man. Scores of skeletons of this type have been turned up, and their distribution extends from all over western Europe to the Middle East, central Asia (Uzbek), and Africa. The earliest of them may go back as far as 150,000 years, and the race disappeared apparently rather suddenly, about 25,000-30,000 years ago, possibly because competing types possessed better weapons or more brain power.

For a long time it was believed that the Neanderthals all but exclusively dominated the world of prehistoric man for nearly 100,000 years, but we now know that plenty of representatives of early Homo sapiens or modern man were living along with them and that there was surely much mixture of these types in the long period of time during which the Neanderthals held sway. Neanderthal man was short in stature, very heavily built, with low forehead and skull, heavy ridges over the eyes, and no chin.

2 This view is not shared by a majority of anthropologists.

By the time that the Neanderthal race disappeared, Homo sapiens had come to dominate the human scene. It was long believed that modern man appeared fairly suddenly, sweeping in rather mysteriously from either western Asia or northern Africa and quickly wiping out the Neanderthals. Many skeletons of this general type had been found, beginning with those discovered in the Cro-Magnon rock shelter in southwestern France in 1868. Hence, early examples of Homo sapiens were rather generally called Cro-Magnon man or the Cro-Magnon race. It was long believed that modern man put in his first appearance from 30,000 to 50,000 years ago.

More recent discoveries have upset all these earlier dogmas about the ancestry and advent of Homo sapiens. This type of man did not appear suddenly but developed gradually with perhaps as long an ancestry as the Neanderthal man. Indeed, some authorities think his remote origins may go back as far as the *Telanthropus*. His ancestry can surely be traced back as far as the Swanscombe man, discovered in a gravel pit at Swanscombe near London by Alvan T. Marston in 1935. This type is thought to have lived around 200,000 to 300,000 years ago. While showing many resemblances to the Neanderthal race, the Swanscombe man also had definite physical traits foreshadowing modern man. The same was true of the Steinheim man that had been found two years earlier at Steinheim, near Stuttgart, Germany, and was assigned an antiquity of less than 175,000 years. Another similar type was discovered in a cave at Fontéchevade in southwestern France in 1947. Believed to have lived at least 150,000 years ago, the Fontéchevade man bore an even closer resemblance to modern man. Further evolution took place between this time and the appearance of the Cro-Magnon peoples some 30,000-50,000 years ago.

The import of all this is that man is an animal who has developed like other animals by an evolutionary process, working through both the selective process and mutations, and that he slowly became progressively less apelike and more human. Man also became erect. Above all, his brain became larger and the cerebrum or frontal lobes of the brain—the thought centers—markedly increased in size.

III. PRELITERARY MATERIAL CULTURE

Our main interest is, naturally, not so much in the physical remains of early man as in his accomplishments. First of all, we must recall the vast time scale, as pointed out in the first chapter, against which we must project this drama.

For an understanding of preliterary history two points must be kept firmly in mind: (1) it has been fully established that, generally speaking, the sequence of culture has been roughly the same for all regions and peoples; and (2) although the races have, on the whole, developed along certain common lines, some groups in certain regions, for environmental or other reasons, advanced more rapidly than others. Some skipped entire cultural stages. Others suffered a catastrophic regression. "It is very likely," writes Professor Georges Renard, "that man first of all used shells, bones, stone, earth, and then, in the order mentioned, copper, bronze, and iron. But it is not right to speak of an age of stone, an age of bronze, an age of iron, unless particular care is taken to localize them, for it is quite certain that one people was still using stone instruments, while another had already learned the art of forging tools and weapons of metal. That can be easily proved. When towards the end of the eighteenth century Captain Cook landed at the Marquesas the natives were still in the stone age, while Europe had arrived at the machine age, and the age of steam and electricity."[3]

As for the Eolithic, or earliest Stone Age, we have nothing but rather dubious beginnings of work on the crudest of stone implements. In fact, this age is technically defined as the period when man did not make stone implements but used only those found in natural designs. There is no evidence that man knew how to strike a fire, that he wore clothing, or lived in human habitations. He must, indeed, have lived during this vast expanse of time much like his simian cousins. The definitive outline of culture in this age still awaits further knowledge. Were the flint stones dating from Eolithic times—which easily fit the hand, are adapted for use as hammers and knives, and are found by the hundreds in river and gravel beds—made by early man? Or were these "eoliths," as we call them, produced by nature alone and never worked by man?

If we are sure that eoliths are man-made, they become the first human tools of which we have any knowledge, since wood and bone implements, which man may have used before taking to stone, have perished. It was the interposition of tools between man and nature that, along with the mastery of articulate speech, marked man off from the rest of the animal world. This was probably the most momentous change in man's cultural life. He became *homo faber*. Hence it is clear that human achievement, on the material side, is mainly a record of progress in toolmaking. Tools have been his civilizing weapons. Yet the first tools, we may say, were the products not of thought, but of accident. Tools were *discovered* before they were *invented*. The epoch-making character of the provision of tools for the further cultural progress of man has been forcefully expressed by Franz Müller-Lyer, who links up the evolution of tools with the momentous progress in human handiness:

Primitive man brought with him into his new environment (a ground habitat) gregarious habits and prehensile hands. The hand, while being itself no tool, is yet the parent of all the most formidable and effective weapons and tools of to-day.

We have already remarked among animals elementary organization and a certain co-operative intelligence; in the same way we find primitive tools among them. Apes walk with the help of sticks, and fling stones, boughs, and prickly fruit on the heads of their enemies. With stones, too, they break nuts and open oysters. The chimpanzee builds himself a little hut out of tree trunks which is very similar to that of many savage men. Thus there exists among apes something like a "wood and stone age."

It was, however, quite other incentives that urged man forward to the use of tools in the course of evolution. Once having become a dweller on the ground, man walked on the soles of his feet like the bears, who easily raise themselves upright; the upper extremities were so differentiated as to be no longer of use for

3 G. F. Renard, *Life and Work in Prehistoric Times*, Knopf, 1929, pp. 13-14.

locomotion and were free to be adapted for new functions in addition to seizing and clinging. Having knocked nuts to pieces with a stone, it was only a small step forward to break other stones into any desired shape with it, and in this manner originated that famous primitive tool, the *coup de poing* of the French archaeologist.

This roughly hewn stone did duty as knife, saw, scraper, hammer, axe, and chisel, but naturally was not the best possible tool for any of these purposes. For this reason men improved it, as time went on, by adding a handle for fighters, teeth for a saw, and so on, until it was gradually differentiated into different tools for each work. In the same way the wrenched-off branch of the tree developed into sticks for throwing, digging or fighting, then into spears and clubs, and later into swords, bows and arrows, and oars and rudders.

The tool or weapon once established, the struggle for existence depended principally on its development, especially with regard to weapons of warfare. The hordes who first brandished the spear or the battleaxe could therewith beat off all others from the field, in spite of superior bodily strength. Thus the struggle for existence changed its sphere from the material to the intellectual; the survivors in the fight were those with the fittest intelligence, those who had elaborated the best weapons of offence and defence. Through the continual recurrence of these results by the development of the tool the minds of men were led to see the superiority of the quick inventive brain over rude force.

In fact, the era of the invention and perfection of the tool marks the most decisive change between the natural and the civilized man. As Noiré puts it: "A knife held in the hand works exactly like a natural organ as long as one needs it, and has the great advantage that, when done with, it can be put away or replaced with another implement." In fact, the hand that clasps a knife is practically another organ to the same hand that holds a paint brush, an auger, a drinking vessel, pen, hammer or pistol. In the hand man has thus a number of organs corresponding to the number of different tools he possesses. If all these tools were part of the physical anatomy, we should have a monstrosity like the Japanese goddess Kwannon, who holds a different object in each of her hundred hands.

Progressive evolution must necessarily leave the organic sphere at a certain point and gradually work along the lines of the processes of civilization. This inevitable transition has been brought about by the above-mentioned causes, and principally by the discovery of the tool, and indirectly by the tool of all tools—the hand.[4]

The fact that stone implements changed and improved in certain ways permits us to distinguish definite stages in preliterary man's advances in culture. In the Eolithic age man probably found most of his tools ready-made. In the Paleolithic and Neolithic periods they were man-made, and slowly but steadily improved in type, variety and finish.

In the Paleolithic age stone implements and weapons were made by knocking and pressing, and were therefore flaked or splintered. Paleolithic culture probably goes back some 600,000 years or more and ends about 15,000 years ago. This long period is divided into three stages: lower, middle, and upper Paleolithic.

4 Müller-Lyer, *History of Social Development*, pp. 54-56. Book II of this work is by far the most stimulating discussion of the role of tools in human cultural evolution.

Though man remained in this period scarcely more than a savage, Paleolithic times provided the true origins of human culture. Cultural advances were, to be sure, extremely slow and gradual. Some notable achievements must, however, be credited to early Paleolithic man, who lived in the last interglacial period mainly by preying on nature. Since the climate in this interglacial period was warm, shelters in natural forests and other protected spots were sufficient. He did not have to build himself a protective dwelling.

In the middle Paleolithic period, the fourth glacial invasion set in. Cold weather forced man to retreat to the caves. Here, perhaps because of custom and habit and also because of climate, many dwelt long after the ice sheet retired. So, during all the middle, and much of upper Paleolithic times, man was a cave dweller. The return of mild weather in the postglacial period made it possible to abandon caves in the final or upper Paleolithic period. A real beginning was made in constructing artificial habitations. Towards the end of the upper Paleolithic era there is evidence of crude huts and shelters.

But there were no agriculture, no domestic animals, except for the dog, who may have domesticated himself, no textiles, and no pottery. Paleolithic man hunted and fished and gathered fruits, roots, berries, and nuts. His only true industries were stone chipping, bone and horn work, and clothes made of animal skins. His chief weapon was the *coup de poing,* or "fist hatchet," which was almond-shaped, about four to ten inches long, three inches wide, one inch thick, with one edge sharper than the others. It could be used as an ax, hammer, knife, scraper, dagger, or awl. An examination of the tools of the middle Paleolithic era shows a much higher skill in flaking—the result perhaps of the new leisure and security man enjoyed while living in caves. In the upper Paleolithic age an abundance of bone and horn tools appear. What early Paleolithic man did with his dead we do not know. Perhaps he gave them formal burial. Only when man retreated to the caves, in the middle Paleolithic age, do we begin to find evidence of human burial.

During the upper Paleolithic period Homo sapiens appeared in Europe. Tools became more varied, more skillfully made. Men began to pay more attention to the adornment of life. There was a concern for the dead, who were buried, as during the middle Paleolithic period, with their tools and implements. Sometimes the bones were stripped of flesh, the skeleton painted red and placed in a flat position on the ground—apparent evidence of the origins of a belief in immortality.

A great cultural revolution occurred in this period. Man learned to make a fire probably by rubbing together two pieces of wood. Fire had surely been used long before this time, but man could now create it. He need no longer wait for the lightning to kindle one, or the hot craters to erupt. The advance from the stage of merely keeping a fire going, to that of lighting a fire, was an enormous stride ahead for humanity. For primitive man fire meant much more than civilized man can imagine. It meant light, heat, protection, and later, it meant that metals could be smelted, and that a new stage in culture might be reached—the metal age. Müller-Lyer has graphically summarized the origins of fire and its significance for the cultural history of the race:

The knowledge of the kindling of fire may be considered as the last great achievement of the primitive age. The evolution of speech and of tools apparently proceeded simultaneously, but the knowledge of the kindling and control of fire must have been acquired considerably later, as it needed great care and complicated labour for its achievement.

Its discovery is probably explained in the following way:

All primitive peoples in manufacturing their wood or stone implements bore holes in them by rotating a pointed wooden stick for hours on end.

In this whirling movement, at which primitive man possesses a dexterity and skill which amazes Europeans, it not infrequently happens that the wood-dust in the hole catches fire from the heat generated by the friction. If these sparks are allowed to fall on dried moss and carefully tended, the whole can be kindled into flame.

Considerable support is given to this theory by the fact that among nearly all primitive people the art of kindling fire is almost identical, that is by rubbing, boring or twirling two pieces of wood; many tribes make use of a bow-shaped instrument to turn the drill. In many places also the first fire may have been supplied by volcanic agency. The glowing lava is utilized to this day by the inhabitants of Oceania for cooking. It is possible, too, that some races discovered fire by the beating together of ferruginous stones. "Fire-beating" is occasionally practised yet by the Terra-del-Fuegians and the Eskimos, who are still in a low stage of culture.

It is almost more difficult to give a reason why man should undertake all the trouble of kindling and keeping a fire in those early ages than to guess how he discovered it. Since the original home of man certainly was not in the frigid zone, warmth could not have been the chief desideratum. Still less could it be its service for cooking, for uncivilized man possesses a very conservative appetite, and shrinks from anything to which he has not been accustomed from his youth up. The destructive power of fire was only realized later, when men hollowed out the trunks of trees with it, and used prairie fires to drive away wild animals. Probably the most attraction was its light, the magic witchery of the flickering, fork-tongued flames, all yellow, red and blue, which consumed everything offered to them, while they whirled upward like things of life. The children of today, as in the childhood of our race, have bonfires simply for the pleasure of looking at them. Especially in the gloom of night the illuminating power must have been very acceptable, and all the more so when it was seen that lions, tigers and other wild beasts shrank away from it in unconquerable fear.

The charm that fire first exercised over man was largely due to the joy in light and terror of darkness that is still evident in our children, and that even our higher civilization cannot totally destroy. This is illustrated by the fine verses in Goethe's *Faust,* and the opinion is confirmed by the philosopher Geiger, who says: "It is not the beneficent results of fire, nor its warmth, which, according to available records, was appreciated in early ages, but its lustre, its red glow; and so far as linguistic designations can be explained with certainty, it is neither its warmth nor its powers of burning, wasting, or of giving pain that provided a name for it, but the glow of red colour. The idea of colour is the oldest that attracted men to fire." [5]

5 Müller-Lyer, *op. cit.,* pp. 56-57.

What, then, had man achieved by the dawn of the Neolithic (New Stone) era? He possessed a considerable variety of tools in several materials, especially stone and bone. He controlled fire, cooked food, wore skin clothing, and lived in settled habitations.'He had some sort of social order, ideas of law, justice, and religion. Perhaps the most striking accomplishments of Paleolithic man were his cave paintings and sculptures, to which we shall devote some attention later. The increment of his material culture was pitifully small, judged by our lofty contemporary standards, but it must be remembered that the initial stages of civilization are the hardest to negotiate.[6] Culture marches on in mathematical progression. It required nearly 100,000 years for man to learn how to bore a hole through a *coup de poing,* put a handle in it, and make an ax of it. Today the whole face of material civilization may be changed by inventions in a single generation.

In the next period, the Ncolithic age, man's advances were infinitely more extensive, but not more impressive than in the metal ages which followed on its heels.

Just how and when the Paleolithic age ended and the Neolithic began is impossible to tell. One probably shaded into the other. Some authorities say that the Paleolithic era is common to all early human history, while the Neolithic is a specifically western phenomenon. Such questions are hard to decide. The evidence is as yet insufficient. There seems to have been a definite intermediary stage between Paleolithic and Neolithic times, called Mesolithic. Its striking cultural characteristics were many small and finely chipped tools called microliths, or pygmy flints.

The Neolithic age began about 15,000 B.C. and ended with the Copper Age. The latter emerged at different times in different places: in Egypt, for example, about 4000 B.C.; in Scandinavia and Britain about 2000 B.C.

The bow and arrow made their appearance early in the Neolithic era, greatly simplifying the food problem. Instead of getting up close to an animal and hacking him to death with a club or stone, or spearing him with a harpoon, one could more safely shoot him down from a distance. The neolithic hunter could kill a bird on the wing, a fleeing deer, a charging tiger, as it sped along. The large hewn-stone ax also appeared in this age, smoothly ground, polished and equipped with a handle. Knives became smoother, and skillfully designed and finished.

But most important, most wonderful, of all, man learned to turn up the ground and to extract some of his food from the soil. Hitherto, he had subsisted mainly on animal flesh and on natural tree-grown or plant-grown products. Now he raised a crop, "tamed" the wild growing grain, and learned to irrigate the soil in a crude way. Neolithic man was acquainted with barley, wheat, millet, peas, lentils, beans, fruit, and flax. He had no animal-drawn plows at first, but cut down branches and logs and whittled them into finely-pointed sticks, dug holes in the ground and grubbed up the sod—the so-called hoe culture.

In this era man also domesticated the common animals. Perhaps this did not come about until he had learned to build a stationary home, clear a piece of

6 The best development of this point remains chap. iii of L. H. Morgan, *Ancient Society,* Holt, 1877.

land, and establish a "farm." Since the soil supplied him with grain, fruits, and vegetables, he no longer had to roam the forests in order to slay elusive animals. Certain beasts like cattle, sheep, swine, goats, were tamed and bred. Man learned to milk cows and goats and fleece the sheep. In time, cattle were yoked together and put to work.

Paleolithic man dressed in crude animal skins, threaded together by strings of beaten bark. Neolithic man wore woven cloth made chiefly of flax and wool. Paleolithic man lived mainly in caves. Neolithic man learned to dig foundations, hew logs, erect walls, raise a roof, and even attempt some kind of interior decoration. He constructed pit dwellings, wattle huts, and many became lake dwellers. Villages were built in lakes on long wooden platforms, with houses bunched together and supported by thousands of piles. This was perhaps the most remarkable of all material advances in the Neolithic era, since it involved a high degree of cooperative labor and a well-developed social consciousness.

Burial now became more formal and elaborate. At first, man raised a mound of earth to indicate a burial. Later he built a "dolmen," a chamber of large upright stones, topped with a flat-lying rock, whose entrance was usually closed by a large loose stone. The whole was covered with earth. Tremendous megalithic monuments, as at Stonehenge, in England, were erected.

Mining and trade were carried on; barter prevailed, but shell money was also used. Property rights developed. Man ceased to be a nomad, settled down to a fixed existence, and began to take on a sense of stability. As early as 4240 B.C.— before the age of metals began—the Egyptians appear to have worked out a quasi-solar calendar of 365 days to a year. Fear of the spirits of the supernatural world produced a system of religious rites and beliefs. Medicine and surgery of a crude kind were practiced. Man not only spoke fluently, but was on his way to learn how to write. He expressed himself in crude pictograms, which eventually became an alphabet.

Following Neolithic times, copper and bronze gradually took the place of stone as the material basis of human artifacts. But this does not mean that stone implements were entirely given up. There was a natural reluctance to abandon a material which had been utilized and venerated for perhaps a half-million years.

It is surprising that iron should not have been the first metal used. Yet, the evidence points to the fact that in most areas man used copper to manufacture his first metal implements. This, we may note, does not mean that there was any universal copper age. In some places man may have known how to make bronze objects, but because he had little tin, he had to use copper. Copper needles, beads, and bracelets are found in Egypt before 4000 B.C. By 3500 B.C., Egyptians were systematically mining the copper deposits in the peninsula of Sinai. Copper culture probably preceded bronze in Italy, England, Scandinavia and Hungary.

The true bronze industry may have originated about 2500 B.C. in the Aegean Islands where there was a natural ore already containing a mixture of copper and tin. In bronze artifacts, man turned out a harder metal than he had ever used before. His weapons became sharper, more deadly. Bronze seems to have come into great demand once its advantages were realized. Sources of tin are rather rare, hence extensive search had to be made for them. This fact probably accounts for the origin of extended commerce. People wandered from the Near East all over Europe—as far as Britain—mainly to discover supplies of tin.

The Bronze Age reached Europe somewhere around 2500 B.C. and persisted till about 1000 B.C. Most of ancient Egyptian, Babylonian, and Cretan achievements were worked out in the Bronze Age. All sorts of articles, both practical and ornamental, were made with this pliant metal. During the earlier part of the Bronze Age man also learned to sail vessels over large bodies of water, developed the art of writing, invented the potter's wheel, developed the plow, and began to wage war on a large and destructive scale. In certain places like Mesopotamia, Egypt, and Crete, he erected imposing buildings. In Switzerland he continued to maintain lake dwellings, and in Gaul pit villages, though the latter began to rise from the ground, contained a thatched roof and had circular clay-plastered walls.

As with other metals, we do not know how iron first came to be used. In Egypt it may have been known as early as bronze, though not widely used at first. Africa with its rich iron deposits never, except for Egypt, had a bronze age. Some students believe that iron metallurgy originated in central Africa and thence spread to western Asia and Europe. We do not know, then, exactly where and when iron was discovered. The Hittites, around 1300 B.C., were working iron deposits on the shores of the Black Sea in Asia Minor. In the thirteenth century B.C. Rameses II asked for a shipment of iron ore to Egypt. A century and a half later iron was used in many places along the Mediterranean. Manufacture of iron in Europe probably began about 1000 B.C. By this time crude smelting furnaces were in existence and a considerable quantity of iron tools from this era have been found. Iron did not displace bronze at once. Bronze, copper, and iron were in many cases used simultaneously. In fact, many parts of the civilized world are still in the Iron Age; there are some races which have not yet reached it.

With iron, tools became infinitely more varied, more durable, and sturdier. We do not have space here to enumerate all the material changes in culture accompanying the introduction of iron implements and weapons. Some of the main changes were the introduction of metallic money (currency), better wheeled vehicles, and more solid dwellings. Iron was used for clamps to bind doorposts and foundations, as well as for hinges. Late in the Iron Age bronze disappeared almost entirely in Europe, except for ornamentation. The wheel was used to make pottery, and a hand-operated rotating mill in grinding grain. Iron plowshares replaced wooden plows. Urban centers flourished. Industry grew by leaps and bounds. Warfare received a great impetus. The Hittites and Assyrians owed their military success in large part to iron weapons, more deadly than those of bronze and copper. As Robert Briffault says: "The chief association of iron is with blood. The coming of the men who wielded metal swords and overthrew the great neolithic culture of Europe marked the final enthronement of physical force and oppression in human society."

By the end of the preliterary era it was apparent that civilization in the Eastern

Hemisphere was headed northward and westward, from Egypt and Mesopotamia to the northern Mediterranean. Civilization first took hold along river valleys, then became seagoing, and, finally, oceanic and world-wide. Before the preliterary epoch closed, the dominant European races—Mediterranean, Nordic, and Alpine types—were not only in evidence but permanently settled in Europe. By this time most of the tools and crude machines that were to prevail until the industrial revolution of the eighteenth century, had been invented. The institution of the family was well established, kinship groupings had appeared, and in some areas rudimentary political life had been established. Economic institutions were taking form. Pastoralism and agrarianism were well developed. Religion, art, spoken language and the pictogram had put in their appearance.

It is not possible to say when recorded or historical civilization began for the West as a whole. By 4000 B.C. Egypt had reached the cultural stage that we call civilization. At this time the Grecian islands, not far away, were inhabited by a people in a low stage of barbarism, and the golden age of Greece did not arrive until about 450 B.C. In 450 B.C. the Teutonic tribes to the north were still in a pre-civilized state.

The vital fact is that around 4000 B.C. man—after several million years on the planet—had mastered the art of writing and could set down literary records. For the purposes of historical writing the ability to record events is all-important. For the life and culture of the race it had less, even if very great, significance. This distinction must be kept in mind as the story of European civilization unfolds.

IV. THE EVOLUTION OF THE HUMAN MIND

In that long expanse of time between *Pithecanthropus erectus* and Homo sapiens —roughly estimated at over half a million years—man's mind as well as his body changed to a marked degree.

As man's habits became more complex and the stimuli to which he was forced to respond became more numerous, there was a selective advantage to having a larger brain. Evidence of such increase in brain size is afforded by the skulls of fossil man. Beginning with *Pithecanthropus erectus* and coming down through the Peking man, Swanscombe man and the like to Homo sapiens, we find the brain case becoming relatively larger and the front of the skull rising. This would seem to indicate that the brain of man has become larger during the process of specifically human evolution and that the cerebrum and frontal lobes, which are related most directly to intelligence, have also grown in size and power.

What bearing does this conclusion have on the psychology of man as he treks his arduous way upward from quasi-bestial life to civilization—from the *Australopithecinae* to the Cro-Magnon? It is implied that there has been evolution in mental patterns as well as in the physiological structure of the brain. Dr. G. E. Partridge, unfolding the sweeping panorama of mental evolution, as conceived of by Granville Stanley Hall, illuminates for us this aspect of history:

The fundamental fact and principle of this biological philosophy is that mind and body have evolved together in the race, and have developed together in the individual, in one continuous process. Not only, therefore, must all mental facts be understood in terms of, or with reference to, physical aspects, but must be studied in relation to the whole history of the race. This evolutionary principle must be applied to all problems of psychology, until we have a complete natural history of the mind. . . .

Genetic psychology assumes as an ultimate fact, and as a background for all its principles, an endless process of time, stretching out into an infinitely remote past and pointing towards an infinitely remote future. Every thing, and every event, must be regarded as the completion of an infinitely long process of development, in terms of which it can be explained; and also as germinal of a future, of which it is in turn to be the cause or genetic origin. Development and change are continuous and unbroken. Nothing is stationary, and man himself is in a stage of active evolution toward a higher form. . . .

The mind stretches far beyond the limited experiences of the individual. It contains within itself all the past and all the future. It has grown up in the race, step by step, and has passed through stages as different from its present form as we can possibly conceive. It is so vastly complex that it is never twice alike in the same individual, nor are ever two minds the same. It is a product of millions of years of struggle. Its long experiences with light and darkness, and with heat and cold, have established many of its rhythms. A long apprenticeship in aquatic and arboreal life has left deep and indelible marks. Sky, wind, storm, flowers, animals, ancient industries and occupations, have directed its fears and affections, and have made the emotions what they now are. It has been shocked and moulded into its present form by labour and suffering, and it shows in every function the marks of the process through which it has passed. Although it is by far the most wonderful work of nature it is still very imperfect, full of scars and wounds, incompletely co-ordinated, and but poorly controlled; in many ways ill-adapted to the practical situations of life. In it barbaric and animal impulses are still felt. Its old forms appear at every turn; and every trait of mind, as well as of body, is full of indications of its origin. So close, indeed, is the past to the present in all we think and feel, that without referring to what has gone before in the race, the human mind, as we know it, is utterly unintelligible and mysterious; while many, if not most, of its mysteries become clear, when the mind is studied with reference to its past.

This point of view is essential for any introduction into the science of psychology. Only thus may one grasp the significance of mind in the world, and be prepared to interpret the common facts of everyday life. One must see that only by studying mind objectively, in its racial manifestations, and in many individuals, can any conception of its range, depth, and meaning be attained. An individual mind is but an infinitesimal fragment and expression of all the soul life in the world. . . .

Such is the conception of man that results from the work of Darwin. His mind is to be regarded as quite as much an offspring of animal life as is his body. The same principles may be applied to both, and both must be investigated by similar inductive methods. . . 7

7 G. E. Partridge, *The Genetic Philosophy of Education*, Macmillan, 1912, pp. 14-28.

V. SOME TRAITS OF PRIMITIVE MENTALITY

Keeping these basic concepts of mental evolution clearly in mind, we may now turn to a brief discussion of the character of the thinking of primitive man.

We have no specific and demonstrable products of truly primitive thinking because, obviously, there were no writings in that age. We can only get some inkling of the primitive mind from observing the thinking of existing primitives who are fully developed in innate mental power—that is, who are representative of Homo sapiens but have not crossed the threshold of civilization.

In discussing the mind of primitive man we are treading on thin ice and few topics of discussion produce more errors or misrepresentations than the attempt to compare primitive and civilized thinking. These misconceptions arise from two basic fallacies. First, most men living in the twentieth century believe that they are civilized by virtue of this fact alone. Secondly, it is assumed that primitive man had a rudimentary and undeveloped brain and was organically incapable of complex thinking.

Perhaps the Neanderthal man, who lived 75,000 or more years ago, had an underdeveloped brain, but Cro-Magnon man who appeared 30,000 to 50,000 years ago, had as good a native mental endowment as we of the twentieth century. As Professor Boas points out, primitive man's mind is not organically inferior to ours. What we have that he does not is a greater accumulation of positive knowledge.

Practically speaking, the primitive mentality is dominated by comparative ignorance, and by a type of attitude we call superstitious, from which the civilized and educated man of today is relatively emancipated. Primitive man also lacks the mental discipline which comes from some training in logic. Consequently, his imagination is more or less unrestrained. He creates and believes in a great number of mythologies. He tries to control nature by magic—that is, by incantations, prayers, rituals, and festivals. Such intellectual advances as civilized man has made have been achieved mainly through release from such naïveté.

But it must not be assumed that primitive man's thinking was all magic and superstition. He could certainly observe nature, and learn from his observations.

The simple objects he invented—his tools, weapons, boats, for instance, or the process of transforming copper and tin into bronze (thousands of instances could be given)—prove that he knew something about cause and effect. To adopt for the moment Professor Goldenweiser's conception of a dual mentality in primitive times—a craft mind and an intuitive mind—we may say that with respect to manifestations of craft mind primitive man gave much evidence of a matter-of-factness and of capacity for cause-and-effect reasoning.

Grant primitive man his premises and he could often draw logical conclusions. He was by no means so absolutely devoid of logic as philosophers like Lucien Lévy-Bruhl have imagined. It is well to remember, as Goldenweiser observes, that "supernaturalism as a system of ideas is in itself perfectly reasonable. When the limitation of knowledge and the theoretical naïveté of aboriginal men are taken

into consideration the unconscious conclusions or hypotheses reached by him with
reference to the world of things and beings are well-nigh inevitable."[8] Altogether
too much stress has been laid on primitive man's mysticism and too little on his
solid scientific achievements in crafts and industries.

If we look rather broadly at the matter of human thinking since we acquired
our present brain equipment, the following facts will become clear. What we call
human culture is essentially an extraorganic or superorganic mechanism employed
by man to control his life and living: i.e., his environment and himself. Primitive
man was unable to exercise a real and direct control over much of his environment because of the undeveloped character of his culture, especially in its technological aspects. Therefore, he was compelled to employ symbolic, that is, fictional, rather than factual means to exercise control over his life and surroundings. This symbolic and fictional system of control is what we call supernaturalism. Primitive man's great mistake, though of course an unavoidable error in
those days, lay in his failure to recognize that it was only a "make-believe" type
of control. Supernaturalism has been outgrown when and as technological progress made possible control in terms of fact instead of fiction. The tool has thus
been, quite literally, the source of new ideas and philosophies.

This may be illustrated by many ready examples. The irrigation engineer has
killed more rain gods and rain magic than all the skeptical philosophers of history.
The telescope, spectroscope, and the like have been the destroyers of the astronomy
of primitive man, of Genesis and of Joshua, by providing factual rather than
fictional conceptions of the astral regions. The microscope, the test tube, and
pathology have revolutionized our ideas of the nature and origin of disease. We
need no longer attribute disease to the wrath of God, malicious magic, or the violation of a taboo. Nor need we have recourse to sorcerers to effect a cure. The
increasing technological control of our environment has rendered many theologies
obsolete. When the further development of industrialism makes possible the complete factual control of our social life, other forms of supernaturalism will disappear.

The rejection of supernatural premises—a process called "secularization"—was
begun by certain Greek and Roman philosophers and has been carried on with
varying fortunes down to our own day. Formal logic was created by the Greeks
and brought to its most intensive development by late medieval theologians. Our
scientific knowledge, begun by the Greeks, has been accumulated mainly since the
thirteenth century.

The ratiocination of a modern scholar like Bertrand Russell or John Dewey,
when contrasted with primitive thinking, is characterized by: (1) a rejection of
the theory of supernatural causation, (2) strict adherence to logical reasoning, and
(3) the possession of a large body of scientific knowledge.

From the intellectual standpoint, then, a man is a modern if he thinks in a
logical fashion and acquires his information through the inductive methods of
observation and experimentation. Insofar as he believes in supernatural causation,
thinks illogically, and does not rely upon scientifically ascertained facts, his think-

8 Alexander Goldenweiser, *Early Civilization*, Knopf, 1922, pp. 410-11.

ing is of a primitive cast, whether he be a graduate of a leading American university in the second third of the twentieth century or an illiterate Australian bushman.

When judged by these criteria, a majority of Europeans and Americans still think much as primitive man did. They simply have a larger stock of information.

It should be kept constantly in mind that one of the fundamental characteristics of human history is that the culture of one era carries over into another. Traits from early periods of civilization linger on into the very latest one. This applies not only to technological achievements but even more to mental habits. There is, for instance, probably no more persistent trait than belief in supernaturalism. It is doubtful that there has ever been a mind entirely free from supernatural leanings. Even in our most brilliant scientific workers there are "vestigial remains" of supernaturalism which come to the fore during individual, social, or intellectual crises. William James's reaction to his experience in the San Francisco earthquake is a good example. The interest shown by a noted scientist in psychic research after he had lost a son in the first World War affords another striking illustration.

The evidences of primitivism in our daily lives are so numerous that, if we think about them, the intellectual distance since preliterary culture seems strangely foreshortened. It is only necessary to catalog a brief list of primitive beliefs which are common property today to realize the powerful hold of primitive thinking on modern society. We shall illustrate this fact a little later by listing some of the more obvious vestiges of primitive religious ideas in our present-day culture.

In summary, it may be well to call to mind the fact that primitive man's brain capacity was not inferior to ours after Homo sapiens appeared. He had considerable capacity for craftsmanship. He also developed many of the social institutions of civilized society. Primitive society was, however, ruled by a rigorous tyrant—custom—which retarded the expression of intellectual independence. Custom kept preliterary man uncritical, and, indeed, it still hangs like a millstone around our necks. In that respect we are still struggling upwards towards an emancipated civilization.

Yet, we must not forget that custom also had a constructive function to perform, especially in primitive society. From the point of view of society it is not so much a millstone as a flywheel. It stabilizes the functioning of the social machinery and keeps it from flying to pieces. Society and the individual frequently have antithetical interests. In such cases, custom may be said to be an evil from the individual's standpoint, but an indispensable advantage to society.

VI. RELIGION IN PRIMITIVE LIFE

It is almost impossible to exaggerate the tremendous role that religion played in the life of primitive man. His conception of the universe rested almost entirely upon supernatural hypotheses. To him knowledge and religion were almost identical. Few of the important daily activities, whether business or recreational, were engaged in except under proper religious auspices. Primitive industry was mainly applied religion. For instance, among the Todas religion centers around their herds of buffalo and dairy activities. Their whole dairy industry is controlled by religion and magical rites. Much time and trouble were devoted by primitive men to propitiating the gods associated with agriculture and industry. Even as late as Roman times, agriculture became a round of religious rituals; there were forty-five holy days a year devoted to placating or venerating agrarian deities. Among the Jews, Yahweh was originally a pastoral god who protected and fertilized their animals. Religion and industry thus went hand in hand among early peoples. So did politics, warfare, and most social activities depend on religion. Social customs were supposed to have been handed down by the gods. Primitive education was scarcely more than initiation into supernatural mysteries.

In brief, the life of early man is cradled in mystery, and matured in the supernatural. The gods attend his birth, safeguard his youth, preside at every milestone of his existence, adolescence, initiation into manhood, marriage, sickness, and death. They shower him with their favors or crush him with their malice. Everything in primitive life is wrapped in supernaturalism. The sun is a god—the Greeks called him Phoebus Apollo, and he was drawn around the heavens in a magnificent chariot. The moon is a goddess—the Greeks called her Artemis. The rivers, forests, winds, waves, flowers are invested with human attributes. The earth and all its phenomena have indwelling secret spirits, invisible, palpable, kind, ferocious, malignant. The primitive mind invests these spirits with romance and drama, with comedy and tragedy. It accumulates a mythology. The popular mythology of Greece, with which we are familiar—perhaps one of the most beautiful and attractive—is paralleled in part among even primitive tribes.

So powerful is the mystical or religious aspect of the preliterate mind that in many respects civilization advances only in the degree to which man frees himself from the spell of the supernatural, puts away his animism, taboos, fetishes, totems —as a growing child puts away its toys—and relies upon his intellect and observations to interpret the varying manifestations of nature and the activities of his own psyche.

How did the supernatural first enter man's mental world? The daily routine of primitive existence left many desires unfulfilled, many questions unanswered about nature and the human psyche. The supernatural hypothesis stepped in, made man feel more at home with nature, provided him with an answer to such simple and yet such difficult questions as: Why does the wind blow? Why does the sun race around the heavens? What makes lightning strike? What causes shadows, images, dreams? What brings on strong bodily sensations, particularly those associated with hunger and sex?

Modern man, equipped with knowledge of the sciences, is able to give a convincing naturalistic explanation of practically everything which puzzled primitive man. We know why water flows, why rocks are dislodged from their natural foundations and crash down hillsides, why the wind blows, what sends the rain down into the ground and stimulates the growth of foliage, why the rivers become raging torrents, what causes bodily changes, and what produces stirring and pleasant sensations when one comes in contact with an attractive person of the opposite sex. Primitive man had to have recourse to the supernatural hypothesis to find plausible explanations of all these—and many other problems.

Goldenweiser divides religious experience into three major phases: (1) the emotional thrill which comes from communion with the supernatural world and from contact with its occult powers; (2) the emotional satisfactions which come from participation in religious ritual, chiefly through worship and the invocation of magic; and (3) the intellectual satisfactions derived from theology, viewed as the conceptional side of religion—the "reasoning out" of the mysteries of supernaturalism.

Primitive man, thus being unable to detect, as we can, the secret workings of nature, and also unable to unravel nature's laws, faced nature with a question mark. This question mark stimulated the production of an endless source of thrill-producing mysteries in the form of supernatural fictions.

Out of the basic hypothesis of a potent mysterious force which creates, controls and replenishes the world arose ghost worship, animal worship, phallic worship, and the worship of nearly all the commonplace phenomena of nature. At the outset, the mysterious essence or force, which was believed to create and guide the world, was not individualized or personified. It was looked upon as a generalized impersonal power which accounted for the activities of the sun, moon, stars, waters, winds, and men. It was believed responsible for a wide range of experiences in savage life.

The name now given to the impersonal supernatural power which furnished the raw material out of which human religion evolved is *mana*—a term applied to it by the natives of Melanesia, among whom such a concept was first discovered by Bishop R. H. Codrington in 1891. Other primitive tribes recognize this vague but tremendous power under the name of *manitou* (Algonquin Indians), *orenda* (Iroquois Indians), *wakan* (Sioux Indians), and so on. The gradual emergence of a belief in spirits from the concept of mana is well exemplified by the Algonquins. Their *manitou* is capable of either a personal or an impersonal interpretation. Religion in this first period of supernaturalism has been called *animatism* by Professor R. R. Marett.

Inevitably, the savage mind in time visualized this supernatural power in terms of man's own daily life and human relationships—where personalities prevail. Once man took this step, he was well on his way to the creation of the personnel and machinery of religion—spirits, gods, devils, and organized cults.

The next stage of religious development has been called *animism*—or the belief that individualized supernatural spirits rule and control the natural world. Once man had invented the world of personified spirits the framework of religion was well laid down. It was only a logical step to assume that most pleasant and beneficial things come through the aid of good spirits, and disasters from evil spirits. In this way the supernatural world was divided into the two contending camps of benevolent and wicked deities.

On earth, early historic man was familiar with established social ranks. Certain classes were servile, others aristocratic. Certain ones were generous and noble, others mean and wicked. These categories were projected into the current interpretation of the gods. Hence, there arose a hierarchy of spirits. Some of the early historic races imagined that the supernatural world is controlled by a supreme benevolent spirit—God. He is continually assailed by a supreme evil spirit—Satan. Each has a host of underlings (angels or devils) fighting for his cause and obeying him as servants obey their master.

Religious thought has rarely, if ever, gone beyond this conception of a hierarchy of good and evil spirits. No great religious system ever developed into a literally pure monotheism. None has ever gone so far as to imagine a supreme God, absolutely isolated, without angels and underlings, alone controlling this vast universe.

Out of this polytheism came an elaborate mythology. Since he was not hampered by considerations of exact scientific knowledge or formal logic, primitive man could ramble on from one absurd fancy to another.

The elevation of this notion of a hierarchy of good and evil spirits into a grand cosmological philosophy, representing the universe as an arena in which the principles of good and evil fought it out until good finally prevailed, was the product of Persian theology, a matter which we shall deal with later.

Along with the hypothesis of a dynamic, creative and all-pervading supernaturalism, primitive man brought into being our ideas of a human soul and human immortality.

The primitive belief in animism implied that all nature including man is animate, that is, possesses a spirit or soul. There seemed to be special evidence to support the idea of a human soul. Man could see his image reflected in a pool of water. He might hear the echo of his voice. He had dreams in which his body seemed to undergo definite experiences and to move from the spot. Yet, on awakening, the body appeared not to have moved. Indeed, some primitive peoples have exceeded the Christians in the matter of postulating a human soul, for they have believed in a plurality of souls.

Closely related to this notion of a soul or spiritual self has been the belief in immortality, of which we have plenty of evidence among primitive peoples—not only among existing primitives but in the burial practices of extinct preliterate peoples. But they rarely believed in a purely spiritual immortality. They shared the orthodox Christian notion of a bodily resurrection. The grounds for the primitive belief in immortality were such things as the notion of a spiritual self which might survive death, the imagery and philosophy growing out of dream experiences, and the rationalized will to eternal existence, whether of the individual or of his relatives and friends.

The notion of rewards and punishments after death was a natural outgrowth of primitive moral codes, with their ideas of compensation, and of the hypothesis of good and evil spirits controlling life after death as well as life on this earth. This conviction grew gradually, but the historical philosophies connected with the elaborate conceptions of heaven and hell maintained by Christians, Muslims and the like were, as we shall see, mainly a Persian contribution.

The activational or behavioristic side of primitive religious experience falls into two categories, namely, magic and worship. A number of the older anthropologists, particularly Sir J. G. Frazer, were inclined to distinguish magic from religion and to represent magic as primitive science. No reputable anthropologist any longer entertains this view of the matter.

Magic is that phase of primitive religious behavior which is devoted chiefly to the immediate realization of certain desired ends or objects. Primitive man imagined that he could gain his ends by coercing the gods according to a definite ritualistic contract that the gods had supposedly revealed and to which they had voluntarily agreed. If these occult formulas were accurately complied with, then the gods, according to the theory of magic, would hand over the desired results to the group. It was even believed by some primitive peoples that these wished-for objects might be obtained, even without the participation of the gods, by virtue of the very potency of the magic rites themselves.

Worship, as distinguished from magic, is the ritualistic and ceremonial expression of man's attitude of awe, reverence, humility, and gratitude with respect to the supernatural world and its dominating powers.

In both early and modern religious behavior, magic and worship have usually been extensively intertwined rather than sharply differentiated, though it is probably going too far to describe magic as the technique of primitive religion. Some writers, especially the eminent French anthropologists Hubert and Mauss, have insisted that the chief difference between magic and worship is that magic is regarded as the bad, or socially disapproved, aspect of religious practices, while worship includes the socially proper manifestations of religious life.

Such a distinction can scarcely be maintained. Magic, by its very nature, had to be more occult, private, and technical than worship, but this does not mean that it was socially taboo. Certain pagan magical practices brought over into Christianity frequently had to be executed under cover, but these were very special cases. The notion, therefore, that magic is bad, or "black," is a late historical view, deeply colored by Christian prejudices. Such a conception rarely prevailed in primitive society. There, magic was distinguished from worship primarily by its more practical and coercive character.

We have traced the evolution of the belief in supernatural power, the rise of a belief in spirits and a spiritual world, the imaginative creation of divisions and hierarchies in the spiritual world, and the modes of approaching these spirits. We may now profitably examine a little more in detail the evolution of gods in primitive and protohistorical cultures.

The traditional notion of the relation between man and God is that man was made by God in his own image. The historical truth would seem to be exactly the reverse. Man has made gods to conform to his own physical image, as well as to his mental imagery. As with religion, in general, so with the deities in particular. Early man accounted for the mysteries of earth by inventing a supernatural realm. He then peopled the heavens and earth with spirits. The gods were no more than such glorified spirits. The whole supernaturalistic structure —the gods, their life and doings—is simply a reflex of the real world—topographically, occupationally, technologically, and the like. Dr. J. H. Dietrich summarizes the evolution of gods out of earlier animistic beliefs in this way:

The recognition of the importance of some spirits over others, in connection with the gradual understanding of certain natural processes, led men to departmentalize and organize their deities, instead of ascribing a spirit to each and every object. Things are grouped together, and one god is thought to preside over a whole group. For example, they no longer think of a spirit in each tree, but of a spirit presiding over all the trees—the god of the forest; there is no longer a spirit in each stream but a god of streams; no longer a god of each sea, but a god of the seas. This stage of thought is best exemplified in the religion of the Greeks and the Romans.

By this time, man had developed a highly organized family and social life and this was carried over into the realm of the gods; so that the gods were related, and special functions and responsibilities assigned to each, and the importance of the god or goddess determined by the importance of the function. Man had also by now attained a much higher degree of culture and there came to be gods of the thought and emotional world, such as the goddess of wisdom and the goddess of love. Thus arose twelve major deities and the countless minor divinities of the pagan world, forming a well-organized pantheon of gods and goddesses.[9]

Man has a tendency to create gods to preside over all the experiences of vital importance to the individual and the group. Consequently, the number and character of the gods devised by any people depend upon the emotional experiences of the members of that group. Some experiences are universal, such as fertility, hunger, life and death, and the like. Therefore, we find certain universal deities among the gods of every race. Many experiences, because of specific differences in geographical environment and the resulting occupations, are common only to particular peoples. This accounts for wide variations in the nature and function of tribal and national deities.

All we can say in the way of a sweeping generalization is that wherever in early civilization there was an emotional experience of great importance to the race man had the raw material out of which a god might be—and usually was—created.

We may consider first those gods who owe their existence to experiences more or less common to all men. One such body of experience grows from the reproductive instinct, which expresses itself in a tendency towards permanent pairing. The sexual urge is responsible for a great number of deities in all pantheons. Household gods are numerous, and have their assigned functions. But reproduction is something which goes far beyond the perpetuation and increase of the human race. It involves all nature. Therefore, man created generalized gods of fertility, of life and death, and rebirth. Noticing that the female seems to be the all-important direct factor in human reproduction, man frequently created female deities or goddesses to embody the generalized concept of fertility and reproduction.

Apart from sexual experiences, every man has to face certain crises in life, such as birth, puberty, marriage, sickness, and death. Gods are usually provided as safeguards in each of these situations. There are also natural occurrences, such as

9 J. H. Dietrich, *How the Gods Were Made*, privately printed, 1926, p. 10; cf. Joseph McCabe, *How Man Made God*, Haldeman-Julius, 1931; and A. E. Haydon, *Biography of the Gods*, Macmillan, 1940.

seasonal changes, and the passage of day into night and night into day, which all men observe. Accordingly, every pantheon has deities for seasons and for light and darkness. Further, strong drink and strong drugs produce strange and powerful reactions in primitive people. Consequently, we find among the Greeks Dionysus, the vine god, and in India a god for Soma, a powerful liquor made from leaves of a mountain plant.

In addition to the gods associated with common human experiences and problems, there are also gods which arise out of special circumstances. Geographic influences have given us gods of the mountains, plains, desert, forest, and sea. Occupations and industries are also recognized. Hunters, shepherds, and agricultural peoples have always invented deities appropriate to their occupations.

Moreover, both shepherds and farmers need rain. The shepherd especially depends on animal fertility, the farmer on weather, the fisherman on the sea. Gods are provided to look after each of these needs. There is also a tendency to deify animals, those upon which for any reason man depends, as well as those he specially fears.

The multiplicity of gods in early civilizations—and of course, among savages— is difficult for us to understand today. Take, for instance, Roman household gods. First there was Vesta, the goddess of the hearth, the center of family worship. Next came the *di penates,* or gods of the family storeroom. Then there was the god of the paterfamilias, the procreative power which continued the family's existence, a sort of symbol of the germ plasm; the god of the door or threshold, called Janus; and finally, the *lar familiaris,* or the spirit of the boundaries of the family domain. Added to these, of course, were the Roman public gods.

Man deifies man as well as nature. Most consciously he tends to give the heroes of the past divine attributes, much as we glorify George Washington and the founders of our country. The political head of society was often deified in early civilizations; so were military heroes.

Not only does man create gods and assign them certain functions, he even invests them with moral attributes. In this process, too, the facts are exactly the opposite of what is usually believed. It is assumed that God created and revealed our moral codes. The Decalogue was handed to Moses on Mount Sinai, right and wrong are decided upon in heaven, and so on. As a matter of fact man has always projected his own moral beliefs on the gods. He has attributed to the gods the origin of the folkways gradually worked out by his social group in the course of its life experiences.[10]

This is admirably illustrated by the Old Testament God, Yahweh, who first appears as a crude supernatural power symbolized by upright stones—a phallic symbol. He then develops into a ruthless tribal divinity of desert nomads, bidding his followers savagely to destroy these enemies who worshiped gods other than Yahweh. He revealed to the Hebrews their elaborate moral code. Ultimately, Yahweh became a universal providence, directing the affairs of nature and man, and controlling the course of history.

10 Cf. W. G. Sumner, *Folkways,* Dover Publications, Inc., 1959, chaps. i-iii.

In preliterary times the gods were the product of man's unrestrained imagination. As culture developed and man learned to write, his deities were given more precise and permanent attributes. We shall have occasion to illustrate this trend as we describe the pantheons of historical peoples.

We may now profitably conclude our treatment of primitive religion by examining some of the basic concepts and practices growing out of the hypothesis of primitive man with respect to the supernatural world.

First and foremost in primitive religious thought is the realm of things sacred, those things which are charged with the power of mana, the vague but potent source of supernatural power. Usually, sacred things can be handled safely only by specialists in mystery, priests or medicine men ("shamans"). In primitive life the sacred—as the source of supernatural power—is both feared and revered. Since nearly all individual, social, and industrial activities were under the spell of the supernatural, it can readily be seen that the shaman, or medicine man, was very powerful in primeval society.

Closely allied to the concept of sacredness are the notions of clean and unclean. In most cases these terms have no relation whatever to considerations of hygiene or aesthetics, but are connected with ideas of safety and danger. A "clean" thing is free of the supernatural or of danger therefrom. It is safe. Contact with it does not expose one to mysterious risks and possible disasters. The unclean is steeped in mystery. Evil forces play around it. Contamination with it may bring tragedy. Only proper religious rites, administered by "authorized" persons, may, at times, make the unclean become clean.

Next we may look at the concept of sacrifice, a highly important rite, combining both magic and worship. The purposes of sacrifice are varied. It may be a way of offering thanks to the gods—one gives them a share of his crops, or cattle. At other times, sacrifice serves to bring gods and votaries together, thereby cementing the bond and renewing the covenant. Sacrifice may also be used to increase the volume of mana or spiritual grace in the community or to bring the social group into contact with its mysterious operations.

Sacrifice takes on varied forms. In "theophagy" a worshiper may eat either the symbol of the god, or actually consume the god's representative, man or animal, thereby imbibing the mana residing in that which is consumed. On the whole, sacrifice usually expresses gratitude and loyalty to the gods, or it is indulged in for the sake of securing supernatural aid in times of stress.

Taboo is a fundamental primitive means of executing social control. It aims to make human life and social activities safe. The gods are supposed to indicate what types of conduct they approve, and what they disapprove. Disapproved acts are taboo—forbidden. If one never violated taboos, he was likely to remain in the favor of the gods, thus receiving and retaining spiritual grace. There may be taboos against marrying certain people, eating certain animals (consider the Jewish dietary laws), working on certain days (the Christian Sunday, for instance, or Jewish Sabbath), coming into contact with strangers (Jewish dislike of Gentiles), and so on. In a word, taboos are the "don'ts" or "red lights" of primitive society.

Fetishism, the worship of certain objects like sticks, stones, or what-not, pervades primitive religion. These objects are believed to harbor spirits and therefore bring good luck. In some cases fetishism does not involve the residence of a spirit in an object. In western Africa, for example, the magical power in the object is looked upon as impersonal and no indwelling spirit is implied.

Primitive religion abounds with rituals, particularly for handling safely crises which are supposed to be specifically charged with mana, and hence peculiarly dangerous. To ward off potential evils during these crucial periods of existence, it was believed that one must indulge in specified forms of magic, thereby propitiating the proper deities. Hence, nearly all primitive tribes invest birth, adolescence, initiation into manhood and womanhood, marriage, sickness and death, with a distinct sense of the sacred and mysterious and evolve specific religious rites to handle them safely. These, as Professor Marett and others have made clear, are the primitive origins of the famous sacramental system of the Roman Catholic church to which we shall later pay attention.[11]

An important concept of primitive religion and social relations is totemism. Most commonly, a group regards itself as descended from some plant, animal or object, towards which it observes an attitude of veneration. Totemism is important as furnishing the basis for marriage taboos—fellow totemites usually may not marry—and in stimulating ceremonial activities.

There are many survivals of these primitive religious notions in cultures so late and recent as our own. This fact may be illustrated briefly by some commonplace superstitions in our own day.

Animism

Personification of nature, which has developed into a philosophy—hylozoism—the theory that all nature is alive.

A poet's invocation of inanimate objects, such as "O nature!" "O river!" "O desert!" and the like; or talking to dice.

Belief in ghosts, spirits, and witchcraft.

Taking an ax or maul and attacking a beam or post on which we have bumped our head.

Symbolism

Veneration for the flag, the cross, and the like.

The belief in the Eucharist or Lord's Supper as symbolic of the Last Supper celebrated by Jesus and his disciples and of the sacrifice of Jesus.

The power of a star or a lily as symbolizing purity.

Observance of Christmas and Easter, symbolic festivals surviving from primitive times.

Magic

Praying for rain, salvation, good crops, health, wealth, luck, and so on.

Planting corn, castrating pigs, and the like in the "dark of the moon."

Power of the cross to bring what one prays for.

11 Cf. R. R. Marett, *The Sacraments of Simple Folk*, Oxford Press, 1933.

Making the sign of a cross over one's body.

Knocking on wood to avoid future bad luck.

Placing image of St. Christopher on the radiator cap of a car.

Fetishism

Good luck charms such as rabbit's foot, horseshoe, four-leaf clover, lucky stones; wearing of the cross; wearing phylacteries; carrying of the Bible; wearing amulets and the like.

Omens

Ominous weather signs. The belief that certain kinds of weather (storms, lightning, etc.) foretell events.

Good luck to see new moon over right shoulder; good luck to find four-leaf clover.

Fear of a black cat crossing the path; fear of lighting three cigarettes on one match; fear of starting a journey on Friday the thirteenth.

Bad luck in breaking a mirror; bad luck for a couple walking to part and go on opposite sides of a post or pole; bad luck to change shirt or waist if put on wrong-side-out in the morning.

Totemism

Emblems taken by athletic clubs, such as Eagles, Tigers, Lions, Braves, and the like.

Mascots adopted by the above.

Emblems taken by lodges such as the Elks and Moose.

Emblems taken to symbolize various countries, such as the American eagle, British lion, Russian bear and the like.

Divination

Flipping a coin to determine action to be taken.

Fortune-telling by tea-leaves, daisy-petals, and the like.

Finally, we must say a little more about primitive "clergy," medicine men, or shamans. They are exalted, ineffable beings, holding special communion with the gods. They alone can deal safely with the supernatural powers and competently handle the sacred, since they themselves are filled with mana.

Two types of shamans are found in primitive society—those who are especially adept in administering rituals and performing ceremonies, and those of a more saintly cast, who dwell mentally in peculiarly mystical regions. The latter are the "holy men." They live apart. Tribesmen come to them for counsel, revelation, and regeneration. In later religions, they became the prophets. The ceremonial shaman became the priest.

Primitive chieftains and kings frequently are supposed to be endowed with mana. On this account they are entitled to high position and great respect. Their special reserve of mana enables them to contact the sacred powers. Hence it is not uncommon to find priest-kings among barbarians. The medieval and modern doctrine of the divine right of kings is no more than a sophisticated vestige of this picturesque bit of primitive speculation.

VII. THE ORIGINS OF SPOKEN LANGUAGE

It is not too much to say that our culture has developed beyond that of other primates in large part because of our mastery of speech. Man left the simian world behind when he created a language. At any rate, human culture is based on man's faculty of speech. This implies that evolution into a human state was intimately connected with the achievement of formal communication. G. Elliot Smith says that "it seems a legitimate inference from the facts to assume that the acquisition of the power of communicating ideas and the fruits of experience from one individual to another by means of articulate speech may have been one of the factors, if not the fundamental factor, in converting an ape into a human being."[12]

Speech, like intelligence, is not, however, a human monopoly. Animals have rudimentary means of communicating with each other. The dog barks, the cow moos, monkeys chatter, the cat has a diapason of sounds. In most cases some sort of meaning is expressed, although one doubts the literal veracity of the Bible when it attributed to Solomon the ability to converse with all the beasts on sea and land.

Animals may thus express well-defined emotions, but as C. K. Ogden says, we must not assume that animals have the ability to name anything specific. An animal utters a cry, expressing a need or desire, or merely giving voice to surplus energy. A naming cry is an interpretive sound. "Plainly naming cannot arise until the animal can respond to situations not merely as eliciting this or that activity, but as possessing this or that character."[13]

Let us pursue the distinction a little farther. All speech, whether animal or human, involves expression. Man's speech involves more than that—it embraces what Ogden calls "objective reference" (interpretation). This objective reference is man's peculiar achievement. How did such an all-important achievement come about?

The thing to remember is that man's higher or differentiated use of speech developed out of the animal's lower or undifferentiated vocal expressions. Even among animal cries—the inarticulate sounds of infants resemble them—there is some sort of objective reference. Before children can speak they have a wide variety of vocal expressions such as a call for food, cry of discomfort, and the like. An infant can communicate long before he utters a definable word. Animals can do much the same. Their cry is a call to action. It expresses an emotion "long before any explicit reflection upon, or recognition of, the situation can have arisen. We must remember, in considering any stage of language, that its use in reflec-

---

12 Quoted by C. K. Ogden, *The Meaning of Psychology*, Harper, 1926, p. 149.
13 *Ibid.*, p. 150.

tion, as an instrument of thought, is a kind of diversion of it from its original uses."[14] The danger cries and other social utterances of animals may be regarded as crude names. What they name is not any specific feature of a situation but the whole situation. A similar phenomenon meets us in human speech if we go back as far as we can into the origin of any given language.

When man had arrived at the stage of forming sentences he too probably first took in a situation as a whole rather than analyzed its component parts. In other words he probably expressed himself as the Eskimo does in saying "sinikatach-pok," rather than the English way of putting it, as "he is ill from having slept too much." There is little doubt whatever that in the beginning language created some of its "ideas" or "words" by imitating natural sounds. English—and every other tongue—has a number of them like "cuckoo," "peewit," "bang," "crash," "plop," "zip." This practice of imitating natural sounds is called "onomatopoeia."

A rival to the onomatopoeic theory of the origin of language is that which holds that bodily movements, or those of hands and feet, were associated with cries which, within the family or community, became standardized in time. In other words, as Fraser points out, all the members of a community agreed to make the same sounds, when, for instance, looking at the sun, peering into a dark place, or kicking an object. After a while the sounds alone would suggest the various actions. This is called the "gesture theory." Probably language actually arose through both imitating natural sounds and putting gesticular meanings into words.

It is not difficult to see how concrete things and events got their names. It is much more difficult to imagine how abstractions—good, bad, true, for instance— arose. It is probable that abstractions began as concrete words and eventually lost their concreteness. Latin *anima*, soul, is connected with Sanskrit, *aniti*, breathes, and Sanskrit *anilas*, wind. The Latin word itself must originally have meant breath. Once the conception of a "spirit" appeared, its presence was located in the body, and it was associated with breathing. In time the word lost its connection with the tangible occurrence "breathing" and came to stand merely for the spirit which was supposed to control the breathing.

We shall probably never know exactly where language originated. Probably it appeared in many places at different times. Our earliest record of speech comes from the valleys of the Nile and Euphrates. But these examples date from—com-paratively—yesterday, when we remember that man has, crudely in the begin-ning, conversed for a half-million years or more. Sumerian, which was spoken about 5,000 years ago in southern Mesopotamia, is one of the earliest languages we know anything about. Nothing, however, would justify our calling the Sumerian dialect a primitive language in the sense that it resembled the language spoken by Heidelberg man, the Brünn man or even the Cro-Magnon peoples.

Little light is thrown on the problem by studying the languages of existing aborigines—from them we only learn that primitive culture seems to go with languages of extremely complicated structure. For instance, the language of the

14 Ogden, *op. cit.,* p. 152.

Eskimo is, to a person who is acquainted with Germanic or Romance languages, one of almost insurmountable difficulties. This will suffice to upset a common notion that primitive man has a very limited vocabulary and a language of simple structure. Such may have been true of the Neanderthal man, but it is not true of existing savages. Professor F. S. Chapin has well stated the cultural importance of the invention of a spoken language:

> Language became the chief vehicle for the transmission and preservation of culture, as well as the most characteristic aspect of culture. Long before written language was invented, oral tradition preserved and handed down from generation to generation the discoveries, the inventions, and the social heritage of the past. Language provided man with a boon without price, the means of storing, externally to any particular nervous system, records of experience having social values to the group. External storage of individual experience in language symbols is a process entirely unknown to any form of life other than man. The importance of this process seems beyond calculation. It reaches its highest development in the alphabet [15]

A spoken language made possible the verbalization of human culture, thus permitting it to be better integrated and more easily transmitted from one generation to another. Human institutions were now supplied with verbal defense, analysis, and rationalization. The very important symbolic representations in human culture now became possible. Human culture depends upon the ability of man to use symbols. It is this fact, more than any other, which separates our culture from the life of the lower forms of primate life. Language also permitted a far more elaborate development of literary culture and institutional life. If our language and its literary products were suddenly taken away from us we would sink back to the cultural level of savages of the cave-dwelling period. We would soon have no greater cultural or institutional equipment than Homo sapiens possessed when he first dominated Europe some thirty thousand years or more ago.

The question naturally arises: do all the families of languages which we can distinguish today go back to a common ancestor? The case for such linguistic monogenesis has been argued by the brilliant Italian scholar, Trombetti, but has received little support in other quarters. This question, like many others involving the origins of man, cannot be answered decisively for the present at least.

VIII. THE ART OF PRELITERATE MAN

The art of Paleolithic man is of peculiar value to us as an index of prehistoric culture. It reveals not only an advanced understanding of artistic form and technique, but also the fact that, thousands of years before man developed an effective written language, thought could be communicated through pictorial means.

Carvings and paintings in caves or beneath rock ledges in certain areas of paleolithic and neolithic France and Spain disclose the concern of early man over the magic of fertility and reproduction problems of the hunt, war, and death. In the art of preliterate peoples in many other parts of the world as well — most

15 F. S. Chapin, *Cultural Change*, Century, 1928, p. 40.

parts of Africa, the Pacific Islands, and several regions in the Americas — similar unwritten records are preserved.

The word "preliterate" or "prehistoric" has different meanings depending upon specific times and places. Most prehistoric art of Europe dates many centuries before the time of Christ. In the American Northwest, on the other hand, and in Australia, such art persisted until quite recent times.

Just as the time and place of preliterate painting and sculpture vary, so do content and quality of expressiveness and technique. It is not positively known whether decorative or "abstract" art precedes naturalistic style. In fact, both geometrical ornament and simple contours of animals have been found within the same parts of caves dating in the earlier division of the Old Stone Age in France. Likewise within the same cavern or among large rocks elsewhere in preliterate regions, some images are found skillfully painted or engraved, while nearby ones may reflect an unsophisticated hand. But in its better examples, prehistoric art reveals a powerful conceptual mastery. During the twentieth century preliterate art has become increasingly widely recognized as an influence upon practicing artists and as a specialized area for scholarly attention.

The question of how man came to express himself artistically is provocative. Certain anthropologists believe that the aesthetic instinct can be traced to animals; others see art as resulting from magical or religious impulses. It is likely that a combination of attitudes, among which was the desire to order forms in space, led to the creation of the first cave or rock painting or sculpture.

The subjects of painting and sculpture of the Paleolithic period in south-central France and northern Spain — the Franco-Cantabrian region — consist largely of cave animals common to that epoch. The human figure occurs less frequently. Franco-Cantabrian painting, perhaps the highest achievement among paleolithic arts, is usually naturalistic. Late paleolithic or possibly neolithic rock-shelter paintings of Levantine or East-Spanish provenience often depict scenes of combat or hunting in which the human figure, stylized in conception, is dominant.

In some cases the symbolical or higher meaning seems to have taken precedence over naturalistic appearance. For instance, certain statuettes discovered at Willendorff, Austria, have strikingly exaggerated pectorals — in general effect not unlike their counterparts in the large female sculptures by Gaston Lachaise. This exaggeration may reflect a naturalistic interpretation of "steatopygy" which occurs as an illness. It may, however, symbolize fertility or motherhood.

But here we are more concerned with the technique or skill of preliterary art, which we can understand, than with its meanings or motives, which we can only guess at. The striking fact is that finished cave art is naturalistic, what is unfinished seems only to be unsuccessful attempts in the same direction.

Sculpture appears to have been executed before painting, and by the Aurignacian period (over 30,000 years ago) it achieved high excellence. We cannot definitely say why human beings should have attempted sculpture before painting or drawing. "It may well be that to represent in three dimensions, that is, in the solid, comes more easily to the mind than registering a mere surface impression in two dimensions, or, in the flat. One notices that a dog understands a substantive shape much better than a picture. Sculpture in relief might act as an educational bridge from the one to the other; though this by no means is certain."[16] Some anthropologists believe that painting and sculpture may very well have originated simultaneously and by the very same act, namely, the painting of the human body.

In work of two dimensions we find so-called arabesques traced with the fingers on the walls of a cave or scratched on the rock with an instrument. Their significance is unknown. True art, however, made its first appearance in outline drawings of animals, formed with monochrome paint, or cut with a graver. Usually the body is in profile. In the earlier drawings of animals only one front leg and one back leg are shown. In the later ones, four legs appear. In the second stage there was, as we may expect, more life in the figures. The perspective of the animal's horns is clear and attention is paid to the shape of legs and hoofs. There were some slight attempts at shading. Furthermore, engraving and painting were now combined. Paint was often thickly laid on top of the engraved outline.

In the next or third phase, engraving was confined to rather small figures, often done with great skill. Painting was in an experimental stage. Attempts were made with a flat wash, red and black in a sort of checkerboard arrangement, with unsuccessful results. In the fourth or final phase of paleolithic art, painting recovered some of the splendor of the second phase, elaborated its methods, and became polychromatic. Sometimes the polychromes were helped out by engraving.

Preliterary art was, on the whole, a straightforward expression. The pictures record, for example, a bison ruminating or on the jump, a boar running, or a horse trotting. If we consider that these paintings date from 20,000 to 30,000 years ago, their finish and accuracy are astonishing.[17]

It is interesting to note that in the art of contemporary primitive peoples the aims of the artist are strikingly similar to those of the Paleolithic period. In many cases the artist is interested in a magical process leading to the success of the hunt. Thus the animal is accurately represented, in all of its realistic details. Opposed to this we find that the representation of human beings among all primitive peoples is much less naturalistic and in many cases extremely stylized. This we can relate to a fear on the part of the hunter that if he were represented in his actual physical character, he would expose himself—his effigy—to the attacks of his enemies. The natives of Haiti today in their voodoo practices offer a striking analogy to this characteristic of preliterary art.

Neolithic art did not reach as high technical proficiency as that of the Paleolithic period. Mural painting declined and disappeared. Some attempts at artistic expression were made in weapons, stone figures, clay figurines of women, pottery decoration, bracelets, necklaces, shell, or bone and stone rings. Chromatic art was negligible in the Neolithic period. Its chief manifestation was of a gruesome character. The flesh was frequently stripped from the skeletons before burial, and the bones then daubed with red ocher and buried. These neolithic peoples ap-

16 R. R. Marett, in J. A. Hammerton, *Universal History of the World,* Amalgamated Press, 1927, I, 253.
17 The finest examples are in the cave of Lascaux in south central France, discovered in 1940.

parently believed red to be a symbol of blood and vitality and, hence, of immortality. The most striking art of the Neolithic period was the great stone monuments. They first introduced the conception of massiveness into human art, thus serving as a forerunner of the building art of the Egyptians and Mesopotamians.

Next to the cave paintings and sculptures of the Paleolithic the most notable artistic products of preliterary peoples were the metal and enamel work and the pottery produced in northern Europe in the Bronze and Iron ages. This is important as proving that the early historical art of the Egyptians and Babylonians was unique neither in time nor in character.

In the Bronze Age the weapons became works of art, and much artistic effort was expended on daggers, dagger handles, sword handles, scabbards, axes, and the like. Designed and ornamented pins for holding clothing in place appeared. Here, then, we find the famous fibulae or brooches, the prototype of our safety pin and decorated brooches, which were not only objects of utility, but became the most characteristic and famous of the ornaments of the Iron Age. Beautifully ornamented bronze bracelets and anklets were made in scroll and spiral designs. Well-designed and artistically decorated vases were produced in abundance.

In the Iron Age, while the weapons came to be made of iron, the handles and other ornamentation were still frequently of bronze. The artistry in the making of weapons, characteristic of the Bronze Age, continued and was improved upon. Special artistic effort was expended on the now prevalent fibulae. These became highly diversified and very beautiful in design and materials. Necklaces of amber, ivory, coral, and glass came into use. Earrings grew common; they were of beautiful design. Polished mirrors, set in metals, and other toilet articles were manufactured. Bronze buckets with sculptured designs were plentiful and highly prized in the early Iron Age. Beautiful vases of curvilinear design and ornamented with bright colors constituted perhaps the highest artistic achievement of the later Iron Age art, especially among the Gallic tribes. Even the making of stained glass was known in Gaul in the Iron Age. Some believe that this was the source of the beautiful stained glass of the Gothic cathedrals in medieval Europe. Jewelry in gold and silver also began to appear.

No verbal description can convey any adequate comprehension of the beauties of the metal work, pottery, and enameled work of the Bronze and Iron ages. The reader must consult such collections of illustrations as those in Joseph Déchelette's *Manual of Archeology,* the guides to the antiquities of the Bronze and Iron ages prepared by the British Museum, or the more accessible material in chapters vii-ix of Professor H. F. Cleland's excellent book, *Our Prehistoric Ancestors.* No one can regard himself as adequately informed with respect to the history of human art and material culture until he has done this. A good illustration of the cultural progress of man in the late Iron Age is provided by the following description of Luernus, a king of ancient Gaul in the La Tène period:

> Greek and Italian travellers saw Luernus advancing along the road at the head
> of a picturesque train of followers including howling dogs of war. A collar and
> bracelets of gold gleamed against the purple and gold of his dress. He rode erect

on a chariot studded with silver. Behind him soldiers bore the Gallic standards, with their device of the wild boar, and at his side, a bard sang his valour to the accompaniment of the lyre. With a grand gesture, which the poet compares to that of a husbandman sowing seed, Luernus threw handfuls of gold and silver coins to the subjects who followed his chariot.[18]

IX. SUMMARY OF HUMAN PROGRESS IN THE PRELITERARY PERIOD

Not very long ago, books on the history of Europe began with the history of Rome. Even after the glory and genius of Greece were recognized, there still remained unappreciated the great achievements of the ancient Orient. Now, we have pushed well behind the scenes of ancient Oriental times. Throwing back the origins of human history into remotest antiquity, anthropology, archaeology, and their allied sciences have revealed a great age that we describe as preliterary. Man is not only discovering his past; he is in truth remaking it.

When man began to record in writing his doings, his achievements, and his beliefs, the preliterary age came to a close and the literary or "historical" age began. This did not happen all at once, the one merged into the other in different regions at various times during the metal ages. By the close of the preliterary age, man had already established the necessary basis for all subsequent culture. True, it took a great period of time—several million years—to accomplish that task. But without the achievements and contributions of the preliterary period, none of the higher cultural attainments of the subsequent literary age would have been possible. In economic activity, in art, in language, in religion, in law, in social organization, preliterary man left an indispensable heritage to his posterity. With respect to material culture, it is not too much to say that human civilization before the industrial revolution more closely resembled preliterary culture than it does our present-day life.

Concepts of property and law, religious institutions, and fundamental economic processes were developed during the preliterary age. In the same period, men advanced from being hunting and fishing food-gatherers to being exploiters who domesticated animals, tilled the soil, and engaged in the metal, textile, and pottery industries. The origins of language, the preliminaries of writing, and rudimentary pictograms during that period mean that the literary age was prepared for in the preliterary. The foundations of art, including the industrial skill and technique which merit the term artistic, were also laid down during this period. First steps in artistic design were taken, and chromatic and realistic art reached high levels. Here, too, we must seek the beginnings of literature and music—that is, oral literature and traditional music, as distinct from literature and music recorded by writing.

We may say with much truth that, by historic times, the European races were distributed to a substantial degree as they are at present. Avoiding all controversial issues, it is sufficient to note that the peoples of Europe fall into three racial groupings: the Mediterranean, the Alpine, and the Teutonic or Baltic (also called Nordic). The first and third belong to the larger Eur-African division, and the

18 **Frantz** Funck-Brentano, *National History of France: The Earliest Times,* Putnam, 1929, p. 57.

second belongs to the Eur-Asian. The longheaded and swarthy Mediterranean race is to be found chiefly around the shores of the Mediterranean. The blond Teutonic, Baltic or Nordic race is located mainly in the north of Europe, especially in Scandinavia. The roundheaded Alpine race—Slavs and Celts—may be placed as occupying the center and eastern area of Europe, forming a wedge of people thrust westward into Europe between the other two races. We must keep in mind that for thousands of years these three racial types have been intermingling with one another, thus making it practically impossible for pure racial types to exist.

We have followed man in his long march from the bestial conditions of Eolithic times to the so-called dawn of history—a period of, roughly speaking, a million years. We shall take up the story of the evolution of material culture once more in connection with the conquest of civilization by the peoples of the ancient Near Orient.

SELECTED READINGS

Barnes, H. E., *Historical Sociology,* Philosophical Library, 1948.

Barnes, H. E., and Becker, Howard, *Contemporary Social Theory,* Appleton-Century, 1940, chaps. ix, xvi.

————— *Social Thought from Lore to Science,* 3 Vols., Dover Publications, Inc., 1961.

Boas, Franz, *Anthropology and Modern Life,* Norton, 1962.

————— *The Mind of Primitive Man,* Macmillan, 1911.

Boule, Marcellin, and Vallois, H. V., *Fossil Men,* Holt, 1957.

Braidwood, R. J., *Prehistoric Men,* Chicago Natural History Museum, 1948.

Broom, Robert, *Swartkrans Ape-Man,* Pretoria, 1946.

Broom, Robert, and Schepers, G. W. H., *The South African Fossil Ape Men,* Pretoria, 1946.

Brown, Harrison, *The Challenge of Man's Future,* Compass, 1956.

Calverton, V. F., ed., *The Making of Man,* Modern Library, 1931.

Carter, G. S., "The Story of Evolution and the Evolution of Man," in *Anthropology Today,* ed. Sol Tax, University of Chicago Press, 1953.

Childe, V. G., *New Light on the Most Ancient East,* Evergreen, 1957.

————— "Old World Prehistory: Neolithic," in *Anthropology Today,* ed. Sol Tax, University of Chicago Press, 1953.

————— *What Happened in History,* Pelican.

Clark, W. E. Le Gros, *The Antecedents of Man,* University of Chicago Press, 1960.

————— *The Foundation of Human Evolution,* Condon Lectures, 1959.

Cole, S., *The Prehistory of East Africa,* Pelican.

Dart, R. A., and Craig, Dennis, *Adventures with the Missing Link,* Viking, 1961.

De Chardin, P.T., "The Idea of Fossil Man," in *Anthropology Today,* ed. Sol Tax, University of Chicago Press, 1953.

————— *The Phenomenon of Man,* Harper, 1959.

Eby, Frederick, and Arrowood, C. F., *The History and Philosophy of Education: Ancient and Medieval,* Prentice-Hall, 1940, chap. i.

Frankfort, Henri, *The Birth of Civilization in the Near East,* Doubleday, 1959.

Frankfort, Henri, *et al., Before Philosophy,* Pelican, 1959.

Fried, M. H., ed., *Readings in Anthropology,* 2 Vols., Crowell, 1959.

Goldenweiser, Alexander, *Anthropology,* Crofts, 1937.
—— *Early Civilization,* Knopf, 1922.
Haddon, A. C., *Evolution in Art,* London, 1897.
Herskovits, M. J., *The Economic Life of Primitive Peoples,* Knopf, 1940.
Hibben, F. C., *The Lost Americans,* Apollo, 1961.
Hooton, E. A., *Up from the Ape,* Macmillan, 1946.
Howells, W. W., *Back of History,* Doubleday, 1954.
—— *Early Man in the Far East,* American Association of Physical Anthropologists, 1949.
—— *Mankind in the Making,* Doubleday, 1959.
—— *Mankind So Far,* Doubleday, 1944.
Hurzeler, Johannes, *Orthepithecus Bambolii Gervais: A Preliminary Report,* Basel, 1958.
Keith, Arthur, *The Antiquity of Man,* Lippincott, 1925.
—— *New Discoveries Relating to the Antiquity of Man,* Norton, 1931.
Korn, Noel, and Smith, H. R., eds., *Human Evolution,* Holt, 1959.
Kroeber, A. L., and Waterman, T. T., *Source Book of Anthropology,* University of California Press, 1922.
Kühn, Herbert, *On the Track of Prehistoric Man,* Arrow, 1958.
La Barre, Weston, *The Human Animal,* University of Chicago Press, 1960.
Lasker, G. W., *The Evolution of Man,* Holt, 1961.
Leakey, L. S. B., *Adam's Ancestors,* Harper, 1960.
Lévy-Bruhl, Lucien, *Primitive Mentality,* Macmillan, 1923.
—— *Primitives and the Supernatural,* Dutton, 1935.
Linton, Ralph, *The Study of Man,* Appleton-Century, 1936.
Lowie, R. H., *Introduction to Cultural Anthropology,* Farrar and Rinehart, 1934.
—— *Primitive Religion,* Grosset, 1958.
—— *Primitive Society,* Liveright, 1947.
Marett, R. R., *Anthropology,* Holt, 1912.
—— *The Threshold of Religion,* Macmillan, 1914.
Mason, O. T., *The Origins of Invention,* Appleton, 1895.
Medawar, P. B., *The Uniqueness of the Individual,* Basic Books, 1957.
Montagu, M. F. Ashley, *An Introduction to Physical Anthropology,* C. C. Thomas, 1960.
Movius, H. L., "Old World Prehistory: Paleolithic," in *Anthropology Today,* ed. Sol Tax, University of Chicago Press, 1953.
Nesturkh, N., *The Origin of Man,* Academy of Sciences, USSR, 1959.
Oakley, K. P., "Dating Fossil Human Remains," in *Anthropology Today,* ed. Sol Tax, University of Chicago Press, 1953.
—— *Man the Tool-Maker,* Phoenix, 1957.
Radin, Paul, *Primitive Man as Philosopher,* Dover Publications, Inc., 1957.
—— *Primitive Religion,* Dover Publications, Inc., 1957.
Roberts, D. F., and Harrison, G. A., *Natural Selection in Human Populations,* Pergamon, 1959.
Rostand, Jean, *Can Man Be Modified?,* Basic Books, 1959.
Scheler, Max, *Man's Place in Nature,* Beacon, 1961.
Schenk, Gustav, *The History of Man,* Chilton, 1961.
Shapiro, H. L., ed., *Man, Culture and Society,* Oxford University Press, 1960.
Simpson, G. G., *Tempo and Mode in Evolution,* Columbia University Press, 1944.

Spuhler, J. N., ed., *The Evolution of Man's Capacity for Culture*, Wayne State University Press, 1959.

———— *Natural Selection in Man*, Wayne State University Press, 1958.

Stewart, J. H., "Evolution and Process," in *Anthropology Today*, ed. Sol Tax, University of Chicago Press, 1953.

Stirton, R. A., *Time, Life and Man*, Wiley, 1959.

Sumner, W. G., *Folkways*, Dover Publications, Inc., 1959.

Swinnerton, H. H., *Outlines of Paleontology*, St. Martin's, 1947.

Tax, Sol, ed., *Anthropology Today*, University of Chicago Press, 1953.

———— *Evolution After Darwin*.

Thomas, W. I., *Primitive Behavior*, McGraw-Hill, 1937.

———— *Source Book of Social Origins*, Bruce Humphries, 1962.

Tylor, E. B., *Anthropology*, Ann Arbor Books, 1960.

Wald, G., *Biochemical Evolution*, Academic Press, 1952.

Weidenreich, Franz, *Apes, Giants and Man*, University of Chicago Press, 1946.

Wendt, Herbert, *In Search of Adam*, Houghton Mifflin, 1956.

White, L. A., *The Evolution of Culture*, McGraw-Hill, 1959.

———— *The Science of Culture*, Grove, 1958.

Woolley, Leonard, *Digging Up the Past*, Pelican, 1950.

III ·

*Oriental Foundations
of Classical Thought
and Culture*

I. BRINGING TO LIGHT A GREAT CIVILIZATION

Before the nineteenth century little was known about the magnificent ancient civilization of the Near East. There were excerpts from Manetho and Berossos, a few stories in Herodotus and other Greek writers, some references in the Bible, a few pyramids and obelisks, some scattered ruined temples above ground, and not much else. Today we have uncovered many extensive ruins, deciphered the languages of Egypt, Babylonia, Assyria and Anatolia, and patiently pieced together a fairly comprehensive outline of the remarkable cultures which flourished along the Nile and in the Tigris and Euphrates valleys from about 6-7000 B.C. to 500 B.C.

Our knowledge of the ancient Near East rests mainly upon archaeology and philology. The archaeologists excavated the remains, the philologists deciphered the languages. The composite picture which has resulted tells us a great deal about man's earliest historic civilization. Not that the picture is complete. There is much excavating still to be done. Some languages of the Near East, especially Cretan and Etruscan, are still waiting to be deciphered.

The beginnings of the recovery of the antique world may be associated with Napoleon's expedition to Egypt in 1798, an expedition futile in a military sense, but very important to history and science. The scientists, engineers and scholars who accompanied Napoleon used their spare time to make a survey of the monuments and inscriptions of ancient Egypt. The results of their work, published between 1809 and 1813, contained the first systematic description of the monuments of the Nile Valley awaiting the excavator's spade.

The earliest important excavations were made after 1840 by the German, Karl Richard Lepsius. His work around Memphis opened the world's eyes to the treasures of the antique Orient which lay buried beneath debris. In 1850 the French government took control of archaeological exploration in Egypt, and Auguste Mariette assumed direction. During the next thirty years the Cairo Museum was filled with the remarkable objects which he and his associates unearthed. In 1880, an even more famous French scholar, Gaston Maspero, took up Mariette's work, but the French monopoly was broken.

Scholars from many countries entered Egypt. The most important of them were the Englishmen, Flinders Petrie and Arthur Weigall, the American, James H. Breasted, the Swiss, Henri Naville, and the Frenchman, Alexander Moret. They penetrated pyramids, excavated tombs and palaces, collected papyri, copied inscriptions, and in every possible way added to our knowledge of the remarkable Nilotic civilization which flourished in the dawn of history, six thousand years ago.

But before the work of excavators could be fully interpreted it was necessary to read the ancient languages in which the Egyptian inscriptions and papyri were written. The first step in Egyptian linguistic exploration was taken when the famous Rosetta stone—inscribed in three languages, Egyptian hieroglyphics, Egyptian demotic writing and Greek, and found by an officer of Napoleon— was deciphered by a French scholar, J. F. Champollion (1790-1832).

The English took the lead in excavating the valleys of the Tigris and Euphrates. C. J. Rich (1787-1820), an East India Company official, was the first to survey the great mounds which covered the ruined cities of ancient Babylonia and Assyria. In 1835-37, General F. R. Chesney led a British expedition which first thoroughly mapped out Mesopotamia for archaeological investigation.

Digging began in 1842 when the Frenchman, Paul Botta, unearthed the palace of Sargon on the ancient site of Khorsabad. He was followed by Sir Henry Layard, who excavated the mound of Nimrod in 1845 and uncovered more Assyrian palaces. Rassam found the famous library of Assurbanipal. In the 1870's the Englishman, George Smith, discovered the Babylonian texts of the biblical stories of the Creation and the Flood. The Frenchman, de Sarzec, uncovered the remains of the palace of Gudea of Lagash, which marked the beginning of our knowledge of ancient Sumerian civilization, thus proving that a pre-Babylonian culture had existed in Mesopotamia. Jacques de Morgan, another Frenchman, discovered the famous Code of Hammurabi at Susa in 1901. De Morgan did much to put archaeology on an engineering basis. In the twentieth century an enormous amount of excavating has been carried on, and vast results accomplished. Professor Breasted and the Oriental Institute of the University of Chicago took the lead, applying efficient engineering and mechanical methods of excavation and using airplanes for exploratory investigation and recording photography.

The difficult task of deciphering the cuneiform script in which the Mesopotamian languages were written was begun in 1765 by the German traveller, Karsten Niebuhr, who pointed out differences in cuneiform characters. In 1802 a German, G. E. Grotefend, deciphered about one-third of the old Persian alphabet. The greatest name in Mesopotamian linguistics is that of Sir Henry C. Rawlinson, who, about the middle of the last century, scaled the rock of Behistun and mastered the old Persian, Susian, and Babylonian languages. Babylonian cuneiform provided a key to Semitic cuneiform. This, together with our existing knowledge of Hebrew and Aramaic, permitted the deciphering of the historical records of western Asia. Not until 1941, however, was the Sumerian language mastered by Professor S. N. Kramer of the University of Pennsylvania.

England created the Palestine Exploration Fund in 1865. Since then Syria and Palestine have been thoroughly excavated. One of the most dramatic of all the episodes in connection with the uncovering of ancient civilization was the excavation, by Heinrich Schliemann, of the site of ancient Troy, which began in 1870. This provided the origins of our knowledge of the great Aegean maritime civilization. Subsequent, and more scientific, work by Wilhelm Dörpfeld, Sir Arthur Evans, and others at Crete and on the mainland of Greece has created a wholly new perspective for our knowledge not only of Aegean, but also of proto-Hellenic, civilization. Perhaps the most remarkable recent achievement has been the unearthing of ancient Hittite civilization in Anatolia, begun in 1906, and carried on by such scholars as Hogarth, Garstang, and Winckler. Many Hittite inscriptions date from the same period as the famous Tel-el-Amarna letters which throw a great deal of light on the administration of the Egyptian empire. Hittite writings were in two languages—one derived from Egyptian, the other from Babylonian cuneiform. They have recently been mastered by scholars. We cannot close this brief summary of the romance of archaeology better than by quoting from James Baikie:

A hundred years ago all that was known, or supposed to be known, about the great empires of the Ancient East could have been printed in the thinnest of duodecimos; and even so, the bulk of it would have been either untrue, or so distorted as to be unrecognisable for truth. To-day all that has been entirely changed. Round these ancient empires, a literature has already grown up which is almost comparable to that existing about Greece and Rome, and which is steadily growing in amount and value year by year. The actual historical outlines of the fortunes of the better known among them—Egypt, and the Mesopotamian kingdoms —are becoming more and more clearly defined; and while there are still great gaps in our knowledge, and much of the chronology is still uncertain, the general course of history in these nations can be, and has been traced with very considerable accuracy. The buried cities themselves have risen again from their dust. We can walk along the Procession Street of Babylon, and tread the great pavement-blocks of red breccia and white limestone over which Nebuchadnezzar's triumphal chariot rolled as he went up to give thanks to Marduk in the vast temple of E-sagila, under the shadow of the actual tower of Babel, E-temenanki, "the Foundation-Stone of Heaven and Earth." We can go down into the tomb of Pharaoh, and see him lying there still, as he was laid in state three and a half millenniums ago, amid the clash of sistra, and the loud lament of the myriads of Thebes. We can read the letters which the king of Babylon wrote to the king of Egypt a hundred years before Moses was born, and can hear these mighty potentates wrangling over questions of tribute or bribe, like bagmen over an order, or horse-copers over a deal. Europeans of to-day have walked through halls where Sennacherib "gloried and drank deep," and have ransacked the library where Sardanapalus, the much-misunderstood, stored for himself the wisdom of all the ages that had gone before in Babylon and Assyria; and the worshippers of the God of Israel can tread the Holy of Holies where the prayers of the great Oppressor of Israel were offered. The very graves have given up their dead to show us, so far as the outward form can show it, what manner of men they were who fought and ruled and legislated before Greece or Rome had been dreamed of; and the code by which men's lives were ordered in Babylonia . . . and the romances and love-songs of Egypt are the common possession of all who care to read them; and we can follow, in the very words in which they themselves gave utterance to it, the thought about God and the universe of men who died five thousand years ago. These are the accomplished facts.[1]

II. THE MILITARY-RELIGIOUS CIVILIZATION OF THE ANCIENT WORLD

Ancient Oriental society—of the Hittites, Sumerians, Babylonians, Egyptians, Assyrians, and Hebrews—grew primarily out of primitive, preliterary culture, which was dominated by supernaturalism, with its belief in the divine origin of social customs and institutions. These Oriental civilizations were created chiefly as the result of centuries of war. Conquest welded the small kinship groups of primitive society into great political states.

Hence it was natural that the dominating psychological traits of the ancient world should be intolerance, and what Professor F. H. Giddings used to call a passion for cultural "homogeneity." Professor Giddings termed this era the "military-religious" stage in civilization. There is much ground for such a designation, since Oriental civilization combined military conquests with a fierce religious intolerance. It was the age of the creation of civil society and large political entities, fused and held together by military force and religious coercion.

There was at first no decrease in the power of supernaturalism as tribal society moved on into civil society. The old gods of those tribal groups which started on a successful career of conquest became the gods of the new territorial states. With the growth in power of their supposed earthly agents, the gods became even more arrogant and brooked less dissent. The conquerors, who believed that they owed their success to the gods, naturally refused to tolerate other religions. To welcome new deities would have been an unspeakable affront to the gods who were supposed to have aided them in their victories.

Since one of the major functions of ancient Oriental civilization was to develop order and unity on a large scale, this unifying psychology proved a valuable aid. It was not, however, in any sense a type of mental reaction adapted to the promotion of philosophical discussion, intellectual freedom, or scientific discovery. Although some beginnings were made in natural science, freedom of thought had to wait for the Greeks.

III. POLITICAL AND LEGAL EVOLUTION

At the close of the preliterary epoch political life revolved about rather small communities. It was based on kinship groups or on local aggregations which had never entered into kinship organization.

[1] James Baikie, *The Life of the Ancient East*, Macmillan, 1923, pp. 4-6.

By the fourth millennium before Christ Oriental peoples began to establish large states, based on military force and territorial organization instead of the so-called blood relationships of preliterary times. The transition from kinship society to political or civil society, involving territorial residence and the principle of citizenship, was very gradual. It came about as the outgrowth of a long series of tribal wars which intervened between the preliterary period and the Oriental empires. Those tribes which were best organized for warfare gradually extended their power until they brought extensive areas under control. War played a larger part in promoting political unity in Mesopotamia than in Egypt, where economic and religious factors were of more significance in advancing centralization. But there was plenty of war even in Egypt.

Usually, the transition from kinship to civil society was achieved by means of an intermediate stage called feudalism, which rested upon the personal relationships of the masses with powerful leaders. Therefore, in the political history which separates the Neolithic from the Iron Age man passed through three political stages: (1) tribal society, based upon kinship; (2) feudal society, founded upon personal relations and allegiance; and (3) civil society, resting upon territorial residence and the principle of citizenship.

In Babylonia, and Egypt to a lesser extent, we find admirable examples of small city-states which were later to be absorbed by expanding empires. City-states reappeared among Greeks and Romans, and in late medieval times among Italians and Dutch.

These city-states represented the earliest stage of civil society in the ancient Orient. They were superseded by the more characteristic political institutions of Oriental antiquity, the kingdoms and empires which grew up as a result of the conquest of other city-states by some powerful city-state or an alliance of such city-states. The great empires were the product of fierce warfare, savage massacres, and much brutality. Their creation was motivated partly by local rivalries, partly by the desire for loot and spoils, and partly by the sheer love of fighting. The latter motive was especially potent among the Assyrians. The administration of the empires was based on the absolutism of the ruling monarch, though in Egypt the power of the vestigial feudal nobility was often strong enough to make this theoretical absolutism difficult to realize in practice. In Mesopotamia also, the particularism of subject city-states at times served to restrict and mitigate royal tyranny.

These new states, with their extensive area, not only provided valuable political discipline for the race; they also supplied training in imperial administration. They may have had some influence upon the later Macedonian and Roman conquerors in setting a precedent for the building up of great empires, in short, in creating the imperial ideal. If so, they exerted a powerful influence upon the political and military tradition in Western life. From Scipio and Caesar to Charlemagne, Otto, Charles V, Napoleon and Mussolini, the Roman tradition of blood, iron, and imperialism has held sway over the minds of men.

We are not, in this book, in any way concerned with conventional political history and its chronology. But it may help to provide a better perspective and understanding if we briefly summarize the sequence of kingdoms and empires which held sway in the ancient East. The Egyptian kingdom and the earliest of the Mesopotamian states, that of the Sumerians, were approximately contemporaneous in their launching of civil society in the East—well before 3000 B.C. The Egyptian empire was established about 1580. The Babylonian kingdom followed the Sumerian epoch and was at the height of its power between 1725 and 1650. The Hittites of western Asia dominated the scene from about 1400 to 1100. The Assyrians ruled from approximately 1150 to 612, when a new Babylonian ascendancy arose with the Chaldeans. The Persians succeeded the Chaldeans about 540. Among the Mediterranean powers, Egypt, which first mastered sea navigation, dominated until the Cretan period from about 2250 to 1200. Crete was the first great maritime empire. Next in order came the Phoenicians, who were at the crest of their influence about 1100. In addition to these military and commercial powers, one should also mention the Aramaeans of Syria, leaders in land commerce and in cultural assimilation, and the Hebrews of Palestine, justly famous for their religious, ethical, and literary contributions.

The supernatural basis of society was, as we have noted, carried over into politics. As the gods were once supposed to preside over the deliberations of tribal assemblies, so now the new and absolute monarchs ruled by divine right. Indeed, they often assumed at their coronation many attributes of divinity. These extensive political entities, ruled by absolute monarchs, were important contributions to civilization and institutional development because they brought in law and order on a large scale. The new states protected life and fostered art, literature, and industry. Property and culture had always been jeopardized by the wars, robberies, and petty violence of primitive society.

But this order and protection were purchased in the Orient at a great sacrifice, namely, the termination of government by discussion—a practice which had characterized to some degree the assemblies of primitive tribes. It remained for the Greeks and Romans to work out on a large scale a passable fusion of law and order with freedom of discussion. Since the major deities presided over all aspects of society, intolerance extended not only to religious beliefs and practices, but also to social institutions in general. The life of the individual was regimented down to the last detail, so as to conform with the accepted mores of rulers and gods.

There was also epochal progress in law during the Oriental period. Law passed from the stage of custom to that of codification. The most famous code that we have recovered is that of Hammurabi, king of Babylon, compiled about 1700 B.C. and first discovered in 1901 in the old Persian city of Susa. It is systematically arranged and deals with a multitude of subjects, personal property, real estate, business relations, agricultural processes, irrigation problems, boundary disputes, family relations, personal injuries, labor control, and protection against unjust oppression. By its references to deeds, leases, wills, partnership agreements, relations between principal and agent, contracts, and promissory notes, it proves that as early as this period commerce had developed to a remarkable extent and a high type of economic morality and integrity had put in an appearance.

Supernaturalism colored jurisprudence just as it did politics. Temples were the law courts, priests were the judges. Law and order were fundamental ideals and received putative support from the gods. The ordeal was still often resorted to in criminal cases.

The Code of Hammurabi represents the first of five great stages in the evolution of jurisprudence; the others were the Justinian Code, the English common law, the Code Napoléon, and the German imperial code of the Hohenzollerns.

Professor Breasted believes that the Egyptians possessed just as advanced a legal code as that of Hammurabi in Babylonia. If they did, there are only the most fragmentary remains of it today. But the theory of Breasted in this regard is supported by reason and logic and by some slight documentary evidence.

IV. THE MATERIAL CULTURE OF THE ANCIENT ORIENT

While we must not overlook the important achievements of preliterary peoples in technology and industry, without which the material culture of the ancient Orient would have been impossible, it is probably true that the outstanding contribution of the Near Orient to human civilization lay in its industry, commerce, and the institutions associated with them. But for these previous achievements and rich resources to draw upon, the civilization of the Greeks and Romans could never have evolved as it did. We shall now proceed to review some of the notable advances made in this field.

In technology the ancient Orient made striking progress. The metal ages began at this time (about 4000 B.C.). Before the close of the ancient Oriental period (about 500 B.C.) all our well-known metals except aluminum were in use. Copper was the earliest, as already noted. The Egyptians seem to have invented copper ware, since we find many copper needles in the Egyptian tombs earlier than 4000 B.C., and copper chisels in Egyptian graves of 3500 B.C.

A harder and tougher metal appeared in bronze, about 2500 B.C., first used, apparently, by the inhabitants of the Aegean islands. Bronze seems to have appeared first where copper and the necessary alloys existed in a natural mixture. Shortly after 2500 B.C. man mastered the more complicated process of manufacturing bronze through mixing tin and other alloys with copper ore.

Though there is some evidence of an early use of iron in Africa, it is generally believed that the Hittites of Asia Minor first manufactured iron around the fourteenth century B.C. Excellent steel was made in Syria before the close of the Oriental period. Work in precious metals and gems had also begun. Egyptians were especially proficient in gold craft, Babylonians in silver craft.

The potter's wheel was invented in this era. Glazed pottery was manufactured, designs became more ingenious and artistic, and ornamentation more beautiful. The potter's wheel foreshadowed the all-important lathe, perhaps the most complicated mechanism which the ancient world produced. It also suggested the drill, which was widely exploited in jewelry work by the Egyptians.

The textile industry rapidly expanded. Finer cloth was demanded and quickly produced. Tapestry weaving began. The Egyptians excelled in the production of linen clothing, while the Babylonians carried the manufacture of woolens to a high degree of technical perfection. Clothing was no longer made exclusively in natural colors but came to be artificially dyed in a variety of shades.

Navigation ranks along with metal work and the origins of writing as one of the most revolutionary advances in the Oriental period. As early as 3000 B.C. the Egyptians and Cretans navigated freely around the eastern Mediterranean. The Cretans in fact laid the foundations of the first great maritime civilization. Canal building developed extensively. As early as about 2000 B.C. an Egyptian ruler had dug a canal connecting the upper end of the Red Sea with one of the branches of the Nile, thus permitting a boat to pass from the Red Sea to the Mediterranean —a forerunner of the Suez canal. Great progress was also made in land transportation through the invention of a wheeled vehicle and through progress in road building, the latter of which attained its highest perfection in Persia.

Architecture and engineering made stupendous strides. Consider the elaborate palaces, and above all, the great temples and pyramidal tombs. Such a structure as the great pyramid of Gizeh would be an impressive achievement even in modern engineering. Millions of tons of limestone blocks were floated down the Nile, and then dragged up to the level of the desert plateau, to be erected into a structure notable for accuracy of construction as well as monumental size. The granite for the chamber linings of the pyramids was brought from a distance of several hundred miles. As the distinguished Egyptologist, Dr. Flinders Petrie, says, in the construction of the great pyramid of Gizeh we find a modern optician's accuracy applied to a structure covering many acres. The remarkable engineering achievements of the lake dwellers and the builders of the huge megalithic monuments of western Europe were now far surpassed.

Besides impressive size and startling precision, Oriental architecture contributed the column and colonnade, which made their appearance in Egypt as early as 2750 B.C. The Babylonians, for their part, invented the arch and the vault, so thoroughly exploited later by the Romans. In building materials, stone and brick replaced the more ephemeral wooden structures of the lake dwellers.

We have been concerned so far chiefly with the pacific arts, but we must not forget that this period witnessed equally remarkable advances in the arts of war. The two were, indeed, closely connected. Stone weapons were replaced by copper and bronze, and still later by iron. The introduction of iron weapons revolutionized warfare and laid the basis for the military supremacy of the Hittites, and later of the Assyrians. The bow and arrow, invented in the Neolithic period, were now widely exploited by Oriental infantry.

The domestication of the horse created a cavalry corps. When harnessed to the chariot, the horse transformed warfare and was one of the reasons for the extended development of Oriental empires. Further, as Professor Breasted notes, the Assyrians, by 800 B.C., had worked out the principles of the "tank," or armored battle-car. This device was actually used, and differed from the modern tank chiefly in the absence of gunpowder and gasoline.

In concluding this brief résumé of technological progress in the ancient Orient we should not overlook the basic fact that man's efforts ceased to be exerted solely for maintaining mere existence, but were directed as well toward the achievement of comfort and even luxury.

Technological advances inevitably resulted in the enrichment of Oriental economic life. Man now made two revolutionary strides to increase his exploitation of the environment. One was the development of human slavery on a large scale. The other was the creation of an international division of labor through commerce.

The new technology increased the volume of manufactured commodities. Improved roads and the domestication of the donkey, camel, and horse, made possible long distance shipments of raw materials and finished products.[2] Division of labor—certain tasks allotted to certain men, instead of one man producing a complete product—increased quality as well as volume. Babylonia produced the first factories or shops, thus providing a better supervision of industry than could be achieved with scattered labor in individual homes. Everywhere we discover notable improvements in the variety and technique of manufacturing.

Agricultural and pastoral industries made enormous strides in the Oriental period. New types of animals, particularly fowls, were domesticated. The donkey was tamed very early in Egypt; the horse around 2200 B.C. by the Kassites in western Asia. We have evidence of selective breeding of domesticated animals in the Orient. Certain beasts ceased to be exploited solely for their flesh, skin or milk, and were used for draught purposes. The plow made its appearance, and hoe culture gradually disappeared. Likewise, the wheeled vehicle, which was designed to play so stupendous a part in subsequent history, was devised by the Sumerians, when they emerged from the Caspian area, possibly about 4000 B.C.

Agriculture was revolutionized not only by the invention of the plow, but in many other ways. More cereals were discovered. Agricultural technique improved, even to the extent of evolving a practicable seed drill hundreds of years before the Christian Era, though the drill was not used in western Europe until hundreds of years later. Men learned to divert and store water. Irrigation was elaborately developed by both the Egyptians and Babylonians. A comprehensive governmental control of the grain trade grew up among the Egyptians. Neolithic farming was carried out on partially cleared lands and on relatively small plots. Settlements, except among the lake dwellers, were frequently abandoned. Now we find large, permanently cultivated estates. Slave labor was widely used in agriculture as well as in manufacturing and building. For the first time in history man accumulated a large surplus of goods for sale. As a result, the ancient Orient witnessed the first widespread commercial activities, an important economic fact which also had extremely significant intellectual results.

Commerce has undoubtedly been one of the chief civilizing influences in history. Merchants carry not only tangible goods for sale but also intangible customs and thoughts. Further, in the Oriental age, commerce did not remain merely landwise and riverwise but emerged into the second great stage—seafaring trade. The Babylonians and the Aramaeans were the most active land traders. The

---

[2] The use of the camel and horse as beasts of burden came very late in the Oriental period. Main reliance was placed on the donkey.

Egyptians, Cretans, and Phoenicians carried trade over the seas and to the borders of the ocean.

As a result of expanded trading relations, commercial credit was greatly improved, particularly by the Babylonians, who invented such indispensable aids as bank checks, promissory notes, leases, contracts, and bills of sale. In the seventh century B.C. the Lydians of Asia Minor first coined money.

We also discover, in connection with the manufacturing and commerce of this era, the true origins of capitalism; namely, the accumulation of pecuniary resources to carry on future economic enterprises and to earn individual profits. Few advances in the Oriental period were historically more significant than this.

While the barter system of exchange prevailed in the early days, the major states of the Orient developed a true money economy even if they did not use coined money. Values were estimated according to the weight of precious metals. Egypt relied on a gold basis for her money system, while a silver standard prevailed in Mesopotamia. Copper, bronze, and iron were used as well for estimating relative exchange values. The Lydian invention of the coined money came too late to be of direct advantage to any of the great empires, except for Persia.

In general, the economic systems of Greece and Rome were inferior to those of Mesopotamia. In fact, classical civilization subsisted largely on the basis of its Oriental economic heritage. Even medieval prosperity was chiefly a retapping of the material sources of the East.

Christian prejudices against Oriental paganism—the "great beast that came up out of the sea"—created a belief that the ancient Orient had a disastrous and demoralizing influence on Mediterranean civilization. The facts are quite the reverse. Greece and Rome not only built on the commercial achievements of Asia Minor and the Nile Valley but the riches of the Orient really sustained Western civilization until the New World was discovered after A.D. 1492. The true situation has been admirably set forth by Franz Cumont:

> It is beyond all dispute that Rome found the point of support of its military power in the Occident. The legions from the Danube and the Rhine were always braver, stronger, and better disciplined than those from the Euphrates and the Nile. But it is in the Orient, especially in these countries of "old civilization," that we must look for industry and riches, for technical ability and artistic productions, as well as for intelligence and science, even before Constantine made it the center of political power.
>
> While Greece merely vegetated in a state of poverty, humiliation and exhaustion; while Italy suffered depopulation and became unable to provide for her own support; while the other countries of Europe were hardly out of barbarism; Asia Minor, Egypt and Syria gathered the rich harvests Roman peace made possible. Their industrial centers cultivated and renewed all the traditions that caused their former celebrity. A more intense intellectual life corresponded with the economic activity of these great manufacturing and exporting countries. They excelled in every profession except that of arms, and even the prejudiced Romans admitted their superiority. . . .
>
> Rome, then, far from having established her suzerainty, was tributary to the Orient in this respect. The Orient was her superior in the extent and precision

of its technical knowledge as well as in the inventive genius and ability of its workmen. The Caesars were great builders but frequently employed foreign help. Trajan's principal architect, a magnificent builder, was a Syrian, Apollodorus of Damascus. . . .

The Hellenized Orient imposed itself everywhere through its men and its works; it subjected its Latin conquerors to its ascendancy in the same manner as it dominated its Arabian conquerors later when it became the civilizer of Islam.[3]

Although the Oriental world may have been psychologically intolerant, its contributions to technology and commerce, then, really created civilization. The wealth and prosperity it produced gave the aristocracy leisure for intellectual pursuits and permitted the Greeks to launch the first great attack on that supernaturalism which had dominated man's intellectual outlook since the earliest days of preliterary society. Professor James Henry Breasted has strikingly summarized our cultural debt to the Orient:

How far would the average citizen go in his day's program if he were to eliminate as of no more use the things which he has inherited from the early Orient? When he rises in the morning and clothes his body in *textile garments,* when he sits down to the breakfast table spread with *spotless linen,* set with vessels of *glazed pottery* and with drinking goblets of *glass,* when he puts forth his hand to any implement of *metal* on that table except aluminum, when he eats his morning *roll* or *cereal* and drinks his glass of *milk,* or perhaps eats his morning chop cut from the flesh of a *domesticated animal,* when he rolls downtown in a vehicle supported on *wheels,* when he enters his office building through a porticus supported on *columns,* when he sits down at his desk, spreads out a sheet of *paper,* grasps his *pen,* dips it in *ink,* puts a *date,* at the head of the sheet, writes a *check* or a *promissory note,* or dictates a *lease* or *contract* to his secretary, when he looks at his watch with the *sixty-fold division* of the circle on its face, in all these and in an infinite number of other commonplaces of life—things without which modern life could not go on for a single hour, the average man of today is using items of an inheritance which began to pass across the eastern Mediterranean from the Orient when Europe was discovered by civilization five thousand years ago.

Even in the world of science it is found, for example, that in the modern study of the moon the observations of the Babylonians furnishing the earliest known data are of great value. Similarly the processes of smelting metallic ores devised by the Egyptians some six thousand years ago, when they became the first smelters of metal, have been employed with little change ever since, until in quite recent years modern chemistry has introduced improvements and changes.[4]

V. SOCIAL DIFFERENTIATION AND THE RISE OF A LEISURE CLASS

Economic changes in the Oriental epoch brought numerous social changes in their train. Improvement in agriculture, greater soil fertility, expansion of commerce and manufacture, all produced a considerable increase in population.

The political integration of society permitted larger social units to develop than

3 F. V. M. Cumont, *Oriental Religions in Roman Paganism,* Dover Publications, Inc., 1956, pp. 2, 8, 10.
4 J. H. Breasted, "The New Past," *University of Chicago Record,* October, 1920, p. 245.

had existed in preliterary times. The kinship basis of social life expanded into relationships based on locality, profession, and economic class. Class differentiation on an extensive and varied scale began to appear. Society was headed towards a division into two extremes—a leisure class, entirely divorced from manual labor, and a slave class, solely devoted to manual labor. The slave class, as a matter of fact, made possible the existence of a leisure class.

This leisure class, while sustained by an often oppressive social system, played a crucial part in the growth of civilization. For the first time in the long course of human history a relatively large number of men were relieved from the burdens of securing a livelihood, and could devote their time to art and science, as well as to display and dissipation. For the first time, too, polygyny was practiced on a considerable scale. The males of this new leisure class were the first group in human history who could support a large group of concubines.

In addition to the ruling and slave classes, there appeared a large number of industrial and professional classes; in fact most of the social classes with which we are today familiar. As early as 2600 b.c. Sumerian documents mention, in addition to peasantry and landowners: (1) learned professions, including priests, teachers, librarians, scribes, publishers, notaries, physicians, astronomers, and musicians; and (2) craftsmen, including fishermen, hunters, weavers, fullers, dyers, brickmakers, potters, smiths, carpenters, boatbuilders, goldsmiths, jewelers, sculptors, and carvers in wood and ivory. The vocational basis of society was already firmly established.

Thoroughgoing social discipline was worked out on a larger scale than ever. Homogeneity, the outstanding trait of Oriental psychology, made, as we have noted, for a rather thorough regimentation of social life.

VI. THE ORIGINS OF NATURAL SCIENCE IN EGYPT AND BABYLONIA

Natural science has been the outstanding factor in the production of contemporary civilization, and it had its origins in the ancient Orient. Practical considerations of everyday life seem to have been chiefly responsible for these remarkable developments. The Egyptians had to be able to compute the rise and fall of the Nile, mark off boundary lines, and lay out pyramids and other enormous structures. The Babylonians needed mathematics for their irrigation projects and commercial computations, while their pastoral duties stimulated the study of the heavens at night.

The Ahmôse papyrus, which goes back to around 2200 b.c.—the oldest known mathematical treatise—reveals that the Egyptians had already mastered elementary arithmetical computations and the principles of rudimentary mensuration. The Egyptians reckoned numbers in terms of units of ten, understood whole numbers and fractions, and could add, subtract, and divide. But they never learned how to multiply directly until the Hellenistic period. Multiplication was achieved by repeated additions. They comprehended the principles of arithmetic and geometric progression. They worked out tables of weights and measures and devised a crude abacus. With later improvements, this was used for practical computations until the Arabic numerals were introduced by the Muslims well along in the Christian Era.

In algebra, the Egyptians went far enough to solve equations of the first degree. Further algebraic knowledge came to them later from India. In geometry, the Egyptians learned how to compute the areas of rectangles, triangles, hexagons, and trapezoids. They also seem to have known how to estimate areas bounded by circular arcs. They could compute approximately the circumference of a circle, giving π a value of 3.16. They made some steps towards elementary trigonometry in their triangulation and plane surveying. They surveyed by means of taut ropes. The Egyptian astronomers observed the heavenly bodies carefully and were close enough in their computations to work out the first calendar—probably by 4241 B.C. —certainly by 2781 B.C. It was based on a year of twelve months of thirty days each, with five feast days thrown in at the end to make a year of 365 days. Each year started on the day (July 19th) on which the dog-star Sirius appeared on the horizon at sunrise—the year thus being of a stellar-solar type.

The Egyptians founded the science of medicine. Careful embalming of the dead gave them a knowledge of anatomy unrivaled in their time. Drawings as far back as 2500 B.C. definitely demonstrate the existence of surgical operations. Much attention was given to the treatment of fractured bones. The dark house interiors of Egypt, and perhaps other causes, made the Egyptians prone to eye troubles and they had their oculists to deal with the problem. One papyrus gives a full statement of the principles of diagnosis, treatment, and cure. An extensive materia medica was accumulated and described. The Egyptians made the first wide use of drugs. Greek medicine was apparently derived mainly from Egyptian experience and achievements. The Egyptian interest in drugs, together with dyeing and metallurgy, enabled them to found alchemy, that esoteric art which ultimately led to chemistry. By the Hellenistic period it was well developed and handed on to the Greeeks.

In mathematics, the Babylonians advanced beyond the Egyptians in devising the multiplication table. They prepared tables of squares and cubes, understood arithmetic and geometric progression, and had a decimal system. As early as 2500 B.C. they had worked out a complicated system of weights and measures. So far as we know, the Babylonians knew nothing of algebra, but they did do important work in geometry. They understood the problems of the right-angled triangle, divided the circle into sixty equal parts, gave π a value of 3, and worked out the principles of the hexagon inscribed in a circle.

The Babylonians were famous astronomers, beginning their observations as early as 2000 B.C. By the sixth century B.C. they could calculate the relative positions of the sun and moon and predict eclipses. Adopting and perpetuating the Sumerian lunar calendar of twenty-nine and one-half days to the month, they put in an extra month when needed. Each year had twelve months. From the Sumerians, also, we obtained our twenty-four-hour day and our seven-day week. The Babylonians later divided the day into hours, minutes, and seconds—which was not done in medieval Europe until the fourteenth century A.D.—and they invented the sun-dial. Both the Egyptians and the Babylonians viewed the cosmos as a great rectangular box, whose floor was the earth. The Babylonians imagined that it had a vaulted roof, held up by four great corner pillars. It was these cosmological views which have been responsible for the persistent phrase about "the four corners of the earth."

The Babylonians invented the pseudo-science of astrology which we shall have many occasions to mention later on. This rested on the assumption that an occult relation exists between the heavenly bodies and the destiny of nations and individuals. The Babylonians were mainly interested in collective destiny, the Greeks being chiefly responsible for the individualization of astrology and its predictions. The golden age of Babylonian astrology came after the Chaldean conquest in the late seventh century. Astrology passed on from Babylonia to Greece and from there to the Romans and to medieval Muslims and Christians.

The Babylonians fell far behind the Egyptians in their medical principles and practices. They regarded disease as the result of evil spirits, a characteristic primitive notion. Hence, they relied upon magicians, incantations, and other forms of magic to effect cures. Medieval medicine embodied both the medical science of the Egyptians and the astrological medicine of the Babylonians—both greatly elaborated, of course, before they reached Christian Europe.

VII. THE PROFUSION OF ORIENTAL RELIGIONS

It is an interesting historical fact that every important world religion has had its birth in the ancient Orient. Even such recent cults as Mormonism and New Thought are, directly or indirectly, of Oriental derivation. No area in the world approaches the Orient for profusion in pouring forth varied systems of supernaturalism. Not even the Greek and Roman religion escaped. The Greek mysteries and their mythology were brought in from the Orient, and the Sibylline Books and emperor worship in Roman religion, as well as the mystery religions of the imperial period, all came in the beginning from the Orient. First let us look at the religions of the ancient Egyptians.

Egyptian religion, like all other historical religions, can be intelligently understood only against the general background of those primitive beliefs which we described in the last chapter. It is not surprising that in Egypt, land of warmth and sunshine, the sun should take a leading place in the pantheon. The sun-god, in fact, under various names, is the most prominent of Oriental deities.

Before dynasties arose in Egypt there was no national religious cult. Each nome —city-state—had its own particular pantheon. When certain cities triumphed over others, their deities were exalted. The priesthood played an important part in systematizing Egyptian religion. The national cult of Egypt in its golden era was, above all, a priest-made religion, a fact which rendered it impossible for religious reformers to gain much headway.

The first step in forming a national religion was made when the priests of Heliopolis brought forward their sun-god Ra and his eight satellites. When Thebes rose to political and military prestige, its god, Amon, had to receive recognition, and so the supreme god of Egypt became Amon-Ra. The effort of Pharaoh

Amenhotep IV, about 1375 B.C., to supplant Amon-Ra by a straightforward monotheistic sun-god failed.

The Osiris myth was extremely influential in Egyptian religion. Involving such factors as the sun, the Nile, soil fertility, and immortality, it dealt with the creation, nature, and destiny of man. Osiris, a wise king who civilized the Egyptians, was killed by his brother Set and his body scattered in bits over Egypt. His wife, Isis, mourned bitterly and searched for her husband's remains. She found them and Osiris returned to life and became ruler over the kingdom of the dead. Horus, son of Osiris and Isis, apprehended Set and caused the tribunal of gods to condemn him.

This myth, obviously, is a representation of life and death, the coming of vegetation in the spring and its disappearance in the autumn, the cycle of night and day, and the like. Osiris was supposed to provide food in this life and immortality in the next world. The god Amon-Ra was pictured as passing through the realm of the dead every twenty-four hours, to be born anew each morning—symbolizing the setting and rising of the sun.

Egyptian religion laid much stress on the future life, holding that the soul persisted after death. Elaborate judgment rites were practiced. The pyramids—the tombs of Egyptian kings—were furnished with miniature replicas of the earthly environment, with symbols of everything a man enjoyed and used on earth, so that when he revived he would find himself at home, and begin life over again in all its splendor and comfort. The Book of the Dead describes in detail the elaborate rites and the inquisition used in the judgment of the dead to determine their destination in the life beyond.

To the Egyptians, immortality did not, however, have the crucial importance it did to the Persians and Christians. Nor was the combat between the powers of good and evil provided with so ingenious and elaborate a philosophical setting as it was in Persian theology and the Christian epic.

The same general religious patterns prevailed in Mesopotamia as in the religious life and ideas of the Egyptians. Marduk was the reigning deity of Babylon. When the Assyrians conquered the city, they exalted their own god Assur, who was symbolized by the sun disc. He fought and conquered the monster Tiâmat, and became the protective god of the Assyrian empire. But the goddess Ishtar was at all times the most important religious deity. As we may suspect, she symbolized "mother earth," fertility, reproduction, and creative power. Associated with Ishtar was her husband Tammuz, the vegetation god, after whom a month in the Jewish calendar is named. There were a number of subordinate deities.

Mesopotamia produced several religious epics woven around its pantheon, which we shall discuss later in this chapter (in the section on Oriental literature). It is important to notice that the Babylonian story of creation and a flood was probably borrowed by the Hebrews. Ishtar's annual descent into the underworld, and her safe and glorious return to the upper world of light and life, was perpetuated in the fertility myths of Syria, Greece, and Rome.

Though they believed in immortality, the Mesopotamians were less interested than the Egyptians in the afterlife. The souls of the dead were imagined as living in a gloomy realm ruled by a grim goddess. And for the most part, these souls remained inert and motionless.

As a consequence of this relative lack of interest in the beyond, Mesopotamian religion concentrated on improving man's fate on earth. The Babylonians employed prophecy, magic, and astrology to control destiny. Divination to foretell the future was carried on by watching the action of the entrails, especially the liver, of slain animals. Through the semioriental Etruscans, this practice was passed on to the Romans.

The Mesopotamians were pastoral people; hence their interest in the heavens. They came to believe that there was a mysterious relationship between heavenly bodies and national destiny—the basis of astrology. The Babylonians and Assyrians worked out an elaborate system of incantations against evil spirits; provided extensive sacrifices to renew contact with the gods and secure regeneration; and devised many hymns and prayers.

Among Oriental religions, the Hebraic is obviously of cardinal significance. Not only did it serve as an important source of Christianity, but its moral code—Hebraic religion and morality were inextricably woven together—is still dominant in Western civilization.

The Hebrews were originally sun worshipers and Jehovah (Yahweh) was a pastoral god of the Kenites of Midian. It is believed that Moses, who married a Kenite girl, took his father-in-law's god over into the Hebrew camp. At any rate, in the Mosaic period, Yahweh underwent a significant change. He became the supreme tribal god of the Hebrews, and he was supposed to have revealed the Ten Commandments to Moses. In due time—especially after the Jewish exile from Palestine in 586 B.C.—Yahweh developed from a tribal deity into a sort of universal providence guiding the destinies of mankind. The Hebraizing of Yahweh gave a moral impetus to the tribes of Israel, a nobler conception of social justice, particularly as expressed by the major prophets such as Amos and Isaiah. Much of Hebrew mythology was, as we have seen, derived from the Mesopotamians.

Before they entered Palestine around 1400-1200 B.C., the Hebrews were a nomadic pastoral race. When they came into contact with the advanced culture of the Canaanites, who had occupied the country for a long time, their cultural development made very rapid strides. Soon the Hebrews abandoned their rude ways and adopted Canaanite civilization. In Palestine they learned to farm and to engage in industry and trade. They lived in permanent dwellings, possessed a written language, and created a crude form of government. Assimilation to civilization did not come all at once. It took three centuries to work off the memories of their nomadic past.

This nomadic heritage was the source of a great deal of the social conflict which is mirrored in the Old Testament history. The desert life implied social equality, coöperative activities, common ownership of property, and absence of extensive wealth. In a settled agricultural and commercial society such conditions were less easily maintained.

About 1000 B.C. the Hebrew kingdom was established out of warring factions, as a result of a movement headed by priests and kings. Under Saul and David, the Canaanites were completely subdued, and all of Palestine was conquered. The kingdom reached its apex of political unity and material property during Solomon's reign (about 960 B.C.). Largely as a result of his ruinous taxation, however —Solomon was apparently not so wise as the Bible would have us believe—the kingdom at his death split into two parts. The united realm was thus less than a century old before it passed away. In Solomon's reign, the Hebrews became important in the inland caravan trade of western Asia. They also had a commercial fleet, commanded by Phoenician sailors. The Hebrews were successful merchants and capable farmers and herdsmen.

When the kingdom split up, a period of decline followed. Israel in the North and Judah in the South were mutually antagonistic. Israel had fertile land, commerce, industry, and an active town life. Judah had only one metropolis, Jerusalem. Its soil was poor and most of the population were shepherds.

The hostility of the two kingdoms was reflected in their religions. The North generally adopted Canaanite agricultural and fertility deities in addition to their desert god, Yahweh. The South execrated the Canaanite gods, who seemed to them to protect especially the town inhabitants, and their hated wealth and injustice to the poor. In the South, Yahweh was the protector of the poor and needy.

Such an attitude concerning Yahweh is found in the lamentations of the early prophets. When the kingdom of Israel was conquered by Assyria about 720 B.C., Jerusalem having escaped, the prophets of Judah exclaimed that Yahweh had punished the Israelites who had forsaken him. This was a sign of his great power and the Judean priesthood made capital out of it.

Around 586 B.C., however, the Chaldeans conquered Jerusalem and the people of Judah, taken to Babylonia as captives, suffered the same fate as Israel. When Persia rose to power about 540 B.C. the Judaeans were permitted to return to Palestine. Two centuries earlier, the northern tribes—the famous ten of Israel— had been transplanted by the Assyrians and lost their identity.

The last step towards relative monotheism was taken during and after the period of exile. Yahweh, originally a simple pastoral deity of a desert tribe, was now turned into an omnipotent God, made in man's image, full of loving kindness and righteousness. The change was far reaching and it vitally affected the later moral and religious history of Europe. In the woeful period of exile, when the Hebrews were strangers in Babylonia, Yahweh appealed to them more strongly than ever, and grew in stature until he became the universal God whom all Oriental nations would some day recognize, worship, and obey.

When, however, they returned to the homeland around 538 B.C., the Hebraic religion contracted into a narrow shell. The Hebrews clung to their God with fierce exclusiveness; in fact, he did not travel beyond the borders of Palestine until the Hebrews migrated somewhat extensively during Hellenistic times.

Hebraic culture, important as it was, played an insignificant rôle in later history, when compared to Hebraic religion. For two thousand years millions upon millions of men worshiped, sacrificed, and martyred themselves for a deity who had sprung from the imagination of this small tribe of shepherds and farmers clustered along the river Jordan. Indeed, it is quite true that no other people— unless it be the Attic Greeks—have exerted an influence on later civilization so disproportionate to their size, wealth, and political strength.

The Jews did not conquer the world, as did the Romans. They did not even make a great impression among their own neighbors. They were indeed a race that, politically, could scarcely hold its own people together. They quarreled among themselves; ten of their twelve tribes were dispersed and assimilated; and the remaining two were carried off into Babylonia as abject captives. But, by virtue of their religion and its notable literature, they did, in a sense, conquer Western civilization.

The last dispersion of the Jews, in A.D. 70, scattered them to all ends of the world and subjected them, for twenty centuries, to persistent cruelties at the hands of the Gentiles—a persecution which, paradoxically, vastly increased the prestige and world-influence of the Jews.

The Philistines, who were probably not a Semitic people, migrated from Asia Minor around 1190 B.C., to the southern coast of Syria and Palestine in what has been called Philistia. They brought many new cultural elements. It seems definitely established that they introduced iron, which they had adopted after having come in contact with the Hittites. They also brought in Aegean pottery and architecture, and the custom of cremating the dead.

There are some traces of Philistine influence on the religion, mythology, and literature of the Hebrews; for instance, the tree and pillar cults of early Israel, calf worship, and probably many famous biblical stories. From the Philistines were apparently derived the Samson and Delilah episodes, Abraham's intended sacrifice of Isaac, Jephthah's rash vow, and, perhaps, the incident of Potiphar's wife and Joseph.

In the realm of religion the Persians, who conquered Asia Minor in the sixth century B.C., made a contribution to Western civilization rivaled only by the Hebrews. Their religion was reformed by the great preacher Zoroaster, who lived some time between 1000 and 660 B.C.

The Persians were apparently the first to carry the primitive conception of a hierarchy of good and evil spirits over into an abstract philosophy. They believed that God created the world as an arena in which the principles of good and evil might engage in a decisive struggle. The Persian god, Ormuzd, led the hosts of the good against the Persian devil, Ahriman. Ormuzd symbolized light and Ahriman darkness. Ormuzd, aided by the savior Mithras, would eventually crush Ahriman and vanquish his army of devils.

Those inhabitants of this earth who were wise enough to believe in and follow Ormuzd would be rewarded with eternal bliss in heaven surrounding the sun. Those who foolishly supported Ahriman would be destroyed in a lake of fire and brimstone. After good had decisively triumphed over evil, and Ahriman and his devilish host were defeated and destroyed, the physical universe would pass away, having fulfilled the function for which it was created.

This Persian conception of an afterlife had a tremendous influence on later European history. The early Jews, as well as the Greeks and Romans, were not greatly concerned with man's existence after death. The Jews thought that the dead gathered in Sheol; the Greeks called this region Hades. Both believed that it was a drab place where virtue received no special reward and wickedness no particular punishment. But the Persians accentuated the beyond. It was of the first importance to them whether a man would dwell in blissful immortality beside the god Ormuzd—or whether he would be damned and hideously destroyed.

These important religious notions of the Persians were adopted by the later Jews, as witnessed by the diabolism and eschatology of the Book of Enoch. They were passed on to the Romans and Christians through the Persian mystery religions, Mithraism and Manichaeism. Christian ideas of the devil, cosmic dualism, and heaven and hell were derived mainly from these Persian sources.

The Hittites seem to have carried to its highest development the typical Oriental fertility religions and fertility myths. Their chief deity was the goddess Kubaba, the great earth mother. Such beliefs and the consequent practices lingered in western Asia long after Hittite ascendancy had waned. It was from Anatolia that the Greeks and Romans derived the mystery religion of the great mother goddess of fertility, Cybele.

Mainly of Oriental origin were the Greek and Roman mystery religions, which became the most important element in the religious life of these peoples.[5] The Sibylline Books, introduced by the Romans during the Second Punic War, had been adapted by the Greeks from Oriental mystery religions and mysticism. The Roman notions and rites of divination came from Babylonia by way of the Etruscans and the Sibylline Books. Oriental contributions as well were the popular mystery religions of the empire—Mithraism, Manichaeism, and the Isis-Seraphis mystery—and the mystery religions of the great mother goddess of Anatolia, Cybele, and of Sol Invictus of Syria.

Philo and other Alexandrian Jews were chiefly responsible for the Platonic strains in later Judaism. Christianity, of course, was originally an Oriental mystery religion, one which was to be profoundly influenced by other competing Oriental mysteries in the later Roman Empire. One of the main Christian heresies, Gnostic Christianity, was a combination of Christianity and Hellenistic Platonism.

The Arabian religion of Mohammed, or Islam, enunciated in the early seventh century A.D., also belongs to the Oriental heritage we have been tracing. The religion taught in the Koran—the sacred book of Islam—relies heavily on the Old Testament, the Persian, and the earlier Arabic religions, particularly those of the *magii* and the Sabaeans. It pays a tribute to Christianity by representing Jesus Christ as one of the major prophets who preceded Mohammed. However, the Christian strains in Islam are derived more from the heretical Gnostic Christianity than from the orthodox creed. The Koran refers to the Old Testament, but not to the New Testament.

Islam is, in fact, a composite religion. Mohammed mixed old ingredients at a time when many religions had penetrated the Arabian peninsula. The basis of the Islamic creed is that "There is only one God, Allah, and Mohammed is his prophet." It laid special stress on the Persian and Christian doctrines of immortality and the future life.

The major religious practices of Islam are the mastery of the many religious

[5] Cf. L. R. Farnell, *Greece and Babylon*, Scribner, 1912.

formulas, obedience to creed, five daily prayers, fasting during the sacred month of Ramazan, almsgiving, and pilgrimages to the sacred city of Mecca. Compared with Christianity, Islam is based on alms and precepts; it is concerned more with obedience to commandments than with devotion to dogmatic "faith."

Islam has a simpler creed than Christianity; it has neither elaborate priesthood nor expensive ecclesiastical machinery. Like the Old Testament the Koran is both a book of religion and a book of law. Its moral code is as high as that of Roman paganism or Christianity. "The equality of all Mohammedans before the law," says Professor J. W. Thompson, "the absence of antagonistic class distinctions, the absence of any priestly caste—for in Islam every man is his own priest—the freedom of Mohammedan society from the evils of an ambitious and avaricious clergy like the bishops and abbots of the Byzantine Empire—these qualities stamp early Mohammedism with a new and refreshing vigor." [6]

VIII. MORAL PROGRESS IN THE ANCIENT ORIENT

From our present knowledge of documentary sources, it seems that the Egyptians were the first to evolve a moral code based on the concepts of justice, truth, individual worth, and personal equality. In short, many of our present ethical ideas are found among Egyptian inscriptions of the second millennium before Christ. The Egyptian legal code, which has been lost, was doubtless based on similar noble ideals. Unlike the code of Hammurabi, justice was not meted out according to the scales of a fairly rigid class system.

The Egyptians were probably the first to develop a consciousness of individualism, and consequently of an individual's rights and worth, as set off against the family, clan, and nation.

Around 2000 B.C. we find Egyptian documents embodying the high moral fervor associated with modern social reformers. This is particularly illustrated in a tractate called by Breasted the "Eloquent Peasant," a discussion, cast in the form of a picturesque Oriental tale, which summarizes the duties of a just official towards the poor and oppressed. This is one of the earliest examples of Oriental skill in illustrating abstract principles by concrete situations, so wonderfully exemplified later in the parables of Jesus.

A peasant, traveling with his small train of donkeys loaded with the produce of the village, is robbed of his animals and all his goods by a petty official. Thereupon, the peasant appeals to the grand steward, of whom it is expected that he will be as fair to the poor as to the rich, to the underprivileged as to the privileged. On the ruling class is placed the responsibility for relief from oppression and for the practice of truth, uprightness, and justice. The nobility are to be the moral lights of society. In the story of the "Eloquent Peasant" the injured man obtains retribution by appealing to the king after the grand steward refused to heed his touching pleas.

The Egyptians had a god of justice, Maat, and they believed that a just man's memory never dies. In the "Eloquent Peasant" the sun-god Ra admonishes man

6 J. W. Thompson, *Economic and Social History of the Middle Ages*, Century, 1928 (Ungar, 1959), p. 193.

to "speak the truth, do the truth. For it is great, it is mighty, it is enduring. The reward thereof shall find thee, and it shall follow thee unto revered old age." Thus we find not only a modern standard of morality as early as 2000 B.C., but we note that the scribes of Pharaoh's court at that time took the trouble to compose moral tracts like the "Eloquent Peasant," that they were propagandists for social justice. Indeed their crusade probably bore fruit, for some time later a certain Egyptian king, Ipuwer, put into dramatic form his own arraignment of the times, and added a sketch of the golden age which he hoped would follow. This tract, dating from the feudal age (2500-1580 B.C.), is called by Breasted the "Admonitions of Ipuwer."

Its author finds moral degeneration and social revolt everywhere. Iniquity triumphs; justice lies fallow; the wicked are becoming rich, the righteous poor:

> Behold, he who had no yoke of oxen is (now) possessor of a herd; and he who found no plough-oxen for himself is (now) owner of a herd. Behold, he who had no grain is (now) owner of granaries; and he who used to fetch grain for himself (now) has it issued (from his own granary.)[7]

The moral situation depicted in this work coincides with our knowledge of social conditions of the times. How is regeneration to be affected? Ipuwer recalls that once in the distant past the sun-god Ra, the ideal king, ruled Egypt, and the peculiar significance of the "Admonitions of Ipuwer" is the noble dream which inspired it, the vision of a benevolent king who will return to vanquish iniquity, reward the virtuous, uplift the poor and spread peace and prosperity. Such a dream is at the heart of the Messianic hope of the Hebrews, of Plato's *Republic*, the sayings of Jesus, and the moral fervor of modern reformers.

The Egyptian crusaders seem to have been more successful than most social reformers. An era, which Breasted calls the "Age of Character," finally dawned. King Amenemhet I inaugurated a policy of social justice which became the very framework of government: "The old days when a man's conduct was satisfactory if it received the approval of father, mother, brothers, and sisters, were passed, there had arisen what may be called a social conscience." [8] On the door post of Amenemhet's front chapel was inscribed the justifiably proud epitaph:

> There was no citizen's daughter whom I misused, there was no widow whom I afflicted, there was no peasant whom I evicted, there was no herdsman whom I expelled. . . . There was none wretched in my community, there was none hungry in my time. . . . I gave to the widow as to her who had a husband. I did not exalt the great (man) above the small (man) in any thing that I gave. Then came great Niles (inundations), rich in the arrears of the field.[9]

Even more rich and mature were the teachings of *The Wisdom of Amenemope,* written by a sage of the tenth century B.C.

Nowhere in Western civilization is there to be found a higher moral code than this. It forms, as Breasted says, the dawn of conscience, it spread into the world

[7] J. H. Breasted, *The Dawn of Conscience,* Scribner, 1933, p. 196.
[8] Breasted, *op. cit.,* p. 23.
[9] *Ibid.,* p. 214.

of western Asia, was absorbed and elaborated by the Hebrews, woven into their glorious literature and handed down as imperishable ideals, to elevate the standards of Europe and the Western World.

From all that can be gathered, Mesopotamian morality was on as high a level as the Egyptian, although it did not produce any notable literature of social protest or social idealism.

While the Code of Hammurabi is partial to the rich and the vested interests, it did offer to the poor and the weak some measure of protection, thus bearing out in part the claim that the code as a whole was designed to prevent the strong from oppressing the weak. This was particularly true in regard to the unusual protection afforded to debtors.

Since Babylonia was a commercial and industrial state, it was natural that much stress would be placed on honesty and dependability in economic relations. A higher development was reached in this field than anywhere else before the time of the medieval guilds. The sanctity of contracts was strongly emphasized. Hence, we find extreme penalties imposed for purchases made without a contract or without witnesses. Breaking a contract was a serious matter. Short weights, shoddy goods, and inferior workmanship were dealt with drastically. If such practical ideals for economic morality embodied no messianic hope or any implicit social revolution, they at least attested to a high development of the sense of integrity and fairness in economic relations and were, perhaps, of more practical value than Utopian dreams which were never realized.

In Mesopotamian literature dating from about the time of Hammurabi (c. 1700 B.C.) we have glimpses of a well-developed sense of justice and a regard for the rights of the humble for whom the gods are solicitous, as is evident from the remarkable pronouncement at the end of the Hammurabic Code:

> It is I that the great gods have elected to be the Shepherd of Salvation, whose sceptre is just. . . . That the strong may not oppress the weak; that the orphan and the widow may be counseled . . . to sustain the feeble. . . . By command of Shamash, the great judge of heaven and earth, justice shall glisten in the land. . . . The oppressed, who has a lawsuit, shall come before my image as king of justice.

The slave finds in this code many considerations which Roman law later denied him.

There was also a nice sense of personal decency and nobility in Mesopotamia reminiscent of many things in the New Testament:

> Set a bridle in thy mouth: watch carefully thy speech.
> As the riches of men let thy lips be accounted rare.
> Let audacity for wickedness be an abomination unto thee.
> Utter not words of arrogance or lying counsel.
> Harm not in any way thy adversary.
> Recompense with good the man who doeth evil to thee.
> Oppose thine enemy with righteous dealing.

The preceding golden precepts emanate from ancient Babylonia, the land which has been defamed by Christian historians as the sink of evil, or, as the author of the Book of Revelation puts it, "Babylon the Great, the Mother of Harlots and abomination of the Earth." This stigma was generally accepted until excavations of recent times revealed a literature which proved how utterly baseless was the accusation.

Babylon was in fact about as sensitive to indecency as we are. Its moral standards were as high as ours and it doubtless had no greater volume of immorality, cruelty, exploitation, dishonesty, corruption, and vice than modern New York, London, or Moscow. The only outstanding difference between moral standards of ancient Babylonia and of modern times was their sanctified religious practice of temple prostitution, the existence of which is acknowledged by Leonard Woolley and other leading authorities on this period, and is inferred from the Babylonian epic, *Gilgamesh*.

But even this fact should not shock us since the Hebrews also clung to this institution, which is in fact frequently associated with the early phases of fertility cults, as the very appellation of the Mesopotamian fertility goddess, "passionate Ishtar," indicates. By the time of the advent of the Assyrians as conquerors of Mesopotamia the character of Ishtar had grown quite civilized. She became the Queen of Righteousness and it is not probable that the crude practice of temple prostitution could have been associated with her. Equally misleading is the bad impression one gets of Assyrian morality, particularly Nineveh, its capital, from the Old Testament. The Assyrians apparently had a high sense of social morality and personal decency, as lofty as the Babylonians or Egyptians.

The noted moral code of the Old Testament was, thus, not a unique and original Hebrew creation but in part an amalgamation of the teachings of the Egyptians, Babylonians, and Assyrians, which were current in the region of Palestine during the existence of the Hebrew nation.

Egyptian armies had marched across Palestine as early as 2500 B.C. Egypt ruled the land from about 1600 to 1200 B.C. The Hebrews reached Palestine around 1200 B.C. For centuries before that Palestine was the home of the Canaanites. The Hebrews, themselves desert nomads when they settled their "homeland," came into contact with the highly advanced civilization of the Canaanites which was largely a composite product of Babylonian and Egyptian elements. Out of this complex culture arose the ethical ideals which have since mainly dominated Western civilization. The Hebrew nation, as we have seen, existed as a political entity from about 1000 to 575 B.C., after which it was humiliated, but it held on one way or another until the first century of our era.

When Hebrew civilization was at its apex both Egypt and Babylonia had fallen into decay. Thus the moral and literary achievements of the inhabitants of north Africa and Mesopotamia were handed on to this Palestinian tribe of desert nomads, who incorporated it, along with their own ideals and mores, into an elaborate and persistent literature, whence it spread to the whole Western World.

The "age of character" of the Israelites was already flourishing by 700 B.C. A good deal of the Bible had already been composed. The old Midianite pastoral god, Yahweh, had become the effulgent deity of the Old Testament, the god of justice and righteousness, who likewise demanded righteousness of his votaries. Long before this time, as already mentioned, Egyptian moral ideas suffused the locality. Yahweh took on many characteristics of the Egyptian god of righteousness, Maat. Moreover, the Hebrew "Sun of Righteousness" probably refers to the Egyptian sun-god Ra, who was also a god of righteousness.

The high morality associated with the people of Israel shines through the prophetic utterances of the prophets of the eighth and seventh centuries. Amos, who probably flourished around 765 b.c., attempted to put the popular religion of Yahweh on a high ethical basis. Religious leaders of his day, apparently, regarded the observance of ritual as being of equal importance in the Lord's eyes with the observance of morals. Amos denounced the empty forms of worship. He protested against the custom of substituting ritual for right conduct, and represented the Lord as exclaiming:

I hate, I despise your feasts, and I will take no delight in your solemn assemblies.
Yea, though you offer me your burnt-offerings and meal-offerings, I will not accept them; neither will I regard the peace offerings of your fat beasts.
Take thou away from me the noise of thy songs; for I will not hear the melody of thy viols.
But let justice roll down as waters, and righteousness as a mighty stream.

Amos not only lifted ethics above ritual; he castigated the economic order of his day, which ground the faces of the poor and depressed the masses into servility. He protested, like a modern socialist, against the maldistribution of wealth and, through the mouth of Yahweh, predicted the most dreadful retribution.

Hear this, O ye that would swallow up the needy, and cause the poor of the land to fail,
Saying, when will the new moon be gone, that we may sell grain? and the sabbath,
That we may set forth wheat, making the ephah small, and the shekel great, and dealing falsely with balances of deceit;
That we may buy the poor for silver, and the needy for a pair of shoes, and sell the refuse of the wheat?

　　　·　　　　　·　　　　·　　　　　　·　　　　　·　　　　　·

Behold, the days come, saith the Lord Jehovah, that I will send a famine in the land, not a famine of bread, nor a thirst for water, but of hearing the words of Jehovah.
And they shall wander from sea to sea, and from the north even to the east; They shall run to and fro to seek the word of Jehovah, and shall not find it.

Such were the penalties prophesied for the exploiters of society, for the economic royalists of that remote era.

Amos stressed man's obligations to his fellows. Hosea, who came after him, was more concerned with man's personal relation to Yahweh, the God of mercy, righteousness, loving-kindness and faithfulness. The moral degeneracy of Israel was regarded by Hosea as an affront to Yahweh, who "desires goodness and

not sacrifice, and the knowledge of God more than burnt offerings." The consequences of impiety, of forsaking the high moral road will be a loss of prosperity,
a dearth of material riches.

> Hear the word of Jehovah, ye children of Israel, for Jehovah hath a controversy
> with the inhabitants of the land, because there is no truth, nor goodness,
> nor knowledge of God in the land.
> There is nought but swearing and breaking faith, and killing and stealing, and
> committing adultery; they break out, and blood toucheth blood.
> Therefore shall the land mourn, and everyone that dwelleth therein shall languish,
> with the beasts of the field and the birds of the heavens; yea, the fishes of
> the sea also shall be taken away.

Isaiah, who flourished towards the end of the eighth century, combined the
missions of his two predecessors, that of social reform and individual regeneration.
The plight of the downtrodden awakened his ardent sympathy and called forth
his thunderous damnation.

> Woe unto them that decree unrighteous decrees, and to the writers that write
> perverseness;
> To turn aside the needy from justice, and to rob the poor of my people of their
> right, that widows may be their spoil, and that they make the fatherless their
> prey:
> And what will ye do in the day of visitation, and in the desolation which shall
> come from afar? to whom will ye flee for help? and when will ye leave your
> glory?

But God, cried Isaiah, is ready to forgive the oppressor. It is not too late to balance the scale. "His anger is not turned away, but his hand is stretched out still."
The decay of morality inspired Isaiah to compose the classical expression of the
ideal of religious faith founded upon personal virtue, which is the special Hebraic
legacy to civilization.

> What unto me is the multitude of your sacrifices? saith Jehovah: I have had
> enough of the burnt-offerings of rams, and the fat of fed beasts; and I delight
> not in the blood of bullocks, or of lambs, or of he-goats.
> When ye come to appear before me, who hath required this at your hand, to
> trample my courts?
> Bring no more vain oblations; incense is an abomination to me; new moon and
> sabbath, the calling of assemblies,—I cannot away with iniquity and the
> solemn meeting.
> Your new moons and your appointed feasts my soul hateth; they are a trouble
> unto me; I am weary of bearing them.
> And when ye spread forth your hands, I will hide mine eyes from you; yea,
> when ye make many prayers, I will not hear: your hands are full of blood.
> Wash you, make you clean; put away the evil of your doings from before mine
> eyes; cease to do evil;
> Learn to do well; seek justice, relieve the oppressed, judge the fatherless, plead
> for the widow.

The burden of Isaiah's song is that no matter how elaborate and costly the ceremonial, it is naught to the Lord if it be not accompanied by nobility of character, lofty and moral living. Micah hammered home the same point. He scourged the iniquitous, the greedy, the expropriators, and forecast national doom as a measure of Yahweh's vengeance for antisocial conduct.

Such were the exalted moral teachings of the prophets of the eighth century. Habbakuk, Nahum, and Jeremiah, who lived amid the stirring events which marked the drooping of Israel's power in the seventh century, reëchoed Amos's and Hosea's blasts at the impious, the wicked, the degenerate, and justified the ways of God to men.

Nahum's patriotic ardor burst into flame at the sight of the downfall of Assyria, Israel's ancient enemy. He regarded it as a singular manifestation of Yahweh's vengeance against the wicked.

Thy shepherds slumber, O king of Assyria; thy nobles are at rest; thy people are scattered upon the mountains, and there is none to gather them.

There is no assuaging of thy hurt, thy wound is grievous; all that hear the report of thee clap their hands over thee; for upon whom hath not thy wickedness passed continually?

Jeremiah painted an extremely dark moral picture of his contemporaries. The kingdoms of Judah and Israel had become examples of unprecedented wickedness. Therefore ruin was close upon them. Destruction would be their just meed. Allowing for exaggerations in Jeremiah's tirades, one may still feel the lofty moral purpose which consumed him, the Utopian dreams which lay unexpressed in his mind.

The Hebrew prophets thus infused greater fervor than the Egyptians into their dream of a world where justice, mercy, tenderness, equality were supreme. But the Egyptian elements were not absent even here. The precepts attributed to Jeremiah seem to be in part a translation from Amenemope's graphic contrast between the virtuous and the wicked man. There are also reminiscences of the Egyptian's thought in the First Psalm, beginning:

Blessed is the man that walketh not in the counsel of the ungodly,
Nor standeth in the way of sinners. . . .

In the Book of Proverbs, in Hebrew law, in Job, Samuel and Jeremiah, Amenemope's wisdom is reflected in ideas, figures of speech, moral standards, and above all in a warmth and tenderness of spirit, a profound feeling of individual worth, with all that is implied of kindness, justice, decency, helpfulness, and the most sensitive and lofty human values.

Breasted emphasizes the fact that the Messianic hope of the Jews was probably derived from the Egyptian "Admonitions of Ipuwer," with its yearning vision of the return of a righteous king who would punish wickedness, reward virtue and restore prosperity. This became a Jewish heritage and an undying gleam of hope in the midst of oppression and conquest.

By 2000 B.C. the Egyptian sages were already preaching the doctrine of asceticism and the futility of material possessions. Says Amenemope:

> Better is poverty in the hand of God,
> Than riches in the storehouse.
> Better are loaves when the heart is joyous,
> Than riches in unhappiness.

The mature wisdom of the Egyptian passed into the Hebrew proverbs, as Breasted shows, almost idea for idea. The Egyptian books containing this social idealism were read in Palestine at a time when the unknown Hebrew writers were compiling their biblical books.

> In receiving a great and inspiring moral and religious heritage from the Hebrews, therefore, we may regard it as a demonstrated fact that we have inherited a two-fold legacy, which is made up in the *first* place in the Ancient Near East, chiefly Egypt, *before the Hebrew nation arose,* and was then in the *second* place marvelously deepened and enriched out of their own social experience by the prophets and sages of Israel themselves.[10]

For nearly two thousand years, during which Europe ignored the ancient literature of Egypt, Babylonia, and Persia, it was believed that the exalted moral code of the Hebrews was an entirely original contribution to man's progress. Now we know that it was not so; that the Hebrews leaned heavily on the social ideals of previous cultures, elaborated them, and sent them forth to guide twenty centuries of Western civilization. .

The Hittites, judging from fragments of their laws recently unearthed, had a sense of international justice. As early as the thirteenth century B.C. a Hittite king admits that he made an unprovoked attack on the Egyptians and recognizes the moral wrong of which he is guilty. A document survives of King Hattusil, in which a sense of legal moderation and justice is embodied. The Hittites probably had some influence on the moral progress of the ancient Orient.

The moral code of the Persians was, like that of the Hebrews, an intimate part of their religion. It had, however, one aspect not found elsewhere in the Near Orient. For the first time it linked up individual morality with cosmic morality and raised the future life to a position of greater importance than this world. The universe was an arena in which the forces of good, led by Ormuzd, fought against the forces of evil, led by Ahriman. Man could not stand aloof from this cosmic duel. Upon his part in it depended his destiny in the future life. Here he would be handsomely rewarded by an eternal life of joy and bliss if he aided Ormuzd, or obliterated in a lake of fire and brimstone if he followed Ahriman. The otherworldly moral sanctions and objectives which dominated Christian morality were derived from this Persian source.

IX. THE ALPHABET AND THE ORIGINS OF WRITING

The origins of writing can be linked with the pictograms which appear on the implements and cave walls of the Paleolithic era. However, before the picture

---

[10] Breasted, *op. cit.,* p. 383.

signs could be regarded as a written language, they had to pass through three well-defined stages.

First, the pictures had to be "conventionalized," so that they always had the same appearance, and represented the same object. Next, it was necessary that they should not only refer to a concrete object, but also become the symbols of abstract conceptions. Finally, the conventionalized symbols had to pass into a stage where they described an abstract concept and the sound of the human voice representing that concept.

The last stage, as may be expected, is the most difficult to attain. It is called "sound writing," and in its most elementary form each symbol represents an entire word. Some languages, like the Chinese, have gone little beyond this stage. Normally, a written language goes farther than the Chinese, each symbol representing not a whole word but a syllable. Then the various sounds of the human voice are analyzed and each is represented by a separate symbol or letter; this constitutes an alphabet.

Around 3000 B.C. the Egyptians had taken an important step in developing an alphabet by using twenty-four hieroglyphic signs to indicate twenty-four consonantal sounds. But they continued to use many additional symbols for words and syllables, and therefore failed to develop a strictly phonetic alphabet.

Our alphabet probably goes back to the Egyptian by way of Phoenician and Greek elaborations. A certain Semite of the nineteenth century B.C., perhaps a Phoenician from Byblos, seems to have invented a true alphabet based on Egyptian antecedents. His alphabet is used in several inscriptions found in southern Palestine. Other inscriptions since discovered at Rasesh Shamra near Latakiyeh in ancient Ugarit (in Syria), are written in an alphabetic cuneiform script of a northern Semitic dialect. Our earliest inscription in a fully developed Phoenician alphabet is the epitaph of Ahiram, king of Byblos, who lived about the year 1250 B.C. The Phoenician alphabet contained twenty-one letters, all consonants.

The Greeks improved the Phoenician alphabet by using some of its signs to indicate vowels. This Greek alphabet, with some modifications, was spread by the Romans to western Europe and by the Byzantines, to eastern Europe. Writing was probably invented in many other places—Anatolia, Crete, Egypt, Babylonia, India, China, and Central America. There were, however, only three great systems of ideographs or picture-forms: (1) the Sumerian or Babylonian cuneiform, which died out about the beginning of the Christian Era; (2) Chinese, with its branches in Korea and Japan; and (3) the Egyptian, from which our alphabet ultimately developed.

When man learned to write he also learned to make writing materials. The Babylonians wrote on clay tablets and stone walls, which, although durable, were clumsy and awkward to handle. The Egyptians solved the problem by using the membrane of the papyrus reed, thin strips which they pasted together at right angles. On this papyrus (whence our word "paper") they wrote with an ink made of water, vegetable gum, and soot.

Papyrus, the first kind of paper, was so widely known that it probably suggested to the Chinese, around 200 B.C., the idea of making a cheaper form of paper from the pulp of a mulberry tree. Peoples who had no papyrus wrote on parchment made from animal skins. The Arabs, about A.D. 750, brought to Spain a paper made from cotton fiber. Five centuries later flax was substituted for cotton and modern linen paper came into use. Rag paper was fairly common in western Europe by the middle of the fourteenth century.

The first pens were pieces of reed which worked like a small paint brush. They were superseded by the quill pen, and later by the modern steel pen.

The invention of writing and a system of keeping records has had a greater influence on man's intellectual development than any other achievement with the exception of speech. Writing made it possible permanently to transmit man's ideas, traditions, and mythology. It permitted the creation of a written literature and enormously aided the growth of learning.

Its great contributions, of course, have been accompanied by certain evils. Although it has enabled us to transmit culture from age to age, it has at the same time kept alive outworn notions and antiquated beliefs whose retarding influences might otherwise never have reached succeeding generations.

Of such importance has writing been for the subject of history that until recent years historians assumed that history began only when man mastered the art of recording his thoughts in writing. This narrow conception we have now fully outgrown.

X. LITERARY ACHIEVEMENTS OF THE ANCIENT ORIENT

1. *Egyptian*

In language and literature the ancient Orient made the great advances from pre-literary culture, first to written folk literature and then to more fully developed literary forms. Long before the Christian Era most of the languages of Western civilization had evolved: Arabic, Semitic, and Aryan; Sanskrit, Greek, Roman, Celtic, and others. They had become written languages in Egyptian hieroglyphic, Babylonian and Persian cuneiform, and Aramaic.

The Egyptians were the first to have what we call books [11]—papyri dating from 4000 B.C. or earlier—and theirs is the oldest literature preserved. The greater part of it was moral and religious. Two of the earliest Egyptian religious works, the *Book of the Dead* and the *Book of Breathings,* were written down about 3300 B.C. or earlier. The first is a collection of formulas compiled by the priests of Heliopolis, and the second contains an interesting group of prayers. The materials of both books had been handed down orally for countless generations before they were written. The many copies that survive provide anthropologists with much valuable information about Ra, Osiris, Isis, and the other primitive gods. The finest product of Egyptian moral literature was *The Wisdom of Amenemope.*

Egyptian literature was not, however, entirely religious. The love of life expressed in Egyptian art finds its counterpart in song and story. Indeed, some

---

[11] Our word book meant originally *beech,* which indicates that a book, among Germanic tribes, was a scrawl on a piece of the inner bark of a beech-tree. In the Orient it was an inscription on papyrus or a clay tablet. The Chinese wrote on silk.

authorities maintain that the Egyptians had an immense secular literature; though little has reached us, and none that can be referred to any individual author. Stories of fantastic adventure and magical experience—among them the original of *Sinbad the Sailor* and others of the *Arabian Nights*—were very popular. There are some moving hymns, and the love songs are in keeping with the lavish brightness of Egyptian painting and tomb furniture.

From the last period of Egyptian history we have the fine *Tale of Two Brothers* which is regarded by some as the source of the biblical story of Joseph and Potiphar's wife. *The Tale of Two Brothers,* apparently, was one of a large body of popular novels which has been lost. Egypt, too, was the source of much amorous literature which was often poetic and sometimes suggestive of the later Song of Solomon. In the twilight of the Egyptian Empire many poetic hymns were produced, one of which was translated by the Hebrew author of the 104th Psalm.

2. *Mesopotamian*

A large and varied Mesopotamian literature has been preserved, most of it prosaic letters and business documents, of first importance to the historian, but of little value as literature. We have recovered, however, from Assyrian tablets at Nineveh, the fragments of two important Babylonian or perhaps pre-Babylonian epics of *Gilgamesh* and of the so-called *Poem of the Creation*.

A dozen bricks contain the extraordinary epic of *Gilgamesh,* the Ulysses of the Mesopotamian world. His story is not a homogeneous composition but a series of myths and folk tales woven into the saga of a supernatural adventurer. Not only is *Gilgamesh* beautiful in its own right, but it contains among other things an analogue to the Bible story of Noah and the flood. In the eleventh tablet, the hero, grown weary and old, remembers that he has an ancient relative, Uta-Napishtim, who knows the secret of making oneself immortal. He visits him, and the old man begins to talk about ancient days. In the course of his story he tells of a deluge of which the gods forewarned him, and how he built a great boat and took his family and a few servants and the seeds of life of all kinds and floated around for six days. We quote this section of the poem because of its striking similarity to the version in Genesis and as a good example of the poetic skill of the Babylonians:

> For six days and nights
> Wind and flood marched on, the hurricane subdued the land.
> When the seventh day dawned, the hurricane was abated, the flood
> Which had waged war like an army;
> The sea was stilled, the ill wind was calmed, the flood ceased.
>
> I beheld the sea: its voice was silent,
> And all mankind was turned into mud!
> As high as the roofs reached the swamp!
> I opened the window and light fell on my cheek,
> I made for shore and stayed seated; I wept:
> Over my cheeks flowed my tears.
> I beheld the world, the horizon at sea;

Twelve [measures] away an island emerged.
Unto mount Nitsir came the vessel.
Mount Nitsir held the vessel and let it not budge. . . .

When the seventh day came,
I sent forth a dove, I released it;
It went, the dove, it came back:
As there was no place it came back.
I sent forth a swallow, I released it,
It went, the swallow, it came back:
As there was no place, it came back.
I sent forth a crow, I released it,
It went, the crow, and beheld the subsidence of the waters:
It eats, it splashes about, it caws, it comes not back.
I sent them forth to the four winds, I poured a libation.
I set an offering on top of the mountain.
I set fourteen adagurru-pots,
Under them I spread reeds, cedar, and myrtle—
The gods scented its savour,
The gods scented the sweet savour,
Like flies, the gods gathered above the sacrifice.

The flood legend probably antedates the epic of *Gilgamesh* into which it was introduced by a late editor. As for the reality of the flood, the ancient Hebrews and the whole Mesopotamian world knew of some unparalleled watery disaster, flood or hurricane in preliterary times, the memory of which was handed down in legendary form; and recent discoveries in the mud clay strata at Ur tend to confirm the ancient story as historical.

The other extant Babylonian epic, the fragmentary *Poem of the Creation,* described the ascent to power of Marduk, the Mesopotamian Zeus, by his victory over Tiâmat, the goddess of the sea—symbolizing the struggle between good and evil—and gives an account of the creation of the world somewhat analogous to the Genesis story. The poem is not without considerable descriptive and narrative power and reveals the existence of a mythology as picturesque as that of the Greeks or of the Norse. The battle itself is an excellent bit of heroic poetry which calls to mind Milton's *Paradise Lost.*

Tiâmat and Marduk, the envoy of the gods, roused themselves,
They advanced to fight each other, they drew nigh in battle.
The Lord cast his net and made it enclose her,
The evil wind that had its place behind him he let out in her face.
Tiâmat opened her mouth to its greatest extent,
Marduk made the evil wind to enter [it] whilst her lips were unclosed.
The raging winds filled out her belly,
Her heart was gripped, she opened wide her mouth [panting].
Marduk grasped the spear, he split up her belly,
　He clave open her bowels, he pierced [her] heart,
　He brought her to nought, he destroyed her life.
　He cast down her carcase, he took up his stand upon it.

After Marduk had slain Tiâmat the chief,
Her host was scattered, her levies became fugitive,
And the gods, her allies, who had marched at her side,
Quaked with terror, and broke and ran
And betook themselves hemmed in, they could not escape.
Marduk tied them up, he smashed their weapons.
They were cast into the net, and they were caught in the snare,
The . . . of the world they filled with [their] cries of grief.

Babylonian prose exists in the form of numerous letters. Like the prose of the Bible, it has a certain terseness and directness and a strong rhythmic quality which proves that the Babylonians did not distinguish rigidly between verse and prose. Here, for example, is part of the epigraph to a long letter from the astrologer Adad-shum-utsur to the king Assurbanipal:

A favourable reign, stable days, years of justice, abundant rains, plenteous floods, high prices. The gods are honoured, the fear of the divinity increases, the temples are prosperous, the great gods of heaven and earth are exalted under the rule of the king, my master. The old men dance, the young people sing, women and maidens are given in marriage, the widows remarry, marriages are consummated, boys and girls are begotten and children are born. To those who have sinned and await death, the king, my master, has given a new life. Those who have been in prison for many years, hast thou set at liberty. Those who have been sick for long days, have recovered their health. Hunger is appeased, the lean grow fat. The orchards are full of fruit. . . . Those who stand in the palace are all, none excepted, without affection for me. I have no friend among them to whom I can offer a present who would accept it and take my cause in hand. May the king, my master, take pity on his servant. Among all these people I pray that none of my slanderers may see the accomplishment of their plans against me.

Not only was there epic poetry and apparently a good deal of written correspondence, but also, as in Egypt and among the Hebrews, what is called "temple literature": psalms, hymns, and prayers. On the whole we may say that the literary arts were developed to a considerable degree in ancient Mesopotamia.

The formation of libraries had already begun in the time of Sargon II (eighth century B.C.), as is indicated by the large collection of books in the temple of Nebo (one of Marduk's fellow gods). Assurbanipal, who ascended the throne in 668 B.C., was doubtless the foremost book collector and patron of learning in the ancient Mesopotamian world. He enlarged the library of the temple of Nebo and was himself not only a learned man but a scribe. The palace library he formed at Nineveh probably contained most of the ancient Babylonian literature. Like the Italian Medici, he sent scribes all over Asia Minor to hunt for manuscripts. Within his own palace was a "scriptorium" where writing tablets were made, inscribed, and afterwards baked; and he himself edited the texts. The library of Assurbanipal contained a system of cataloguing and each of the tablets bore a colophon inscribed with the king's name. We have recovered from the ruins of this extraordinary library works on history, literature, law, grammar, chronology, geography, astrology, and documents relating to commercial and official life.

3. Hebraic

Among the literatures of the ancient Orient the Hebraic was easily the finest. Not all of it, however, has survived, and we cannot help wondering whether what is lost may not have been equal in merit and abundance to what we have. The loss to literature, in any case, must be great indeed, for the Old Testament is surely superior in its imaginative scope and its power of expression to anything else in the Near Orient. Into its sentences flowed the religious fervor of the Hebrews, their moral aspirations, love poetry, narrative gifts, folklore, theology, historical works, and legal codes; and in its pages we may find the still-living spirit of a great people.

Though modern scholarship has made it extremely difficult to believe the old doctrine of the unique inspiration of the Old Testament, it has nevertheless tended to enhance its interest as literature. Scholars have established, on the basis of language and textual criticism, an acceptable chronology for the different parts of the Bible. We now realize, for example, that it is unlikely that the earliest prophets, Amos and Hosea, made any written contributions. In the seventh and sixth centuries b.c. the more interesting sayings of the prophets began to be written down by admirers, much as Plato composed the dialogues between Socrates and his friends, and the moral fervor of the prophets and their followers expressed itself in many a striking metaphor:

> Ah sinful nation, a people laden with iniquity, a seed of evil-doers, children that deal corruptly! they have forsaken Jehovah, they have despised the Holy One of Israel, they are estranged and gone backward!

The better historical writings in the Bible, such as the Book of Samuel, are admirable as history and often equal in literary quality to the poetry and prose of the prophetic books and the Psalms. The latter clearly were imitated from the Babylonian penitential psalms and may have been composed during or after the return from Babylon (c. 538 b.c.). Some of the Hebrew psalms, Psalm 13, for example, are among the most magnificent didactic poems in all literature:

> How long, O Jehovah? wilt thou forget me forever?
> How long wilt thou hide thy face from me?
> How long shall I take counsel in my soul,
> Having sorrow in my heart all the day?
> How long shall mine enemy be exalted over me?
> Consider and answer me, O Jehovah, my God:
> Lighten mine eyes, lest I sleep the sleep of death;
> Lest mine enemy say, I have prevailed against him;
> Lest mine adversaries rejoice in thy salvation.

A few of the Psalms were uninspired compilations similar to those found in the religious literature of many Oriental civilizations.

One must be able to read the Old Testament in Greek or Hebrew to be able to appreciate fully how much of the beauty and music of the English Bible was contributed by the King James translators. Not only were these men masters of the

great English prose and verse of the age of Shakespeare, but they possessed a
unique gift for apprehending the spirit and imagination of the Hebrew people.
Such a combination of powers could hardly fail to contribute immeasurably to
the literary quality of the Bible stories. Tolstoy, a master of the short story, considered the incident of Joseph and Potiphar's wife a model of literary form; and
the same might be said of a number of other biblical narratives—Esther, Ruth,
Baalam, Jonah.

The Book of Job, one of the great examples of literary tragedy, is in many ways
the finest piece of Hebrew literature. As tragedy, it is a masterpiece of concentration, struggle, and reconciliation; as brief epic, it served as a model for Milton's
Paradise Regained. But even more important, perhaps, is the historical and social
significance of its ethics. For it illustrates the finest of the Hebrew attitudes
toward Jehovah, and at the same time it bears witness to the universality of that
idea of struggle between man and fate which is the center of Greek tragedy:

> *Job:* I was at ease, and he broke me asunder;
>   Yea, he hath taken me by the neck, and dashed me to pieces:
>   He hath also set me up for his mark.
>   His archers compass me round about;
>   He cleaveth my reins asunder, and doth not spare;
>   He poureth out my gall upon the ground.

The Psalms, the short stories, and the epic and dramatic passages are sufficient
indications of the abundant variety of the Bible. It contains other literary types as
well. There is, for example, the exquisite love poetry of the Song of Songs:

> I am the rose of Sharon,
> and the lily of the valleys.
> As the lily among thorns,
> so is my love among the daughters.
> As the apple tree among the trees of the wood,
> so is my beloved among the sons.

There is the great stoic music of Ecclesiastes which has moved many a later writer:

> Also when they shall be afraid of that which is high,
> And fears shall be in the way,
> And the almond tree shall flourish,
> And the grasshopper shall be a burden,
> And desire shall fail;
> Because man goeth to his long home,
> And the mourners go about the streets:
> Or ever the silver cord be loosed,
> Or the golden bowl be broken,
> Or the pitcher broken at the fountain,
> Or the wheel broken at the cistern.

The wisdom of the Proverbs has long since passed into common currency as
part of the language. And the richness of their concrete imagery seems to have
suffered no loss of richness despite countless repetition:

> Happy is the man that findeth wisdom,
> And the man that getteth understanding,
> For the gaining of it is better than the gaining of silver,
> And the profit thereof than fine gold.

Modern scholarship has made clear that the tales and ideas of the Old Testament were not the unique possession of the Hebrew people. They sprang in large part from the primitive literatures of Egypt and Babylon and Assyria. But the Hebrew language was responsible for the form in which they are preserved and which has given them a kind of permanent life. Hebrew was not a philosophical tongue; it was extraordinarily weak in abstract words. But in compensation it was rich in the vocabulary of nature and the daily life of man. What distinguishes the Semitic languages from the Aryan, as Renan once said, is that the "primitive union of sensation and idea persists—so that in each word one still hears the echo of the primitive sensations which determined the choice of the first makers of the language." Perhaps the basic reason for the excellence of our Bible is that this observation is also true of English. As Professor Lowes says, "No less than Hebrew, the native English is the language of the eye, the hand, the heart." Modern English, of course, differs greatly from early English because of the continued influence of Latin and French. It is for this reason that modern translations of the Bible lack the rhythm and flavor of the King James version.

The experience of the Hebrew nation, as it preserved through centuries of hardship its unity and hope, and the vivid imagination which shaped its thoughts and its stories rendered the Old Testament the best of pre-Christian literature. The transformation of these ancient books into the language of Elizabethan England produced a work which has been justly called "the noblest monument of English prose."

4. Sanskrit

The only serious rivals of the Jews in early literary achievement were Indo-Europeans who invaded India and Persia. The Indo-Europeans produced notable Sanskrit epics and the *Vedas* as early as 1400 B.C. The oldest of these is the *Rig-Veda,* a collection of some thousand hymns, virtually all religious and representing a multitude of authors and a long period of authorship, like the Bible. Originally composed orally, these hymns were not written down until shortly before the Christian Era, for India did not have a written language before the invasion of Alexander the Great. The religion of the *Rig-Veda* is nearer to animism than to the spirit-personification of later and more sophisticated theories or to the contemporary religion of Homer. The civilization reflected in the *Rig-Veda* is of a low order and such a matter as cow stealing is of major importance.

Next in time in ancient Sanskrit literature were the *Brahmanas* and the *Upanishads*. The *Brahmanas,* for the most part written in verse, dealt mainly with sacrificial rituals; they were filled with mystical reflections. The *Upanishads* were theological speculations about Brahma, "the world soul." (The word *upanishad* means "a sitting-down at the feet of an instructor.") In many cases the instructor expounded the so-called "forest philosophy" which emphasized the notion of withdrawing from the household life after one's family has been raised. As we shall see, the Buddha owed much to the primitive doctrines found in the *Upanishads*.

In the *Atharva-Veda* we find a marvelously complete picture of Hindu private life as it was, embedded in magical formulas, charms, and penitential, theosophic, and ritualistic hymns. The parts of *Atharva-Veda* vary greatly in age; some of them go back to preliterary times, and some to the time when writing was first introduced.

All these works constitute the pre-Buddhist religious literature of India. Some of it is subtly philosophical and comparable to early Greek philosophy with which it was contemporary; some is simply hieratic (pertaining to sacred uses) and mainly unintelligible to modern Occidental readers. Although it is extremely difficult to work out a satisfactory chronology, the literature which came after the *Rig-Veda* on the whole reflected a more advanced culture and more highly developed religious beliefs. Examples of this would be the *Sutras,* written mostly after the Buddha's time. They were short mnemonics (aids to memory) in the fields of religion, philosophy, law, and grammar; and they were accompanied usually by learned commentaries for the use of the student.

Of the two great Sanskrit epic productions the *Mahabharata* is the longer. It is a work of composite authorship, a collection of tales woven together through centuries of oral tradition. It recounts the long story of the struggle between the Kurus·and the Pandavas for the country around Delhi and weaves into the episodes philosophical and religious matters which give a serious tone to the whole poem. One episode of the *Mahabharata* has had a kind of separate existence: the *Bhagavad-Gita* which forms part of the sixth book. It tells of the meeting between Arjuna, leader of the Panadavas, with Krishna who instructs him in the work of a warrior. Krishna passes from war to ethics and religion and finally reveals himself as the Lord of Creation. In spite of certain confusions of pantheism and monism, the *Bhagavad-Gita* is the greatest ethical product of Hindu philosophy.

The other Sanskrit epic, the *Ramayana* (saga of Rama), greatly differs from the *Mahabharata,* being the literary product of a single author—it is generally attributed to Valmiki. The *Ramayana* appears to be older as well as shorter than the *Mahabharata*. The central character was Rama-Chandra, a kind of wandering hero. His wife Sita was captured by a giant who ruled over Ceylon. Rama's conquest of the giant and rescue of his wife provides the main action.

The most important intellectual contribution of ancient India was the religious philosophy of Buddhism. Gautama, called the Buddha (Enlightened One), flourished in the fifth century B.C., and early in life became dissatisfied with the theory and practice of the Brahmans. Through long meditation he developed his own religion. He succeeded in winning many disciples; and, though they were soon corrupted, his teachings spread over most of the Eastern world until Buddhism became the most popular of all religions.

Buddha's teachings were recorded long after his death from the oral tradition handed down by his disciples. They were written in both Sanskrit and Pali, a dialect spoken in the province of Magadha from about the sixth century B.C. (Pali has often been related to Sanskrit as Italian is related to Latin.) Scholars are now confident that the genuine doctrines of the Buddha are those preserved in this language.

The greater part of the Pali Canon consists of dialogues (*Suttas*) between the Buddha and his disciples, or mnemonic verse passages of which the best known is the *Dhammapada*. In the dialogues the Buddha set forth his doctrines of the Four-fold Path away from sorrow. His central teaching was detachment from all objects, for the cause of suffering is attachment and desire. The end of Buddhism is a state in which all desire has been suppressed and the self becomes extinct (Nirvana).

The *Dhammapada* (Path of Virtue) was a sort of elementary textbook, and it is still the best introduction to Buddhism. Written in a kind of rhythmic free verse, it lends itself well to memorization. The repetition is so subtly managed that the effect is never one of tediousness:

> The monk, full of delight, who is firm in the doctrine of Buddha will reach the quiet place, cessation of the mortal and transitory, and happiness.
> The young monk who applies himself to Buddha's teaching, lights up this world like the moon freed from clouds.

The Buddhist writings relied much upon the imagery of nature and daily life in a manner often remarkably similar to that of the Hebrew prophets. The following passage, from the *Sutta-Nipata,* is a good illustration of the style of the Pali books and expresses, too, the core of Buddhist teaching:

> The wise man who fares strenuously apart,
> Who is unshaken in the midst of praise or blame,
> Even as a lion that trembles not at noises,
> Or as the wind that is not caught in a net,
> Or as the lotus that is unstained by the water—
> A leader of others and not by others led,
> Him verily the discerning proclaim to be a sage.

5. Persian

On the fringe of Babylonia lived the Persians, Indo-Europeans existing in a pastoral state of culture. They were influenced by the intellectual activities of their neighbors and probably about the tenth century B.C. began to produce a literature, the great landmark of which is the *Zend-Avesta* (the Bible of Zoroaster). This work consists of twenty-one books of ritual, liturgy, hymns, paeans of praise to Ormuzd, theology, predictions about the end of the world (eschatology), and fragments of history. The earliest sections may go back to the eighth century B.C. Zoroaster was a religious reformer, who, says Professor Lynn Thorndike, "had the great idea that to be able to distinguish truth from falsehood is divine, and that man must strive to attain this goal by 'good thoughts, good words, good deeds,'—Good Thought, Right Order, Excellent Kingdom, Holy Character, Health and Immortality." The Gathas included in the *Zend-Avesta* are a series of primitive hymns, with as intense an ethical note as the Hebrew Bible. The literary quality of the *Zend-Avesta* is in general not as high as that of the *Vedas*. The great epic of the Persians was the *Shah-Namah* (Book of Kings), a poem of about 60,000 lines composed in the tenth century A.D. by Firdusi. Rustam and other ancient heroes are its main characters. Although a literary rather than a folk epic, it contains the stories of the ancient Persian gods and heroes, and is in some ways similar to the *Mahabharata*.

6. Historical Writing in the Orient

With the exception of the Hebrew, historical writing in the ancient Orient was an undeveloped art until very late times, when the region was deeply affected by Greek culture. Historical material consisted mainly of inscriptions which described building operations, military victories, and hunting exploits. It showed no critical sense whatever; nothing was included which would in any way disparage the monarchs or gods who were supposed to guide the people. With the exception of a few fragmentary annals, such as the Palermo stele and the Turin papyrus, there is no known Egyptian historical work of any importance before the Hellenistic period, when an Egyptian scribe, Manetho, about 275 B.C. at the order of King Ptolemy Philadelphus, compiled a narrative history of his native land. This seems to have been of a high order, but little is preserved of his work except garbled excerpts in later writers like Josephus, Julius Africanus, and Eusebius.

The Babylonians and Assyrians compiled somewhat better historical documents than the Egyptians, but there was no Mesopotamian historian comparable to Manetho until a Hellenized Babylonian priest, Berossos, produced his history of Babylonia in the third century B.C. The earliest sources of Babylonian history, dating from the third millennium B.C., are the votive inscriptions, giving the names of kings and their genealogies and descriptions of the buildings they erected. For the Sumerian period the cylinder inscriptions of Gudea of Lagash (2070 B.C.) are a rich historical source. About four centuries later came the Code of Hammurabi, an invaluable source for Babylonian social and legal history.

For Assyrian history there are three types of sources: "display inscriptions" written mainly on slabs of stone, intended for architectural adornment, and bearing little relation to accuracy of fact; royal annals, giving a brief chronological account of the events of each year—these are the most important sources of Assyrian history; and the *Eponym Canon*, which gives a list of the limnii and the year of their appointment. Some attempt at historical·narrative was made in the *Synchronous History* and the *Assyrian Chronicle*. The former is ostensibly a history of the relations between Babylonia and Syria from c. 1600 to c. 800 B.C., but in reality it is an elaborate "display inscription" glorifying Assyria and disparaging Babylonia. Though the *Assyrian Chronicle* is a dry compilation of the names of officials and annual events, it has considerable chronological value.

From the later Babylonian or Chaldean Empire emanated one first-rate historical narrative. The *Babylonian Chronicle* was written about the time of the fall of Assyria in 608 B.C.; it began with about 745 B.C., covered an unusual range of interests, and was amazingly impartial. Berossos' *Babyloniaca*, the work of a Hellenized Babylonian priest, was almost the only source of Babylonian and

Assyrian history known to the Greek and Roman world. Its text has now all but disappeared, and as to its specific character we can only vaguely conjecture.

The royal annals of the Babylonians and Assyrians were continued by the Persian kings. One of the most important, that of Darius on the great rocky crag at Behistun set down in Persian, Susian, and Babylonian script, has proved of special significance in reconstructing our modern knowledge of ancient Oriental history and languages.

The honor of having first produced a truly historical narrative of considerable scope and veracity must be accorded to the Hebrews of ancient Palestine. Because of its signal importance in Western history we may fittingly go into some detail here about the actual composition of the Bible.

In the first place, the very term Pentateuch (five books) is a misnomer, since the Pentateuch really consists of a block of eleven books—the first twelve books of the Bible minus the book of Ruth, which is a late product of the Persian or Greek periods. Far from being the creation of a single author, the Pentateuch was actually compiled by at least four groups of authors writing from about the close of the tenth to the middle of the fifth century B.C. None of the four foundation documents, called "J," "E," "D," and "P," of the Pentateuch exists as it was written down; all were revised in different degrees by subsequent editors. Nor is the Pentateuch arranged in chronological order; these sources were combined by later editors in an almost inextricable fashion. Professor Shotwell has given an excellent, brief account of the matter:

> "J" is the earliest, a product of the late tenth or early ninth century, so-called because the writers call the Hebrew God "Jahveh." Next in order is the "E" source, about the eighth century, so-called because the authors call the deity "Elohim." The third in time (c. 650 B.C.) is the Book of Deuteronomy: scholars refer to it as "D." The final document is the so-called priestly or "P" source, dating from about 506-450 B.C.

The first appearance of true historical narrative of which any record has been preserved anywhere is found in the "Jahvist" sources of the Pentateuch, Joshua, the Books of Samuel and the opening of the first Book of Kings. The Jahvist narrative reaches its high points in II Samuel ix-xx, which is probably the best example of early Oriental historical writing.

The remaining historical books in the Old Testament were the Book of Kings, written about 560 B.C., and Chronicles-Ezra-Nehemiah, written about 300 B.C. The author of the former tried primarily to convince his people of the value of religious fidelity by citing historical illustrations of disasters suffered by Hebrews when they deserted their religion. Chronicles-Ezra-Nehemiah were written mainly by one man, a priest of Jerusalem, who, by means of genealogies and narrative, surveyed all Hebrew history, with the aim of glorifying through exaggeration the splendor of the kingdom of David and Solomon. He also emphasized the moral of deserting the true religion. Both Kings and Chronicles-Ezra-Nehemiah are distinctly inferior to "J" in accuracy and literary charm.

One of the ablest products of Hebrew historiography was the first book of Maccabees, which was not included in the Protestant canon of the Bible. Written about 125 B.C., this narrative tells the stirring story of Hebrew history from the conquest of Palestine by Alexander the Great in 332 B.C. to the accession of John Hyrcanus. The critical attitude maintained by the author is unique for his time. He maintained that the Hebrew victories resulted from the personal ability and courage of the Asmoneans and not from direct intervention of God on behalf of the Jews. Unfortunately, Christian historians of the Middle Ages did not take as their model the brilliant narrative of First Maccabees, but tried to strengthen their followers' zeal and terrorize their opponents by imitating conventional Hebrew stories about the miraculous interference of God in rewarding the faithful and punishing the faithless.

The national historian of the Jews was Flavius Josephus (A.D. c. 37-105), author in Greek of the *War of the Jews* and *Antiquities of the Jews.* Writing mainly after the destruction of the Hebrew power in A.D. 70, he tried to compensate for contemporary distress by emphasizing the glories of the past, and was led to exaggerate more than the author of Chronicles-Ezra-Nehemiah. Josephus' treatment of the Old Testament period is highly unreliable; but his discussion of the post-Maccabean era is in general free from exaggeration and superstition. Josephus has been called the "Livy of the Jews," but his accuracy did not surpass that of the Roman historian.

Although the Hebrews created realistic historical narrative, their work did not affect the general current of historiography until after the Christians had taken over the Old Testament and used it not only as the basis of much of their mythology, but also as the foundation of their chronology and synthesis of pre-Christian events.

XI. THE ACHIEVEMENTS IN ART

1. *Egyptian*

If the hieroglyphics had never been deciphered, if we had no secular Egyptian literature, no *Book of the Dead,* the life and thought of ancient Egypt would nevertheless be revealed to us through its art. Egyptian wall paintings—*Songbirds in a Tree, Wandering Geese, Cat Among the Papyrii*—are eloquent poems of the field. Relief sculptures [12] of the hunt, boating trips, girls playing ball; of domestic scenes, of cattle- and donkey-herding, of dairying, all attest to the Egyptians' zest for life. On the other hand, the colossal, enduring, Egyptian temples are impressive records of what must have been a powerful and strictly organized religious hierarchy. Egyptian tombs, monumental storehouses of treasure and richly decorated inviolable sarcophagi, need no *Book of the Dead* to reveal the Egyptians' certainty of a life continuing after death. The fact that almost all the surviving buildings are either temples or tombs shows that an overwhelming importance was attached to religion.

---

[12] *Relief sculpture* is indisseverably part of a background. It may be modeled so high that it is practically three-dimensional, or so low as to have almost no depth. When low, it is called *bas relief* (French *bas =* low). A medal is a familiar example. *Sculpture in the round* is three-dimensional sculpture which stands independent of a background; sculpture which we can walk around and see front, back, and sides. It is frequently called "free standing sculpture."

There can be little question that the ancient Egyptian civilization was highly developed before the date of its first important manifestation, the Pyramids of Gizeh (c. 3000 B.C.). The amount of planning and organization necessary to the construction of such gigantic edifices, the scientific knowledge indispensable for the manipulation of huge masses of stone, the complicated structure of the interiors, the mummification of the person for whom the tomb was built—could we ask for more convincing evidence of cultural development?

These pyramids, designed as tombs for the Pharaohs of Egypt, were planned to ensure the maximum in permanence and impressiveness. Their lines, like those

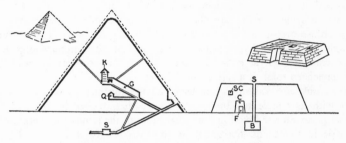

CROSS SECTION OF A PYRAMID AND A MASTABA

Pyramid (left): *K* King's chamber, *G* grand gallery, *Q* Queen's chamber, *S* subterranean chamber. Note air-shafts to *K* and *G*. Mastaba (right): *S* shaft in which sarcophagus was lowered, *B* burial chamber for sarcophagus, *SC* statue chamber, *C* chapel, *F* false door.

of all Egyptian architecture, stress the formal and the geometric. Power and immovable force were expressed in their huge, simple forms. To the Egyptians it was supremely important that the body of the deceased be permanently preserved, to enable the soul (*ka*) to return to its original abode whenever it desired. This accounts for the elaborate precautions taken in burial. The body was carefully embalmed. The size of the tomb and the hidden position of the burial chamber were designed to protect the body from violation, to shield it from robbers whose vandalism might expose it to the elements and to decay. Outside the pyramid proper was a chapel where services for the dead were held, and within the pyramid itself spread a complicated series of misleading tunnels intended to prevent the discovery of the tomb chamber.

The second type of tomb, the *mastaba,* like the pyramid, was geometric in form —pyramidal with the upper section removed. These smaller tombs were built for the nobility and the upper classes. The mummy was placed in a subterranean chamber cut off by a deep vertical passageway filled with broken stone and masonry, and the entrance to the tomb chamber was just as carefully masked as in the pyramid. In addition to the subterranean mortuary chamber, the mastaba contained a chapel and a statue chamber. The latter housed a sculptured effigy of the deceased, the effigy providing a substitute haven for the soul, if by chance the mummy should be destroyed.

The third type of tomb, the *hypogeum* (below ground), is the product of a later phase of Egyptian civilization when it became customary for the upper classes to bury their dead in chambers hollowed out of the rock cliffs facing the Nile. These rock-cut arrangements had chapels as well, but placed at a considerable distance from the cliff, nearer to the bank of the river. Within the tomb enclosure a square room was fashioned, covered with a flat ceiling supported by columns. The columns, as well as the room itself, were decorated with paintings and bas-reliefs representing the noteworthy accomplishments of the deceased. At the far end of this decorated room, one entered the effigy chamber, and below it space was provided for the sarcophagus in which the mummy was placed.

The precise preparations and careful deceptions practiced by the builders of pyramids, mastabas, or hypogea did not restrain marauders from looting them a few generations after the body had been interred. The discovery today in Egypt of an unviolated tomb is a rare event indeed.

The massive and enduring character of Egypt's funerary architecture was consistent with its temple structures. These were characterized by the use of the same large stone units found in the construction of the tombs and were similarly geometric in shape and horizontal in emphasis. Confronted by an Egyptian temple, we are amazed at the tremendous amount of space covered by this imposing and mysterious-looking building. The approach led through an avenue of small sphinxes ending in a pair of stone obelisks which were decorated with carved inscriptions and capped with bright metallic points. The façade or entrance to the temple consisted of an elaborate trapezoidal doorway, flanked by a pair of larger, similarly shaped sections known as pylons. These three units were constructed with sloping sides so as to shed the desert sand. In front of the pylons the builder placed a pair of colossal stone effigies.

The visitor, after passing between the two pylons, entered a large open courtyard, square in shape, which was surrounded by row upon row of columns. (If he were a member of the lower strata of Egyptian society, this was as far as he could go, for the social demarcations were strict; no one could enter close to the deity but the king and the priest.)

From the open court the privileged Egyptian could proceed to the next section, known as the hypostyle hall, which consisted of an endless number of columns arranged in rows. The two central rows of columns were higher than the outside rows, an effect which we shall find later approximated by the Christian church with its nave higher than its aisles. The builder took care of the lighting in the hypostyle hall by perforating the thin stone walls above the high central columns. This arrangement is known as a clerestory and we shall encounter its use later in the Christian churches.

Beyond the hypostyle hall the privileged Egyptian passed through chamber after chamber, each more diminished in height and in the quantity of light admitted, until he reached the sanctuary proper: a tiny and dark room where the most secret and intimate rites of Egyptian worship were performed.

A curious sense of indestructibility results from the even, horizontal design of the temple, heightened by the approach through the double row of sphinxes and the progression through simple but powerful geometrical forms such as the trapezoids of the doorways and the cylinders of the columns. Yet the straightness of line which harmonizes so well with the Egyptian landscape is relieved to a certain extent by a decoration of hieroglyphic inscriptions, either narrative or religious, which cover every available inch of wall space and column space.

The most famous Egyptian temples are at Karnak and Luxor. They are truly overwhelming in size. The hypostyle hall of Karnak was approximately four hundred feet long by one hundred and seventy-five feet wide and over eighty feet high. The twelve columns of the central section are each as tall as the Vendôme Column in Paris; indeed the entire hall could easily contain an ordinary Gothic cathedral. Both temples seem to suffer from hasty building, for they are neither entirely straight nor are the masonry joints as carefully measured as they could be. Luxor and Karnak, however, are not typical of the unified Egyptian style. They were rather testimony to the vanity of successive Pharaohs who delighted in multiplying the various parts of the temples even at the cost of unity of design and faultless workmanship.

The Egyptians appear to have invented the use of columns in architecture. They employed different types, each varying considerably in the shape of the capital (the portion between the column proper and the superstructure it supported). Most popular of all were the plain cylinder and the beveled columns.[13] For the shapes of the capitals the Egyptian architects adapted vegetable and flower forms—the lotus flower, the papyrus reed—as well as the inverted bell and the human head; but the lotus was the overwhelming favorite.

The Egyptian's simple arrangement of verticals and horizontals—commonly called the column-and-lintel—is the fundamental system in architecture. Driven by the necessity for permanence to using stone blocks, the Egyptian architect limited himself to large unwieldy masses. Once he chose such materials, he was virtually forced to use the column-and-lintel system.

In addition to the tombs for the dead and the temples for the gods, the Egyptians must have enjoyed a highly developed residential architecture, but unfortunately there are no surviving examples. Like the Mohammedans of the East, the Egyptians apparently had a strong prejudice against living in a house where someone had died. This habit of abandoning old homes—even palaces—in favor of new ones inevitably led to the practice of building only temporary residences.

Egyptian sculpture was inextricably part of the tombs and temples and took on their characteristics. The large stone figures, most of which survive to this day, are among the most striking remains of ancient Egyptian civilization. We find reflected in them the same impressiveness and rigidity, the same formalism and symmetry, that were displayed in Egyptian architecture. The sculpture, too, aimed

---

[13] This type of column with eight or sixteen sides must be the ancestor of the Greek Doric form with its simple severity and the very neat flat block inserted between the column and the superstructure.

at durability to provide a permanent haven in effigy for the soul if by chance the
mummy should be destroyed. The sculpture was simple in design just as the
architecture was simple and geometric. For the Egyptian chose to carve in
the most permanent stones—granite, diorite, basalt. It would have been difficult
indeed to cut elaborate details into such hard materials even if he had wished to.

It is true that he used other, softer materials, particularly during the earlier
dynasties, when wood served as one of the most important media for sculpture.
These early figures were colored atractively to simulate a degree of naturalism
which was accentuated by brightly colored stones set in for the eyes.

One of the earliest examples of monumental sculpture is the famous "Sphinx,"
located near the Pyramids of Gizeh, which shows a curious combination of animal and human form that became popular in the entire ancient world, particularly in Mesopotamia and Persia. During the second great period of Egyptian
history, the Middle Period (Theban dynasties), when the great temples of Karnak
and Luxor were built, granite became the most widely used material for sculpture.
Karnak was filled with a veritable portrait gallery of the Pharaohs who were its
benefactors. So many of these figures were produced that successor kings were
occasionally forced to clear away the figures of their predecessors. In some of the
older Egyptian buildings many badly mutilated figures have been found, most
frequently lacking the head and sometimes other important parts of the body.
This happened particularly in the case of kings who had been cordially hated
during their lifetime for deeds that inspired their successors to go to the tremendous trouble of disfiguring practically indestructible granite. We emphasize
the hard quality of the stone because it was probably one of the most important
factors responsible for the style of Egyptian sculpture.

One of the first things we notice about this art is the rigidity of the postures.
The arms and legs almost never extend far from the body and the indentations
of the sculptor's chisel are seldom very deep. These phenomena are conditioned
by the stubborn character of the stone plus the fact that the vast majority of
Egyptian sculptures were made for funerary-religious purposes which imposed a
set of rigid conventions upon the artist. All art has rules of this type, particularly
in the Orient, but few countries have conformed as consistently as the Egyptians.

Of the large stone figures there are two human types to consider: the standing
figure and the seated figure. Their most significant characteristic is their essentially blocklike form. The base upon which the person sits or stands is usually
the outside limit of the figure, thus ensuring a minimum of protruding parts and
preventing unfortunate accidents. For the same purpose, a large section of stone is
left uncut behind the head to act as a support and to make willful damage difficult. Although the seated figures show the legs held rigidly together with the arms
posed stiffly at the sides of the body, the standing type usually varies to the extent
of permitting one foot to move a few inches in front of the other; as well as
allowing a similar liberty for the corresponding arm. In both cases the idea of
symmetry and absolute rigidity is emphasized by the fact that the shoulders, hips,
and feet are arranged in parallel horizontals. This "frontality" is one of the distinguishing marks of Egyptian sculpture and is extended to such a relatively in-

formal sculpture as the cross-legged seated figure (the *Scribe* in the Louvre). Even this presumably casual representation reveals all the formalism and convention of the Buddhas of the Far East.

In all the sculptured figures we have discussed, there was a cleavage between the treatment of the body, which was stylized in almost all cases, and of the head, which was more realistic and individualized. It must be remembered that these sculptures were meant to be portraits of the deceased and that their efficacy would depend upon their degree of accuracy. There can be little doubt that, compared with the other civilizations of the ancient Orient, the Egyptians produced the greatest portraiture of antiquity. Such celebrated examples as the *Sheik of the Village* (Cairo), *Seated Scribe* (Louvre), and the *Nefertite* (Berlin) are ample proof. The inherent naturalism of their portrait art is manifest in that we are able to discern the racial characteristics of the ancient Egyptians from these figures; the round face, low forehead, thick lips, wide shoulders, and exaggerated pectoral muscles.[14]

In addition to such a pronounced conventionalization as the "frontality" of these figures, other exaggerations were practiced to ensure a high degree of compositional unity. The normal length of a thigh, leg or foot might be increased, and sometimes all of the fingers were made the identical length. Here again, the idea of geometrically related proportions (as in Egyptian architecture) was stressed.

Another type of human sculpture in the round—the charming Egyptian figurines, usually carved of wood—was placed in the tomb with the mummy to reproduce the deceased one's everyday activities. Thus, the landed noble would order carved models of his dairy, butchery, etc., with the appropriate workmen at their duties, to accompany him to the world beyond where his life, uninterrupted, could continue forever. Like most lower class subjects, these figurines, although much more naturalistic in attitude, still retained a good many of the rigid qualities of the more monumental sculptural forms.

Between the purely human and the animal types there was an intermediate group of hybrid forms, typified by such a monument as the Sphinx. Usually this type of sculpture showed a lion's body, capped with a man's head arrayed in ceremonial wig and beard. Sometimes this was varied by the use of a bull's head, but in either case the sculpture was a religious or possibly royal symbol, or both, since in Egypt royalty and religion were far from incompatible. Composite figures were not limited to the sphinx type, but extended to cow-headed goddesses (Hathor), lion-headed goddesses (Sekhmet), and others. Here, too, it is safe to assume that the animal attribute is not merely decorative but serves to indicate an important relationship of ideas. It is unquestionably a form of preliterary survival.

In animal sculpture proper, we find much less conventionalized treatment than in the representation of human beings; particularly is this true in the rendering of animals that apparently served no specifically religious purpose. This difference in artistic approach is one that only a civilization with the long history of Egypt,

[14] When the *Sheik of the Village* was first dug out of the ground, the modern Egyptian peasants helping the archaeologists gave the figure its name when they began to shout "The Sheik of our Village!"—so well did it resemble a modern Egyptian.

and its direct if slow evolution from an early and preliterate period, could show. In the Paleolithic and Neolithic periods we found a similar distinction in artistic representation. There it was bound up with a totemistic fear of accurate delineation of one's own body, whereas animals were most carefully and naturalistically represented in order to "facilitate" the hunt. Perhaps this Neolithic heritage can account for the unwavering conventionalization of the bodies of the human effigies; while the bodies and heads of animals show a unified and consistent naturalism.

In addition to sculpture in the round, the Egyptians practiced relief sculpture. They frequently used this technique for the elaborate narratives with which they decorated the walls of tombs and the columns, the walls and the façades of the temples. These sculptured reliefs were similar to the painting of the time for, not only were most of them painted in the characteristic flat colors used in Egypt, but the rules of perspective, outlines, and arrangement were applied to both arts simultaneously. Apparently the artists working in painting and relief sculpture were unable to adapt their highly conventionalized ideas to the necessities of a narrative art. The result was a lack of perspective in which figures were placed above one another in registers instead of behind one another as is the practice in modern times. To indicate the importance of a particular person (the Pharaoh, let us say), the artist exaggerated the figure's size, a device that grew out of the hierarchical nature of Egyptian society. The reliefs and the wall paintings usually read from the top down, with the bodies of men colored red and those of women a light yellow.

Individual figures here, as in sculpture in the round, were subject to a series of strict conventions: the head was presented in profile while the eye was rendered fullface, the legs in profile and the trunk fullface. As with the modern cubist artist, it was the aim of the Egyptian artist to show as much of the body as he could at one time. Disregarding these naturalistic paradoxes (which are obviously "frontal" conventions), we find the line quality of the painter or bas-relief sculptor extremely sophisticated and modern; in no sense could it be regarded as crude or uninformed. Egyptian portraits and animal sculpture prove conclusively that when he was so minded the Egyptian artist could be as naturalistic as anyone else, but that the long uninterrupted evolution that Egyptian civilization had undergone from primitive times naturally imposed the conventions we have seen.

It must be observed, finally, that the Egyptians produced one of the finest industrial arts the world has ever known. A casual glance at the jewelry collections of the large museums convinces us of their superb treatment of precious stones, metals, wood, alabaster, ivory, etc. Their products were eagerly sought after in the markets of antiquity and were one of the means of disseminating Egyptian ideas and forms.

2. Mesopotamia

The valley between the Tigris and Euphrates rivers in Asia Minor produced a culture which was about as old as Egypt's, but not nearly so progressive. Most of the early monuments which the Mesopotamians constructed have disappeared, for, possessing very little stone, the builders were forced to use the much more perishable brick. Frequent floods and terrific rainstorms did not help to preserve these buildings. The years 3000 to about 1700 B.C. marked the period of development from which emerged the customs and arts of the Assyro-Babylonian valley.[15]

In the early or Sumerian-Akkadian phase of Mesopotamian art appear sculptures and decorative objects, usually smallish and sometimes in precious metals. Among the more spectacular discoveries in royal Chaldean graves are craft objects, including the gold harp of Queen Shubad of Ur (c. 2800 B.C.) and a finely worked gold helmet. Copper plaques and inlaid shell patterns from this period demonstrate an advanced mastery over decorative techniques. Somewhat later comes a more monumental type of sculpture, the "Gudea of Tello" (c. 2400-2250 B.C.) in both seated and standing poses. These likenesses of Gudea, a prince or governor, are carved from extremely hard stone. As portraits they lack the finished plastic quality of Egyptian masterpieces of similar date. But such sculptures are among the most powerful expressions of earlier Mesopotamian art. They possess a convincing simplification of form. The skirt of the robe of these figures is incised with written legends which lend textural interest to the broad surface. Although the Sumerians believed in life after death, their art does not disclose the preoccupation with this theme common to Egypt. The Mesopotamian palace rather than the tomb or temple-tomb was, along with the *ziggurat*, the outstanding building form. The *ziggurat* was a stepped tower whose different levels were connected by inclined ramps. The uppermost stage was probably occupied by an altar which was used by priests during rituals. In basic design the *ziggurat* is not unlike the Egyptian step pyramid. It was handed down to the Assyrians who incorporated it within the royal palace enclosure.[16] This early Chaldean civilization (Abraham is supposed to have been associated with Ur of the Chaldees) also produced ingenious cylinder seals, some figured with animal forms, others with cuneiform or wedge-shaped written characters. The art of glazed tile was known in this period, but did not reach the perfection seen in later phases.

The second stage of Mesopotamian civilization transferred to the Assyrian Empire which absorbed the culturally superior Babylonians through their highly developed military machine. Assyrian architecture, very much like that of the Chaldeans (early Babylonians), can be more easily examined in such an extant example as the Palace of Sargon at Khorsabad (722-705 B.C.). This edifice in its location on a high platform, reached by a series of ramps, resembles a fortified encampment. At the entrance to this imposing enclosure is an elaborate gateway, flanked by composite monsters similar to those of Egypt. This gateway, like the palace walls, was faced with brilliantly colored enamel tiles.

Within the palace enclosure, the huge building spread out under the Mesopotamian sun. Light entered only through the many open courtyards. The walls

---

[15] It is customary to distinguish between an earlier period, the Chaldean (c. 2000-1000 B.C.—Chaldea was located in the lower part of the valley, in the portion usually designated as Babylonia) and the later period, the Assyrian (beginning c. 1500 B.C. and culminating in 1100 B.C. with the conquest of Babylonia). After a short interlude, during which the entire valley was overrun by nomads out of the desert, the Assyrian Empire proper was established (c. 900-607 B.C.).

[16] Among the later Mohammedan peoples of the Mesopotamian region, the tower as a religious structure became very important, e.g., minarets used at the four corners of a mosque.

themselves contained no window openings. In the Near East the problem was rather to exclude the sun than to admit it. Although at first the tremendous number of rooms present a relatively confused picture, the Palace of Khorsabad organizes itself into a series of clearly separated sections; the public rooms, the central section dedicated to the apartments of the king, the harem apartments, and finally, the quarters for the slaves and other attendants.

Since stone was very scarce in this part of the Near East, the Assyrian builder used brick. This had its advantages for, unhampered by unwieldy stone, he was not limited to the vertical-horizontal system—as had been the Egyptian builders. To roof the distances between walls, he used the rounded arch as his basic struc-

Left, column-and-lintel construction as illustrated in Egyptian architecture. *Right,* arch construction as illustrated in Assyro-Babylonian architecture.

tural principle. Although the Egyptians had known this scheme (had probably invented it), it remained for the Assyro-Babylonians to develop its use in a widespread and practical fashion.

The same necessity that led him to hide the rough brick surface of his exterior walls, now led the Assyrian builder to embellish the interior of the palace with stone slabs upon which he carved as fine a series of relief sculptures as has ever been produced. Artistically these sculptures are the main contribution of this part of the ancient Near East (sculpture in the round was rare in Assyria), exceeding by far the production of the Egyptians in this field. The great majority of the scenes represented on these bas-reliefs are concerned either with the hunt or with war, the two favorite occupations of this nation. Working in a softer stone than the Egyptian, the Assyrian artist was able to express, particularly in his animal representation, a degree of energy and realism that can stand comparison with the art of any age. The Assyrian sculptor, too, was subject to a great many conventions. He still represented heads in profile with eyes in fullface. He still used the same flat-footed method of posing his figures as did his Egyptian colleagues: the full-front shoulders and hips that contrasted so vividly with the profiled head and feet. Obviously this is stylization, but with a much more powerful result than anything the Egyptians ever produced in relief sculpture. When the artist ventured into animal portraiture (*The Dying Lioness*) he was incomparable.

3. Persia

By the end of the sixth century B.C. the Assyro-Babylonian Empire yielded to the Persians. Their kingdom (c. 550-330 B.C.) covered most of the Iranian plateau, from the Tigris to the Indus River and was better organized than any other empire in antiquity from both the military and administrative points of view.

In its development, the character of Persian art followed the military expansion of the empire. First it showed a series of Mesopotamian and Ionian (Asiatic Greek) borrowings and then, with the conquest of Cambyses, a series of influences from Egypt. It is customary to speak of the art of Persia as eclectic, as formed by the various borrowed elements from its conquered territories. In Persia, as in the earlier Mesopotamian Empire, the important art manifestation was the palace of the Great King, placed upon a terrace approached by monumental staircases whose sides were ornamented with elaborate bas-reliefs analogous in style to those of Assyro-Babylonia. Not only does the relief sculpture repeat the artistic characteristics of its Assyrian predecessors, but the gigantic winged monsters flanking the elaborate entrance portico to their palace platforms are similarly reminiscent.

The architecture of Persia (i.e., palaces and audience halls) was, unlike that of Assyro-Babylonia, generally columnar in arrangement, because the building stone necessary for this type of construction was available. Persepolis ("city of the Persians") was the most important center. Here stood the palaces of Darius, Xerxes, and Artaxerxes III, all built in the typical Persian arrangement of a large square-columned hall surrounded by small rooms and preceded by an ample portico. In addition to Xerxes' palace, the site of Persepolis shows the remains of his audience hall, a magnificent building analogous in shape to the palace, with columns spaced thirty feet apart and almost as tall as those of the great Hypostyle Hall at Karnak, Egypt, whose influence it clearly shows.

The eclectic character of Persian art is most evident in the shape of the columns: tall fluted (channeled) shafts placed upon a floral base. For the capitals it was customary to use the foreparts of a pair of bulls, set back to back, while immediately below them a series of volutes (curved sections in the shape of scrolls) led down to a number of palm leaves, lotus forms, etc. Some of these elements, the flutings and the scrolls, indicate a contact with Asiatic Greece, while the use of the bulls' heads, floral motives, etc., are part of the Egyptian heritage. The total effect is rather disorganized and composite. Other evidences of the cultural borrowing in this civilization are the royal tombs at Naksh-i-Rustam, where, as in Egypt, a series of burial chambers have been hollowed out of the rock.

The well-known bas-reliefs of Persepolis, which decorate the impressive staircases, while reminiscent of the Assyrian, differ from it in feeling. They have none of the cruelty and harshness so often expressed in Mesopotamian narrative sculpture. Persia's contact with the Greek world appears to have softened the contours of the figures and to have eliminated the tightness which was characteristic of the outlines of the Assyrian figures. The enameled tiles (*Frieze of the Lions, Frieze of the Archers* (Susa)) are a similar adaptation of a borrowed style. We have not spoken of Persia's temples, for with the exception of a number of fire altars, there does not seem to have been any.

4. *The Mediterranean and Aegean*

Another important culture of the Near East, generally referred to as the Minoan, developed on the island of Crete in the Mediterranean. Like that of Mesopotamia and Persia, Minoan culture was dominated by the palace of the king. Early Minoan development coincided with the Bronze Age (c. 3000-2200 B.C.). The first great Minoan palaces, Knossos and Phaistos, were produced c. 2000 B.C.[17] The arrangement of these palaces is large and rambling, even confused.

A high degree of civilization was reached here at an early period, judged by Minoan painting, sculpture and minor arts, all of which are extremely well developed and beautifully stylized. Such frescoes as *The Cup Bearer* from Knossos are most elegant in design and strikingly colored in a modern manner, although they still adhere to the customary Near-Eastern tradition of using a profile head with a frontal figure. In their representation of natural forms, animals, plants, etc., the Minoans reached a degree of verisimilitude that is higher than that of other contemporary civilizations. This is so true of their small enameled tiles of fish, etc., that they were once believed to be fossils rather than works of art. Their *repoussé* (beaten out) bronze vessels, decorated with representations of animals, are another eloquent witness to the skill of Minoan artists in depicting living forms. Here, as in Egypt and Mesopotamia, a distinction in treatment between human beings and animals was made; the human representations express a high degree of conventionality while the animals are almost completely liberated from stylization, e.g., *Vaphio cups, Harvester vase.*

One of the most important Minoan productions is their pottery. Beautiful in shape and color, it was the most outstanding pottery in the field before the work of the Greeks. Here again they employed naturalistic motifs, sea plants, and sea animals, adapted most skillfully to the shape of each vessel.

The later stage of Minoan culture developed on the mainland of Greece, at Mycenae and Tiryns (c. 1400-1100 B.C.) and at Troy on the coast of Asia Minor. It coincided with what we know as the Homeric Age, during which the mainland cities were dominated by imposing palace fortifications usually built on the top of a hill (acropolis). The palace of the king was built in a style that clearly anticipated the shape and construction of the later Greek temple.

In their painting, sculpture, and minor arts, the cities of the mainland betray an outgrowth of the culture of Crete proper and therefore should still be classified in the Near-Oriental category. This Minoan-Mycenaean period came to an end about 1000 B.C. with the Dorian invasion of the Greek peninsula which destroyed the palaces of Mycenae and Tiryns, and ushered in the dark age of Greece

---

17 The Palace of Knossos is known as the labyrinth (i.e., palace of the labrys or double-ax, one of the religious symbols).

(c. 1000-700 B.C.). Many of these pre-Greeks were forced to emigrate by the invaders and found their way across the Aegean into Asia Minor where they came into contact with Persia.[18]

SELECTED READINGS

Baikie, James, *The Life of the Ancient East*, Macmillan, 1923.

Barnes, H. E., *History of Western Civilization*, 2 Vols., Harcourt, Brace, 1935, Vol. I, chaps. iii-v.

────── Becker, Howard, and Barnes, H. E., *Social Thought from Lore to Science*, 3 Vols., Dover, 1961, Vol. I, chaps. ii-iii.

Botsford, G. W., *Source-Book of Ancient History*, Macmillan, 1912, chaps. i-v.

Breasted, Charles, *Pioneer to the Past*, Scribner, 1943.

Breasted, J. H., *The Conquest of Civilization*, Harper, 1938.

────── *The Dawn of Conscience*, Scribner, 1933.

────── *The Development of Religion and Thought in Ancient Egypt*, Harper, 1959.

Caphart, Jean, *Egyptian Art*, tr. by W. R. Dawson, Stokes, 1923.

────── *Lectures on Egyptian Art*, University of North Carolina Press, 1928.

Childe, V. G., *New Light on the Most Ancient East*, Grove, 1957.

Clark, R. T. R., *Myth and Symbol in Ancient Egypt*, Grove Press, 1960.

Davis, W. S., *Readings in Ancient History*, 2 Vols., Allyn and Bacon, 1912-14, Vol. I, chaps. i-iii.

Delaporte, L. J., *Mesopotamia: The Babylonian and Assyrian Civilization*, Knopf, 1925.

Dhalla, M. N., *Zoroastrian Civilization*, Oxford Press, 1922.

────── *Zoroastrian Theology*, privately printed, 1914.

Durant, Will, *Our Oriental Heritage*, Simon and Schuster, 1935.

Eby and Arrowood, *The History and Philosophy of Education*, chaps. ii-iii.

Erman, Adolf, *Life in Ancient Egypt*, Macmillan, 1894.

────── *Literature of the Ancient Egyptians*, Dutton, 1927.

Farnell, L. R., *Greece and Babylon*, Scribner, 1912.

Finegan, Jack, *Light from the Ancient Past*, Princeton University Press, 1959.

Forsdyke, E. J., *Minoan Art*, Oxford Press, 1931.

Frankfort, H. A., *et al., The Intellectual Adventure of Ancient Man*, University of Chicago Press, 1946.

────── *Art and Architecture in the Ancient Orient*, Penguin, 1955.

Garrison, F. H., *Introduction to the History of Medicine*, Saunders, 1929, chaps. ii-iii.

Glanville, S. R. K., *The Legacy of Egypt*, Oxford University Press, 1942.

Glotz, Gustave, *The Aegean Civilization*, Knopf, 1925.

Hammerton, J. A., ed., *Universal History of the World,* 8 Vols., Amalgamated Press, 1927-29, Vols. I-II.

Handcock, P. S. P., *Mesopotamian Archaeology*, Putnam, 1912.

Hauser, Arnold, *The Social History of Art*, Knopf, 1951.

Hertzler, J. O., *The Social Thought of the Ancient Civilizations*, Russell, 1961.

Hitti, P. K., *History of the Arabs*, St. Martin's Press.

18 Recently, the English philologist, Leonard R. Palmer, has questioned the traditional view that Minoan-Mycenean culture was destroyed by invaders from the mainland. See *Time*, July 18, 1960, p. 52.

Huart, C. I., *The Ancient Persian and Iranian Civilization*, Knopf, 1927.

Jastrow, Morris, *Aspects of Religious Belief and Practice in Babylonia and Assyria*, Putnam, 1911.

—— *The Civilization of Babylonia and Assyria*, Lippincott, 1915.

Keller, Werner, *The Bible as History*, Hodder Stoughton, 1956.

Kramer, S. N., *History Begins at Sumer*, Doubleday, 1959.

Larson, M. A., *The Religion of the Occident*, Philosophical Library, 1959.

Lods, Adolphe, *Israel*, Knopf, 1932.

Mason, W. A., *History of the Art of Writing*, Macmillan, 1920.

Maspero, G. C. C., *Art in Egypt*, Scribner, 1912.

Moret, Alexandre, *The Nile and Egyptian Civilization*, Knopf, 1928.

—— and Davy, Georges, *From Tribe to Empire*, Knopf, 1926.

Muller, H. J., *The Loom of History*, Harper, 1958.

Murray, M. A., *Egyptian Sculpture*, Scribner, 1930.

—— *The Splendor That Was Egypt*, Philosophical Library, 1949.

Myers, B. S., *Art and Civilization*, McGraw-Hill, 1957.

Myres, J. L., *The Dawn of History*, Holt, 1912.

Neilson, Francis, *From Ur to Nazareth*, Robert Schalenbach Foundation, 1959.

Olmstead, A. T., *History of Assyria*, Scribner, 1923.

—— *History of Palestine and Syria*, Scribner, 1931.

—— *History of the Persian Empire*, University of Chicago Press, 1948.

Pavry, J. D. C., *The Zoroastrian Doctrine of a Future Life*, Columbia University Press, 1929.

Peet, T. E., *Egypt and the Old Testament*, Small, Maynard, 1923.

Petrie, W. M. F., *Arts and Crafts of Ancient Egypt*, McClurg, 1910.

—— *Religious Life in Ancient Egypt*, Houghton Mifflin, 1924.

—— *Social Life in Ancient Egypt*, Houghton Mifflin, 1923.

Rogers, R. W., *Cuneiform Parallels to the Old Testament*, Abingdon Press, 1912.

Sedgwick, W. T., and Tyler, H. W., *Short History of Science*, Macmillan, 1917, chaps. i-iii.

Sidhanta, N. K., *The Heroic Age of India*, Knopf, 1930.

Sigerist, H. E., *Primitive and Archaic Medicine*, Oxford University Press, 1951.

Smith, E. B., *Egyptian Architecture as Cultural Expression*, Appleton-Century, 1938.

Smith, J. M. P., *The Moral Life of the Hebrews*, University of Chicago Press, 1923.

Steindorff, George, and Seele, K. C., *When Egypt Ruled the East*, University of Chicago Press, 1957.

Taylor, H. O., *Ancient Ideals*, 2 Vols., Macmillan, 1913.

Ullman, B. L., *Ancient Writing*, Longmans, 1932.

Wallis, Louis, *A Sociological Study of the Bible*, University of Chicago Press, 1912.

—— *By the Waters of Babylon*, Macmillan, 1931.

—— *God and the Social Process*, University of Chicago Press, 1935.

Webster, Hutton, *Historical Selections*, Heath, 1929, Part I.

Part Two

CLASSICAL THOUGHT AND CULTURE:
THE BEGINNINGS OF SKEPTICISM

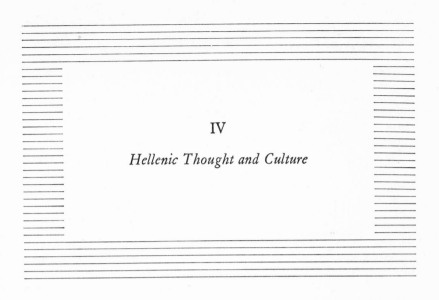

IV

Hellenic Thought and Culture

I. THE GREEK HERITAGE FROM THE ORIENT

With the entrance of Greece on the world's stage, civilization took a new turn, and the Hellenic peoples reached in almost double-quick time a cultural preeminence which has profoundly impressed the Western World ever since.

The query arises: did Hellenic culture involve a break with the Oriental civilization which preceded it? Or did one emerge out of the other as a seed emerges from a plant?

Historians used to draw a sharp line between Oriental and Hellenic civilization and regarded the latter as a spontaneous and unique growth. This is no longer done. We know now that Hellenic culture owed a great deal to the Near Orient. Throughout Greek history, there was a continuous interaction between Hellas and its Oriental neighbors.

The knowledge and achievements accumulated by those who had preceded the Greeks served as a basis for many of the latter's accomplishments. Finally, during Hellenistic times, from about 300 B.C. until the early Christian Era, Greek and Oriental civilization merged in a brilliant synthesis that fused the two cultures.

Modern scholarship, although it fully recognizes Greece's debt to the Orient, in no way belittles the special Hellenic contribution to civilization. The Greeks, after all, did in some measure release man from the dead hand of tradition and the incubus of superstition. They introduced the scientific frame of mind and a thoroughly secular way of looking at life. Furthermore, they produced notable types of literature and the fine arts, and evolved political ideals that have in many ways never been surpassed.

Yet it may be fairly said that Greece would not have taken all these forward steps if Egypt and Mesopotamia had not cleared the road and set up the cultural and intellectual signposts.

When we speak of Hellenic civilization, we must be careful to point out that not all of Greece shared in the glory. Parts of the peninsula and many of the Aegean Islands were under a pall of darkness while Ionia and Attica were enjoying a golden age. Sparta was an actual liability to Greek civilization and did much to lessen its glamor. Thebes was little better. And a number of Greek city-states never emerged at all from the obscurity which they richly deserved.

The Greece into which philosophy was born was much larger than the Greece of today. It consisted of all the coasts and islands washed by the Mediterranean from Asia Minor to Sicily and southern Italy, and from Cyrene to Thrace. The peninsula itself at first played an insignificant rôle. Leadership was held by the Ionians, who had colonized the coasts of Asia Minor. By the seventh century, when the first Greek philosophy appears, Ionian trade and colonies extended over the entire Mediterranean world. Miletus became the wealthiest of these, and the cradle of Greek science. For more than a hundred years before it was destroyed, in 494 B.C., Miletus was the intellectual leader among Hellenic cities.

After 480 B.C. the center of gravity was shifted from Miletus to Athens, or, from the islands to the mainland. The history of classic Greece then became for a time almost entirely the history of Athens. Among the large cities of Hellas, such as Corinth, Aegina, Sparta, and Thebes, Athens quickly became the center of Greek civilization after her successful leadership in the Persian Wars.

The Greeks who settled Attica were a mixed race and very versatile. Before the Persian Wars Athens had been disciplined by the benevolent tyrant, Pisistratus, who took the first steps toward founding the Athenian empire. Between 490 and 480 Themistocles built the Athenian fleet and thereby made Athens the naval and maritime leader of Greece. There were other reasons why this particular city should become the focal point of Hellenic civilization. Sparta was too oligarchical and unintellectual. Thessaly was too luxurious and stagnant. Thebes was not fired with zest for wisdom and knowledge; she was too aristocratic and indolent. When Athens formed and controlled the Delian Confederacy (after 480 B.C.), she used its fat treasury to enrich herself culturally. She drew scholars and artists from all Hellas, and practically drafted the talent of the peninsula. Consequently, like Florence in the fifteenth century, she became the hub of Hellenic culture, the cyclopean eye of its civilization.

In Hellenistic times (300 B.C. et seq.), however, Alexandria surpassed Athens and all other cities in wealth and culture. Nothing else in antiquity could rival the wonders of Alexandria. Its museum and library were in many ways like a modern university. Scholars of all nations were entertained, often at public expense. There was a large botanical garden, a zoölogical collection, an anatomical museum, an astronomical observatory and a library of at least 750,000 volumes. In Alexandria, Euclid wrote his geometry, Eratosthenes presided over the great library and pursued his astronomical labors, and Apollonius wrote his treatise on conic sections. Here Ptolemy and his school formulated a system of astronomy which was accepted for 1,500 years, here Jewish philosophy took on a Platonic cast with Philo, here Neoplatonism was born, and here Christian theologians were educated. Literature, art, history, philosophy, and criticism flourished. All religions were welcomed. For five hundred years or more Alexandria was the intellectual capital of the Western World, the most polyglot, most tolerant of cities. In its streets mingled Buddhist, Hebrew, Greek, Egyptian. Nothing like it was seen again until the rise of Paris in the later Middle Ages, or of Florence in early modern days.

II. THE ORIGINS OF THE LIBERAL-LEGAL STAGE OF CIVILIZATION

The brilliance of Hellenic culture could not have been achieved unless it had reached what Professor Giddings called the "legal-liberal" stage of civilization. This was based on intellectual freedom and a respect for law and personal rights.

We have described the Oriental empires of Mesopotamia and Egypt as a military-religious civilization, where allied races or tribes were forcibly brought together in one political organization. The machinery of government was improved. Causes of antagonism within the race were eliminated. Centralization put an end to innumerable forms of local conflict, and to untold and unnoticed wastes of energy, thereby liberating potent physical and mental forces for leisure-time activities. These activities produced literature, art, and a rudimentary science, besides adorning and adding to the amenities of life.

The diversity and liberalism of the second stage of civilization were thus prepared for in the first stage. Homogeneity of thought, as in Egypt, prepared the way for later freedom. A successful political organization, as in Babylonia and Assyria, released a store of energy for all kinds of nonmilitary enterprises. With no more worlds to conquer, men could turn their thoughts to other things.

But the human intellect can make only limited progress under a military-religious regime, which is autocratic in essence and acts as a cultural steam roller, enforcing like-mindedness on the population.

In the liberal-legal stage, best represented in this period by Athens at its apex, the race learned to appreciate unlike-mindedness. It came to understand the value of doubt and skepticism, of individual initiative and voluntary organization. It learned that *variation* and *criticism* constitute the life blood of man's progress. All this the Hellenes, and particularly the Athenians, realized.

On the political side, the liberal-legal state replaced despotic authority, and the "divine right" of kings was supplanted by a constitutional government and freedom of thought and action.

Under the liberal-legal dispensation men could begin to make internal or domestic changes. They studied their institutions and their laws. A rebellion against authority occurred; individual freedom became an important condition of existence. Many of the people acquired a plastic mind, in contrast to the static mentality of a military-religious culture. Because of previous war, conquest, slavery, and trade, there was a large admixture of diverse elements among the inhabitants, who were alert and versatile. The investigating, critical and philosophical spirit arose.

The instinct of curiosity was now promoted for its own sake and not for purely material or economic reasons. Geography, history, and science became serious intellectual pursuits. As the critical scent, so to speak, became sharpened, the idea of possible improvement was conceived. The protestant, the reformer, now became influential, and the self-conscious community undertook to reorganize and improve itself. In other words, a Hellenic Hosea or Isaiah did not beat the air vainly with his fiery words. Society was eager to hear the indictment—and to do something about it. A protestant nation is a progressive nation, and therefore it faces the problem of achieving unity and stability without curbing freedom.

The demand became insistent that the government should cease exercising arbitrary powers and that liberty of thought and action be guaranteed within reasonable limits to every citizen. Therefore, charters and guarantees were wrested from tyrants, whose claim to divine right was no longer taken seriously. Little by little, legislation and precedent were interwoven, and the strong fabric of constitutional law evolved. Autocratic powers were curbed and governmental duties defined. Freedom of contract between individuals was taken for granted. Political absolutism, such as characterized Oriental civilization, was ended.

Greece was the first society to enter the legal-liberal stage of civilization. Athens developed the critical and philosophical—the liberal—features, but she failed relatively in the constitutional and legal aspects, a failure in part traceable to the problem of maintaining a strong military organization for protection against numerous enemies. Rome did better on the legalistic side of the picture, but was not so successful in maintaining liberalism in the face of an increasingly orientalized imperial despotism and the dominion of the military arm. A true liberal-legal state was not achieved until the developments in England after the revolution of 1688-1689.

III. THE CITY-STATE PERSPECTIVE OF GREEK CULTURE

The liberal-legal stage of civilization was facilitated in Greece because things were done on a small scale. Quality was achieved because quantity was either not desired or could not be secured.

Attica was a trifle smaller than the state of Rhode Island and Sparta was less than three-quarters of the size of Connecticut. The population was equally small, judged by modern standards. Athens in Pericles' day had about 40,000 citizens, not counting women, slaves, and aliens. The total population ran somewhere between 200,000 and 300,000.

Within this small territory political life reached functional perfection. The citizenry possessed complete self-government. The chief political bodies were the council and the assembly. Each *polis,* or city-state, also had a public meeting place where free discussion of political and other matters was carried on. In all cases, the polis and city proper ruled the countryside, containing the villages and hamlets upon which it depended for its food supply.

Each city-state was a completely independent entity. It had its own laws, religion, currency, calendar, and system of weights and measures. Civic pride ran deep and dominated the psychology of every citizen. It was more than mere patriotism. It was a *raison d'être* and a philosophy of existence combined.

Athenian democracy offered the fullest opportunity for public service. A citizen might serve in the council or assembly, become a judge, or do jury duty. He could participate in various current public problems. The small city-state offered a direct and immediate participation in politics, which is not possible in large-scale modern democracies.

A man was an Athenian or Spartan or Theban first, and an individual afterwards. This did not mean that he was unconscious of his individuality, but that the welfare of the commonwealth suffused and lessened selfish desires. To understand Hellenic civilization at all this primary fact must constantly be borne in mind. Professor Hutton Webster gives us an admirable summary of the character and traits of the classical city-state, which was so important a factor in Greek civilization:

> A Greek or Roman city usually grew up about a hill of refuge (*acropolis, capitolium*), to which the people of the surrounding district could flee in time of danger. This mount would be crowned with a fortress and the temples of the gods. Not far away was the market place (*agora, forum*), where the people gathered to conduct their business and enjoy social intercourse. About the citadel and market place were grouped the narrow streets and low houses of the town. Thus an ancient city was closely built up and lacked the miles of suburbs that belong to a modern metropolis.
>
> Each of these numerous cities was an independent self-governing community. It formed a city-state. Just as a modern nation, it could declare war, arrange treaties, and make alliances with its neighbors. Such a city-state included not only the territory within its walls, but also the surrounding district where many of the citizens lived. It was usually of small size. Aristotle once said that "a city could not consist of ten men, nor again of one hundred thousand." By this he meant that a city ought not to be so small that no community life was possible in it, yet not so large that a man could not know many of his fellow-citizens.
>
> The members of an ancient city-state were very closely associated. The citizens believed themselves to be descended from a common ancestor and so to be all related. They were united also, in the worship of the patron god or hero who had them under his protection. These two ties, the tie of supposed kinship and the tie of a common religion, made citizenship a great privilege which came to an individual only by birth. Elsewhere he was only a foreigner without legal rights—a man without a country.
>
> To the free-born inhabitant of Athens or of Rome his city was at once his country and his church, his club and his home. He shared in its government; he took part in the stately ceremonies that honored its patron god; in the city he could indulge his taste for talking and for politics; here he found safety and society.[1]

The independent nature of the city-state had its drawbacks. It led to pointless and endless wars, and eventually paved the way for Alexander's conquest of Hellas. But there were many compensations. Each city had its own character and

[1] Webster, *Ancient History*, Heath, 1913, pp. 165-66, 562-63.

personality. Through its institutions and laws, its religion and festivals, its monuments and heroes, its particular interpretation of the economic, political, moral and intellectual principles of civilization, each city helped to give that civilization an infinite variety of expression.

The character and ideals of Greece—and particularly of its brightest star, Athens—received their classic description in the funeral speech put into the mouth of Pericles in Thucydides' *History of the Peloponnesian War:*

> . . . The freedom which we enjoy in our government extends also to our ordinary life. There, far from exercising a jealous surveillance over each other, we do not feel called upon to be angry with our neighbor for doing what he likes, or even to indulge in those injurious looks which cannot fail to be offensive, although they inflict no positive penalty. . . .
>
> . . . We cultivate refinement without extravagance and knowledge without effeminacy, wealth we employ more for use than for show, and place the real disgrace of poverty not in owning to the fact but in declining the struggle against it. Our public men have, besides politics, their private affairs to attend to, and our ordinary citizens, though occupied with the pursuits of industry, are still fair judges of public matters . . . and instead of looking on discussion as a stumbling-block in the way of action, we think it an indispensable preliminary to any wise action at all. Again, in our enterprises we present the singular spectacle of daring and deliberation, each carried to its highest point, and both united in the same persons. . . . In generosity we are equally singular, acquiring our friends by conferring, not by receiving, favors. Yet, of course, the doer of the favor is the firmer friend of the two, in order by continued kindness to keep the recipient in his debt; while the debtor feels less keenly from the very consciousness that the return he makes will be a payment, not a free gift. . . .[2]

While the political individualism and separatism of ancient Greece must be stressed to reproduce the historical fact, yet we must recognize the importance of certain bonds which united all Hellenes in a cultural sense, even if political unity proved a transient dream. Among these bonds were the common historical and literary tradition, similar artistic ideals, a common language, the political ideals of the city-state which were shared by all Hellenes, periodic athletic games, culminating in the Olympics held every fourth year, and national religious shrines. This cultural and psychological unity went far to offset the political diversity and the spirit of separatism and provincialism.

IV. THE BIRTH OF FREE THOUGHT

In such a wholesome atmosphere the dead weight of superstition, which effectually choked off intellectual progress in the Orient, could not persist. Moreover, Hellenism offered a marked psychological contrast to Orientalism. The Orient was characterized by a love of homogeneity and by intolerance of diversity and dissent. The Hellene had a supple, alert mentality; he was buoyed up with the energy of cultural youth, and felt, in Wordsworth's phrase, that

[2] Thucydides, *History*, Everyman Ed., 1910, pp. 121-25.

> Bliss was it in that dawn to be alive,
> But to be young was very heaven!

The great contribution of the Greek to civilization—and one not to be under-estimated—is that he inaugurated free thought. He thus provided the indispensable foundation for scientific progress. Man himself became free for the first time from the restraining tentacles of the primitive supernatural obsession. To change the metaphor, he was like a person walking blindfolded through a flowery lane, who suddenly has the blinds removed, and is dazzled by the beauties which he has never before observed.

The social and political pattern of Greek life promoted, as we have noted, intellectual freedom and philosophical discussion. The city-state, with its small compass and diverse occupations and population, inspired self-expression and free thought more naturally and readily than did the priestly and dictatorial empires of the Orient.

The Hellenic priesthood never became a powerful caste, as among the Egyptians or Hebrews. It never tyrannized the community as did the medieval Christian clergy. Nor was it able to silence criticism. Public worship was kept under control, and though some priestly families came to have considerable influence, their civic duties preceded religious considerations. Just as each member of a symphony orchestra bends his will to that of the director, so every phase of a Greek's existence was subservient to the state's needs. Religion was one of these subservient things.

Again, it may be remarked that the Greeks were not a home-loving race. They were roving and restless, like the Vikings, traveled everywhere, and everywhere planted colonies. This created the cosmopolitan spirit essential to free thought. If a man never passes beyond his own country, his native folkways and mores are always highly satisfactory to him. When he travels abroad and experiences the impact of strange customs and alien ideas, he develops the critical eye and the comparative method. These tend to weaken authority, to raise questions, and to test all issues at the bar of reason.

The Greeks invented the skeptical method. They questioned everything. Xenophanes, for instance, in the sixth century, went from city to city, subverting the popular mythology, laughing at the anthropomorphic deities which were collected in the Greek pantheon.

This sort of thing culminated in Socrates' famous vindication of individual conscience. In Plato's *Apology,* Socrates maintains that the individual must refuse, at all costs, to be coerced by human authority or any tribunal, to do anything, or think anything, which his own mind condemns as wrong.

Socrates also pointed out the public value of free discussion. How eloquently and sadly do his words fall upon many countries today where free thought is at such a premium:

> In me you have a stimulating critic, persistently urging you with persuasion and reproaches, persistently testing your opinions and trying to show you that you are really ignorant of what you suppose you know. Daily discussion of the matters

about which you hear me conversing is the highest good for man. Life that is not tested by such discussion is not worth living.[3]

Free thought in the Socratic sense, unknown in the Oriental world, has since become an essential element in any real civilization. To the literate, upper class Greek—the masses, as everywhere, wallowed in superstition—skepticism came naturally because he rejected the supernatural interpretation of life. He believed that the chief business of existence was complete expression of the personality here and now.

He was a pagan in the best sense. Beneath the warm sun, and overlooking the blue Mediterranean, he could only accept a philosophy which exalted the joys of this world. Unlike the Egyptian and the Persian, the hereafter did not seem to interest him profoundly until late days when the Oriental mysteries had gained a hold.

Accepting this highly secular view of life, the Greek was in a position to speculate freely about human problems and social issues. He was able to discover what the "good life" was really like. Such a humanistic outlook was an absolutely new thing in the world, and has remained, through ages of darkness, turmoil, tyranny, and defeat, a perpetual inspiration. It is the morning star lighting up the course of Europe's subsequent chequered intellectual history.

V. EARLY GREEK THOUGHT

Among the Greeks, intellectual curiosity began by claiming that both nature and human experience may be explained by pure reason better than by supernatural causes. In the course of that explanation, they created the intellectual discipline we call philosophy. The able historian of Greek philosophy, John Burnet, says, "Unless we are to use the term in so wide a sense as to empty it of all special meaning, there is no evidence that philosophy has ever come into existence anywhere except under Greek influences." [4]

The earliest Greek philosophy was based on natural science. It has been called the cosmological period of early philosophy, since most of the thinkers tried to explain the nature of the universe. The Milesian thinkers of Ionia, among whom philosophy originated, were "scientists" rather than "philosophers," in our use of the terms. Science and philosophy were, indeed, not yet differentiated, and the answers to the fundamental philosophic question, "What, amid the changes of the physical world, is permanent?" were first given in physical terms.

Students of Greek philosophy agree that Thales was the founder of Greek thought. The only date connected with him is 585 B.C., since tradition says that he predicted a total eclipse of the sun, which is known to have taken place in that year. Thales, in answering the query as to the source of all things, asserted that water is the first principle of the universe. What precisely was implied by this we can only imagine. Many things disappear by being dissolved into water. Many others, including rocks, plants, and animals, apparently owe their existence to

[3] Quoted by Bury, *History of Freedom of Thought*, p. 34.
[4] In R. W. Livingstone, *The Legacy of Greece*, Oxford, 1921, p. 58.

the presence of water. But, to say that water is the ultimate reality, does not solve the problem of existence. It is neither philosophically nor scientifically exact.

And yet Thales was a philosopher, and his stab in the dark yielded highly important results. It suggested a method for solving the problem of ultimate reality. That method was reason and experience. And even the crudest of mechanistic hypotheses marked a real step in advance over the credulous supernaturalism of primitive society and the Orient.

Thales opened the way for Greek philosophy, and each of the four then-recognized elements, earth, air, fire, and water, was in turn selected as the ultimate reality. Thales had suggested water, Anaximenes named air, Xenophanes earth, and Heracleitus fire.

With Thales' immediate successor, the Milesian, Anaximander, the interpretation took a different turn. He said that the universe was derived neither from water nor any other single element, but from the *infinite*—a portentous conception which he first introduced in philosophy. Anaximander grasped at least one of the ultimate scientific truths; something like what we now call conservation of energy: "That from which things take their origin, into that again they pass away, as destiny orders." [5]

With the third and final of the Milesian thinkers, Anaximenes, who flourished about 550 B.C., we find a return to the monistic or single-track interpretation which Thales had suggested. Anaximenes held that the ultimate substance is air. But he anticipated the synthesis of Empedocles by stating that in a condensed form air manifests itself as water and earth, while in more rarefied form it becomes fire. This was the last important cosmological contribution of the school of Miletus. In 494 B.C. the city was destroyed by the Persians and philosophy found other homes.

The next group of Greek thinkers flourished in the Italian Peninsula. Three of them, Xenophanes, Parmenides, and Zeno, lived in Elea; Pythagoras, at Crotona; and Empedocles at Agrigentum in Sicily. Heracleitus, who may be connected with them as their major opponent, came from Ephesus in Asia Minor.

Pythagoras is a half-legendary figure, but we are sure that he was an historic personage, that he was born in the first half of the sixth century on the island of Samos, in Ionia, that he founded the notable school in Crotona, and that he died there. Yet we have nothing that can be definitely attributed to his pen.

The Pythagoreans introduced an important novelty in philosophy, the system of opposites. They compiled a table of what A. W. Benn called "antithetical couples":

The Limited	and Unlimited
The One	and the Many
Rest	and Motion
Light	and Darkness
Good	and Evil

This notion of contrasts exerted a powerful influence in Greek thought.

The Pythagoreans also launched the mystical notion that numbers and geo-

5 C. M. Bakewell, *Source Book in Ancient Philosophy*, Scribner, 1939. p. 3.

metrical figures (mathematical forms) are the immediate patterns from which all things are made. They held that the ultimate reality is a being that endures through all apparent changes. Being has a seemingly dual existence in the form of unlimited space and numbers. The Pythagoreans solved the dilemma by holding that this unlimited space may be reduced to mathematical forms. "Unlimited space furnishes the material; numbers or mathematical forms furnish the mould; the result is a material thing." [6] The Pythagoreans are important in the history of religion because of their introduction into Western intellectual tradition of the doctrine of the transmigration of souls. We shall deal later with the remarkable contributions of the Pythagoreans to mathematics, astronomy, and medicine.

With Xenophanes (c. 530 B.C.), a native of Asia Minor and a contemporary of Pythagoras, who in his wanderings stopped at Elea and may have founded the school known as Eleatics, we go back to the Milesian way of thinking. He believed that earth is the fundamental substance, and at the same time, like Anaximander, he conceived this primordial element as infinite in nature. Xenophanes seems also to have been the author of a common theory in Greek geology and cosmology, namely, that of successive creations of the earth. He had a clear idea of the age of the earth and appears to have grasped the true significance of fossils. He predicted that the earth would sink into the sea, that men would disappear, and that a new creation would begin. [7]

Of all religious thinkers in history, Xenophanes was certainly one of the most remarkable. In almost the spirit of the eighteenth-century deists he distinguished between a noble monotheism and the crude anthropomorphic cults and superstitions of the masses:

There is one god, supreme among gods and men; resembling mortals neither in form nor in mind.

The whole of him sees, the whole of him thinks, the whole of him hears.

Without toil he rules all things by the power of his mind.

And he stays always in the same place, nor moves at all, for it is not seemly that he wander about now here, now there.

But mortals fancy gods are born, and wear clothes, and have voice and form like themselves.

Yet if oxen and lions had hands, and could paint with their hands, and fashion images, as men do, they would make the pictures and images of their gods in their own likeness; horses would make them like horses, oxen like oxen.

Ethiopians make their gods black and snub-nosed; Thracians give theirs blue eyes and red hair.

It is just as impious to say that the gods are born as to say that they die. For it follows from either view that at some time or other they do not exist.

Homer and Hesiod have ascribed to the gods all deeds that are a shame and disgrace among men; thieving, adultery, fraud.

The gods did not reveal all things to men at the start; but, as time goes on, by searching, they discover more and more.

There never was, nor ever will be, any man who knows with certainty the things

[6] H. E. Cushman, *A Beginner's History of Philosophy*, Houghton Mifflin, 1918, I, 50.
[7] Bakewell, *op. cit.*, pp. 10-11.

about the gods and about all things which I tell of. For even if he does happen to get most things right, still he himself does not know it. But mere opinions all may have.[8]

Here we find a Greek thinker, only a little after the middle of the sixth century b.c., sizing up the major religious issues about as well as they have ever been described right down to our very day. It would put a contemporary modernist to the test to state the case better in the same number of words today. This extract from Xenophanes reveals the fallacy of the conventional view that the Hebrews had a monopoly on religious insight at this period—about the time of the return from the exile.

Properly to appreciate the later Eleatics, we must first consider the speculations of their opponent Heracleitus, one of the most original of the early Greek philosophers, who flourished about 500 b.c.

So far, three elements—water, air, and earth—had been suggested as the ultimate reality. Heracleitus claimed this virtue for the fourth, fire. The idea may have come to him from Anaximander, who suggested that the heavenly bodies are merely sky openings under vast revolving rings of fire. At any rate, Heracleitus said, "This universe, the same for all, no one, either god or man, has made; but it always was and is, and ever shall be an ever-living fire, fixed measures kindling and fixed measures dying out." [9] It is important to notice that for Heracleitus the primordial element, fire, kept its identity throughout all external transformations. This crudely anticipated the electronic theory of modern physics. And this idea led him to the still more general principle, that of the creative capacity of conflict. For instance, he said, "Opposition brings men together, and out of discord comes the fairest harmony, and all things have their birth in strife." [10]

Most important of all the Heracleitean doctrines is that of change or flux. His principle "that all things flow; nothing abides" has been vindicated by modern investigation in every field of science. How accurate is his statement: "One cannot step twice into the same river. . . . Into the same river we step and we do not step; we are and we are not." In the belief that there is no being, but becoming, Heracleitus made the most momentous of all contributions among the early monists (those who would find ultimate reality in a single substance or concept). But in so doing he neglected one category—namely, rest, which can not superficially be reconciled with eternal motion. In this, however, Heracleitus was in harmony with modern thought, which recognizes that seemingly inert matter is in a high state of agitation and electronic motion. The contemporary physicists have finally proved that there is no such thing as rest.

Parmenides (c. 475 b.c.) of the Eleatic school upheld exactly the opposite view. He proclaimed that the world was not only finite, as the new Greek astronomy seemed to prove, but it was "continuous, homogeneous, eternal," and always at rest. And not becoming, but being, is the ultimate reality. Parmenides declared that all existence is really space, "continuous, homogeneous, transparent, and im-

---

[8] Bakewell, *op. cit.*, pp. 8-9.   [10] *Ibid.*, p. 31.
[9] *Ibid.*, p. 30.

movable." In other words, he refined existence down to extension, and then proceeded to identify it with pure thought or being: "for one thing are thinking and being." In so doing he only followed the lead of Xenophanes and other early Greek philosophers, who, because of the survival of primitive animism, held that nature is alive and attributed to the primordial substance some kind of spirit or consciousness—an attitude which is known in philosophical terms as *hylozoism*. Parmenides further denied that difference and duality can exist. Body and soul, he said, are one and the same. To boil down his thought, the major significance of Parmenides lies in the fact that he was, along with the Pythagoreans, the philosophical father of Plato's theory of immutable and eternal universals as the seat of reality. As Cushman puts his attitude: "The senses show us only the many and the changing. The reason shows us nothing of the sort, but only permanence and unchangingness."

Parmenides' paradoxes produced a good deal of ridicule, and his younger friend, Zeno (c. 465 B.C.), came to the rescue with a number of intriguing arguments and controversial paradoxes which seemed to disprove the reality of either space or motion. One of the most famous was his attempt to prove that space does not exist: "If space is, it will be in something; for everything that is is in something; and to be in something is to be in space; space then will be in space, and so on *ad infinitum*. Therefore, space does not exist." [11] Another of them was the famous puzzle of Achilles and the tortoise. Achilles, the swiftest, and the tortoise, the slowest of beings, run a race, the animal being given a head start. Achilles cannot overtake him since there will always be a margin between the two racers. In the same way, it can be said that when we start for a destination, we never reach it, because a fixed space is infinitely divisible. We cover, say, half of it, then half of the remainder, half of that remainder, and so on indefinitely. There will always be a margin not covered.

Greek thought thus came to a deadlock in the Parmenidean and Heracleitean philosophies. But the ingenuity of the Hellenic mind was not exhausted, and a number of thinkers, sailing on a new tack, delivered it from the dilemma of monism by postulating a pluralistic explanation of the universe.

We have seen that water, air, earth, and fire had each been successively proposed as the original source of all things. Empedocles, who flourished about 470 B.C., held that all four are coexisting entities. Hence, he performed a great service to philosophy by being the first thinker to declare that what we call creation and disintegration are really nothing but the union and separation of pre-existing elements. Consequently one could reconcile Heraclitus and Parmenides by thinking of nature as a permanent substance persisting through a series of never ending changes. And behind these changes Empedocles saw something like a pure spirit, "a sacred and unutterable mind, flashing through the whole world with rapid thoughts." [12]

The four elements, as envisaged by Empedocles, Aristotle, and their successors, were not precisely the earth, air, fire, and water which we find and use in daily

[11] Bakewell, *op. cit.*, p. 22.
[12] A. W. Benn, *Ancient Philosophy*, Putnam, 1912, p. 33.

life. In our earthly experience with them, we find these elements only in mixtures. For example, the water that we know is, according to the theory of the elements, mainly made up of the element water, but it also contains some earth, air, and fire. The elements are to be found in pure form only in special parts of the universe. Earth is purest when found nearest to its center. The area of pure water is in the region of the clouds. Next comes the realm of the air. Finally, in the most remote regions, near to the fire of the heavenly bodies, we find the zone of pure fire.

Neither Empedocles nor his predecessors had discovered the ultimate reality, in spite of their ingenious guesses. It remained for Leucippus, an Ionian of Abdera, who was a contemporary of Empedocles, to suggest a more plausible explanation of physical nature. In short, Leucippus suggested the atomic theory. He declared that there are hard, solid particles of matter, indivisible, invisible, and eternal which enter into the composition of all earthly masses, from the smallest to the largest.

According to Leucippus, the atoms differ in shape and size, these differences leading to a corresponding variety of movements. The convergence of these atoms brings all things into existence. The atomic theory implied, as a corollary, the concept of a void in which the atoms can move freely. Leucippus thus bridged the gap between being and becoming, the one and the many. He denied the concept of not-being. Everything is being in the process of becoming. It is one and many. Everything is composed of atoms, which are mobile and invisible, whirling in a void which is itself immobile and visible.

In this way, the atomic theory seemed to reconcile the Eleatic philosophy of Parmenides and Zeno with common sense, and at the same time explained the endless flux which Heracleitus had assumed. Leucippus had a worthy successor, Democritus of Abdera (460-361 B.C.). Windelband calls Democritus "the greatest investigator of nature in antiquity."[13] He was no closet philosopher but traveled very widely, closely observing nature and its varied manifestations. Democritus carried the atomic theory to its most complete development in antiquity. He agreed with Leucippus that atoms form the ultimate physical reality. The atoms differ among one another in shape and size and move freely about in space. They have an infinite number of forms and a great variety of sizes. Creation consists solely in the fortuitous concurrence of these atoms, and death is but their separation and dispersion after a particular concurrence. "Atoms differ only in form and size, and in their union and separation all events are to be explained." The quality of motion dwells inherently in the atoms, which are normally and continuously in flight through empty space, save when they collide and form the aggregations which make up all bodies in the universe.

Atomism, unfortunately, had little success among ancient philosophers; Aristotle, lamentably and to the great disadvantage of scientific progress, chose to adopt and sanctify the doctrine of Empedocles relative to the four elements. But atomism was victoriously revived in the sixteenth and seventeenth centuries, and in more precise interpretations, forms the basis of modern chemistry.

13 Wilhelm Windelband, *History of Ancient Philosophy*, Dover Publications, Inc., 1956, p. 155.

It is worth mentioning that Democritus, although he propagated a system of philosophic materialism, was one of the loftiest moralists of the ancient world. Among his "golden sayings" we find these:

> If one chooses the goods of the soul, he chooses the diviner [portion] of the goods of the body, the merely mortal.
> He who does wrong is more unhappy than he who suffers wrong.
> One should emulate works and deeds of virtue, not arguments about it.
> Strength of body is nobility in beasts of burden, strength of character is nobility in man.
> Neither art nor wisdom may be attained without learning.
> It is better to correct your own faults than those of another.
> Fame and wealth and wisdom are unsafe possessions.
> Making money is not without its value, but nothing is baser than to make it by wrong doing.[14]

Anaxagoras, born about 500 B.C., was a thinker who apparently tried to mediate between the revolutionary atomic theory and the conventional opinion of the time. The atomists had affirmed that only the primary qualities of matter—extension, shape and resistance—are real. What are known as secondary qualities—temperature, color, or taste—have only a subjective or imaginary existence. Anaxagoras accepted no such distinction. He believed that all material qualities are "equally real and equally eternal." Based on the abstract principle that nothing can come from nothing, his contention was logically defensible. To call one category real and another unreal evades the issue.

Anaxagoras declared that in the beginning there was a primordial chaos—"an infinite aggregate of infinitesimal particles," in each of which all qualities were indiscriminately mingled. Out of this chaos the cosmos arose by what we may call in modern terms evolution; that is by integration and differentiation—a doctrine elaborated by Herbert Spencer. The agency which caused this differentiation Anaxagoras called *Nous,* or mind, by which he meant immaterial reason. He describes it as "the thinnest of all things and the purest, and it possesses all knowledge and the greatest power. And whatsoever things are alive, the largest as well as the smallest, over all is mind the ruler." [15] We may note here a survival of primitive animism as in the Parmenidean concept of thought, or pure being.

Anaxagoras is an important figure in the history of culture, since he was the first philosopher who chose Athens as his abode. Like Socrates he was eventually prosecuted for impiety—for stating that the moon is made of earthly substances and shines by reflected light—but escaped by fleeing the city. The Athenians clung to supernaturalism, even if less strongly than other parts of the Greek world, and they resented Anaxagoras' belief that the heavenly bodies were not divine constellations, made of the mysterious fifth element, but masses of earth and stone. The moon, he affirmed, is a dead body, and causes eclipses of the sun by interposing her dark orb between us and the sun. It shines by the reflected light of the sun.

[14] Bakewell, *op. cit.,* pp. 60-61.
[15] *Ibid.,* pp. 51-52.

With Anaxagoras we come to the end of what Professor H. E. Cushman calls the "cosmological period" of Greek philosophy. After the Persian threat disappeared in 480 B.C., the second stage of Greek philosophy, the "anthropological period," began. Athens became its center, Socrates the first striking personality, and the study of man and the state replaced the study of the physical universe.

The contributions of these earlier thinkers to the course of subsequent philosophy and science are important. They outlined most of the basic scientific and philosophical notions followed down to modern times. They also launched metaphysical discussion. They set up skepticism and opposed it to emotionalism and religious dogma. They initiated the long debate between the monists and the pluralists. They stated clearly the opposing doctrines of evolutionary naturalism and teleology—the idea that things are planned and created with a definite purpose in mind. They originated, if they did not name or define, the seven liberal arts. Their work laid the basis for subsequent philosophical discussion and scientific investigation.

VI. THE SOPHISTS, SOCRATES, PLATO, AND ARISTOTLE

Thoroughgoing skepticism and realism first entered human thinking with the Greek Sophists of the period from about 450 to 350 B.C. Until recently, the Sophists have been in ill-repute, as has the attitude of "sophistication," which is literally derived from the Sophists. A number of reasons for this antagonism is apparent. Most of the Sophists were strangers to Athens and suffered from the well-known influence of provincialism, with its hostility to outsiders. They were cosmopolitan rather than narrowly Greek or Attic. Being a learned professional class, they encountered the perennial bias against the "highbrow." They taught the relativity of knowledge and right, and were thus hated by those who believed in dogmatic certainty and rectitude. They taught practical subjects and were on that account assailed by pedants who lived in the intellectual clouds. They popularized the existing knowledge and this exercise has always been opposed by the professional scholar. A few irresponsible members of the group helped to discredit the abler Sophists. Finally, the Sophists have been presented mainly by their enemies. The chief ancient authority on their work was Plato who, as we shall see later, stood at the opposite pole from them, on fundamentals. In contemporary times, the main authority on Greek philosophy was the German writer, Eduard Zeller. He was a disciple of Hegel and, hence, vigorously opposed to any notion of the relativity of knowledge. Zeller, with his penchant for absolutes in thinking, portrayed the Sophists in an unfavorable light.

Of late, however, students of history have come to appreciate the real merits and services of the Sophists. The truly modern attitude towards most questions singularly resembles the general point of view of the Sophists. It has taken humanity well over two thousand years to recover from the influence of post-Sophistic thought and to get back into this salutary frame of mind. We differ from them chiefly in the higher esteem we place on natural science. Gilbert

Murray has well stated this contemporary trend towards a more discerning and appreciative attitude towards the Sophists:

> Their main mission was to teach, to clear up the mind of Greece, to put an end to bad myths and unproven cosmogonies, to turn thought into fruitful paths. Many of them were eminent as original thinkers: Gorgias reduced Eleaticism to absurdity; Protagoras cleared the air by his doctrine of the relativity of knowledge. The many sophists to whom "wisdom" meant knowledge of nature, are known to us chiefly by the Hippocratic writings, and through the definite advances made at this time in the various sciences, especially Medicine, Astronomy, Geometry, and Mechanics. Cos, Abdera, and Syracuse could have told us much about them; Athens, our only informant, was thinking of other things at the time—of social and human problems. In this department Protagoras gave a philosophic basis to Democracy. The mass of mankind possesses the sense of justice and the sense of shame—the exceptions are wild beasts, to be exterminated—and it is these two qualities rather than intellectual powers that are the roots of social conduct. Alkidamas, a disciple of Gorgias, is the only man recorded as having in practical politics proposed the abolition of slavery; in speculation, of course, many did so. Antiphon the sophist represents, perhaps alone, the sophistic view that a wife is a "second self" and more than any friend.
>
> In history, Hippias laid the foundations of a national system of chronology by publishing the list of Olympian victors. The whole science of language rests on the foundations laid by such men as Prodicus and Protagoras: the former insisting on the accurate showing that language is not a divine and impeccable thing, but a human growth with conventions and anomalies. As to morals in general, most of the Sophists were essentially preachers, like Hippias and Prodicus; others, like Gorgias, were pure artists. The whole movement was moral as well as intellectual, and was singularly free from the corruption and lawlessness which accompanied, for example, the Italian Renaissance. The main fact about the Sophists is that they were set to educate the nation, and they did it. The character of the ordinary fourth-century Greek, his humanity, sense of justice, courage, and ethical imagination, were raised to something like the level of the leading minds of the fifth century, and far above that of any population within a thousand years of him. After all, the Sophists are the spiritual and intellectual representatives of the age of Pericles; let those who revile them create such an age again.[16]

We have space here only for a presentation of some of the more representative doctrines of the leaders of the Sophist movement. Protagoras, who was born about 480 B.C., was the first important Sophist. He was influenced by the doctrines of Heracleitus and Democritus. He proclaimed the relativity of all knowledge and contended that there is no absolute or eternal truth. The sense-perception of the individual is the sole source of our knowledge. Man is the measure of all things, and the only reality is that experienced by the human individual. These latter doctrines were to become immensely popular in the days of Italian humanism two thousand years later.

The most erudite, and also the most vain, of the Sophists was Hippias, who was flourishing around 425 B.C. He was immensely learned in a showy fashion in

16 Gilbert Murray, *Ancient Greek Literature*, Appleton, 1897 (University of Chicago Press, 1956), pp. 163-64.

all the branches of knowledge of his day. He looked upon social conventions and law as running counter to human nature. Anticipating Rousseau, he advocated a return to nature as the best path to happiness and contentment.

The most complete skeptic among the Sophists was Gorgias, a contemporary of Hippias. He contended that one could not attain certainty in any field. His argument, which resembled some of the doctrines of Zeno, was to the effect that nothing really exists, that its existence could not be known to man if it did exist, and, finally, that even if reality exists and could be known to the individual, no knowledge of it could be generally communicated. The skepticism of Gorgias extended to complete agnosticism as to the Greek gods and religious beliefs. While all this may seem silly to some, Gorgias hit upon a profound truth: that a thing in itself is different from our perception of the thing, and our knowledge of it is difficult to put into words precisely descriptive of our own impressions.

Prodicus, at the close of the fifth century B.c., was the chief Sophist student of morals. He expressed doubt as to the possibility of formulating any absolute notion of virtue or good conduct. He maintained that good and right are relative terms. He anticipated the Epicureans by contending that a major test of right conduct is how it actually works out in human experience. Thrasymachus, in the same generation, anticipated Nietzsche and other modern philosophers in maintaining that might is right in actual practice. The strong make the laws and the weak must obey them. An early hedonist, he held that the basic law of nature is the gratification of individual desire. Thrasymachus was also one of the first important teachers of rhetoric, which came to play so important a rôle in Greek intellectual life and literary expression. Polus presented a sort of rudimentary foreshadowing of the felicific calculus of Bentham by suggesting that a shrewd calculation of ends is the surest way to happiness.

One of the major Greek dramatists, Euripides (d. 406), showed much sympathy with the attitude of the Sophists. His plays emphasized the element of relativity by presenting differing opinions and viewpoints—they resemble Bernard Shaw's in raising questions but failing to settle them in dogmatic fashion. He well illustrated the skeptical, urbane, and cosmopolitan attitude of the Sophists. Professor Cushman has well summarized the major doctrines of the Sophists:

> Laws are made by the strongest, represent their will, and must be obeyed if they cannot be disobeyed; it takes a strong man to make a law, but a stronger to break it; the laws are only conventions invented either by the many to restrain the powerful few, or by the few to enslave the many. Even religions are devices of the crafty to enchain the people. Obedience to law is therefore a matter of personal interest. Happiness is the most important consideration of the individual. Sometimes personal interest conflicts with law and law does not then bring happiness, for criminals are often the most happy. It is not obedience to law that brings happiness but a shrewd calculation of ends with no regard to right or law. The Sophists made no attempt to put their theories into execution. They expressed the sentiments of the Greek people, and Greek public opinion then pointed to segregation and individualism. Plato said that, after all, the Greek public was the great Sophist.[17]

[17] Cushman, *A Beginner's History of Philosophy*, I, 71-72.

The first major figure in Greek intellectual life was Socrates (c. 469-399 B.C.). Since he wrote nothing, or at least nothing that he wrote has survived, we have to get our information about him from commentators. Fortunately, both his friends and his enemies left observations upon his work. Plato, his disciple, frequently brings him into his *Dialogues,* and Xenophon speaks kindly of him in his *Memorabilia.* On the other hand, the dramatist, Aristophanes, scathingly satirized him in his play, *The Clouds.*

Socrates followed the Sophist, Prodicus, in introducing the skeptical and inquiring mood into the consideration of moral conduct. But his purpose and results were entirely different. Instead of using skepticism to prove the relativity and subjectivity of moral judgments and codes, as had Prodicus, Socrates sought to discover eternal principles of right and good, which would hold equally well for all times and places. Socrates believed that knowledge is absolutely essential to sound and rational behavior. Man cannot behave correctly without knowledge, save by rare accident. But it is equally true that man never knowingly acts wrongly or wickedly. As Aristotle interpreted the thought of Socrates, "he contended that no one acts contrary to what is best, but by reason of ignorance of what is best." [18] Hence, the indispensableness of reliable knowledge if we are to act rightly and, consequently, be happy. Therefore, Socrates tackled the question of whether or not this saving knowledge might actually be acquired and taught.

> The judgments of individuals differ greatly as to the concept of "good," of "bad," of "beautiful," of "ugly." These differences have arisen from the lack of clarity in thinking. By methodical analysis through discussion, by isolation of the essential elements of each concept, by agreement upon these essentials, the underlying truth of each judgment might be obtained. Concepts thus attained Socrates held to be valid, and eternally so. Knowledge, therefore, could be both learned and taught.[19]

Since these eternal principles of right conduct can be discovered man can know what is right, act accordingly, and achieve human happiness, which Socrates held, is the real purpose of philosophical analysis and teaching.

In his opinion, right is not relative to time, place, or social conditions. It is absolute and eternal. What incensed Socrates in the Sophistic doctrine was the notion that such things as morality and justice could be considered mere conventional matters which might vary with circumstances. He held that morality and justice must, in their essence, be the same for all time and under all conditions. He contended that the essence of things must be separated from mere transient "accidents," such as their applications according to time and place. Socrates thus provided the germinal principle for Plato's doctrine of ideas. He freed generalizations from dependence upon particulars. To Socrates William James's remark that we can see no further into a generalization than our knowledge of particulars permits, would have been meaningless or repugnant.

It was from reasoning along this line that Socrates formulated for the first time the notion of a superior and binding natural law, which existed before man

[18] M. M. Dawson, *The Ethics of Socrates,* Putnam, 1924, p. 5.
[19] W. L. Westermann, *Greek Culture and Thought,* Encyclopaedia of the Social Sciences, I, 25.

and may exist after man has disappeared. This doctrine was later revived, elaborated, and applied with disastrous social consequences. Since any such notion as this has long since been revealed to be palpably untrue, Socrates really placed a nasty stumbling block in the way of those who would seek a sane and accurate guide to moral conduct. Thus he defeated the purpose to which he was sincerely devoted. His pupil, Plato, made this retreat from concrete reality and actual experience the basis of his philosophical system and gave it currency through the ages.

Though the results of Socrates' discussions may thus have been disastrous for the human race, his method of approaching the problems of knowledge was helpful and ever useful. He refused to accept any preconceived notions or current dogmas, maintaining that all matters must be analyzed with care and errors in reasoning detected and eliminated. The method he relied upon has been called dialectic, or argument and discussion for the sake of arriving at the truth. This stands in contrast with the methods of "eristic," or argument for the sake of winning a case or downing an adversary, which was common to many Sophists and was revived in the grand manner by the modern Jesuits, and which still dominates courtroom arguments and intercollegiate debating.

The works of Plato (427-347 B.C.) represent the first extended literary product of a single author which has been preserved in a fairly complete fashion. Much of his philosophical writing was urbane and untechnical. In fact in antiquity only Cicero, a popularizer, could match Plato in the matter of appeal and attractiveness to the general reader. And in modern times not until the advent of Montaigne was there another philosopher who wrote so charmingly.

The reason for this appeal was that Plato sought to find a large reading public for his *Dialogues*. He had a serious and practical political purpose. He hoped that enough people would read his works and be affected by them so that a sane political revolution might be achieved in Greek institutional life. If this were brought about, he believed, Hellenic civilization might be extended and preserved. His discontent with existing laws and institutions was intensified by the shock which came to him as a result of the death sentence imposed on his master, Socrates.

Plato's dialogue technique was well adapted to further his goal of popular consumption. He even frequently introduced dramatic and colorful material which was not always relevant to his argument, in order to create reader interest. His dialogues present several conflicting points of view and his characters espouse various sides. Rarely does he arrive at any dogmatic conclusion, though usually it is easy to discover where Plato considered the weight of argument to lie.

The quest for popularity and political effect was not the only, or even the major, reason for Plato's use of the dialogue. The conversational device was a continuation and extension of the Socratic method of philosophical discussion. Plato believed that well-directed conversation may stimulate and clarify our thinking, organize our knowledge, and promote the discovery of truth. His unwillingness to end up in dogmatism is also understandable, since he believed that sensible and well-argued "opinion" is about all that even intelligent conversation could produce. But he never fell into the error of confusing even the most enlightened opinion with philosophical certainty.

We may pause to mention a few of the more important Platonic dialogues. The *Apology* deals with the accusation, trial, conviction, and conduct of Socrates. The *Protagoras* is chiefly concerned with the problem of the teachability of virtue, an issue which is argued out between Socrates and Protagoras. In the *Phaedrus*, one finds an outline of the fundamentals of Plato's famous doctrine of the reality of universals and his notion of the world of pure ideas. This basic conception of Platonic philosophy is also presented in many other works, particularly, the *Philebus*, the *Theatetus*, the *Parmenides*, and the *Sophist*. In the *Theatetus*, Plato devotes himself to an examination and criticism of the skeptical position, starting his argument with an analysis of Heracleitus. In the *Phaedo*, he goes into the matter of theology and religion, having Socrates reaffirm the doctrine of preexistence and immortality during his last hours on earth. There is implied a view of the eternity of the mind and truth.

The *Symposium* is devoted, in part, to Plato's views of aesthetics. The nature of love is discussed and it is contended that the contemplation of the beautiful is the real beginning of philosophy. The *Timaeus*, a mystical and semi-poetical analysis of the universe, calls in the imagination to supplant reason, when the latter fails to bridge the gulf between the ideal and the actual. Since the *Timaeus* was the inspiration of the Neoplatonists, it has been one of the most influential books in all history. Its indirect influence, exerted through Neoplatonism, the *Celestial Hierarchy*, medieval mysticism, and the Jewish *Cabala*, rivaled the direct influence of Aristotle's logic, Pliny's *Natural History* and Donatus' Latin grammar on medieval thought and culture. Plato's stimulating and original political and social theory is embodied, for the most part, in his *Republic*, *Laws*, and *Statesman*.

The core of Plato's contribution to systematic philosophy and metaphysics was his doctrine of Ideas. This particular term—Idealism—has caused much confusion, for Plato's notion was much different from the idealism of the romanticist philosophers of the eighteenth and nineteenth centuries. Moreover, in the Middle Ages the Platonic conception received the label of Realism, though it stands at the very opposite pole from the realism (as we understand the term) of such a nineteenth-century writer as Émile Zola. What the medievals meant by realism was that reality exists only in the ideal or universal concepts of the Platonic philosophy.

Plato's idealism was a philosophical revolt against both Heracleitus' view of eternal flux or change, and the contention of the Sophists that truth is relative and that knowledge is to be circumscribed by practical issues of everyday experience. Plato found his inspiration mainly in Parmenides and Socrates. The former had argued against the dogmas of Heracleitus relative to the notion of change and flux. As Professor Edman puts it, "Parmenides found pure unity, an immutable reality, against which the whole world of phenomena became merely the world of illusion, the world of appearance, an invalid mirage of the senses. On the one hand was the absolute world of the One, unchanging, unified, and

eternal, on the other hand the shifting world of appearances, ceaselessly changing, eternally unreal, the realm of non-being." [20] Against this latter world Plato
rebelled. He could not endure, as he put it, any such conception of the universe
as one like "a leaky pot, or a man running at the nose."

From Socrates, Plato received another impulse to find absolute and unchanging reality. Socrates had striven to arrive at a final definition of such concepts as
Truth, Justice, Wisdom, Beauty, and the like, which would hold good at all times
and places and under all circumstances. Plato felt that Socrates had failed and
died because he had not gone far enough in divorcing the ideal from the actual.
Socrates had too much faith in the possibility of harmonizing the actual laws of
man with the ideal of abstract justice. He had not sufficiently distinguished between the methods and pitfalls of discussion by means of human language and
the lofty domain of universal reason. Plato resolved to plant his feet firmly on
the ground of pure theory and thus be able to arrive at substantial philosophical
and scientific truth. We now know that Plato reversed the processes by which
truth may be discovered, but our awareness is irrelevant to the present purpose—
to explain the method and aspirations of Plato.

In preparing for his scientific and philosophical studies, Plato had been influenced not only by Parmenides and Socrates, but also by the Pythagoreans, from
whom he had derived the belief that the laws and postulates of rigorous mathematical demonstration present the best formal technique for pursuing truth effectively. In mathematics, we have the most evident possibility of achieving the essential divorce of intellectual pursuits from the changing phenomena of the
world of the senses. Plato sought in his metaphysics to create a world of valid
ideas which would be both intelligible and yet independent of the superficial
appearance of things, of the flux of eternal and accidental matters, and of the
biased interests and warped desires of man. The reality apprehended by the bodily senses is made up of only half-truths, which are but imperfect reflections of
the realities existing in permanent and perfect fashion behind the flux and flow
of the phenomenal world. As Professor Edman expresses the Platonic notion,
"things are the shadows of ideas thrown upon the screen of experience."

Back of the world of things and experiences, apprehended by the senses, there
is thus another and more fundamental world of eternal forms and types. In
everything there is an essence or unchanging reality, quite independent of the
mere material "accidents" which surround it in everyday experience.

These eternal realities, transcendental truths, universal forms, or "ideas,"
should be the true goal of the philosopher. Philosophical analysis consists in dis-
engaging these universals or essences from their accidents, that is, from their
partial embodiment in the external world of sense phenomena. "The business of
education is to turn the eyes of the soul from the seductions and illusions of sense
to those divine eternal patterns bound together in the 'empire of the gods' by the
Idea of the Good, which transcends all thought and all being, and is the goal
of both." [21]

[20] Irwin Edman, ed., *The Works of Plato*, Tudor Publishing Co., 1934, Introduction, p. xxxv.
[21] *Ibid.*, p. xxxvii.

According to Plato, then, there is no reality in any individual or concrete example of a horse, house, table, city, a beautiful woman, or what not. The only reality exists in the universal concept, type, class, or idea of a horse, table, or beauty. As one facetious commentator has observed, to Plato the only things that exist are those which do not exist. The latter are "eternal, they are absolute, they constitute a divine order of reality transcendent to human knowledge or earthly existence . . . it is their being which informs and constitutes empirical and understandable and livable reality."

This Platonic abstraction of reality from concrete experience and the observation of phenomena was unscientific and misleading. Modern science has made headway chiefly by reversing the Platonic approach. Man can never hope to attain any eternal truth or absolute reality. Any progress on the way to truth must be made by observing the commonplace things of everyday life—those particulars which Plato despised. From such observations we may derive tentative generalizations, which are as far as the simian mind of man can hope to advance. But Socrates and Plato effectively launched a major philosophical discussion which reached its height in the medieval struggle between realism and nominalism and has not ceased even to this day.

Plato's theology was intimately connected with his philosophy. To Plato, the soul is the connecting link between the world of sense-impressions and ordinary daily experiences—in which birth and death follow each other in unending regularity—and the eternal and unchanging world of absolute reality. While the individuals who make up this cycle of life are not permanent, the soul itself supplies an eternal and dynamic attribute which gives undying permanence to the whole. This eternal soul of Plato's imagination was, however, the universal soul. He was less explicit and dogmatic about the immortality of individual souls, but most commentators agree that he believed that even individual souls never wholly perish.[22] At any rate, Plato believed in preëxistence, a notion which he derived from the Pythagoreans, who had, in turn, borrowed the idea from Eastern philosophies. Plato developed the doctrine and argued that as the finer souls turned to philosophy they would thereby purify themselves and recover some dim recollection of their knowledge of eternal "ideas" in an earlier existence. Indeed, the philosopher has already lived with these universals in his mind "in the discarnate existence before birth."

It has been maintained by leading authorities that Plato was motivated primarily by a desire to reform Greek politics and to train rulers. He is said to have wished to train the finest minds in philosophy so that they might rule in the true interest of humanity. Others believe that he was more interested in the quest of abstract justice. There is, however, no denying his practical interest in political reform. He wished to gain disciples, teach them sound philosophy, and install them in positions of authority. He believed that only by so doing could he preserve Athenian integrity and civilization. In order to teach the philosophy which he believed so essential to sound statesmanship, Plato opened the Academy, a

---

22 Cf. A. E. Taylor, *Plato: The Man and His Work*, Dial Press, 1929 (Meridian reprint), pp. 191-306, for Plato's discussion of immortality.

school of philosophy, on his estate in Athens. Upon his death he willed the estate to the Academy. That his interest was by no means wholly academic is to be seen in the fact that three times he made the perilous voyage to Syracuse in order to try to persuade the ruler of that state to adopt his legislative program.

The most famous of Plato's writings on politics and society is the *Republic,* which is as much a work on sociology as on politics, so broad is its scope and so fundamental is its analysis of human society. The announced purpose of the book is a quest for principles of social justice. The foundations of this justice Plato believed he discovered in the process of the social division of labor among the crafts and the major social classes. He worked out a hierarchy of social classes—the workers who supplied material needs, the guardians or warriors who protected the state, and the rulers, preferably philosophers, who directed political life. On the foundations of the social division of labor and the hierarchy of the social classes Plato sought to establish a true political equilibrium that would produce the highest civic good. He would promote unity among the rulers and guardians who were in a minority in the population, while permitting strife and discord to continue among the lower or working classes so that they would never be able to unite and overthrow the ruling minority. His scheme was an application of the "divide and rule" plan.

The original and daring social proposals which have been associated with the *Republic* and have led to its being called the first great Utopia in human literature, were reserved for the upper classes of guardians and rulers. Desiring unity above all else here, Plato believed that the chief threat of discord arose from private property. Hence, he recommended communism for the rulers and guardians. It was among them also that Plato's ingenious plan of selective breeding—one of the first statements of the eugenics principle—was to apply, in order to produce a super-race to guard and rule the state. The lower classes could own private property, quarrel among themselves about it, breed promiscuously, and deteriorate physically and mentally.

Plato seems to have realized that his sweeping plan of political reconstruction, as set forth in the *Republic,* was too advanced for man to adopt, at least in his day. So he wrote an even longer work on politics, *The Laws,* devoted to describing the best form of political organization that seemed to have some chance of practical adoption. It was far more conventional and stereotyped than the program of the *Republic.* The state was placed under the solicitude of the gods and an authoritarian political system was proposed which would have delighted Benito Mussolini or Adolf Hitler. In his *Statesman,* Plato analyzed with much acumen the problems of political leadership and critically appraised the various forms of government.

Plato was the first to set forth clearly what became the typical classical theory of the cycles of government, from kingship to tyranny, from tyranny to aristocracy, from aristocracy to oligarchy, from oligarchy to democracy, from democracy to anarchy, and from anarchy back to kingship again.

In his *Republic,* he expounded what may be regarded as his most valuable and enduring contribution to a theory of civilization, namely, his emphasis on the primary importance of nonmaterial elements in civilization—a eulogy of the "supra-pig" activities of man.

In the course of describing the craft basis of the ideal state in the *Republic,* the argument gets to the place where all the material needs of man are cared for. It is then suggested that an ideal civilization has now been provided. But a devastating answer is given to any such idea by countering that nothing has yet been done except to insure a "city of happy pigs." Even pigs should have their material necessities taken care of. A true human civilization begins only at this point and builds from the pig level upward. Accordingly, the description of the ideal state proceeds to unfold and to indicate the higher ranges of activity which must be provided for through the emergence of scientists, philosophers, artists, musicians, actors, athletes, and the like. These latter make possible a truly human civilization which accords proper place to beauty, wisdom, truth, happiness, and physical self-expression. This thought is particularly relevant for our own day, for we are the first to have within our grasp the mastery of the material needs of man—the pig-level of existence—and the first to face the problems of large-scale leisure, the leisure which sets before us the panorama of supra-pig existence.

Several rather conflicting intellectual traditions came down from the teachings and writings of Plato. His skepticism was perpetuated by the Academy which remained in existence until the Emperor Justinian closed it down in the sixth century of the Christian Era (A.D. 529). Out of the influence of his retreat from concrete reality and the mystical teachings of the *Timaeus* and the *Epinomis* (the Platonic authorship of which is questioned by some) there developed the very influential Neoplatonism, elaborated by Plotinus (A.D. 204-270) and others. This became the most popular of all philosophies in the ancient world during the period of the establishment of Christianity, and kept its hold on the Middle Ages and the humanists. Neoplatonism discarded not only science but also dialectic, and placed complete reliance upon irrational intuition, visions and ecstasy as the means of reaching communion with the absolute. The mythology of the *Timaeus* was very popular in the Middle Ages, when Christian writers tried to harmonize it with the historical tales of the Old Testament. All in all, only Aristotle and Augustine have rivaled Plato in their intellectual influence on humanity.

Plato's general philosophical contribution—his theory of ideas and his repudiation of experience—helped to retard adoption of the empirical methods of natural science. Even more deplorable was the credulous and mystical Neoplatonism, as has been emphasized by writers, such as Professor Warner Fite in his book, *The Platonic Legend.* Today, with the rise of advanced electromagnetic physical science that depends on mathematics, scientists are returning to Plato's method of using conceptual constructs to orient themselves in the world of the unknown.

The more admirable traits of Plato's thoughts were his urbanity, his tolerant and skeptical analysis of the problems of knowledge and social relations, his devotion to the common good of humanity, and his emphasis upon the notion that civilized humanity should be chiefly concerned with the nonmaterial issues of life, provided, of course, that material needs are taken care of. This last principle is coming to be regarded as the major contribution of the Greeks to the cultural life of man—a theory of the good life conceived in aesthetic terms.

Plato's most famous pupil was Aristotle (384-322 B.C.), one of the most distinguished and influential intellects in the whole history of human learning. Only Leonardo da Vinci has excelled him in intellectual versatility, only a few like Leibnitz, Newton, and Helmholtz have rivaled him in mental power, and no philosopher to date has matched him in the scope and number of his writings. The intellectual prestige of Aristotle through the ages has been thoroughly in keeping with his intellectual distinction. Some competent authorities believe that he easily occupies first place among those who have influenced the scholarly attitudes and mental exercises of humanity.

Yet the world came very near being deprived of his contributions. But for a lucky accident, his works would have been lost and Aristotle would have been little more than a name, as was the destiny of the great Roman compiler, Varro, whose scores of works have disappeared. Many of Aristotle's manuscripts were taken to Asia Minor and hidden in a pit for some two centuries. They were discovered by chance on one of Sulla's expeditions and brought back to Rome where they were copied under the supervision of Tyrannion. About 70 B.C., the new copy was edited and arranged by Andronicus of Rhodes. And it is through Andronicus' edition that we have come to know Aristotle's works and their traditional arrangement.

From this time onward, Aristotle's writings were available in Greek in the East until the age of humanism. Boëthius and others translated portions of them into Latin in the later Roman Empire, and after the thirteenth century most of them were rendered into medieval Latin. But not all of Aristotle's writings, by any means, have been preserved. Two major groups are missing: (1) his popular works, written in dialogue form in imitation of Plato; and (2) the compilations which he used as the basis of his systematic books. Of the latter, only the *Constitution of Athens* has been recovered—and that only two generations ago.

In spite of the fact that many of Aristotle's works have disappeared, the list and range of those that have been preserved are staggering. The large two-column page of the *Encyclopaedia Britannica* is required merely to list and identify their titles. He ranged from astronomy to aesthetics, and from anatomy to theology. His learned writings fall mainly into eight major fields: logic, metaphysics, ethics, aesthetics, biology, psychology, physics, and political philosophy. Outstanding among his many works are his *Organon,* or logical treatises; his *Historia animalium,* embracing his biology; his *Nicomachean Ethics;* and his *Politics* and *Poetics.* Those most likely to have permanent value are the *Organon* and the *Ethics.*

Some of the major intellectual innovations in the history of human thought and culture date from Aristotle. He was the first technical philosopher. Philosophical nomenclature and its esoteric ways began with him. He was the first to reduce logic to a technical and formal system of thought. Once he had done this, it could be taught as a mental discipline. He was the earliest of our true encyclopedists. Aristotle not only mastered all learning; he also classified it in thorough fashion for the first time. He recognized and differentiated the various branches of learning and assigned an appropriate content and method to each. In the course of mastering all existing knowledge he incidentally examined most of the writings which had dealt with any subject before his day. He thus knew all that anybody else had known in every field of knowledge and was, hence, the first to cite authorities in systematic fashion. He reduced his vast learning to written form, devoting one or more formal treatises to each branch of learning. In this way, he may be said to have first launched what we have come to know as "book learning."

We have already implied that Aristotle abandoned the free and easy discussion and the conversational methods of Socrates and Plato and formulated a technical and professional approach to philosophical problems. Though he seems to have written popular works in the form of the Platonic dialogues, in his systematic philosophy he relied upon logical processes of reasoning, instead of formal discussion, as the approach to truth.

Aristotle's logical treatises, embodied in the collection known as the *Organon,* were divided into several sections. The *Categories* and *On Interpretation* set forth the preliminary conditions and nomenclature of logical reasoning. The *Prior Analytics* dealt with an analysis of the syllogism. The *Posterior Analytics* treated particularly scientific modes of reasoning. The *Topics* and *Sophistic Refutations* discussed the distinctions between logical correctness and true scientific thought.

His logic was his most enduring and important legacy to intellectual history and it had a wider influence upon posterity than any other phase of his work. Indeed nonmathematical logic has made relatively little progress since his day.

Aristotle also founded what we have come to know as metaphysics, though he did not apply this term to his fundamental philosophy. In his metaphysics, he took up Plato's theory of ideas and universals and set forth his famous theory of causation. In treating of the problem of universals, Aristotle moved toward what came to be known as Conceptualism, as distinguished from the philosophical realism of Plato. He denied Plato's notion that reality exists only in universals, and asserted that universals are only convenient intellectual concepts. He held that reality resides only in the observed and the concrete—in individual examples of things or particulars. Yet these things or particulars have permanent worth and significance chiefly as representations of the general class or type to which they belong. Before they take on any specific form, things exist in nature only as energy and potentiality. Some form of motion is the dynamic and creative principle in the process of transforming them into any concrete actuality. As a result of motion the thing produced then falls within some type representation as a man, house, vehicle or whatever it may be.

Aristotle was the first to work out a synthetic doctrine of causation.[23] He maintained that, in the processes of nature which produce any completed thing, there are four basic causes: the material, the formal, the efficient, and the final. The first relates to the material involved; the second to the particular class or type within which the thing falls; the third to the maker; and the fourth to the pur-

23 Cf. W. D. Ross, *Aristotle,* Methuen, 1930 (Barnes and Noble, 1955), pp. 71 ff.

pose in mind. To illustrate by a marble statue, the material cause would be marble, the formal cause a statue, the efficient cause the sculptor, and the final cause the promotion of an appreciation of beauty. His notion of purpose in the final cause is held to indicate that Aristotle believed in a purpose in the cosmos, or, as philosophers would put it, that he espoused the *teleological* point of view.

Aristotle's theology was wholly compatible with his general philosophical attitude. Since disciplined reasoning, logic, is the master key to knowledge, God must be viewed as a reason-loving being. Since motion is the primary element in creation, God must be regarded as the prime mover, the first cause and the source of all motion. Aristotle believed that rational and logical thinking is the highest form of human activity. Hence, it was natural that he would conceive of God as a being who puts reason before all other things. The most godlike activity must be pure thought, and the highest form of pure thought, must be thinking about God. Therefore, having brought motion into being, in his capacity as the prime mover, God spends his time in contemplating himself.

Aristotle's conception of ethics was sane and practical and his ethical theories rank along with his logic as his most valuable and enduring intellectual gift to mankind. He maintained that the chief human good and the end of life is happiness. And happiness is to be judged in relation to this life rather than with respect to salvation and rewards in a life to come. The best life is well-rounded, guided by reason and virtue. The latter implies that intellectual restraint which guides an individual into a happy mean between irrational indulgence and ascetic denial. In addition to this generalized virtue, viewed as the happy mean, there are special virtues, such as liberality, courage, justice, temperance, veracity, insight, cleverness, and an appreciation of beauty. The speculative life of wisdom was looked upon by Aristotle as the most perfect and divine, but he thought that it should be tempered by a discreet cultivation of the social graces and the satisfaction of normal human desires. Such moderns as John Dewey, H. G. Wells, and Bertrand Russell would qualify as practitioners of the Aristotelian conception of the good life.

Few books have been more widely or persistently studied than Aristotle's *Politics,* in which we find his political and sociological views. He declared that man is by nature a social animal; he traced in brief and brilliant fashion the genesis of the city-state, outlined the foundations of political relations and legal control, analyzed concisely and ingeniously the importance of economic factors in politics, and described in penetrating fashion the psychology of revolution. His *Politics* is surely one of the major landmarks in the history of political theory. But it is of slight value as a guide to modern political life, since its generalizations were based upon a study, albeit a wide one, of conditions in the antique city-state, and his economic views were circumscribed by the relatively elementary economy with which he was acquainted.

Aristotle was not only the first great technical philosopher, applying his philosophy to every field, but he was one of the oustanding figures in the history of natural science. He ranged from astrophysics to embryology. He was at his best in observing nature and in recording the results; in short, as a descriptive scientist.

Particularly in descriptive biology did he distinguish himself, anticipating the doctrine of organic evolution, adding much of value to the existing knowledge of the anatomy and habits of animals, and making solid contributions to embryology. He was the first to outline clearly the nature of sex, heredity, nutrition, growth, and adaptation, and may justly be called the father of comparative anatomy. His theoretical work, especially in physics, was all too often erroneous, in which respect he contrasted markedly with the great Hellenistic physicist, Archimedes.

Aristotle conceived of the universe as having the earth—a stationary sphere—at its center. Around it revolve some fifty-five concentric and transparent spheres, on which the moon, sun, planets, and moving stars are placed. All is surrounded by the great sphere or *primum mobile,* beyond which God dwells among the fixed stars. God, as prime mover, set the whole in motion, and all heavenly motion is circular and eternal.

Aristotle's physical theories were based upon the doctrine adopted from Empedocles that all earthly objects are composed of the four fundamental elements—earth, air, fire, and water. The heavenly bodies are made of the mysterious fifth element, ether. This dogma held back the development of both physics and chemistry, and was not finally obliterated until the time of Boyle and Stahl in the seventeenth century. Aristotle held that all motion on the earth is rectilinear and, hence, inferior to the circular movements of the heavens. His conceptions of dynamics were awry, since he believed that the speed of falling bodies is proportional to their weight, a view that lingered until the days of Galileo. He had no idea of the law of gravitation. His theories of "light and heavy" were mystical and aesthetic rather than scientific. Even in the field of biology, Aristotle often fell into serious error. For example, he denied the sexuality of plants, a fact not fully established until the experiments of Camerarius in 1694. He thought the heart to be the seat of human intelligence, the function of the brain being to pump phlegm into the heart, to keep it from overheating in periods of active cerebration.

Aristotle was not only the intellectual giant of his day; he exerted, as we have noted, a tremendous influence upon human thought from his age to our own. His philosophy and some of his scientific efforts were carried along by his students, the Peripatetics, in the Lyceum until 529, when Justinian closed all the Athenian schools, including the Platonic Academy. The Greek Neoplatonist, Porphyry, and the Latin scholar, Boëthius, translated parts of his logical treatises and kept alive an interest in them in the Latin West during the Middle Ages.

Most of his major works which have survived, were, of course, preserved and well known in the Greek or Eastern Empire. The Muslim scholars translated many of them into Arabic and maintained a vigorous interest in Aristotelianism during the medieval period. But the intellectual omnipotence of Aristotle developed in the Christian West after Abelard, in the twelfth century, had made logic indispensable to Christian theology. From the thirteenth century to the so-called Renaissance, when Plato became more popular, Aristotle was the most revered secular authority in all western Christendom. With the rise of modern science the prestige of Aristotle's antiquated scientific notions justly waned. But the influence of his logic, ethics and politics deservedly lingered on. Even those who, like Peter Ramus, bombastically assaulted Aristotle's logic in their rhetoric, came back to it in their sober philosophy. A contemporary school of thinkers, the conservative Humanists, have in our own day called for a return of Aristotle, though they have shown themselves to be not too well acquainted with his learning or his methods. In Catholic theology and in Catholic university instruction Aristotle still holds a higher place than any other single secular thinker. President Robert Maynard Hutchins and Professor Mortimer J. Adler formerly of the University of Chicago rivalled the medieval scholastics in their reverence for Aristotle.

The sources of Aristotle's great and lingering influence are not difficult to understand. In the first place, he opened the era of bookmaking. He was very learned and preserved this vast knowledge in formal treatises which could later be consulted and revered. He was the greatest intellectual light down to Leonardo, Newton, and Leibnitz, and the comprehensiveness and logical arrangements of his writings appealed to the academic mind of the medieval period. He brought a vast range and variety of facts to the conscious attention of mankind. He set the example of examining authorities and of subjecting scientific facts and theories to thorough analysis.

Being the greatest of all logicians, his works were eagerly sought when medieval Christians came to believe logic essential to the elevation and preservation of the "queen of sciences," theology. His teleology and its implied theology made his works palatable to the Christians. God was the prime mover. The heavens, with their circular motion and their derivation from the mysterious "fifth element," were superior to the earth. His fourth cause implied that there was a divine purpose in the universe. Hence, the medieval Christians could accept Aristotle with much more relish than they could have an anti-religious writer like Lucretius.

VII. GREEK THOUGHT AFTER ARISTOTLE

With the death of Aristotle, the theoretical side of philosophy, so successfully completed by the great Greek masters, became subordinated and almost completely lost to view. Metaphysical speculation was neglected, except insofar as it threw light on ethics and the natural sciences.

In the preceding stages of Greek philosophy ethics and politics were, practically and theoretically, two sides of the same question. Even the pragmatic Sophists did not separate ethics and politics, though they paved the way for the divorce of the two. Now, for the first time, ethics were considered mainly with reference to the individual, and with less regard for the political situation. This new orientation of philosophy was perhaps the result of the decay of the Greek state. There was less possibility of finding moral assurance and consolation as a member of the city-state when political conditions became unstable. Moreover, life had become cosmopolitan. Nations were commingling. Ethics had to meet the needs of human beings—not merely of Athenians, Spartans, or Romans. Vices and virtues also had to be either cosmopolitan or intensely individualistic.

The main schools of post-Aristotelian philosophy were the Skeptics, found mainly among Plato's followers in the Academy; the Cynics; the Cyrenaics; the Stoics; the Epicureans, and the Eclectics.

The more important Skeptics were Pyrrho (365-275 B.C.), Timon (320-230 B.Ç.), Arcesilaus (c. 315-240 B.C.) and Carneades (c. 213-128 B.C.). They continued the skeptical analysis which had received its finest earlier expression in the dialogues of the master, Plato.

The founders of the Cynics were Antisthenes (c. 444 B.C.) and Diogenes (c. 412-323 B.C.). This group of thinkers sought happiness and complacency by a stark return to nature and a renunciation of both physical pleasures and the involvements of social conventions. The Cyrenaics, launched by Aristippus (c. 380 B.C.), took the opposite stand from the Cynic renunciation. They also desired mental serenity, but they believed that man could rise superior to human appetites only by tasting all possible human pleasures, from complete corporeal indulgence to spiritual ecstasy.

Stoicism, founded by Zeno (c. 336-264 B.C.), Cleanthes (c. 265 B.C.) and Chrysippus (d. c. 206 B.C.), was a logical development out of Cynicism. It gave to the latter a more sophisticated and broadly philosophical content. Epicureanism, the most notable Greek exponent of which was Epicurus (342-270 B.C.), was a product of the ethical attitudes of the Cyrenaics and of the mechanistic cosmology of Democritus. The Eclectics, of whom the major representative was the Roman, Cicero (106-43 B.C.), aimed to select the best from all these philosophies.

As will be evident from what we have said, all of these schools had one common and fundamental aspiration—to free the human individual and the mind from the worries and uncertainties of life. As Cushman puts it, they all aimed at "the withdrawal of the individual from the world and his exaltation above his environment." Their differences arose solely from divergent frames of reference as to how this common goal might be achieved. They went at the same problem in different ways. After this brief orientation, we may proceed to examine more closely the various solutions which each school offered for the dilemma of a calm life in a distracted world.

The Skeptics elaborated and synthesized the agnostic attitude of the Sophists. The Old Academy was made up chiefly of the immediate disciples of Plato. Its leaders were Pyrrho and Timon.[24] They directed their attack chiefly against the finality of Aristotelian logic and metaphysics. They sought mental peace and calm, but doubted the adequacy of Aristotelian thought to bring about this result in philosophical terms. They held that all we can know is what is revealed to us through sense impressions, which merely tell us how we feel in response to stimulation. They do not reveal reality to us.[25] Hence, the way to imperturbability is to suspend judgment on all matters. This attitude represented the most completely imaginable renunciation of dogmatism.

The next attack on Stoicism was made by the Middle Academy. Here the leadership was taken by Carneades, one of the ablest of the post-Aristotelian philosophers. This group of Skeptics frankly adopted the agnostic (not-knowing)

24 Pyrrho had great repute with early modern skeptics who called themselves "Pyrrhonists."
25 The Skeptics here anticipated Hobbes, Hume, and critical English philosophy of modern times.

attitude and directed it against the self-assurance of the Stoic dogmas. They took special delight in exposing the inconsistencies in the Stoic notion of anthropomorphic deities as personified natural forces. They showed the absurdity in the attribution of human qualities to a deity who is devoid of bodily senses and social relationships. They also indicated the manner in which the noble ethical ideals of the Stoics fade out in the crises of life, where the law of self-preservation submerges all other considerations.

So far as the Skeptics had any constructive contribution, it lay in the recommendation of a sort of rudimentary pragmatism, namely, a workable theory of probability. This would be sufficient to guide the practical activities of man in daily life. Absolute certainty as to ultimate reality is something which may not reasonably be expected.

The founders of the Cynic philosophy were contemporaries of Plato and Aristotle. They accepted the Socratic thesis that virtuous living and the highest good depend primarily upon knowledge. All else should be spurned. Especially should we have contempt for ignorance, social involvements, and corporeal indulgence. We should satisfy our animal needs only to the degree necessary to keep us alive and thus be able to carry on the quest for saving knowledge. The wise man can in this way alone keep himself independent of all external circumstances and realize mental serenity.

The Cyrenaics took an attitude directly opposed to the Cynic asceticism. They placed major emphasis on the value of complete sensual indulgence, thus actually advocating the attitude which has so long and inaccurately been ascribed to the Epicureans. They held that the value of sensual experiences stands in proportion to their intensity. For this reason, bodily sensations are to be preferred to mental experiences. Man may be trusted to choose and determine his sensual pleasures because of human poise and insight. Only by experiencing the whole gamut of human sensations and forming our own personal judgment about them, can we rise superior to them and attain that inward calm for which all these schools of Greek philosophy sought. Man can literally be "the lord of his appetites."

The Stoics took up the crude Cynic notion of a return to nature in the sense of ascetic renunciation and gave it a broad philosophical justification. They approached the problem of human serenity from the standpoint of an exaltation of the human personality. The key to this was their conception of the reality and function of the individual soul. The soul transforms our sense-impressions into intelligent perceptions and projects our feelings into will and action. The soul, in short, brings about reasoned action. Only through this reasoned action can we rise above the confusions and complexities of the social environment. Rationality brings us to the highest good, namely, apathy towards life experiences. This notion of apathy does not mean that we should surrender all our feelings; it implies, rather, that we shall not surrender to our feelings. In other words, we must not be controlled by our emotions. The man who attains to this saving apathy is the wise man. Few, however, can do so. The majority of men are foolish. They are the slaves of ignorance and their emotions.

Curiously enough, the Stoics linked up this eulogy of the free and rational personality with a doctrine of complete materialistic determinism. They identified nature with matter. Matter alone is real: "it alone acts and is acted upon." Even God is matter. They were, thus, thoroughgoing materialists. But this is not all. They were also consistent determinists. Everything in the universe is strictly determined by a chain of naturalistic causation.

This suggests the problem of how the Stoics harmonized such a doctrine with their emphasis on the free and worthy personality which rises above all material things. How can a determined personality and determined personal action be free? How can rational freedom and strict determinism be reconciled?

The Stoics had two answers which satisfied them. In the first place, they identified nature with God and with cosmic reason. Hence, reason dominates both the cosmos and the individual personality. Man and God both being a part of a rational nature, man is, like God, free. The other solution they suggested for the dilemma was the contention that man's very knowledge of the deterministic action of nature and natural law sets him free. He adapts himself to nature through an intelligent comprehension of its character and its laws. In this way the Stoics imagined that they could embrace determinism and yet escape a mechanistic view of the world. The Stoic doctrine thus, obviously, ended up in rationalization rather than rationalism. And the Skeptics lost no time in driving this fact home.

The Stoic view of ethics grew logically out of their deterministic doctrines. Since all is determined by nature, which is also God and cosmic reason, we may assume that anything which happens is both reasonable and according to the will of God. Hence, we should resign ourselves to the expression of God's will and make the best of it. Duty thus became a universal law, and responsibility a cosmic obligation. Virtue exists for its own sake, not for any hope of reward.

The Stoics best expressed the cosmopolitan ideals of the age. They had little interest in particular states. Their ideal was a universal government; moreover, the wise man does not need the state to control him. The Stoics emphasized the brotherhood of man. But it was to be a brotherhood solely of the wise men who had attained to Stoic enlightenment and apathy. They felt no kinship with the foolish majority, whether their own countrymen or foreign fools. But they did stress the brotherhood of all wise men, however divided by political boundaries. There is much to be said for their view that a wise man has more in common with an informed and intelligent foreigner than with an ignorant and mediocre compatriot.

In Epicureanism the individual was raised to supremacy in his own right. The Epicurean cosmology and ethics were both built up around the primacy of individual self-interest. And this individualism required no elaborate philosophical or cosmological justification. It stood on its own feet, quite independently.

Epicurean individualism was grounded in the thesis that the happiness of the individual is paramount and in the corollary that pleasure is desirable and pain is to be avoided. This had led many to hold that the Epicureans believed in the extreme hedonism and sensationalism of the Cyrenaics. But such an interpretation is not accurate. Whereas the Cyrenaics had valued pleasurable sensations in proportion to their intensity, the Epicureans ranked them according to their duration or permanence. This enabled Epicurus to maintain that mental experiences are the highest form of pleasure because they are most enduring. "When, therefore," says Epicurus, "we say that pleasure is a chief good, we are not speaking of the pleasures of the debauched man, or those which lie in sensual enjoyment, as some think who are ignorant, and who do not entertain our opinions, or else interpret them perversely; but we mean the freedom of the body from pain, and of the soul from confusion. For it is not continued drinkings and revels, or the enjoyment of female society, or beasts or fish and other such things as a costly table supplies, that make life pleasant, but sober contemplation, which examines into the reasons for all choice and avoidance, and which puts to flight the vain opinions from which the greater part of the confusion arises which troubles the soul." [26]

This shows how far from the truth is the common allegation that the Epicureans recommended, above all else, gross corporeal indulgence. The highest good, to Epicurus, was not so far different from Aristotle's ideal of the perfect life of intellectual reflection and contemplation. But Epicurus was in no sense ascetically inclined. He held that one should fully experience the pleasures of the senses, since mental life is a product of the senses. An important part of mental pleasure is the contemplation of physical pleasures previously enjoyed.

Whereas, to the Stoics, God permeates nature, indeed, is nature, the Epicureans excluded the gods from any part in the material universe or human affairs. They took over from Democritus his mechanistic theory of causation and made it the basis of their cosmology. There is an automatic mechanistic process which rules out any active rôle of the gods. Nor do the gods have anything to do with man and society. There is no need of fear of an afterlife, since the atoms of the soul are automatically scattered at death. Epicurus did not deny the existence of the gods. In fact, he believed that they exist, and even accepted the conventional gods of the time. But he held that they disported themselves in a sort of perpetual celestial picnic, taking no cognizance whatsoever of the earth and its inhabitants. The Epicureans thus did away with what they believed to be the chief causes of human worry and anxiety—fear of the gods and fear of a life to come.

The Epicureans cleared the way for a purely utilitarian theory of ethics. They did not have to please the gods or to be subject to any categorical imperative. They held that the Stoic view of virtue for its own sake was pure nonsense. Worse than nonsense was the Stoic contention that we should resign ourselves to painful and unpleasant experiences as an unavoidable part of the natural and divine order of things. Good conduct is that which gives a particular individual the most pleasure. Self-interest is the dominating motive and guide. But this has its reasonable limitations. Unless a man is able to have some consideration for his fellow men, his very selfishness will in the end reduce his own prospect of increasing pleasures. Friendship is the most commendable of all social relations, but, as Windelband emphasizes, even friendship, according to the Epicureans, is motivated by the consideration of how far friends can promote our happiness. Social relations as a whole, including the state, were viewed by the

[26] Bakewell, *op. cit.*, p. 300.

Epicureans as merely a matter of convenience. In this connection, they suggested that the state had its origins in a conscious governmental contract. The personal and social ethics of the Epicureans were, thus, wholly compatible with their extreme individualistic assumptions.

The Eclectics, later represented by Cicero, tended to pick and choose as they thought best from the varied philosophical offerings of the post-Aristotelian world. Some inclined towards Stoicism and others towards Epicureanism; but more of them, and Cicero was one of these, were inclined to a moderately skeptical point of view. Indeed, Eclecticism implied a skeptical approach in the very nature of the term.

We shall deal with Neoplatonism later, when we consider the intellectual influences contributing to the decline of pagan thought and culture in a later chapter.

Since the history of educational theory and practice will receive our attention throughout this work, we should say a word about the nature of education among the Greeks. There were the same marked contrasts in Greek education that we find in the culture of the various states. In Sparta, the education of youth was almost entirely physical and military training. The boys were thrown into barracks at an early age and given rigorous physical training. Then they learned the arts of war. There was little literary education beyond chanting ancient laws and passages from Homer. Bravery, brutality, and loyalty to the state were the essentials of Spartan education, and a harsh disciplinary system prevailed.

Athens made provision for both physical and cultural education. Athenian boys received extended instruction in physical education on the exercising fields, and were taught music (singing and playing the flute or lyre), reading, and writing in the so-called music schools. The broad interpretation given to music among the Greeks accounts for its content in medieval education and for its inclusion as one of the seven liberal arts. Selections from the more important Greek authors were copied and committed to memory. At the age of eighteen the citizen boys entered the army where they went through two years of military training.

With the coming of the Sophists literary education gained at the expense of physical training, though the latter was by no means abandoned. Education of mature youths was designed primarily to fit them for a public career. Therefore, much stress was laid upon rhetoric, dialectic, and literature. Sophistic education was highly individualistic and practical. The work of the Sophists was gradually absorbed by the schools of rhetoric, of which one of the earliest and best was founded by the famous rhetorician, Isocrates (436-338 B.C.). These rhetorical schools were likewise devoted chiefly to training for public life, in which rhetoric came to play an ever larger rôle. But the rhetorical studies grew more artificial and formal, facility in the use of sonorous phrases and appropriate literary embellishments taking the place of original ideas and sound thinking. A smattering of general information was given, and here we may, perhaps, detect the origins of the so-called orientation courses which, in more substantial form, have become deservedly popular in our day.

More active intellectual life was kept alive in the two main organizations which perpetuated the teachings of Plato and Aristotle, the Academy and the Lyceum, respectively. The former was mainly interested in promoting skeptical dialectic and the latter in pursuing researches in the natural sciences and expounding Aristotelian teachings in the scientific field. These establishments lasted until the sixth century of the Christian Era.

There were a number of important universities which sprang up after the close of the fourth century. The first of these, and the most important until Hellenistic times, was the University of Athens. After 300 B.C. it was displaced in primacy by the famous University (Museum and Library) of Alexandria, the intellectual center of the Western World for many centuries. Other important universities existed at Rhodes, Pergamum and Rome. Post-Aristotelian philosophy, rhetoric and natural science dominated the intellectual life of these institutions.

The Greeks made important contributions to educational theory. The Sophists held that knowledge must be brought down to earth and related to social needs. We are only now beginning to appreciate the soundness of this doctrine. Socrates introduced the notion of arriving at truth through well-directed questioning of current dogmas. Through protracted logical analysis we may come upon the truth. Plato emphasized the sane notion that education should be suited to the mental capacity of students, giving the abler ones the greatest opportunity for advanced studies. The supremely capable youths were to receive prolonged training so that they might take responsible positions in the government. We are coming to see that the Platonic notion was more sensible than the democratic practice of the last century or so which prescribed much the same education for all, irrespective of general ability or special talents. Aristotle's treatise on education has survived only in part. In the fragment which remains he emphasized the importance of thorough physical training. From our knowledge of his intellectual interests we may infer that he must have laid much stress upon training in logic, ethics, and natural science.

VIII. SCIENTIFIC ACHIEVEMENTS OF THE GREEKS

We have already dealt incidentally with several phases of Greek science. We analyzed the doctrines of the early cosmologists, and described the origins of the atomic theory and of the doctrine of the four fundamental elements. We referred casually to the Pythagorean interest in mathematics and to its influence on Plato. Finally, we described the scientific work of Aristotle. Let us now look into those Greek scientific achievements which call for more thorough treatment.

Before turning to the important groups we may mention Hecataeus of Miletus (c. 550-475 B.C.), who is generally regarded as "the father of geography." His *Circuit of the Earth* summarized Ionian geographical knowledge. The first passable map of the Mediterranean regions—one which was used by Herodotus—is supposed to have been provided by him.

Perhaps the earliest important group of real Greek scientists were the Pythagoreans, founded by Pythagoras of Samos (d. 497 B.C.) at Crotona in southern Italy. They combined an interest in rigorous mathematical theory with a mystical view of numbers and the universe. It was from them that we have derived the mathematical group of the seven liberal arts—the *quadrivium*—arithmetic, geometry, astronomy, and music.

The Pythagoreans started with the mathematical knowledge of the Egyptians and the Babylonians and carried it much further. They distinguished and named the various kinds of numbers—odd and even, prime and composite, and so forth. They understood arithmetic and geometric progression and other numerical series, and compiled tables of squares and cubes. They also seem to have been the first to have some inkling of incommensurable quantities. They founded mathematical acoustics and discovered the musical octave.

With these sound arithmetical beginnings, the Pythagoreans combined mystical notions as to the alleged properties of numbers. As Professor Arnold Reymond says: "He [Pythagoras] and his school came to the conclusion that number and its properties constitute the basis of all things. Hence, number is not a pure abstraction, it is a concrete reality, although our senses cannot directly apprehend it. Numbers have each spatial, physical and even spiritual properties, clearly defined. By their combinations they give birth to the beings and the things we see." [27] This mysticism exerted a powerful influence well down into modern times. Plato embodied it in his *Timaeus*. The Neoplatonists adopted the theory and helped to spread it.

In geometry, the Pythagoreans defined fundamental postulates and entities, such as line, surface, angles and the like. They carried out elementary exercises in triangulation. They solved the famous Pythagorean theorem, namely, showing that in the case of a right-angled triangle with sides equal to 3, 4, and 5, the square on the hypotenuse is equal to the sum of the squares on the other two sides.

Their astronomical theories, best represented by Philolaos and Hicetas, were especially interesting. The Pythagoreans held the center of the universe to be a great ball of fire about which the earth and all the planets, as well as the sun, describe orbits circumscribed by the appropriate hollow sphere which enclosed each. The earth also turns on its axis daily. This was not quite the later Copernican theory, since the sun was not placed at the center but revolved about the hypothetical central fire.

The Pythagoreans founded theoretical medicine, anticipating Hippocrates in their notion of a crisis of the disease and the critical days through which it is approached. Their most capable early physician was Alcmaeon (c. 500), the real "father of medicine" and an able anatomist. He carried on dissections and recognized that the brain is the center of intellectual life.

The most important advances in mathematics may be traced to the Sophists, Hippias and Hippocrates of Chios. The former dealt with the quadrature of the circle and the trisecting of angles. Hippocrates first reduced geometry to a system, and suggested the theorem that the areas of circles are proportional to the squares of their diameters. The latter problem was solved by Eudoxus of Cnidos (c. 408-355 B.C.), one of the ablest of Greek mathematicians and astronomers. He also showed that the volume of a pyramid and a cone is equal, respectively, to one

---

27 Arnold Reymond, *History of the Sciences in Greco-Roman Antiquity*, Dutton, 1927, p. 35.

third of the volume of the circumscribing prism or cylinder having the same base and altitude. He also carried on investigations in mechanics and acoustics. In astronomy, Eudoxus worked out a scheme of the heavenly spheres, claiming that there must be twenty-seven of them to account for the planetary motions. He also seems to have been the first to suggest a star catalogue and the notion of a leap year.

Plato carried further the Pythagorean mathematics and transmitted their mystical arithmetic through his *Timaeus*. His associate, Archytas, solved the duplication of the cube. Mecaechimus, a student of Eudoxus, anticipated Apollonius in dealing with conic sections. The scientific work of Aristotle was carried on by his disciples, the Peripatetics of the Lyceum, the most renowned of whom, Alexander of Aphrodisias, became head of the Lyceum in Athens about A.D. 200. He is looked upon as the ablest of all classical commentators on Aristotelian scientific works.

The immediate successor of Aristotle in the Lyceum was Theophrastus (372-287 B.C.), author of *The History of Plants* and *The Causes of Plants,* and the foremost botanist in all antiquity. The brilliant descriptive zoölogical and botanical work of Aristotle and his successors was greatly aided by the new flora and fauna brought back from the eastern conquests of Alexander the Great. Another student of Aristotle, Heraclides of Pontus (c. 350), contended that the earth turns on its axis from west to east once in every twenty-four hours and anticipated Aristarchus by suggesting the heliocentric theory. Aristoxenus (c. 325), another of Aristotle's students, carried the mathematical study of music further along than any other person in classical antiquity.

Greek medical science was ably promoted by Hippocrates of Cos (c. 460-c. 380 B.C.). He divorced medicine from the more crude and vulgar of the ancient superstitions and tried to place it on a secular and empirical basis. Systematizing existing medical knowledge, he gave it this new scientific and professional slant. The main flaw in his system was his theory of the four humors which make up the body—blood, phlegm, yellow bile, and black bile—whose proper mixture produces health and whose disturbances induce disease. The whole was involved with astrological lore, the heavenly bodies exerting an occult influence on the mixture of the humors. Aside from this fantastic theory, which was basic in the physiology of the time, the medical concepts of Hippocrates were sane and scientific. He accurately described the major diseases and gave a faithful clinical report of his cases. He advocated the close study of special symptoms and emphasized the theory of a crisis in each disease. He was especially famous for surgical operations on major bone dislocations. So high was the conception of medical ethics held by Hippocrates that the Hippocratic oath is still administered to our medical graduates before they receive their diplomas. We shall deal later with Hellenistic medicine.

We now come to the most important period in the development of natural science before the later Middle Ages and the origins of modern times—the Hellenistic age after Alexander the Great. Alexandria was the center of this astonishing intellectual activity. It lasted from about 300 B.C. until the fourth century of the Christian Era, when fanatical Christians destroyed the greatest glory of pagan scholarship, the library and museum at Alexandria, with its 750,000 volumes—an act of vandalism long unfairly ascribed to the Muslim caliph, Omar. So prolific were the scientific achievements in this age that we will do best to treat them by fields of science in order to avoid confusion. First we may turn to Hellenistic mathematics.

Arithmetic received the least attention from Hellenistic mathematicians. In fact, there were only two writers of importance on the subject in seven hundred years, Nicomachus of Gerasa (A.D. c. 100) and Theon of Smyrna (A.D. c. 130). *The Introduction to Arithmetic* by Nicomachus is the first treatise on record in which arithmetic was handled as an independent body of knowledge. It summarized the Pythagorean arithmetic and divorced it to some extent from mysticism. It dealt especially with the general properties of numbers, particularly the problems of proportion and ratios. Freely translated into Latin by Boëthius, it became the basic text in arithmetic for a thousand years. Less important was the manual by Theon, who also wrote treatises on the other scientific subjects among the seven liberal arts which came to be known as the quadrivium.

Algebra had but one important expositor in the Hellenistic age, but he was one of the ablest algebraists of all time, Diophantus of Alexandria (A.D. c. 275), who, curiously enough, called his great treatise on algebra, *Arithmetic*. It was the first important book on the subject and rightly earned for its author the title of "the father of algebra." Not until the time of the Muslim algebraists were there any advances made beyond his achievements. He introduced algebraic notation, and many symbols, such as those for minus, unknown quantities, powers, and the like. He stated and solved a large number of problems, among them the solution of the cubic equation, a feat not duplicated until early modern times by Tartaglia and Cardan.

In geometry the name that is best known is, of course, Euclid (c. 300 B.C.). Few persons have had so long and honorable an influence on the history of mathematics and the teaching of geometry. He seems to have received his inspiration from the Platonic tradition while still a student in the Academy. His *Thirteen Books of Elements* was a constructive synthesis of the existing knowledge and achievements in the field of geometry, and has remained the foundation for the teaching of elementary geometry to our own day. Most of his life was spent in Alexandria.

More original was Archimedes (287-212 B.C.), the ablest scientific genius of the whole Hellenistic period and, save for Leonardo da Vinci, perhaps the greatest scientific genius of all time, when his limited equipment of knowledge and instruments is taken into consideration. Usually regarded as a physicist, Archimedes was one of the most competent mathematicians of the age—more direct and independent in his work than any of the other Greek scholars. He had great facility in numerical computations and geometrical measurements. He was especially noted for his work on circle measurement, the quadrature of the parabola, spirals, and the relations of the sphere and cylinder and their mutual projections.

Apollonius of Perga (c. 262-c. 200 B.C.), the third great figure in Hellenistic geometry, founded the systematic study of conic sections and projective geometry. Of his eight-book treatise on the subject about half is taken up with a generous and accurate historical account of what had been achieved in the field before his time. He demonstrated all the main properties of conic sections, showed that all conics can be considered as sections of the same cone, introduced the names parabola, ellipse, and hyperbola, and dealt with three and four line loci, thus foreshadowing analytical geometry. More closely than any other Hellenistic scientist did he approach the value of π. He contributed to astronomy the theory of epicycles which was adopted by Hipparchus and Ptolemy to supplement the concentric spheres of Eudoxus as an explanation of planetary motion.

Further work in conic sections was carried on by Pappus of Alexandria (A.D. c. 300), whose *Mathematical Collection* also provided the best historical account of classical mathematical achievements. He handled such novel problems and theorems as curves of double quadrature, the focus of the parabola, the interpretation of conic sections in terms of the directrix, and the involution of points. He was on the track of analytical geometry, and his famous problem of geometrical loci was the starting point of the researches of Descartes which led to the establishment of analytical geometry in the seventeenth century.

It was the distinction of Hipparchus of Rhodes and Alexandria (fl. c. 150-125 B.C.) that he took over the slender earlier work in trigonometry and brought into being through his own constructive genius both plane and spherical trigonometry. He prepared a table of chords similar to present tables of natural sines and was the first to provide a method for solving spherical triangles. Hero (or Heron) of Alexandria (c. 100 B.C.) made certain practical applications of trigonometry to surveying, especially in his problems of triangulation. Menelaos of Alexandria (A.D. c. 100) was the first to separate trigonometry from stereometry and astronomy and to handle it as an independent branch of mathematics.

The next important figure was Ptolemy of Alexandria (A.D. d. c. 165), the famous systematic astronomer of the Hellenistic age. The ninth and eleventh books of his *Almagest* contain the clearest and most complete exposition of trigonometry in antiquity. Ptolemy was especially important for his theory of approximate calculations which is the basis of applied mathematics. Pappus also contributed in important ways to trigonometry, particularly in indicating its uses in astronomical calculations.

Trigonometry represented the furthest advance of Greek mathematics. aside from the above-mentioned anticipations of analytical geometry by Apollonius and Pappus, and Archimedes' brilliant intuitions relative to the nature of the infinitesimal calculus. The latter came out in Archimedes' discussion of the number of grains of sand in a great ball of sand with a radius as long as the distance from the earth to the starry firmament. But Archimedes lacked the algebraic notation, and any true anticipation of the calculus was out of the question.

The Greeks carried astronomy to heights of achievement which were not equaled until the time of Copernicus. Aristarchus of Samos (c. 275 B.C.) actually anticipated the Copernican theory in a very literal fashion by holding that the earth rotates daily on its axis and moves in a yearly orbit around the sun. By emphasizing the fact that the universe is vastly larger than the orbit of the earth around the sun, Aristarchus envisaged a cosmos far greater in extent than that imagined by any of his predecessors. He attempted to estimate the comparative distances and size of the sun and moon by mathematical methods. While his results were far short of the reality, the method suggested was an original one.

Eratosthenes of Cyrene (c. 273-192 B.C.) is correctly known as the first important scientific geographer of antiquity. But he is so known primarily because he applied astronomical methods to terrestrial problems. He was thoroughly grounded in astronomy and applied it to earth measurements and also to historical chronology.

Probably the ablest of the Hellenistic astronomers was Hipparchus. He applied trigonometry to astral measurements and computations, was the first to divide the circles of his instruments into 360 degrees, constructed the first celestial globe and astrolabe on record, was an accurate observer and prepared the best star chart known until modern times, computed with accuracy latitude and longitude, and discovered the obscure and elusive fact of the precession of the equinoxes. He also introduced the theory of epicycles and eccentrics to explain planetary motion. But for his intellectual cowardice the whole future of astronomy might have been far different. He was familiar with, and recognized the accuracy of, Aristarchus' heliocentric theory of the universe. But this challenged the conventional scientific, philosophical, and religious beliefs which were all based on the geocentric theory. So Hipparchus put his authority behind the latter theory and was therefore mainly responsible for the fact that it dominated astronomical thinking until the time of Copernicus.

Ptolemy's *Almagest* systematized and perpetuated the Hellenistic astronomy, with its geocentric hypothesis, and handed down the idea to future centuries. It was the classic summary of Greek astronomy. His only original contributions related to the motions of the moon and the planets. His star chart, based on that of Hipparchus, was the most valuable one passed on from antiquity, since Hipparchus' was lost. It was the only adequate description of the heavens down to the fifteenth century.

In the realm of physics, Archytas founded the study of mechanics. Euclid laid the basis for the scientific study of optics. He seems to have understood the principle of the propagation of light in straight lines and the laws of the reflection of light. Archimedes appears to have devised ingenious burning glasses. The best Greek work in optics occurs in a book on the subject ascribed to Ptolemy. It contains an account of elaborate experimental research in the field of the refraction of light. Indeed, it is the best example of experimental research in all antique science. It included a study of atmospheric refraction. By these experiments Ptolemy found that the angles of the incidence and refraction of light are approximately equal.

The most memorable work in physics in the antique world was that by Archimedes in static mechanics and hydrostatics. He laid down the fundamental principles of the equilibrium of weights, worked out a theory of the center of gravity, and elaborated on the principles of the wedge, lever, pulley, and screw. In hydrostatics, he discovered the famous law of floating bodies or specific gravity, incidental to his attempt to detect the debasement of the gold in the crown of

King Hiero of Syracuse. Archimedes applied his physical theories in ingenious fashion to practical mechanics. They exerted some influence on contemporaries and were prized and preserved by the great Roman architect and engineer, Vitruvius. Archimedes thus qualified as the first important mechanical genius.

Probably the greatest mechanical genius of antiquity was Hero of Alexandria, around 100 B.C. He did some work in theoretical physics, such as a study of the comparative flow of water in pipes, the discovery of the reflection of the light ray in a path of minimum length, and his mathematical theories of plane surveying. But he is more noted for his many brilliant inventions which included siphons, fountains, a fire-engine, a water-organ, an air pump, a thermoscope, and a steam engine. The latter was a true anticipation of the steam turbine, a more advanced conception than that of James Watt. Had the Greeks been practically minded and more interested in labor-saving devices, men like Hero might have brought them an industrial revolution and an empire of machines nearly two thousand years before they came to western Europe.

Rudimentary chemistry came into being at this time through the foundation of alchemy. We have already pointed out how the Egyptian pharmacy and metallurgy had first suggested the material basis of alchemy. The mystical elements were contributed by the Pythagoreans and by Plato's theory of matter as set forth in his *Timaeus*. In Hellenistic times the practical and mystical elements were combined to found historic alchemy, devoted as it was to transmuting the baser metals into gold and to discovering the principle of human rejuvenation, all of which could be accomplished, if one could only isolate and utilize the mysterious fifth element.

The eminent Hellenistic authority on the materia medica, Dioscorides, embodied in his encyclopedia a considerable survey of Greek alchemy and elementary chemistry. The first Hellenistic writer to deal specifically with alchemy was Democritus (Pseudo-Democritus), whose appropriately titled *Physica et mystica* was probably written about A.D. 100.[28] Far more important was Zosimus of Panopolis (A.D. c. 300) who compiled an encyclopedia of the alchemistic arts in twenty-eight books. While little of it was original, it brought the alchemistic lore together in comprehensive fashion. It was particularly valuable in its treatment of metallurgy. There was no advance beyond its contents until the time of the great Muslim alchemists.

The most important achievement in general biology, botany, and zoölogy was the descriptive work of Aristotle and his school, notably the Peripatetics and Theophrastus. The latter we have noted to be the greatest botanist of antiquity. In addition to invaluable description and classification, this work of the Aristotelian group laid the basis for the theory of organic evolution and the principles of genetics. The latter was hampered, however, by the failure to recognize the sexuality of plants.

Even more important was the work in anatomy and physiology, in which Herophilus (fl. c. 300 B.C.) and Erasistratus (b. c. 300 B.C.) took the lead. They car-

[28] Possibly as late as A.D. 200.

ried these subjects to a level not again matched until the time of Leonardo da Vinci and Vesalius and his followers.

Herophilus of Chalcedon was the founder of scientific anatomy and the ablest anatomist of antiquity. He gave admirable descriptions of the brain and nervous system, the vascular system, the organs of digestion and the genital organs. He did particularly good work on the anatomy of the eye. He rejected Aristotle's theory that the heart is the center of thought and accepted the doctrine of the supremacy of the brain. He recognized that there is a direct relationship between the strength of the pulse beat and that of the heart. His terminology gave greater precision to anatomical nomenclature.

Erasistratus of Ceos was second only to Herophilus as an anatomist and much abler as a physiologist, in which field he ranks as the greatest figure of antiquity. He was the first to discard, root and branch, the theory of the four humors as the basis of physiological chemistry. His researches relative to the brain, the nervous and vascular systems and the heart were particularly important. He carried on the best investigation of the brain in classical anatomy and physiology, distinguishing carefully between the cerebrum and cerebellum and the functions of each. He also differentiated between the motor and sensory nerves. He contended that every organ is connected with the rest of the body through arteries, veins, and nerves. He came very close to a discovery of the circulation of the blood.

Eudemus of Alexandria (c. 250 B.C.) went even further in his studies of the nerves, bones, and embryology. He was the discoverer of the pancreas and of some of its functions. Marinus of Alexandria (A.D. c. 100) brought together Greek anatomical knowledge in a comprehensive treatise which was widely used and highly praised by Galen. Rufus of Ephesus, in the second century A.D., carried the anatomical study of the eye and the liver further than any other anatomist of the ancient world and was the ablest physiologist dealing with the nature and functions of the nervous system.

Eratosthenes was the first scientific geographer of Greece. By an ingenious mathematical device he first made a relatively exact measurement of the circumference and diameter of the earth, which he estimated at 24,662 miles and 7,850 miles, respectively. He also wrote on the history of geography, mathematical and physical geography, and scientific map making. The astronomer, Hipparchus, was even more successful in applying astronomy to geographical measurements, providing, as we have seen, the first accurate determination of latitude and longitude.

Crates of Mallos (c. 175 B.C.) constructed the first terrestrial globe of which we have any record. Posidonius of Rhodes (c. 133-49 B.C.) was the most intelligently observant traveler of antiquity and gathered a large volume of geographical information. He was the first to maintain that the tides are caused by the attraction of the sun and moon. His estimate of the size of the circumference of the earth, much below Eratosthenes', had a disastrous effect on later geography, for it was adopted and transmitted by Ptolemy to the Middle Ages. It had one good result, however; it made more feasible the proposed voyage of Columbus who, on this account, greatly underestimated the distance westward to the Indies.

The most comprehensive work on geography in antiquity was the *Geography* of Strabo (c. 63 B.C.-c. 15 B.C.)—mathematical, physical, political, historical, and human geography. It contains a vast amount of information on physical features and the customs of inhabitants. Strabo suggested many ingenious theories as to the formation of earth features, laying stress on internal pressures, volcanic eruptions, earthquakes, and water erosion. He noted the apparent rise and fall of earth masses.

Marinus of Tyre, who flourished in the first half of the second century A.D., made an earnest effort to construct a more accurate map of the world. He greatly increased the extent and precision of the extant knowledge of Asia and Africa, and his materials were the chief source of information used by Ptolemy in his maps. Ptolemy is usually looked upon as an astronomer and mathematician, but his *Geographical Treatise* was as influential on the subsequent course of geographical knowledge as was his *Almagest* on later developments in astronomy. He made wide use of his knowledge of astronomy in his geographical work and was the first to employ the terms parallels and meridians. His maps of the world were the best transmitted to the Middle Ages by antiquity. The first scientific travel guide prepared in antiquity was the *Description of Greece* by Pausanius (A.D. c. 150). It is the best source for ancient Greek topography and antiquities, and has proved invaluable in the reconstruction of our knowledge of Greek culture in modern times.

In Hellenistic medicine the great names are those of Herophilus, Erasistratus, Asclepiades, Themison, Soranus, Rufus, Galen, and Dioscorides. Herophilus developed the empirical or observational approach to disease further than Hippocrates, improved the methods of diagnosis and prognosis, and experimented widely with drugs. He also relied heavily on bloodletting. His work on obstetrics was especially original. Through his repudiation of the theory of the four humors, Erasistratus should probably rank as the most original of all ancient physicians. Unfortunately, Galen followed Hippocrates and handed down the fantastic theory of the humors to posterity. Erasistratus distinguished between hygiene and therapeutics, placing primary stress on the former. Hence, he advocated strict attention to diet, exercise, bathing, and the like. He was skeptical of the careless use of drugs and excessive bloodletting.

The first Greek physician to introduce Hellenistic medicine in Rome was Asclepiades of Bithynia (b. c. 125 B.C.). He deserves much credit not only for having rejected the preposterous Hippocratic theory of the four humors but also for having substituted in its place the atomic theory of Democritus. He held that disease is caused by a disturbance of the atoms in the body. His great weakness was his contempt for anatomical studies. Themison of Laodicea (c. 50 B.C.) was the first notable disciple of Asclepiades. He founded the so-called methodist school of medicine, holding that health and disease arise from the general state of the body as a whole. While this hypothesis had some virtue, it tended to encourage the neglect of a careful study of special symptoms. Soranus of Ephesus (A.D. c. 125) was the outstanding representative of the methodist school. He was also far and away the greatest gynaecologist of antiquity. His description of the womb is the best provided in antiquity. He introduced the use of the speculum and the obstetric chair. We have already mentioned the work of Rufus of Ephesus on the anatomy of the eye. He was the ablest exponent in ancient medicine of the theory that pathology should be based on anatomy and physiology. He was also the first to suggest boiling suspicious-looking water before drinking it.

The most influential physician in antiquity, not even excepting Hippocrates, was Galen of Pergamum (A.D. 129-199). He was not only a great medical writer but an able practicing physician. He unified and systematized Greek anatomical and medical knowledge, put it in clear language, in about 150 treatises, and transmitted it to posterity. He also carried on a large number of anatomical and physiological observations, proving, for example, that the arteries contain and carry blood. His empirical medicine was, however, mingled with a vast amount of magic and some astrological medicine. Coming to Rome he enjoyed great popularity and prestige as a physician. His influence was greatly increased as a result of the fact that his work was widely used by the Muslims and rivaled the *Canon* of Avicenna as a textbook on medicine in the Middle Ages in both Muslim and Christian regions. Indeed, the *Canon* was, in part, a Muslim adaptation of Galen, combined with Indian, Persian, and Muslim medical lore. It was from Galen that the later world gained most of its knowledge of Hippocratic medicine. The most unfortunate fact in this situation was that Galen's faithful following of Hippocrates led to the transmission of the latter's grotesque theory of the four humors.

The great authority on the materia medica in antiquity was Dioscorides of Cilicia (A.D. c. 150). He wrote an encyclopedia on the subject which embraced all extant Greek knowledge of pharmacy and applied botany. It also gained popularity because of its admirable arrangement. The book contained, as well, a good summary of ancient chemistry and alchemy. It was the standard work on the materia medica for fifteen hundred years, rivaled only in the later Middle Ages by the great Muslim manual by al-Mardini.

This brief review of Hellenistic science will suffice to give some indication of the magnitude and novelty of the achievements. Nothing like it took place again until the period from the thirteenth to the seventeenth centuries of the Christian Era. The advance of science in this age was due in part to the great library and museum at Alexandria, which permitted coöperative scientific effort and also facilitated research into the previous achievements in any special field of work.

IX. THE RELIGION OF THE GREEKS

Basically, there were important resemblances between the religion of the Greeks and the cults of Egypt and Mesopotamia. The three systems had certain myths in common. The myths of the Egyptian Osiris, the Babylonian Ishtar, and the Greek Persephone were wrought out of the same raw materials of fertility, vegetation, and seasonal changes. This attests to the fact that all three races went through a long period in which life was chiefly pastoral and agricultural.

The history of Greek religion, then, falls into the familiar patterns of religious growth. When the Hellenes appeared on the historical stage, they had a fully developed mythology and a picturesque pantheon. But there were still traces of a primitive belief in an impersonal supernatural power or mana.

Like their Oriental neighbors, they divided their gods into classes as good and evil. But they did not believe in a clear-cut cosmic dualism, in a struggle between the forces of light and darkness, a conception which the Persians first projected and later handed on to Jews and Christians.

Mount Olympus, where the Greek gods dwelt, was a naturalistic place and its mythical inhabitants led human-like lives. Indeed, in religion as in everything else, the imaginative creations of the Greeks were permeated with a certain humanity, as it were. The members of the Persian and Christian pantheons were super-natural personifications of good or evil. The Olympians are amiable, lifelike creations. We would recognize them, if we were to meet them, and indeed they are as real and human as our friends. The gods of no other race so capture our imagination, or appeal to us so powerfully.

On the throne of Olympus sat Zeus, or Jupiter. In later times he moved his residence to a region above the sky, where the source of all light was supposed to be located. Zeus had a wife, Hera, who was also his sister. (Incest among the Olympians was a frequent occurrence.) All the blessings of nature emanated from their union, and when they met, as on Mount Ida, flowers sprang up around them. Homer describes Hera as jealous, angry, and quarrelsome, but lofty, proud, and somewhat frigid.

Athena was the ingratiating personification of mind, a virgin goddess, but really sexless in nature, suggesting that mind is not an attribute of sex, but an independent power at work through all creation. Ares, or Mars, was the terrible god of war, the gore-loving divinity, depicted with a shield and lance, who, when he was wounded, according to Homer, fell to the ground with a thundering crash, like the noise of ten thousand warriors engaged in battle.

Apollo was the sun-god, and was portrayed as a beautiful youth. He was also the god of music (hence his golden lyre), of the herds that graze on the fields warmed by him, the god of prophecy, revealing all secrets, as the sun lights up the darkness and dispels nocturnal gloom. Artemis, or Diana, the sister of Apollo, was originally the moon-goddess, and later goddess of the chase and of wild life.

Aphrodite, or Venus, was the incomparable goddess of love, and almost the pa-tron saint of poetry and art to many post-Greek poets and artists who frequently invoked her. All the sublimest physical traits of womanhood were molded in this goddess, who appears to us in innumerable statues as serene and compassionate, ever young and ever beautiful.

Hephaestus, or Vulcan, the son of Hera and Zeus, was the god of fire, the trouble maker. Homer tells us that once, when Hephaestus took Hera's part against Zeus, his father seized him by the heels and cast him out of Olympus. Through the air he sailed for a whole day, and at evening, when the sun went down, he fell upon the island of Lemnos near the crater of Moschylus, where some mortals found him and gave him friendly care. The place afterwards became the principal center of his worship.

Poseidon, or Neptune, was one of the three sons of Cronus (the supreme god whom the Titans had cast off out of Olympus). Zeus and Hades were his brothers. Poseidon was ruler of the sea, depicted, with his three-pronged scepter, as forever riding the waves in his chariot, driven by two sea horses. Hermes, or Mercury, the fleetest of the gods, was the messenger of the Olympians, announcing the will of the gods to men.

The "jolly god," Dionysus, or Bacchus, "ever fair, and ever young," as Dryden describes him, was the god of life, particularly of vegetable life. His power over the sap of vegetation made spring a season of gladness and joy, and winter a season of sorrow. He was also the god of wine and intoxicated abandon.

The great mother-goddess of the soil and of fertility was Demeter, or Ceres, around whom was woven one of the most picturesque of myths. Pluto, or Hades, carried off her beloved young daughter Persephone, and she, with a mother's sorrow, lit her torch, mounted her cart, drawn by winged snakes, and swept through all the lands, searching for her. Whenever she rested, she was hospitably received, and hence whenever she departed, she left a blessing in the form of instruction in the art of agriculture. Finally, Demeter prevailed upon Zeus to let her have her daughter back for six months (the summer months) out of each year. During the remaining six months Persephone continued to live underground with her husband, Pluto.

Pluto, the brother of Poseidon and Zeus, was the god of the dead, but there was no such rivalry between him and Zeus as there was between Persian Ahriman and Ormuzd, or between Satan and the Christian God. Pluto was on relatively good terms with the divinities of the upper world, simply ruling over the dead, with his queen, Persephone (Proserpina) of whom Swinburne sings,

> Thou art more than the day or the morrow,
>   the seasons that laugh or that weep,
> For these give joy and sorrow, but thou,
>   Proserpina, sleep.

Persephone, as we have noted, spent only half the year in the underworld, and the rest in the realm of the living, promoting the processes of fertility.

Thus we see that the Olympians were preëminently human, and always ready to help mortals out of their difficulties. For example, a man in love could invoke Aphrodite or Eros; a woman in the pangs of childbirth, Artemis; a soldier facing the dangers of war, Ares; an athlete about to enter the contests, Hermes; a citizen puzzled by the arts and industrial problems, Athena and Hephaestus. When confronting the perils of travel one could call on Hermes; when faced with hunger, Demeter; when in need of pleasure and distraction, Aphrodite, Eros and Dionysus; when suffering from disease, Aesculapius and Apollo. In anticipation of the complexities of marriage, one could invoke Demeter, Aphrodite, and Hera. If one wished to assure himself of good crops, he could turn to Demeter and Dionysus. If his flocks needed protection he would call on Apollo, Pan, and Hermes. And if he found himself facing danger at sea, he could pray to Poseidon—and, since the Greeks were a seafaring people, Poseidon enjoyed extreme importance.

Therefore, there were few life situations in which the Greeks could not feel sure of divine interest and assistance.

Surrounding the Greek gods and the myths were many legends as to the origins of the universe, man, animals, plants, and the arts and sciences. Hesiod worked out a cosmogony comparable to that of the Hebrews in Genesis. He also suggested the progressive degeneration of the cultures of the world in his theory of the five ages of man, which began with the age of gold and ended with the evil age of iron. This roughly resembled the Hebrew story of the decline of man prior to the Flood. The Greeks also had a very definite deluge myth almost identical with the story of the salvation of Noah in the ark. The legend of Prometheus, dealing with the origin of the arts and the methods of civilized life, reminds one of the biblical reference to Tubal Cain.

The Greeks, like other races, elaborated their mythology in order to overcome their fear of nature, and to gain supernatural aid amid human crises. But they did not imagine that any mortal could coerce a god. It was prudent to be on good terms with the gods. If one could not force them to do one's bidding, one could at least keep them in countenance through appropriate rituals, especially through sacrifice.

There were many religious festivals in Greece, the most important being dedicated to the agrarian deities, Dionysus and Demeter. The festival of Dionysus was celebrated in winter as a symbolic effort to awaken the sleeping god who ruled over plant life and the vine. The great festival of Demeter, connected with the Eleusinian mysteries, was held each autumn and lasted nine days. It was designed to assure the return of the goddess Persephone and the restoration of vegetation and of animal fecundity. Later on, the Eleusinian mysteries assumed an esoteric character, and were associated with a kind of occult belief in the abstract principle of life after death.

Although the Greeks did not imagine that they could directly control the gods, they were sure they could discover the intentions of the gods, and be guided by them. For this purpose they resorted to omens, oracles, and divination—deriving the latter from the Orient.[29] The behavior of sacrificial animals, and the condition of their entrails when exposed, were sinister or propitious omens. So were dreams, thunder, lightning, storms, the flight of birds, the accidental occurrences of daily life.

The manifest will of the gods was also revealed through oracles, the fortune-tellers of Greece, to whom special sanctuaries or temples were erected, the most famous of which was the one to Apollo, at Delphi in Phocis. There priests transmitted oracular wisdom in the form of more or less ambiguous phrases and scraps of verse.

The Greeks thus got along well with their gods. They did not live in terror of them, as did Persians, Jews, or Christians. If they could discover the divine will—the Olympians were always ready to make themselves audible, and if the gods seemed silent, it was only because of faulty transmission, like static on the radio—and adapted their behavior accordingly, all was bound to be well.

[29] Cf. Farnell, *Greece and Babylon.*

The Greek deities did not intimidate their earthly followers. The gods lived independent lives and exacted from man no terrifying faith, like the Oriental gods, but only cheerful belief and occasional sacrifice. In other words, morality was not associated with the pangs of conscience and a sin-complex. As G. Lowes Dickinson says, "The function of a (Greek) religion was rather to quiet the conscience by ritual than to excite it by admonition and reproof." [30] The Greeks were thus brought into harmony with the world, and were free to eat, drink, and be merry, without feeling that the possible tortures of hell hung upon their slightest move.

The Greeks believed in a future life spent in the realm of the dead ruled over by Hades (Pluto). Compared to the Persian and the Christian heavens and hells, the realm of the dead in Greek mythology was a rather gray, drab, and indifferent abode. There were special punishments only for those who deliberately violated the wishes of the major gods. Later some faint resemblance to the Persian and Christian views appeared in the notion of the joys of Elysium and the sufferings of Tartarus. But the Greek religion never really developed a conception of the future life which would offer adequate consolation for the sorrows and disappointments of life on earth. This was one of the main incentives of the Greeks to make the life here and now worth while to man.

It was this absence of a notion of a blessed future in Greek religion that led to the popularity of the later mystery cults which contained the promise of a personal immortality of deep significance to the individual. This explains the enthusiasm of the Greeks for the later developments in the Eleusinian mysteries, which embodied the idea of immortality derived from the earlier and crude fertility myth of Demeter and Persephone. It also makes clear the great zeal of the Greeks at a later date for Mithraism and Christianity, the two mysteries which laid most stress upon their promise of immortality. As the conditions of life on earth became more harsh in later Greek history there was much more ardent longing for the compensations of the hereafter.

Greek religion was less a ritualistic system than a way of life. Social institutions were believed to have been invented by the gods, who, as we observed, led very human lives. They lived *en famille,* loved, wedded, procreated, ruled, hated, and rebelled, thereby justifying and typifying social institutions and human situations. Hence, the sweet reasonableness of Greek ethics, with its joyous acclaim of the good things of the world, which, later, the Christians denounced as pagan and vicious.

The amalgamation of religion and society was best exemplified in the relation of the Greek church to the state. Church and state were one, religion and patriotism were intertwined, piety and reverence were civic duties. Atheism, heresy, and sacrilege were treasonable. Priests were public officials.

While the Greek religion was satisfactory for the mass of the people, it was obviously ill equipped to oppose the inroads of philosophical speculation. It broke down quickly under skeptical analysis. Therefore we find the first metaphysicians,

30 Dickinson, *The Greek View of Life,* Doubleday, 1926 (Ann Arbor Books, 1958), p. 214.

long before Plato, poking holes in the popular religion, especially in its anthropomorphic tendencies. Xenophanes, for example, held that if oxen had gods they would create them in the form of oxen.

Plato and the Stoics rejected the popular view of the gods and conceived of an abstract divine intelligence which was communicated to man in the form of the logos. In the thought of Plato, the logos was the messenger of wisdom mediating between God and man. With the Stoics the logos was the direct emanation of divine wisdom. For minds which recoiled at abstract speculation in religion but could not accept the popular supernaturalism, the Hellenistic Greeks provided an appropriate philosophy in the form of Neoplatonism, which extolled the virtues of complete faith in regard to all matters connected with the gods and religion. It also held that the supreme religious experience lay in an ecstatic communion with the supernatural, from which all elements of reason and logic were absent.

Epicureanism developed a complete indifference to the celestial powers. While not rejecting belief in the gods, the Epicureans held that the gods had no interest in or concern with mankind. Thus these thinkers hoped to free man from the worries of religion and from the vast waste of time connected with the propitiation of supernatural powers that were completely oblivious to humanity.

As we shall point out later in greater detail, Christianity was deeply influenced by Greek contributions. From Greek philosophy Christians derived their theology. From the Neoplatonists they secured their reliance upon justification through faith. Greek rhetoric gave the Christians their models for successful preaching. Finally, from the common meal in the Eleusinian mysteries they derived the basic sacrament of the Mass or Lord's Supper.

In view of this account of the prevalence and thoroughness of supernatural religion among the Greeks, one might legitimately ask, Why can one point to Greece as the home of free thought?

The reply is that, though the masses, as everywhere, fell prey to supernaturalism, a small band of philosophers and scholars, from the sixth century B.C. onward, rid themselves of all trammels on free thought, and in their emancipation, created philosophy, brought pure science to birth, and made some progress in applied science. Their courageous speculation constitutes the beginning of the secularization of the human intellect, a secularization which has suffered many rebuffs through the centuries and left many martyrs in its path.

X. GREEK LITERATURE

1. *The Heroic Age*

To the Greeks we attribute virtually all our literary forms. From them we derive historical writing, literary criticism, the scientific monograph, rhetoric, lyrical poetry, the pastoral, the philosophical dialogue, the tragic drama and comedy, the character sketch, and the oration. What important literary forms did the Greeks not invent? Satire, as a form, apparently was invented by the Romans, and the prose novel by the modern world, although the latter had its Greek prototype in the romances of the later Greek world.

Greek literature, like Greek art, may be divided into periods:

I The epic or heroic age, dating from the beginning to about 600 B.C.
II The lyrical age, 600-475 B.C.
III The Attic or golden age, 475-300 B.C.
IV The Alexandrian or Hellenistic age, 300 B.C.-A.D. 200.

Greek (and European) literature begins with the Homeric poems, the origins of which are shrouded in mystery. It is not even known that there was a blind bard named Homer, nor when he lived. The German critic Wolf in the last century introduced the theory that the epics are of patchwork authorship, like some books in the Bible. Opposed to this is the theory that Homer was a person who, stringing together a number of "lays" (short poems), composed the magnificent epics in their present form. The tendency today is to agree that the *Iliad* is the work of a single poet, and so is the *Odyssey,* though each was probably written by a different man. At all events, the Homeric poems, which constitute only two out of many Greek epic cycles which have been lost, seem to have assumed oral form in the Ionic dialect about 1000 B.C., and were written down about two hundred years later. The *Iliad* deals with some legendary events in the last portion of the ten years' siege of Troy; and for the Trojan War there is probably a basis of historical fact in occurrences during the decline of the Minoan and Mycenaean culture.

The theme of the *Iliad* is the wrath of Achilles: the hero had come to Troy, a man of destiny. He had been given the choice of a long life with dishonor or a short life with honor. He had chosen honor and a short life. But now "honor," symbolized by his prize, the captured maiden Briseis, is being taken from him. He withdraws from the battle and sulks in his tent. And so the Greeks are driven back until Achilles' good friend Patroclus implores Achilles to aid them and, failing this, to lend his armor to Patroclus. The death of Patroclus draws Achilles again into the battle and leads directly to the tragic climax in the death and mutilation of Hector.

But no brief outline can presume to convey the charm of the poem. We have spoken of the Homeric epics as a beginning. In one sense we may regard them as an end—as the climax of a particular form of society—the tribal. Already in the Homeric poems we have the hexameter developed as a magnificent poetical instrument. We have a technique of storytelling seldom excelled and we have a developed and conscious literary art. One or two points may illustrate this. The Homeric epithet is clearly a literary convention but an effective one. Every hero, every god, even every place, has its appropriate descriptive summary—there is swift-footed, noble Achilles, there is Hector of the nodding plume, there is Agamemnon, king of men, and godlike Priam. The goddess of wisdom is the gray- or flashing-eyed goddess and the wife of Lord Zeus is known as the ox-eyed lady—blessed with the large, luscious, limpid, brown eyes of a cow.

Our poet (or poetical syndicate) knows, too, the value of pictorial embroidery.

The action is helped along by many a descriptive simile—by similes of size and force, of strength or swiftness, homely pastoral scenes or vivid analogies. A closely fought battle is like two men contending with measuring rods about the boundaries of a field or like a thrifty woman who carefully weighs wool in the scales. A hero is driven back by his enemies like a donkey being driven from a field by small boys, and the restlessness of Odysseus is like a sausage turning on a spit before the fire.

The influence of Homer has been incalculable. It is a striking fact about European literature that it makes its debut with epics of such excellence—the plot of the *Odyssey,* said Coleridge, is one of the three greatest in the world. The Homeric poems are easily in the first rank of epics. Moreover, they have the benefit of being first in the field (they are at least the earliest survivors of popular epic), which means that they possess a freshness and bloom which later epics cannot quite match.

The second great name in Greek literature is that of Hesiod, who flourished probably about 775 B.C. His extant poems are *Works and Days,* a sort of farmer's almanac, with advice both professional and moral to farmers and sailors; and the *Theogony,* a poem which describes the origin of the gods and the universe. Though not a great poet, Hesiod was widely read in antiquity and created the so-called "georgics," poems of farm-life, of which Vergil is probably the greatest master. There could be no sharper, clearer contrast than that between the poems of Homer and of Hesiod. The one poet is interested in the Zeus-nurtured heroes, the "kings" or leaders of tribes. If the common people appear, as once in the case of Thersites, they are greeted with bitter scorn. But Hesiod seems to represent the dispossessed. His poems have an undercurrent of gloom and complaint; "The earth is full of ills, of ills the sea." Justice has fled from the earth and dwells now only among the gods. The poems of Hesiod have therefore less appeal, but they unquestionably represented a very real aspect of Greek life in the period.

2. *The Lyric Age* (600-475 B.C.)

Greek lyric poetry was choral, either accompanied by the lyre (hence the term "lyric" poetry) or by a chorus in religious ritual. Lyric poetry had its origin in Ionia, but we find lyrics in all three Greek dialects: Aeolic, Doric, and Ionic. The term lyric was applied to any poetry of an *emotional* character, whether mournful, like the elegy, or sentimental, like the love song.

Some of the outstanding authors of the lyric age are Archilochus of Paros, who lived about 660 B.C. and invented the iambic measure (a foot of two syllables, a short unaccented, followed by a long accented) which he used for satiric purposes; Solon (about 600 B.C.) the great Athenian lawgiver who used the elegy to express his political philosophy; and Simonides of Ceos (c. 556-c. 486 B.C.) who is famous for his elegiac epitaphs on the heroes who fell in the Persian Wars. Of these poets only about 300 lines of Solon, a handful of the verses of Archilochus, and some fragments of Simonides survive.

The other great names among Greek lyric poets are Sappho, Alcaeus, Anacreon, and Pindar. Sappho of Lesbos lived in Solon's day. Though only a few of her poems are extant we get from them an impression of the purest lyric ecstasy. It is as though her words were "tipped in fire." We have here the clearest and simplest communication of personal passion in language of exquisite simplicity and grace, with a poignancy and an insight never excelled. One or two examples must convey a suggestion of this simple beauty. A girl who failed to get married is compared to an apple that ripens out of reach—"Like an apple that reddens on the tip of the bough, yes on the very tip—for the gatherers had forgotten it; no they had not forgotten it but they were unable to reach it."

Or the evening star that brought "all desired and timely things." "Evening star you bring back again all that the shining morn had scattered. You bring back the sheep, you bring back the goat, you bring back the child to its mother."

Alcaeus (620-580 B.C.), also a native of Lesbos, sings zestfully of love and war. His work, like Sappho's, exists only in fragments. Anacreon lived around 530 B.C. and his surviving snatches are tender and graceful songs about wine and women. Some of the Anacreontic odes which have come down to us are probably not by him, although written in the measure he invented. In fact, Sappho, Alcaeus, and Anacreon all gave their names to the stanzaic forms (sapphics, alcaics, and anacreontics) in which they wrote and which were imitated by Roman poets.

Greatest of Greek lyric poets, however, is Pindar of Thebes (about 470 B.C.) who wrote choral odes—whence our "pindarics"—commemorating the victorious athletes in the Greek games. Poetry was a part of Greek religious ceremonials. Pindar was the luckiest of all Greek lyrists, since about one-fourth of his work remains, four books of *Epinician Odes* (*Odes to the Victors*). The pindaric ode was chanted by a dancing chorus. One stanza, the *strophe,* was accompanied by a movement from right to left; in the next, the *antistrophe,* the movement was reversed; during the third, the *epode* (literally, after-song), the chorus stood still. This triplicate pattern could be repeated indefinitely. Pindar is more of a poet for poetry's sake than other Greek lyrists. His genius resides in his imagery and orchestral effects, virtually untranslatable into another language. Pindar had an important influence on modern literature, though his strict form was not followed, partly because the melodic and dancing elements disappeared, and partly because the regularity of his verse was difficult to reproduce. Ronsard and the Pléiade imitated him in the sixteenth century; many English poets attempted pindarics in the seventeenth and eighteenth.

In the lyric age of Greece, poetry became less a matter of group sentiment and more a vehicle of individual expression. Pindar, for example, like the sculptors of the Parthenon, sings of beautiful bodies and spirited action, all regulated by admirable restraint. He is not a deep poet, but like Homer, the tribulations of men move him to a simple and affecting expression.

It may be possible perhaps to indicate the appeal of this earliest lyric poetry in the period of man's first consciousness of himself as an individual: bitterly like Archilochus, poor and dispossessed, scornfully rejecting the patriotic appeal ("Throw away my shield, I can get another as good," or the Spartan mother exhorting her son to come back *with* his shield or *on* it!), fawningly like Pindar who sang of the "glorious" achievements of the wealthy or powerful; or just simply and sensuously like Sappho or Alcaeus or Anacreon, awaking to the delights of the external world around them, telling of the joys of love and wine or describing the simple things they see—shepherds who tread down bluebells on the hillside, the young girl who cannot mind her loom for thinking of her lover, or down by the seashore the seagull, the bird that rides on the blossom of the swell, the sea-purple bird of spring.

3. Greek Tragedy (475-300 B.C.)

In the Attic or golden age of Greek literature, the lyric is less important than those more ambitious literary forms, the poetic drama and prose history. Prose at this time achieves perfection as a vehicle of expression.

The Greek drama originated in Greek religious festivals. Hence it was essentially religious and musical in nature. Its subject matter was consequently restricted to stories of the gods and the heroes who ran into conflict with them.

The dramas were produced at the great spring festival; they were chosen in open competition. Performances were undertaken by the citizenry, a practice, we shall see, more or less common in the medieval religious drama. They were held in outdoor amphitheaters nestling in the beautiful hills. Since the playwright was writing for a religious festival and a communal undertaking, he was perforce restricted in expression, and his ideas usually reflected the prevailing mores.

Greek dramas, then, were quite different from ours. They approximated somewhat to Wagner's music-drama, but with this difference: that although written by an individual, they were more the product of the folk mind. The text was only a part of the whole in which music and ballet were vitally linked.

Drama emerged from the Dionysian "dithyramb" in which a chorus sang and danced out a lyrical poem around a wooden altar. In its earliest stages the drama consisted of popular mimicry and the collective buffoonery of simple folkways. In time, one of the chorus stepped out of rank, mounted the altar, and recited something. Later he began to wear a mask and costume and impersonated some character in the narrative. Then he would enter a booth, change his costume, and come out to impersonate another character.

This change of personality is the germ of drama. The first playwright we hear of is Thespis, who flourished in Attica about 550 B.C. and composed a "drama" which was more like an oratorio, and in which there was no action. One character delivered formal speeches at intervals. As the drama developed, the chorus played a less important rôle and the speechmakers evolved into what we call dramatis personae. Aeschylus (525-456 B.C.) introduced a second actor on the altar or stage and reduced the size of the chorus. He thus became the first true dramatist in European history, for drama implies conflict of wills and this cannot be depicted unless two characters are brought into verbal collision. We must remember that because the actors wore masks in Greek drama, two people could act out a play of many characters. Nevertheless, the plays of Aeschylus read like a recited narrative interspersed with lyrical passages. The conversation of modern plays, with the flash of action and events, does not come till Sophocles. In Greek drama the chorus always plays a vital part and is endowed with a knowledge of the will of the gods not granted to the protagonist. The chorus and hero discuss the story in lyrical dialogue.

Seven of Aeschylus' seventy plays survive. His subjects, as in most Greek tragedy, deal with gods or heroes. Behind the gods is Nemesis or Fate, who deals out justice or retribution, and from whom there is no escape. The plots of Greek tragedy can be epitomized almost as follows: a god or a mortal—Prometheus, Medea, Agamemnon, or Orestes—has committed a crime, and a struggle ensues to escape just punishment. Justice inevitably triumphs and the mortal goes to his death, like a fly caught in Fate's web.

The plays of Aeschylus are *The Suppliants, The Persians, Seven against Thebes, Prometheus Bound,* and the trilogy called the *Oresteia.* Of special interest is *The Persians,* the only extant Greek tragedy which deals with contemporary events— in which, incidentally, Aeschylus was a participant. The battle of Salamis is depicted with the eye of an observer. The *Prometheus* narrates the legend of the god who, when Zeus decided to destroy mankind, stole fire from heaven and taught men how to kindle it, thereby permitting them to learn crafts and to be lifted up to the level of civilization. For this Prometheus is chained to a crag and is tortured by wind, weather, earthquake, and birds.

The *Oresteia* is the familiar story of Agamemnon's victorious return from Troy, his murder at the hands of his wife Clytemnestra and her paramour, Aegisthus, and the vengeance taken upon Clytemnestra by Agamemnon's son, Orestes. It will be well to indicate here how Greek tragedy differs from modern tragedy. Modern drama, of Shakespeare or Molière, for example, is based upon the conflict of egos; individual strives with individual, or with himself. Hamlet, for instance, is at war with his mother, with Claudius, with Polonius, and in lesser degree, with others. Classic tragedy is based on a different formula. That the world is out of joint, is indeed the basic theme of all tragedy. But in modern tragedy, the world is out of joint usually because the protagonist is out of joint with himself, either because of a crime he hesitated to commit, like Hamlet, or a crime he did commit, like Macbeth; or because his emotions and happiness are thwarted, like Molière's Misanthrope, by the world's lack of sympathy. In Greek tragedy the world is out of joint because an individual has committed a crime against society. It is not the individual who counts, not Clytemnestra, who murdered Agamemnon, nor Orestes, who murdered Clytemnestra, but society, to whom a great wrong has been done first, when Clytemnestra violated her marriage vows, and secondly, when she brutally murdered her husband.

The conflict in classic Greek tragedy, then, is a conflict between the individual and the mores. Euripides gets away somewhat from this conception of tragedy and comes nearer to modern drama. He is less concerned with the mores and more absorbed in the individual as an independent and self-conscious entity. To Sophocles and Aeschylus the individual is an entity only as part of the group.

In Aeschylus we see raised and treated with great power the problem of justice (and the Homeric Lord of Olympus, the very human Zeus of the Homeric poems, becomes the divine repository of an eternal principle), the problem of transgression and the retribution which *ought* to follow this transgression. These are problems which were obviously becoming more and more pressing as Greek society evolved and developed and as the struggle between landowner and merchant and between rich and poor became more menacing and absorbing.

The language of Aeschylus was marked by a kind of titanic, torrential energy, mountain piled on mountain; Mt. Ossa on Mt. Pelion. Yet he was capable of passages of exquisite beauty and quiet emotion—"When on his mid day couch, windless and waveless Ocean sank to rest," or "a dream treading upon the ways of sleep."

Sophocles (496-406 B.C.) wrote over a hundred plays; eighteen times he won the first or second prize. Drama, we should mention, continued as a state function and the successful dramatist was voted a state prize. Only seven survive, *Antigone, Ajax, Oedipus Rex, Oedipus at Colonus, Trachiniai, Electra,* and *Philoctetes.* Their subjects, as one may notice, are traditional. In fact, Greek drama differed from the modern in another important way. It did not invent plots. The themes were familiar to the audiences. The novelty resided in the treatment. Sophocles advanced the drama by introducing a third actor and developing the more theatrical elements, suspense, climax, and conflict. The result has told with posterity, since at least three of his plays, *Antigone, Electra,* and *Oedipus Rex,* have held the stage right down to our times, and have been translated successfully into English, German, and French.

The greatness of Sophocles lies in the fact that he gave universal significance to individual emotions. That is, whatever facet of emotional experience he handled, he regarded it from the point of view of society as a whole, not from that of an isolated human being. This, as we observed on a previous page, was the general drift of classic tragedy, and indeed of Hellenic art as a whole. Sophocles does not create portraits but types, just as Phidias does not model individual but generalized heads. Sophocles' leading theme is the ethical relation of man to the gods, of individual ethics to the unwritten moral code by which all men must abide. Sophocles is therefore an illustrious example of the "universal poet." He wrote, like Shakespeare, truly not for an age, but for all time.

The most powerful of Greek dramas is probably Sophocles' *Oedipus Rex* in which the well-known legend of the king doomed to wed his own mother, unfolds in what we may call a sculpturesque manner. As told by Sophocles, the story of Oedipus, moving, through the curse of the gods, from disaster to disaster, is one of the most gripping in all literature. The English actor, Sir Martin Harvey, in our generation, has acted this play to innumerable audiences. It is as effective in the reading as on the stage. The style of Sophocles again reminds us of Phidian sculpture. It is simple, dignified, and serene.

Euripides (480-406 B.C.) has been luckier with posterity than his fellow dramatists. No less than nineteen of his tragedies survive, the chief of which are *Alcestis, Iphigenia Among the Taurians, Iphigenia at Aulis, Medea, Hippolytus,* and *The Bacchae.* Euripides may be called the romantic, the rebel, among classic playwrights; by which we mean that he broke away from the traditional moods and treatment and introduced a modern note. He had imbibed the skepticism which was sweeping over Athenian society during the disastrous Peloponnesian

War, and being a man of the times, he saw that his own generation wanted
something rather different from the high and lofty morality characteristic of
Sophocles and Aeschylus.

People had become more introspective than they used to be and Euripides
provided them with plays in which they could recognize themselves. In other
words, he made his characters behave more like men and less like gods. He depicted more normal emotions and personages than did Sophocles and Aeschylus.
His favorite themes remind us of Shakespeare. He probed the conflict between
love and duty, between loyalty and love, as they affect an individual's character,
as they tear a spirit asunder, and send a man to his doom. Euripides thus presents
the social ideals and realistic thinking of the Sophists in terms of tragic drama.
Tradition asserts that Euripides paints men as they are, Sophocles as they should
be.

The treatment of traditional religion in Euripides is negative, skeptical, and
critical. The important problem in his drama is not whether gods exist, whether
there is a really existent object for the emotion that men call worship, but rather
what is the effect of belief and the mood of veneration on the individual spirit.
This can be seen most clearly in the *Bacchae* in which the new cult of Dionysus
is introduced into Thebes. Many and various types of humanity are brought
within the range of its influence—the professional religionist, the cynical old man
of the world, the ardent young king and statesman who fears that a new and
ecstatic cult will undermine the unity and sanity of his state; on the other hand
the women who are caught up in an ecstasy of adoration, and Agave, the mother
of the king, who is left shattered and quite mad as a result of the clash of contending forces within her. In all this the problem of Dionysus' nature and existence is a matter of only secondary importance.

Euripides is interested in the common man and draws full-length portraits
of peasants and slaves whom previous dramatists had slighted or omitted.
Euripides is at his best in portraying women—a sex which did not play a great
rôle in Athenian society—and thereby becomes the first great dramatist who
depicted the emotion of love adequately. He has the supreme ability, granted to
few male writers, of making his female characters, for instance Phaedra and
Clytemnestra, utterly real. In other words, Euripides is more of a naturalist than
either Aeschylus or Sophocles. He, as it were, humanizes the stock characters of
Greek tragedy. That is why Euripides is popular in modern times, as the success
of Gilbert Murray's English translations attest.

4. Greek Comedy

We know very little about the origin and early development of Greek comedy,
which was also cradled in religious festival, and can be traced to the wild dances
and ceremonials in honor of the god of the vine, Dionysus. (Euripides in his
Bacchae describes such a ritual.) Greek comedy, like tragedy, is musical and
choral, but its spirit is exultant, satiric, ribald, and farcical.

Greek comedy is usually divided into three stages: old comedy, which flourished
until about 400 B.C.; middle comedy, which flourished from about 400 to 336 B.C.;

and new comedy, which flourished from 336 to 250 B.C. The greatest writer of old comedy was Aristophanes (448-380 B.C.), eleven of whose pieces have survived in written form. The modern reader may be surprised at the spirit, vigor, wit, and contemporary relevance of these dramas. Aristophanes was primarily a social and political satirist and dealt with the absorbing controversial issues of his day with a quite engaging freedom.

As described elsewhere in this volume, the age of Aristophanes was a period of great crisis in the affairs of Athenians and Greece. Athenian commercial expansion and unrestrained imperial adventures had come to its logical end in violent and widespread warfare. And the ferment of ideas that had come in the train of Athenian imperialism seemed to many conservatives to be undermining every one of the old sanctities on which the Athenian society had reposed. It was to this conservative temper that Aristophanes appeals. He attacks imperialism and aggressive expansion: in the delightful fantasy of the birds he depicts an imperial colony or outpost built on the great strategic highway between earth and heaven; thereby the imperial power can levy tribute on the gods and interrupt their illicit commerce with human maidens. War he hates as the Attic countryman must have hated war, seeing year by year his crops destroyed, his homestead ravaged, and burnt. In one hilarious and broadly farcical play (*Lysistrata*), Aristophanes suggests that women have the remedy in their own hands; they can bring peace by withholding themselves from the love of men: the men would soon come to terms.

The Athenian popular leaders responsible for aggression and violent expansion Aristophanes despises as low-born blustering braggarts. In the *Knights* he brings a parade of them across the stage—a leatherseller and a hempseller, and, most ridiculous of all, a sausageseller, who sets up his trestle table in the market place (agora) and surveys the whole actual and possible dominions of Athens (twisting his head rapidly from Carthage to Caria) as a field for his illiterate and scanty talents.

The "new thought," too, Aristophanes distrusts. *The Frogs* (which we may regard as the beginnings of literary criticism) represents his views on the changes in the drama that had been introduced by Euripides. Dionysus (here represented as a potbellied, drunken, gluttonous figure of fun) sets off for the lower world to bring back a good poet. After many adventures he arrives and Aeschylus and Euripides are pitted the one against the other; the poet's preference very clearly rests with the conservative Aeschylus rather than his rival, the radical and innovator.

New and radical tendencies in thought, too, Aristophanes hates—the Sophists—materialists and Skeptics whose work (he thought) destroyed the basis of the old religion. In *The Clouds* Socrates is picked on as a representative Sophist (Socrates turned idealistic and conservative later in life) and the unhappy philosopher is pictured hanging aloft in a basket peering into the nature of the heavens and the physical universe. The comic effect must have been irresistible and later in life when Socrates was on trial for his life before the restored democracy (after a repressive interlude) he cleverly blamed the conservative Aristophanes for creating this prejudice against him.

No comic dramatist has ever displayed such a versatile control of all the devices of comic and satiric art—spirit and swiftness of movement (what the critics call "comic power"), lampoon and execration, witty abuse and subtle rapierlike thrusts, unexpected situations and unforeseen turns of events, slapstick farce, and wild burlesque, as well as a high-spirited and Gargantuan use of obscenity. As a consequence his plays still make fascinating reading and his humor shines through the quiet and euphemistic paraphrases of English country clergymen who have "translated" him.

But that is not all. Swinburne speaks of "the half divine humorist in whose incomparable genius the highest qualities of Rabelais were fused and harmonized with the supremest gifts of Shelley." Aristophanes was not only a political satirist, an incomparable master of parody, satire, and burlesque; he was also a lyric poet of superb skill endowed with a gift of exquisite expression that compares favorably with the finest lyrical passages in the entire history of literature. This is not a phase of his talent that can be adequately indicated in English: the reader may care to turn to Swinburne's attempt (inadequate as it is) to render the Grand Chorus of *The Birds* into English poetry. For this reason, and for many others, to be effective on the modern stage, Aristophanes has to be pruned and edited to fit our conception of choralless drama. The last two plays of Aristophanes, which are somewhat more shapely in plot and less stinging in satire, probably exemplify the middle comedy, about which little else is known.

The chief dramatist of the New Comedy is Menander (c. 300 B.C), whom we know mainly from the translations by Plautus and Terence. Menander is the Molière or Congreve of ancient Greece. He deals in stock characters taken from Athenian life, but is noted for his polished phrase, his sophisticated outlook. The New Comedy plays with wit instead of situation, and appeals to the intellect, as the Old Comedy appealed to the raw sense of fun. Menander's plots, though complicated, are important, since they were copied not only by Latin dramatists, but by Ariosto, Shakespeare, and Molière, and hinge on false identities, misunderstandings, misrepresentations, and the like. A good example of this kind of plot is Shakespeare's *Comedy of Errors.*

5. *Greek Historical Prose*

In the writings of Herodotus (c. 484-425 B.C.) we have the first work that can be described as history. Herodotus exhibits a remarkable blend of historical acumen and naïve, amiable, credulous garrulity. He obviously appreciated the need for effort as the first qualification of a historian. He traveled widely and enquired carefully and jotted down everything he discovered, sometimes with manifest reservations; then again his simplicity laid him open to jocular treatment as when the priests in Egypt told him that the inscriptions on the pyramids conveyed the amount of radishes and garlics and leeks that had been paid to the workmen who built them. Religions, customs and manners, governments and people, and institutions and priests—he collected an immense mass of material and set it down with an engaging frankness and a seeming absence of prejudice. The father of history is also the father of anthropology.

And so at first sight the work conveys an impression of incoherence, of gossip, of anecdotes and description all strung together. But closer examination discloses the presence of an organizing idea. Everything leads to the great clash between Greek and barbarian, the Persian Wars that had so captured the Greek imagination. To explain how this clash came about he must write a history of Greece and a history of the rise of the Persian Empire, its ruthless suppression of all rivals, its ascent to hegemony over Asia. He is forced far afield but returns to the central theme which comes to its dramatic climax in Marathon and Thermopylae and Salamis.

But the great victory of Greek over Persian is also an exemplification of the divine and essential nature of things. Herodotus' ideal was the traditional Greek ideal of measure, balance, harmony, the "golden mean." And this principle the Greeks embodied, just as the "barbarians" embodied excess—size, arrogance, and overwhelming force—the human monarch who vaunted himself against nature and the gods; who flogged the Hellespont as a revenge for wrecking his fleet, and lowered fetters and branding irons into the sea; who led his fantastic Oriental multitudes against the devoted little band of Greeks. In this conflict between the golden mean and arrogant excess, god must be on the side of the mean and the Greeks. And so justice is vindicated and Herodotus succeeds in justifying the ways of god to man.

As we pass from Herodotus to Thucydides (c. 456-396 B.C.) we move from one intellectual climate into another. The moral and supernatural idea around which Herodotus organized his work is quite lacking in Thucydides, who tried to make of history a science. Thucydides, too, quite evidently distrusted the sheer charm of his predecessor's work; he did not want readers to be coaxed from the serious business of analyzing and understanding society to the trivial and childlike occupation of listening to fairy stories. Thucydides gives an impression of painstaking research and labored investigation about the workings of society and the meaning of social law. He writes not for a time but forever in the hope that as similar problems recur he might be able to make a contribution of permanent value to their solution. He is the first writer to grapple with the central problems of historical writing, the meaning of "cause" in history, the interrelation, and relative value, of economic factors and personal factors in explaining a historical event. It has been suggested that in his attempt to get at the meaning of "cause," he took over valuable suggestions from the medical school of Hippocrates, men who in the island of Cos were striving to work out a technique of medical diagnosis and scientific medicine.

But Thucydides is more than the founder of the "science" of history: he also treats historical interpretation as an art and constructs his history like a tragic drama, the tragedy not of an individual but of a state, of a political idea; it is the tragedy (in a strict sense) of Athens and of imperialism. Just as in the drama of an individual (Aristotle thought) the hero must be a great man, a man of really heroic stature, but must have a fatal "flaw" in his character that brings him inevitably to destruction—a process that is the inevitable consequence of the flaw in his character—so it was with Athens. Athens was great and it was imperialism that had made her great. Her cultural achievements, based on the success of her imperialism, were tremendously impressive. There is no more splendid picture of the creative and cultural significance of Athens than that which Thucydides puts into the mouth of Pericles in the famous "Funeral Oration." But imperialism has a fatal flaw: an empire must expand or perish. The creative ideal of Pericles is deliberately counterpoised to the ruthless, brutal reality. The necessity for expansion means the inevitable conflict and overthrow of the imperial power. The overthrow of Athens was swift and very terrible. It is always difficult to realize the "tragedy" of a group. We are more poignantly moved by the death of friend or neighbor than by a million Chinese overwhelmed by flood or famine. Thucydides succeeds in conveying the sense of national tragedy and its inevitability. There are few things more moving than his account of Athenian downfall and overthrow.

The last of the major Greek historians was Polybius (c. 198-117 B.C.), who was perhaps as profound as Thucydides and whose standards of accuracy were equally as high. Polybius, however, while equal to Thucydides and superior to Herodotus in scholarship, did not have their literary gifts. His style is labored and diffuse, and that is why his popularity has been far less than theirs.

Polybius' *History,* in forty books, was an ambitious attempt to narrate the expansion and development of Rome down to 146 B.C. Herodotus was the historian of early Greece, Thucydides of the golden age of Athens, Polybius of Hellenic decline and the ascent of Rome.

A native Greek who spent most of his life in Rome—he was one of the literary group which surrounded the younger Scipio—Polybius was a more impartial recorder of Greek and Roman history than any other writer of antiquity. He tried, in a well-organized treatise, to explain the rise of Rome, and his sixth book is the best existing ancient analysis of Roman political and military ideals. He was a keen student of events and personalities, and his character sketches, as, for example, of Hannibal, are often masterpieces.

Polybius advanced the methodology of history even more than Thucydides. In his critique of the antiquarian Timaeus, in the twelfth book, Polybius provides us with the first great treatise on scientific history. Like Thucydides, he had a pragmatic conception of history; an accurate knowledge of the past should help to guide the present administration of the state. But he rarely allowed the teacher in him to displace the historian. He carefully considered the reliability of the sources which a historian must use, denounced partisanship, and was a relentless foe of rhetoric, which was already debauching Greek and Roman historical writing.

As Croiset observes: "It was in his work that there was defined the idea of continuity of human life, of an intimate logic of things, and of an interdependence among nations, which until then had been able to appear isolated." [31] All in all, one can agree with the late Professor G. W. Botsford that a careful reading of

31 Croiset, *Hellenic Civilization*, Knopf, 1925, p. 218.

Polybius is the best possible introduction to the spirit and method of sound historical writing.

The remaining Attic historian to be mentioned is Xenophon (b. c. 431 B.C.), the friend of Socrates, a memoir of whom he wrote in his *Memorabilia*. He composed a *Hellenica,* a sequel to Thucydides' *History,* of no great inspiration, which carried Hellenic affairs down to 362 B.C. Xenophon's famous *Anabasis,* a sort of war-correspondent's memoirs, is on a higher level. It describes the romantic retreat of the 10,000 Greek mercenaries who marched into Asia under Cyrus, the Persian prince.

In Xenophon's life of Agesilaus we have the best historical biography in Greek literature, and in his *Ways and Means* the only example among Greek historians of a thorough consideration of economic factors in politics. On the whole, we may agree with Bury that Xenophon is a journalist, a pamphleteer and war-correspondent rather than a scholarly historian, and that he owes his reputation in part to the fact that his works survived while finer writings perished..

An important incidental contribution of the Greeks was their development of historical chronology. Timaeus (c. 350 B.C.), whom Polybius criticized, introduced reckoning according to Olympiads, the four-year interval between Olympic games. Eratosthenes of Cyrene in the next century first fixed the major periods of Greek history mainly by means of astronomical calculations. The work of Eratosthenes was carried on by Apollodorus of Athens in the second century B.C., Castor of Rhodes in the first century B.C., and later by Julius Africanus, Eusebius, and St. Jerome in making Christian calculations of world history. But it was not used by the major Greek historians.

Greek prose, which developed later than Greek poetry, reached perfection in Herodotus and Thucydides. It was further amplified by the Sophists, particularly Gorgias, who popularized the ornate and antithetical—what we call the "Ciceronian"—style. The rhetoricians fashioned Greek prose into one of the most subtle and expressive verbal vehicles in history. Demosthenes (c. 383-322), the greatest of Greek orators, has probably never been equaled except by Cicero in glow of passionate language. The eloquence of his prose is continually amazing.

Demosthenes' *Philippics* were a clarion call to the Greeks, particularly the Athenians, to unite against the barbarian, Philip of Macedon, who was about to swallow Hellas in his maw. Demosthenes wields an electrical scourge, as it were, flaying dishonesty, meanness, tyranny, and political cowardice in words which still ring in our ears.

6. *The Hellenistic Age* (300 B.C.-A.D. 200)

The last or Hellenistic phase of Greek literature contains no great names. While Hellenistic art moved to new types and produced masterpieces in a novel manner, literature reached a level of mainly undistinguished mediocrity. Alexandrian or Hellenistic writers achieved important results in the less creative phases of belles-lettres. Grammar and lexicography were studied, classic writers edited and commented upon. Education and scholarship flourished.

Chief among the latter was Theocritus (third century B.C.), who created the pastoral, a series of poetic vignettes (little stories) of country life, beautiful, sincere, and somewhat oversweet. The pastorals of Theocritus have enjoyed perennial favor, and have been imitated by countless poets in the ancient and modern world, notably Vergil and Tennyson.

The First Idyll, which contains the "Lament for Daphnis," has prompted a long line of elegies. Bion of Smyrna, a contemporary of Theocritus, wrote a "Lament for Adonis," and Moschus (c. 140 B.C.) wrote a "Lament for Bion."

The last important Greek writer in antiquity was the brilliant satirist, Lucian (A.D. 120-180), a true and worthy forerunner of moderns like Rabelais and Swift. He was the Aristophanes of Greek prose. Among his best works were *Dialogues of the Gods, True History, Sales of Lives,* and *Timon.* He was probably the outstanding wit among the ancients, and was ever an enemy of pretense, pedantry and hypocrisy.

We cannot close this story of Greek literature without a few words about the famous *Anthology,* a collection of 4,100 short Greek poems on innumerable subjects, representing in their composition a period of about 1,700 years. The *Anthology* (literally *Garland*) was collected by several people, the first of whom lived in the first century B.C., the second in the first century A.D., the third in the sixth century A.D., the fourth about 950 and the fifth in the fourteenth century. Many of the poems in the *Anthology* are minor masterpieces. Nearly all have the virtues of Greek poetry at its best: directness, lucidity and technical proficiency.

XI. HELLENIC ART

If we wish to arrive at a reasonably accurate estimate of the rôle of the fine arts in the lives of the ancient Greeks, we must not begin with exaggerated notions derived from overwrought poets and essayists. Although it is tempting to think in terms of an ideal state of society in which people have enough leisure and taste to discuss arts and letters and to philosophize on the merits of various abstract ideas, we must try to think of the Greeks objectively even as we hasten to acknowledge the debt we owe them. There can be little doubt that the vocabulary of Western art and literature was, in a great measure, invented by the Greeks, but by the Greeks we mean that very limited group who constitute the poets, philosophers, and artists of any civilization. Unfortunately the more romantic modern critics have transferred the virtues of this intellectual stratum to the mass of Greek society—as great an error as to say that every member of twentieth-century society knows what mechanical processes are involved when he turns on his radio or starts his automobile.

Although the preliterate and ancient Oriental worlds have contributed significantly to Western civilization, the most far-reaching influences upon us begin with the Greeks. From the end of the Minoan-Mycenaean period (c. 1000 B.C.) to about the seventh century B.C. the mainland of Greece went through a period of slow evolution during which the religious and social customs of a newer culture were crystallized. The relatively abstract divinities of Mycenae and Tiryns gave way before the more concrete and humanized gods of the Indo-European races (from which the invading Dorians derived). Although many inhabitants of the peninsula still visited the ancient acropolises (fortified palaces) for sentimental and traditional reasons, the former dwelling place of the king came to be used as a temple for the newer gods in human form, while the structure itself retained most of its former physical characteristics.

The period of transition (archaic) from c. 700 to c. 500 B.C. offers many tangible artistic remains but these are relatively primitive. Many examples remain of a massive form of pottery (known as "Dipylon ware") which was used for funerary purposes—as one can judge by the crude designs painted on the surface. These representations of funeral games (the chariot races, etc., which are described in Homer's *Iliad*) are most awkward and casually executed; they show some of the physical proportions of earlier Mycenaean ware but none of the suavity and elegant stylization associated with the older culture.

The sculpture of the archaic period was stiff and badly proportioned, but a considerable quantity of it was sculptured in the round. (We will remember that Mycenaean, Assyrian, and Persian sculpture was predominantly carved in relief.) Archaic Greek sculptures (c. 700-c. 500 B.C.) were either funerary figures or representations of deities. The latter type resulted from the necessity of showing the gods in human shape and consequently was widespread.

That early Greek sculpture derived a great many ideas from Egypt is apparent in a comparison between the archaic *Kouros* and a typical standing Egyptian figure. Both are frontal and rigid, with the arms close to the sides and one leg slightly advanced. The figures are still blocklike because the sculptor in carving has removed relatively little from the original stone mass, and the carving of the surface shows as little detail in the archaic Greek figures as in the Egyptian. There is small attempt at portraiture, however, in the Greek work, and where the artist attempted to infuse some expression into the face, the result is a curiously insipid grin known as the "archaic smile."

The early Greek sculptor confined himself to few types: the standing nude male, the standing draped female, the seated draped female, the flying draped female (Victory), but within the space of a century and a half he made truly remarkable progress. Sculpture in quantity was scarcely found before 600 B.C. but by 475 B.C. we are able to speak of important individual artists.

Although sculpture existed among the later Greeks as an "art for art's sake" phenomenon, its early development was linked primarily with religion. "Sculpture and painting, in fact, to the Greeks, were not merely a medium of aesthetic pleasure; they were means of expressing and interpreting national life. As such they were subordinated to religion. The primary end of sculpture was to make statues of gods and heroes; the primary end of painting was to represent mythological scenes; and in either case the purely aesthetic pleasure was also a means to a religious experience." [32] We must turn, then, to the earliest Greek temples for a representative cataloging of early Greek plastic art. Not only were standards established in these buildings for sculptural decoration of all types, but architectural standards were set which became a precedent for the classical world (and for modern adaptations).

[32] Dickinson, *op. cit.*, p. 214.

Greek architecture may be divided into three periods: an archaic period from the first Olympiad (776 B.C.) to the end of the Persian Wars (479 B.C.), a central period from 479 B.C. to the time of Alexander the Great (c. 330 B.C.), and a Hellenistic period from the time of Alexander to the sack of Corinth by the Romans (146 B.C.). During the archaic period the technical vocabulary of Greek architecture was determined; the orders (moldings, ornaments, and superstructure attached to the columns), the various types of buildings, and the use to which these buildings were put.

Probably nothing in Greek artistic creation has had as much influence as the orders of architecture: the simple Doric (used for the most part on the mainland proper), the more delicate and ornamental Ionic (primarily employed in Asiatic Greece), and the later Corinthian style (raised to its greatest height by the Romans). For our purposes it is sufficient to observe that these orders were religiously adhered to by the Greeks, and were transmitted to the Romans who added very few types to this relatively small collection. This material was revived during the fifteenth century in western Europe when handbooks on architecture preserved it and made it a permanent part of modern architectural practice.

Today, the most complete collection of Greek buildings may be seen in the so-called sanctuary cities of Olympia, Delos, or Delphi, where the various Greek city-states gathered periodically to celebrate the rites of the regional deity. The most famous of these sanctuary cities was Olympia, where the great Olympian or Olympic games were held at four-year intervals, an event that we have revived in our own day.

Each city represented at the festival had its individual headquarters with accommodations for its athletes and for its funds. The latter, treasuries, were small versions of the larger temple architecture. The athletic events themselves were held in a stadium shaped like a hairpin, open at one end to enable the sprinters to run beyond the finish line. Along the rim of the stadium, ascending tiers of seats accommodated the spectators. Down the center were placed a row of commemorative stone slabs (stelae) erected in honor of previous contest winners. (Not only were stelae dedicated to the hero but prizes were given him and upon his return home we are told that men carried him into the city through a breach made in the wall for that purpose.)

In addition to treasury buildings and stadia the sanctuary cities contained theaters where performances were given during the festival. The Greek theater was usually built against the side of a hill that served as a support. The theater was semicircular in shape, and like the stadium, edged with ascending tiers of stone seats for the spectators. Its straight side was closed by an elaborate backdrop of permanent stone scenery known as the *skene* (our word "scene"). The drama was acted on a stage in front of this stone backdrop. Directly below the stage, in the orchestra pit, moved the opposing sections of the chorus whose function was to comment poetically upon the action and to foretell what would follow.

The most important building in the sanctuary enclosure was the temple, a large rectangular building surrounded by columns spaced at equal intervals and capped by a gabled roof. Greece was unusually fortunate in its building materials, for a plenitude of fine marble was available which gives Greek architecture its amazing color, even today. If we think of these Greek buildings as heaps of sad ruins, we would be pleasantly surprised by a visit to the ancient cities, for time has lent them a handsome gloss or patina which reflects the sun brilliantly against the Mediterranean blue sky.

The low triangular section under the gable of the roof is known as a pediment and was planned with the intention of filling it with sculpture in the round. This involved careful composition of the sculpture group so that the figures would taper gracefully to fit the low angles of this wide triangle. These figures

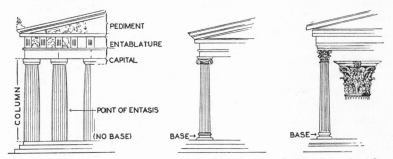

The orders of Greek architecture: Doric (*left*), Ionic (*center*), Corinthian (*right*).

were colored, as was most Greek sculpture, to make them stand out from the relative darkness of their background. The background was painted a contrasting color.

The series of decorative horizontal elements, arranged successively below the pediment and leading to the columns, is known as the entablature. This section varies in the character and arrangement of its component parts from the Doric style (Zeus at Olympia or Parthenon at Athens) to the Ionic style (Nike Temple, Acropolis at Athens) and the Corinthian style (Monument of Lysicrates, Athens). Differences among the three orders become most striking in the columns themselves. In the Doric, a severely fluted (channeled) column was set directly on a base, and the capital consisted of a very simple convex shape that was separated from the entablature (superstructure) by a simple flat block. The Ionic column, much slenderer in its proportions, stood upon an elaborately molded base, and its capital consisted of a series of moldings which were climaxed by a pair of spirally curved cushions known as volutes. In the Corinthian order we find the base and column were very similar to the Ionic. The main difference lay in the more elaborate Corinthian capital which consisted of a double row of acanthus leaves accented by a thin volute at each corner. This order was not extensively used by the Greeks but found its full development in later Roman architecture where its florid possibilities were fully realized.

In plan, the typical Greek temple consisted of a series of upright walls within a rectangular columnar arrangement. The structure was divided into three separate parts, a shallow portico, a long sanctuary chamber in which the image of the god was placed, and a smaller section used as a robing room for the priests and as a depository for treasure and sacrificial vessels. The Greek temple had no windows, the only light admitted coming in through the open doorway. Let us remember that these buildings, like the Egyptian temples, were not used by the populace. In Greece this was not the result of a privileged social scheme as in Egypt. The people did not use the temples because their religious ceremonies were usually conducted out-of-doors, and only the priest entered the sanctuary where the statue of the god was kept.

Let us return to our discussion of sculpture. The end of the archaic period is exemplified in such figures as the group called *Harmodius and Aristogeiton,* sometimes known as *The Tyrannicides.* By this time the sculptor has managed to free the limbs of the tyrant killers to the extent of showing wide spaces between the legs as well as between the arms and the body. While the absolute rigidity of such earlier works as the *Archaic Apollo* is considerably improved upon in this work, there still remain the stolid expression in the faces, badly proportioned heads, and a weakly defined anatomy.

The sculptures in the pediments of the Temple of Zeus at Olympia, showing the famous combat between the *Centaurs and the Lapiths* and the story of *Pelops and Hippodomia,* mark the final stage in the development of temple group sculpture before the golden age (the middle of the fifth century B.C.). Not only is there more animation in the representation of these interesting stories, but the anatomical knowledge has considerably improved. In the story of the *Centaurs and the Lapiths,* that presumably exciting attack of the centaurs upon the brides of the lapiths, the centaurs are permitted great latitude in unrestrained emotions, but the young women retain an admirable if slightly disconcerting calm in the face of what is happening to them.

By the beginning of the fifth century B.C. individual artistic personalities such as Myron and Polycletus begin to emerge. The work of Myron is particularly interesting for the lesson it teaches about the possibilities of bronze as a medium for sculpture. Myron was very much interested in the representation of the nude male athlete, such as his celebrated *Discus Thrower* (Discobolos). Here was no simple, relaxed athlete such as the archaic sculptors of the sixth century had produced. It was a design conceived and executed at the moment of greatest physical strain. It is dangerous to carve an active representation like this in such a relatively brittle material as marble, for the contorted position assumed by the figure makes the composition top-heavy and increases the danger of the body's snapping off at the ankles or elsewhere. In bronze, however, the artist works with a hollow medium, where he can pour more weight into the legs and leave the top of the figure relatively light—consequently much safer and more permanent.

Polycletus must be remembered for his complete knowledge of the human figure, crystallized in such a work as the *Lance Bearer,* an epitome of the youthful athletic type, so perfect in its proportions that it was known in antiquity as the canon by which all other male figures were measured. The quiet bearing of the young athlete as he leans forward with the lance on his shoulder has become typical for us of the ideal Greek sense of equilibrium, a balance that is both mental and physical.

By the end of the Persian Wars (479 B.C.) a combination of circumstances brought Athens into the most prominent political and intellectual position in the Greek world. Under the leadership of Pericles, her great statesman, the arts and sciences were encouraged to such high achievement that the period of his influence (about forty years) has always been called the golden age of Greece. He formed advantageous alliances, fostered trade, and drew a great many artists to Athens through his avowed policy of beautifying and replacing buildings which had been partly destroyed during the wars. Some of the greatest minds in the Greek world were drawn to the city of opportunity, hence this period takes on a broader significance than might be implied if merely Athenian. It would not be an exaggeration to say that the activity in literature, art and science which flourished during the major part of the fifth century B.C. in Athens was, for the most part, due to Pericles. As an ancient historian expressed it, "Athens wore his face for a time, as one wears a mask, and then wished to put it aside."

Artistic activity during Pericles' administration was focused upon the ancient Acropolis of Athens and involved the rebuilding of the old temple and the construction of various new buildings as well. The approach to the Acropolis hill was dominated by an imposing, ceremonial gateway which, in form, resembled an ordinary temple building. At the side of this entranceway there was placed a small temple built in honor of the victorious Athena (Athena Nike) in the delicate Ionic style, noteworthy for the beautiful bas-reliefs on its balustrade. The most famous of the sculptures found on this tiny building is the figure of *Victory Tying Her Sandal* which shows a delicately carved feminine form clad in amazingly transparent draperies gracefully bending forward as she raises one foot.

Along the sacred way of the Acropolis enclosure the spectator encountered the *Erectheum,* built on the site of the old temple which had been destroyed by the Persians. It was dedicated to the legendary ancient king of Athens, Erectheus, as well as to Athena and Cecrops. Though the Erectheum was, to be sure, a somewhat irregularly planned building, it was undoubtedly one of the most charming pieces of Greek architecture, particularly for its famous *Porch of the Maidens.* This section, dedicated to Pandragea, the daughter of Cecrops, possesses a characteristically Ionic arrangement of columns in the form of human figures, in this case beautifully proportioned maidens. These columns are known as caryatids and are one of the most interesting Greek architectural inventions. They combine stability with movement; the young women stand with one leg rigid and the other relaxed, the whole conveying an actual sense of support as the entablature of the porch rests upon their heads.

In contrast to the delicacy of the Erectheum stands a building called the *Parthenon* (Temple of Athena Parthenos—the Virgin Athena), one of the artistic marvels of the ancient world. This celebrated edifice was constructed under the direction of Phidias, the most famous of the Greek artists. He was not satisfied with supervising the construction and embellishment of the Parthenon, but he himself created the most important thing in it, the gigantic ivory and gold figure of the goddess Athena. The statue has survived only in small copies, although the original was supposed to have been forty feet high. For the general plan of the building, we are indebted to two imported architects, Ictinus and Callicrates, who designed it in the Doric style with eight columns front and rear and seventeen down each side. The building was completed during the years 448-437 B.C. and represents the finest achievement in architecture of the ancient world.

Looking at the sad ruins of the Parthenon today, it is difficult for the average person to understand the fervid enthusiasm of the ancient writers, among them Pausanius and Plutarch. But if we could roll into one the perfections of all other temples and if we could add to this a series of subtle optical adjustments such as architecture has never shown elsewhere, we should only begin to approximate the exquisite proportions of the Parthenon, the delicate balance of line and mass.

In line the Greek temple represents a series of transitions from the verticals of the columns to the horizontals of the entablatures. The Parthenon architects noticed that horizontal lines with vertical accents coming down upon them tended to appear bent downward. They hastened to compensate for this optical illusion. They adjusted the line of the base upon which the columns rested, so that it curved slightly upward, and the downward thrust of the columns made it appear perfectly straight. Similarly, if the column was made with perfectly vertical sides, it nevertheless had the appearance of caving in at the center. In order to compensate for this optical illusion, the architect gave the column an outward swelling at the center (called *entasis*).

In addition to the gigantic figure of Athena, the Parthenon was decorated with a wealth of sculptural detail, both inside and outside. The sculptures on the pediments portray at one end the *Birth of Athena,* full-grown from the head of Zeus, and on the other the conflict between *Athena and Poseidon* for the privilege of protecting Athens. These compositions, like most of the pediments of Greece, have been reconstructed from the pitifully few fragments that remain of their original splendor. Enough survives, however, to give us a very clear idea of their superhuman beauty and strength.

We must remember that the gods of ancient Greece were great heroes in the form of human beings. The sculptors' aim "was not merely to reproduce but to transcend nature. For their subject was gods and heroes, and heroes and gods were superior to men." [33] Such a sculpture as *Theseus,* a reclining figure of a young male god, is a miracle of quiet strength. Larger than life-size, he is a gentle giant belonging to a superhuman race. The famous figure of *Adam* by Michelangelo (Sistine Chapel, Rome) is the only other artistic creation that compares in monumental strength with this piece of marble. The female figures, as was customary in Greek sculpture of the classical period (through the fifth century B.C.), were draped, but in such a way that they revealed the Amazonian beauty of their bodies. There is nothing involved about either the poses or the modeling

[33] Dickinson, *op. cit.,* p. 217.

of these works, yet with their extreme simplicity they achieved a majesty that is one of the glories of all time.

Under the porticoes of the Parthenon, we find one of the most famous friezes of bas-relief in the world, the *Panathenaic Procession*. This was a representation of an annual ceremony during which a new robe was brought for the goddess and in which all of the citizens of Athens are shown participating. Here was a radical departure in Greek sculpture, for this work was the first in which everyday material was permitted to grace so important a monument. The frieze is over five hundred feet long and, when one considers the tremendous number of figures involved, the artist or artists have admirably succeeded in achieving a high degree of variety. No figure or pose is repeated among the hundreds of young, middle-aged and old men and women. Some walk, others ride horses and still others are seen leading cattle. All move toward the east side of the building where the priest is shown receiving the robe. Above this eastern doorway (the entrance to the temple) the frieze breaks and we are carried to a section above it where the gods are shown on Olympus looking down on the scene as it occurs. How many of these sculptures Phidias was responsible for personally is difficult to say, but it is certain that he supervised the entire production. If the Parthenon is the homogeneous and harmonious whole that criticism acknowledges, it is undoubtedly because one individual was responsible for the entire direction.

Lest we be carried away by our enthusiasm for these unquestionably beautiful things and be led to imagine a paradise on earth that was ancient Athens, it must be observed that even before the sculptures on the Parthenon were finished, Phidias was imprisoned, charged with appropriating some of the gold for the statue of Athena for his own purposes. This was the climax of a process of opposition to Pericles. It might well be taken as an indication that the fundamentally conservative mind of the Athenians was not as much interested in the idea of making Athens the most beautiful city in Greece as was Pericles and his small group of intellectuals, most of whom had been imported from outside cities. The city that attempted to force Pericles to abandon his wife because she was a Greek from Asia Minor (and not an Athenian), that imprisoned its most famous artist and that finally forced Socrates to drink the hemlock may not be the ideal state we would perhaps like to think it, but it is well to remember these things if we wish to achieve a complete picture of Athens. This is, in no sense, a condemnation, just as we do not necessarily condemn nineteenth-century French society because it did not treat its artists well. Such behavior is common in a highly developed commercial society and it must be remembered that the great period of Athenian art and culture was made possible only by prosperity.

The political stability which had formed the background of the golden age came to an end in 431 B.C. with the beginning of the disastrous civil war between Athens and Sparta. In 429 B.C. Pericles, who had recently been removed from his position and fined as the result of an unsuccessful campaign, died of the plague. The following year Plato was born and it is to his philosophy that we may turn for a complete comprehension of the troubled times in which he lived.

In the same way that Plato responds to the disturbed state of society with such a book as his ideal *Republic,* the art of the fourth century B.C. presents an emotional character far removed from the serenity of the golden age. Instead of the Olympian objectivity of the Parthenon pediment figures we encounter the sentimental art of Praxiteles, the turbulent emotionality of Scopas, and the nervous elegance of Lysippus. These are the three great sculptors of the fourth century. In their art we find a reaction against the relatively severe style of Phidias toward a taste for grace and delicacy. New qualities in sculpture supplanted the idealized virility and Amazonian robustness of Phidias' men and women.

With Praxiteles, we move from the ideally conventionalized schools of art toward an extremely individualized form of expression. This was not only the result of Praxiteles' personal idiom, but was largely caused by economic supply and demand. There was no longer a demand for heroic religious sculpture because there was no longer available the wealth of the previous period. Elaborate public works such as the Acropolis buildings were abandoned for private commissions such as tombs and other commemorative monuments of simple character. The most famous of Praxiteles' sculptures are the *Hermes and Dionysus* and the *Cnidian Venus.* In the former, the sculptor has shown the youthful messenger of the gods resting in the course of carrying the infant Dionysus or Bacchus. The left hand supports the child while the right holds up a bunch of grapes toward which the infant reaches, but this apparent playfulness is mitigated by the dreamy expression of the handsome youth which brings to mind later Madonnas who absent-mindedly toy with the children they hold. The *Hermes,* like all of the sculptures of Praxiteles, has a creamy white surface quality that is extremely sensuous, and conveys a quality of indolence in the negligent posture which forms the body into an "S" curve. The hip is thrown out slightly as the weight rests on one foot. Here, the athletic bearing of a nude like the *Lance Bearer* of Polycletus is supplanted by the quiet introspective and relaxed position of the *Hermes.* It is interesting that this sculpture is one of the few figures from the art of ancient Greece that we are sure has come down in its original state and not in the usual form of a later Roman copy. What is even more startling is the fact that this is the only piece of sculpture that we can, with relative certainty, attach to the name of a specific ancient artist. But even this has recently been questioned.

The *Cnidian Aphrodite* (done for the Island of Cnidos) was the prototype for many Venuses during the fourth and later centuries. Here, for the first time, the artist ventured to unclothe a feminine figure. Its kinship with the *Hermes* is evident, both in the pose and surface texture as well as in the thoughtful mien associated with the work of Praxiteles. The ancient writer Pliny tells us that not only was this the finest work of Praxiteles, but of the entire world as well.

The second of the famous sculptors of the fourth century was Scopas in whose extant production we are not so fortunate, since most of it has disappeared and we are forced to have recourse to second or third-hand copies, or to fragments ascribed to him. Certain it is that his style was the most emotional produced during this period and that its tragic intensity, seen in such a work as the *Maenad,* was the inspiration for many later sculptures such as the mournful *Niobe and Her Daughter,* etc. The ecstatic madness of the *Maenad* as she holds up the kid to be sacrificed to Pan is the most extreme manifestation of Scopas' characteristic qualities. Scopas apparently was one of the last important sculptors to decorate a temple pediment. We learn from Pausanius that the Temple of Athena Alea near Tegea was ornamented by him. Fragments found on this site consist of heads with painful expressions and bulging eyes which affirm the work of Scopas.

The change in the sphere of activity in art from the fifth to the fourth century is indicated by a work with which Scopas was associated, the famous *Mausoleum of Halicarnassus,* a memorial built by Queen Artemisia for her husband Mausolus (whence the name) and decorated with a series of figures expressing quiet but intense sorrow. Tomb sculpture in general became very important during the fourth century. We have evidence in a series of beautiful headstones very much like ours in shape, decorated with quiet representations of the departed. The dead are shown as they perform some simple act in life, such as a woman dressing and putting on her jewels, etc., of which the *Stele of Hegeso* is the most famous example.

The last member of the group was Lysippus, the official portraitist of Alexander the Great, who brings us to the end of the fourth century. Lysippus is known for a refined naturalism that never became gross no matter what subject he treated. He is also important as the first Greek artist to attempt to bring out the personality of individuals in portraits such as *Alexander the Great,* whom he always showed as a beardless young man. His most famous statue is known as the *Scraper* and shows a youthful athlete scraping the mixture of oil and dirt from his body after he has come from the stadium. Although related to the tradition of Polycletus' *Lance Bearer,* this work is typical of Lysippus in the greater expressiveness of the face, in the more lithe and nervous quality of the body, and in the changed proportions of the figure. The other notable work ascribed to Lysippus is his statue of Agias, a masterpiece of poised alertness.

An account of Greek art in the fifth and fourth centuries would be woefully incomplete without some mention of Greek pottery. Words cannot convey the perfection of the many styles. Like the architecture, the pottery was a beautiful combination of utility and exquisite shape. Keats' famed *Ode on a Grecian Urn* vividly brings to mind what these forms have meant to generations of art lovers.

It is to the pottery of ancient Greece that we must turn for the only extant idea of what their painting was like, for most other evidences have disappeared. We learn of fine and precise drawing, economical in the number of lines used and tight in its outlines. The ingenious way in which the patterns were made to fit the variable shapes of the pottery is parallel with the taste displayed in the composition of the sculptures of the period. Judging from the accounts of contemporary writers, painting was as important in Greece as sculpture, to which painting was related. The temples, for example, always had some painting on them, either in the niches of the metopes or in the backgrounds of the pediments. Apart from this simple use, however, murals were painted in newly invented techniques, some of which are still in use today; mosaic, fresco, tempera, encaustic, etc. Although we know the names of the celebrated painters of Greece: Polygnotus, Apelles, Zeuxis, etc., it would be fruitless to go into details here about works that have perished. From what we are able to gather, the painting of Greece was often a figure art executed in a sculpturesque manner which will reappear in Roman painting. But it was not limited to this form.

We might mention, at this point, the Greek facility for making coins—miniature bas-reliefs. Everything to which the Greeks turned their attention became fine in its production, and their minor arts such as pottery and coinmaking are just as significant aesthetically as their sculpture and architecture. Pottery and coins have been found far from their place of origin. Most Greek pottery in existence today was found in the Etruscan tombs in Italy, an indication that it was an important item of export. Greek coins have been found along the coast of Spain, France, Italy, even as far as the shores of the Black Sea, which shows the tremendous trade radius of the Greeks and their colonial expansion in many parts of Europe, as Marseilles (Massilia), Tarragona (Tarraconensis), etc. Artistically the coins of ancient Greece are fine examples of the sculptor's art and are composed with truly monumental conception. Furthermore, a good deal of our information concerning Greek statues which have disappeared (although written about in ancient times) is derived from the representations found on coins, for an important statue became the symbol of the city in which it was kept. For example, the *Cnidian Venus* of Praxiteles is found on the coins of the city of Cnidos.

The period of internationalism ushered in by the world-wide conquests of Alexander the Great marked a new epoch in the spread of cultural ideas. No longer was the leading culture that of a small city-state or even a nation. The conquest of Greece by this young man from Macedonia naturally placed Athens in a weaker position as a cultural center. Interest was shifted to Alexandria in Egypt, Pergamum, and Rhodes. The Greek spirit was spread to many parts of the Asiatic world where it had previously been unknown. Culture followed the flag and Alexandria (founded by the "young god") became a new and more magnificent Athens, more luxurious in its habits and much more important as a point of distribution for ideas, even though some of these were not its own. In the Near East proper, Greek ideas were spread through Parthia and Persia with repercussions felt as far as the Indus River.

After the death of Alexander in Babylon (323 B.C.) his gigantic empire fell apart, and although for some time it was divided by his generals into three large sections, various small independent principalities formed themselves, such as Pergamum and Rhodes which became important cultural centers together with Ephesus and Alexandria. The average Hellenistic city (note difference between the term "Hellenic"—i.e., classical Greek, and "Hellenistic—i.e., later Greek) was much more carefully planned than the earlier Greek cities, for it frequently was laid out in a systematic manner which foreshadowed modern town planning; at Priene, for example, we find a covered passageway or portico along the sides of the main square which enabled citizens to cross that space without exposing themselves to the sun. Most of the cities of the time enjoyed this convenience. In certain instances the portico was elaborated into two stories. In this form it was known as a *basilica* (place of contracts) and became the focal point of the town's civic and commercial affairs. In addition to the basilica, the public square usually contained a municipal library (learning was much more widespread during the Hellenistic period than ever before) and a *gymnasium* (secondary school). Most cities at this time also possessed large theaters, entirely out of proportion to the size of their population and more a matter of pride and competition than anything else. The temples of the period usually conformed with the Hellenic tradition.

The character of religion, however, changed considerably from the regional view prevalent in classical times (Athena for Athens, Zeus for Olympia, etc.) to one that was more pantheistic in character, with the entire notion of godhood compressed into one figure or idea. To this end, gigantic altars were built at Pergamum, Magnesia, Syracuse, etc.

Pergamum is the only large center of which we have exact information, although it was, itself, only the chief city of a small state in Asia. Under the wise administration of its art-loving rulers, it produced one of the most important schools of sculpture in the Hellenistic period. Such figures as *Gaul Slaying Himself and His Wife* or the *Dying Gaul* (Byron's *Dying Gladiator*) are examples of the human pathos with which the artists of Pergamum could invest their sculptures. It is at this center that the most famous of the Hellenistic altars was built, the *Altar of Zeus and Athena*, constructed in honor of the victory of the Pergamines over the invading Gauls. This monument is important for the elaborate frieze that decorates its base for a distance of four hundred and thirty feet, comparable to the great Panathenaic frieze of the Parthenon. A comparison between the two shows the distance we have traveled from the quiet dignity and serenity of the fifth-century work to the restlessness and emotional agitation of the Hellenistic frieze. This composition, known as *The Battle of the Gods and Giants*, symbolizes the conflict just completed between the Pergamines and their enemies. Not only is the tumult of the struggling adversaries extremely impassioned but the muscles are swollen and strained to match the emotion on the faces.

The adjacent school at Rhodes is distinguished for a work that is very similar in feeling, the celebrated *Laocoön* in which the dramatic quality typical of the Pergamine frieze reaches new heights. Here three figures, an old man and his two young sons, are shown being crushed to death by serpents. It was the artist's problem, therefore, to show not only the physical agony of death but the mental anguish with which the doomed and afflicted Trojan priest sees his sons about to die. This work is very important because, rediscovered in the early part of the sixteenth century, it exerted considerable influence upon the incipiently baroque and exaggerated style of many artists including Michelangelo.

In Alexandria we have one of the most important cities of antiquity. Unfortunately for clear definitions and classifications it was a melting pot of all the current influences of the time. One can observe well-defined erotic tendencies, for example, in the Venuses produced here, for the figures tended to become increasingly plump and physically attractive. Alexandria, moreover, was important for creating a type of allegorical figure such as the *River Nile* which became a model for the Hellenistic world as well as for later Roman art. Although the allegory is not a very high form of intellectual expression, it has great interest from the narrative point of view. The *River Nile* is a huge masculine bearded figure (of the Neptune type) outstretched with sixteen children sporting about him, representing the number of cubits the river rose and fell each season. Religious representations here became different from those of the past. Either they were such curious combinations as the typical Jupiter-Serapis figure (mixture of two early Egyptian gods, Osiris and Apis, to whom the characteristics of the great Zeus have been added) or they took on such abstract religious form as the *Praying Youth* who symbolizes the worship of a Supreme Being. Both these types of sculpture were an expression of the broader scope, the pantheistic implications in Hellenistic religion.

Alexandrian art also produced a series of figures that may best be classified as "idyllic": *Two Children Kissing* or *Child Struggling with Goose*. This was undoubtedly part of a naturalistic development that expressed itself in a preference for everyday subject matter. One of the results was a new school of portraiture which carried further the earlier simple ideals of Lysippus. Take, for example, the figures of *Demosthenes* or *Sophocles* where the artist attempted to indicate the true personality of these historical characters. Another indication of this taste for naturalism was a preference for ugly subject matter, sometimes taken directly from the teeming streets of the capital: *Drunken Woman, The Old Market Woman,* etc., as well as urchins and street singers of all sorts.

Of particular importance for the later development of art was the Hellenistic tendency toward exaggerated elegance, symbolized by such a figure as the famous *Apollo Belvedere* whose postures and lines will be revived during the seventeenth century in Italy and elsewhere.

One of the most charming manifestations of the early Hellenistic period is the group of terra-cotta figurines from Tanagra (Asia Minor). These show everyday subjects such as women conversing or doing up their hair in attitudes which are lifelike and attractive. These Tanagra figurines in the smallness of their size, lovely surface coloring and charming mood, were very likely manufactured for home use, much as are our modern book ends or fine ash trays. They tell us more of the spirit of Hellenistic art than any elaborate piece of sculpture might.

As a transition between the classical Greek world and the Roman world, the Hellenistic period fulfilled its destiny. Many of the ideas the Romans will use were already begun at this time. The merger was very gradual and in many cases almost imperceptible.

XII. GREEK MUSIC

Unlike architecture and sculpture, the music of Greece was not a native creation, but was imported for the most part from Asia Minor. The Greeks took crude tonal materials and fashioned them into a musical art which, like the other Greek arts, has made its influence felt through the ages. Our music, like our literature, art, and science, traces its ancestry back to ancient Greece.

The word "music," although of Greek origin, has a more circumscribed meaning for us today than it had for the Greeks. For them music was more than an independent art with its own aesthetic values. It was the inseparable counterpart of poetry, drama, and dancing, and thus of tremendous cultural significance. Music accompanied every drama. The oracles gave forth their utterances to an accompaniment of musical strains. Competitive singing and playing were major parts of the festival contests. Every cultured Greek was expected to be able to pick up the *kithara* (a precursor of the harp) at a banquet and accompany himself extemporaneously while he sang. Men, women, and children all participated in large choral singing groups which acted as narrators at dramatic performances and public celebrations.

Because music was thus bound up with emotion-stirring arts and occasions, the Greeks regarded it as having more a physiological-moral than an aesthetic significance. Music was supposed to produce definite physical effects on the listener, which made him in turn brave, sorrowful, masterful, elated, depressed, or gentle.

Significant of the musical scene in Greece was the fact that everybody whether of high or low degree participated in the actual music-making. This contrasted with the later custom of Oriental countries where music-making was entrusted to professional singers and players—to employees of the temples, wandering street musicians, hired court orchestras, and, in the home, to slaves. To be sure there were also professional performers in Greece; but young men of the cultured classes were expected to achieve in the course of their education some proficiency in playing not only the *kithara*, but also the wind instrument of the day—the *aulos*. Children learned the old hymns and paeans, and later the newer tunes for use at social gatherings.

Greek music was predominantly single-line music, that is, it consisted of unaccompanied melody. (A melody consists of a meaningful succession of tones.) Harmony, the combination of tones, was practically unknown to the Greeks. The tone system which the Greek theoreticians evolved was based on groups of four tones called tetrachords. The tetrachords in turn could be joined to produce larger series; two tetrachords, for example, produced an octave—a scale of eight tones. These octave scales, which eventually became the most important of the tetrachord groupings, unlike our modern scales, were conceived as a descending series and included intervals smaller than those nominally in use today, for example, quarter tones. Known as "modes," the octave scales were named after groups of cities in western Asia Minor—Dorian, Phrygian, Lydian, Aeolian.

Actual specimens of Greek music and Greek musical notation are extremely rare today. For the modern scholar only a few inscriptions on stone, some fragmentary scraps of notation on papyri, and a few manuscripts remain. Our knowledge of the nature and significance of Greek music derives chiefly from the writings of various theorists and philosophers of the time. The earliest studies in acoustics and the mathematical aspects of tone relationships have been attributed to Pythagoras. Plato and Aristotle made occasional references to music in connection with its moral influence and its place in the educational scheme. But of all the numerous Greek writers on music, the most outstanding was the philosopher Aristoxenus, a pupil of Aristotle.

While Greek music perished with Greek civilization, the Greek theories of the art were of incalculable influence on the music of the Middle Ages. The tone system of the Greeks was transmitted to western Europe by the treatises of two sixth-century Roman scholars, Cassiodorus and Boëthius. The *De musica* of Boëthius retained its preëminence as a source of information for medieval musicians for over a thousand years.

XIII. THE DEBT OF WESTERN CIVILIZATION TO HELLENIC CULTURE

To begin with, it is necessary to remember that when we use the term "Greeks" or "Hellenes" in relation to civilization, we mean chiefly the people of Ionia, Doris, Aeolis, Athens, some Greek colonies in the Mediterranean, and the more important cultural centers of Hellenistic times. The majority of the Greek city-states made no more contribution to the progress of civilization than the Hottentots.

The outstanding cultural contributions of Greece were of an intellectual or emotional cast. In material things, few significant advances can be attributed to them. In this respect the Orientals and the Romans were superior to them. Progress in applied science came only in the Hellenistic era, which was far more Oriental than Hellenic.

If the Greeks added little to culture materially, intellectually they reached a height which few other races have ever approached. They were the first to emancipate man in any degree from the supernaturalism and intolerance of the Orient. They challenged the traditional superstitions which were inherited from pre-literary ages, and flung out bold hypotheses about the origins of the universe and the facts of nature. Free thought, intellectual tolerance, and urbanity were the great gifts of the Greeks to the Western World.

Their spirit of free inquiry explains their scientific achievements, although these were mainly in the realm of mathematical and speculative science. There was no general inclination to carry on that long and patient examination of commonplace things on which experimental science depends. Yet they made many contributions in astronomy, mechanics, and biology; contributions which, for the most part, were not improved upon until the seventeenth century.

Acute insight and clever observation, however, were mingled with curious fancies, as exemplified by Aristotle's physiology and Hippocrates' four humors. The Greeks had little enthusiasm for technology and were more at home disputing in the market-place than in the laboratory.

In philosophy, to use a slang phrase, they set the world on fire. They created systematic philosophy, metaphysics, and formal logic. In fact, in abstract thought, the Greeks were about as far advanced as we are today. Their political thought also was notable, although their political institutions were a failure in the end. In economics, Plato and Aristotle made important beginnings.

With the Greeks formal education made its first appearance both as an intellectual discipline and as a social institution. Before the Hellenic age, education had been a group or family matter, and its content was mainly the transmission of customs and traditions. The Greeks broadened the "curriculum" until it embodied the acquisition of new information in the form of science and philosophy, systematically taught. The chief defect in this educational system was a love of rhetoric, thus encouraging carelessness in observation and in logic.

We hardly need to mention the Greek legacy in plastic art. Literature, both prose and poetry, reached heights of excellence which have rarely been equaled or surpassed. Systematic historical writing was their creation.

But, all things considered, the greatest of their legacies is the Hellenic theory of life, embodying not only a fervent devotion to the principles of truth and beauty, but a secularization of the human mind, which made the basis of conduct a mundane instead of a supernatural matter. This manifested itself in a rationalism the like of which has only occasionally been seen in the Western World. So important was their philosophy of life that some authorities regard Greek aesthetics as one of the two major advances since man reached civilization. The other is the industrial revolution since 1750. The one created the spiritual, the other the physical mold of civilization.

The major weakness of Hellenic culture was its failure to develop a technology and an economic system equal to its intellectual and political attainments. In other words, the material foundations of Greek life were inadequate.

If the Greeks could have developed a stable and less militaristic political organization, a machine age, and a richer economic life, they would have solved nearly all human problems. The Greek challenge to the modern world is contained in the fact that a rich cultural life is possible in a rather backward and impoverished economic era. We now have superabundant material wealth, but culturally we are inferior to the Greeks. Looking at the matter in a broad way, we may say that Greek civilization perished because Greek culture and social institutions outdistanced Hellenic science and machinery. In our day, civilization is endangered because we have pushed our science and machinery far beyond our institutional development.

SELECTED READINGS

Anderson, W. J., and Spiers, R. P., *The Architecture of Greece and Rome* (revised by Dinsmoor and Ashby), 2 Vols., Scribner, 1927, Vol. I.

Antcliffe, Herbert, "Music in the Life of the Ancient Greeks," *Musical Quarterly*, April, 1930.

Bakewell, C. M., *Source Book in Ancient Philosophy*, Scribner, 1939.

Becker and Barnes, *Social Thought from Lore to Science*, Vol. I, chaps. iv-v.

Benn, A. W., *Ancient Philosophy*, Putnam, 1912.

Bonnard, André, *Greek Civilization*, Macmillan, 1959.

Botsford, G. W., and Sihler, E. G., eds., *Hellenic Civilization*, Columbia University Press, 1915.

Bury, J. B., *The Ancient Greek Historians*, Dover, 1958.

Clagett, Marshall, *Greek Science in Antiquity*, Abelard-Schuman, 1956.

Croiset, Maurice, *Abridged History of Greek Literature*, Macmillan, 1904.

—— *Hellenic Civilization*, Knopf, 1925.

Cushman, H. E., *Beginner's History of Philosophy*, 2 Vols., Houghton Mifflin, 1918-1920, Vol. I, chaps. i-xiii.
De Ridder, A. H. P., and Deonna, Waldermar, *Art in Greece*, Knopf, 1927.
Dickinson, G. L., *The Greek View of Life*, Ann Arbor Books, 1958.
Durant, Will, *The Life of Greece*, Simon and Schuster, 1939.
Eby and Arrowood, *The History and Philosophy of Education*, chaps. iv-x.
Gardner, E. A., *The Art of Greece*, Studio, 1925.
Gardner, Percy, *The Principles of Greek Art*, Macmillan, 1914.
Garrison, *Introduction to the History of Medicine*, chap. iv.
Gomperz, Theodor, *Greek Thinkers*, 4 Vols., Humanities Press.
Goodell, T. D., *Greek Tragedy*, Yale University Press, 1920.
Greene, W. C., *The Achievement of Greece*, Harvard University Press, 1923.
Gulick, C. B., *The Life of the Ancient Greeks*, Appleton, 1902.
Hadas, Moses, *Hellenistic Culture*, Columbia University Press, 1959.
Hamilton, Edith, *The Echo of Greece*, Norton, 1957.
―――― *The Greek Way*, Norton, 1942.
Hammerton, *Universal History of the World*, Vols. II-III.
Harrison, J. E., *Prolegomena to the Study of Greek Religion*, Meridian.
Licht, Hans, *Sexual Life in Ancient Greece*, Dutton, 1934.
Livingstone, R. W., ed., *The Legacy of Greece*, Oxford Press, 1921.
Murray, Gilbert, *Five Stages of Greek Religion*, Anchor Books, 1955.
Nilsson, M. P., ed., *Greek Folk Religion*, Harper Torchbooks, 1961.
Oates, W. J., ed., *The Stoic and Epicurean Philosophers*, Random House, 1940.
Powers, H. H., *The Message of Greek Art*, Macmillan, 1925.
Prentice, W. K., *The Ancient Greeks*, Princeton University Press, 1940.
Randall, J. H., *Aristotle*, Columbia University Press, 1959.
Reymond, Arnold, *History of the Sciences in Greco-Roman Antiquity*, Dutton, 1927.
Robin, Léon, *Greek Thought and the Origins of the Scientific Spirit*, Knopf, 1928.
Ross, W. D., *Aristotle*, Barnes and Noble, 1955.
Sarton, George, *Science through the Golden Age of Greece*, Harvard Univ. Press, 1952.
―――― *Hellenistic Science and Culture*, Harvard University Press, 1959.
Shotwell, J. T., *Introduction to the History of History*, Columbia University Press, 1922, Section III.
Singer, Charles, *et al.*, eds., *A History of Technology from Early Times to Fall of Ancient Empires*, Oxford University Press, 1954.
Swain, J. W., *The Ancient World*, 2 Vols., Harpers, 1950, Vol. I.
Swindler, M. H., *Ancient Painting*, Yale University Press, 1929.
Tarn, W. W., *Hellenistic Civilization*, Longmans, 1959.
Taylor, A. E., *Plato: The Man and His Work*, Meridian.
Thompson, J. W., *A History of Historical Writing*, 2 Vols., Macmillan, 1942, Book I.
Torr, Cecil, "Greek Music," *Oxford History of Music*, Vol. I, Oxford Press, 1929.
Tucker, T. G., *Life in Ancient Athens*, Macmillan, 1906.
Van Hook, Larue, *Greek Life and Thought*, Columbia University Press, 1923.
Walters, H. B., *The Art of the Greeks*, 2d rev. ed., Macmillan, 1922.
Warþeke, J. M., *The Searching Mind of Greece*, Crofts, 1930.
Windelband, Wilhelm, *History of Ancient Philosophy*, Dover Publications, Inc., 1956.
Winspear, A. D., *Who Was Socrates?*, Russell, 1958.
Zeller, Eduard, *Stoics, Epicureans and Sceptics*, Russell, 1962.
Zimmern, A. E., *The Greek Commonwealth*, Oxford Press, 1931.

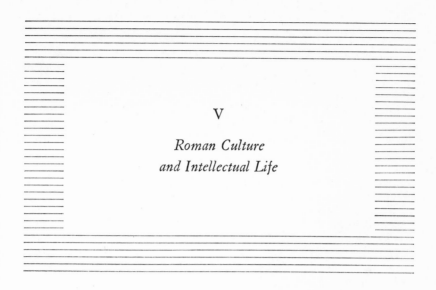

V

Roman Culture
and Intellectual Life

The close racial resemblance between the ancient Greeks and Italians may be used as an admirable warning against a racial interpretation of history. The conclusion may be drawn from a study of the racial composition of Greeks and Romans that the progress of civilization depends more on the mixture of cultures and races, which occurs through numerous contacts between them, than on the special gifts of a single race. Race itself does not seem to influence greatly the direction of culture; contacts and interbreeding may do so.

The Greeks and the Romans had approximately the same racial heritage. That is, they were mainly a mixture of longheaded Mediterraneans and roundheaded Alpines. Yet their civilizations show the sharpest contrasts. The Greeks never achieved political unity. They were "separatists" and each city-state guarded its independence jealously. The Romans had marked military and political capacity and they created an immense world-empire. The Greeks were culturally creative and made remarkable headway in science, philosophy, and the arts. The Romans were culturally imitative, and showed more interest in engineering, government, and law than in science, philosophy, literature, or art.

The earliest inhabitants of the Italian peninsula were a longheaded Paleolithic race. The only remnant of them in classical times were the Ligurians. The next inhabitants of Italy were a longheaded Mediterranean people, who may have come from Africa in the late Paleolithic era. Traces of them are found today in southern Italy and Sicily. They were followed by the Etruscans, also probably a Mediterranean race (and probably related to the Philistines) who, around 1000 B.C., came from Asia Minor or the Aegean. By 800 B.C. the Etruscans were established in the west-central plain of Italy called Etruria.

The invasion of Italy by the roundheaded Alpine race began in Neolithic times. The Terremare peoples, a pile-dwelling group, began to settle in the peninsula after 2500 B.C. By 2000 B.C. we find them ensconced in the southern part of the Po Valley. The so-called Italian tribes, also roundheaded, came from central Europe about 1500 B.C. They overran the peninsula, assimilated the natives, and eventually separated into the Samnites, living in the southern part, or foot of the boot of Italy; the Latins, living along the "calf"; and Umbrians in the north and center, or between "calf" and "knee."

The Italians were later displaced from the eastern and western coasts and huddled towards the center of the peninsula. The Etruscans drove them from the western coast above the lower Tiber. Around 800 B.C. the colonizing Greeks occupied the "toe," the "sole" and "heel" of Italy—that is, the southern coast line, both east and west. The last invaders before the Germans were the Gauls, who appeared in the sixth century and were established in the Po Valley around B.C. 400.

The Romans of antiquity were thus a mixture of many types, Gauls, Greeks, Etruscans, Italian tribes, Terramares and Ligurians, all mainly of Mediterranean and Alpine blood.

The Roman period in history represents, broadly speaking, an attempt by a nation consisting mostly of farmers to capture and control the Western World. The attempt had been made thrice before on a smaller scale by Assyria, Persia, and Macedonia. All three enterprises ended in failure.

Rome began as a rudimentary feudal society of large landowners, with something roughly like the medieval manorial system. As she branched out from a small city-state on the banks of the Tiber into a world power her social composition underwent vital changes. Gradually Roman society split into two classes besides the ever-present slaves—large farmers or *patricians,* and free peasants, or *plebeians.* Continuing wars and added territories multiplied the wealth of the patricians, who began to command vast acres and large estates farmed by slaves. The conduct of these wars, however, depended vitally on the brawn and loyalty of the plebeians. Hence, the plebeians were granted political concessions. But the irrepressible trend towards great estates crowded them out and ended their independence. They entered the army or crowded into the cities, and in the empire helped to create the *colonate,* made up of those who were legally free but economically dependent.

For a time a new aristocracy, the business and office-holding class, vied with the patricians for political and social supremacy. They were mainly merchants, contractors, usurers, publicans, and businessmen. From the days of the consul-general Marius, who flourished around 100 B.C., to the reign of Marcus Aurelius Antoninus, more than two centuries later, they formed a vital middle class.

The unjust taxation system of the later empire, however, destroyed them, and the plutocratic landlords rose again to the top, refused to pay their taxes, shirked their civic duties, and snubbed the government. Political and legal turmoil ensued, the western empire succumbed to the invading Germans, and western Europe slipped into feudalism and a cultural decline. Had Rome been able to develop a large and free peasant class in the East, had she been able to keep afloat the free peasantry of the West, and had the middle class not been destroyed, the empire might have survived.

This, all too briefly, is the generalized story of Rome's social and economic failure. The picture would not be complete without some idea of her psychological and intellectual deficiencies. The Roman intellect was at bottom a farmer's intellect. It not only lacked imagination and flexibility—the two seem to go together—but it did not have sufficient commercial enthusiasm and financial wisdom to carry the load of world-empire.

Why then, it will be asked, did Rome undertake imperial expansion? The answer is that Rome did not set out consciously to conquer the world, like Alexander the Great or Napoleon Bonaparte. Rome's expansion was the result of a series of accidents. It began, as Monroe Smith once observed, in the necessity of dealing with nuisances on the local frontiers. Once the warriors and plutocrats had tasted the spoils of conquest, however, they were avid for more.

The chain of conquests was difficult to stop. Augustus, for instance, advised his successors in his will not to seek more territory. Yet there were greedy Romans who did not want to check expansion. Eventually, the empire fell because of inadequate facilities for travel and communication, turmoil among social classes, and the inability to create an administrative machine which, like that of modern Britain, could administer empire efficiently. Essentially, the Roman mind was conservative and provincial, and could not sufficiently adapt itself to the colossal task of ruling vast territories inhabited by polyglot races, with their strange customs and un-Roman ways of thinking.

II. THE INFLUENCE OF ROMAN POLITICS AND IMPERIALISM ON ROMAN CULTURE

The tiny city-state of Rome in the boot of Italy began to push out around 400 B.C. The first inspiration to expand came, as we have noted, from the need of beating off enemies on the border. The Etruscans were the first to be suppressed. Their fleet had been utterly destroyed by Hiero of Syracuse in 475 B.C. and they later were defeated by the Gauls streaming into Italy through the northern mountain passes. In 390 B.C. Rome nearly expired at the hands of the savage Gauls who swarmed into the city as far as the citadel on the Capitol hill. The barbarians were bought off with gold, however, turned back and settled in the Po Valley where they remained a menace for a time.

Around 350 B.C. Rome became mistress of Latium by absorbing the Latin League through a process of both granting Roman citizenship to its inhabitants and planting her own colonies among them. By 290 Rome controlled the peninsula from about the "shin bone" to the "knee" or from the Greek cities in the South to the Arno. By 275 B.C. the Greek cities in southern Italy were also under Rome's domination, but only after a bloody struggle with King Pyrrhus of Epirus (a state just across from the "heel" of Italy) in which Carthage was called upon for assistance. Rome was now master of the boot. Her nearest rival was Carthage, with which at this time, and for centuries before, she had been on good terms.

Until recently, historians of Rome slighted the importance of this African power. Preoccupied with Italian and Roman history, scholars usually ignored the importance of Carthage, just as Greek historians used to slight the rôle of Hellenistic Alexandria in their desire to make more explicit the greatness of Athens.

Carthage was historically more than a mere Roman adversary, more than simply an obstacle in Rome's path to empire. As a matter of fact, Carthage, which had started as a Phoenician colony about 875 B.C., had created by the time of the First Punic War in 264 B.C. the most opulent and powerful civilization in the western Mediterranean. Only Hellenistic Alexandria, a little later, could equal Carthage in trade and military strength. Carthage was strategically situated, near present-day Tunis, opposite Sicily, on the northern tip of the African promontory. It could expand by sea, both eastward and westward. Moreover, its harbor was deep, its fortifications seemingly invulnerable, and its Semitic inhabitants were shrewd and active traders.

At a time when Italy was mostly a land of uncivilized farmers, Carthaginian ships sailed the Mediterranean and Atlantic from the coasts of Africa to Europe. They were found as far north as Britain and the Baltic, and as far south as Guinea. Carthage monopolized the Gibraltar route, well-nigh dominated the Mediterranean, and traded in Spanish silver, British tin, Baltic amber, and African gold. Although principally a mercantile state, Carthage practiced agriculture and created great estates in North Africa. Carthage probably devised the most scientific methods of farming in antiquity. Mago's book on agriculture, translated into Latin, became a classic in Italy. The luxuriance of Carthage, her exotic Oriental culture, has been depicted in masterly detail in Gustave Flaubert's romance, *Salammbo*.

At the time of the First Punic War, Carthage was far richer than Rome, and had probably twice as many inhabitants. Rome had, however, a more unified political fabric, a more dependable army, and a more loyal population. Carthage was an oligarchy, dominated by merchant princes, even less patriotic and generous than the band of senatorial farmers who controlled Roman policies. Ostensibly a senate of 300 and two elected judges were at the head of the Carthaginian polis. Actually, the country was ruled by a clique of thirty senatorial plutocrats who were more interested in commerce and profits than in preserving the Carthaginian state. In the Second Punic War, for example, the Carthaginian oligarchy shamefully abandoned the heroic Hannibal, and withheld the reinforcements and supplies which ultimately forced him to retreat from Italy.

The military system was a feeble link in the Carthaginian state. There was no great body of patriotic peasants from which to recruit an army. War was undertaken usually by mercenaries, who frequently proved unreliable on the battlefield. The merchant-oligarchy feared that the generals might encroach on politics, and the more brilliant they were the more the government was loath to support them, as the treatment of Hannibal proves. Such was Carthage, Rome's great rival, when the latter emerged as mistress of Italy. Could the two powers live at peace and as allies, as they had done for centuries?

Historians believe the Punic Wars to have been inevitable. Carthage had willingly helped Rome to conquer the Greek cities in Italy, because the Greeks and Carthaginians were commercial rivals. Rome considered Carthage a menace because Carthage with its fleet could close the Adriatic. 'Carthage considered Rome a menace because the Latins now were in a position to grasp Carthaginian markets in the western Mediterranean and Sicily. The rivals were rather well matched. Rome had no navy, but possessed, as we indicated, a more reliable and tested army. The First Punic War dragged on for twenty-three years. Rome built a fleet and landed soldiers in Africa. The war was waged mostly in and around Sicily. Finally, in 241 B.C., peace was negotiated. Sicily was ceded to Rome and Carthage paid a heavy indemnity.

The Second Punic War began in 218 B.C., motivated by the same general conditions which had created the first. Rome and Carthage were now enemies to the death. In this phase of the struggle Hannibal crossed the Alps by superhuman efforts and reached the gates of Rome. Had the Carthaginian nobles sent in time the available supplies and men, Hannibal would probably have vanquished Rome and arrested the course of empire. What the fate of the world would have been in that event, no one can say.

The peace of 201 B.C. left Carthage a weakened power. A crushing indemnity, deprivation of its fleet, confinement to African territory—this was Carthage's lot. But Carthage revived and made a last and futile stand against Rome 149-146 B.C. This defeat meant extinction. Rome harkened to Cato's perennial cry, *Cartago delenda est* ("Carthage must be destroyed!"), and razed the city to the ground.

As a matter of fact, the Third Punic War was a needlessly cruel enterprise engineered by a small group of Italian landowners who were adversely affected by Carthaginian trade in wine and oil. When Carthage became a province these Roman vintners and olive growers lost a competitor and profited hugely. Between the Second and Third Punic Wars Rome marched irrepressibly ahead on the path to empire. Certain intrigues among Greek and Syrian powers gave her the excuse to inaugurate a series of wars which resulted in her control over the eastern as well as western end of the Mediterranean.

Philip V of Macedon had been Hannibal's ally in the Second Punic War, at the close of which he and Antiochus III of Syria planned to invade Egypt, then a politically forlorn land. This inspired Rome to invade the Balkans and defeat Philip. No Greek territory, however, was annexed at this time. Antiochus of Syria was the next victim, in 190 B.C. Again no territory was annexed. In 166 B.C. Egypt voluntarily became a tributary of Rome. In 167 Macedonia had suffered another defeat. In 148 a Macedonian uprising was again suppressed and the country became a Roman province, as did Greece in 146 B.C. Rome was soon in control of much of the vast realm in Europe and Asia over which Alexander the Great had once reigned. In addition, she had annexed northern Africa and was queen of the Mediterranean.

So great was Rome's power at this period that when Attalus III died in 133 B.C., he willed his kingdom of Pergamum in Asia Minor to Rome. It was designated as the Province of Asia. Spain had been occupied as early as 206 B.C., Narbonese Gaul fell into Rome's web in 118 B.C. Mithridates, king of Pontus, tried to drive

Rome out of Asia, and endeavored to occupy Greece and Macedonia. Sulla stopped him after 86 B.C.; Pompey crushed him in 67 B.C. and proceeded to clear the Mediterranean of pirates.

The ball of empire rolled on amid civil war and colonial uprisings. Between 100 B.C. and the era of Trajan and the Antonines (A.D. 98-180), Rome acquired Dacia, the territory between the upper Rhine and upper Danube, the larger part of Gaul, and a good slice of Britain, Mesopotamia, and Arabia. Alexander the Great had ruled over the eastern Mediterranean and western Asiatic peoples. Rome ruled over much of the empire of Alexander plus the western Mediterranean and northwestern European regions. Rome welded this enormous realm, extending from Britain to the Black Sea, into a unity which was a new phenomenon in human history.

The result had profound effects on civilization. It established the tradition of world conquest by force of arms, a tradition which has been the curse of mankind ever since. It is true that the kings of the ancient Orient ennobled themselves by military victories, but Rome far surpassed their achievements. She was the premier militaristic state. The sound of the Roman legions echoed through three continents. Rome symbolized the glory of war. She popularized and left as an ineradicable heritage the tradition of conquest, of subjecting races to the rule of an alien conqueror. The Roman ideal inspired countless generals and kings in the succeeding centuries, and recently we had European dictators who, with the political philosophy called Caesarism, attempted to revive the militarism of Rome in a world that appeared to have outgrown it and seemed ready in many ways for the establishment of a world society.

The concept of the brotherhood of man ultimately became a part of the political philosophy of Rome. When Rome was building an empire in the last two centuries before Christ, the Western World was permeated with Greek ideas. Conspicuous among them was the philosophy of Stoicism, which, as enunciated by its founder Zeno, promulgated, as we saw in the last chapter, the brotherhood of man, and preached the cosmopolitan spirit.

The Greek civilization brought forth at first a political philosophy based on loyalty to the *polis* (city-state), a concept which was already too narrow for Alexander the Great, whose political tenets envisioned a *cosmopolis,* a world-state, in which all men would be equal. "We should not live in cities and demes, each distinguished by separate rules of justice," said Zeno, as recorded by Plutarch, "but should regard *all* men as fellow-demesmen and fellow-citizens; and there should be one life and order [world] as of a single flock feeding together in a common pasture." [1]

The empire of Alexander was transitory. After his death it split up and declined. Rome, at length, having welded together a world far greater even than Alexander's, could make the cosmopolitan ideal a fact. A common culture had been spreading over the Mediterranean world for centuries before the Roman Empire was established, and this common culture made easier Rome's task of ruling so many diverse races.

[1] Quoted in Cyril Bailey, ed., *The Legacy of Rome,* Oxford Press, 1923, p. 52.

As a result of praetorian legal practice and contact with so many cultures there developed in Rome what was called the *jus gentium,* which was considered to be valid for all free men everywhere, and in practice softened the fate of even the slave. From the *jus gentium,* which was ultimately accepted in part by the Roman citizenry in dealing among themselves, there developed the *jus naturale,* literally, "natural law" or the principles of justice, regarded as common to all mankind.

By this time, we have traveled far from the Hellenic subdivision of mankind into Greek and barbarian, and the Hebrew distinctions between Jew and Gentile, with all the inequalities implied therein. In the *jus naturale* there is implicit a principle enunciated long before by the Hellenistic thinker, Eratosthenes, that men are neither Greeks nor barbarians, friends nor foes, but simply good and bad. The omnipotent power of the Roman Empire, which had created a world-state, could incorporate such a remarkably advanced idea into its legal code and give it a currency which it has never wholly lost in Western civilization. We must add that the idea of the brotherhood of man, cast into relief by the basic fact of a world-empire, passed into Christianity, where it became, in democratized form, a foundation stone of its theology.

The expanding Roman Empire in the centuries before Christ encountered three important intellectual currents: first, there were Hellenistic monarchies built on the political embers of the dying city-states which had lost their feeling for autonomy and were not too unwilling to be incorporated into a monarchy in which they could usually retain municipal government but leave foreign relations to an omnipotent king. These monarchies consisted not only of politically weary city-states but also of tribes which had not acquired political ambitions. Secondly, there was Stoicism, preaching human brotherhood and cosmic fatalism at the same time. Thirdly, a strong religious trend from the mystery cults of Greece and the East was sweeping over the Western World. In general, there was a revival of religion and a powerful movement towards the belief, afterwards forcibly embodied in Christianity, in a God who ruled over the universe.

Roman imperialism accommodated and wove together all three currents. "A Roman development meets a Greek conception. That is the genesis of the Roman Empire." [2] A modern scholar, Mr. Ernest Barker, thus brilliantly sums up the situation. Let us see how the marriage of the two worked out.

The democratic spirit which infected Athens in Periclean times was dead in the Mediterranean world. A feeling of acquiescence in whatever rulers there be, was in the air. We have noted that the strong instinct of "separatism" which characterized the Hellenic polis had vanished. The time was ripe for making uniform in both East and West the idea of divine monarchy which prevailed in Oriental civilization, and, as we pointed out in an earlier chapter, was a survival from primitive society.

The titles of Augustus were, in addition to his name, Octavius, "the August," "Princeps" (the "First" among citizens), and "Imperator" (whence our word "emperor") which meant "commander." Augustus regarded himself in Rome as a plain civil head of the state, which he ruled as a *dyarchy,* in conjunction with

[2] In Bailey, *The Legacy of Rome,* p. 60.

the senate. Whatever he may have meant to the Romans, the East understood that his titles denoted divine monarchy. Egypt conferred on him the salutations addressed to their former rulers, the Ptolemies, "Autocrat, Son of the Sun, Lord of the Diadem, Caesar, living forever, beloved of Ptah and Isis." In Greece he was called "God, the son of God, Augustus, the Benefactor."

When Augustus died, the emperor was elevated to the position of *divus* (the deified) and a cult of emperor worship arose. This emperor worship, like the homage which is paid to the British king, was a cement of empire. In the polis, the citizenry was united by the common love of the city, by an ardent civic pride. In the Roman Empire the citizenry was united by the common bond of emperor worship.

The concept of empire was further deepened when the valuable right of citizenship was extended to provincials. Claudius (A.D. 41-54) admitted even Gallic chieftains into the senate. By his time the citizenry included provincials and freedmen as well as Italians and freeborn. With Trajan (A.D. 98-117) the office of emperor itself was opened to provincials. The cosmopolitan idea reached its summit in the edict of Caracalla in A.D. 212, which granted citizenship to *all* freeborn inhabitants of the empire.

There was now a three-fold unity in the Roman world—unity in citizenship, unity in law, and unity in government. An important trait of the Roman legal structure may be noted here, namely, that it harmonized absolutism of government with the guarantee of constitutional rights to its citizens. This, too, was a novelty in Western civilization.

With Aurelian (270-275), the Roman emperor began to turn into an Oriental despot. He ordered his subjects to worship him in Oriental imagery as "The Vicar and emanation of the Unconquered Sun." With Diocletian the last vestiges of the dyarchy which had long ceased to be more than an empty formality disappeared. The senate was turned into a municipal council with jurisdiction over Rome and the suburbs. The distinction between provinces nominally ruled by the senate and provinces ruled by the emperor, also vanished. The absolutism of Aurelian, with its Oriental flavor—he adopted a throne and a footstool and allied himself with the Syrian Sun cult—existed side by side with a fiction of liberty and constitutionalism. But this only presaged another revolution in the concept of empire. The next step was to make the dominant motive of the monarch not solely political or secular, but ecclesiastical as well. When Christianity became the Roman state religion the change was complete.

It used to be believed that the Orient enervated the Roman Empire, and brought it to an end centuries before its time. It was customary to contrast the virile and virtuous West with the degenerate East. The Belgian scholar, Franz Cumont, began the assault on this theory in *Oriental Religions in Roman Paganism* (1911). He and others have proved that without the wealth of the East the inefficient and corrupt imperial machine would have collapsed centuries before it actually did.[8]

The truth seems to be that the western empire tottered first, and that when it

[8] See above, pp. 72-73.

was on the verge of collapse the emperors wisely established a capital in the East, at Constantinople. Whatever culture and material resources had escaped Roman plunder kept this eastern empire going for more than a thousand years, or until the Turks overthrew it in 1453.

We have just noted how the relationship of the East to the empire as a whole has long been misunderstood. The rôle of Gaul in the imperial system has not been misunderstood—it has generally been overlooked entirely. Gaul was more than a stage for the display of Caesar's military genius. Its conquest, as Guglielmo Ferrero has indicated, was of the first importance for the future of the Roman Empire. Gaul was a productive source of linen, wheat, pork, and other merchandise and provided a market for Roman materials. It helped to balance the West against the riches of the East.

If Caesar had not crossed the Alps, the western empire might have toppled centuries earlier. Culturally, Roman Gaul was a vital agent in diffusing civilization in northwestern Europe, thereby laying the foundation for medieval civilization and ultimately for the discovery of America and the spread of culture to the New World. If the German Arminius (Hermann) had not defeated the usually invulnerable Roman legions in A.D. 9, Rome might have penetrated beyond the Rhine and civilized the Germanic tribes as well. In that event, the culture of medieval Europe, in which the Germans played so large a part, might have started on a higher level.

III. THE IMPORTATION OF HELLENIC THOUGHT AND CULTURE

The Romans made it a point to trace their origins to Troy, to Aeneas, son of Anchises, so proud were they of the Hellenic tradition which they had adopted and later Romanized and transmitted to the Western World. There is also a famous line in Horace which epitomizes the impact of Greece on Rome:

Graecia capta ferum victorem cepit.
Greece, conquered by Rome, took captive the conquerors.

The influence of Hellenic culture upon Rome can be traced as far back as the sixth century B.C., when we find the first known attempt to write Latin—and it was in an alphabet borrowed from Greece. About 450 B.C. the first Roman code of laws was engraved on the so-called Twelve Tables—and they too are in an alphabet borrowed partly from the Greeks, and partly from the Etruscans, who probably adopted theirs from the Phoenicians.

The earliest channel of cultural interaction was chiefly mercantile. Goods passed back and forth between Rome and the Greek colonies to the south of her. And so, doubtless, did slaves. These slaves not only introduced Greek words but also Greek customs and ideas. Between the Roman merchants who had come in contact with Hellenic life and the Greek slaves who had lived it, Rome, itself uncultured, absorbed a good deal of Hellenic culture before she became an imperialistic power.

As late as the fourth century B.C. the Romans, on the whole, were still an illiterate race. The civilizing process began in the next century, with Greek aid. And that brings us to the second channel of Greek influence—literature. In 272 B.C. a certain Greek, Andronicus, from the city of Tarentum in the heel of Italy, was brought to Rome to live in the household of the general Marcus Livius, and was assigned to teach his children. Since there were no Latin books, he had to translate Greek into the native tongue.

From this time onward, for a few centuries, the infiltration of Hellenic culture into Rome through literary channels was steady. At first, naturally, the Hellenizing process was confined to the upper classes. For instance, Scipio Africanus the younger (c. 185-129 B.C.) and his family were Graecophiles. Scipio even transferred to his own home a Macedonian library. Philosophers and poets (Terence was one of them) surrounded him and wrote dramas on Greek models and everywhere spread Greek ideas.

Besides the Greek epic, Andronicus introduced Greek drama to Rome. Naevius (264-194 B.C.), the first native Latin poet, a little later established Greek tragedy on the Latin stage. Plautus (c. 254-184 B.C.) and Terence (c. 195-c. 159 B.C.) Romanized Greek comedy. Ennius (c. 239-c. 170) was the first important Roman writer to popularize Greek culture. He stirred an interest in Greek narrative and tragic poetry. It is curious to observe, by the way, that Terence's translation of the Athenian New Comedy made Rome acquainted with a Greek skepticism reflected in that comedy. Every antique moral dogma was undermined and humanistic ideals were emphasized, as in Terence's immortal line,

Homo sum: humani nihil a me alienum puto.
I am a man: and nothing human is outside my interests.

Religion was another Hellenizing influence. A number of Hellenic deities were appropriated by Rome centuries before she expanded into the full sphere of Greek influence. We find the Italians early invoking Proserpina as a curse against enemies, much as we say today, "Go to Hades!" Hercules was worshiped as a protector of trade and travel as far back probably as the days of the kings. Almost as old as the cult of Hercules were the cults of Castor and Pollux, to whom a temple was built in the capital, and of Apollo, the god of light, the oracle whose shrine at Delphi was patronized by Romans.

In 212 B.C., we find at Rome games in honor of Apollo, who was thought to have sagaciously counseled the Romans during the Second Punic War. In 208 B.C. the games were made an annual event, and the next year, after Hasdrubal, Hannibal's brother, had been defeated, the oracle at Delphi sanctioned as an act of thanksgiving the worship of a new Greek deity, the Great Mother Goddess, Cybele, whose home was on Mount Ida, near Troy. In 205 B.C. there were picturesque ceremonies in Rome when the meteoric stone in which the Goddess was supposed to have lived was brought from her temple at Pessinus. After that she was honored by annual ceremonies. About the same time, the Greek Sibylline Books were brought to Italy.

The Greek conception of political liberty made a lasting impression on the

Roman governing class, in whom there was by nature a sort of Hellenic love of independence. The war against Philip V of Macedon was undertaken by commanders like Flamininus with something of Byron's ardor when he went to aid the Greeks in their fight for liberty. Rome was anxious to overthrow the Macedonian despot, not to annex his realm, but to restore the political freedom of the Greek cities. This is attested to by the fact that for almost fifty years after her first victories in Greece Rome annexed no Greek territory.

That the ideals, however, say of Pericles or Themistocles, were not entirely congenial to the Roman "Tories," as we may call them, is illustrated by Cato the Censor (234-149 B.C.). The political philosophy of Greece assumed a degree of individual freedom and social enlightenment which the Tories believed would weaken the solidarity of Rome. Yet even Cato condemned the Greek despots of his own day and exalted the benevolent rulers of a previous golden era, Pericles, Epaminondas, or Themistocles. And in his old age he, who had been set against Greek fashions and ideas all his life, studied Greek himself and explored Greek literature, as all literate Romans, statesmen perhaps most of all, were doing.

Among the members of the Scipionic circle, already alluded to, there was a Greek philosopher, Panaetius, who was destined to be one of the leading Latinizers of Stoicism, that philosophy which is most closely associated with Rome. Greek thinkers were systematically visiting Rome by the middle of the second century B.C. In 155 B.C. Cato proposed that certain Greek philosophers, among them Carneades the Skeptic, whom we discussed in the last chapter, should be ejected from Rome. His reason was the same that had been trumped up against Socrates centuries before—"they were corrupting the Roman youth."

But Cato could no more keep Greek philosophy than Greek literature from inundating Rome. Carneades and his friends, one of whom came to spread the doctrines of Stoicism, attracted enthusiastic audiences. Stoicism, indeed, seems to have been made to order for the Romans. Its cardinal tenet, that man's purpose is not pleasure but duty, including duty to one's country, was particularly acceptable to the Romans. One of Cicero's chief works, a century later, was an adaptation of a book by the above-mentioned Panaetius. It was called *De officiis* ("On Duties"). At all events, Stoicism made great headway in Rome in the generation which followed Cato's. It is another interesting fact that Cato's great-grandson, Cato the Younger (95-46 B.C.) became the most famous Stoic of his time.

When Augustus inaugurated an era of peace after the battle of Actium (31 B.C.) Stoicism was given new life, and this time it became more than merely the philosophy of the elite. We can observe the growth of Stoicism in Rome from Panaetius, through Vergil, Seneca, Epictetus, Marcus Aurelius, and Christianity.

But we must not suppose that Stoicism, so popular among the upper classes, conquered the middle classes as quickly. Epicureanism, another Greek philosophy, was more to their liking. Its emphasis on pleasure made a peculiar appeal in the last century of the Roman Republic. The philosophy of Epicurus also found many expounders, the most illustrious, Lucretius and Horace, to whom we shall return in a later section of this chapter.

Most representative of the Hellenizers was Cicero, who had traveled widely in the classical world, sampled many brands of Greek thought, philosophical, ethical, and religious, and endeavored to transmit them to his countrymen. His eclectic mind permitted him to extract, as a bee extracts nectar from flowers, the best from all phases of Greek culture. Most of his philosophical works are in fact Latin adaptations of Greek material.

Rome depended on Greece for things material as well as spiritual. There is scarcely a phase of the arts or crafts which was not borrowed from Hellas. We have already spoken of the drama, a Greek art, transplanted, stagecraft and all, to Rome. Most of the architects who contributed to the rebuilding of Rome under Augustus, Nero, Trajan, and Hadrian, were Hellenistic Greeks and Syrians. The architectural models were of course also Greek—Attic or Hellenistic.

Rome drafted many Greek engineers, boat builders, sailors, astronomers, actors, musicians, bankers. Little by little Greek professions and arts found a footing in Rome. Yet the Romans did not carry ahead the scientific work of the Greeks. The interesting technological advances of Hellenistic times stopped still, not to be resumed until the seventeenth century.

Greek and particularly Alexandrian science was made good use of in practical fields such as surveying, building, medicine, cartography, and navigation. But among Romans we look in vain for an epitomizer of scientific knowledge on the level of Aristotle, for an astronomer as original as Aristarchus or Hipparchus, an inventor like Archimedes or Hero, a pioneer in medicine like Hippocrates.

IV. ROMAN SCIENCE

Some idea of the relatively insignificant scientific achievements of Rome can be gleaned from the fact that in a standard history of science [4] fifty-four pages are devoted to Alexandrian science and only eight to Rome. The Romans, a practical but rather uncreative race, did not seem to be interested in scientific research or in pure science. Alexandrian science, which flourished under the Ptolemies, was merely adopted and epitomized under Rome.

When we think of Rome we think of splendid achievements in law, building, engineering, literature, and government. When we think of Greece we think of philosophy, science, art, ethics, and literature. Roman history is not studded with brilliant philosophers like Heracleitus, Democritus, Socrates, Plato, or Aristotle; mathematical geniuses like Euclid or Archimedes; scientific investigators like Hippocrates or Eratosthenes, or inventors like Hero.

The significance of Rome is that it applied the scientific knowledge of its predecessors, thereby developing the conveniences of life to a level which in many ways has been surpassed only in the last century. Hence we may safely conclude that, although it may have been more stimulating mentally to live, for instance,

[4] W. T. Sedgwick and H. W. Tyler, *A Short History of Science*, Macmillan, 1917.

in Athens in Periclean times, it was far more comfortable to dwell in either the Roman capital or in a major provincial city in the days of, say, Trajan.

The lack of achievements in science may have resulted partly from the rather prosaic cast of the Roman's mind, and partly from his outlook on life, as illustrated by the predominant upper-class philosophy, Stoicism. The latter, we may recall, accepted nature as it was, as a part of the great chain of being—the universal system—created by God. It provided little impetus for discovering new facts, deducing new scientific laws, and making new syntheses of knowledge.

Not that there was a lack of observation of nature. Latin literature was the first to give copious expression to the love of plant life and animal life. But the Roman did not seem to have the architectonic mind which derives general laws from an infinite observation of small facts. He regarded nature as the sensitive farmer does, as a beautiful and lovely thing. That it is part of a scientifically-arranged universe operating according to complex laws and processes seldom occurred to him.

Hence the Roman was at his best not in speculations about science, but in the practice of medicine, provisions for health and hygiene, engineering projects, cartography, and general application of astronomical knowledge.

No man of Roman blood ever wrote an original medical treatise, yet a great deal of what we know about ancient medicine is contained in works written in the Roman Empire. Among them we may mention Soranus of Ephesus (second century A.D.) who wrote books on midwifery, medicine, and anatomy; Dioscorides of Cilicia (discussed in the last chapter), a military surgeon under Nero, the author of the standard pharmacopoeia of the Middle Ages; and Celsus, who left us the only important medical work written in Latin—it incorporates the surgical knowledge of Alexandria, and is probably a free translation from the Greek.

Roman genius contributed to civilization the hospital and the medical school. Somewhere before A.D. 40 Asclepiades of Bithynia came to Rome and began the systematic teaching of medicine. At first it was a loose kind of school, the master taking his students on visits to his patients. This developed into formal societies with a definite meeting-place and a board of officers. Eventually the government built lecture halls for them and in the time of Vespasian (A.D. 69-79) the faculty began to be paid by the state. The *schola medicorum* were not research centers, like some modern medical schools, but served mainly as training places for army surgeons.

The needs of the army as well as a sense of social service were instrumental in creating the institution known as the hospital. The Greeks had private surgeries where doctors treated their patients. But they had nothing like a public health service. Their nearest approach to the hospital system were the temples of Aesculapius, the god of healing, where no medical treatment, however, was given.

In the first century A.D. Rome had its *valetudinaria,* or infirmaries, where the poorer classes, notably slaves, were treated. There were also at this time something like private hospitals, which eventually were opened to the public and came under the patronage of the state. The army established military hospitals at strategic places in order that sick soldiers need not be sent all the way home for treatment. The excavation of such a hospital near Düsseldorf revealed a building arranged very much like our modern hospitals, with ample facilities for drainage and sanitation. Private hospitals for use of government officials and their families were also erected in the provinces and these led finally to a system of charity hospitals, which survived into the Middle Ages, when they came under ecclesiastical domination.

There is a great deal of talk nowadays of socialized medicine, but few people know that the ancients were pioneers in this form of public service. Herodotus tells us that many Greek city-states had public physicians. Under the Roman Empire, every town had a corps of medical men, paid by the state for their services to the poor.

The Romans were familiar with devices for indicating time, ideas for which were probably borrowed from the Greeks. Vitruvius, the great writer on architecture, gave easy directions for making sundials and water clocks.

Our present months, with their Roman names, go back to a time when the Romans had a lunar calendar of twelve "lunations," or 355 days. Julius Caesar reorganized this calendar by adopting, on the advice of Sosigenes, an Alexandrian, a solar year of 365 days with an extra day added in February every fourth or leap year. The Julian calendar, as it was called, modified in 1582, prevails at present in the Western World.

Romans like Pliny, for instance, were aware of the curved surface of the earth, as had been taught by Eratosthenes. There were also individuals who accepted the theory of Aristarchus that not the earth, but the sun is the center of the universe. In general an intelligent Roman's conception of the cosmos was that of a *finite* world, regulated by mechanical laws and bounded by a flaming rampart. Combined with a disbelief in the supernatural religion, this was a source of the pessimism so common in the later empire, a pessimism which made fertile soil for the mystery cults and led to the final triumph of Christianity.

The Romans had a certain skill in cartography. They put together an excellent map, showing all the roads in the empire, which was so large that a special building had to be erected to house it. From it were produced so-called strategical maps like the "Peutinger Table" (named after the man who discovered it in the sixteenth century), indicating the imperial army routes. In conjunction with their road making, which will be discussed below, the Romans devised the milestone or road marker, which, like modern highway signs, indicated distances between important places.

Accurate cartography was not, however, a Roman forte. Tacitus, who might have known better, believed, for instance, that the Pyrenees ran north and south instead of east and west, and a map constructed from his description gives quite an erroneous picture of the relative location, say, of Spain and Britain.

The haziness of Roman geography is quite manifest in the work of the popularizer, Pomponius Mela. To him the world consists of three continents: Africa, Asia, and Europe; Asia is as large as Europe and Africa combined; central Europe is almost a blank; Britain and Ireland are oblong-shaped and stretch beyond modern Denmark.

Among Roman mechanical instruments we find the crane, worked by a human treadmill and a system of pulleys, the "steelyard," a balancing instrument, and the "groma," a surveying device. Vitruvius describes a curious and complicated affair for marking road distances which resembles our taximeter. Seneca seems to have known about the magnifying power of glasses.

The majority of Roman scientific works were devoted to compilations of current scientific and pseudo-scientific lore. To these we shall pay attention in a moment. But there were a few important and relatively original works by Roman authors. Far and away the most valuable and influential was the work of Marcus Vitruvius, who lived in the reign of Augustus (31 B.C.-A.D. 14), *Ten Books on Architecture*. This treatise was not only the outstanding work on architecture in all classical antiquity but also an encyclopedia of the physical and technical knowledge of the Augustan age. It contained, incidentally, the first-known analysis of the principles of architectural acoustics. The revived knowledge of the book in the later Middle Ages was a powerful stimulus to the growing popularity of Roman architecture in the fifteenth and sixteenth centuries. Along with Vitruvius, we might mention Marcus Vipsanius Agrippa (63-12 B.C.) and his collaborator Cocceius Auctus, two of the most famous and competent of Roman engineers. Agrippa is usually regarded as the ablest and most prolific of the engineering geniuses of Rome. He was also a great geographer, completing the official survey of the Roman Empire and putting the results on the great map of the world which was placed in the Porticus Octaviae by order of Augustus. Among his construction projects was the famous aqueduct at Nîmes. The other important Roman geographer and map maker was Pomponius Mela (A.D. c. 50). He understood that the world is a globe, and he laid out the climatic zones.

Other Roman works of some originality were those on husbandry. They derived much from the writings of Mago, the Carthaginian (c. 200 B.C.), the ablest writer on the subject in classical times. The first was the *De agricultura* of Cato the Censor, a general and very patriotic tract on Roman farming, gardening, and horticulture. The best of all these works was the *De re rustica* of the encyclopedist, Varro (116-27 B.C.), which was preserved in part in Augustine's *City of God*.[4a] The last of such books was the *De agricultura* of Rutilius Palladius (A.D. c. 330). It was written in the form of a farmer's calendar, giving the duties of each month. It contained valuable suggestions on the grafting of trees, soil drainage, and fertilization, and on determining the age of horses. The foremost writer on veterinary science was Flavius Vegetius (383-450), also an expert on military science.

The Romans compiled the most complete treatises on astrology in antiquity. The first important Roman astrologer was Publius Figulus (d. 44 B.C.). Another influential work was the long astrological poem of Marcus Manilius (A.D. c. 15), the *Astronomicon*. But the most comprehensive textbook on the subject prepared in ancient times was the *Matheseos libri viii*, by Firmicus Maternus (A.D. c. 335).

In the field of astronomy the most popular Roman writer was Julius Hyginus (c. 25 B.C.). His *Poeticon astronomicon* was an elementary treatise dealing mainly with the myths concerning the twenty-four major constellations. It was based

[4a] Since recovered, in large part.

chiefly on Aratos and Eratosthenes. Hyginus also wrote on agriculture and geography, and he produced the first Roman treatise on the care of bees, a very important industry among the Romans.

The leading Roman writer on medicine was Aurelius Cornelius Celsus who flourished in the reign of Tiberius (A.D. 14-37). His *Artes* was really an encyclopedia of the learning of the Roman world—a prototype of Pliny's *Natural History*. It dealt with rhetoric, philosophy, law, military science, agriculture and medicine. Since only the medical sections of the work have survived, Celsus has usually been treated solely as a physician and a writer on medicine. Celsus wrote with stylistic brilliance and scientific precision and the section of his work dealing with medicine was the most important Latin work in the field. It ranks next to those by Hippocrates and Galen among all ancient writings on the subject. It gives the best summary of Alexandrian medicine. The treatise is especially important for its sections on anatomy and surgery. It contains the best classical account of the human skeleton. In surgery it describes, for example, operations to remove cataracts from the eyes and to remove tonsils. Lost during the Middle Ages, it was recovered by Guarino Veronese in 1426 and exerted a wide influence on humanist medicine.

The Roman compilers of scientific knowledge, aside from Celsus, did not reach a high level of accuracy. Marcus Terentius Varro was a prototype for the medieval writers in the liberal arts. In his *Disciplinarum libri novem,* he separated knowledge into nine compartments: grammar, rhetoric, dialectic, geometry, arithmetic, astronomy, music, medicine, and architecture. The Middle Ages dropped the last two.

Varro's writings, of which only two books have been preserved even in fragments, the *De re rustica* ("On Agriculture") and the *De lingua Latina* ("The Latin Language"), were inspired, like Cato's, by the patriotic motive of building a monument to Latin learning and setting it against the Greek. Varro's facts are mainly taken from books and embody little personal observation—in this way, too, setting an example for medieval compilers with their sublime trust in the written word rather than in the observed fact. His seventy-four or more works, in over 600 books, deal with historical, antiquarian, biographical, critical, philosophical, geographical, and practical scientific subjects. His work on agriculture was the best compendium on the subject produced in the Latin world. Varro condensed the conventional scientific knowledge in his treatises on the arts, and seems to have had some considerable mathematical information. But he showed most originality in dealing with farm animals, plants, and animal diseases.

Another encyclopedist was the philosopher Lucius Annaeus Seneca (3 B.C.- A.D. 65), whose picturesque suicide (by opening his veins) forestalled Nero's vengeance. Seneca was a rhetorician and philosopher rather than a scientist and his *Natural Questions* is even more of a secondhand job than Pliny's. Seneca was less prone to accept superstitions than Pliny, but he utilized his material to show that nature in its various manifestations acted out a moral or philosophic drama. By associating this moral pageant with Christian doctrine, medieval theologians found Seneca very much to their taste.

Of all the works on ancient science far and away the most widely read and copied was the fearful and wonderful *Natural History* of Pliny the Elder (23-79). Aristotle certainly had a wider subsequent intellectual influence than did Pliny, but it is doubtful that the purely scientific works of Aristotle, outside of technical scholarly circles, enjoyed anything like as protracted and extensive a popularity as did the encyclopedia of natural science compiled by Pliny. It was the accepted compendium of science for the literate Romans of the empire, was the major arsenal of facts used by the Christian writers who compiled the bestiaries in the patristic period, was the basis of the scientific information of all the medieval compilers from Isidore of Seville until the ascendancy of Aristotle in the period of scholasticism, and even contested Aristotle's popularity in scientific matters. It was surpassed only by the Bible, Aristotle and Augustine's *City of God* for popularity among the educated classes down to the period of declining medievalism.

Pliny was a state official and naval officer who had to give most of his time to official duties. He had little save his nights to devote to the acquisition of scientific data. But he gave over his spare time with great gusto to this quest. He had scientific tracts read to him while he ate, and often dictated his materials from his bath. He stated that he had read two thousand books in the course of his investigations. He died at the age of fifty-six in the famous eruption of Vesuvius in A.D. 79. In spite of the fact that he had by no means completed his researches at the time of his death, his *Natural History* is much the most complete repertory of antique learning, scientific and cultural, which has been preserved. Varro probably gathered more information but most of his works have been lost. Professor Lynn Thorndike says of the *Natural History*:

> Pliny's *Natural History,* which appeared about 77 A.D. and is dedicated to the Emperor Titus, is perhaps the most important single source extant for the history of ancient civilization. Its thirty-seven books, written in a very compact style, constitute a vast collection of the most miscellaneous information. Whether one is investigating ancient painting, sculpture, and other fine arts; or the geography of the Roman Empire; or Roman triumphs, gladiatorial contests, and theatrical exhibitions; or the industrial processes of antiquity; or Mediterranean trade; or Italian agriculture; or mining in ancient Spain; or the history of Roman coinage; or the fluctuation of prices in antiquity; or the Roman attitude towards usury; or the pagan attitude towards immortality; or the nature of ancient beverages; or the religious usages of the ancient Romans; or any of a number of other topics; one will find something concerning all of them in Pliny.[5]

What is the value of this vast collection of antique lore? Any compilation of ancient scientific beliefs, even if made by very critical writers, would have been bound to include much that was fanciful. Pliny, whatever his zest for searching after information, was certainly not critically-minded. Nor did he have the scientific training to enable him to sift with discrimination the information he collected. He was honest, stated his authorities fully, had an excellent memory, and was an assiduous compiler. But the result was a strange admixture of facts and wonders. It well illustrated his aphorism that no book is so bad as not to be able

[5] Lynn Thorndike, *A History of Magic and Experimental Science,* 2 vols., Macmillan, 1923, I, 42-3.

to yield up something of value. As Thorndike says: "The *Natural History* is a great storehouse of misinformation as well as of information, for Pliny's credulity and lack of discrimination harvested the tares of legend and magic along with the wheat of historical fact and ancient science in his voluminous granary." In addition to the large element of often humorous fancy in it, the book is also rather rambling and discursive. But when all is said and done, it is certainly the most complete and representative of all extant collections of what passed for scientific knowledge in classical antiquity:

> On the whole, while to us today the *Natural History* seems a disorderly and indiscriminate conglomeration of fact and fiction, its defects are probably to a great extent those of its age and of the writers from whom it has borrowed. If it does not reflect the highest achievements and clearest thinking of the best scientists of antiquity—and be it said that there are a number of the Hellenistic age of whom we should know less than we do but for Pliny—it probably is a fairly faithful epitome of science and error concerning nature in his own time and the centuries preceding. At any rate it is the best portrayal that has reached us.[6]

We have no space here to illustrate in detail Pliny's humorous credulity. Those interested in the intellectual history of Europe should certainly dip into his work, particularly into Book VII, which deals with man. A few samples will reveal the flavor of his work. He tells us, citing authorities to support his statements, of such things as the following: a savage race whose feet all turn backwards; an Indian tribe which has heads like dogs; a race in Albania whose hair is white from birth; a race where females conceive in their fifth year and die at the age of eight; another race which is bisexual, the individuals alternately performing the functions of each sex; another tribe whose people have no neck but have eyes in their shoulders. Mrs. Dionne was far outshone by a woman of the Peloponnesus, who gave birth to quintuplets four successive times. Remarkable feats of strength, courage, and eyesight, for example, are recounted. One man supported a whole wagonload of wine on his back until the casks were emptied; another was in the habit of carrying his mule to work. A famous gladiator fought 120 battles, was wounded 45 times in the front of his body but never in his back. One man had such acute eyesight that he wrote the whole of Homer's *Iliad* on a piece of parchment so small it could be enclosed in a nutshell. Another man was able to distinguish objects at a distance of 135 miles. And so on.

These were only some of the wonders of mankind, which go on through sixty chapters. To these were added the wonders of the animal and plant kingdom and the magic of gems, stones, and the like. While Pliny presumed to rebuke magicians as impostors, his own work is filled with magical lore—the magical qualities of animal habits, certain stones, many plants and herbs, medical remedies, and so forth.

Such was the work which was ransacked for more than a thousand years by every important seeker after scientific data. It is one of the great landmarks in the intellectual history of Europe. No other work gives us so comprehensive and

⁶ Thorndike, *op. cit.*, I, 51.

faithful an impression of the scientific and cultural equipment of the cultivated classes of classical antiquity. If Pliny seems credulous to us, he was not more so than the average literate Roman of his day. Even the great physician, Galen, was equally prone to dispense magic and wonders. As Thorndike observes: "Where should Pliny turn for sober truth? The Stoic Chrysippus prated of amulets; treatises assigned to the great philosophers Democritus and Pythagoras were full of magic; and in the works of Cicero we read of a man who could see for a distance of 135 miles, and in Varro that this man, standing on a Sicilian promontory, could count the number of ships sailing out of the harbor of Carthage." [7]

The chief Roman scientific compilers after Pliny were Aelian, Solinus, and Horapollo. About the beginning of the third century, Aelian of Praeneste wrote his work *On the Nature of Animals* in seventeen books. Though a Roman, Aelian composed his treatise in Greek. He leaned rather heavily on Pliny but showed some originality. His work was a hodgepodge in arrangement, having much less order than that of Pliny. Aelian was much given to moralizing on the habits of animals, contrasting them with human habits to the detriment of the latter. For example, he laid much stress on the alleged chastity of doves, who never divorce each other, and contrasted their virtue with the notorious incontinence of partridges. His moralizing tendency made him popular with the church fathers who dealt with biological topics, especially influencing Ambrose. He was particularly industrious in collecting elephant lore. No other Roman writer was so eloquent in portraying the alleged wonders and marvels of animal behavior.[8] Magic abounds in his writings. His Greek text made him particularly prized by later Byzantine writers on natural science and its theological implications.

Solinus' *Wonders of the World* was primarily a work on historical geography, written probably in the third century and revised by some patristic writer in the sixth century. Beginning with Italy, the authors dealt with the major regions of the known world. After a history of each region, Solinus recounts the religious miracles and the natural marvels associated with the area in the traditional folklore. It was thus true to its title of "wonders." He derived much of his information from Pliny. Solinus laid great stress on Alexander the Great, telling how his mother vainly tried to get for him a nobler father than Philip by having intercourse with a dragon. The book had much to commend it to later compilers. As Thorndike remarks: "It would be rash to conjecture which quality commended the book most to the following period: its handy size, or its easy style, or its emphasis on marvels." Beginning with Augustine, the compilers drew much from Solinus, Isidore of Seville making special use of his work in compiling his encyclopedia.

Horapollo was an Alexandrian of the fourth century, who is traditionally supposed to have written his *Hieroglyphics* in the Egyptian language. But it has survived only in the Greek text. He wrote this treatise on the nature and habits of

[7] Thorndike, *op. cit.*, I, 50.
[8] For illuminating and amusing details, see Thorndike, *op. cit.*, I, 323 ff.

animals in order to clarify the use of animal signs in the Egyptian hieroglyphic writing. Horapollo used mainly Aristotle's *History of Animals,* Pliny, and Solinus, as well as drawing on popular Egyptian pseudo-science. Particularly rich in magical lore, his treatise is one of the more edifying of the treatises on magical zoölogy. It was popular in the Byzantine realms during the Middle Ages.

V. TYPES OF ROMAN PHILOSOPHY

Lucretius' *De rerum natura* ("On the Nature of Things") is the greatest didactic poem in Latin, and it survived by a thread, like the Anglo-Saxon epic, *Beowulf,* in a single manuscript. Lucretius, Epicurus' chief Roman disciple, was convinced that his master has delivered mankind from two of the greatest evils, fear of gods and fear of death. How had Epicurus done this?

The gods, whose existence Epicurus did not deny, are freed from responsibility for human actions. They led a jolly Olympian existence, paying no heed to man. As for death, Epicurus taught that the soul does not survive the body, which, according to his teachings, decomposes into constituent atoms. Body and soul, mind and matter, are composed of the same irreducible atoms. An individual life is merely a combination of atoms which existed in a different combination before that individual was born and will exist in another combination after his death. To fear death is foolish because consciousness is "snapt asunder" and we shall no longer be able to feel.

The true liberation of man is to observe the principles of natural science and realize that nature is a dynamic process in which life and death are part of the same cycle, and matter is indestructible: "For verily matter does not cohere inseparably massed together, since we see that everything wanes and perceive that all things ebb as it were by length of time and that age withdraws them from our sight, though yet the sum is seen to remain unimpaired by reason that the bodies which quit each thing, lessen the things from which they go, gift with increase those to which they have come, compel the former to grow old, the latter to come to their prime, and yet abide not with these. Thus the sum of things is ever renewed. . . . Some nations wax, others wane, and in a brief space the races of living things are changed and like runners hand over the lamp of life." [9]

This is the Lucretian theory of physical nature and does not jar with the views of modern science. From it he builds up a story of physical creation based on Democritus and a ladder of life, like Aristotle's. Everything in nature consists of tiny, mobile particles. The origin of the world is explained by the interaction of atoms, an occurrence which took place without the help of deity or "creative intelligence." The genesis of life is the same for all organic creatures. Earth produces first plants and then animals. Simple organisms evolve into more complex species. Only the fit survive. Lucretius unfolds by sheer imaginative intuition a panorama of evolution which modern archaeology, anthropology, and paleontology have shown to be not far removed from the facts. He throws himself back

---

[9] Munroe's translation in Bakewell, *op. cit.,* pp. 306-7.

into preliterary times and sees the earth thick with tropical forests. All kinds of species emerge and fight for survival in the stifling climate, and the weak go down,

> Enshackled in the gruesome bonds of doom,
> As prey and booty for the rest, until
> Nature reduced that stock to utter death.[10]

Among the numerous species which arise and become extinct we perceive the human race—primitive man, who has not learned to speak or wear clothing. Weaker than the animals around him, he prowls for food amid the sheltering forests, and takes it to his cave dwelling. From the cave-dwelling state, Lucretius traces the race through a poetic recreation of the Stone, Bronze and Iron ages.

If we consider that Lucretius had seen nothing of savage life and that hardly anything was known in his day about earthly origins and the earliest history of man, the poet's intuition becomes almost incredible. Conspicuous among his adumbrations of modern science are not only the doctrine of survival of the fittest, but his theory of light, which anticipated Newton and his theory of chemical affinities, which foreshadowed Lavoisier.

Lucretius was more interested in the physical than in the ethical views of his master, Epicurus. Epicurean ethics were peculiarly congenial to one side of the Latin temperament and received classic expression in the poetry of Horace (68 B.C.). Faced with the assertions of Epicurus that there are no meddling gods and no afterlife, Horace accepts the consequences with the urbanity of a man of the world, and counters, as it were, with the catch phrase, "Let us eat, drink and be merry, for tomorrow we may die!"

> Postumus, postumus, alack-a-day,
> The years, how swiftly do they glide away!
> No piety keeps wrinkles from the brow,
> Nor makes old age his near approach delay,
> Nor never-mastered death more time allow.

We must go the way of all flesh, prince or pauper, master or slave, and leave one day, forever, the good things of life.

> Earth must thou leave, thy home and charming wife,
> Nor though, thou tendest many, shall one tree
> Of all that thou didst own in this brief life,
> Except the hateful cypress, follow thee.[11]

Horace's skepticism does not inspire bleak despair, but on the contrary, he impels us to accept, or embrace with gay equanimity whatever pleasures there may be:

> Soon must you leave the woods you buy,
> Your villa, wash'd by Tiber's flow,
> Leave,—and your treasures heap'd so high
> Your reckless heir will level low.

---

[10] Book V, lines 875-77, trans. by William Ellery Leonard.
[11] Horace, *Odes,* ii, 14, trans. by Coutts.

Whether . . .
In wealth you lived beneath the sun,
Or nursed in beggary and scorn,
You fall to death, who pities none.
One way all travel; the dark urn
Shakes each man's lot, that soon or late
Will force him, hopeless of return,
On board the exile-ship of Fate.[12]

And since we are doomed to but one life, one brief spasm, as it were, of joy, Horace cries, in words which have echoed again and again in European literature:

Pile on the hearth the chill-dispersing brands,
Pour out the Sabine wine, four winters old;
Leave to the gods all else. . . .
Count as gain each day
That Fortune grants; but never think to tease
Its secret from tomorrow.[13]

The philosophy of Horace is called *carpe diem* (literally, make the most of today). But it must not be confounded with sensuality. Horace is Greek enough to know that temperance is the essence of happiness.

Who makes the golden mean his guide
Shuns miser's cabin, foul and dark,
Shuns gilded roof, where pomp and pride
Are envy's mark.

We may fittingly take leave of Roman Epicureanism with this bit of advice from Horace, perhaps as civilized a man as the ancient world produced:

In sadness hope, in gladness fear,
'Gainst coming change will fortify
Your breast. The storm that Jupiter
Sweeps o'er the sky
He chases. Why should rain today
Bring rain tomorrow?
Be brave in trouble; meet distress
With dauntless front; but when the gale
Too prosperous blows, be wise no less,
And shorten sail.[14]

The Horatian philosophy reflects Roman civilization at its mellowest, after it had emerged from the provinciality and hardness of Republican times, and before it toppled over into the decadence of the generations after Horace.

We have seen how Greek philosophy was formally brought to Rome in the famous embassy from Athens of 155 B.C., among whom was Diogenes the Stoic bearing a credo which was very congenial to the Roman temperament. In time Stoicism, along with Epicureanism—there was no Epicurean in the embassy of

[12] *Odes,* ii, 3, trans. by J. Conington.   [14] *Odes,* ii, 10, trans. S. Conington.
[13] *Odes,* i, 9, trans. Coutts.

155 B.C.—became the leading philosophies in Rome. Among the intellectuals, Stoicism supplanted religion—that poverty-stricken Roman religion, as Franz Cumont calls it—as the guiding spiritual force in life.

In the last chapter, we gave an analysis of the philosophy of Zeno, the founder of Stoicism. Here we shall briefly discuss the modifications given to that philosophy by the three great Roman Stoics, Seneca, Epictetus, and Marcus Aurelius.

It is one of the most curious things in the history of thought that the name of Seneca, a man, apparently, of little conscience, should be associated with the doctrine of conscience and the moral regeneration of the ancient world. Seneca was a Spaniard of noble family who became a well-known courtier in Caligula's reign. After being exiled by the Emperor Claudius, on the charge, it was said, of being the favorite paramour of the emperor's sister, he returned to favor seven years later when Agrippina married Claudius.

Agrippina obtained for him the quaestorship (public treasurer) and made him tutor to her son Nero. When Nero became emperor at the age of seventeen Seneca was one of the two "regents" of the empire. As with Francis Bacon sixteen hundred years later, an exalted moral philosophy apparently did not prevent Seneca from sharing in the prevalent graft, and he amassed a fortune of about fifteen million dollars. The fortune, he said, was forced upon him. At any rate, Seneca, whose influence upon his pupil was enormous, did not protest too much against Nero's brutalities. Yet he was implicated in Piso's plot against the emperor and even before that had fallen out of favor and was forced to retire to private life. We have already indicated how he met his fate, like a Stoic and a man of honor.

In Seneca, as far as we can judge, a low sense of private morality was allied to a high conception of abstract justice and individual worth. He was one of the most copious writers on morality in the ancient world. Although a great number of his works are lost, many have survived, doubtless, because of the piety of medieval Christians who regarded him as one of their propagandists.

Seneca also wrote tragedies, more to satisfy the ardent theater-goer Nero than to suit himself. Seneca's are the only Latin tragedies which have come down from antiquity, and formed the models for the tragic writers of the sixteenth century.

The era in which Seneca lived was not one to make a moral philosopher comfortable. The life of the ruling classes reached a level of degradation which became a classical example for subsequent moralists. Whether Seneca took part in it willingly or not, it is hard to say. But, very likely, he found in philosophy the only escape, the one consolation for a disappointing existence. He was thus *in* the world, but not a part of it.

The titles of his treatises cover most of the important aspects of morality—"On the Shortness of Life," "On Clemency," "On Anger," "On Peace of Mind," "On Giving and Receiving Favors," "On Consolation." Seneca accepts the fatalism of the Stoics, but combines it with a genuine yearning for God. But his god is not the God of the Christians, much as later Christians would have liked to believe it was. He has no conception of a narrow and petty-minded anthropomorphic deity. His god is the divine logos—the benevolent abstract righteousness. In line with his conception of duty is his idea of conscience—a power within us, which makes for righteousness. And conscience becomes to him the voice of duty, which thereby shows us how to take part in the universal goodness for which the world was created.

Seneca therefore becomes the great preacher of self-examination, the conscience-stricken sinner who first gave to European philosophy the moral accent of the Old Testament prophets. "We have all sinned," he cries, "some in greater measure, some in less; some on purpose, some by accident, some by our own fault, some by the fault of others; we have not kept our good resolutions; in spite of our will and our resistance we have lost our innocence." [15]

In these sentences we can hear, already, the distant lamentations of self-torturing Christians, the wild threnodies of despair uttered by men like Augustine who spent their existence in plaguing themselves for sins real and imaginary. Is it any wonder that a Christian writer said, *Seneca saepe noster* ("Seneca is frequently one of us")?

Epictetus (A.D. c. 60-c. 120) elaborated the Stoic emphasis on duty. Epictetus was a Greek slave who was given his freedom and afterwards taught philosophy, first at Rome and later in Epirus. His discourses were taken down by a pupil, Arrian, who in the second century published them in Greek with the title *Encheiridion* or "Handbook."

Epictetus stresses the godhead in man, exhorting us to make ourselves more aware of that godhead. His philosophy is a sort of moralistic pantheism. "When you are in the company of women, when you are conversing, when you are exercising, when you are disputing, do not you know that it is the Divine you feed, the Divine you exercise. You carry a God about with you, poor wretch, and know nothing of it." [16]

The God of Epictetus is a sort of moral watchman, though we must not confuse him here or elsewhere in Stoic philosophy with the Christian providence. The latter is a personalized being, the former is more of an abstract force. Epictetus' God hears and sees all. We must not, consequently, profane him with impure thoughts and unclean actions. In brief, this godhead who dwells within us demands obedience. Duty is the key to the ethics of Epictetus.

Pragmatically this amounts to the command, "follow nature!" We are urged to accept our lot in life, to observe that we are part of a world-scheme, a world-harmony, and warned that we must not be in opposition to the circumstances arranged for us by a benevolent and impersonal providence. The core of Epictetus' teaching is found in Fragment CXXXI of the *Encheiridion:*

> All things serve and obey the [laws of the] universe: the earth, the sea, the sun, the stars, and the plants and animals of the earth. Our body likewise obeys the same, in being sick and well, young and old, and passing through the other changes decreed. It is therefore reasonable that what depends on ourselves, that is, our own understanding, should not be the only rebel. For the universe is powerful and

[15] Quoted from Hammerton's *Universal History*, III, 1907.
[16] Bakewell, *op. cit.*, p. 321.

superior, and consults the best for us by governing us in conjunction with the whole. And further, opposition, besides that it is unreasonable and produces nothing except a vain struggle, throws us into pain and sorrows.[17]

This passage prepares us to understand the saying of Epictetus, *bear and forbear,* which A. W. Benn called the most momentous of its length in the whole literature of morality. If the command of Epictetus is *follow nature,* we must amend it, as Dean Inge suggests, to *follow nature and resist nature.* To know our place in the universal scheme, whether it be as shoemaker, banker, baker, or candlestick maker, is part of the essence of wisdom. We must also subdue our desires, and make the most of things.

The philosophy of Epictetus and Stoicism in general may be criticized for its bareness, its denial, as we shall note, particularly in Marcus Aurelius, of natural sentiments, of the warm human affections. When Seneca found his wife weeping for their child who had died, he comforted her by saying, "He is either happy or non-existent."

By its very nature, Stoicism could not make a wide appeal to the masses. It was an intellectual philosophy and religion, supported by reason and nourished as it were by repression. As such it passed into Christianity which in its earlier and purer phases possessed a great deal of the ascetic philosophy.

Epictetus reveals moods of religious yearning which remind us of many Christian saints, though we cannot define him as exactly a mystic. We might liken him, rather, to those modern scientists who, enthralled by the perfect mechanism of the cosmos which astrophysics is revealing to us, deduce from it that some rational, all-powerful being is at the basis of the universe. But it is easy to see how here, too, Epictetus may have given an impetus to Christianity. The following is an anticipation of many doxologies which appeared later in Christian literature:

> If we had understanding, ought we to do anything else than praise God and sing of his benefits? While we are digging and ploughing and eating, ought we not to sing this hymn? Great is God, who has given us these implements to till the earth; great is God, who has given us hands, and organs to breathe and digest our food. What else can I do, a lame old man, than sing hymns to God? If I were a nightingale, I would do the part of a nightingale; if a swan, I would do like a swan. But as I am a rational creature, my work is to praise God, and I will not cease to do so. I exhort you to join in the same song.[18]

Marcus Aurelius (A.D. 121-180) is the last of the great Stoic sages. In Marcus we have finally that which Plato yearned for, a philosopher-king. That he was an efficient ruler, we know, and had he lived in an earlier era he might have been another Augustus. He reigned in a melancholy time, and not all the sagacity and energy at his command could do much to stem the forces which were undermining the far-flung empire which his predecessors had conquered.

[17] Bakewell, *op. cit.,* p. 324.
[18] Quoted in Hammerton, *Universal History,* III, 1907.

Dean Inge calls him "dreamy, sensitive, hopeless." That he was sensitive we may agree, that he was dreamy or hopeless we deny. His book of *Meditations,* written in Greek, in the secrecy of his study, or in the privacy of his tent when he was on march with the Roman legions, is a work which the world has cherished, as it will always cherish the sensitive remarks of a man who saw civilization crashing all around him, but who did not break down and cry defeat. The *Meditations* have a message for mankind, and it can be summed up in a word, *Resignation.*

The doctrine of Marcus Aurelius takes its cue from some lines in Homer:

> Like the race of leaves
> The race of man is:—
> The wind in autumn strows
> The earth with old leaves; then the
> Spring the woods with new endows.

We should resign ourselves to the fact that men come and men go, and that after death, as Seneca said, we are either happy or nonexistent. But that does not matter. Marcus is an agnostic and what concerns him is the here and now. Therefore he says, with the logic of Stoicism, "Whatsoever is expedient unto thee, O World, is expedient unto me. Nothing can either be unseasonable unto me, or out of date, which unto thee is seasonable. Whatsoever thy seasons bear shall ever by me be esteemed as happy fruit and increase. O Nature! from thee are all things, in thee all things subsist, and to thee all tend." [19]

Marcus emphasizes the transiency of life, but he does not follow it with the advice to rush therefore into a round of pleasure and sip the wine while it lasts. He stands on the opposite side of the gospel of the Cyrenaics. Dean Inge says that in the *Meditations* everything in Stoicism has disappeared except the duty of resignation. It is, however, the resignation not of an unfeeling soul but of an extremely human person, one who accepts things as they are and who is, in his words, "kindly affected toward men."

Another point to notice in Marcus is that he slights the body, treating it somewhat like a corpse: his desire being to prepare for the annihilation of self which comes with death, and the return to the primordial essence of the universe.

It is easy to see that the philosophy of Marcus Aurelius could not appeal to the masses. It is too ascetic. Furthermore, people were craving for mystical faith and immortality in those days of a crumbling empire when unemployment, servility, and cruel taxes were making life unendurable for an increasing portion of the population.

The most representative mind in the intellectual history of Rome was that of Marcus Tullius Cicero of Arpinum (106-43 B.C.). He fell far behind Lucretius in intellectual brilliance and originality and he did not match Varro or Pliny the Elder for encyclopedic knowledge. But he presents the best example of what the Roman character could produce when subjected to Hellenic cultural influences. Roman intellectual life was chiefly a composite imitation of Hellenic learning, and Cicero was by both nature and education perfectly equipped to illustrate the

[19] Bakewell, *op. cit.,* p. 327.

Latin assimilation of Hellenism at its best. He was greatly enamored of Hellenic literature, learned quickly, had a very retentive mind, and excellent opportunities for wide travel and study. All this enabled him to absorb an unusual volume and variety of Greek and Hellenistic learning.

Joined to this was a remarkable felicity of expression which enabled him to set forth this Latinized Hellenism with charming ease. One of the leading historians of Roman literature, Wilhelm Teuffel, put the matter in a nutshell when he wrote that "Cicero possessed, to a wonderful extent, the power of appropriating and assimilating to his own individuality foreign ideas, and of dressing them up anew in an easy and pleasant style."

Cicero was the son of a Roman business man, or knight, as they were called, but he lined up politically with the aristocratic senatorial class. In order to train himself as an advocate and for a public career, Cicero plunged deeply into Greek learning and rhetoric at an early age. While a youth he was tutored by the able Greek poet, Archias, who lived in Rome. At this time, he read widely in the Greek poets and rhetoricians. There was a considerable influx of Greek scholars and teachers to Rome after 87 B.C. because of the wars of Mithridates. Cicero took advantage of this to continue his Greek studies intensively under representatives of the Platonic Academy, the Stoics, the Skeptics, and the Eclectics who expounded all varieties of Greek philosophy. About six years later Cicero left Rome for a period of travel and study in Athens, western Asia, and the various centers of Hellenistic learning. At the end of this travel-study expedition he was thoroughly versed in every aspect of Greek philosophy, rhetoric, and literature, and his retentive mind and facile style enabled him to make the most of his erudition.

While some of his works have been lost in whole or in part, we have more of Cicero's writings than of any other Latin author. They fall into three major divisions: (1) rhetorical; (2) philosophical; and (3) personal. Of the first, we have over fifty speeches, either delivered or written for delivery, and several treatises on rhetoric which were used for the instruction of Roman youth. His *De oratore, De inventione,* and *Topica* exercised a great influence on medieval rhetorical studies.

Cicero's philosophical writings cover such subjects as post-Aristotelian philosophy in Greece, Greek views on religion and theology, and ethics, practical philosophy, and political philosophy. From Cicero's *Academy,* the *Tusculan Disputations,* and *De finibus (On the Supreme Good)* has been derived most of what is today known of Greek philosophy after the age of Plato and Aristotle. Greek religious thought is best reflected in his books on *Divination* and *The Nature of the Gods.* The latter is far and away the best source of our knowledge of classical religion and theology. It presents the diversities of Greek religious philosophies and theologies in clear and tolerant fashion. There is no better way of driving home the contrast between pagan and Christian attitudes towards the supernatural world than by reading in succession Cicero's *The Nature of the Gods* and Augustine's *City of God.*

The best exposition of Cicero's views on ethics is contained in his *De officiis (On Duties).* In the realm of practical philosophy and moral aphorisms, Cicero is best known for his essays on *Friendship, Old Age,* and the *Tusculan Disputations.*

Cicero's political philosophy was contained mainly in his books *On the Commonwealth* (*De re publica*) and the *Laws.* His political theory was a compound of Stoicism and the views of Polybius, the Greek historian of Rome. From the Stoics he derived the notion of natural law as the norm by which to test the excellence of laws and political institutions. This view was handed down from Cicero to the church fathers and from them to the medieval writers on political theory, among whom the natural law doctrine was of prime importance. Polybius contributed the idea of the cycle of governmental changes—a common classical notion—and the dogma that Rome escaped from this cycle as a result of combining monarchical, aristocratic, and democratic elements in her constitution. Cicero is especially noted in political theory for his emphasis on the fact that justice is the core of the state and that the doing of justice is the chief political obligation. This view was an elaboration of Stoic moral and political philosophy.

Cicero was a parvenu and a social climber. Like so many of this type, he repudiated his own economic and social background and outdid even the aristocratic landlords in his social snobbery and his contempt for labor, industry, and trade. In a classic passage he wrote:

> All gains made by hired laborers are dishonorable and base, for what we buy of them is their labor, not their artistic skill: with them the very gain itself does but increase the slavishness of the work. All retail dealing too may be put in the same category, for the dealer will gain nothing except by profuse lying, and nothing is more disgraceful than untruthful huckstering. Again, the work of all artisans is sordid; there can be nothing honorable in a workshop.

Cicero's writings were otherwise urbane, tolerant, and undogmatic. They were a mosaic of Hellenic thought and learning. His extraordinary ability in gathering up Hellenic thought and interpreting it to Rome was the result of his tolerant interest in conflicting points of view as well as of his unusual assimilative powers. No one has succeeded better than Cicero in expressing the admirable attitude of urbanity and tolerance: "We who search for hypotheses are prepared both to refute without prejudice and to be refuted without resentment." It was not until the time of Erasmus, Montaigne, Bayle, Anthony Collins, and early modern freethinkers that such tolerance reappeared in human thought. Little wonder that the urbane Erasmus proposed to designate him as "Saint Cicero" and praised his tolerance as against the acrimony and dogmatism of medieval scholastic philosophers. Cicero stood at the opposite pole in mental outlook from the theological and philosophical wranglers who dominated European thought from the decline of Rome to the triumph of rationalism in the eighteenth century.

Cicero was one of the very few Latin prose writers who were relatively well known during the Middle Ages. Only a few of his writings were in circulation, however, and they related to rhetoric, education, and philosophy, subjects of direct interest to medieval schoolmen. When classical literature was revived by the humanists of the so-called Renaissance, Cicero enjoyed almost unrivaled popularity. This was mainly because of the clear and easy character of his thought and his polished and elegant style. At present, there is a tendency to deplore the fact that the florid Ciceronian Latin gradually displaced the clear and direct medieval Latin after the age of the humanists.

Roman education was as deeply influenced by Greek models as were other phases of Roman culture. Before the Hellenization of Rome began in the late third century B.C. most Roman education had been carried on in the homes. It was mainly physical, moral, and occupational education, based on the stern ideals of the virile days of the republic. By the second century the Greek influence had become preponderant in Roman education.

The elementary school which sprang up was known as the *ludus*. Here were taught the "three R's," reading, writing, and the elements of calculation. This school made practical use of popular historical tales and the laws of the twelve tables. Some Greek literature was read, especially the Latin version of the *Odyssey*. Harsh discipline prevailed.

Next above the ludus was the grammar school. Here the basic instruction was in grammar, rhetoric, and literature, with some attention to arithmetic, astronomy, geometry, geography, and music. Hence, the curriculum was very similar to that which came to prevail in the Middle Ages under the name of the seven liberal arts. There were both Latin and Greek grammar schools, and all Roman boys who wished to regard themselves as truly educated attended a Greek grammar school, even if they also went to the Latin school.

The main professional school was the rhetorical school, which was copied after the Greek model. Here the fundamental instruction was in oratory, on which subject Quintilian came to be the great authority. Enough literature was introduced to furnish a broad illustration of oratorical and rhetorical types. Rhetoric was the basic preparation necessary for public life until imperial despotism settled down upon Rome. In the later empire rhetorical instruction became more artificial, stereotyped, and threadbare than it had been in declining Greek society. There were no professional law schools. The prospective Roman lawyer first went through a rhetorical school and then listened to the public legal arguments and expositions of the eminent jurists. The Romans who wished a higher education attended the same universities as did Greek students, namely, those at Athens, Alexandria, Rhodes, Pergamum, and Rome. There were no Roman contributions to educational theory comparable to those made in Greece by the Sophists, Plato, and Aristotle. The only item worthy of notice here was the persuasive defense of rhetorical training by Quintilian and Cicero. Varro systematically classified and described the liberal arts, but added nothing to their content. An important contribution of the Romans to education was their dissemination of this Hellenized educational system, with the emphasis on rhetoric, throughout the length and breadth of the vast Roman Empire.

VI. RELIGIOUS BELIEFS AND PRACTICES OF ANCIENT ROME

Roman religion, like Roman civilization in general, was an amalgam, derived from the experiences of centuries (Rome had an active civilization for more than eight hundred years) and the cultures of many races.

Roman paganism was at first a primitive rustic cult. It was exposed to Hellenic paganism and Greek philosophy and borrowed ideas from both; then it came under the influence of Oriental mysteries, from which it adopted emperor worship, and the cult of the Great Mother Goddess of Asia Minor. In the later empire the Eleusinian mysteries, Mithraism, Manichaeism, Neoplatonism, Gnosticism, orthodox Christianity and others competed with the older Roman religions for popular favor. Christianity triumphed and finally extinguished them all.

The earliest Roman religion we can discern had reached the animistic stage of personified spirits, ranged into a hierarchy of good and evil types. Some traces, however, of preanimism with a belief in *mana,* the impersonal supernatural power of primitive religion, lingered. When employed as an adjective, *numen* seems originally to have meant something like mana, but when used as a noun denoted a supernatural being.

The earliest religious rites in Rome were connected with the family and the farm. They attempted to secure the gods' protection for an individual's domestic life and livelihood. The Roman peasant asked directly for security against evil spirits and demons and prosperity for crops and flocks. There was scarcely a philosophical undertone. Early Roman religion was a practical agrarian religion.

The genius or divinity of the paterfamilias (the head of the household) was believed to inhabit every dwelling. It was the procreative, life-giving power which made sure that the family perpetuated itself.

Important crises in family life required special rites. Great care was taken to prevent a child from coming under the influence of evil spirits at birth. In its second week of existence a baby was purified and adopted into the family. From this and similar rites elsewhere Christian baptism arose. Marriage and death had their special rituals. A bride was received by her husband according to certain ceremonials, particularly when she crossed the threshold of his house. A corpse was carried out with its feet forward, so that the ghost could not find its way back. The dead had to be thoroughly buried, else the ghosts would wander about the earth full of evil intentions. In such ways were the crises of life protected from the malice of supernatural spirits.

The center of early Roman religion was the home, where there were three places particularly sacred to the gods. In the hearth dwelt Vesta, the spirit of fire. To honor and placate her a piece of sacred cake was thrown into the hearth after the chief course of a midday meal. In the *penus* or storeroom dwelt the *di penates,* the storeroom guardians. The door or threshold required special rites, in order to keep the good spirits in the house and prevent ghosts and evil spirits from entering. Rituals for birth, death, marriage; ceremonials in honor of family ancestors, of Vesta, of the di penates, and of the door spirits assured the individual a prosperous and safe domestic existence.

Other aspects of early Roman religion revolved around the forces of fertility and the spirits associated with the family estate. First among these was the *lar familiaris,* the guardian spirit of the *heredium* (the plot of ground owned by a given family) and its productive power. The great festival of the *compitalia,* held shortly after the winter solstice, paid particular honor to the lar familiaris. Other rites celebrated the fixing of farm boundaries, thus insuring divine benediction on family property. The boundary points themselves were sacred spots, and were honored with due ceremonials.

In addition to rites which exhorted the gods to shower the family, the dwelling, and the estate with good luck, the Romans had a large number of vegetation festivals. In the spring the supernatural powers were supplicated in order to make the planted seed bear fruit. In the summer there were festivals expressing gratitude for the harvest, and hope that the grain would be gathered and stored successfully. In the autumn rites were celebrated in connection with preparing the soil for new seeds and another crop. Altogether, there were about forty-five agrarian festivals in early Rome.

Our information about the earliest Roman deities is vague. Most of it is derived from the calendar of festivals, on which we can distinguish about thirty-three *numina* or divine beings. The numina represent a kind of transition between animism and polytheism. Jupiter, Janus, Vesta, Tellus, and Mars were apparently the most important of the early personified spirits. Jupiter (Greek Zeus) was the benevolent protector of the physical universe, the ruler of the forces of nature. If properly propitiated Jupiter offered safety from the unseen and mysterious powers of nature.

Tellus was Mother Earth, the goddess of fertility, of the first importance to farmers, and worshiped at the vegetation festivals, as well as in marriage rites. Janus was originally a guardian spirit, first of the threshold and later of the entrance to the city of Rome itself. In later times, Janus became the god of a good beginning, and hence we get January, the first month. On New Year's Day in Rome there was fittingly a celebration in honor of Janus.

Mars originated as a wild woodland sprite, and later became the god of war. Vesta, at first a hearth spirit, became goddess of fire and at Rome there was a circular temple to her, with an altar in the center, in which was a fire that was never allowed to die. The attendants or priestesses in the temple of Vesta were called Vestal Virgins, and were chosen by the high priest, the pontifex maximus. Their duty was to feed the sacred flame of her temple, and offer sacrifices and prayers for the state's welfare.

Contact with the Greeks added to the Roman pantheon. Diana was a Roman equivalent of Artemis, Neptune the Roman Poseidon, Bacchus the Roman Dionysus, Ceres the Roman Demeter, and Mercury the Roman Hermes. Some authorities believe that not all these deities were naturalized Greeks, but that Rome developed them independently of Hellas.

As in the Greek pantheon, the chief Roman gods had definite services to render, services associated with human life and nature, guaranteeing safe contact with the physical universe, safe passage over the crises of existence, and prosperity in earning a livelihood.

As Rome developed and war became an important part of life, the early family religion broadened to meet new conditions, and supernatural protection was invoked for military as well as agricultural undertakings. In March, the month named after him, when military operations were about to begin, elaborate rites were offered to Mars the war god. In October, when the campaigns were usually over there were ceremonies for cleansing the soldiers from the taint of foreign blood, and from the alien and perhaps malevolent spirits with which they came in contact when they fought the hostile strangers. There were then military and agrarian festivals and on their days of celebration, *dies nefasti,* work or business was taboo. Altogether there were 109 holidays on the calendar and this, as Lucretius pointed out, meant a considerable waste of time, for which religion was mainly responsible.

The Romans, like the Greeks, practiced divination, in order to ascertain the will of the gods. As Rome became more warlike the practice increased. The gods' approval was requisitioned before the start of a campaign, as well as for any important public action. The Etruscans probably helped to develop the art of augury and divination among the Romans, who, before they adopted the Oriental method of examining the entrails of slaughtered beasts, took their omens from the flight of birds. In the Second Punic War, when Hannibal was on the point of crushing Rome, new ways were sought for discovering the will of the gods. Then the Romans turned to the Sibylline Books of the Greeks.

The augurs or diviners were organized into a corporation or college. This marked the emergence of a state religion, paralleling the old family cult. The augurs or priests controlled jurisprudence as well as divination. Their power was immense, since early Roman law comprised chiefly religious customs and precepts, a knowledge of which was the monopoly of the priesthood. The appearance of the laws of the Twelve Tables about 450 B.C. indicated that law and religion were being divorced. In fact, the priesthood slowly lost its legal monopoly, and in time was completely superseded by the local magistracy.

Contact with Greek civilization influenced Roman religion profoundly. Not only were Hellenic gods Romanized, but Hellenic theology was borrowed, particularly the Stoic rationalization of the supreme power which ruled nature. Stoicism appealed especially to the Roman intellectual because it permitted him to be pious and rational at the same time. For the Roman masses, Greece provided the Asiatic mystery cults with their interest in the afterlife.

Greek influence in fact insinuated an Oriental flavor into Roman paganism. The Sibylline Books suggested that the Romans should appropriate the Great Mother Goddess of Asia Minor. When she was Romanized after the Hannibalic War the preliminary step was taken in exposing Rome to Oriental cults, a step which had great consequences, and paved the way for the triumph of Christianity. The Romans, like the Greeks, had vague ideas about the afterlife, and believed in immortality as a sort of drab and indefinite existence. Their concern was with burying the dead thoroughly, so as not to expose themselves to mischief-minded ghosts. The Oriental mystery religions had more definite ideas about life after death and brought forth a vivid heaven and hell, conceived originally in ancient Persia.

As the republic wore on there was an increasing popularity of Oriental religions which in time almost completely deluged the older Roman paganism. Hellenistic astrology also became a fad, and many a wealthy Roman had his private astrologer, as in the Middle Ages many a baron had his private chaplain. Then came the cult of emperor worship, as already observed, with sun worship in its train.

The Oriental mysteries began their triumphal march in the later republic. The old Roman religion had lost some of its appeal; it had grown moribund and less able than in the old days to furnish emotional satisfaction.

As economic conditions grew worse in the empire and life became more difficult for an increasing number of people, any religion which offered an attractive afterlife, as Roman paganism did not, was bound to make a strong appeal. If life here and now offered so little, why not enroll in a cult which repudiated the here and now and extolled the pleasures of the hereafter? Who would not exchange a wretched mortality—and it became increasingly wretched as the empire began to crack up—for a blessed immortality? Furthermore, the ritual and pageantry of the Oriental mysteries were far more seductive than pagan ceremonials.

Consequently, the four leading Oriental religions in the empire, Persian Mithraism, the Egyptian cult of Isis and Serapis, Palestinian Christianity and the cult of the Great Mother Goddess of Phrygia gradually crowded out Roman civic and family cults. Long before Christianity triumphed, in the fourth century, it became obvious that the Oriental religions were superseding Roman paganism. Even the efforts of Augustus could not save the native *lares* and *penates*. It was only a question as to which mystery would become supreme.

Of course, to many enlightened Romans, particularly the Epicureans, any religion was obnoxious. Or was the intelligentsia's aversion to Roman religion explicable, somewhat at least, by the poverty of that religion? The great Belgian authority, Franz Cumont, laid down the verdict that "never did a people of advanced culture have a more infantile religion."

Ennius (c. 239-c. 170 B.C.) had translated from Greek into Latin *The Sacred History of Euhemerus* which declared that the gods were only deified human beings. In his dramas Ennius propagated the view of Epicurus that the gods paid no attention to human problems and lived in Olympian isolation. Lucretius and Horace took an aggressive stand against religion and argued that the foolish fears and anguish it produced were very costly to society.

We thus observe how, in the course of about seven hundred years, Roman religion passed from a rustic family cult, whose chief business was protection against evil spirits, into a multiplicity of world religions with a marked mass appeal based on the offer of blessed immortality.

VII. ROMAN LAW

A Frenchman has said that "Rome's mission was war and her vocation law." It was in the field of legal theory and practice that Rome made some of its most enduring contributions to the civilization of western Europe. In the course of the thousand years of its legal development, Rome succeeded in creating both a science and an art of law. The body of legal theory and practice which was one of Rome's great gifts to the future history of mankind has provided the regulations by which a considerable part of the human race has governed itself.

The influence of Roman law has been far-reaching indeed. It was the basis of the law in all Romance lands throughout the Middle Ages. It provided the framework for canon law—the law of the Roman Catholic church. It became of extreme importance in political life and discussion throughout western Europe towards the close of the Middle Ages. Its influence is apparent in the legal codes of modern European countries since the close of the eighteenth century, and in English law—especially the law merchant. The place of Roman law in the history of civilization can scarcely be exaggerated.

The Romans evolved, in their long contact with many races and diverse psychologies, an eminently workable philosophy of law, which in a nutshell may be defined as the art of justice. What, then, is jurisprudence (the science of law)? It is, according to the Romans, a knowledge of justice and injustice.

A jurist's business was to bring the two litigants together, to practice the art of justice by knowing what is right and what is wrong according to the broadest social viewpoint. And who, after all, sets the norm in standards of justice? The Romans concluded that justice is not a revelation from heaven. Human nature is a constant, and the test of justice is that which an honest man of common sense would always deem to be right. Moreover, justice is not a static affair the principles of which may be formulated once and forever. Human nature may be a constant, but the environment changes, times change. And here the Romans made another great contribution to civilization; they regarded law as something always subject to change and in a state of development, and held that the practical applications of justice must be continually restudied in the light of new conditions.

In other words, no body of law may be permitted to exist unchanged for long, but must be constantly improved and brought up to date, in order to meet changing conditions, new forces in the environment. In this respect, our present-day reactionary opponents of efforts to modify antiquated legal concepts and methods are pitifully behind the times. They have not yet caught up with a legal philosophy which the Romans were practicing two thousand years ago.

Broadly speaking, there were no *a priori* principles upon which the whole body of Roman law was erected. Roman law, having slowly developed out of practical demands, was distinctly not a product of any formal preëxisting legalistic conceptions. It evolved slowly as a means of dealing with practical problems. Secular law came to be regarded as the mode of social control par excellence in Rome, and the Roman jurists insisted upon the subordination of all citizens and their activities to the reign of law. Roman private law rescued the individual from the associations of one kind or another in which he had been obscured, and recognized him as a distinct entity. The Roman lawyers derived from imperialistic experiences and international contacts a theory of the universality of fundamental legal principles which they believed to be common to all rational men.

One of the most important sources of Roman law was primitive custom. Since the earliest regulation of custom was intrusted to the priests, for many generations law was hardly distinguished from religion. It was at first entirely a matter of ritual, and religious elements were dominant in the origins of Roman law. The religious law—*jus divinum*—was for some centuries about the only law the Romans knew. Its chief aim was to keep the peace with the gods, and a violation of taboos was the chief crime. The law was in the hands of the priests and this fact gave the priestly class great power. The impact of the Etruscans seems to have been the vital influence in breaking down this priestly monopoly, secularizing Roman law and opening the way for its evolution.

Yet, important as it may have been, religious custom was only one of the sources from which the body of Roman law grew. The jurists themselves recognized that statutes, plebiscites, decisions of the Senate, decisions and edicts of magistrates, imperial decrees, and the interpretations of jurists all entered into its derivation. The sources that gave Roman law its most original characteristics, and explain at the same time its fertility and flexibility, were the *leges* or statutory enactments, the edicts of the magistrates, and the interpretations of the lawyers. Obviously enough, all these influences did not always operate with equal effect at the same time, nor did they all persist throughout the thousand years of Roman legal development. They made themselves felt at different times and in varying degrees.

The laws of the Twelve Tables (c. 450 B.C.) constituted the first step in the development of written law. The civil law—*jus civile*—which appeared in the Twelve Tables was suited to a relatively simple society not far advanced economically, and it contained many primitive elements. Nevertheless, it remained the written law which regulated the life of the Romans until the last quarter of the second century B.C. This was made possible by the fact that the provisions of the laws of the Twelve Tables were not entirely rigid, but were constantly being modified and expanded by the interpretations of trained jurists who adapted them to new conditions. This made for an extremely flexible and practical body of law.

Before a lawsuit was tried, both parties to the case consulted students of the law, who rendered advice to the litigants which was supposed to be wholly impartial in nature. Many of these legal experts kept records of their cases and there thus developed a body of practical legal literature. After having received advice, the parties to the suit appeared before the praetor. This magistrate did one of two things: he either settled the case then and there by handing down his final interpretation of the law involved, or he passed the case on with instructions to a trial judge (*judex*), usually a senator, who then determined its outcome. In a broad way, it may be said that the praetor ruled on matters of law and the judge on the facts of the case.

As Rome expanded by conquest and became a cosmopolitan city, necessity demanded the creation of a new magistracy. The office of *praetor peregrinus* was instituted (247 B.C.) to take care of cases in which a foreigner was a participant. The praetor peregrinus, unlike the older *praetor urbanus,* was free from the restraints of the laws of the Twelve Tables, and he was able to introduce new principles in the settlement of lawsuits. In time, it became customary for the praetor to issue an edict when he asumed office. In this he enunciated the working rules which were to guide him in settling disputes. These edicts were sometimes modified by the succeeding praetor and sometimes reissued without change. They made up in time a considerable body of legal theory and practice. Not until the time of Hadrian did this process of modification and interpretation cease. The governors in the provinces usually followed the legal concepts and procedure of the praetor peregrinus in Rome.

In this new legal procedure that developed and was applied in cases involving foreigners, the magistrates were not averse to adopting legal practices of non-Roman origin, especially when the latter were better suited to problems arising from more mature economic conditions than were the provisions of the Twelve Tables. In many ways, the legal practice covering cases that involved foreigners was thus far in advance of that which obtained in disputes between Roman citizens.

Toward the close of the second century B.C., the mode of procedure of the peregrin praetors was transferred to the urban praetors—an existing remedy was thus adopted to meet changing conditions—and many dogmas and methods of the Twelve Tables were thus given their deathblow.

As a result of this praetorian legal theory and practice, and of the contact with the many cultures of the empire there developed what is known as the *jus gentium*—the composite law common to peoples of the eastern Mediterranean world [20]—which was distinguished from the jus civile, the law of Rome and its citizens. In time the more advanced jus gentium was occasionally accepted by Roman citizens in their dealings among themselves, and in a few instances it became an integral part of the jus civile. From it there also developed the notion of the *jus naturale,* those basic legal principles believed to be common to all mankind. The jus naturale was more of a legal philosophy than a body of formal law. In the process of assimilating foreign law to Roman usage, the contribution of Greece was, as Vinogradoff has suggested, very important.

Under the empire new sources of law arose. Such were the *edicta,* the true legislative enactments of the empire; *decreta* or imperial judgments; *rescripta,* the answers to petitions involving points of law; and the *mandata,* orders issued to provincial governors to guide them in the conduct of public affairs.

A most important rôle in the development of Roman law was played by the jurists with their close reasoning and their examination and interpretation of legal problems. They advised both judges and practicing attorneys, as well as private individuals. Briefly, the function of the jurists was to relate the law to concrete

---

[20] Not to be confused with what we now know as international law—the principles governing the relations between states.

cases, to see clearly how the law should be applied in order to bring about what was "good and fair." The most outstanding of the early jurists was Sextus Aelius Paetus, who was consul in 197 B.C. The really great names in Roman law, however, date from a later time. Sabinus, Julianus, Papinian, Paulus, Gaius, Ulpian, and Modestinus all lived under the empire. The later jurists incorporated into their legal thought, along with the Roman elements, the Stoic conception of a natural law governing all mankind. The particular function of the jurists, as well as the fundamental achievement of Rome in the field of law, is set forth in the following sentences:

> No people have drawn a clearer distinction than the Romans between the absolute and the relative, or better understood that every legal solution belongs to the sphere of contingency. Their endeavour was to make apparent in each particular case what appeared to them to be Law, and then, better still, what with greater moral refinement they called Equity.[21]

The Roman jurists also indirectly supplied instruction in law. They argued important cases and legal problems in public. Persons interested in the law would gather to listen to the exposition. Principles of jurisprudence and case analysis were thus supplied. Students tended to follow one or another type of interpretation of Roman law, and thus different schools of law arose.

Our law of contract is that part of the modern law which is most definitely Roman in essence. In Roman law a man was bound to carry out his promise or contract, regardless of the circumstances which influenced the making of the contract. Fraud, ignorance, or force was not an excuse for annulling a legal promise. However, the praetor or judge could step in and, after listening to the pleas, might nullify the contract on the basis of the facts presented. This, substantially, is modern legal practice. The concept of "good faith," which is an integral part of our law, was also worked out by Roman jurists.

Just as the transition from city-state to empire is reflected in the development of Roman law, so the appearance of an absolute emperor stimulated the tendency towards codification. Two compilations of imperial legislation were undertaken at the close of the third century A.D. Then, in A.D. 438, the first part of the code of Theodosius II appeared. This showed very clearly the influence of Christianity. The most important and complete codification of Roman law was the product of the extensive labors initiated by the Byzantine Emperor Justinian. This enterprise resulted in: (1) the *Code*, in 529 (a revised edition appeared five years later), in which the earlier codes were recast and brought together; (2) the *Digest*, in 533, consisting of cogent excerpts from juristic writings and legal opinions; and (3) the *Institutes*, a concise manual of Roman law, in the same year. The name *Novels* is given to the laws of Justinian which were promulgated after the Code was completed. The codification by Justinian, while it put an end to the further development of Roman law, at the same time served as one of the most important agencies procuring its preservation for subsequent ages.

Roman law was of the greatest importance for later European history. As has

21 Joseph Declareuil, *Rome the Law-Giver*, Knopf, 1926, p. 25.

been already noted, it furnished the basis for the canon law of the Roman Catholic church. At the height of the Middle Ages, Roman law was revived and exploited by the secular monarchs in their struggle against the church. Roman law laid great stress upon the supremacy of imperial authority over all contending groups and classes. Hence it buttressed the claim of the monarchs to dominion over the church when the two came into conflict. Roman lawyers flocked to the courts and were patronized by the monarchs whom they served. Law schools, of which the most famous was the one at Bologna, developed to give adequate training in Roman law. Even the Christian church was rent by a great dispute (the Conciliar Movement) which, in part, turned on the application of Roman law to the principles and problems of ecclesiastical administration.[22] Finally, Roman law became a powerful bulwark of secular absolutism when the latter came into being along with the rise of the national state in early modern times. The conception of popular sovereignty in Roman law was a powerful impulse to the later development of representative government.

VIII. LATIN LITERATURE

1. *The Periods of Latin Literature*

Roman literature in its early development was thoroughly native in subject matter, in treatment, and in sentiment. It seems to have arisen from the social interests of primitive religion and primitive legal arrangement and finds its culmination as a purely Roman and native art with so thoroughly practical a work of everyday advice as Cato's book on farming. What Roman literature might have been if it had continued to develop as a purely native art under the stimulus of purely Roman forces we can hardly guess. But it was not allowed so to develop, for in the third and second centuries B.C., its course was deflected by the influence of a thoroughly mature, many-sided, and even sophisticated art—the literature of Greece, whose outline we traced in our last chapter. Roman writers, frequently with the encouragement of wealthy and powerful Romans, set themselves to translate, adapt, and rebuild their Greek models.

We may, for convenience, distinguish four stages in the history of Latin literature:

    1. Formative period: from the beginning to 83 B.C.;
    2. The golden age: 83 B.C. to 14 A.D. (death of Augustus);
    3. The silver age: 14 A.D. to 117 A.D.;
    4. Age of decline: A.D. 117 to the fall of the Empire in the West.

The golden age may be subdivided into the "Republican" and "Augustan" ages. The first is a period of great names: Catullus, Lucretius, Cicero, Caesar, and Sallust; the second, of names that are hardly less great: Vergil, Horace, Livy, Tibullus, Propertius, and Ovid. Conventionally the silver age is regarded as a time of decline. However, it produced one of Rome's greatest prose stylists in Tacitus; the Roman master of the epigram in Martial; a writer of graceful prose in the

[22] See below, pp. 512-13.

younger Pliny; the satirist Juvenal; the polished cynic Petronius; the rhetorician, Quintilian; and attempts at the epic, dull and unconvincing, to be sure, by Statius and Lucan.

With the second century the decline of Roman society set in and this decline was reflected in the literature of the period. The creative impulse grew dim; there was little enthusiasm either in letters or in life; the empire was on the defensive and its writers were driven back into themselves. The professor succeeded the poet, the critic and rhetorician held sway. An excessive individualism led to an excessive interest in problems of conduct, to an insipid and rhetorical sermonizing or to the development of a talent for scandal and gossip. Subject matter became more sensational, as in the spicy *Lives of the Caesars* of Suetonius. The chief authors of this era included, in addition to Suetonius, Fronto the rhetorician, and Apuleius the novelist.

After the Antonine emperors the best Latin literature is Christian literature, since by that time the sect was sufficiently Romanized, and contained enough educated converts to inaugurate a literary tradition of its own. This literature will be discussed in Chapters VII-VIII.

2. *Latin Poetry*

In the first period we find the development from early religious chants and lays to the beginnings of a rude native verse scheme—the Saturnian meter, and so thoroughly Roman a work as that of the elder Cato on "Farming."

We find, too, the beginnings of Greek influence: translations from the Greek, the development of a Roman comedy on Greek models, the creation of the Latin hexameter and the Roman epic, and the growth of a purely native genre, the satire, which Lucilius made into a weapon of biting and incisive comment on men and society.

There is much to support the convention which regards a Greek slave, Titus Andronicus, as the founder of Latin poetry: he translated the *Odyssey* into a primitive Roman meter to use as a textbook in his teaching. We have a few remaining fragments which enable us to contrast the breadth, spaciousness, rapidity of the original with the stilted, pedantic, and cramped rendering of the Roman copy. Fortunately, perhaps, this slave and schoolmaster did not create a mold for Latin poetry, which took a different direction, drank deeper draughts from Hellenic springs, and set itself to copy, naturalize, and adapt Greek rhythms and meters as well as Greek themes. The attempt to use native Roman measures did not emerge again until the age of affected and self-conscious archaistic revival in the period of decline.

Naevius (264-194 B.C.) was a significant figure in several ways. He wrote the first Roman epic, the *Bellum Punicum,* on the great historical conflict between Rome and Carthage. This work, in native Saturnian meter, was widely influential; it was mentioned by Horace as a textbook of his school days and it inaugurated a tendency very congenial to the Roman temperament to glorify the patriotic Roman past. In many ways an event of equal significance was his attempt to adapt to Roman conditions the old social and political drama that had once flourished under Aristophanes. In the course of his work he made a sharp attack on the powerful family of the Metelli, and was promptly disciplined for his daring. It will be, perhaps, not fanciful to trace to the failure of this attempt the relatively insipid development of Roman comedy as a comedy of manners and stock characters.

Roman comedy was a crude and undeveloped instrument until it was caught up in the full tide of Hellenic influence. We may regard Plautus (254-184 B.C.) as responsible for the real genesis of Roman comedy. He seems to have risen from humble origin, to have been a manual laborer before he became a playwright. A certain earthy homeliness characterizes his work to the end. His life seems to have been hard and impoverished and we can detect a frequent undertone of bitterness in his writings. There can be little question that Plautine comedy suffered from the "censorship" that the fate of Naevius imposed on later poets. In Plautus the times and the man conspired to produce a comedy of vigorous social satire, not conservative as in the case of Aristophanes, laughing at any innovation, but radical and critical of Roman mores (ways of thought and life) and the governing class. But this he could not attain. He laughed at Roman institutions, Roman foibles, and Roman weaknesses, but was careful to keep over all a Greek veneer. In his work the plot and setting is always Greek, but in harmless and nonpolitical matters a kind of rollicking, good-humored criticism of things Roman constantly breaks through. He was a man of the people throughout, his language was the language of the vernacular and the streets; his humor and his talents were ribald and earthy. It is something of a literary tragedy that this genius of the people should have been so thwarted and deformed, forced to manipulate stock situations and stereotyped characters, his genius channeled off into such sickly and insipid themes.

Twenty-one of his plays survive—adaptations and combinations from the "new comedy" of Philemon and Menander—and within the limitations that the social situation imposed on him they run the gamut of personal and social comedy. It is no accident that the comedy of manners of the French, English, and Italian "Renaissance" should have drawn so heavily on Plautine comedy and themes.

The other great Roman comic poet of the period, Terence, presents a tremendous contrast. He was a member of an aristocratic circle and wrote for a cultivated and sophisticated audience. He has nothing of Plautus' exuberance and productivity; but his few plays show a polish that Plautus quite lacks. Plautus wrote "for the galleries," Terence for the boxes and the pit. Plautus' plays were a hilarious success when acted. The plays of Terence carry their appeal in the quiet of the study; they were failures on the stage. Furthermore, Plautus had used his Greek originals with discretion, had adapted freely and combined carelessly, infusing everything with his own native and boisterous humor. Terence follows his originals with slavish fidelity and obtains his effects by concentrating on wit and polish and purity of diction.

With Terence begins the process by which literature becomes divorced from the interests of the people to become the exclusive possession of a jaded and wealthy class. With Terence begins the tendency to emphasize purity of diction, correctness of sentiment, appropriateness of taste. The people, their interests, their outlook, even their speech—spoken Latin hereafter hardly enters the field of written literature—more and more were elbowed out of the field of vision of the playwright and the poet. This fact will perhaps account for the rapid exhaustion and increasing insipidity of Latin literature after its brief period of bloom, in the brief heyday of Roman and national patriotism, the creation of the Empire and the rise of the bourgeoisie. This, too, will perhaps account for the relative failure of drama as an art form after Terence. It lost its popular appeal, became an aristocratic preserve and a playground of preciosity. It could no longer hold its own against the gladiatorial combats with their saltier and more direct appeal.

We may mention one other poet from this early period, not because there is any likelihood that because of this mention he may be again extensively read (only 600 lines of his work survive), but because of his great influence on a succeeding generation of Latin writers. Quintus Ennius (c. 239-170 B.C.) was the first great Latin writer. He translated Greek tragedy. He set the fashion for the patriotic epic (his *Annales* were immensely popular and widely quoted in Rome and, in fact, became the great national epic until they were supplanted by Vergil's *Aeneid*). He created the Roman hexameter, the poetical instrument of Lucretius and of Vergil, which Tennyson regarded as "the stateliest measure ever molded by the lips of man." Both Cicero and Lucretius speak of Ennius with profound respect—father Ennius, our own Ennius, who "first brought down from lovely Helicon the garland of leaf undying."

3. The Poetry of the Republic

Two great poets will represent for us the poetry of the Roman Republic—to the taste of many the greatest of Roman poets, Lucretius and Catullus. No two poets could be more different. Lucretius brought to Rome the didactic poem, and his theme was a mature one—physical reality and the external universe, which he treats in a mood of the most austere, scientific enthusiasm. The Latin hexameter, a relatively crude and imperfect instrument in the hands of Ennius, becomes in Lucretius' *De rerum natura* a poetical vehicle of marvelous flexibility and power, with a finish almost equal to Vergil's but with infinitely more masculinity and vigor.

Lucretius made it his aim to expound for Roman readers the philosophy of Epicurus, thinking that in this he had a weapon capable of destroying religion, superstition, and the fear of the gods. Only by so doing, he believed, could the way be clear for man to live free from fear and tranquil in spirit.

When human life lay foully prostrate before our eyes, crushed to earth beneath the dire weight of Religion, which showed its face from Heaven scowling at mortals from above with grim visage, a man of Greece first dared to raise his mortal eyes against her, first to stand against her; and him neither myths told of the gods nor thunderbolts, nor heaven with threatening crash could dismay, but all the more aroused the eager valor of his spirit so that he longed to be first among mankind to burst through the close bars of nature's portals. And so the living power of his mind prevailed and he marched far beyond the flaming ramparts of the universe and traversed the whole immense in spirit and in mind.

With religion Lucretius dealt faithfully if not lovingly. He recounts the foul deeds it has induced, in language of exquisite pathos, telling the fate of the maid in Iphigenia sacrificed by an ambitious father to appease the gods and assure fair sailing for his fleet. *Tantum religio potuit suadere malorum*—a line that is almost a sob—"That's the kind of monstrous deed that religion could induce." He details the origin of religion: man's helplessness in the face of natural powers and the majestic panorama of natural phenomena; the visions of superhuman figures that man has always seen in sleep or wakefulness. "And they placed in heaven the habitations and abodes of the gods because night and the moon seemed to move through the heavens, the moon and day and night and the austere constellations of the night, the sky's night wandering torches and flitting flames, clouds, and sun, showers and snow, winds, lightning, hail, the swift moving noise of thunder and its great noise of threats." No translation can possibly do justice to the incomparable majesty of this march of natural phenomena. And so, Lucretius insists, humanity made its profoundest error when it saw the hand of the gods behind natural phenomena and connected with that hand the purely personal resentments of human will. As a weapon against this error and in order to remove fear and to provide the objective prerequisites for a peace of mind, he valued the "golden" words of his master, the philosopher Epicurus, whom he held to be half-divine. It is for this struggle against the gods that Lucretius values the study of physical nature and with enthusiasm and poetical skill expounds his atomic theory.

But his austerity and scientific enthusiasm is relieved by an extraordinary tenderness for the tiny helpless things of earth—colts with their tottering legs, little lambs who frisk intoxicated in their "new little minds" with their mother's milk, the dog who crouches to the ground expecting blows, the bereaved cow whose calf is taken away for sacrifice. Here he strikes a new note in Latin, and perhaps all ancient, literature. His sympathy is not with the god who sniffs with appreciation the savor of a burnt offering, nor with the man who bargains with his deity, but with the mother who is bereaved and mourns and cannot be comforted by fresh grass or flowing stream because her child is no more.

Lucretius manifests, too, a most extraordinary sharpness of observation and a fine concreteness of visual imagery. He observes the shells on the seashore "painting the bosom of earth," the flapping of colored awnings on the theater, clothes that will not dry by the seashore, the cock that flaps the light out with his wings, dogs who sleep by the fire and dream of the hunt, a woman's stealthy skill that wears down a man's resistance like the quiet persistence of water dropping on a hard rock.

He has an extraordinary sense of the rush and life and movement of natural things—the upsurge of trees and shrubs, the "ice of brass" that melts in the flame, flowers that burst into a "flame" of color. And all these qualities of high poetry are subordinated to his central task: to free men from fear, to show that death is oblivion, to induce the quiet mind by an exposition of his scientific philosophy! [23]

No poet could provide a sharper contrast to Lucretius than Catullus. In him we have a poet who gave lyrical [24] expression to a purely personal emotion, expressed with a poignancy and beauty that makes Gaius Valerius Catullus (84-54 B.C.) worthy to be mentioned in the same breath with Sappho. Catullus was at his best when writing of Lesbia (in all probability) the notorious Clodia, a lady of fashion, the wife of Metellus Celer and sister of Clodius, Cicero's great enemy, and herself the object of bitter and scornful language from Rome's foremost orator. Never perhaps has the course of true love run so stormily and never has emotion been so well reflected in its every shade. The Lesbia series begins with the playful tenderness of the first ode to his lady's sparrow—light, boyish, and gay—the half serious mourning for the death of the sparrow—"A curse upon you, you cursed shades of hell, who gulp down every pretty thing; so pretty is the sparrow that you have taken from me. Fell deed! Poor little sparrow! For you now my lady's eyes are red and swollen with weeping." But playfulness gives way and recklessness takes its place (we paraphrase rather than translate):

> Life, Lesbia, life and love
> And as for growls of grim old greybeards
> Let's hold them all together at just about a nickel's worth.
> The suns can rise and set to rise again forever.
> But we, when once our brief day is set—
> Night is eternal—one long, long sleep time.
> Pile on your kisses thousand on thousand, hundred on hundred.
> And then we'll wipe the slate clean
> So that no envious tongue may bewitch
> Through knowing the score of our kisses.

The affair proceeds through every phase of ardor, quarrel, and reconciliation. The devotion is on one side; on the other perhaps a thin, sensuous attraction and perhaps a sense of gratification that such a talent as Catullus' should be laid at her feet. She bullied him in the presence of her husband—a most humiliating position for ardent and illusioned youth!—and flitted from one affair to another. Catullus pleads with her lovers, thinking this may help to keep her faithful; but disillusionment finally arrives in the person of his own best friend. And so he comes to view her with mixed emotions:

> I love her and I hate her. Perhaps you ask how that can be. How I don't know; but I know that it is so and I am torn on the rack.

Our poet reasons with himself: "Poor Catullus, cease your folly and what you see is dead, count dead." In time he comes to take a man's clear view of the present and the past:

---

[23] The reader may care to refer again to Tennyson's poem "Lucretius," where is reproduced the old polemical legend that Lucretius died in madness as a result of a love potion from his jealous wife.

[24] Roman lyric poetry is lyric in the modern sense—that is, unaccompanied by music; in Horace much mention of harp and lyre is kept as a literary convention.

If there is any pleasure for a man to recall his earlier kindnesses, when he reflects that *he* has been loyal, has never violated the sanctity of honor, has never abused in any relationship the power of god to cheat his fellowmen, then many joys await you in the years to come, Catullus, from this unhappy love of yours.— Why, then, torture yourself more? Strengthen yourself in soul and draw your footsteps home, all the way home. O cease to grieve: god asks no grief from you.— O god, if it is yours to pity—look upon poor me and as I have lived in purity take this plague, this pest from me. Alas it crept like languor into my marrow bones and drove all gladness from my heart. I now no longer ask that she should love me in return: or the impossible that she should want to be chaste and true. For myself I pray, health, to lay aside this foul disease. O god, grant me this if I have ever served you!

The gods granted his prayer but with the perishing of his love all that was poignant and sensitive and beautiful perished too. Outside of this extraordinary sequence of love poems there was little of first-class merit in Catullus' work. There was an enthusiastic poem in praise of Sirimio—gem of islands and peninsulas where he had his villa—"Sweet Catullus all-but-island, Olive silvery Sirimio." There was a poignant poem on his brother's death—"Atque in perpetuum, frater, ave atque vale." (And forevermore, my brother, I greet you and say farewell.) There were marriage hymns of a rather academic sort (marked by occasional flashes of extraordinary tenderness); there was an attempt at an epic, and many poems of coarse and bitter lampoon directed against political and private enemies. But the story of Catullus as a great lyric poet is almost commensurate with the story of Clodia, the lady who "made a poet out of a man," and this experience raised Catullus to the lyric heights.

We have perhaps sufficiently indicated that Roman lyric poetry had reached a high state of development and had even produced in the poems of Catullus work that might merit the epithet "masterpiece." Quintus Horatius Flaccus was not, in spite of his own rather boastful words, the first to adapt Aeolian lays to Latin measures. Nor did he possess any of the lyrical passion and direct feeling that marked the poetry of Catullus. Horace's work was marked rather by wit, polish, good taste, and urbanity. Of genuine feeling he manifests little and when Rome, his one enthusiasm, moves him to fervor, he tends to draw back, to whistle his little Muse home again, and take refuge in good-natured and skeptical banter.

Horace was the son of a freedman. His father was probably an auctioneer's clerk and we find very touching references to his father's careful supervision of his education. Horace received, we are told by the poet himself, the education that any knight or senator would give his own offspring. So that nothing might be lacking to his education, Horace's father himself acted as *paidagogos* or escort to and from school, improving the occasion with simple moral admonitions and examples. After he had imbibed grammar and literature at the hands and the ruler of Orbilius ("the man of many blows") Horace was sent as an undergraduate to Athens to steep himself in philosophy and the customary higher education. The civil wars interrupted his undergraduate days. He served in command of a legion under Brutus at Philippi, where, he tells us, he ingloriously threw aside his shield and ran. Returning to Rome he experienced the hardship of "Grub Street days": the life of a literary man without adequate patronage. His earlier work bears the marks of this experience, particularly the *Epodes* and first book of the *Satires* which are strongly satirical in our modern sense. Fortunately he was rescued from poverty by an introduction to Maecenas (Vergil introduced him and Horace amusingly described the scene: his blushing, stammering embarrassment could hardly have convinced the great man of his worth). Maecenas gave him a country house—the famous Sabine farm in the hills some miles east of Tivoli and Horace set to work to cultivate simple tastes and the life of a country gentleman.

His life was, from hence forward, uneventful. Once he was nearly killed by a tree falling on his head and the occasion of his escape was made into a second birthday. The incident also provided the theme for two poems of mild mockery and skillful moralizing. From this perhaps we can gather something of the measure of the man.

The three books of *Odes,* appearing in 23 B.C., may be regarded as his best work. Horace has been described as an Epicurean but an Epicurean he was in only a modified and eclectic sense. He has nothing of the intellectual breadth that characterized Lucretius: he cared nothing for the study of nature, of the heavens, the physical universe, the origin of man, or the baleful influence of religion. His Epicureanism gave him the excuse for trite moralizing and the regurgitation of old commonplaces. It gave him a chance to preach his favorite doctrine of the simple life—simplicity as it is understood by the comfortable suburbanite. For the deeper scientific enthusiasms of the Epicureans he cared nothing and even its moral outlook he could lay aside on occasion like a well-worn cloak, when he wanted to evoke the old thrill of Roman patriotism, warn his countrymen against the impending dangers of civil war, make a graceful genuflection before the traditional religion of the countryside, or flatter the great and powerful in terms a little too fulsome to be (from an Epicurean point of view, at least) quite nice. He even suggested that Augustus was present on earth as a god (Mercury, the traditional patron of traders—and thieves). No good Epicurean could have been guilty of such a lapse.

But in spite of these obvious limitations Horace's poetry has a wide appeal. It is not simply an accident of the curriculum that for centuries generations of schoolboys have found in him stimulus and amusement. It is partly that every temperament from patriot to puritan, from cynic to sensualist, can find some doctrine of consolation expressed in the most quotable and epigrammatic Latin, and so fortify his own prejudice by an appeal to hoary tradition. It is much more the extraordinary skill and facility with which Horace expressed himself. He is the most quoted and most quotable of poets and dozens of his lines have passed as proverbs into every modern Western tongue. Horace himself tells us his secret—it is the *labor limae*—the toil of the file, the constant process of polishing and finishing which brings perfection. It is the beauty of the miniature and the filigree rather than a great canvas or impressive piece of statuary.

Publius Vergilius Maro (70-19 B.C.) has from the beginning been fortunate in his public. He became almost immediately a literary textbook and his pages have provided an exercise book for schoolboys from the grandsons of Augustus to our own William Ellery Leonard! [25] For this purpose he is eminently suitable. By temperament gentle and retiring, with a profound sense of the tragedy inherent in human things, he was a lover of peace and yet preached patriotism; he hated the anguish and pain involved in war, but was proud of Rome's imperial mission and exhorted his countrymen to war down the proud. This prescription is in itself perfect; but add to this the fact that the medieval church recognized him as an *anima naturaliter Christiana,* admitted him along with Isaiah as one of the prophets who had foretold the coming of Christ. Add to this the fact that in his major works there is not the slightest trace of the coarse and the obscene, that even the intrigue of Aeneas with Dido is handled with perfect delicacy and restraint, and one can recognize why in spite of an almost feminine sensibility, a verse that lacks the power, the virility, and the passion of Lucretius, the influence of Vergil has been so profound.

Vergil was born in the neighborhood of Mantua, in that part of Italy north of the river Po, which the Romans called cisalpine Gaul. His father was a man of comfortable circumstances but in the confusion of the civil wars lost his patrimony. Vergil's patron, Pollio, appealed to Maecenas and the family was restored to the position of comfortable security that befitted a member of the landed gentry. The first "eclogue"—cast in the mold of Theocritus—represents this experience of Vergil's earlier years. The poignant lamentations of the shepherd who goes into exile is contrasted with the rather fulsome gratitude of the shepherd who is restored. The shepherds are stock characters borrowed from the Sicilian idyl, well representing the romantic nostalgia of jaded city dwellers for country life—about as real as Dresden china shepherds or as Marie Antoinette playing at milkmaid in the Trianon palace. But Vergil had real feeling for the Italian countryside and the native landscape; and the peace of the pictorial conclusion was admirably conveyed: "Yet you could rest this one night with me—the green shade above. I have ripe apples, mealy chestnuts, and cheese aplenty. And now the rooftops of the distant cottages send up smoke, and longer shadows fall from the high hills."

The fourth eclogue is perhaps equally famous. It describes in language of hope and excitement the golden age that will be ushered in with the birth of a boy (it is this poem that admitted Vergil into the charmed circle of those who had foretold the coming of the Christ). Man will no longer—by the sweat of his brow—eat bread, but earth will spontaneously produce all things in abundance. The exquisite close of this poem, too, is worth quoting for its imaginative representation of the tiny infant on its mother's knee.

> Begin, tiny boy, to recognize your mother with a smile [or by her smile]. To your mother ten months have brought weariness; on whom his parents have not smiled, no god shall grace his table, no goddess grace his couch.

The great "home secretary" of the Emperor Augustus, Maecenas, was well aware of the value of poetry to glorify the ideals and achievements of the new

---

[25] Leonard in his poem "The Dawn" describes the effect produced on him as a schoolboy, of Vergil's first eclogue, "How in the breast of a lad, love of the Muses began."

regime. Vergil, like Horace, became a valued member of the court circle and his two great poems are for better and for worse "court poems" in the sense that they consciously supported and advocated and embellished the program of the regime.

The *Georgics,* on which Vergil spent seven years, is a didactic epic (modeled on Hesiod's *Works and Days*) in praise of the country, farming, and the life of the farmer. It is a conscious idealization of nature and the life of the Italian countryside and as such represents the conservative side of the Augustan reconstruction: the attempt to revive the old way of life, rustic prosperity, and the simple faith of an earlier day. The Italian farmer had been pressed hard by the shifting economic forces that had brought on the civil wars and had created the empire; and the march of economic forces could not be stopped by a poem no matter how charming. There was consequently an air of brooding and romantic unreality about Vergil's advice on the varied interests of the farmer—the planting and tending of the vine, care of livestock and horses, the breeding of bees, the tilling of the soil, observations on the weather and the worship of the old gods. There was an even greater unreality about his prescription for the breeding of bees—leave a dead calf in the fields and bees will spontaneously emerge—reads a little like an attempt to teach the facts of life to young bees.

The poem ended originally with a panegyric to Cornelius Gallus, Augustus' prefect of Egypt, but the unhappy Gallus rebelled and committed suicide. And the unhappy poet had hastily to change his plans and substitute the present conclusion—the idyllic story of Orpheus and Eurydice.

In the *Aeneid* Vergil's work represented the more dynamic side of the Augustan age. In spite of much talk of the Pax Romana, Augustus was a leading Roman imperialist, and the Augustan age was a period of notable imperial expansion. The *Aeneid* is the epic of empire, the tears and toils that had gone into its founding, its achievements, and its "manifest destiny." And yet, here is the central paradox of Vergil's work; the theme, involving as it did, war and bloodshed and the ruthless subordination of all human emotions to the imperial will, was less congenial to the temperament of the brooding, sensitive, almost tearful, poet than the idyllic pictures of his own well-loved Italian country. In the famous episode with Dido, when Aeneas was faced with a conflict between Roman destiny and personal feeling, the hero heroically submits to destiny, but the poet, perhaps in spite of himself, shows manifest sympathy with the unhappy queen crushed by hopeless love and driven to suicide. As a consequence, the horror of war rings true, its heroism sounds false. Never was a hero less heroic than Aeneas, never were scenes of battle more labored and less convincing.

The appeal of the *Aeneid* to later generations has, therefore, been more subtle than it was to Vergil's contemporaries. It has survived because of its revelation of a remarkable personality with a haunting sense of the pathos of human destiny, his sense of a quest which becomes at times almost a spiritual mission, the untiring pursuit of a Holy Grail, a longing for some higher vision of the meaning and purpose and sense of human life.

With the circle of Maecenas, of which we have discussed the two chief figures, we may contrast the circle of Messala: Ovid, Tibullus, and Propertius are the leading representatives of this group. The writers who made up Maecenas' circle put their tongues, their pens, and their talents at the disposal of the new regime. In an individualistic and decadent age they responded to the new emotional and intellectual impulse of the new regime and became in a literary and artistic sense its chief exponents and apologists. There was no such response in the circle of Messala. Its members remained individualists to the end, self-absorbed and self-complacent, delighting in the pleasures of the passing hour, and striving in refinement to find the anodyne for the ever-present menace of sheer boredom. Augustus gave great thought to the reform of morals, the restoration of decaying family life. Horace, in spite of his flippant freedom, supported him. But not the elegiac poets. Love was their all-absorbing theme, not the earthy human passion of Plautus, or the rending, tearing, vitalizing emotion of Catullus, but love as the meretricious adornment of an empty and oversophisticated life. In this sense they were children of their times and pictured the gay, cynical, sensuous life of the gilded youth of the Augustan day. All that Augustus tried to do could not stem the tide. He was finally forced to expel his own daughter from Rome for licentious conduct and in this scandal, gossip involved the name of Ovid.

We need not then be surprised to find that Ovid wrote about "Love"—the technique of seduction and dreams of fair women. He wrote not with ardor or abandon but with a cold cynicism that does not need to satirize and exaggerate in order to bring the point home.

This is his dominant theme but he is also the master of narrative. In the *Metamorphoses* he presented a whole gallery of stories, great or trivial, cosmic in their scope or merely contemptible, always swift-moving, absorbing, and rapid. His seems to have been a pictorial imagination; he viewed the cosmos as would a Hollywood producer—if *he* ever attained a cosmic sweep; and his imagination is not crisp, incisive, and accurate like that of Lucretius, but soft and romantic, shedding a pink haze over the sharp contours of things. It need not surprise us to learn that when such a temperament suffered exile (in the aura of strict Puritanism that surrounded the older generation of the court, his conduct and his views could not go unnoticed forever) he should take refuge in the most contemptible lamentations and the weakest kind of whining.

The two other members of this circle may be quickly characterized. They shared Ovid's interest in sex and kept to the tradition of the elegy as love lamentation. Both Propertius and Tibullus were markedly individualistic and markedly decadent. Both were self-absorbed. Propertius complained that he was specter thin— "as to my whole body I am nothing"—no wonder, he abused his body and flogged his brains. There was a strong touch of the neurotic about him—a kind of de Musset of Latin antiquity. "There are so many pretty women," he sighed, "in the world below." It is difficult to feel much sympathy with a man who feels frustrated in this reflection. In the same way Tibullus pictured himself dying at Corfu. "Here lies Tibullus slain by death's fell hand, accompanying Messala over sea and land," and writes his own epithet. The imaginations of both poets tend to run to the macabre. Cynthia appears to Propertius in a vision, rising from the dead "and the garment from her side was burned away."

All three poets produced a barren dead sea fruit. They lack conviction and for them life has no meaning. The poetry of a decadent aristocracy is ready to wither away.

Of the later epic there is little need to speak. Lucan is its least insignificant exemplar and he represents a man torn between his political convictions and his real self-interest, "willing to wound yet afraid to strike." He wrote the *Pharsalia,* a romance of the civil wars, mingling a romantic nostalgia for the vanquished Republican side with the most abject flattery of the present representative of the victors—the ruling emperor, Nero.

When the imperial impulse that Augustus had represented and fostered began to pass over into an oppressive and ruthless despotism, as Rome came to the end of her period of expansion to set foot on the long, agonizing road of her decline, there was little left for poetry to do except to write polished and witty epigrams of sycophantic flattery or to thunder denunciations against the moral decline— as though Rome's troubles were the result of a moral decline!

Of the first tendency Martial (Marcus Valerius Martialis, A.D. c. 40-104), was the consummate representative. The picture he conveyed of the life of a literary man in the early empire is nauseating. The only requirement was wit and a facility for turning out epigrams. This ability Martial had and was conscious of it. His own description of his art has been paraphrased as follows:

> The qualities all in a bee that we meet
> In an epigram never should fail,
> The body indeed should be little and neat,
> With a sting in the end of its tail.

The sting, Martial knew how to inject and he combined with this a talent for fawning, for tail-wagging self-abasement that must have been unique even in that self-abasing age. Nonetheless flashes of the old capacity for genuine feeling still shine through, in his description of his country place, in his devotion to the little home-born slave girl Erotian.

With the next generation the moralizing, satirical, nostalgic tendency and tradition in Roman poetry reaches its apogee in Juvenal (Decimus Junius Juvenalis, A.D. 60-140). Juvenal lashed the vices and foibles of his age with a quite enthusiastic unrealism and even seems to have had the conviction that by so doing he was saving Rome from decay. In this he was not unique. It is the supreme example of Roman unrealism, the intellectual failure of a highly practical people, that they saw in moral forces the dynamic behind social movements. Juvenal only carries to its logical conclusion the point of view of Horace, Vergil, Livy, and Tacitus.

4. *Latin Prose*

Prose was a congenial vehicle to the practical Roman: it developed out of his need for exposition, for transmitting instruction about practical things. It was influenced, too, by his need to plead, to speak in the law court or senate, to win adherents and influence votes. Thus, when poetry was feeling the influence of Greek models, Cato (Marcus Porcius Cato, the "Censor," 234-149 B.C.) was writing and speaking—a perfect torrent of production—of which only one characteristic work survives—a treatise on agriculture, *De re rustica,* written with a dry wit in copybook style—like the epigrams of Shakespeare's Polonius, or Tupper's Proverbial Philosophy.

In Cicero, whom we have already discussed in connection with Roman philosophy, Latin prose reached a kind of perfection. In his hands the Latin language, in spite of many deficiencies, as compared to Greek, for example, began to rank high in flexibility and expressiveness. Cicero, in fact, created classical Latin prose.

The Ciceronian style has left its mark in subsequent European languages. Our oratory, for instance, even now is Ciceronian. You have only to put a speech by a contemporary orator like Senator Borah beside an oration by Cicero to perceive the close relationship. The prose of Cicero has an orchestral variety. It achieves the grand, impassioned manner, an organlike full voice, in the *Orations,* with their rhetorical mannerisms, repetitions, antitheses, and explosive piling up of effects. In the *Essays* he comes down to a pianolike tone of quiet contemplation and reflective analysis. In his letters he writes in an easy, familiar, and conversational style.

Emotionally Cicero was also a master of many words. He could bring a courthouse audience to tears with his tenderness. In the Senate he could fulminate in the grandest theatrical manner against blackguards like Catiline. He could write dialogues in a style supple and lucid. He was capable of irony, bombast, paradox, tenderness, earnestness, and familiarity. He was, also, by no means superior to a little hypocrisy. But who among the world's prose writers has sounded so many notes, and so well? If Cicero was not the greatest of prose masters, Latin and modern, he was at least the most versatile, and centuries of men have imitated him, consciously or not, since he has been the uninterrupted schoolmaster of the Western World; for even after the modern languages were turned to literary purposes the style of Cicero's prose still haunted them. But his style has its defects and drawbacks, too. His keenest admirers would admit that Cicero was verbose; he took a page to tell what Tacitus would convey in a sentence; Cicero, too, runs to exaggeration and the superlative. His parade of superlatives sometimes sounds a little like the Pope of the Ingoldsby Legends.[26] Cicero tended to substitute persuasion for clarity, emotion for truth. He was an orator and an advocate more concerned with winning a case than with finding the facts. The influence of his style has not been, therefore, entirely beneficial and happy.

Some of the finest classical prose was expended on the art of Roman history, which includes four important names: Caesar, Sallust, Livy, and Tacitus. Down to the second century B.C. most Roman historical writing was done in Greek. The first major historian to write in the native tongue was Julius Caesar (100-44 B.C.). His *Commentaries on the Gallic War* and *Civil War,* generally accurate and always clear, forceful and direct in style, are the best historical memoirs of the ancient world. They both gain and lose from being the *apologia* of the principal participant in the events they portray. They gain in directness, vividness, and truth; they lose in that they are at times a most ingenious piece of special

[26] *O turpissime, vir nequissime, sceleratissime, issime, quissime.*

pleading. By maintaining subtle restraint, and by keeping to understatement, he cleverly brought his case home. At the same time he demonstrated his genius with full effect.

Gaius Sallustius Crispus (c. 86-34 B.C.) has been called the Roman Thucydides, but that is to flatter him. His chief work, a history of Rome from 78 to 67 B.C., is lost, but from his monographs, the *Conspiracy of Catiline* and *Jurgurthine War,* we can taste the flavor of his vigorous, dignified style, and his power of biographical and political analysis. Ancient critics praised his impartiality; moderns suspect that he has written in his *Catiline* a clever defense of Julius Caesar. But he made no attempt to conceal his despondent attitude towards Rome's future, as the late republic sank farther and farther into chaos.

Sallust never fully appreciated the underlying trends in contemporary Roman politics—but this is to criticize him unfairly—for what ancient historian did? Sallust's chronology and geography, however, were sometimes careless, and therein he lapsed from the best standards of the ancient historians.

Titus Livius (59 B.C.-A.D. 17) is unsurpassed as a storyteller, easily the peer of Ovid, and probably of Homer. His *History of Rome,* much of it lost, was a prose counterpart to the *Aeneid,* an epic of the growth of Rome. His genius as a prose stylist ranks him next to Cicero. To style he subordinated even accuracy of statement. In brief his model was not Thucydides but the Greek rhetoricians. The high literary merit of Livy's work, which has given it wide popularity, does not, however, conceal its deficiencies as history.

Livy wrote frankly to glorify Rome, to flatter national vanity, and to inspire Roman youth with patriotic ardor and affection. His piety was second only to his patriotism. The supernatural returned to history with a vengeance. Few medieval historians outdid him in assigning historical events to the interference of the gods. He used sources carelessly, and failed to reject fables and legends, particularly in his treatment of Roman origins, when he made a veritable synthesis of myths, marvels, and portents. And, unfortunately, the earlier part of his work has been preserved, the later has been lost. The contrast between the patriotic and the scientific historian was never better illustrated than in the two histories of Rome by Livy and Polybius.

The best of the major Roman historians, Publius Cornelius Tacitus (A.D. c. 55-120), was an ardent admirer of the aristocratic Roman Republic and showed a very marked bias against several of the emperors, against Tiberius Caesar in particular. These loves and hates may perhaps find their explanation in the political relations of Tacitus' own day; in his aversion to the gloomy tyranny of Domitian, and in the aversion of the activists and expansionists of his day—Agricola's son-in-law probably shared these views—for the cautious policy of the stay-at-home emperors. After the famous defeat of Varus in the Teutoburg forest in 9 A.D., Augustus had left in his will the advice to keep the empire within its present limits. Tacitus adds with characteristic innuendo, "It is not certain whether because of envy or fear." Tiberius tried conscientiously to apply this advice and carry out this policy, but he was bitterly opposed and the opposition tended to center around the person of Germanicus. We have in consequence a highly colored dramatic contrast drawn between the elderly, suspicious, overcautious "ogre of Capri" and the young, brilliant, dashing Germanicus—a veritable second Alexander—constantly thwarted and checked by unreasonable and suspicious authority.

This bias makes Tacitus a little open to the suspicions of the scientific historian, and his work displayed an even more serious flaw. He wrote not to analyze the essential dynamic, social forces that induce the movements of history (as Thucydides had done) but rather for moral ends, to edify and instruct; he held that history's highest function is "to let no worthy action be uncommemorated, and to hold the reprobation of posterity as a terror to evil deeds and words." He lamented that the period with which he had to deal lacked the nobility of Rome's past—a sordid tale of intrigue and cowardice. His work, too, suffered from the lack of a broad plan, an integrating, organizing idea such as we noted in the works of Herodotus or Thucydides. The central process of development is obscured by too many personal, episodic details, by complicated intrigues, and the struggle of factions. He does not appreciate at all the complicated economic, social, and political interests that underlie these factional struggles. And yet his views have been widely influential. The picture of the early Roman Empire which he painted in the *Annals,* the lurid stories of the Flavian empires in the *Histories,* have created a picture of the Roman Empire which endures in the popular mind until this day—a picture of senseless intrigue, of pointless slaughter, and a city and state quivering under the sway of a tyrant and trembling at the ever-present informer and spy. The contrast drawn in the *Germania* (one of the few ancient works on descriptive sociology) between the early Germans and the decadent Romans has tended to reinforce the analysis of Rome's decay in terms of moral causes and has thus indirectly provided material for the pulpit and pamphleteer even to this day.

But what Tacitus lacked as a historian, he made up for as a stylist. His work is brilliant and studded with epigrams—"They create a wilderness and call it peace"; "By universal consent he was capable of rule, if only he had never ruled" (*capax imperii nisi imperasset*); "Let them hate so long as they fear," and epigrams which have become part of the common heritage of the Western World. His work moves with a quite breathless rapidity. Let the reader scan the account of the end of Messalina in the eleventh book of the *Annals* (beginning with chapter 26) and ask himself whether any account was ever more rapid, whether more information was ever packed in a shorter space, and whether suspense was ever more breathlessly sustained. Tacitus has, too, a power for incisive characterization and clear portraiture. No writer has greater power over the completely damning innuendo (a comparison with Lytton Strachey comes irresistibly to mind). His work is to the reader a delight, if to the historian an infuriation and a challenge.

The last Roman historian of much consequence was Suetonius Tranquillus (A.D. c. 75-160), a secretary of the Emperor Hadrian and consequently an important imperial official. His racy *Lives of the Caesars* is one of the earliest examples of history debunked. He is rich in personal description, anecdotes, gossip, and scandal, and has influenced posterity's verdict on all his subjects, from Julius

Caesar to the Flavian emperors. Suetonius avoided the current rhetorical fads and told history simply, letting the poisoned arrows fall where they might. His chief significance has been just this: that he became to the later Humanists the model in style and arrangement for historical biography. Far more important was the history of the Roman Empire by the Greek historian, Ammianus Marcellinus (A.D. 330-401), who wrote in Latin in the hope of securing a Roman reading public.

It may be fitting now to turn to the famous work of Fabius Quintilianus (A.D. c. 35-c. 95), the *Institutio Oratoria* (*Education of an Orator*), which is the most exhaustive textbook of its kind ever undertaken in ancient times. It provided a full course of training to the orator, down to the most practical detail of style and delivery. The technical parts of Quintilian's book do not interest us so much as the survey of Greek and Latin literature which he furnished to the budding orator. His discussion of education is still interesting. In sum, Quintilian is a master of Ciceronian style—he has been called the first of the followers of Cicero—and a valuable critic, who surveyed the history of classical Latin literature with something like the insight of a contemporary, providing many incisive and compressed judgments which posterity still regards with challenged interest.

Plinius Caecilius Secundus (A.D. c. 61-c. 113)—Pliny the Younger—was one of the last prose writers of the silver age, and this means that he was one of the last to write in classical Latin. He has a place in Roman literature as a graceful writer of letters, a position he consciously cultivated. Although a busy man of affairs, leader of the bar, consul, and governor, he was a voluminous letter-writer, and wrote with an eye to publication. Fate was not unkind to him, and though much has been lost in Roman literature, Pliny's letters, full of valuable information about private and public affairs have survived—there is a most significant correspondence between Pliny while an official in Bithynia and the emperor Trajan about the treatment to be accorded to the Christians.

5. *The Roman Novel*

We have seen in the last chapter that the novel was one of the few literary types which the Greeks failed to invent. Some kind of storytelling was practiced by Hellenistic writers, however, and they at least made experiments in novel writing. Credit for the first prose Roman romance must probably go to Gaius Petronius who was also called Petronius Arbiter (Arbiter of Taste), a pro-consul in Bithynia, who, like Seneca, committed suicide by command in A.D. 66.

Petronius' *Satyricon* was a long work in about twenty-four books, verse interspersed with prose, a sort of picaresque novel, a realistic study of middle-class and plebeian life. It recounts the adventures of Encolpius, the narrator, his attendant Giton, and friend Ascyltus, a Roman knight. There is no plot, the story moves from episode to episode without much connection, and keeps to a high level of excitement. Petronius was one of the few classical writers to interject colloquial Latin in his work. His book is a mixture of dignified literary prose, popular slang, and the dialect of mixed Greek and Latin spoken in some parts of the empire. Among them is the inimitable dinner of Trimalchio, "whose details vividly recreate an extravagantly vulgar dinner party given by a wealthy *parvenu* of the freedman class to people of similar standing and to uninvited guests." [27]

About a century after Petronius there appears the *Metamorphoses* of Lucius Apuleius, a rhetorician and a follower (though at a respectful distance) of Plato. He was incidentally a priest of the Egyptian goddess Isis and gives us valuable material for reconstructing at all events the preliminary stages of the process of initiation into the mystery cults. In Apuleius we see the fading of classical Latin. His language is not that of Cicero or Livy. Colloquialisms have crept in and there is marked Hellenistic influence. The novel of Apuleius, based on a Greek original, is a picaresque account of the traveler Lucius who was turned into an ass. It is partly phantasy, partly a realistic study of "low" life, and contains many interpolated novelettes, among which the story of Cupid and Psyche is the most famous.

IX. ROMAN ENGINEERING AND ARCHITECTURE

If we could take an imaginary walk through a Roman city we should be struck by many things which are usually assumed as belonging exclusively to our modern world. We should find that the better Roman houses contained glass windows, indoor plumbing, cisterns and taps, steam baths, central heating (where the climate, as in Britain, demanded it), and a drainage system. The water, drawn through aqueducts from enormous distances, was purified and made available in ample quantity. The city of Rome had a supply of 300 million gallons a day, enough for a population of 10 million people. Water was piped into the houses through an underground system and drained by lead pipes into a system of sewers. The streets of a Roman city, in sharp contrast to those of Athens, were well surfaced, and the dwellings were consciously laid out in a unified design. Town planning was the Roman fulfillment of a Hellenistic experiment. Fountains, temples, theaters, forums, public baths, arcaded sidewalks, and shops were zoned off as in a model American town. Wheeled traffic was not permitted during the daytime.

The Roman city plan provided a rectangular network of streets enclosing squares of uniform size, with intersecting arteries leading to a spacious plaza. Not crossed by any thoroughfare, the plaza contained the principal edifices: the local temple, basilica, or public hall, the offices of the magistrates, and sometimes a library. The magnificent villas of the city were inhabited by the wealthy, and balconied apartment houses of durable brick, by the middle classes. The poor, as in the modern metropolis, lived for the most part in crowded tenements.

Passing from this Roman city for a visit to the countryside, we might take one of the admirable roads which were always in good repair and which measured twelve feet or more in width. Such roads literally covered the empire, usually running in straight lines and easy gradations along open ridges, thus avoiding ravines which might require bridging. It was part of the Romans' sense of the practical that led them to connect every part of their empire in this way. No matter where we desired to go in the empire, we would find good roads, comfort

27 J. W. Duff, *Literary History of Rome*, Barnes and Noble, 1960.

stations, steam baths, hospitals, amphitheaters (usually charging no admission fee), and temples of favorite Roman deities.

If we cared to travel by water, we would find at our disposal deep harbors, canals, and lighthouses. We could sail along the rivers and under graceful, vast, arched stone bridges, some of whose massive piers, made to withstand the ages, exist even to this day. Across the Tagus River in Spain, in modern Alcántara, for instance, the bridge was more than 180 feet above the surface of the water, and measured 617 feet in length. The Pons Fabricius at Rome, now called the Ponte dei Quattro Capi (Bridge of Four Heads), still serves traffic, with only a modern parapet added to the original structure. Some of the finest bridges were in the provinces. At Merida in Spain, at Rimini in Italy, at Sommières in Provence, and elsewhere, bridges still stand as monuments to the Roman genius for construction. Indeed, modern engineering has not improved on Roman bridgebuilding except for the use of steel girders and the cantilever and suspension principles.

As we sailed along on our imaginary Roman journey, we might see the endless arches of an aqueduct—carrying the water in concrete channels built with numerous shafts for ventilation—rolling across the countryside like an elevated highway. Some might have tanks or reservoirs alongside. Where today we find arid deserted tracks in northern Africa, Asia Minor, and Syria, in Roman times flourishing cities and towns stood, thriving largely because of an artificial water supply.

The city of Rome had fourteen aqueducts, whose total length was 265 miles. Water was conveyed to Roman Carthage over a distance of ninety-five miles. There were low-pressure and high-pressure aqueducts. The pipes were made of stone or lead—never of cast iron—with large bores. Many Roman aqueducts are still in use, as the one in Segovia, Spain, where peasants wearing modern costumes instead of the Roman toga walk beneath towering arches two thousand years old.

If on our imaginary journey we returned to the capital, we would be surprised by the splendor of the public buildings, which unlike the Greek, frequently had domed ceilings. For the Romans had learned how to enclose vast spaces by means other than the flat roof which, as we have seen in the Egyptian architecture, necessitated the use of far too many supporting columns to allow spaciousness or light. Taking over devices originated in the Near East, the Roman builders produced three chief systems of roofing their large buildings: the barrel vault, the groin vault, and the dome. Stone, brick, and concrete comprised the building materials. When he used concrete, the Roman builder constructed a wood form into which the flowing mass was poured; and he removed the form after the mass had hardened, in much the same manner that is followed today. When he used brick, cement served as the binding substance; the dome of the Pantheon, for example, 142 feet across, was built of horizontal layers of brick embedded in thick cement, and supported by ribs joined at the crown. The basilica of Maxentius, measuring 80 feet across, was roofed by three groin vaults.

An examination of the barrel vault and the groin vault brings to light their common origin in a single principle: the rounded arch. The stone barrel vault had been introduced by the Etruscans, and by the time of Sulla it had been elaborated into the groined vault. Fundamentally, the barrel vault is merely a rounded arch extended in depth; and the groin vault, two barrel vaults crossed. We begin to recognize that the basic principle of all Roman architecture was the rounded arch, familiar to the civilized world through the countless photographic reproductions of the Colosseum. Unlike the basic principle of Greek building, the column and lintel, the Roman arch provided the means for extensive adaptation and development, not only in Roman but in later architecture as well.

In republican times wood was chiefly used in constructing bridges, buildings, and boats, but by the first century A.D. it seems to have become scarce and expensive. Meanwhile the soft volcanic rock of the peninsula was discovered to be excellent building material. It was made into bricks and when coated with stucco not only offered a bright appearance but possessed great durability as well. More imposing structures, such as public buildings, were built with "travertine," a hard

Roman vaulting systems: barrel vault (*left*), groin vault (*center*), groin vault seen from below (*right*).

white limestone, or with "pozzolana," a soft volcanic stone. The walls were covered with stucco or marble and marble was used for the floors.

Expert masons, the Romans worked in a kind of guild system, handed their craft secrets on from generation to generation, and thus transmitted their skill to the Middle Ages. The Romans approached construction much in the modern manner, that is, as a functional rather than aesthetic project. But we might add that if the Romans, like us, usually built their public or private structures primarily for use and secondarily for beauty, they had a fine appreciation of quality; and unlike us, apparently were not jerry-builders. The continents of Europe, Asia, and Africa are strewn with Roman remains. Many of them, bridges, aqueducts, and roads, are still usable; others are picturesque and sturdy fragments, like the Colosseum in Rome. Will American public buildings last so well? Will any of our municipal stadia be as remarkably preserved two thousand years from now as the Roman Colosseum is today?

Rome borrowed its ideas of decoration from Greece; but applied them with a lavishness typically Roman. It is significant that although they used all three Greek orders—Doric, Ionic, Corinthian—the Romans preferred the Corinthian, the most elaborate one. Roman constructional ideas were a Roman development of the simple, powerful Etruscan vaulted architecture. Roman building skill improved as time went on, but Roman decoration degenerated in the later empire because of its careless profusion. This may have been the result of a division in labor: the masons and laborers worked independently of the architect, who, as with us, scarcely did more than design the building and produce the blueprints. In Greece a man like Phidias had charge of the construction as well as the architectural planning. It is for this reason that Greek decoration and Greek construction are organically interrelated whereas, with the Romans, decoration became a nonfunctional and inorganic something that was superimposed.

Rome's great contribution to art lies in architectural engineering—in skillfully raising the vault and dome to magnificent proportions. To be sure, the Romans used the Greek column and entablature but only as a decoration, not for support. A Greek building conveys a sense of quiet power and delicate perfection while a Roman building, by virtue of its vault and dome much larger than the Greek, creates an impression of magnitude and grandeur. The early Greek dedicated his art to religion but the Roman expressed himself in eminently utilitarian creations such as baths, courthouses, amphitheaters, libraries, etc. Typical were the Baths of Caracalla, an extensive establishment equipped with facilities for baths of various temperatures, for exercises, and for reading and recreation. An even better-known example was the Colosseum, the huge amphitheater, where multitudes gathered to watch the gladiatorial combats. Such public structures, perhaps more than anything else, proclaim the lavishness and splendor of Roman culture.

When the Romans diverted architectural practice from the column-and-lintel system (used by the Greeks and Egyptians) to the vault and dome system, they performed an inestimable service to future builders, as we shall see in Byzantine, Romanesque, and Gothic churches. During the period of the so-called Renaissance, the decorative and structural values of Roman architecture passed into the secular architecture of that age, and have been a living tradition ever since. Public buildings in Europe and America, particularly those built before the World War, reveal a slavish dependence upon the forms of Roman antiquity, a dependence which shows signs of relaxing only now in modern functional and nontraditional architecture. The modern industrial world, particularly in the nineteenth century, repeated the Roman mistake of using in a nonfunctional manner decorative details borrowed from the past: the Woolworth Building in New York City applies the stone decoration of a Gothic cathedral on the structural steel skeleton of an office building!

From our discussion so far one might gather the impression that religion played no rôle in the cultural life of Rome. It is true that temple architecture was less vital to the Romans than to the Greeks. Romans, for the most part, worshiped their gods privately in their own households. In Europe Roman temples were usually small, like the Maison Carrée at Nîmes which followed Greek design and construction except that it was built on a high platform reached by a flight of steps, an influence of Etruscan architecture. A notable departure, however, was the Pantheon in Rome, whose colossal proportions we have already mentioned. In Asia, probably because of Egyptian and Parthian influences, Roman temples were generally massive (for example, the temple at Baalbek).

In addition to developing secular and religious buildings, Rome invented several original architectural forms, best described as commemorative. These include the triumphal column and the triumphal arch, designed for the home-coming of a victorious general. Both types have been revived since the fifteenth century for analogous purposes (l'Arc de Triomphe de l'Étoile of Napoleon in Paris, the

Washington Square Arch in New York City, and the Place Vendôme column in Paris). Both columns and arches were decorated with relief sculptures which graphically recorded the successful military campaign. On the arch these were modeled in horizontal plaques, but on the column (Trajan's Column, Rome) the figures in spiral arrangement climbed the full height of the shaft. Ancient examples of triumphal arches are the Arch of Titus at Rome (late first century A.D.) and the Arch of Trajan at Benevento (early second century).

X. ROMAN SCULPTURE AND PAINTING

While our emphasis so far in this chapter has been on Rome's original contributions, for example, architectural engineering, and on Rome's original forms, such as commemorative arches, amphitheaters, baths, law courts, aqueducts, we must not fail to acknowledge the debt Roman art owed to Etruscan and Greek influence. The Romans were not only influenced by Greek art, but they went to the trouble of importing its figure art in large quantities, especially when Greek cities were captured. Since the demand soon exhausted the supply of these works, the vogue for making copies developed. We owe the survival of many Greek masterpieces to these Roman copies made for the decoration of palaces and rich men's villas.

It was the capture of the Greek city, Syracuse, Sicily, in 212 B.C., that brought the excellences of Greek art to Rome's attention. In 161 B.C. hundreds of wagonloads of sculpture and other works of art were transported from Macedonia to Rome. At the sack of Corinth (146 B.C.) the Roman contractor whose duty it was to cart the marbles from Corinth to Rome warned his workmen that if they damaged one single piece of sculpture he would compel them to replace it! The same procedure of conscientious spoliation has been followed by modern conquerors, among them Napoleon, whose Italian plunder formed the foundation of the Louvre collection. Rome despoiled Greece not from some basically artistic urge but from a desire to manifest her own power, much as the modern millionaire frequently buys celebrated paintings.

It is not surprising, then, that the Roman taste for literalness soon asserted itself. Rome patterned itself not on the idealized art of the Greek golden age but upon Hellenistic art, which showed a preference for naturalism and portraiture. From this Hellenistic beginning, Rome developed portrait sculpture to its first western European stage of perfection.

A preoccupation with portrait sculpture is the obvious expression of a vain, power-loving civilization. However, we may be grateful for faithful representations of such great Romans as Caesar, Augustus, Trajan, Hadrian, and Marcus Aurelius, for the Romans believed in portraying the individual with photographic realism. In no other art do we feel the same sincerity in representing meanness or dignity. The portraits extended to busts, half-length figures, full-length figures, equestrian portraits, and relief sculpture on tombs and sarcophagi. The form of equestrian portraiture was transmitted to a few sculptors of the Middle Ages, to many in the fifteenth century (among them Donatello and Verrocchio), and so on to modern times.

The high point of Roman sculpture was reached in the first century A.D. in the reign of Augustus. At this time the Roman mingled his own inherent desire for naturalism with the more sedate and noble ideas of the Greek school. This resulted in as fine a statue as the full-length *Augustus Haranguing His Troops*. This work retains all the excellencies of a Roman portrait head and adds to the figure the fine proportions and noble bearing of a Polycletus. During this same period the art of relief sculpture reached a magnificent height thereafter never attained by Roman art. The famous *Altar of Peace* built by Augustus introduced the allegorical relief sculpture, a sober and dignified anecdotal representation which served as a model for many painters and sculptors of later centuries. From this Augustan height Roman sculpture began a slow retrogression, though Roman relief sculpture was at its best in Trajan's time. It was a relatively decayed Roman art that influenced the sculptural productions of the early church.

Although our knowledge of Greek painting is confined to the forms outlined on Greek vases, firsthand evidence is available of Roman painting in the frescoes at Pompeii and Boscoreale. It is fairly certain that the Roman painter, like the Roman sculptor, derived his inspiration from the Greeks. Thus we are also able to learn something of late Greek painting from the Roman works at hand. Roman homes of the wealthier classes were liberally decorated with paintings that were not always of the best quality, since much of this production was obviously commercial.

A good many Roman paintings strived for naturalistic effects. The painter tried to simulate the appearance of stone materials in paint, for instance, of marble, or he attempted to reproduce a deep architectural expanse on the wall, to enlarge the room, creating much the same effect as the familiar vaudeville backdrop which though painted on a flat surface conveys the illusion of tremendous depth. For this purpose *linear perspective* (the method of using converging lines to represent a three-dimensional object on a two-dimensional surface) was used. In the painting of landscape (the *Odyssey Landscapes* in the Vatican) the Roman painter showed that he was familiar with atmospheric effects. He was able to indicate distance by a successive diminution of color intensity in objects which were intended to appear farther away from the spectator. This device is known as *aerial perspective* and is one of the many technical devices which were lost during the Middle Ages only to be rediscovered during the so-called Renaissance. Many Roman figure paintings revealed an attempt to reproduce rounded sculptural effects; here the artist modeled rather carefully, if academically, and showed a familiarity with the possibilities of light and shade to indicate roundness.

In the best Roman wall painting, the figure predominates. A fine example is the Boscoreale representation of *A Woman and Her Maid* in the Metropolitan Museum. The figure subjects are distinguished by an impressive sculptural quality, the forms taking their place in the composition with monumental dignity. They frequently convey a high emotional content since many of them are religious or narrative in character. Another type reveals great charm in imaginative subject matter such as cupids playing, bucolic scenes, etc. A third shows a penchant for fanciful and impractical architectural ornament, used to break the space and form a background for figures, birds, or landscapes.

In minor arts the Romans produced a number of fine examples, among them "thousand flower" bowls,[28] skillfully cut gems and cameos, as well as furniture and household utensils. With marble they were able to make useful and good-looking stone benches, candelabra, etc.

The specific contributions of the Romans may be summarized as the development of an elaborate and practical architecture, the perfection of portrait and narrative sculpture, and the development of technical devices in painting. All of these contributions were destined to have repercussions in subseqeunt generations.

XI. THE LEGACY OF ROME

After this brief discussion of Roman culture, it will be well to summarize by way of answer to the questions: What did the Romans do for the world? What are their lasting contributions to that process of civilization which might be compared to the task of Sisyphus, in the fable, who was compelled to roll a stone up hill incessantly because it was always slipping down just as it got to the top. Rome brought many phases of civilization almost to the top—and then Western man slipped down into barbarism and the Dark Ages. But in the twelfth century he began to roll the stone up hill again until now, perhaps, it is on the brink of another descent into barbarism and darkness.

The leading trait of Roman culture was its imitativeness. It shone by borrowed light, as the moon does. The light came from Greece. That is only the most general of truths, however. Becoming more specific we see that one of the major heritages bequeathed by Rome is the tradition of military conquest. Whether because the Romans were inherently a bellicose race, or because accident forced them, as it forced England, into imperialism, the fact is that Rome's long series of brilliant victories created a military tradition which has cursed the world ever since. More than anything else, Rome stood in later times as a symbol of war, and from Charlemagne to Mussolini, rulers have longed to imitate the military feats of Scipio, Caesar, Sulla, or Augustus.

In the political realm, Rome extended the imperial ideal inherited from Egypt, Assyria, Persia, and Macedonia. Rome carried the city-state one step farther than Greece, and merged it, on a large scale, and for a few centuries, with world-empire. Essentially the Roman Empire was a fusion of city-states. It was long believed that one of the glories of Rome was its genius for organizing and administering an empire. Modern research, however, has proved that nothing could be further from the truth. Rome had great military genius which was useful in carving out an empire, but she was far less talented in administering the empire, once it was conquered. Down to the time of Augustus, the administration of the Roman Empire was incredibly corrupt, brutal, and inefficient. A really efficient administration was not provided until the reign of Diocletian (284-305) when the empire was already going to pieces socially and economically, and the provinces had been so well ransacked that they could not contribute enough taxes to meet

[28] Made of *millefiori* glass which when held up to the light reveals threads of countless colors fused in the glass.

the cost of the new machinery. Moreover, by the time of Diocletian the treachery of the army and the greed of the bureaucracy had left its finger marks, as it were, deeply embedded in the neck of its victim, the provinces. It is well, however, to be discriminating and to point out that it was mainly on the financial side that Rome fell down in her imperial system. A lofty conception of empire developed and the political and legal aspects of imperial administration were of a high character. It was the graft connected with imperial taxation and finances which helped to undermine the Roman Empire.

Whatever Rome's weakness as ruler of empire may have been, it cannot be denied that her conquest of the Western World contributed a great deal to subsequent civilization. It accustomed the Western races to the idea of a world-state, and by the *pax romana* (Roman peace) it demonstrated the benefits of a long absence of war, even if the price was the loss of political independence by most of the races of the world.

The presence of one sovereign power over vast areas enabled peoples to merge their contributions to culture. There was a constant exchange of ideas between the Italian, Greek, Mesopotamian, Syrian, and Gallic parts of the empire. This was the most successful and extensive assimilation of culture so far achieved in man's history. The localism of Hellenic civilization was supplanted in Roman days by at least a healthy beginning towards a true league of nations and a brotherhood of man. Because peace and order reigned on a large scale, many activities which were impossible during the endless wars from almost 2000 B.C. to the beginning of the Christian Era were undertaken in the first two centuries of imperial rule. Even Rome's incompetence as financier of empire could not completely kill the cultural benefits to be derived from peace and order.

Specifically, Rome made its greatest contribution to civilization in the field of law. Here, as we have seen, she established the theory that the state is the fountain of justice, and is supreme over individual or group. If the state was supreme, however, it exercised that supremacy, in theory at least, in order to protect the rights of the individual or the group. For the first time in history, the individual's rights were fully put into constitutional form, and he was given legal immunity from the despotic acts of a governing power. Roman law also extended those rights to the corporation.

Roman lawyers perfected legal procedure and codified legal principles, and in their conception of the jus gentium Rome tried to bring together and harmonize into one code of law the ethical practices of many races, just as England in her common law tried to synthesize the legal knowledge of the people in her local areas. Roman law became medieval church law and with the rise of strong monarchies at the height of the Middle Ages it encouraged kings to challenge and destroy the tyranny of church over state, of the ecclesiastical over the secular arm of society.

If Roman law made for royal absolutism in the Middle Ages, it made for popular rebellion in modern times. The theory of Roman law that the state's sovereignty rested on the consent of the people sowed the seeds of modern revolutions.

The influence of the Latin language and literature was, and still is, enormous. Finally, it must be recalled that Rome passed Greco-Oriental civilization on to Christianity and the Middle Ages. And so, if Rome ultimately helped to undermine many aspects of medieval Catholicism, she also made many important contributions to the medieval Catholic church in provincial organization, law, terminology and festivals.

Why, it may be asked in conclusion, did Roman civilization decline? Generally speaking, Rome declined because the perspective, ideals, and economic system of an agrarian civilization, with its grasping avarice and its crude methods of communication and transportation, could not hold a world-empire together.

SELECTED READINGS

Adcock, F. E., Roman Political Ideals and Practice, University of Michigan Press, 1959.
Anderson and Spiers, The Architecture of Greece and Rome, Vol. II.
Bailey, Cyril, ed., The Legacy of Rome, Oxford Press, 1923.
—— The Mind of Rome, Oxford Press, 1926.
Bakewell, Source Book in Ancient Philosophy.
Carcopino, Jérôme, Daily Life in Ancient Rome, Yale University Press, 1960.
Carter, J. B., The Religious Life of Ancient Rome, Houghton Mifflin, 1911.
Cumont, F. V. M., The After Life in Roman Paganism, Dover, 1959.
—— Astrology and Religion among the Greeks and Romans, Dover, 1960.
Declareuil, Joseph, Rome the Law-Giver, Knopf, 1926.
Duff, J. W., Literary History of Rome, 2 Vols., Barnes and Noble, 1960.
Durant, Will, Caesar and Christ, Simon and Schuster, 1944.
Eby and Arrowood, The History and Philosophy of Education, chaps. xi-xii.
Fowler, W. W., The Religious Experience of the Roman People, Macmillan, 1911.
—— Social Life at Rome in the Age of Cicero, Macmillan, 1915.
Grant, Michael, The World of Rome, Weidenfeld and Nicholson, 1960.
Greene, W. C., The Achievement of Rome, Harvard University Press, 1934.
Grenier, Albert, The Roman Spirit, Knopf, 1926.
Hamilton, Edith, The Roman Way, Norton, 1932.
Hammerton, Universal History of the World, Vols. III-IV.
Haverfield, F. J., Ancient Town-Planning, Oxford Press, 1913.
Homo, Leon, Roman Political Institutions, Barnes and Noble, 1962.
Kiefer, Otto, Sexual Life in Ancient Rome, Barnes and Noble.
Laistner, M. L. W., The Greater Roman Historians, Univ. of California Press, 1947.
Mackail, J. W., Latin Literature, Collier Books.
Peterson, Torsten, Cicero: A Biography, University of California Press, 1920.
Preston, H. W., and Dodge, Louisa, The Private Life of the Romans, Putnam, 1893.
Rivoira, G. T., Roman Architecture, Oxford Press, 1925.
Shotwell, Introduction to the History of History, Section IV.
Singer, Charles, From Magic to Science, Dover Publications, Inc., 1958.
Strong, E., Art in Ancient Rome, 2 Vols., Scribner, 1928.
Swain, The Ancient World, Vol. II.
Teuffel, W. S., History of Roman Literature, 2 Vols., Macmillan, 1891-92.
Thorndike, Lynn, A History of Magic and Experimental Science during the First Thirteen Centuries of our Era, 2 Vols., Macmillan, 1923, Vol. I.
Tucker, T. G., Life in the Roman World of Nero and St. Paul, Macmillan, 1910.

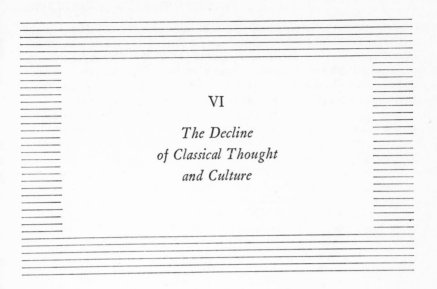

VI

*The Decline
of Classical Thought
and Culture*

I. THE MATERIAL BASIS OF THE DECLINE

In the preceding chapters we have described the thought and culture of ancient Greece and Rome. We have observed that a major part of Rome's civilization was derived from the civilization of the Greeks. In this chapter we shall trace briefly the causes of the decline and collapse of ancient pagan culture, which was followed by the establishment of the Christian civilization of the Middle Ages.

Economic conditions in the Roman Empire became progressively worse after the Antonines (end of second century). Depending largely on Gaul and the Orient for its sustenance, Rome developed the attitude and policies of the parasite and spendthrift. The senseless waste which characterized the upper class pauperized the proletariat as well.

The provinces were sucked dry by administrative grafters, and the sources of imperial revenue were slowly but surely depleted before the time of Diocletian, who became emperor in 284 and tried in vain to salvage the empire. The cities became less prosperous and populous. The basis of Roman civilization slowly shifted back to an agrarian pattern. The earlier era of peasant landholding was replaced by a system of great landlords, slaves, and a semiservile peasantry (the colonate).

Poverty increased and the cost of living rose, in spite of efforts at regulation by the government. The Roman coinage system was debased and depleted. Payment in kind became common; even taxes were often collected in kind in the fourth century. The urban middle class—the backbone of Roman society—was crushed by the unjust burden of taxation thrown on it, and gradually declined to a semiservile level, where it merged with the oppressed peasantry.

The later Roman world in the West became a quasi-feudal regime, lacking only the military element, which was to be supplied by Charles Martel in the eighth century. In the later Roman Empire a marked centralization of governmental powers and an attempted increase of political functions made their appearance. But these trends came at a time when it was least easy to raise revenue and when the administrators could be most readily defied by the powerful group of landlords who were laying the basis for the medieval feudal system.

Anarchy, confusion, and disorder grew rampant and were further stimulated by the barbarian invasions. Not until the ninth century were conditions even partially stabilized. And not until the twelfth century did there emerge some kind of economic, political, and social order.

There has thus been a general tendency to discover in the fall of Rome not a cataclysm, precipitated by the barbarian invasions, but a slow process prepared by centuries of internal political, social, and economic decay. It is probable that the barbarian invasions of the fifth century were no more formidable than those of the third, which were triumphantly repelled by the Illyrian Caesars, or those of the fourth, which were thwarted by Julian and Valentinian. Why did the invasions of the fifth century succeed, while the earlier ones failed?

The answer, as Sir Samuel Dill has suggested, can be found in a study of the imperial edicts. In the voluminous enactments issued, from Constantine (d. 337) to Majorian (457-461), we find an illuminating but tragic account of the maladies which sapped the strength of Roman society.

Municipal liberty and self-government died out. The upper class was set off from the masses by sharp distinctions of wealth and privilege; yet it was forbidden to bear arms and it lost any real interest in public affairs. Not only had an Oriental monarchy usurped the system of Augustus, but an almost Oriental caste system made every social grade and every occupation practically hereditary, "from the senator to the waterman on the Tiber."

Poverty steadily increased, wealth became more insolent and aggressive. The impoverished and disinherited carried looting and brigandage to the very gates of Rome. Parents sold their children into slavery. Public buildings fell into decay. Service on the great post roads became disorganized. Frontier posts were abandoned at a time when every frontier area was threatened. There were wholesale desertions from the army. Freemen refused to enlist and the army had to be recruited from slaves and barbarians.

The largest fissure in the empire, however, lay in its financial system. The collection of revenues in kind opened the door to every species of corruption. The official municipal class—the *curiales,* who were charged with the collection of taxes in their district—was crushed under its responsibility at the same time that it was looked upon by others as a shameless oppressor.

By the time of Theodosius (who became emperor in 379), the last bars seem to have been lowered, Roman society was in a state of moral decay resembling France on the eve of the revolution. Fraud and greed were prevalent. The rich grew richer, the poor grew poorer, and the imperial government, in spite of good intentions, had lost all control of the vast political machine.[1]

1 Dill, *Roman Society in the Last Century of the Western Empire,* Macmillan, 1906 (Meridian reprint), pp. 227-29.

II. POLITICAL ANARCHY AND MILITARY DICTATORSHIP

There was, as we have just made clear, in the closing centuries of the Roman Empire a distinct decline in loyalty to public institutions and obligations. The lack of patriotism, loss of interest in public office, and absence of political integrity among all classes undermined the Roman state.

The army—once the main prop of the empire—had undergone fundamental transformations. It had to resort to compulsory conscription, as mentioned above. In the fourth century the difficulty of providing soldiers made it necessary to put the military arm among the hereditary professions. At the same time, more barbarians were entering the army. By the end of the third century the words barbarian and soldier were used interchangeably.

The army, in fact, became a real menace to the existence of the state. It assumed a major rôle in the government as political and social conditions disintegrated. It made and unmade emperors at will. The praetorian guard became ever stronger, and under Tiberius it was concentrated in Rome where it exerted a constant pressure on politics. In the provinces, the great armies of the Rhine, the Danube, and the East split off from central control and became autonomous. In the third century this military machine threatened to annihilate the empire. The legions elected emperors by caprice and capriciously destroyed them. During the fifty years that followed Alexander Severus (225-235), to be elected emperor was equivalent to being given a decree of death.[2]

Consequently, the government grew more unstable. The emperor was usually the puppet of the army. No matter how honest and competent, he could not provide the protection and security which were needed to keep the far-flung empire orderly and coherent. The graft and exploitation in the imperial finances in previous centuries made it impossible even for an able and public-spirited emperor like Diocletian to rule effectively.

III. INTELLECTUAL DECADENCE UNDER PAGANISM

The disintegration of the economic life, social structure, and political administration of the empire had profound intellectual effects. Paganism was extensively modified. Scientific curiosity and philosophic speculation were being slowly deluged by an emotional bath which poured into Rome from the warm and luscious East. From the East emotion-bearing religions, with antiscientific trends, were imported by the Roman legions and sailors. There was thus a widespread interest in supernatural faith and dogma in the empire even before Christianity appeared on the scene. Scholarship markedly decayed. Intellectual life degenerated and a widespread acceptance of credulity and supernaturalism arose. There was a growing reluctance to face reality and to solve the mounting problems of living. The classical world had, as Gilbert Murray puts it, "lost its nerve."

The Greeks had made remarkable progress in the realm of natural science, beginning with Thales and the Milesian group in the sixth and fifth centuries B.C.

2 Cf. Ferdinand Lot, *The End of the Ancient World,* Knopf, 1931 (Harper Torchbooks, 1961), pp. 8 ff.

Then had followed the introduction of the atomic theory of Leucippus and Democritus' mechanistic theory of causation; Aristotle's comprehensive work in scientific description and classification; the origins of medical science with Hippocrates; and, above all, the astonishing achievements of the Hellenistic scientists —Theophrastus, Euclid, Eudoxus, Apollonius, Aristarchus, Eratosthenes, Archimedes, Hipparchus, Herophilus, Hero, and Ptolemy.

This was an imposing advance from the crude beginnings of the Egyptians and Babylonians. Looking at it purely from the standpoint of the development of science, it is difficult to see why the process did not keep on after Hipparchus (d. c. 125 B.C.) and Hero (c. 300 B.C.). Why did not applied science develop and produce the modern scientific and industrial world two thousand years earlier than it was actually attained in England after 1750?

The explanation usually has been found in the disintegration of Greek political life in the Hellenistic period. But, as historians have made clear, political conditions in Greece were more disturbed during the period of maximum scientific activity than during its decline.

Actually, when the historian views the intellectual life of the classical and patristic periods, the enigma that confronts him is, not why ancient science perished but why it was able to persist as long as it did. He finds that nearly all phases of intellectual life, the prevailing attitudes of mind, and social and economic conditions during the Roman Empire either openly opposed the scientific viewpoint or obstructed those tendencies which would promote scientific activity.

IV. WEAKNESS OF HELLENIC SCIENCE

The very character of Greek science was unprogressive. Aristotle well illustrates this point. He had a penchant for finality and definiteness. Hence he spent a good deal of time classifying and arranging data. This process, clarifying as it was, savored of logic quite as much as of science. Aristotle also sanctified Empedocles' conception of the four fundamental elements, and thereby prevented the adoption of the more sensible atomic and mechanistic theory of Democritus. This sanction by Aristotle held physics and chemistry in bondage until the time of Paracelsus (1493-1541), Libavius (1540-1616), and Boyle (1627-1691).

Aristotle's false notions of dynamic mechanics, and his fantastic cosmology, tended to obscure the accurate work done by the later Hellenistic scientists. Moreover, because the scholastics swallowed Aristotle's system uncritically, it proved an obstruction to the growth of early modern science as well.

Aristotle's compiling tendency, valuable, perhaps, in his own hands and in those of Ptolemy, became, as early as Pliny the Elder (A.D. 23-79), a vehicle for incorporating into scientific works vast masses of pseudoscientific materials—many accepted on the strength of mere tradition or gossip. Astrology further complicated this growth of true science by spreading many grotesque errors of thought and method, and it also hindered the development of astronomy.

Physiological chemistry, resting on the false theory of the four "humors," constituted the scientific basis of medical practice. Since it was associated with the illustrious names of Hippocrates and Galen, this quaint notion barred progress in medical science. To the doctrines of humors were added innumerable magical ideas and practices. Galen was especially guilty here.

Even the remarkable science of the Hellenistic period had its limitations. Archimedes, Hipparchus, and Ptolemy carried it about as far as was possible with the existing techniques of research. Of precise instruments, such as the microscope, balance, stop watch, and thermometer, they had few or none.

In general, the Greeks were unwilling to observe commonplace things and occurrences, an attitude which derived partly from the Platonic enthusiasm for the transcendental, and partly from the contempt of aristocrats for mundane matters associated with servile labor. Enthusiasm for absolutes and transcendentals led to disinterest in the changing and dynamic phenomena of the real world. Hence, the evolutionary concepts of the Greeks and of Lucretius, which required vindication by observation of minute changes in nature, made no headway and were lost sight of until the later Middle Ages.

Finally, we must note that the Greeks were unable to apply the scientific knowledge they actually possessed. Hero, for example, had produced the turbine engine a hundred years before Christ, but he could think of nothing more relevant to do with it than to furnish amusement to the queen by automatically opening the temple doors. Archimedes, as well as Hero, invented many practical devices, especially the lever and pulley, which might have had great industrial significance, but he used them mainly to edify King Hiero of Syracuse.

James Harvey Robinson admirably summarized the reasons why Hellenic science came to a dead stop and the age of machines was delayed by two thousand years:

> After two or three hundred years of talking in the market place and of philosophic discussions prolonged until morning, such of the Greeks as were predisposed to speculation had thought all the thoughts and uttered all the criticisms of commonly accepted beliefs and of one another that could by any possibility occur to those who had little inclination to fare forth and extend their knowledge of the so-called realities of nature by painful and specialized research and examination. This is to me the chief reason why, except for some advances in mathematics, astronomy, geography, and the refinements of scholarship, the glorious period of the Greek mind is commonly and rightfully assumed to have come to an end about the time of Aristotle's death. Why did the Greeks not go on, as modern scientists have gone on, with vistas of the unachieved still ahead of them?
>
> In the first place, Greek civilization was founded on slavery and a fixed condition of the industrial arts. The philosopher and scholar was estopped from fumbling with those everyday processes that were associated with the mean life of the slave and servant. Consequently there was no one to devise the practical apparatus by which alone profound and ever-increasing knowledge of natural operations is possible. The mechanical inventiveness of the Greeks was slight, and hence they never came upon the lens; they had no microscope to reveal the minute, no telescope to attract the remote; they never devised a mechanical timepiece; a thermometer, nor a barometer, to say nothing of cameras and spectroscopes. Archimedes, it is reported, disdained to make any record of his ingenious devices, for they were

unworthy of the noble profession of a philosopher. Such inventions as were made were usually either toys or of a heavy practical character. So the next great step forward in the extension of the human mind awaited the disappearance of slavery and the slowly dawning suspicion, and final repudiation, of the older metaphysics, which first became marked some three hundred years ago.[3]

Roman science, like nearly everything else Roman, was mainly an inferior Greek imitation. While the Romans certainly made notable contributions in structural engineering, they hit upon these more by intuition and ingenuity than by mastering the science of mechanics. Or they drew upon the assistance of Hellenistic engineers and the mechanical theories of Archimedes. They did little or nothing to advance natural science. On the other hand, they did much to degrade science and to block strictly scientific impulses by compiling vast pseudoscientific works like Pliny's *Natural History*.

Ancient science thus bore within itself the seeds of its own decline. But much more important in impeding scientific growth were various nonscientific or antiscientific intellectual currents which dominated the later classical world.

V. THE POPULARITY OF HELLENIC METAPHYSICS AND NEOPLATONISM

A major discovery of Greek thinkers was metaphysics. They did not call it by that name, but they lost themselves, nevertheless, in its endlessly fascinating mazes. Consequently, it prevented them from observing the concrete, the minute, and the essential. When Socrates turned philosophy from fact to truth, as it were, the Greek mind became entranced by its own fanciful creations. Plato gave this mental attitude both respectability and immortality. The philosophers fled from particulars and took refuge in generalities.

So obsessed were the Greek thinkers with abstract speculation that Aristotle's notion of God was that of a being eternally absorbed in contemplation and introspection. The Stoics followed this general tendency and refined it in ways even more deadly to science.

One of the most influential and fatal of these flights into abstractions was Plato's idealism. Turning away with his master, Socrates, from the Sophists' emphasis on the relativity of knowledge and the significance of the concrete and specific, he sought reality in the transcendental. He concluded that reality exists only in the *ideal* type, form or pattern—the universals—of which concrete specific examples—particulars—are but lowly, imperfect, and ephemeral manifestations. This attitude tended to discourage a truly scientific approach towards natural phenomena.

Even more antiscientific were the later Neoplatonists who took their cue from the most abstruse and mystical of Plato's dialogues, the *Timaeus*, a mystical cosmology. The realm of sense impressions—the sole source of information for the scientists—was utterly spurned as unworthy of man's consideration by the Egyptian mystic, Plotinus (A.D. 204-270), founder of Neoplatonism. The concrete and material were, at best, he argued, only a necessary evil. Reflecting the extreme

[3] J. H. Robinson, *Mind in the Making*, Harper, 1921, pp. 111-13.

asceticism of Neoplatonism, Plotinus is said to have expressed shame, humility, and embarrassment at possessing a physical body. The metaphysical contemplation of pure being—Plato's and Aristotle's ideal and divine world—was somewhat more highly esteemed by Plotinus than the concrete and changing world of sense impressions. Plotinus focused his attention, however, on the regions of the absolute, which could be reached only through vision and ecstasy, where neither observation, nor reason, nor analysis had any part.

We find, therefore, in Neoplatonism three ascending levels of experience: (1) sense impressions, (2) logical reasoning and metaphysical analysis, and (3) intuitive grasp and mystical visions. The third and last was incomparably superior to the other two and the only possible way of coming upon reality, especially religious reality.

The intellectual bankruptcy of this Neoplatonic approach to knowledge was itself thus a kind of absolute. According to Adolf Harnack:

> The contempt for reason and science, and these are contemned when relegated to the second place, finally leads to barbarism, because it results in the crassest superstition, and is exposed to all manner of imposture. And, as a matter of fact, barbarism succeeded the flourishing period of Neoplatonism. . . . The masses grew up in superstition, and the Christian Church, which entered on the inheritance of Neoplatonism, was compelled to reckon with this and come to terms with it. Just when the bankruptcy of the ancient civilisation and its lapse into barbarism could not have failed to reveal themselves, a kindly destiny placed on the stage of history certain barbarian nations, for whom the work of a thousand years had as yet no existence. Thus the fact is concealed, which, however, does not escape the eye of one who looks below the surface, that the inner history of the ancient world must necessarily have degenerated into barbarism of its own accord, because it ended with the renunciation of this world. There is no desire either to enjoy it, to master it, or to know it as it really is. A new world is disclosed for which everything is given up, and men are ready to sacrifice insight and understanding, in order to possess this world with certainty; and, in the light which radiates from the world to come, that which in this world appears absurd becomes wisdom, and wisdom becomes folly.[4]

In the works and teachings of some of the followers of Plotinus, the intellectual degradation proceeded much further. With Iamblicus (A.D. c. 300) there developed the thesis that unbounded credulity with respect to things religious is a moral principle, and that the chief purpose of philosophy is to teach the essential wickedness of questioning anything relating to the gods and their supposed actions. Magic and theurgy were looked upon as the noblest of human practices. The mental collapse represented by Iamblicus, the complete surrender to mysticism, prepares us for the Christian thinkers. Taylor has admirably set forth the intellectual degradation of well-developed Neoplatonism as expounded in the writings of Iamblicus:

> There was no conflict, but complete surrender and happy abandonment in Iamblicus the Divine (θεῖος) who when he prayed might be lifted ten cubits from

4 Harnack, *History of Dogma*, 7 vols. bound as 4 vols., Dover Publications, Inc., 1961, I, 337-38.

the ground—so thought his disciples—and around whose theurgic fingers, dabbling in a magic basin of water, Cupids played and kissed each other. His life, told by the Neo-Platonic biographer, Eunapius, is as full of miracle as the contemporary Life of St. Anthony by Athanasius. Iamblicus floats before us a beautiful and marvellously garbed priest, a dweller in the recesses of temples. He frankly gave himself to theurgy, convinced that the Soul needs the aid of every superhuman being— hero, god, demon, angel. He was credulous on principle. It is of first importance, he writes, that the devotee should not let the marvellous character of an occurrence arouse incredulity within him. He needs above all a "science" which shall teach him to disbelieve nothing as to the gods. For the divine principle is essentially miraculous, and magic is the open door, yes, and the way up to it, the anagogic path.

There is no lower depth. Plotinus' reason-surpassing vision of the One (which represents in him the principle of irrationality) is at last brought down to the irrational act, the occult magic deed or word. Truly the worshipper needs his best credulity—which is bespoken by Iamblicus and by this book. . . .

So low sank Neo-Platonism in pagan circles. Of course it did not create this mass of superstitious fantasy. It merely fell in cordially, and over every superstition flung the justification of its principles. In the process it changed from a philosophy to a system of theurgic practice. The common superstitions of the time, or their like, were old enough. But now—and here was the portentous fact—they had wound themselves into the natures of intellectual people; and Neo-Platonism represents the chief formal facilitation of this result.[5]

It is difficult to exaggerate the great influence which Neoplatonism exerted on the western mind for more than a thousand years after Iamblicus. It not only provided the general intellectual atmosphere of the pagan world during the triumph of Christianity, it also specifically influenced Christian thought very directly for over a thousand years. If Hellenistic metaphysics, especially Aristotle's writings, shaped the formal Christian theology of the medieval period, Neoplatonism inspired that more intimate personal Christian religion of the Middle Ages, mysticism—an intuitive apprehension of supernatural experience. The most influential of the church fathers, Augustine, was steeped in Neoplatonism. It profoundly affected his theology which was supreme until the time of Aquinas, and the latter was by no means free from mysticism.

A Syrian monk, falsely called Dionysius the Areopagite, wrote in Greek in the fifth century A.D. a vastly influential work, the so-called *Celestial Hierarchy*. The author was a Christian Neoplatonist. He adapted Neoplatonism to the exposition of Christianity so that pagans who were much taken with Neoplatonism might find it easier to accept Christianity. They would find the same general intellectual concepts and religious truths in the latter. In this way, the author hoped both to promote Christianity and to check the growth of pagan Neoplatonism. Christianity would become the substitute for the latter. The author faked an apostolic date for the book, thus representing it as having appeared long before the work of Plotinus, the founder of Neoplatonism. This work was translated into Latin

[5] H. O. Taylor, *The Medieval Mind*, 2 vols., Macmillan, 1925, I, 47-48.

by John Scotus Erigena in the ninth century and exerted a deep influence on medieval Christian mysticism.

The three stages of salvation according to Neoplatonism were: (1) the discovery of the soul and its union with the oversoul, and the shuffling off of all material attributes; (2) pure contemplation, expressing the communion of the soul with the mind; and (3) mystical communion with the absolute through vision and ecstasy. These were all but identical with the medieval mystical religious interpretations. The medieval mystics, like Hugo of St. Victor, Meister Eckhart, and the others, were much influenced by the *Celestial Hierarchy*. Finally, as we shall see in due time, Neoplatonism dominated the Platonic revival in the days of the humanists and laid the foundations of much of humanist philosophy and pseudo science.

The pagan mind thus returned to the void, after extraordinary achievements in the realm of the abstract, and after laying a foundation for natural science. The Western World had to wait for many centuries to recover from this intellectual cataclysm. It required a millennium to bring philosophy down from the clouds, where Aristophanes, in his satire, had placed it in the person of Socrates, and to put it to work observing, analyzing, and synthesizing the lowly sense impressions whose data nourish science and sound philosophy alike.

VI. THE SUBSTITUTION OF RHETORIC FOR THOUGHT

Another phase of the decadence of pagan thought was the popularity of rhetoric and the love of flowery language and sonorous phrases. This not only corrupted historical writing, but also diverted philosophical attention from the concrete realities with which science deals. It encouraged satisfaction with words and phrases instead of facts and achievements. "Well-said" was substituted for "well-done."

This was about as fatal to scientific endeavor as the Neoplatonic preoccupation with the mysteries of the absolute, the miraculous, and the supernatural. "It is not easy for us to realize," wrote Professor J. B. Bury, "the importance which the art of rhetoric possessed for the Greeks as a purveyor of esthetic pleasure. . . . For the later Greeks, the declamations of rhetoricians, which we find intolerably tedious to read, had as intense an esthetic value as the Homeric poems for their remote ancestors." [6] People went to hear a rhetorical display as we go to a symphony. This interest lasted down to late Graeco-Roman times.

Among the Romans, rhetoric, having its great expositors and defenders in Cicero and Quintilian, came to be even less original than among the Greeks. Writers speedily lost interest in reality and preposterous fictions flourished like the green bay tree. The laws of human life did not seem to interest them, character and situations were despised. They lapsed into vapory dreams, and created a "wonderland" in which cause had no relation to effect, in which men did such things as were never seen on land or sea, and in which the magic of words acted as an opiate, putting not only the reason but observation to sleep. The slavery to

6 J. B. Bury, *The Ancient Greek Historians*, Dover Publications, Inc., 1958, p. 174.

the music of words, to cadences, and to verbal ingenuity among the Romans is hard for us to understand. As Professor A. C. Clark writes: "The ears of the Romans were almost incredibly sensitive to such points. We are told that an assembly was stirred to wild applause by a double trochee."

During the Roman Republic, as Taylor points out, rhetoric had been a great civilizer of provincials. The rhetorician went wherever the legions penetrated, taught the provincials Latin literature, and fostered oratory and the art of turning neat Latin proverbs. But under the empire, oratory, whether practiced at home or in the provinces, was emptied of its real purpose, which was to stir action and generate thought. Outside the business of law, oratory became hollow and insincere. It shied away from real life. "Well-said" again triumphed over "well-reasoned" and "well-done." Oratory was the foundation of education, and the more it fled from reality, the more incapable the Romans became of taking hold of themselves and ruling the world.[7]

VII. MARTIANUS CAPELLA AND THE RISE OF THE SEVEN LIBERAL ARTS

Nothing could better illustrate the decline of science in later paganism than the accepted curriculum in the schools—the "seven liberal arts"—the trivium (grammar, rhetoric, and dialectic), and the quadrivium (geometry, arithmetic, astronomy, and music).

These subjects had been for the most part developed, differentiated, and classified as early as Plato and Aristotle. Varro and Cicero, among the Romans, had written about them. The definitive exposition of the seven liberal arts was, however, the work of an African Neoplatonist, Martianus Capella, who lived sometime during the fourth or early fifth century. His work, one of the most widely used textbooks in the Middle Ages, bore the quaint title of *The Satyricon* or *The Marriage of Philology and Mercury*. It was written in verse and prose, the *chantefable* form. The false nuggets of dubious learning were embedded in allegory, and formed, in Taylor's phrase, a "sterile union of fantasy with pedantry." This became for centuries the intellectual pabulum of the medieval schools. Boëthius and Cassiodorus wrote typical medieval textbooks on the arts to meet the needs of the curriculum. The concentration of the learned on such studies definitely diverted attention from science and the scientific attitude.

Of the two divisions, the trivium was the more important during the Middle Ages and received the bulk of attention from students. The quadrivium itself did not contain the more promising and practical sciences, but merely the more logical and formal. Furthermore, geometry, arthmetic, and astronomy did not mean to the Middle Ages what they meant to the Greeks, or what they mean now. They were chiefly concerned with formal definitions, and with the magic qualities of celestial phenomena, numbers, formulae, geometric figures, and the like.

There was, consequently, nothing in the seven liberal arts to promote science, but much to discourage it.

7 H. O. Taylor, *The Classical Heritage of the Middle Ages*, Macmillan, 1925, pp. 34-36.

The medieval mania for compilations and epitomes was inherited from the decline of pagan culture. Tradition, gossip, and hearsay were packed willy-nilly into these alleged scientific tomes. While some of the best of the earliest compilations unquestionably contained scientific knowledge as then accepted, they invariably amalgamated with it much that was not scientific in any sense of the word.

Even the very best epitome, as a means of extending scientific knowledge, is necessarily inferior to the poorest of laboratory investigations. Most of the actual compilations, however, embraced little of the Athenian or Hellenistic science. Aristotle's epitomizing came from the genuine scientific impulse. This was inevitably superseded by wild guesses, by crude superstition, or by Christian miracles, much of the material being allegorical and anagogical.

Representative pagan compilations, some far better than others, were Ptolemy's *Almagest,* much the best of the lot, Varro's works on Roman antiquities and on agriculture, Pliny's *Natural History,* Seneca's *Natural Questions,* Aelian's *On the Nature of Animals,* Solinus' *Wonders of the World,* and Horapollo's *Hieroglyphics.* In the Dark and Middle Ages, this sort of literature was continued in Isidore of Seville's *Etymologies,* Rhabanus Maurus' *De universo,* Alexander Neckam's *De natura rerum,* and Vincent of Beauvais' *Speculum majus.*

Christian theological controversies tended to give a fresh tone to intellectual life for a time, but even these soon became dry, arid, and reminiscent. For the Latin West the creative patristic epoch closed with the death of Augustine (A.D. 430). There followed a period of intellectual sterility. Men translated from the Greek, wrote commentaries on older writings, or expounded the philosophic systems of their predecessors with a change of emphasis. Epitomes and compendia multiplied, and knowledge was brought down to a more barbarous level. The chief representatives of the postpatristic period of transition were the contemporaries, Boëthius (c. 480-524) and Cassiodorus (c. 490-c. 583), Gregory the Great (d. 604) and, lastly, Isidore of Seville (d. 636).

All these, still clinging to Latin culture, were transmitters of antique and patristic thought. They originated little, and put together materials congenial to their retrospective minds. They remained intellectual authorities well into the medieval period, to be slowly thrown aside only when the real light of science began to rise dimly above the horizon in the twelfth century.

What historians of culture regard as the most important psychological change occurring during paganism took place in the first centuries of the Christian Era. The old, stereotyped, and relatively unemotional pagan religion which flourished in the early days of the Roman republic was gradually superseded by the Oriental mystery cults. These cults were found in the Near East by the Roman legions and sailors, who brought them to Italy where they soon achieved a great vogue.

From Phrygia, came Cybele, the great mother goddess; from Syria, the god of the invincible sun (*sol invictus*); from Egypt, the cult of Isis and Serapis; from Persia, the mysteries of Mithras and Manes (Manichaeism). All were designed to play upon the emotions, and to bring a consciousness of sin, a desire for salvation and purification, and a promise of eternal life in a future world. In earlier days, the Roman intellectuals, for the most part, had remained aloof from the traditional religion and particularly from the popular cults. The Oriental mysteries seduced many of the learned as well as the mass of the illiterate. Christianity only carried this transfiguration farther and eventually conquered the Western World for its simple cosmology and dogmatic theology.

The fact is that the religion of antique paganism had dried up. Its roots were sapped. In Cumont's words, "It became a thing devoid of sense, whose *raison d'être* was no longer understood; it embodied dead ideas and an obsolete conception of the world. In Greece as well as Rome it was reduced to a collection of unintelligible rites, scrupulously and mechanically reproduced without addition or omission because they had been practised by the ancestors of long ago." [8]

The Oriental mysteries, lacking solid intellectual substance but overlaid with emotional rites, carried away first the masses and then the classes. Their imposing ritual and pageantry and their reassuring worship comforted the humble and oppressed, while their doctrines, freighted with the rich wisdom of the old and distant Orient, captivated the literate and opulent. Women fell prey to the orgiastic cults of Isis and Cybele. Men particularly worshiped Mithras, which subjected them to a rigid moral discipline.

Roman gods and Oriental deities existed side by side. Devotion to the Roman gods was an empty civic duty, worship of the Oriental deities was a glamorous emotional feast which satisfied intimate feelings and moral aspirations. The new Oriental religions seemed to answer the problems of existence, while providing a spiritual life whose intensity made all material happiness appear insipid and vulgar and promising a blessed immortality. In this way, antiquity expired and a new intellectual era was born. As Cumont puts it:

. . . The Oriental religions acted upon the senses, the intellect and the conscience at the same time, and therefore gained a hold on the entire man. Compared with the ancient creeds, they appear to have offered greater beauty of ritual, greater truth of doctrine and a far superior morality. The imposing ceremonial of their festivities and the alternating pomp and sensuality, gloom and exaltation of their services appealed especially to the simple and the humble, while the progressive revelation of ancient wisdom, inherited from the old and distant Orient, captivated the cultured mind. The emotions excited by these religions and the consolations offered strongly attracted the women, who were the most fervent and generous followers and the most passionate propagandists of the religions of Isis and Cybele. Mithra was worshipped almost exclusively by men, whom he subjected to a rigid moral discipline. Thus souls were gained by the promise of spiritual purification and the prospect of eternal happiness.

The worship of the Roman gods was a civic duty, the worship of the foreign gods the expression of a personal belief. The latter were the objects of the thoughts,

[8] Cumont, *Oriental Religions in Roman Paganism*, p. 31.

feelings and intimate aspirations of the individual, not merely of the traditional and, one might say, functional adoration, of the citizen. The ancient municipal devotions were connected with a number of earthly interests that helped to support each other. They were one of various forms of family spirit and patriotism and guaranteed the prosperity of the community. The Oriental mysteries, directing the will toward an ideal goal and exalting the inner spirit, were less mindful of economic utility, but they could produce that vibration of the moral being that caused emotions, stronger than any rational faculty, to gush forth from the depths of the soul. Through a sudden illumination they furnished the intuition of a spiritual life whose intensity made all material happiness appear insipid and contemptible. This stirring appeal of supernatural life made the propaganda irresistible. The same ardent enthusiasm guaranteed at the same time the uncontested domination of neo-Platonism among the philosophers. Antiquity expired and a new era was born.[9]

X. PERSIAN DUALISM AND SHIFTING INTELLECTUAL INTERESTS

One of the major contributions of paganism to the medieval world appeared in the cosmic philosophy and otherworldliness of Christianity. The idea of the universe as an arena where God and evil spirits fought against each other for man's soul, entered the classical world from Persia with its belief in the duel between Ormuzd and Ahriman. The Christian borrowed these picturesque figures and elaborated them into a complicated philosophy—the philosophy of diabolism and cosmic dualism.

Ormuzd was the Persian god (a sun god), who led the hosts of righteousness. Aiding him was the Persian savior, Mithras. Opposing Ormuzd and Mithras was Ahriman, the Persian devil, assisted by a body of evil spirits. Their duel constituted the core of the Persian theology.

The struggle of Ormuzd and Ahriman, passing on the one hand through the channels of Judaeo-Christian literature, and on the other, through the Oriental cults of Mithraism and Manichaeism, provided inspiration for the endless nightmares involving hell and the devil which tormented the orthodox of the Middle Ages.

Intimately related to this cosmic tableau was the Persian belief in a final cataclysm which would end the cosmic duel. Ahriman and his followers would be vanquished. The powers of darkness would be routed, Ormuzd would reign triumphant, and a world of eternal bliss would unfold. And here the faithful who had supported Ormuzd and believed in his savior, Mithra, would enter and enjoy everlasting bliss. The wicked followers of Ahriman would be destroyed in a lake of fire and brimstone.

The Greeks and Romans had no very clear idea of immortality. They were not particularly interested in "last things." But with the wide acceptance of this Persian fantasy, attention was directed to preparing for death rather than for life. Assurance of immortality became more important than success here and now. This culminated in the patristic attitude, best reflected in Augustine's famous *City*

[9] Cumont, *op. cit.*, pp. 43-45.

of God. Here the joys of earthly existence are despised and life is portrayed as a severe test of fitness for blessed immortality in the hereafter.

XI. THE GRADUAL TRANSITION TO MEDIEVALISM

With the disintegration of the empire and the intellectual and cultural changes we have just described, Western civilization moved slowly but surely into what is generally known as the Middle Ages.

The transition was more gradual than used to be believed, and no final statement can be made as to just exactly when the pagan world ended and the Middle Ages began. Some historians have suggested the year 325, when the Council of Nicea was convened by the Emperor Constantine, as the beginning of the medieval period. Others would put the date as late as 622, when Mohammed fled from Mecca. Still others would advance it to Charlemagne's coronation in 800.

Medieval scholars themselves, for the most part, regarded the Middle Ages as a continuation of the glorious Roman Empire. The humanist historian, Flavius Blondus (1388-1463), was the first to look upon the Middle Ages as a distinct period. The first historian to divide history into the segments we now recognize was the Dutch humanist, Cellarius (1634-1707). He terminated "ancient history" with Constantine the Great, who died in 337, and "medieval history" with the fall of Constantinople in 1453. It hardly needs to be added that these divisions are arbitrary and misleading. Around dates in a single restricted area, the Byzantine Empire, were organized the achievements of Western civilization. The Christian chronologers' organization of universal history about the framework of Jewish history was hardly more absurd.

A fanciful theory grew up in the so-called Renaissance to the effect that the Middle Ages in many ways represented a discontinuity of civilization, a dreary void, a millennium of intellectual darkness and social anarchy. Then the romanticists of the eighteenth and nineteenth centuries went to the other extreme and exalted the Middle Ages as a period of "faeried story," of gaily caparisoned knights and lovely ladies, of chivalrous sentiments and high valorous deeds.

The truth is that, after the decline of Rome, western European culture retrogressed to the level of the Cretan and Mycenaean civilization which had preceded "the glory that was Greece" and the Etruscan civilization which had ushered in the "grandeur that was Rome."

Between the time of Clovis (481-511) and the advent of the Tudors in 1485, northern Europe went through a sweeping development from tribalism to feudalism, and then to the modern civil state. Culturally, it had climbed again to a point partly comparable to, and partly surpassing, the civilization of the classical world.

Nevertheless, the more we learn about the Middle Ages, the less "dark" they appear. All the lights did not go out. Their story is not an unending tale of barbarism and stagnation. The cultural gleams from the traditions of Greece and Rome, however dim and hazy they may have become, always pierced the gloom.

The medieval period was, rather, a period of gradual change, a slow uphill process of cultural recovery from about the eighth and ninth centuries onward, with a notable acceleration in the twelfth century. The really constructive period of medievalism did not set in until the vestiges of classical civilization, which remained in what used to be Gaul, fused with the crude culture of the Germanic barbarians and the archaic learning of Christianity. This amalgam we call medievalism.

The years from about 500 to 1100 may perhaps rightly be termed the Dark Ages. With Charlemagne (800) there was a definite renaissance. The invasions of the Northmen, along with other confusion, however, produced a considerable regression in the late ninth and tenth centuries. From about 1100 onward the lights were slowly turned on until, around the year 1500, in Italy at least, they reached a notable effulgence.

Most of western Europe was culturally relatively backward before the thirteenth century when compared to the Byzantine Empire whose capital was Constantinople. In the East, the Greek language and Hellenistic learning and literature persisted. Byzantine civilization was noticeably different from, and in many ways superior to, the Latin culture of the Christian West.

Not all medieval Europe, however, was Christianized. In Spain, across the Mediterranean, and in western Asia, there was a highly cultivated Muslim civilization: While their Christian rivals were slaughtering each other, the Muslims created a brilliant material civilization and intellectual life. Neither did they have to take a back seat in respect to political and military achievements.

In the chapters immediately following, we shall first consider the rise of Christianity and its otherworldly philosophy, enforced by the power of the greatest international state the world knew down to modern times—the Roman Catholic church. Then we shall turn to the thought and culture of the first clearly Christian age in Western history, the Dark Ages from about 500 to about 1100. Next we shall deal with the intellectual and cultural developments of the height of the Middle Ages in the twelfth and thirteenth centuries. Finally, we shall trace the decline of medievalism and its gradual emergence into modern times in the period between Roger Bacon and Petrarch.

SELECTED READINGS

Allbutt, T. C., *Greek Medicine in Rome*, Macmillan, 1924.

Arragon, R. F., *Transition from the Ancient to the Medieval World*, Holt, 1936.

Atkins, G. G., *The Making of the Christian Mind*, Harper, 1928.

Bakewell, *Source Book in Ancient Philosophy*, chaps. xxii-xxiii.

Bark, W. C., *Origins of the Medieval World*, Stanford University Press, 1958.

Burr, G. L., "Anent the Middle Ages," *American Historical Review*, July, 1913; "How the Middle Ages Got Their Name," *Ibid.*, July, 1915.

Cochrane, C. N., *Christianity and Classical Culture*, Oxford University Press, 1940.

Cumont, Franz, *Oriental Religions in Roman Paganism*, Dover, 1956.

Dill, Samuel, *Roman Society in the Last Century of the Western Empire*, Meridian Books.

——— *Roman Society in Gaul in the Merovingian Age*, Macmillan, 1926.

Dopsch, Alfons, *The Economic and Social Foundations of European Civilization*, Harcourt, Brace, 1937.

Foligno, Cesare, *Latin Thought during the Middle Ages*, Oxford Press, 1929.

Funck-Brentano, Frantz, *The Earliest Times*, Putnam, 1927.

Glover, T. R., *The Conflict of Religions in the Early Roman Empire*, Beacon, 1960.

Guérard, A. L., *French Civilization from Its Origins to the Close of the Middle Ages*, Houghton Mifflin, 1921.

Halliday, W. R., *The Pagan Background of Christianity*, London, 1926.

Haskell, H. J., *The New Deal in Old Rome*, Knopf, 1939.

Hatch, Edwin, *The Influence of Greek Ideas and Usages on the Christian Church*, Harper Torchbooks, 1957.

Heitland, W. E., *The Roman Fate*, Cambridge University Press, 1922.

Hyde, W. W., *Paganism to Christianity in the Roman Empire*, University of Pennsylvania Press, 1947.

Inge, W. R., *The Philosophy of Plotinus*, 2 Vols., Longmans, 1919.

Jones, A. H. M., *Constantine and the Conversion of Europe*, Macmillan, 1949.

Laistner, M. L. W., *The Intellectual Heritage of the Early Middle Ages*, Cornell University Press, 1957.

————— *Christianity and Pagan Culture in the Later Roman Empire*, Cornell University Press, 1951.

Lot, Ferdinand, *The End of the Ancient World*, Harper Torchbooks, 1961.

Mackail, *Latin Literature*.

Murray, *Five Stages of Greek Religion*.

Parkes, J. W., *The Foundations of Judaism and Christianity*, University of Chicago Press, 1960.

Rand, E. K., *Founders of the Middle Ages*, Dover, 1957.

Robinson, J. H., *The New History*, Macmillan, 1912, chap. vi.

————— *Readings in European History*, 2 Vols., Ginn, 1904, Vol. I, chaps. ii-iii.

Showerman, Grant, *Rome and the Romans*, Macmillan, 1931.

Singer, Charles, *From Magic to Science*, Dover, 1958, chaps. i-ii.

Starr, C. G., *Civilization and the Caesars*, Cornell University Press, 1954.

Stewart, H. F., *Boethius*, London, 1891.

Taylor, H. O., *The Classical Heritage of the Middle Ages*, Macmillan, 1925.

Thorndike, *History of Magic and Experimental Science*, 2 Vols., Macmillan, 1923, Vol. I.

Whittaker, Thomas, *The Neo-Platonists*, Cambridge University Press, 1901.

Part Three

THE MEDIEVAL SYNTHESIS

VII

The Christian World View

I. THE CULTURAL BACKGROUND OF THE TRIUMPH OF CHRISTIANITY

Religious conditions in the later Roman Empire were very favorable to the spread and triumph of Christianity. The ancient pagan cults of Greece and Rome had gradually lost their grip through contact with skeptical philosophies, the clash of varied cultures, and the impact of disintegrating social and economic conditions. The primitive rural cults, which had flourished during the republic, decayed after centuries of exposure to economic changes, an expanding empire, and the infusion of new peoples, of foreign religions, and of critical attitudes. The state cults also lost their former hold on the Roman populace. Even emperor worship—an exotic cult which had failed to have any great attraction for the Roman citizen—never aroused much popular enthusiasm. On the whole, the old pagan religions were in a state of impending dissolution about the time when organized Christianity appeared on the scene.

Some pagan intellectuals seemed to get along fairly well without the comforts and assurances of any supernatural religion, but the majority of people ardently yearned for a "personal" god with an overpowering appeal, to whom they could entrust their destiny. Their old heathen idols no longer offered them much solace or reassurance.

The quest for a new religion was naturally intensified by the growing political anarchy and economic misery. As we have seen in the last chapter, the lower class was always in a desperate condition, and the middle class was gradually being pushed down to the level of the miserable peasants and city rabble. For all but the wealthy minority of profiteers and great landlords, life on earth was agonizing and haphazard. It came very near to matching Hobbes' description of the life of man in the state of nature—"poor, nasty, brutish, and short." As life here lost its attractions, people looked to "the bourne whence no man returns" to compensate them for their miseries.

When the empire cracked up and the older political and intellectual certainties lost their grip and prestige, even philosophers looked around for a religion that offered reassurance. Any new cult which held out hope of personal regeneration in this life and salvation in the hereafter was bound to evoke a hearty response. These conditions account for the great popularity of numerous mystery religions which competed for the favor of the Mediterranean world after the Roman Republic fell.

When Christianity appeared with its splendid doctrinal accouterments and unshakable self-confidence, it had for a long time to combat the rival mystery cults, as well as Gnosticism, which explained Jesus and his ministry in terms of Hellenistic metaphysics, and Neoplatonism, which (like nineteenth-century Positivism) was a sort of Catholicism without the Christianity.

Why did Christianity triumph over its many powerful rivals and eventually suppress them all? The answer is complex, indeed, and involves a wide knowledge of conditions in the Roman Empire during the first three centuries of our era. Chiefly, however, Christianity triumphed because it was better organized than its competitors and pushed its roots down deeper among the masses, particularly in the urban areas. This enabled it to preserve discipline, and hold all the ground it gained.

Of all the rival religions, Mithraism came closest to Christianity in coherence of organization and it also made the most spectacular emotional and doctrinal appeal. But it had several defects. For one thing, it excluded women, the more religious of the sexes. Had it taken cognizance of how impressionable women are to religion, it might have won out over Christianity. Another significant weakness of Mithraism was its limited appeal. It seemed to make most headway among the classes, the army, and officialdom, while Christianity appealed more to the masses (the underdogs), and met the average man more on his own ground. Christianity indeed became the popular religion par excellence for which the citizenry of Rome had yearned.

Slaves and freemen looked with envy upon the riotous life of the upper class, which carried on its levantine frolics and indulged in its purple vices while the multitude suffered, sank deeper into debt, drifted into servility, and were otherwise deprived of the good things of life. Christianity, with its scorn for luxury and wealth, seemed to offer the masses a magnificent opportunity to oust the wealthy from their lofty perch and to do away with the exasperating spectacle of glaring social and economic inequality. Social scores could be evened up here and now.

Christianity, in other words, tempered its program to the needs of the "shorn lamb." Instead of material riches, which the masses could not obtain, Christianity exalted moral worth and high ethical ideals, which were within the grasp of everyone, rich and poor alike.

Christianity had still another important feather in its cap. It not only attracted the suffering masses, but also made many recruits among the urban middle class.

The Roman economic system in the later empire was, as we have seen, especially hard on middle-class officialdom—the *curiales*. As time went on, taxation well nigh threatened this group with extinction. To them, too, Christianity seemed a way out of intolerable oppression. It offered the possibility of a social revolution here and now, and the certainty of a happy future life as well.

Paul quickly saw the value of concentrating Christianizing efforts on the urban middle class.[1] Their widespread conversion was a tower of strength to the struggling Christian cult. Roman civilization was primarily an urban civilization. Therefore, a religion that had triumphed in the cities was likely to subdue the empire as a whole.

There were other factors favoring the success of Christianity, which can only be summarized here. Among them were:

The certainty and profound assurance of Christian dogma.

The belief in an afterlife compensating for the sorrows and disappointments of this life.

The messianic hope of the Jews which led many to accept Jesus.

The transformation of Jesus from an earthly to a heavenly messiah.

The preparation for Christian attitudes in such pagan philosophies as Stoicism and Neoplatonism.

The Christian notion of the equality of men before God.

The persecutions and martyrdoms, which drew attention to the Christian sect.

The austere character of many early Christian leaders.

The divorce of Christianity from national and local politics, giving it a universal appeal.

The development of mutual aid and charitable work among the early Christians.

Christianity, then, triumphed because it possessed most of the advantages of rival religions, and in addition, possessed special features which none of the others could match. Above all, it had the missionary vision and the organizing genius of Paul, without which it might have remained an obscure and ephemeral mystery cult. Paul transformed it from a local Jewish sect to a universal religion, mapped out a systematic plan for converting the Roman world, and devoted his life to promoting this enterprise.

Paul was the architect of Christianity, the blueprint maker who laid out the structure and got the workmen into action. He originated the admirable discipline and government of the church. He established the fundamental Christian rite, the Eucharist. He freely reinterpreted and adapted the words and views attributed to Jesus in order to advance his own program. When Paul died (between A.D. 62 and 67) there was a faith and an organization which could stand on its own feet and did not need to yield to any other cult. As conditions in the Roman world grew worse, the religion of Paul went on to steady triumphs.

---

[1] Indeed, the word "heathen" originally meant "one who lives in the country."

II. THE EVOLUTION OF THE CHRISTIAN RELIGION

It was once generally believed that the underlying doctrine of Christianity was "the faith once for all delivered unto the saints." Not until the eighteenth century was it admitted, or even known, that Christianity owed a great deal to religions which had preceded it, and to beliefs and institutions existing in the Roman world when Christianity arose.

Critics constantly remark that historical Christianity has had little relation to the teachings of Christ; that there has been little "Christliness" in the history of the church. But the fact remains that, if the Christ cult was to travel far beyond the borders of Palestine, it necessarily had to depart from the shadowy and provincial teachings of Jesus.

At the beginning, it was hardly imagined that among the numerous mystery cults which Roman soldiers, merchants, and travelers brought back from the picturesque East, Christianity would vanquish all the others. That it did so was in part a result of its syncretic nature, of the process whereby Christianity brought together most of the active religious elements in the intellectual and emotional ferment of the Roman twilight.

The fundamental doctrines in Christianity were common to all religions. Primitive man had furnished them all with the basic beliefs essential for dealing successfully with the supernatural world. Primitive man had provided the doctrine of supernatural power, and had classified its agents into good and evil spirits. He had originated various rituals—worship, magic, sacrifice, baptism, birth, death, initiation, and purification rites—which indicated man's fear and gratitude with respect to the supernatural powers who were believed to control the world. These were at the root of Judaism and other eastern prototypes of Christianity, and most of them still persist in orthodox Catholicism and Protestantism.

The religion of the Jews, developed over hundreds of years, made many obvious contributions to Christianity. Christians measured historical time by means of the Jewish chronology, which ran back to the Creation. Jewish history provided the framework of the Christian historical perspective and the heroes of the Christian past—Moses, Joshua, Samson, David, Solomon, and the like. Even Enoch and Lot crowded out Pericles. The Christian cosmology—the theory of the origin and development of the universe, the earth, and its inhabitants—was derived primarily from Genesis.

The Jews also gave the Christians their particular deity. Their tribal God, Yahweh, became the Christian God, and his putative son, Jesus, became the Christian savior. Finally, the Jews contributed Jesus himself, whom they later disowned.

Jewish scriptures supplied the specific literary basis for the expected coming of Christ—namely, the so-called messianic hope. Much of early Christian morality was also obtained from the Old Testament. God's revelations in respect to good conduct, and his manifest will in such matters, as illustrated by Old Testament examples, were accepted by Christian readers. The historical basis of the Christian epic was provided by the Old Testament.

Pre-Christian asceticism was found in certain Jewish cults which preached the doctrine of vanity and futility to be found in the literature attributed to Solomon, and urged withdrawal from the world. John the Baptist presumably belonged to such a sect, the Essenes.

The sacred works of the Jews, not only the Bible, but the Talmud, and later the Cabala, similarly exerted a deep influence on Christianity. Hence, there were many Jewish legal and religious beliefs, not found in the Old Testament, which were worked into Christianity by scholarly Jewish converts.

Some Jewish lore which the Christians took over, such as the legends relative to the Creation and the Deluge, originally came from Babylonian sources, while it is believed by the late Professor Breasted and others that the messianic hope originated in Egyptian social philosophy, whence the Jews borrowed it.

The Greeks left innumerable impressions on Christianity. Scholarly Greeks converted to Christianity could not rest satisfied with the real Jesus, portrayed as an unlettered village workman, whose intimates and disciples were fishermen. They had to exalt him to high metaphysical rank, where he could rival the Platonic logos, the source of truth. Hence, Christian theology became essentially Greek metaphysics, restated and revalued in relation to the person and mission of Jesus. In Gnosticism, a logical but extreme development of this metaphysical interpretation, Jesus all but ceased to be a person and became an abstract philosophical principle, an illuminating and redeeming revelation. Most of the great heresies of the early church were little more than varying unofficial Hellenic views of Jesus' nature and mission.

The moral austerity of Christianity drew heavily upon the Stoic eulogy of moral earnestness. The Stoics also contributed their cosmopolitan outlook, and their attitude of resignation to the all-pervading will of God, as expressed in nature and the life experiences of man. Neoplatonism gave Christianity its general mental atmosphere—the belief that faith and credulity most befit a religious person; that they are the only avenue to true contact with the infinite. It thus stimulated Christian mysticism. Finally, when Aristotle was rediscovered by the Middle Ages, Hellenic thought supplied the logical foundations for the completed body of Catholic doctrine—scholasticism.

Christian ritual was borrowed in part from the Greek mysteries. The holiest of Christian rites, the Eucharist, was invented by Paul as an imitation of the sacred meal of the Eleusinian mysteries. Baptism and the colorful Christian liturgy and ritual were drawn primarily from Hellenistic orientalism. Greek rhetoric furnished the models for Christian preaching, and the original name of a Christian church—*ecclesia*—was of Greek origin.

From the Persians came perhaps the most influential of all the elements that entered into Christianity—namely, the notion of the preponderant importance of the life to come. The Persians were the first to provide elaborate and dogmatic answers to the eternal question: Why had the universe and man come into existence? They believed that God had created the universe as an arena where the principles of good and evil could engage in decisive combat, and where the triumph of good over evil might be overwhelmingly demonstrated. Those who had been wise enough to believe in the principle of good represented by Ormuzd, the

Persian God, would be rewarded by a life of immortal happiness in the world to come. Those who had been foolish enough to pin their hopes on the forces of evil, championed by Ahriman, the Persian devil, would be thrown into a lake of fire and brimstone.

For the first time in human history, the future life became a matter of all-absorbing interest. The Greeks and Romans had, until influenced by the Persians, believed in a sort of drab and indifferent afterlife, in which men were neither sad nor glad, though certain specially hideous criminals might receive appropriate punishment. The Persian eschatology made the next world a challenge to our conduct in this world. Indifference was no longer possible, since the good would be forever blessed and the wicked forever punished.

Christianity thus derived its idea of immortality from Persia, partly through direct contact with competing Persian religions like Mithraism and Manichaeism, and partly from the Jews of pre-Christian days. These Jews had taken over the Persian beliefs, as is particularly evident in the book of Enoch.

The Persians, through Mithraism, contributed, in addition, the famous light and darkness symbolism, associating the former with good, the latter with evil. Incidentally, they supplied the particular date chosen for Christmas. The twenty-fifth day of December was the day of the great Mithraic feast celebrating the returning strength of their sun-god. From Mithraism also, rather than from the traditional Jewish sabbath, was derived Sunday, with its taboo on work. Many Christian rites, such as the use of bells, candles, and the like, were imitated from Mithraic usage; whence likewise came blood symbolism in baptism.

Into Christianity were drafted elements of Manichaeism, a strange compound of Persian, Babylonian, and Buddhist religions, founded by Manes of Ctesiphon (A.D. 215-272). It laid special stress on renunciation of the flesh, the vividness and reality of heaven and hell, and the symbolism of light and darkness. Manichaeism, we may note, persisted down to late medieval times among the Cathari of Italy, the Albigenses of southern France, and certain Bulgarian sects, such as the Bogomiles. The philosopher, Pierre Bayle (1647-1706), thought well of it in modern times.

Rome brought to Christianity its genius for organization and administration. Roman law, adapted to religious cases, became the famous canon law of the medieval church. When the Christian church spread about the Mediterranean world it took over the system of administration used by the Roman emperors. It even adopted many of the administrative districts and titles. The title of bishop, for example, had been that of the leading civil officer of the Roman municipalities in the East.

The Romans, moreover, made important contributions to Christian ritual. Roman rites dealing with the more critical milestones in life—birth, puberty, marriage, and death, which were especially safeguarded in Roman religion—passed over into Christian baptism, confirmation, the sacramental wedding, and the ecclesiastical funeral. Roman notions of *religio,* embracing attitudes of awe, anxiety and piety, and Roman conceptions of the sacred, as something holy and made over to God, also exerted a real influence on Christian doctrine.

Finally, when Christianity was taken among the barbarians of northern Europe, the primitive beliefs, rites, and festivals of these backward peoples were carried over into their new religion and a fusion between the two resulted. The antique primitivism in Christianity, which had survived from the preliterary period, was thus merged with the freshly primitive culture of the new barbarian converts.

This catalogue does not exhaust the accretions to Christianity consisting of elements drawn from many sources. But it does show how the composite character of the new religion gave it a potential appeal to many areas, cultures, sects, and linguistic stocks. It was the most syncretic, and therefore the most attractive, of all the cults which competed for favor in the later Roman Empire.

III. THE VICTORY OF CHRISTIANITY OVER ROMAN PAGANISM

At first there was a tendency to regard Christianity as a religion which would appeal only to Jews. It is said that a special vision was required to convert Peter to the idea that Christianity should be spread over the whole pagan world.[1a] This attitude is mirrored in the Gospel according to Matthew, and the conflict it engendered in the book of Acts. Paul dispelled that belief once and forever. This wider purpose appears in the Acts, the Pauline Epistles, and the Gospel according to Luke, written under Pauline influence.

The Christians made the most of their missionary opportunities. One of the great advantages of conversion to Christianity in the early days was that it offered a chance to live normally in a pagan society and at the same time claim communion in the kingdom of God and look forward to salvation in the world to come. The idea that all Christians in the first and second centuries lived like terror-stricken refugees, is quite false. Only during periods of persecution were they driven underground—and then only in certain places.

Christianity inevitably aroused the suspicion and animosity of the Roman Empire. The independence which the Christians arrogated to themselves clashed at times with Roman law, which assumed that the state was sovereign, and could not tolerate the defiance of any lesser group. Moreover, in addition to emperor worship, there was a Roman state religion, and both of these conflicted with Christianity. The Roman government tolerated many different religions within its boundaries, but it insisted upon an annual show of deference to both the emperor and his cult. This formal gesture the Christians stubbornly refused to execute. It was this, together with some unorthodox social views, which specifically provoked the persecutions by the Romans.

To the Roman authorities, the Christians thus appeared as heretics and traitors. Hence the periodical persecutions, in spite of the attempts of Peter and Paul to reassure Rome that Christianity recognized the necessity and divine origin of secular government. The persecutions began with Nero in A.D. 64 and continued sporadically through the reigns of Trajan, Decius, Marcus Aurelius, Valerian, and Diocletian (284-305).

[1a] Acts, chap. 2.

This "bloodletting" served on the whole to stimulate rather than check the growth of Christianity, since for the lower classes a speedy martyrdom for the sake of Christ and a blessed future life was no worse than being ground down for a lifetime under the ruthless economic system. The Christian soon developed an ineffable zeal for martyrdom which defied the cruelty of imperial Rome. "Let cruelty, envious or malignant," cries Cyprian, "hold you here in bonds and chains as long as it will; from this earth and from these sufferings you shall speedily come to the Kingdom of Heaven. . . . The body is cherished with the refreshment and solace of Christ." [2]

No torture Rome could devise, and the Latins have been past masters in the art, could halt the flow of converts. By A.D. 300 there were so many Christians that persecution seemed pointless. Christianity had become an organized defiance of imperial law. In 311 the Emperor Galerius revoked the edict of persecution of 303 and introduced an era of tolerance. In 313 Constantine issued the famous Edict of Milan which legalized Christianity, and in 325 he called the great Council of Nicea, which settled for a time the doctrinal dispute between the Arians and the Athanasians by deciding in favor of the latter.

After Constantine's death, paganism was practically doomed. Christians were favored over pagans, and finally, under Theodosius the Great (379-395), Christianity became a religious monopoly defended by the state. The worship of heathen gods was forbidden. Then the Christians turned the tables on their enemies and soon more than evened the old score through vigorous persecution of the pagans.

IV. THE ELABORATION OF WORSHIP AND CHURCHLY ORGANIZATION

We have already noted that the chief props of early Christianity were its superior discipline and organization. In the days of the Apostles there had been little need for extensive organization. Believers were few, and they expected Christ to return soon and bring earthly matters to a close. Therefore, they set up a simple and primitive communistic society: "As many as were possessors of lands or houses sold them, and brought the prices of the things that were sold, and laid them at the apostles' feet: and distribution was made unto every man according as he had need." [3]

Jesus, however, did not return promptly, and meanwhile converts multiplied. Some kind of organization was needed to teach, direct, and aid the newcomers. Besides, heresies were arising, which, if allowed to flourish, might destroy the new religion virtually at its birth.

Organization therefore arose to satisfy the needs of worship and charity among small bodies of believers. Walter Pater, in *Marius the Epicurean*, has graphically described the church convert of the days of Marcus Aurelius. The novitiate was enamored of the ethical grandeur of the new religion, its strong sense of family ties, its peaceful industriousness, its doctrine of chastity and continence. The very

[2] Cited in C. H. Dawson, *The Making of Europe*, Sheed and Ward, 1932, p. 29.
[3] Acts, IV.

air in Cecilia's house, where Pater's Christians gathered, was like balsam, "full of mercy in its mere contact, like a salve on aching flesh." [4]

Eventually, the simple familylike organization was outgrown, and formal leadership was necessary. Originally, all believers residing in a particular locality met in a small room, sat around a table during the sacred meal, and listened to the words spoken by the more important or older members of the group. As the Christian community grew, there was no longer room for all the believers at the table. From this time on, seats at the table were reserved for local church officers and visiting prophets. The others sat about the room and the deacons moved among them, distributing the consecrated bread, and taking up contributions for the impecunious votaries in the district. This marked the first differentiation between the clergy and the laity in the Christian church. The officers who sat at the table came to be called the clergy. Those who sat around the room were the laity.

At first the chief officer was called an "overseer." Under him were elders or presbyters and deacons. Presently, the overseer evolved into a bishop and the presbyters into priests. The deacons always remained subordinate. The names of the more important officers were taken over from civil officers in pagan society. Thus, as we have noted, *episcopus* was the title of a municipal officer in Asia Minor, and the very word used for church, *ecclesia,* was the name of an ancient Greek assembly.

Beginning mainly as a village and rural cult, with an appeal to workers, fishermen, shepherds, and peasants, Christianity, as we noticed, soon spread to the cities, where organization necessarily become more complex. The bishop [5] became the pivotal officer. He administered the basic rite, the mass or Eucharist, which symbolized Jesus' sacrifice for the sins of the world. Out of this simple responsibility, the bishop's position expanded into one of great power:

> In addition to his religious authority, and his prestige as a representative of the people, he possessed recognized powers of jurisdiction not only over his clergy and the property of the Church but as a judge and arbitrator in all cases in which his decision was invoked, even though the case had already been brought before a secular court. Consequently, the episcopate was the one power in the later Empire capable of counterbalancing and resisting the all-pervading tyranny of the imperial bureaucracy. Even the most arrogant official feared to touch a bishop.[6]

Corresponding to the civil province of the empire was an ecclesiastical province governed by a metropolitan, who resided in the capital of the province. There was also a tendency to build up an exarchate to match the civil diocese or group of provinces that was controlled by a vicar in the Roman imperial system. The whole church system eventually culminated in the papacy, or the elevation of the bishop of Rome to supreme command. At the same time, the ecclesiastical capital was ultimately established in Rome, the old center of the secular empire.

As the chief imperial city, Rome had considerable influence in raising the Roman church to supremacy. Moreover, when the stronger emperors removed to

---

[4] Cf. Pater, *Marius the Epicurean,* chap. xxii, for the description of a church at this time.
[5] This term was first used in A.D. 63.
[6] Dawson, *op. cit.,* p. 36.

Byzantium, not only was the Roman bishop freed from the direct control of the emperors, but there was nobody left in Rome who could wield greater power. As the empire grew weaker, the church had to assume many of the functions of civil government. These and many lesser factors combined to make Rome the mother church, and its bishop the pope. The primacy of Rome was recognized as early as 381. Professor Flick thus portrays the majesty of the pope:

> At the head of the hierarchy stood the all-powerful and absolute Pope as God's agent on earth. . . . He was the defender of Christianity, the Church, and the clergy in all respects. He was the supreme censor of morals in Christendom and the head of a great spiritual despotism. He was the source of all earthly justice and the final court of appeal in all cases. . . . He might, if he so wished, set aside any law of the Church, no matter how ancient, so long as it was not directly ordained by the Bible or by nature. He could also make exceptions to purely human laws and these exceptions were known as dispensations." [7]

While in this work we are not concerned primarily with the personal side of history, one cannot adequately summarize the triumph of the New Rome without some reference to the great Greek and Latin fathers who shaped administrative policy and church doctrine and led in ecclesiastical strategy. They defended the unity of dogma and fought for the preservation of orthodoxy. They advanced the doctrine of theocracy, or the supremacy of the church in human society. They preached the wickedness of this world and extolled the blessedness of salvation in the next. They upheld the glories and promise of that most holy of all types of Christian life, asceticism, and thereby promoted and guided the development of monasticism. They shaped the growth and organization of the church and led in the strategy that ultimately put the New Rome in a position of ascendancy over the Old Rome.

Among the leading Greek fathers, Origen (185-254) was especially notable for his battle against the Gnostic heresy (that is, the extreme Hellenization of Christian doctrine), and for his assimilation of Greek philosophy to Christian theology. He was a master of the allegorical method. He did much to interweave Hellenistic paganism and Philonic Judaism with Christianity. Athanasius (296-373), bishop of Alexandria, was the great defender of orthodoxy—the Nicene creed—against the Arian heresy, which refused to accept the orthodox view of the Trinity. His views were adopted by the Council of Nicea. Basil (329-379) fought valiantly for Christian orthodoxy and monasticism. He attacked the paganism of the emperor, Julian the Apostate, as well as the Arian heresy within Christianity. His writings on the Trinity and on the Christian liturgy were particularly well known. He also compiled one of the first guides to monastic life. Gregory Nazianzen (c. 329-389) was notable for his theological labors in behalf of orthodoxy, being a leading opponent of Arianism. He not only warmly recommended but personally practiced the severe ascetic life. John Chrysostom (c. 347-407), archbishop of Constantinople, was the great preacher of the Eastern church. Better than anyone else, he adapted the canons of Greek rhetoric to the effective exposi-

---

7 A. C. Flick, *The Rise of the Medieval Church*, Putnam, 1909 (Burt Franklin, 1959), pp. 575-76.

tion of Christian doctrine. He was an able administrator and organizer as well.

Among the Latin fathers, Ambrose (340-397), bishop of Milan, was a great clerical administrator and a leading exponent of theocracy and Christian charitable work. Possessing the courage of his convictions, he even disciplined the powerful emperor, Theodosius the Great. He fought Arianism vigorously in the West. Jerome (c. 340-420) was a leading scholar among the Latin fathers. Famous for his Latin translation of the Bible, the so-called Vulgate, he was an eminent theological writer and one of the most eloquent defenders of the virtues of the ascetic life. Augustine (354-430), bishop of Hippo in North Africa, was the most influential figure in the entire history of Christian theology down to the time of Thomas Aquinas. His *City of God* is the most important book in the history of patristic Christian literature. An authoritative formulation of early Christian theology, it contains, as well, powerful propaganda against paganism. Augustine wrote widely on other subjects, including guidance for the Christian life in general and for the ascetic life in particular.

Gregory the Great (c. 540-604) was perhaps the most eminent ecclesiastical administrator in the West. Together with Ambrose, he consolidated the ecclesiastical organization and did much to advance theocratic doctrines and practices. He described graphically the devil and the horrors of hell, as well as writing very effectively for the guidance of the life of the monks.

Though it is true that the rise and domination of Christianity were determined primarily by the state of material culture and intellectual life from 100 B.C. to A.D. 300, historical forces nevertheless operate only through personal agents. These early fathers were the main personal instruments through whose varied and diverse efforts Christianity emerged as the prevalent religion of the West in the fourth century of our era. It is they who were responsible for the establishment of unity and orthodoxy, for the encouragement and guidance of asceticism, for the perfection of church administration, and for the launching of the view of the supremacy of the church over the state.

V. THE SACRAMENTAL SYSTEM OF THE CATHOLIC CHURCH

The main function of the Christian church, as of all other forms of revealed religion, was to provide for the well-being and safety of its communicants through proper mediation with the supernatural powers. But Christianity was rather less concerned, in theory at least, with securing economic betterment for its membership than certain earlier religions had been. For example, it had no rites so immediately connected with the increase and safeguarding of crops as did the old Roman agricultural religion. Christianity did not guarantee man an increase of material well-being on this planet. Indeed, in its earlier forms and doctrines it condemned power and riches and upheld meekness and poverty. Its main promises concerned man's fate in the next world. The only material betterment that it assured was charity for the helpless. It was not inclined to disapprove too seriously of earthly misery and anguish. Human suffering here on earth might help to concentrate attention upon religion and the hope of salvation in the world to come. Therefore, the oustanding protection that Christianity offered was the safe-guarding of its members against the mysterious forces of life and against the malicious evil spirits headed by the devil himself.

In all supernatural religions it has been deemed desirable not only to provide divine protection and support in the life struggle as a whole, but to supply par-ticular sustenance in the major crises of human existence, which were always viewed by prescientific peoples as full of special mystery and danger. As examples of such crises one may cite birth, adolescence, the beginning of professional life, marriage, imminent death, and special lapses into sin. Even in primitive society extensive religious rites were worked out to tide man over these crises with a maximum of safety and success. It is not surprising, therefore, that the Christian church provided a most elaborate scheme of belief and practice designed to secure God's aid in correct living, His protection against the crises of life, and His assur-ance of salvation to the righteous. This scheme was the so-called sacramental system, the pivotal factor in medieval Christianity.

According to mature Catholic Christianity there were seven basic sacraments: (1) the Eucharist or communion, which is given in the ceremony of the Mass; (2) baptism; (3) confirmation; (4) ordination; (5) marriage; (6) penance; and (7) extreme unction. The third and fourth of these can be administered only by a bishop. In the early Middle Ages the full seven sacraments had not yet emerged. The groundwork for the complete doctrine was laid down in the twelfth century in the works of Hugo of St. Victor and, especially, of Peter Lombard. The latter, in his *Book of Sentences,* defined the seven sacraments. Other acts of piety that had earlier been called sacraments were now called "sacramentals." Though the seven sacraments were generally accepted thereafter, there was no authoritative pro-nouncement on their number until 1439.

In the celebration of the Holy Eucharist or Lord's Supper it was held, according to the doctrine of transubstantiation,[8] that the bread and wine of the symbolic holy meal were miraculously transformed into the very flesh and blood of Jesus. There was thus a continual renewal of contact between the church and its sacri-ficed Savior God, a resulting spiritual regeneration, and an indwelling of the po-tent grace of God. The Eucharist, then, was not so much designed to protect man against special crises of life as to give him added strength and power to resist evil in his every thought and act. It symbolically reproduced the function of the sacri-fice, as expressed in the earlier religions, in the way of bringing together God and his worshipers and renewing divine grace. The Eucharist was the most vital ele-ment in Christian worship; a duly consecrated priest was required for its adminis-tration.

It will be obvious that the other sacraments offered protection against life's crises and against the results of man's sinful nature. Baptism, by wiping away the stain of original sin, was designed to safeguard birth and early years. Infants who died unbaptized were consigned to limbo (*limbus infantum*). Confirmation threw the blanket of spiritual protection about adolescence. Ordination corresponded to earlier rites that protected one against disaster in assuming the responsibilities

[8] Not officially confirmed until the Fourth Lateran Council in 1215.

of adulthood and professional life. In the service of the medieval church it spread the special benediction of God upon the young priest about to assume holy orders.

Sex relations and marriage had been looked upon from primitive times as peculiarly charged with mystery and danger. In the Christian belief there was the added notion that in the procreation of children the destiny of a human soul was involved. Hence, it is not surprising that the Christian church made marriage a sacrament. With the Romans marriage had come to be a civil contract to be terminated freely at the will of the participants. Under Christianity it became a sacred act to be ended only with ecclesiastical approval under the most unusual and extenuating circumstances. Indeed, in the formal theory of the church, the marriage bond, if consummated, can be dissolved by death alone. What the curia declares, when it dissolves a marriage, is that the marriage was invalid because of impediments that are applicable even if discovered after the marriage. The marriage is, accordingly, annulled. No divorce is granted or sanctioned by the Roman Catholic church.

Extreme unction was the sacrament provided in the presence of imminent death. It was useful either in restoring the person to health or in tiding him over safely into the great beyond. Penance provided the possibility of absolving one of sinful conduct after baptism and the entry into membership in the holy church.

Persistent and obedient reception of the sacraments of the church not only gave assurance of safety in this world but also guaranteed salvation in the next. Catholic theologians presented elaborate technical interpretations of the sacramental system, best embodied in Peter Lombard's *Book of Sentences,* written in the middle of the twelfth century.

This brief analysis will indicate the comprehensive character of the sacramental system of the Roman Catholic church and its significant position in the life of the faithful believer. To administer the sacraments, and thus bring about ultimate salvation, was the primary business of the Christian church. Everything else was subordinate and incidental in the scheme of salvation.

As has been noted, only a bishop could ordain or confirm, but a priest could administer the other five sacraments. In exceptional cases all of these five, save the Mass, could be administered by a layman. Marriage without a priest, where solemn promises were exchanged by a couple, was valid if a priest could not be obtained. The couple was expected, however, to acknowledge the compact before a priest at the earliest opportunity.

VI. THE REPRESSION OF HERESY

Inevitable divergencies arose from the orthodox interpretations of the complex doctrines of Christianity, bitter disputes over the person and nature of Christ, the purpose of His ministry, and the character and results of the Christian life. It soon became obvious that some method must be devised for checking these so-called heresies, or Christianity would be split into irreconcilable sects, and perish from internal dissension, if not from imperial persecution and from the competition of other cults.

A Christian heresy was a new or special brand of Christian doctrine that did not conform to the theology approved by those in official authority within the church.[9] Inasmuch as salvation depended upon precise belief in the official version of Christian doctrine, heresy was a serious matter—treason to God and the church-state. It threatened innocent converts with future damnation. It might also break up the church. The latter had to organize to stamp out heresy and preserve unity.

Most of the early Christian heresies were of a doctrinal and metaphysical character, growing out of the tendency to reinterpret Christian origins in terms of Greek philosophy. The majority of them revolved around philosophical efforts to reconcile the divine and human elements in Christ's personality and to determine the relative position of the three members of the Trinity. They usually turned on abstruse doctrinal differences that might today be regarded as relatively trivial.

For example, the greatest of all the Christian heresies was Arianism, which started in the first quarter of the fourth century as the result of the teachings of one Arius (256-336), a presbyter of Alexandria. The approved doctrine of the Trinity, upheld by Athanasius (296-373), contended that Christ was made of substance identical with God (*homoŏusios*, ὁμοούσιος). Arius claimed that he was made of similar substance (*homoiousios*, ὁμοιούσιος). Over this doctrinal difference, revolving about a single letter in a Greek word and involving the question of whether God and Christ were cosubstantial and coeternal, a mighty controversy was waged for years and thousands of persons lost their lives or freedom in the conflict. Joseph McCabe says: "The quarrel made five or six times as many martyrs in fifty years as the pagan emperors had made in two hundred and fifty years; and to these we might add the massacre of the Goths in 378."

But we must not judge the nature or significance of these heresies in terms of our modern outlook. What may seem to us trivial was taken very seriously in those days, when it was believed that a slight divergence of belief was as effective in producing damnation as a complete repudiation of the whole body of Christian doctrine.

There was an economic as well as a doctrinal basis for heresy. An effort might be made to dislodge a rich bishop by accusing him of heresy or by starting a heresy through which it was hoped to capture his following, undermine his power and dissipate his possessions. Such a procedure was a sort of racketeering in heresy. But this economic cause of heresy became important only after Christianity was well established and thoroughly organized. It had little or nothing to do with those earliest heresies which indirectly contributed to the need for Christian organization.

Arianism was the most important of the early heresies, but there were many others. Gnosticism represented an extreme Hellenization of Christian doctrine in which Jesus was reduced to an approximately impersonal agent of metaphysical revelation. At the opposite pole from Gnostic intellectualism was Montanism, launched by Montanus of Phrygia in the second century. This heresy was eminently practical. It preached the immediate return of Jesus and recommended a severe asceticism and complete celibacy in preparation for the second coming.

[9] On the heresies see A. C. McGiffert, *A History of Christian Thought*, 2 vols., Scribner, 1933, vol. I.

Three heresies, the Ebionite, Elkesaite, and Clementine, were an extreme development of the tendency, already evident in the Gospel of Matthew, to represent Christianity as a religion for the Jews and to emphasize the similarities between Judaism and Christianity. At the opposite extreme stood the heresy of Marcion, who lived in the middle of the second century A.D. He rejected the Judaistic elements in Christianity, even those derived from the Old Testament, and based his teachings upon the doctrines of St. Paul.

Macedonianism, started in the fourth century by Macedonius, bishop of Constantinople, was a further elaboration of the Arian heresy. It held that the Holy Ghost was inferior to both the Father and the Son and was a creature on a level with the angels. The Monarchian heresies, which appeared mainly between A.D. 175 and 300, constituted sincere and ingenious efforts to explain the divine element in Jesus' personality without violating the unity of the Godhead or introducing the logos Christology. The most elaborate development of Monarchianism was what is known as the Sabellian heresy, which maintained that God is both one person and one substance. The Father, Son, and Holy Ghost are only three manifestations or energies of this unified God. In the Middle Ages Abelard was wrongfully accused of Sabellianism.

Apollinarianism, founded by Apollinarius, bishop of Laodicea, in the late fourth century, was devoted to a reconciliation of the divine and human elements in the personality of Jesus. It stressed the divine element at the expense of the human, and was thus believed to make difficult the doctrine of redemption. The extreme reaction to Apollinarianism appeared in the Nestorian heresy of the early fifth century, led by Bishop Nestorius of Constantinople. It emphasized the human element in Jesus as he had lived on earth. Jesus had two distinct natures—the human and the divine. The former alone had been born, lived, suffered, and died. A variation of the Nestorian heresy was what came to be known as Adoptionism. It developed in the eighth century in Spain under the leadership of Bishop Felix of Urgel and Bishop Elipand of Toledo. According to this doctrine, Jesus was originally the son of God solely in his divine nature. In his human nature, he became the son of God only through adoption by divine grace.

The Donatist heresy was a fourth-century movement in North Africa which held that the ministerial functions performed by an immoral or heretical priest were invalid—in other words, that the efficacy of the clerical office depended upon the personal character of the priest or bishop.

The threat offered to church unity and strength by the heresies led to the institution of a vigorous policy of repression. As early as the middle of the second century we find writers of the Epistle to Jude and the Second Epistle to Peter denouncing heretics in very intemperate language. A century later, Cyprian (d. 258) expounded the famous dogma that outside of the Catholic church and the orthodox faith there is no salvation for anyone, no matter how pure his moral life or how saintly his character.

In the fourth century Christianity became the state religion, and soon imperial legislation was directed toward enforcing obedience and conformity to official Christian doctrine. A man might be put to death, for instance, if he failed to

admit the accepted view of the Trinity expounded by Damasus of Rome and
Peter of Alexandria. In 438 Theodosius II published a collection of Roman imperial laws. These included edicts on religion. The following quotation well illustrates the triumph of Christianity within the Roman system as well as the out-
lawing of the pagan cults:

> We desire that all those who are under the sway of our clemency shall adhere
> to that religion which, according to his own testimony, coming down even to our
> own day, the blessed apostle Peter delivered to the Romans, namely, the doctrine
> which the pontiff Damasus (bishop of Rome) and Peter, bishop of Alexandria,
> a man of apostolic sanctity, accept. According to the teachings of the apostles and
> of the Gospel we believe in one Godhead of the Father, Son and Holy Ghost, the
> blessed Trinity, alike in majesty.
>
> We ordain that the name of Catholic Christians shall apply to all those who
> obey this present law. All others we judge to be mad and demented; we declare
> them guilty of the infamy of holding heretical doctrine; their assemblies shall not
> receive the name of churches. They shall first suffer the wrath of God, then the
> punishment which in accordance with divine judgment we shall inflict.[10]

For some twelve hundred years heresy remained a capital crime. It became
veritably true that reason was in prison. The autocratic Roman state was succeeded
by the equally autocratic medieval church-state. This church, extending its control
over the secular arm of kings and princes, brooked no opposition whatever.
Heresy was treason against God himself and against Church authority, compared to which murder was a minor offense. The "Christian epic," therefore, as it
was finally elaborated, did not have to rely for perpetuation on its intellectual
plausibility or traditional authority. The Church, with its powerful influence over
civil authorities, tried to make sure that its beliefs were neither questioned nor
revised.

It took centuries of heresy, and it cost thousands of lives, to break the tyran-
nical hold of Christian doctrine. The medieval church was a colossal giant crushing all heretics in its tremendous maw, cowing skeptics with its transfiguring
gaze. Heretical books were burned. The houses of heretics were destroyed. As
an intellectual weapon, intolerance prevailed from the code of Theodosius down
to almost recent times, reaching its most perfect organization in the inquisition
of the thirteenth century and thereafter. James Harvey Robinson has admirably
summarized the medieval Christian attitude towards heresy:

> Heresy was looked upon as a contagious disease that must be checked at all costs.
> It did not matter that the heretic usually led a conspicuously blameless life, that
> he was arduous, did not swear, was emaciated with fasting and refused to partici-
> pate in the vain recreations of his fellows. He was, indeed, overserious and took
> his religion too hard. This offensive parading as an angel of light was explained
> as the devil's camouflage.
>
> No one tried to find out what the heretic really thought or what were the merits
> of his divergent beliefs. Because he insisted on expressing his conception of God in
> slightly unfamiliar terms, the heretic was often branded as an atheist, just as to-day

[10] Cited in J. H. Robinson, *Readings in European History*, 2 vols. Ginn, 1904, I, 23-24.

the Socialist is so often accused of being opposed to all government, when the real objection to him is that he believes in too much government. It was sufficient to classify a suspected heretic as an Albigensian, or Waldensian, or a member of some other heretical sect. There was no use in his trying to explain or justify; it was enough that he diverged.[11]

VII. THE MONASTIC MOVEMENT

During the Middle Ages an individual's only logical goal was to assure himself of heaven and avoid hell. Life was like the visions of Anthony, terrible with temptation and sin; withstanding them gained immortal salvation, yielding to them meant eternal damnation.

The church fathers emphasized the supreme importance of securing a valid passport to the next world, and warned men of the difficulty of retaining it. It is not surprising, therefore, that, beginning in the East, a large number of believers in early Christian days separated themselves from normal social relations and devoted their lives to those spiritual exercises designed to insure salvation. The monks became veritable "spiritual athletes."

The intensity of emotion which accompanied the otherworldly outlook that encouraged monasticism can be discerned in Jerome's exhortation to a friend to flee the dangerous attractions of mundane joys and to retire to the monastic cell: "Though your little nephew twine his arms around your neck," he writes, "though your mother, with disheveled hair and tearing her robe asunder, point to the breast with which she nourished you; though your father fall down on the threshold before you, pass on over your father's body. Fly with tearful eyes to the banner of the cross." [12]

Christian monasticism grew out of an indifference to this world in view of the imminent approach of the kingdom of God. Receiving encouragement from Paul, from the Gnostics, and from Neoplatonism, the renunciation of the flesh and the world developed into a mania with many. Pleasure was a mirage, a delusion not worth the pursuit. In Plotinus the pagan, in Origen the church father, and in Anthony the most famous of ascetics, self-mortifications are convulsive, the longing for translation into the next world, with all its beatitudes, becomes lyrical.

The anchorites—solitary monks—soon became too numerous for the Church to permit each to do as he pleased. Simeon Stylites, perched for thirty years on top of his pillar, was exaggerating the Christian ideal and overdoing the mortification of the flesh. The church had to corral the hermits and force them to submit to a more orderly existence. The energetic Eastern father, Basil, in the fourth century, was one of the first to lay down a cenobitic rule, ordering the monks to live together, practice chastity, renounce family ties, and perform useful labor.

The monastic ideal soon took hold in the West as well. When Christianity was legalized and Christian life became safer, there was a tendency to dip again into sensualities, to recoil from the austerities practiced in the days when the

[11] J. H. Robinson, *Mind in the Making*, Harper, 1921, p. 133.
[12] Cited in Robinson, *Readings*, I, 86.

Christian sect was hunted and persecuted. The otherworldly ideal was in danger if the world, the flesh, and the devil were not frequently renounced.

So long as the persecutions lasted, it was easy for a communicant to secure an assured entrance to the other world. Many gave themselves up to the Roman authorities and were glad to be thrown to the lions. When the church was legalized, and grew rich and powerful, multitudes of Christians fled to monasteries in the wilds in order to guard themselves against temptation and to assure themselves immortal bliss.

More complete and perfect rules and regulations for the lives of the monks were developed in the West. The Western monks were more temperate and practical, and the Western peoples appeared to have greater talent for organized activity and systematic government. Harsher climatic conditions also helped to make communal monasticism more necessary in the West. The great Latin fathers, Ambrose, Augustine, and Gregory the Great, all worked ardently in behalf of western monasticism and its more perfect regulation. Towards the close of the life of Augustine, Cassian, a Christian compiler in the West, wrote two important books on monasticism. They reviewed the character of monastic life in the East, pointed out its evils, and recommended remedies.

A century later there was set forth the most influential of all rules for monastic life, the long-famous Benedictine rule, worked out by Benedict of Nursia (c. 480-550), who founded the monastery of Monte Cassino about 530. Making use of earlier writings, particularly those of Basil and Cassian, he brought out a complete, clear, explicit body of rules for the control of monkish life. Most of the Benedictine rule is given over to very precise regulations of monastic life for all hours of the day and the night. It had no official or mandatory sanction, and Benedict did not, as has so often been supposed, found an order of monks. But his rule became almost universally adopted for the control of monastic life during the Middle Ages. Its popularity grew out of its timeliness in meeting the great need for a satisfactory body of regulations for the Western monks, and its intrinsic excellence. It was given an added impetus by the spreading fame of Benedict's own piety and miracles, and by the effective recommendation of the rule by Pope Gregory the Great. Professor James Westfall Thompson presents the following excellent summary of the daily life and regimen of the monks under the Benedictine Rule:

> The daily order in a monastery was thus: After having been present at the service of Prime, the monks assembled in the chapter house. The prior assigned to each individual the amount and the kind of labor on which he was to be engaged during the day. A few short prayers asking for a blessing upon their work were next offered up. The tools were then produced and the brethren marched two and two and in silence to their allotted tasks in the fields. From Easter to the beginning of October they were thus occupied from six o'clock in the morning, in some instances until ten; in others until noon, the duration depending upon the season. St. Benedict had no patience with the excesses and fantastic austerities of eastern monasticism. He was too level-headed a Roman for that. The food was abundant, though simple. Flesh food was restricted, certainly no great deprivation in a

Mediterranean country. There was no limitation upon fish or oil or butter. The monk had two meals per day, at which he was allowed eight ounces of bread, a pint of wine, two dishes of vegetables, with fruit. His clothes were made of wool, adapted to the season. Naturally as monasticism spread into the northern countries, some changes of diet became necessary. The most notable was that beer was drunk instead of wine in countries where wine-growing was climatically impossible.[18]

The cenobites of the new monastic communities were not cowards. For the sake of the holy light and the world to come, they mortified the flesh, worked hard, prayed much, fasted long, and frequently, like that Augustine who converted the Angles, undertook dangerous journeys to distant lands and barbaric peoples.

The secular clergy, from the archbishops down to the lower orders, were busy carrying out various duties connected with saving souls and rendering praise unto God. But the perfect religious life in the Middle Ages was believed to be that of these "regular" clergy, namely, the monks and nuns who fled from this world to devote themselves to the contemplation of the awful nature of sin and the glory and graciousness of God.

One can only understand this extraordinary phenomenon in the light of the great moral revolution, particularly in regard to sex, which Christianity introduced. While there were some examples of asceticism and the impurity-complex in ancient times, pagan society was generally open-minded and took sex expression as a matter of course, to be controlled rationally by social, economic, and aesthetic principles.

Christianity came to look upon sex as the worst form of evil, and the greatest temptation to which man is heir. This belief, as it finally crystallized, was a product of orthodox Judaism, pre-Christian asceticism, the purification trends in the mystery cults, the general supernatural orientation of Christianity, and the abnormal personal experiences of Paul and Augustine.

Paul's prejudices against pagan views of sex are abundantly illustrated in his Epistles. Augustine was converted after a licentious youth and swung so far to the other extreme as to argue that the original sin in the Garden of Eden had consisted of the beginning of sexual intercourse. The resulting fall of man, caused by a woman, was pictured by him as the cause of all the miseries and evils which had since befallen the human race. Women came to be regarded as inherently dangerous because of their sex appeal. This fear of sex entrancement sent hordes of salvation-bent men flocking to monasteries.

Theoretically, the monkish life was the most holy because it was dedicated to poverty, chastity, and obedience. Poverty would protect men against fatal entanglement in riches and the sin of covetousness. Chastity would save men from the curse of sex. Obedience would preserve discipline and protect them from the sins of pride and vanity.

In practice, the monks were more successful with obedience than with poverty or chastity. They became the best farmers, winegrowers, and innkeepers of the Middle Ages. Money rolled in and they found it extremely hard to maintain

[18] Thompson, *An Economic and Social History of the Middle Ages*, p. 146.

actual poverty and the mental attitudes supposed to accompany it. Nor were they able to resist sexual lures in many cases. Even in the early days of monasticism, when they lived a rather abstemious life, the records indicate that many monks gave quite as much time to contemplating the temptations of sex as to observing the glories of God. In the later Middle Ages, as Henry Charles Lea abundantly revealed, all semblance of chastity was abandoned in many areas.

Nevertheless, the Christian exponents of monasticism aimed high, and the monastic ideal, according to Taylor, was a personality "faultless in humility and obedience to God . . . knowing neither pride nor vanity, nor covetousness nor lust, nor slothful depression; grave and silent with bent head, yet with an inner peace, even an inner passionate joy; meditative, mystic, an other-world personality; one that dwells in spiritual facts, for whom this world has passed away and the lusts thereof; one that is centered in God and in eternal life, and yet capable of intense activities. A man who will not swerve from orders received, as he swerves not from his great aim, the love of God and life eternal." [14]

Prominent among the activities of the monks was their learning and scholarship. The secular clergy was engaged in worship, administering sacraments, and in ecclesiastical politics and diplomacy. The regular clergy, among other ways, advanced the business of the church with the laity by acquiring a near monopoly on education and by preserving and promoting learning.

The most important figure in giving a literary cast to monasticism was the statesman-monk, Cassiodorus (c. 490-c. 583). Retiring to his estates after a busy life in the service of King Theodoric, he set up a monastery and put his monkish followers to work copying ancient manuscripts, paraphrasing classical knowledge, and writing manuals for instruction in both pagan and Christian knowledge. Later we shall have more to say of the important scholarly and educational work of Cassiodorus and his circle.

The monks became the literati of the Middle Ages. Every monastery had a scriptorium, a sort of publishing (manuscript) house and printing (copying) plant combined. From it emerged homilies, catechisms, poetry, allegories, nearly all the manuals and books of the medieval world.

The monasteries also transmitted Roman methods of raising crops, breeding cattle, and cultivating fruit, and also added improvements of their own. The monks cleared forests, drained swamps, practiced artificial fertilization of soil, built dikes, cut roads. In every way that industry, knowledge, and intelligence could devise, they improved their landholdings. In a rather short time many became relatively rich.[15] At the height of the Middle Ages they were employing serfs and agricultural laborers extensively, and with increased wealth came monastic leisure, sloth, indolence, vanity, and pride.

To summarize the conclusions of Flick and others on monasticism: On the positive side, the monastic movement saved the church from spiritual decay

<hr>

[14] Taylor, *The Classical Heritage of the Middle Ages,* p. 182.

[15] "The nunnery of Gandersheim, the favorite foundation of the Saxon house, was started in 956 with an endowment of 11,000 manors; Hersfeld in thirty years accumulated 2,000 manors scattered in 195 localities; Tegernsee in Bavaria . . . owned 11,886 manors; Benedictbeuren . . . owned 6,700 manors. Fulda possessed 15,000; Lorsch, 2,000; St. Gall, 4,000." Thompson, *op. cit.,* p. 604.

during the period when paganism collapsed and Christianity had not reached its mature organization. It introduced lofty social ideals—poverty, obedience, chastity, and amelioration of man's vicious impulses. It maintained some kind of democracy within the clerical and secular hierarchy of the Middle Ages. Above all, it was the agency which not only preserved something of pagan learning but also created a new, Christian culture. It gave to the world the best agricultural science of the time, besides contributing notably to industry, commerce, and finance.

On the negative side, monasticism might be condemned as "escapism." It ran away from sin instead of meeting it and overcoming it. It exaggerated the sinful nature of human activities and created an artificial separation between the secular and religious world. It disrupted social ties and, by idealizing the celibate, encouraged "race suicide." It took many of the ablest men out of public life and consecrated them to otherworldly activities. It sacrificed patriotism to spirituality. And, while helping with religious education, it doomed real secular education, and thus retarded the growth of science and secular learning. Finally, in practice, it often encouraged idleness, laziness, and sanctimonious begging.

VIII. CHRISTIAN OTHERWORLDLINESS, THE DEVIL, HELL, AND THE LAST JUDGMENT

What was the intellectual foundation of this tremendous new religion which inspired such missionary zeal and monastic fervor? What was the emotional spring whence it flowed to permeate every corner of Europe, subduing serf and baron, Roman and Viking, Gurth the illiterate swineherd, Alfred the intellectual king, Charlemagne the burly and brusque warrior, and Bede, the gentle and credulous scholar?

As we suggested above, Christianity did not guarantee man greater prosperity on this planet. It even seemed at times to encourage earthly misery and argued that through adversity one might better prepare for the Kingdom of God. What Christianity offered to do was to safeguard its believers against the evil spirits led by the devil. That offer was irresistible if one accepted the belief that the whole cosmic process was one encompassing conflict between the forces of good and evil. God "moved in mysterious ways his wonders to perform," but so did Satan, who was everywhere, and turned up where he was least suspected.

The Christian church was thus a great organized effort to help God in this supreme struggle against the devil. In the heavens above, God was aided by the archangels and angels. On earth, the church was the champion of God in the conflict that was to lead to the ultimate triumph of good. It was the great stronghold that guaranteed to the pious the prospect of protection against earthly evils, and definite assurance of eternal salvation. The church was like a well-lighted house, looming in the darkness to a man wandering, terror-stricken, in a dark and stormy night. The Christian citadel offered comfort, safety, and surcease from all mundane cares.

So important a figure was the devil in medieval Christian thought that it is worthwhile briefly to summarize the origins of the Christian conception of the devil. It is a well-established fact that the Christian idea of the devil was derived

from the Persian dualism, and its leaders, Ormuzd and Ahriman. The latter was
the Persian devil. As Franz Cumont points out:

> In his treatise against the magi, Theodore of Mopsuestia speaks of Ahriman as
> Satan. At first sight there really is a surprising resemblance between the two. Both
> are heads of a numerous army of demons; both are spirits of error and falsehood,
> princes of darkness, tempters and corrupters. An almost identical picture of the pair
> could be drawn, and in fact they are practically the same figure under different
> names. It is generally admitted that Judaism took the notion of an adversary of
> God from the Mazdeans along with portions of their dualism. It was therefore
> natural that Jewish doctrine, of which Christianity is heir, should have been closely
> allied to the mysteries of Mithra. A considerable part of the more or less orthodox
> beliefs and visions that gave the Middle Ages their nightmare of hell and the devil
> thus came from Persia by two channels: on the one hand Judeo-Christian literature,
> both canonical and apocryphal; and on the other, the remnants of the Mithra cult
> and the various sects of Manicheism that continued to preach the old Persian
> doctrines on the antagonism between the two world principles.[16]

The idea of a devil was unknown to the early prophets and leaders of Old
Testament times, such as Moses and his successors, who had not so much as
heard of the devil.[17] Indeed, the devil is specifically mentioned only three times
in the canonical books of the Old Testament. In the prologue to the Book of
Job the devil is referred to as a son of God, but is portrayed as the black sheep
of the divine family, causing much parental solicitude over his wayward actions.
In Zechariah iii the devil appears more malign in the rôle of a persecutor of
Israel and Joshua. In I Chronicles, xxi, the devil plays the part of a tempter,
urging David to take a census of the Israelites. These are the only allusions to the
devil in the Old Testament. There were many other lesser Old Testament
demons, some of them females.

In the Jewish apocryphal literature, which grew up between the Old and the
New Testament, the devil is frequently mentioned, and he dominates the Book
of Enoch, which was deeply influenced by Persian eschatology and demonology.
The devil was, thus, well known among the Jews in the time of Jesus as a result
of this infiltration of Persian lore. The specific name, devil, was derived from
the Greek, *diabolos,* by which term Satan, or the devil, was rendered in the
Greek translation of the Old Testament, the famous Septuagint. Beelzebub, a
name sometimes applied to the devil, was originally the god of the Philistine city
of Ehron.

The accepted hierarchy of good and evil spirits among the Christians, culminating in the Trinity and the devil, was worked out chiefly in the late Hellenistic
age. Persian influences were strong here, as was Neoplatonism. The devil now
was provided with lieutenants: a supreme council of hell, a general staff, and, as
it were, many noncommissioned officers, along with innumerable imps. The
Alexandrian father, Origen, helped to formulate such notions. Among the church

---

[16] Cumont, *Oriental Religions in Roman Paganism,* p. 153-54.
[17] They were, of course, familiar with the idea of evil spirits.

fathers, Gregory the Great was, perhaps, the most influential in popularizing devil lore and arousing the fear of hell.

The medieval idea about God and the devil attributed the greater power to God but assumed that the devil was far the more active and aggressive. If God was the greater, the devil tended to make up for this by a more constant devotion to business. God's attention had to be called specifically to the needs of the Christian, but the devil went out briskly and cheerfully to waylay the faithful without having to be prodded into activity. This conception of the greater alertness of the devil, incidentally, helped to make reasonable the need of God for the help of the individual Christian in battling against the devil and securing the triumph of the kingdom of God.

The first important attack upon orthodox views of the devil was made by a Dutch clergyman, Balthazar Bekker, in his *The Enchanted World* (1693). Pointing out the lack of harmony and logic in the scriptural references to the devil, he showed that the medieval views of the devil, in turn, often diverged markedly from the scriptural notions. However, it is the modern study of Persian theology which has enabled us to explode the devil-myth as a result of our knowledge of just how the whole idea developed in Western civilization.

It is hard for us in this twentieth century to project ourselves back into the medieval intellectual atmosphere and to realize how far thoughts and fear of the devil engrossed the minds of men. The French scholar, Albert Réville, tries in the following paragraph to drive home this fact, which is so important in any effort to understand the medieval frame of mind:

> The absorbing nature of the belief in the devil during the middle ages is the point we wish to make clear. Those who have still this faith can hardly imagine to what a degree it then controlled men's whole lives. It was the one fixed idea with every one. A fixed idea tends, among those whom it possesses, to center everything in itself. When, at the present day, we observe closly those of our contemporaries who devote themselves to spiritualism, it is surprising to see how fertile their imagination becomes when they are busy in interpreting, in favor of their hobby, the most trifling and unimportant circumstances. The unlatching of a half-closed door, an insect describing arabesques in its flight, the fall of a badly-balanced article, the creaking of furniture at night-time, any of these petty accidents suffices to give wing to their fancy. If we generalize such a mental state, by substituting faith in the incessant interventions of the devil for the harmless illusions of our spiritualists, we shall get a fair notion of what took place in the middle ages.[18]

Closely related to the history of diabolism is that of eschatology—the Christian notion of last things, the final judgment, and the future life. Christian eschatology resembled its diabolism in being primarily a Persian product. Both were, in fact, derived from the same sources.

Early Jewish thought had no more idea of hell-fire than it had of an aggressive devil. There was no clearly developed notion of retribution after death. Sheol was merely the place of the dead, retribution having already taken place in this life. Gradually, however, the doctrine of the afterlife became related to the mes-

[18] Albert Réville, *The Devil, His Origin, Greatness and Decadence*, Scribner, p. 37-38.

sianic hope. The belief arose that the righteous in the dreary Sheol would rise from the dead and share in the restored prosperity and prestige of Israel. In the postexilic period, after the Jews had been exposed to contact with Persian religious thought, the notion of future punishment in an afterlife became more common and popular.

The Jewish conception of a final day of judgment also underwent a gradual evolution. At the outset, it was held that in "the Day of Yahweh" the latter would use natural cataclysms—earthquakes and the like—to destroy his earthly enemies. Next came the idea that in this day Yahweh would also punish the heathen nations. To this was soon added the doctrine that after the enemies of Israel had been crushed on the last dread day, the righteous would be blessed. In the Book of Joel (c. 400 B.C.), we find the first actual evidence of a Jewish notion of a definite day of judgment. Here Yahweh judges his people in the valley of Jehoshaphat. Finally, in Deuteronomy, chapter 12, we discover the first reference to a judgment day which deals with the dead as well as the living.

By the time of the apocalyptic literature (200 B.C. et seq.), the Persian idea had fully taken root and the Jewish views roughly resembled those held by the Persians and later by the Christians. But they were colored by the messianic hope. It was widely believed that after the Messiah had destroyed the enemies of Israel and all evil spirits he would set up as an eternal kingdom on this earth. This has led to the dispute among scholars as to whether Jesus shared this Jewish messianic notion of an eternal and ideal kingdom on earth, or held to the Persian view of the destruction of this earth and the setting up of a kingdom of God in heaven. The early Christians certainly accepted the messianic belief in an earthly kingdom and eagerly awaited Christ's second coming to set up his earthly utopia. They were disappointed.

The official Christian eschatology is embodied in the Book of Revelation. This accepts pretty thoroughly the Persian views of the Day of Judgment and heaven and hell. The Persians had first asserted that the wicked would be consumed at once in a lake of fire and brimstone. But in due time their theologians seemed to feel that this was letting the followers of evil off too lightly. So they invented the dogma of eternal punishment in hell-fire. The Christians adopted the latter interpretation.

The eschatological program of the Book of Revelation ran as follows: There are signs and portents—wars and rumors of wars, convulsions of nature, and the like. Then two witnesses of the impending return of Jesus, Enoch and Elijah, make their appearance, but are slain by the antichrist. Christ then returns in the rôle of judge and warrior. The antichrist and the false prophets are overcome and cast into a lake of fire and brimstone. The devil is bound and thrown into a pit for a thousand years. Then there comes the millennium, in which Christ reigns with the saints and martyrs who have been raised from the dead. At the end of the millennium, the devil is let loose and he gathers all his evil followers from the four corners of the earth to do battle against the hosts of righteousness. The final test comes at the great and decisive battle of Armageddon (which Theodore Roosevelt popularized in the Bull Moose campaign of 1912). The devil and his hosts are defeated, in part by fire from heaven. The devil is thrown into hell, and the Day of Judgment follows. Those whose names do not appear in the book of life are thrown into hell along with the devil, their master. The old heaven and the old earth then pass away and the new heaven and the new earth come into being. The New Jerusalem, let down from heaven, is the metropolis of the heavenly dispensation. Here the saved souls dwell with God and Christ throughout eternity, casting down their golden crowns upon the glassy sea.

The church fathers accepted this view, embellishing it with certain symbolism taken from the scriptures; for example, Jerome's vision of the four great beasts which came up out of the sea—the Assyrian, Persian, Macedonian, and Roman empires. They also made ingenious guesses as to how long it would be before the millennium. Augustine believed that the Christian church would last for a thousand years, after which would come the events as portrayed in Revelation. This notion is what led certain historians to imagine that there was a great panic in Christendom as the year A.D. 1000 approached. That there was nothing of the sort we shall later make clear.

The church fathers and the theologians of the Dark Ages were zealous and prolific in portraying the horrors of the Christian hell. The latter probably represents the supreme achievement in human morbidity in the history of the race.

During the thousand years which separated Rome's fall from early modern humanism, the power of religion was paramount, as it had been among primitive races. This resulted in part from fear of what the devil might do to man on earth, but far more from terror of diabolical temptations which might lead to eternal damnation and land a person in hell. Devout men readily preferred death to anything that would definitely ignore, alienate, or defy the celestial deity. Religious rites came before bread itself. It was considered far better to starve with reasonable assurance of salvation than to live riotously and face hell-fire. Though supernatural vengeance did not strike a man down in the middle of his earthly journey, it was sure to torment him in the other world. The wrath of God and the wiles of the devil assailed man on every side.

To the man of the Middle Ages, the other world was a reality so vivid that Dante and his vision were a fair expression of his age. Ideas of heaven, purgatory, and hell may not always have corresponded exactly to Dante's famous outline, but they were made amply real and horrifyingly detailed in the literature of the time. The following quotation from a medieval theologian will provide some inkling of the horrors of the Christian hell:

> Hell is wide without measure, and deep and bottomless; full of incomparable fire, for no earthly fire may be compared therewith; full of stench intolerable for no living thing on earth might endure it; full of unutterable sorrow for no mouth may, on account of the wretchedness or the woe thereof, give an account nor tell of it. Yea, the darkness therein is so thick that one may grasp it, for the fire there gives no light, but blindeth the eyes of them that are there with a smothering smoke, the worst of smokes. And nevertheless in that same black darkness they see black things as devils, that ever maul them and afflict and harass them with all kinds of tortures; and tailed drakes, horrible as devils, that devour them whole

and spew them out afterwards before and behind. At other times they rend them in pieces and chew each gobbet of them, and they afterwards become whole again, such as they previously were, to undergo again such bale without recovery, and full well they see themselves very horrible and dreadful; and to increase their pains the loathsome hell-worms, toads, and frogs that eat out their eyes and nostrils, and adders and water-frogs, not like those here, but a hundred times more horrible, sneak in and out of the mouth, ears, eyes, navel and at the hollow of the breast, as maggots in putrid flesh, ever yet thickest. There is shrieking in the flame and chattering of teeth in the snowy waters. Suddenly they flit upon the heat into the cold, nor ever do they know of these two which is worst for them, for each is intolerable. . . . And this same wanhope is their greatest torment, that none have any more hope of any recovery, but are sure of every ill, to continue in woe, world without end, even in eternity. Each chokes the other, and each is another's torment, and each hateth another and himself as the black devil; and even as they loved them the more in this world, so the more shall they hate them there. And each curseth another, and gnaws off the other's arms, ears, and nose also. I have begun to tell of things that I am not able to bring to any end, though I had a thousand tongues of steel, and told until they were all worn out.[19]

Medieval people were naturally interested in food, clothing, shelter, and other needs of the flesh, but staring them ever in the face, following them like shadows, were their devil-fixation and hell-neurosis. The more they became absorbed in earthly problems, the more they betrayed the Christian theory of life, and heightened the possibility of being thrown, after death, into burning lava, or devoured by tailed drakes. Few had the temerity to face such dire consequences.

There have been many organized efforts to provide man with guidance in meeting the problems presented by the hypothesis of a supernatural world and a future life, but the Christian church of the Middle Ages was perhaps the most impressive of them all. In the Western World it provided the most pervasive influence, the most elaborate organization, and certainly the most seductive propaganda.

IX. THE AUGUSTINIAN SYNTHESIS AND THE CHRISTIAN EPIC

The Christian philosophy of history, of man's creation, destiny and redemption, was gradually evolved from the days of the Apostles to its culminating expression in Augustine's *City of God* and Orosius' *Seven Books of History against the Pagans*.

As Aristotle summed up Hellenic learning and Cicero most clearly and completely reflected the impact of Hellenism on Latin culture, so the greatest of the church fathers, Augustine (A.D. 354-430), may be regarded as the writer who brought together in the most thorough fashion the major currents of thought in Christendom during the age in which Christianity triumphed over paganism. He worked out the first complete Christian philosophy of history—the Christian epic—and he systematized what remained the authoritative theology of Christendom until Augustinian dogmas were merged with Aristotelianism in the thir-

[19] Cited in S. M. Brown, *Medieval Europe*, Harcourt, Brace, 1932, pp. 358-59.

teenth century to form the scholastic theology of Thomas Aquinas. But not even Aquinas left any such enduring impression upon Christian thought as did Augustine. If Aristotle has been the greatest single secular influence upon human thinking in the West, a comparable priority must be assigned to Augustine with respect to his prestige in the religious thought of Christendom.

We have seen that Christianity itself was a compound of Jewish, pagan, and Pauline elements—that it brought together and blended the religious beliefs and philosophies of most of the cultures which had preceded its triumph. Augustine illustrated in his own personality these same synthesizing experiences and qualities. He united in himself many pagan traditions with a deep and sincere Christian religious experience.

Augustine was born in northern Africa of a pagan father and a Christian mother. As a young man he studied and taught rhetoric in Carthage. He indulged in the typical fleshly pleasures of the youth of his time, and was especially enamored of the pagan theater. A reading of Cicero's *Hortensius* at the age of nineteen first aroused his interest in philosophical speculation. He read widely and sought consolation in philosophy and religion. First he tried the theology of the Persian sect of Manichaeism, and was for some years a member of that religious group. It did not satisfy his intellectual or emotional longings. So he turned to Hellenic philosophy, flirting first with the doctrines associated with the Platonic Academy and then more seriously with Neoplatonism. From the latter he derived much of the mysticism which permeated many of his later Christian writings. In 384 he went to Milan to teach rhetoric. There, under the influence of Bishop Ambrose, he took to reading the Epistles of Paul and decided to espouse Christianity. He was converted in 386 and baptized in 387, shortly before the death of his mother. He went into retirement for several years and in 395 he was made bishop of Hippo in northern Africa, an office which he held until the time of his death in 430.

Augustine thus inextricably combined within his intellectual experience both pagan and Christian elements. They remained mingled in his intellectual equipment and in his writings throughout his life. Even when he was most fiercely denouncing pagan culture in his controversial writings, he unconsciously used the tricks of argumentation, the learning, and much of the philosophy which he had acquired in his pagan youth. He put the City of the Devil to work in promoting the City of God. His personality itself was a complex combination of opposites. This has been well stated by Teuffel, the historian of Roman literature: "Augustine combined in his character qualities seemingly opposite: an abundant imagination, and penetrating intellectual vigor, a passionate want of regard and affectionate tenderness, a tender heart and zealotism, a blind belief in superior authority and originality of thought, zeal for the unity of the Church and individual piety, romanticism and scholasticism, mysticism and sophistry, poetical talent and philosophical genius, rhetorical pathos and grammatical pedantry— himself a psychological mystery."

One other element in Augustine's mental make-up must be noted, and that was his zest and talent for systematization. This trait has been well described by the late President Hibben of Princeton: "Augustine's type of mind is essentially that of a great systematizer of doctrine. He could rest content with no form of knowledge unless it could be reduced to a *schema* in which part fitted to part in an exact and inflexible manner." It was this power as a systematizer that enabled Augustine to construct an impressive synthesis of Christian doctrine.

In spite of his busy life as the administrator of an important bishopric, Augustine became a prolific writer in defense of the new religion he had espoused. He was the author of a number of heated controversial tracts, attacking especially his old friends, the Manichaeans, and the Donatists and the Pelagians. He was particularly bitter against the latter, who contended that human efforts were more important than divine grace in insuring salvation. Few writers, not even excepting John Calvin, were as vehement as Augustine in emphasizing the indispensable omnipotence of the grace of God and the inherent depravity and corruption of mankind. Augustine also compiled a number of doctrinal works, of which the most important was the long treatise on the *Trinity,* which took many years for its composition. His *Confessions,* written in 397, was the first great Christian autobiography and is an important source for Augustine's religious development and exaltation, and for an understanding of his complex personality.

But the outstanding literary product of Augustine's pen was his *City of God* which occupied him from 413 to 426. It was a veritable encyclopedia of Christian learning, doctrine, and instruction. In addition, it presented a philosophy of history and of the state. In the latter respect it added little to existing patristic political theory, but the philosophy of history was original and immensely influential well down into modern times. It embodied a sweeping theological interpretation of history, which we have come to know in our day under the label of the Christian epic. It revealed to man the divine panorama and depicted the temporal unfolding of the plan of the Creator from Adam to the Day of Judgment.

The *City of God* starts off with a long refutation of the charge that Rome had been conquered by the barbarians because of the demoralizing influence of Christianity. Augustine pointed out how earlier empires had been destroyed in Oriental antiquity before the origin of Christianity. He called attention to the fact that Rome had been more completely devastated by the Gauls in 390 B.C. than by Alaric in his own day. Indeed, Augustine contended that Alaric had been restrained by his respect for Christianity. Otherwise, his sack of Rome would have been more destructive and brutal. Augustine laid much stress on the refutation of this allegation, for he induced his younger disciple, Orosius, to prepare an historical work contrasting the horrors of the pagan past with the glories of the Christian age.

The latter portion of Augustine's magnum opus is devoted to a contrast between the City of God (*Civitas dei*) and the City of the Devil (*Civitas terrena*). The City of God embodied the Christian heritage and the Christian church. Its members were the angels, the saints and elect, and all God-fearing Christians. To the City of the Devil were consigned the pagan cultural heritage, the ancient pagan empires, and all existing states and peoples who rejected Christ. Over against the glories of the City of God were set the evils of the unspeakable

heathendom which slumped down in the City of the Devil. Augustine portrayed the clash and conflict of those two cities from creation to the impending
Day of Judgment. This historical conception had a tremendous influence upon
historical philosophy. Under its spell, Orosius compiled the first medieval work
on ancient history, and Otto of Freising, one of the foremost historians of the
Middle Ages, wrote his major book on the subject of the "Two Cities." The first
great modern universal history, that of Bishop Bossuet, was based faithfully upon
the Augustinian premises.

The *City of God* is also rich in doctrinal material. In it Augustine deals fully
with such basic theological matters as freedom of the will, faith, divine grace,
redemption, the sacraments, the Trinity, churchly leadership, and the like. The
whole field of ethics is reviewed and a new theory of morality stated in terms of
Christian supernaturalism. The virtues of the heathen were declared by Augustine
to be in reality vices, since the pagans did not know the true God. The conventional classical virtues, as formulated by Aristotle and others, are restated in Christian terms. Temperance becomes keeping one's self whole and incorruptible for
the service of God. Fortitude is bearing all things cheerfully for the sake of God.
Justice is serving God alone to the exclusion of all else. Prudence is discrimination
between what helps and what hinders God. The things of this world are not to
be enjoyed by the true Christian; they are only to be exploited in order to promote entry into eternal bliss.

The upshot of the Augustinian outlook upon theology and morals was that it
made theology the "true queen of the sciences." If salvation was the all-absorbing
goal of human life, then the science of salvation—theology—naturally stepped to
the forefront among the branches of human knowledge. History, natural science,
rhetoric, dialectic, and the like were looked upon as valuable only insofar as they
further illuminated the Scriptures and promoted a redeeming understanding of
the Christian life. Augustine suggested that a new compendium of human learning be worked out which would give theology this primary place and properly
subordinate the other fields of knowledge. This wish was gratified in due time
through the work of Cassiodorus, Isidore of Seville, and Rhabanus Maurus.

In one phase of his reconstruction of morals, in particular, Augustine left a
potent heritage to European thinkers: his violent reaction against sexual indulgence. He had, as we have seen, in his youth led a wild and dissolute life, judged
by Christian standards, and he had been loath to abandon this life. His prayer
on this point—"O Lord, make me chaste, but not quite yet!"—is a classic. But
when he was finally converted his conduct and attitude in such matters changed
violently. He became very bitter on the matter of sex and denounced it. He suffered acutely from what modern psychologists call "overcompensation." He traced
all human ills to sexual indulgence and redefined original sin in such terms.
Original sin was thus portrayed as the origin of sexual intercourse, the blame for
which was thrown upon Eve. These morbid eccentricities of Augustinian
thought, growing out of his own erratic personal experience, were able to pervert
human thinking on sexual matters for a thousand years, and their influence is still

strong with millions. Augustine's personal sex neurosis was elevated to a dominant position in western European ethical theory.

Augustine's theory of the state and government shows no great originality. In general, it conformed to the views of the Stoics and the earlier Christian fathers. The state is rendered necessary because of sin. Its services are required to guide and restrain sinful men. It has the sanction of God because it is essential to suppress and punish sin and make life safe for the godly. But the state is markedly inferior to the church, which is an instrument for promoting the glory of God and securing the salvation of man. Augustine departed from Cicero by holding that justice, which Cicero believed to be the cornerstone of the state, is possible only in a Christian state. These political theories were later eagerly exploited in the fierce medieval struggles between church and state. Augustine's intellectual perspective naturally inclined him to lay little stress on earthly political and social reforms. Interest in such affairs on the part of man only distracts attention from the all-important matter of salvation in the world to come. Earthly inconveniences and misery might better be tolerated than jeopardize the destiny of immortal souls.

Augustine thus brought the conceptions of triumphant patristic Christianity to their logical culmination. The import of such thought has been admirably portrayed by the eminent philosopher, George Santayana, in his eloquent summary of the Christian epic. This unfolds the Christian intellectual panorama of the Augustinian dispensation in unrivaled fashion:

There was in the beginning, so runs the Christian story, a great celestial King, wise and good, surrounded by a court of winged musicians and messengers. He had existed from all eternity, but had always intended, when the right moment should come, to create temporal beings, imperfect copies of himself in various degrees. These, of which man was the chief, began their career in the year 4004 B.C., and they would live on an indefinite time, possibly, that chronological symmetry might not be violated, until A.D. 4004. The opening and close of this drama were marked by two magnificent tableaux. In the first, in obedience to the word of God, sun, moon, and stars, and earth with all her plants and animals, assumed their appropriate places, and nature sprang into being with all her laws. The first man was made out of clay, by a special act of God, and the first woman was fashioned from one of his ribs, extracted while he lay in a deep sleep. They were placed in an orchard where they often could see God, its owner, walk in the cool of the evening. He suffered them to range at will and eat of all the fruits he had planted save that of one tree only. But they, incited by a devil, transgressed this single prohibition, and were banished from that paradise with a curse upon their head, the man to live by the sweat of his brow and the woman to bear children in labour. These children possessed from the moment of conception the inordinate natures which their parents had acquired. They were born to sin and to find disorder and death everywhere within and without them.

At the same time God, lest the work of his hands should wholly perish, promised to redeem in his good season some of Adam's children and restore them to a natural life. This redemption was to come ultimately through a descendant of Eve, whose foot should bruise the head of the serpent. But it was to be prefigured by many partial and special redemptions. Thus, Noah was to be saved from the deluge, Lot from Sodom, Isaac from the sacrifice, Moses from Egypt, the captive Jews from Babylon, and all faithful souls from heathen forgetfulness and idolatry. For a certain tribe had been set apart from the beginning to keep alive the memory of God's judgments and promises, while the rest of mankind, abandoned to its natural depravity, sank deeper and deeper into crimes and vanities. The deluge that came to punish these evils did not avail to cure them. "The world was renewed and the earth rose again above the bosom of the waters, but in this renovation there remained eternally some trace of divine vengeance. Until the deluge all nature had been exceedingly hardy and vigorous, but by that vast flood of water which God had spread out over the earth, and by its long abiding there, all saps were diluted; the air, charged with too dense and heavy a moisture, bred ranker principles of corruption. The early constitution of the universe was weakened, and human life, from stretching as it had formerly done to near a thousand years, grew gradually briefer. Herbs and roots lost their primitive potency and stronger food had to be furnished to man by the flesh of other animals. . . . Death gained upon life and men felt themselves overtaken by a speedier chastisement. As day by day they sank deeper in their wickedness, it was but right they should daily, as it were, stick faster in their woe. The very change in nourishment made manifest their decline and degradation, since as they became feebler they became also more voracious and blood-thirsty."

Henceforth there were two spirits, two parties, or, as Saint Augustine called them, two cities in the world. The City of Satan, whatever its artifices in art, war, or philosophy, was essentially corrupt and impious. Its joy was but a comic mask and its beauty the whitening of a sepulchre. It stood condemned before God and before man's better conscience by its vanity, cruelty, and secret misery, by its ignorance of all that it truly behoved a man to know who was destined to immortality. Lost, as it seemed, within this Babylon, or visible only in its obscure and forgotten purlieus, lived on at the same time the City of God, the society of all the souls God predestined to salvation; a city which, however humble and inconspicuous it might seem on earth, counted its myriad transfigured citizens in heaven, and had its destinies, like its foundations, in eternity. To this City of God, belonged, in the first place, the patriarchs and the prophets who, throughout their plaintive and ardent lives, were faithful to what echoes still remained of a primeval revelation, and waited patiently for the greater revelation to come. To the same city belonged the magi who followed a star till it halted over the stable in Bethlehem; Simeon, who divined the present salvation of Israel; John the Baptist, who bore witness to the same and made straight its path; and Peter, to whom not flesh and blood, but the spirit of the Father in heaven, revealed the Lord's divinity. For salvation had indeed come with the fulness of time, not, as the carnal Jews had imagined it, in the form of an earthly restoration, but through the incarnation of the Son of God in the Virgin Mary, his death upon a cross, his descent into hell, and his resurrection at the third day according to the Scriptures. To the same city belonged finally all those who, believing in the reality and efficacy of Christ's mission, relied on his merits and followed his commandment of unearthly love.

All history was henceforth essentially nothing but the conflict between these two cities; two moralities, one natural, the other supernatural; two philosophies, one rational, the other revealed; two beauties, one corporeal, the other spiritual; two glories, one temporal, the other eternal; two institutions, one the world, the other

306 THE MEDIEVAL SYNTHESIS

the Church. These, whatever their momentary alliances or compromises, were radically opposed and fundamentally alien to one another. Their conflict was to fill the ages until, when wheat and tares had long flourished together and exhausted between them the earth for whose substance they struggled, the harvest should come; the terrible day of reckoning when those who had believed the things of religion to be imaginary would behold with dismay the Lord visibly coming down through the clouds of heaven, the angels blowing their alarming trumpets, all generations of the dead rising from their graves, and judgment without appeal passed on every man, to the edification of the universal company and his own unspeakable joy or confusion. Whereupon the blessed would enter eternal bliss with God their master and the wicked everlasting torments with the devil whom they served.

The drama of history was thus to close upon a second tableau: long-robed and beatified cohorts passing above, amid various psalmodies, into an infinite luminous space, while below the damned, howling, writhing, and half transformed into loathsome beasts, should be engulfed in a fiery furnace. The two cities, always opposite in essence, should thus be finally divided in existence, each bearing its natural fruits and manifesting its true nature.[20]

On this "magnificent illusion" medieval Christians pinned their faith and their hope. Its veracity they did not, dared not, question. Its lyrical simplicity appealed to everyone.

In a world torn with warfare, a world where tyranny reigned with an unchecked hand, men needed the assurance of a dogmatic otherworldly religion. They needed the splendid vision of the *civitas dei* to bolster them amid backbreaking toil, amid sickness, want, famine, plague. That it might all be an illusion, a poetic figment, did not occur to them. It is hard for us to understand how literally they interpreted the Christian epic. It is as if we took Milton's *Paradise Lost* as scientific history. More than a thousand years were required to undermine the Christian epic, and it is a tribute to man's intellectual valor that ultimately he shook off the tyranny of an absolutist way of thinking, that he questioned the veracity of the epic and broke the spell it exercised on the lives of millions. To the story of how this spell was broken we shall return in a later chapter.

X. THE INTELLECTUAL PATTERNS OF EARLY CHRISTIANITY

The doctrine of otherworldly salvation profoundly altered man's orientation to life. By that we mean that the transition from paganism, with its emphasis on the here and now, to Christianity, with its accent on the beyond, is one of the major revolutions in all intellectual history. As Professor J. T. Shotwell suggests, the achievements of thinkers and workers, of artists, philosophers, poets, and statesmen, were given up for the shadowy revelations of prophets and an overwrought gospel of worldly renunciation.

Henceforth, there was only one acceptable theory of the creation, of nature and of the mission of man; one moral code; one standard of social relations; and one

20 George Santayana, *The Life of Reason: Reason in Religion*, rev. ed., Scribner, 1954, chap. vii.

chronology of history, based upon the alleged dates of the creation of man and birth of Jesus. The whole scheme was wrapped in supernaturalism. Christian cosmology and ethics emanated not from a human but from a divine source; and the goal of both was not this world but the next—the "divine event towards which the whole Creation moves." Neither in primitive nor in Oriental society, except Persia, had there existed an otherworldly approach so omnipresent and so precise. The interpretation of every phase of human existence was colored by this basic otherworldly frame of reference.

Secular judgments of conduct were speedily banned. The tolerance and intellectual freedom which had characterized paganism disappeared. Free discussion might provoke heresies, and heresies would mean the damnation of souls, since there was but one true road to salvation.

Religiosity became the motif of a whole civilization. Some of the greatest Romans had been religious, but many of the intellectual leaders were either irreligious or antireligious. Even pietistically inclined philosophers, like the Stoics, took their piety in an intellectual rather than an emotional sense. Apart from the formal and superficial cult of emperor worship, the Roman government had never tried to enforce uniformity in religious beliefs. Indeed, one strength of Rome was its tolerance towards competing religions. As for scholars, their interests were centered on natural more than on supernatural phenomena. And even the popular Roman cults were chiefly concerned with making man's earthly journey brighter.

Christianity encouraged intolerance, bigotry, and religious persecution. It destroyed all conflicting cults with an incredible ferocity. Peasant and scientist, literate and illiterate, all had to share, willingly or not, the same basic beliefs. Nothing less than rigorous conformity was demanded.

The church was the only power which could adjust man to the spiritual world and assure him of a heavenly reception. For this purpose it provided him with an elaborate theology—his guide or textbook in the arduous business of placating God and outwitting the devil. The practical appeal of Christianity—a religion inspired by a lonely carpenter who could not endure the injustices of the world, the selfishness, and viciousness of mankind, to whom the formal Jewish religion was an abomination—was greatly enhanced by its beautiful allegory and its haunting symbolism. That the parables and symbols were not original, did not matter. Wafted from all ends of the earth, as we have pointed out, drawn from all the cults of the known European and Asiatic world, the new religion was presented with such persuasiveness and infused with so much emotion, that its appeal was irresistible.

The allegory and symbolism with which Christian thought is so heavily freighted were no innovation. Hellenistic Judaism and Neoplatonism had both employed them extensively. Christianity, however, supplied additional impulses. Interpreting Scripture presented the pressing problem of explaining away obvious discrepancies, excusing conduct not in harmony with Christian ethics, and disguising literal impossibilities in the Old and New Testament stories. In short, Christian theology and religious texts made allegory and symbolism absolutely imperative. We must look behind the temporal veil for God's seal, for a deeper and loftier meaning than is at first apparent. Neoplatonism exerted a powerful influence on Christianity in this mode of thinking. The Alexandrian father, Origen (c. 185-c. 254), was the most effective early exponent of the allegorical method. Shotwell and Conybeare have well stated Origen's justification of this procedure:

> Interpretation of the scriptures by allegory is not, in Origen's eyes, an unwarranted liberty. The scriptures themselves sanction it—allegorically! "There is a hidden and secret meaning," he says, "in each individual word. The treasure of divine wisdom is hid in the vulgar and unpolished vessels of words; as the apostle also points out when he says, 'We have this treasure in earthen vessels.'" Quaintly naïve as such reasoning seems when based upon a single text, its weakness becomes its strength when sufficient texts are adduced to convey the impression that the scriptures themselves do really proclaim their own symbolic character. This Origen endeavors to do. "If the texts of Moses had contained nothing which was to be understood as having a secret meaning, the prophet would not have said in his prayer to God: 'Open thou mine eyes and I will behold wondrous things out of thy law' (Psalms, 119. 18)." What, he asks, can one make out of the prophecy of Ezekiel except allegorically? Prophetic literature implies allegory in its very structure. But the strongest proof of the legitimacy of allegorical interpretation is its use in the New Testament, and so largely by St. Paul.[21]

> Wherever, he [Origen] argues, we meet with such useless, nay impossible, incidents and precepts as these, we must discard a literal interpretation and consider of what moral interpretation they are capable, with what higher and mysterious meaning they are fraught, what deeper truths they were intended symbolically and in allegory to shadow forth. The divine wisdom has of set purpose contrived these little traps and stumbling-blocks in order to cry halt to our slavish historical understanding of the text, by inserting in its midst sundry things that are impossible and unsuitable. The Holy Spirit so waylays us in order that we may be driven by passages which taken in their *prima facie* sense cannot be true or useful, to search for the ulterior truth, and seek in the Scriptures which we believe to be inspired by God a meaning worthy of Him.[22]

The allegorical method can, perhaps, be best illustrated from a typical passage in the *Epistle of Barnabas:*

> Now what do you suppose this to be a type of, that a command was given to Israel, that men of the greatest wickedness should offer a heifer, and slay and burn it, and that then boys should take the ashes, and put these into vessels, and bind round a stick purple wool along with hyssop, and that thus the boys should sprinkle the people, one by one, in order that they might be purified from their sins?

> Consider how He speaks to you with simplicity. The calf is Jesus: the sinful men offering it are those who led Him to the slaughter. But now the men are no longer guilty, are no longer regarded as sinners. And the boys that sprinkle are those that have proclaimed to us the remission of sins and purification of heart. To these He gave authority to preach the Gospel, being twelve in number, corresponding

---

[21] J. T. Shotwell, "Christianity and History," *Journal of Philosophy, Psychology and Scientific Methods,* Feb. 26, 1920, pp. 115-16.

[22] F. C. Conybeare, *History of New Testament Criticism,* Putnam, 1910, pp. 14-15.

to the twelve tribes of Israel. But why are there three boys that sprinkle? To correspond to Abraham, and Isaac, and Jacob, because these were great with God. And why was the wool [placed] upon the wood? Because by wood Jesus holds His kingdom, so that [through the cross] those believing on Him shall live for ever. But why was hyssop joined with the wool? Because in His kingdom the days will be evil and polluted in which we shall be saved, [and] because he who suffers in body is cured through the cleansing efficacy of hyssop. And on this account the things which stand thus are clear to us, but obscure to them, because they did not hear the voice of the Lord.[23]

Equally interesting as an allegorical interpretation of Scripture is Gregory's commentary on the scriptural statement that Job possessed, among other property, five hundred yoke of oxen and five hundred she asses:

We have said above that by the number fifty, which is completed by seven weeks and the addition of an unit, rest is signified, and by the number ten the sum of perfection is set forth. Now, forasmuch as the perfection of rest is promised to the faithful, by multiplying fifty ten times, we arrive at five hundred. But in Sacred Writ the title of oxen sometimes represents the dullness of the foolish sort, and sometimes the life of well-doers. For because the stupidity of the fool is represented by the title of an ox, Solomon says rightly, "He goeth after her straightway, as an ox goeth to the slaughter." Again, that the life of every laborer is set forth by the title of oxen, the precepts of the Law are a testimony, which enjoined through Moses, "Thou shalt not muzzle the ox when he treadeth out the corn." And this again is declared in plain words, "The labourer is worthy of his hire."

By the title of asses, too, we have represented sometimes the unrestrained indulgence of the wanton, sometimes the simple-mindedness of the Gentiles; for the inertness of fools is imaged by the designation of asses, as where it is said through Moses, "Thou shalt not plough with an ox and an ass together." As though he said, "Do not associate fools and wise men together in preaching, lest by means of him who has no power to accomplish the work you hinder him who has abundant power." The unrestrained indulgence of the wanton is likewise set forth by the appellation of asses, as the prophet testifies when he says, "whose flesh is as the flesh of asses."

Again, by the title asses is shown the simplicity of the Gentiles. Hence, when the Lord went up to Jerusalem, he is related to have sat upon a young ass. For what is it for him to come to Jerusalem sitting upon an ass, except taking possession of the simple hearts of the Gentiles to conduct them to the vision of peace, by ruling and ordering them? And this is shown by one passage, and that a very easy one, in that both the workmen of Judea are represented by oxen, and the Gentile peoples by an ass, when it is said by the prophet, "The ox knoweth his owner, and the ass his master's crib." For who appears as the ox saving the Jewish people, whose neck was worn by the yoke of the Law? And who was the ass but the Gentile world, which was like a brute animal readily seduced by every deceiver, for he did not resist by exercise of reason? [24]

Allegory and symbolism were even applied to natural science. Since God had created all things, and through them all a divine purpose runs, stones, plants, and

[23] "The Epistle of Barnabas," in *Apostolic Fathers,* Ante-Nicene Christian Library, I, 114-15.
[24] Selection from Gregory's *Moralia* in Robinson, *Readings in European History,* I, 79-80.

animals are supposed to hide within their corporeal forms sacred verities and spiritual values. The following passage from Taylor's paraphrase of the *Physiologus,* a popular type of allegorical natural-history book during the early Middle Ages, will furnish an adequate conception of the allegorical zoölogy which was so common for more than a thousand years:

> The lion has three characteristics; as he walks or runs he brushes his foot-prints with his tail, so that hunters may not track him. This signifies the secrecy of the Incarnation of the Lion of the tribe of Judah. Secondly, the Lion sleeps with his eyes open; so slept the body of Christ upon the Cross, while his Godhead watched at the right hand of the Father. Thirdly, the Lioness brings forth her cub dead; on the third day the father comes and roars in its face, and wakes it to life. This signifies the Lord's resurrection on the third day.
>
> The Pelican is distinguished by its love for its young, as these begin to grow they strike at their parents' faces, and the parents strike back and kill them. Then the parents take pity, and on the third day the mother comes and opens her side and lets the blood flow on the dead young ones, and they become alive again. Thus God cast off mankind after the Fall, and delivered them over to death; but He took pity on us, as a mother, for by the Crucifixion He awoke us with his Blood to eternal life.
>
> The Unicorn cannot be taken by hunters, because of his great strength, but lets himself be captured by a pure virgin. So Christ, mightier than the heavenly powers, took on humanity in a virgin's womb.
>
> The Phoenix lives in India, and when five hundred years old fills his wings with fragrant herbs and flies to Heliopolis, where he commits himself to the flames in the Temple of the Sun. From his ashes comes a worm, which the second day becomes a fledgling, and on the third a full-grown phoenix, who flies away to his old dwelling-place. The Phoenix is the symbol of Christ; the two wings filled with sweet-smelling herbs are the Old and New Testaments, full of divine teaching.[25]

It is obvious that the medieval churchmen left little to be desired in the art of uncovering Christian meaning in secular things and the written word. To bring this art to full fruition, language had to be used in extraordinary ways. Simplicity and clarity were eschewed. The vaguer the statement, the more ingenious interpretations one could attach to it. Augustine set forth the general intention when he wrote in the *Confessions:* "Were I to write anything of eminent worth, I should desire to write, so that whatever truth one might later find regarding these things, my words might resound on the side of the prevailing opinion at the time, rather than that I should state one true opinion regarding the matter so clearly that I should exclude other opinions, the falsity of which could not injure me." [26]

The phase of patristic learning which was probably most directly opposed to the scientific point of view was the all-pervading belief in miracles and supernatural intervention.

Since Christianity itself was founded essentially upon a complex of alleged miraculous occurrences, it was but natural that the Christian fathers would expect a continuance of these miraculous acts. To be sure, pagan thinkers, particularly

[25] Taylor, *The Medieval Mind,* I, 76-77.
[26] *Confessions,* XII, 31.

the Neoplatonists, had contended that divine action is essentially miraculous, but the Christians developed the zest for the miraculous much farther than the Neoplatonists. The miraculous was the surest proof of divine intervention in the interests of the faithful and to the embarrassment or discomfort of the devil and his sinful followers. But the devil himself was also prolific in miraculous acts, and it was often difficult for the good Christian of the Middle Ages to be certain whether God or the devil had performed the miracle in question. Taylor has well summed up this patristic enthusiasm for miracle mongering:

> Here are fundamental principles of patristic faith. The will of God is the one cause of all things. It is unsearchable. But we have been taught much regarding God's love and compassionateness, and of His desire to edify and save His people. These qualities prompt His actions towards them. Therefore we may expect His acts to evince edifying and saving purpose. All the narratives of Scripture are for our edification. How many mighty saving acts do they record, from the Creation, onward through the story of Israel, to the birth and resurrection of Christ! And surely God still cares for His people. Nor is there any reason to suppose that He has ceased to edify and save them through signs and wonders. Shall we not still look for miracles from His grace?
>
> Thus in the nature of Christianity, as a miraculously founded and revealed religion, lay the ground for expecting miracles, or, at least, for not deeming them unlikely to occur. And to the same result from all sides conspired the influences which had been obscuring natural knowledge. We have followed those influences in pagan circles from Plato on through Neo-Platonism and other systems current in the first centuries of the Christian era. We have seen them obliterate rational conceptions of nature's processes and destroy the interest that impels to unbiassed investigation. The character and exigencies of the Faith intensified the operation of like tendencies among Christians. Their eyes were lifted from the earth. They were not concerned with its transitory things, soon to be consumed. Their hope was fixed in the assurance of their Faith; their minds were set upon its confirmation. They and their Faith seemed to have no use for a knowledge of earth's phenomena save as bearing illustrative or confirmatory testimony to the truth of Scripture. Moreover, the militant exigencies of their situation made them set excessive store on the miraculous foundation and continuing confirmation of their religion.[27]

This absorption in the expectancy and contemplation of the miraculous also reflected the Christian idea of God and the mode of his manifestation in nature. Since the days of the deists we have come to conceive of God as manifesting himself, if he does so at all, in the orderly workings of nature. Natural law and divine law have been assimilated, and no one of a scientific turn of mind expects or wishes any deviation from the norms of nature. But in the patristic period God was expected to express himself primarily through aberrations and eccentricities in nature—the great prototypes of which were Moses' parting of the Red Sea and the stopping of the sun in the interest of Joshua's military strategy. This Christian conception of God has been called by Harnack the belief in the "God of arbitrariness." Professor Robinson has well described this conventional patristic attitude towards God.

[27] Taylor, *The Medieval Mind*, I, 74-75.

The medieval Christian was essentially more polytheistic than his pagan prede-cessors, for he pictured hierarchies of good and evil spirits who were ever aiding him to reach heaven or seducing him into the paths of sin and error. Miracles were of common occurrence and might be attributed either to God or the devil; the direct intervention of both good and evil spirits played a conspicuous part in the explanation of daily acts and motives.

As a distinguished church historian has said, the God of the Middle Ages was a God of arbitrariness—the more arbitrary the more Godlike. By frequent inter-ferences with the regular course of events he made his existence clear, reassured his children of his continued solicitude, and frustrated the plots of the Evil One. Not until the eighteenth century did any considerable number of thinkers revolt against this conception of the Deity and come to worship a God of orderliness who abode by his own laws.[28]

The classic portrayal of the "God of arbitrariness" is that set forth by Mark Twain in his work, *The Mysterious Stranger:*

A God who could make good children as easily as bad, yet preferred to make bad ones; who could have made every one of them happy, yet never made a single happy one; who made them prize their bitter life, yet stingily cut it short; who gave His angels eternal happiness unearned, yet required His other children to earn it; who gave His angels painless lives, yet cursed His other children with biting miseries and maladies of mind and body; who mouths justice and invented hell; who mouths mercy—and invented hell; who mouths morals to other people and has none Himself; who frowns upon crimes, yet commits them all; who created man without invitation, then tried to shuffle the responsibility of man's acts upon man, instead of honorably placing it where it belonged, upon Himself; and, finally, with altogether divine obtuseness, invites this poor, abused slave to worship Him.

XI. THE PATRISTIC ATTITUDE TOWARDS SECULAR LEARNING

The problem of secular learning, that is, human knowledge not directly related to the Christian religion, created difficulties for the church fathers. Augustine had only reflected the general sentiment of the fathers when he designated all the learning of the pagan past as an integral part of the City of the Devil.

Yet the pagan learning was all the learning there was to be had in the period of Christian triumph, save for the Jewish learning. And the latter was equally repugnant because the Jews had rejected Jesus. But Christians could not be con-verted, instructed, and disciplined without the use of spoken and written words. Moreover, the pagan cults that competed with Christianity were manned by learned scholars. Illiteracy would have put the Christians at a sad disadvantage. So the Christian fathers, whether they liked it or not, had to tolerate the acquisi-tion of this pagan learning—reading, writing, philosophy and the like. They jus-tified this on the ground that it would promote the Christian faith just so much more effectively. The leaders in this rationalization of Christian literacy were Tertullian, Jerome, and Augustine.

[28] Robinson, *Mind in the Making,* p. 124-25.

This attitude towards learning naturally elevated theology to the rank of "the queen of the sciences," from which she was not dislodged until the time of the Italian humanists and Francis Bacon. All other forms of learning and literature were merely the handmaidens of theology. The chief of these handmaidens were the seven liberal arts. We have pointed out in the preceding chapter the pagan origins of these arts and we shall later indicate how they were taken over into the Christian educational system. The first three of the arts, the trivium, or grammar, rhetoric and dialectic, were most prized. There was less interest in the quadrivium: arithmetic, geometry, astronomy, and music. As for philosophy, it was utilized chiefly in constructing Christian theology. We have already made clear how the latter was literally a restatement of the major tenets of the Christian faith in terms of various types of Greek metaphysics.

Indeed, there was little philosophy which was not theology. From the time of Boëthius to the medieval realists and nominalists there was only one true philosopher, John Scotus Erigena of the ninth century, and his philosophy was entirely concerned with theological problems. Philosophy was not divorced from theology until the time of Montaigne, Francis Bacon, and Thomas Hobbes.

As for natural science, it was studied and valued exclusively for its possible services to theology in illustrating religious truths, chiefly in an allegorical manner. The typical attitude of the fathers towards natural science was perfectly expressed in the *Hexaemeron* of Ambrose:

> The patristic attitude towards cosmogony and natural science plainly appears in the *Hexaemeron* of St. Ambrose. This was a commentary on the first chapters of Genesis, or rather an argumentative exposition of the Scriptural account of the Creation, primarily directed against those who asserted that the world was uncreated and eternal. As one turns the leaves of this writing, it becomes clear that the interest of Ambrose is always religious, and that his soul is gazing beyond the works of the Creation to another world. He has no interest in physical phenomena, which have no laws for him except the will of God.[29]

The Christian fathers studied Pliny's *Natural History,* Solinus' *Wonders of the World,* and the popular bestiaries. They took from these the fanciful examples of scientific marvels and wonders and tried to find in them edifying religious truths. Taylor's paraphrase of sections from the *Physiologus,* which we cited above as illustrating the Christian use of scientific allegories, is a good example of this procedure. As to the *Physiologus* itself, Professor Lynn Thorndike points out that it is now difficult to tell whether it was originally a Hellenistic bestiary, written in Greek about 125 B.C., or whether it was a collection of later writings by the Christian fathers based upon these animal allegories.[30] Whichever it was, the result admirably illustrates the patristic attitude towards natural science and its uses.

The fathers were no longer even interested in making their own scientific compilations as Pliny had done. They simply took the pagan encyclopedias which were at hand and bent them to their allegorical needs and religious aspirations.

29 Taylor, *The Medieval Mind,* I, 72-73.
30 Thorndike, *History of Magic and Experimental Science,* I, 497 ff.

All semblance of critical sense was left behind. In addition to allegorical zoölogy, the fathers made wide allegorical use of geography, astronomy, and mathematics. Geographical areas and earthly wonders, the movements of the heavenly bodies, and numbers were prized for their allegorical and magical significance.

It goes without saying that the fathers accepted the scriptural version of the universe and its creation. Ambrose characteristically deprecated any discussion of this sacred cosmology. Take it on faith and leave it at that:

> To discuss the nature and position of the earth [says he] does not help us in our hope of the life to come. It is enough to know what the Scripture states, "that He hung up the earth upon nothing" (Job 26:7). Why then argue whether He hung it up in air or upon the water, and raise a controversy as to how the thin air could sustain the earth; or why, if upon the waters, the earth does not go crashing down to the bottom? Not because the earth is in the middle, as if suspended on even balance, but because the majesty of God constrains it by law of His will, does it endure stable upon the unstable and the void. . . .

And again Ambrose asks, "Why argue as to the elements which make the heaven? Why trouble oneself with these physical inquiries? Sufficeth for our salvation, not such disputation, but the verity of the precepts, not the acuteness of argument, but the mind's faith, so that rather than the creature, we may serve the Creator, who is God blessed forever." [31]

To the authoritative Jewish account of creation in the Scriptures, the fathers and later writers added the Neoplatonic notion of mystical beauty in the universe and the idea of a close affinity between the universe as a whole and man. This led to the popular macrocosm-microcosm analogy of the Middle Ages. We shall have more to say on the subject of early Christianity and natural science in a later chapter on the Dark Ages, and these brief characterizations will suffice in this place.

The interest of the fathers in history was similarly founded upon religious values. They divided history into two branches: (1) the higher or sacred history, which dealt with religious developments; and (2) the lower or profane history, which treated of secular affairs. But even their profane history—insofar as they wrote any—had a religious purpose and import. The famous *Chronicle* of Eusebius, read in the West in Jerome's Latin version, used the familiar and relatively unimportant Hebrew history as the framework upon which to hang a chronological summary of all world history. This remained the practice well down into modern times. Eusebius wrote the great sacred history of the period, his valuable *History of the Christian Church*. Augustine's disciple, Orosius, compiled the one important example of profane history in the patristic age, the *Seven Books of History against the Pagans*. Orosius had little interest in historical facts. He used such of the latter as he cared to gather in order to prove that the world was worse off before the Christian Era than it had been since. The remaining historical work of the period fell into the category of sacred history, the lives of the saints, of which Jerome was the chief compiler in that age.

There was little interest in social science. With the fathers its place was taken

<hr>

[31] Taylor, *op. cit.*, p. 73.

by the Christian epic. The past development of man was comprehended in the doctrine of the fall of man, while the future of mankind was provided for in the Christian eschatology which we have described. The only real concern of the fathers for literature was their zeal for the Hebrew scriptures and the writings of other fathers. They had no interest in classical literature as such. They exploited it solely for its possible aid in propagating Christianity. Any such thing as literary criticism and textual science was rendered impotent by the prevalent esteem of allegory and symbolism. Absurd and dubious passages in sacred texts were neither doubted nor critically investigated. They were the more highly prized because they were believed to hide within themselves a more precious allegorical message.

From all of this we may safely concede that James Harvey Robinson did not pass too harsh a judgment when he wrote of the patristic era that "No form of ignorance or perversity of thought was left for the Middle Ages to discover."

XII. ART AND ARCHITECTURE

1. Catacomb Art (I-IV Centuries)

We find the most impressive artistic remains of this period in the catacombs on the outskirts of Rome, where the Christian community buried its dead. Here lay the bodies not only of those who had died natural deaths but of the martyrs as well—which may help to explain why later generations came to build churches above these underground passageways and why they were ransacked for relics. The catacombs themselves consist of an intricate maze of narrow tunnels running in all directions. Frequently intersecting, they formed an opening suitable for the construction of a chapel dedicated to some martyr or bishop. These tunnels were really abandoned building quarries; and it was in such forsaken places that the early Christians sought refuge for the bodies of their dead and occasionally even for themselves.

The shrouded bodies rested in rectangular horizontal niches cut into the sides of the narrow passageways. These niches are known as "shove" tombs from the manner in which they were filled. Frequently the square chamber formed by intersecting tunnels reveals a curved or gabled ceiling covered with fragments of painting. If we remember that these vaults were probably painted by men totally untrained in art and executed under extreme conditions of darkness and cold, we are less inclined to compare them with the Roman paintings done at that time— paintings for the upper classes, created under the most favorable circumstances. In addition to his technical lacks, the catacomb painter had to fight against darkness and consequently he had to paint as quickly as possible. This accounts in some measure for the very ideographic and loose technique of these works. Consider further the emotional intensity under which the artist was moved to carry out his work, and the agitated and expressionistic features of the paintings take on added significance.

What were the subjects of the catacomb frescoes and why were they chosen?

Upon casual examination we find a considerable number of representations of both Old and New Testament miracles, particularly those that show people being saved: Jonah and the Whale, Noah and the Ark, Daniel in the Lion's Den, The Three Hebrews in the Fiery Furnace, Susanna and the Elders, Christ Healing (various types and examples), etc. We need only read the texts of the early Christian prayers for the dead to appreciate the relationship between the painted scenes and the usual formulae recited at the burial service. The worshiper begs the Lord to save his soul just as He had accomplished the above-represented miracles—in themselves fine examples of imminent destruction followed by miraculous intervention and rescue. Viewed in this light the catacomb paintings are illustrations of very old prayers, and their importance and significance are heightened by the frequent appearance of praying figures of both men and women with arms raised high in attitudes of worship. A figure of this type is known as an *orans*. That the orans very often was intended to signify a particular personage of the time is indicated by the names found inscribed beneath them.

Perhaps the most interesting aspect of these works, from the purely sociological viewpoint, is their generally ambiguous meaning. For the Christian worshiper of the time they signified one thing, and for the casual pagan visitor they signified something entirely different—something recognizable only in terms of what he already knew. This meant, of course, that the Christian artist consciously adapted those artistic motifs, common at the time, which could serve symbolically to represent the thoughts and beliefs of the new faith. The advantage of this double-meaning symbolism for purposes of secrecy may be readily appreciated, particularly when a scene such as that of Daniel in the Lion's Den can make a twentieth-century observer think of classical representations of Orpheus among the Beasts. Of course this method of ambiguous symbolism could not always be applied. But there is no mistaking the general impression made by a typical catacomb chapel chamber with its multitude of pagan ornaments: garlands, cupids, floral motifs of all sorts, and with such apparently "harmless" subjects as a young man carrying a lamb over his shoulder—the Christian Good Shepherd "in disguise."

It is perfectly understandable that any artist working in the first to the third centuries in Rome would think in terms of Rome's artistic vocabulary. But catacomb painting presents a serious departure of its own. While Roman painting (at Pompeii, Boscoreale, etc.) shows a meticulous adherence to fine craftsmanship and to the representation of tiny details, shadows, and the like, the work of the untrained, rapt Christian artist displays a high degree of simplification—not only in the sense of rendering a scene in shorthand but in the way in which single figures were painted—with abrupt and loose strokes of the brush. The surface shininess of many pagan Roman works pales before the more fluid and modern style of the catacomb paintings, before their dynamic emotional power.

To be sure many of these paintings impress the observer as little more than mediocre—interesting more for content than for style. But occasionally, in such representations as the so-called "Isaiah, Virgin and Child" or in the finer examples of the female *orans*, a tremendous degree of emotional vitality is achieved—and in a manner which today would be called "expressionistic." Not only is the subject matter distorted by reducing an elaborate story—such as Moses striking water from the rock, to merely a man, stick, and rock—but the very manner of applying both color and line conveys a similar feeling of condensation and abruptness. Highlights are hastily applied to the tip of the nose and the cheekbones; powerful lines frequently outline the figure, changing in thickness as they move about the subject; backgrounds tend to disappear, and the subject seems to be standing in a vague space, or on nothing. All of these stylistic elements depart sharply from the calmly photographic character of Roman painting, to create a new art that is definitely emotional in content and in treatment.[32]

Although Rome shows a vast number of remains of these first two centuries, it must not be thought of as the only center of catacomb production. Paintings of the same general character are found elsewhere as well, although ordinarily underground burial places, such as in Alexandria and Syracuse, have lost their embellishments. At Palmyra, in Asia Minor, there are still some early tomb paintings in the form of grave portraits.

2. Church Architecture

With the stabilization of the Christian religion under Constantine the church emerged from underground and a furious period of building activity ensued. In all parts of the empire churches sprang up, decorated either with paintings or mosaics and representing the "arrival" of the new religion. Some of these churches are still standing today, some outside the walls of Rome—Saint Paul and Saint Lawrence Outside-the-Walls—and many within its confines.

Here again, as in the case of catacomb art, the architects, painters, mosaicists, and sculptors, now working for the greater glory of God, naturally expressed themselves in the current language of Roman art. For example, the most important of all the architectural types of this period, the basilican church, represents a combination of various Roman elements, as do the sculptures and the mosaics found in connection with these buildings. An examination of the nature of these buildings should be rewarding, since they embody the entire tradition of church architecture in Europe from the earliest period to the present.

The plan of old St. Peter's (a basilican church rebuilt in the sixteenth century) reveals a number of the fundamental elements present in churches down to modern times. There is a broad spacious central aisle (nave) flanked on either side by one or two side aisles. The nave rises a considerable height above the aisles, offering the builder an opportunity of piercing the upper part of the nave walls with windows. These form the clerestory. At the lower end of the church there lies a crossing (transept) at right angles to the nave, which creates the cross-shaped plan. Beyond the transept is the semicircular apse before which the altar was

---

[32] If catacomb painting may be regarded as a variant of the current pagan mode in painting (and since some solidity for the figure remains, this is relatively true), ancient pagan art up to the second century A.D. displays two fairly modern phenomena: (1) aerial perspective, such as that shown in the famous Odyssey Landscapes, and (2) "distorted" and "expressionistic" painting. This does not imply that these elements have any immediate effect upon the development of art. They are interesting, however, in the sense that two significant modern painting ideas were fairly well known at an early period in human evolution.

usually placed. The early Christian basilica had a rather large atrium added to its entrance side: a hollow square enclosed by a double row of columns and corresponding to the part of the Roman house after which it was named. In a later period of church building (the Romanesque) the atrium was transferred to the side to serve as a cloister for the monks or nuns. During the early Christian period, it was used as an approach to the church, not only in the physical sense but in the spiritual as well, since those who were either penitents or aspirants to church membership were usually detained there.

Beyond the atrium an elaborate portico (or narthex) was usually placed as the entrance proper to the church. (Here again we find a correspondence in terminology to the Roman house.) Passing from the narthex to the interior, the worshiper

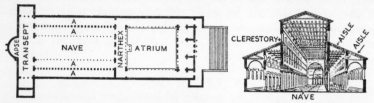

Left, floor plan of an early Christian church (Old St. Peter's); *right,* sectional view of the same church, looking toward the apse.

found himself in the nave (*navis,* i.e., "ship of the church") where a double row of columns, arranged in a processional fashion and topped with either a classical entablature or a series of arches, led in the direction of the transept. (Most of the churches of this period had no transepts; old St. Peter's is an exception.) The main body of worshipers would gather in the side aisles, the neophytes occasionally being admitted to the rear of the nave. Usually the apse was occupied by the bishop's throne and directly in front of it was the altar on which the mass was celebrated.

In essence this architectural scheme does not markedly differ from most of the later church developments except for elaboration and structural changes. The early Christian basilica must be regarded as an extremely simple architectural type, with a simple column-and-lintel system. The roof was divided into three parts: wooden ceilings over each aisle and a wooden gable above the nave. If the basilican church was simply constructed it was rather elaboratedly decorated with ornate marble floors and fine classical columns—usually borrowed (stolen) from some luckless pagan building. Since the class of society now interested in Christianity was considerably wealthier than the poor Christians of the catacomb period, it is not surprising to find the church of these "triumph" days a rich building decorated with fine mosaics (a design composed of small pieces of colored stone or glass inlaid in cement).

The most prominent type of sculpture from the period beginning with the fourth century appears in the sarcophagi in which wealthy Christians were entombed. Frequently, these sarcophagi were embellished with a portrait of the deceased placed upon such a classical motif as a conch shell; sometimes the face of the spouse was added. Their main feature of decoration grew out of the same sources as the pictures found in the catacombs, that is, scenes of miraculous saving eloquent of the coming to life in the world beyond. If we remember that by the fourth century pagan Roman sculpture had deteriorated considerably from the crisp freshness of the Augustan age, we shall not be surprised at the frequently empty characterizations on these sarcophagi. Besides the very unfortunate crowding together of scenes that often defy comprehension, the concept of the human figure, in the majority of cases, is a rather sad affair.

There are exceptions, to be sure—the so-called columnar sarcophagi, where the scenes are separated by columns covered with alternating gables and arches, in such a famous work as the *Junius Bassus Sarcophagus,* executed for a rich Roman of that name. In this latter work the anatomical conception strikes us as unusual by contrast to the majority of sarcophagi. But it is still a far cry from the typical examples of Greco-Roman style of the Augustan era, and must be regarded as an indication of the decay of classical art. Too few examples of sculpture in the round survive to enable us to make any generalized judgment. Probably there were few figures executed, since one of the sensitive points of the new religion was its abhorrence of "idols." Except for the well-known "Good Shepherd" (again a catacomb subject) and the effigy of St. Peter in the cathedral of that name, there remains little free-standing sculpture of the period.

Not only were the early basilicas embellished with elaborately inlaid marble pavements and fine marble columns, but the walls of the nave and other parts of the building displayed colorful, splendid mosaics. Here again the reminiscence of classical style is strong and lasting (as, for example, in the church of Santa Maria Maggiore in Rome). The artist has made a definite attempt to convey a feeling of depth by using a rather schematic type of landscape and an awkwardly represented architecture. The figures stand firmly on the ground; their draperies give a feeling of the third dimension. Emotionally they are somewhat stereotyped and not too convincing. Thus classical qualities are evident to a minor degree, and, as in the case of sculpture, they point to the drying up of classical inspiration. The one really convincing example of sculpturesque feeling and architecturally convincing background is the well-known apse decoration in Santa Pudenziana in Rome showing Christ and the Apostles. Here the landscape is suggested, then a solid architecture, and finally in the foreground the truly majestic figure of the Savior flanked by two groups of senatorial figures in striped Roman togas. It shows us for once a complete, if temporary, assimilation of the best Roman technique.

XIII. EARLY CHRISTIAN LITERATURE

In the early days, when Christianity was fighting against persecutions and the threat of extinction or was carrying on unending controversies with older religions, there was little opportunity for the development of an atmosphere conducive to the production of any real literature. Likewise, after the victory was won there was need to consolidate the gains and lay down the doctrines of the new dispensation. Therefore, a period of dogmatic theological and didactic writings followed upon the age of apology and controversy. For this reason, most of the literary activity of Christian scholars in the first four centuries of the Christian Era was devoted to matters immediately connected with the defense and establishment of the faith.

The first Christian writings appeared when the church was very much in the minority. Hence, the literature was apologetic in character, relatively meek and defensive in tone. It tried to explain and defend Christianity. Among the more representative writers were Ignatius, Papias, Justin Martyr, and Minucius Felix.

As the church grew a little stronger, its champions dared to lash out more vigorously against opponents, whether pagan or Christian. Thus, we find in the period from about 150 to 325 a prolific literature of heated religious controversy between different groups of Christians, between Christians and heretics, and between Christians and pagans. Some of the leading controversial writers of this age were Irenaeus, Hippolytus, Cyprian, Tertullian, Arnobius, and Lactantius.

Then came the period of triumph and the age of dogmatic religious literature—both theological and didactic—designed to unify the faith and guide the discipline of Christians. Here we find the writings of the great church fathers—Athanasius, Basil, and Chrysostom in the East and Ambrose, Jerome, Augustine, and Gregory the Great in the West. Of these, by far the most influential was Augustine.

The earliest of this Christian literature was composed in Greek. The first Christian work in Latin was the *Octavius* of Minucius Felix, written about 190. Latin gradually triumphed in the West, but Greek was the usual language employed in the East throughout the Middle Ages.

When Christianity gained headway and security, along with some leisure for contemplation, there was an opportunity for true literary activity to begin.

Origen (c. 185-c. 254) was one of the best of early exegetists, a master in applying the allegorical method to the Bible. He maintained that Scripture had a threefold meaning: *somatic* (which was the body), *psychic* (which was the soul) and *pneumatic* (which was the spirit). In practice he was rarely able to show all three meanings in a given passage, and was usually content with two: one referring to Christian life on earth, the other to the next world.

This sort of exegesis was deeply influential upon the church fathers and won the support of such men as Ambrose, Jerome, and Gregory the Great. Ambrose (c. 340-397) is one of the most interesting personalities in early Christian literature, one of those who bridged the gap between classical and Christian thought. He Christianized Roman ideas, just as Cicero and Lucretius Romanized Greek ideas. Like most literary men of his era—Augustine was perhaps an exception—St. Ambrose was more of an ecclesiastic than a literary artist. In his treatise *De officiis ministrorum* he showed that the pagan virtues, the Roman ideas of exemplary conduct, were abundantly illustrated in both the Old and New Testament, in the history of the church from the beginning, and in the lives of Christians in his own time.

Ambrose was not wholly intolerant of pagan ethics. By juxtaposing Christian and heathen moral ideas he proved that the Christian was immeasurably superior.

Above all, he was a mystic. He combed the Bible for hidden meanings, figurative and allegorical. He performed this sleight-of-hand, however, with a good deal of charm, as the following passage addressed to young people preparing for baptism shows:

> Perhaps when you hear this, my daughters, you who are tending towards the grace of the Lord, you may be tempted to get your ear-rings and bracelets and say to me, "Why do you forbid us, Bishop, to have what Rebecca accepted as a gift and yet exhort us to be like Rebecca?" Ah, yes, but Rebecca did not have the kind of ear-rings and bracelets that are wont to show disputes in the Church, the kind that often slip off. She had other ear-rings—and would that you had them too!—and other bracelets. The ear-rings of Rebecca are the symbols of pious attention. The bracelets of Rebecca are the ornaments of good works. She had the kind of ear-rings that do not oppress the ears but soothe them. She had the kind of bracelets that do not burden the hand with material gold but lighten it with spiritual deeds.[33]

Ambrose's *Hexaemeron* (*Six Days*), a series of nine sermons on the six days of creation, is a remarkable scriptural commentary, ingeniously combining natural science with the allegorical method. His notions of atmospheric composition and animal habits, for example, are curious indeed and remind us of the *Physiologus* or bestiary quoted on page 310. The polypus, for instance, symbolizes fraud to him, the phoenix, resurrection, the sea is the gospel, and the fishes are men.

Ambrose's senses were not entirely blunted by indefatigable moralizing. His sermons could contain such an exquisite vignette as this:

> [The sea] when it whitens with the caps of its rising waves and bedews the cliffs with snowy spray or when on its crisping surface, as gentler breezes blow and the sky is calm and cloudless, it takes on purple colors which spread and merge as you see them from the distance. And when it beats the neighboring shore not with the madness of its billows but with quiet salutations and peaceful caresses, how sweet is its sound, how pleasant the breaking surf, how grateful and harmonious its ebbing flow![34]

Not many later Christian moralists revealed such sensitivity to nature.

Many church fathers, while relishing the literature of Greece and Rome, felt uncomfortable about it, and feared that it interfered with the quest for salvation. Jerome (c. 340-420), the greatest literary figure in early Christian literature, illustrates this divided allegiance between the heathen artist and the Christian propagandist. When he withdrew to Antioch, he took along the classical works he had collected in Rome. One day in a vision a figure appeared to him and exclaimed *Ciceronianus es, non Christianus*—"Thou are a Ciceronian, not a Christian!" This occurrence threw Jerome into consternation and he vowed that the lover of Christ should never again love Cicero.[35]

Jerome's extremist attitude toward pagan letters held sway down to the time of Petrarch (1304-1374), when it was again possible to be both a good Christian

33 Translation by E. K. Rand, *Founders of the Middle Ages*, Dover Publications, Inc., 1957, p. 89.
34 E. K. Rand, *op. cit.*, p. 97.
35 See below, p. 559, for Erasmus' attitude on this subject.

and a devotee of pagan literature. How irreconcilable the two were in the Dark Ages may be seen in Gregory the Great's destruction of a classical library in Rome. Gregory, when he heard that one of his bishops was giving lectures on classical literature, reminded him that to sing the praises of Jupiter was blasphemy. As Gregory went on to add in the same epistle, the reading of secular literature was a frivolity, an impropriety, and a sin.

Jerome's greatest contribution to the church was his translation of the Old Testament into vernacular Latin, upon which the modern Vulgate Bible is based. As a master of three languages, Hebrew, Greek, and Latin, and a keen textual critic, he was eminently fitted for the task. Jerome was also one of the best of the early letter writers, possessing a remarkable style, keen wit, a stinging tongue, and a nice sense of irony. His long and exciting life which varied from that of an upper-class missionary in the feverish capital of Christendom, Rome, to that of a desert hermit, his ardent piety, knowledge of classical authors, and unusually bright intellect prepared him to make a significant contribution to the epistolary art.

His epistles provide a good picture of Roman life in the fourth century, as the following excerpt from a letter to his pupil Eustochium reveals:

> Give a wide berth to those who remain widows from necessity, not inclination. Though they change their raiment, their schemings are as of old. Their Basternian litters are preceded by a cohort of eunuch couriers. They redden their cheeks and fill in the skin so neatly that you would think they had not lost husbands but were on the hunt for them. Their houses are full of flatterers, full of feasts. The clergy, too, are there, who ought to have been employed in their duties. They kiss the heads of these matrons, and then hold out their hands—to pronounce a benediction over them, you would imagine, if you did not know that they receive in their palms the tip for their sacred salutation. . . . They are called chaste and nuns—and after a seven course dinner, they dream of apostles.[36]

Among Jerome's multifarious labors was the *Vitae Sanctorum* (*Lives of the Saints*), the earliest example of one of the most popular types of medieval litera-ture. Indeed, saints' lives were the thrill literature, adventure stories, of the Middle Ages. Jerome's lives of Paul the first Hermit, Malchus, and Hilarion were not unworthy of Jacopo da Voraigne who many centuries later wrote the master-piece of that genre, the *Golden Legend*. Jerome's aim in writing these lives was to provide Christians with light reading which would be amusing and edifying at the same time. Jerome also compiled the *De viris illustribus,* a kind of encyclo-pedia of well-known Christians, and translated the chronicle of world history by Eusebius.

Among lesser Christian prose writers of the early Middle Ages was Sulpicius Severus (c. 362-c. 425) who wrote a *Chronica* or summary of sacred history from the dawn of time to his own era, omitting the occurrences mentioned in Scripture. Severus emphasized the misdemeanors of kings, princes, and church dignitaries. He lashed out particularly against the bishops who were involved in the shame-less murders of the Priscillian heretics of Gaul and Spain. The value of Severus' work lies in the picture he gives of his own age.

[36] E. K. Rand, *op. cit.,* p. 113.

Salvian (c. 390-470) wrote an important if one-sided account of life in Gaul in his century, entitled *De gubernatione dei*. Salvian was a puritanic Christian zealot and maintained that the chaos of the century was the result of prevalent immorality and violation of God's will. The most remarkable section of his book is the description of Romans and barbarians, with the dice loaded in favor of the latter. The feebleness and decadence of the Romans are contrasted with the strength and ignorance of the Germans.

The two most renowned histories of the era were the *History of the Christian Church* by Eusebius of Caesarea (c. 260-340) and the *Seven Books of History against the Pagans* by Paulus Orosius (compiled between 415 and 418). The work of Eusebius, which brought the story down to 324, was scholarly, systematic, and relatively impartial. But it was compiled without literary skill and it made extremely superficial analyses of the underlying causes of the great social and religious movements. If not a profound thinker, Eusebius was an industrious scholar who plodded through an enormous amount of material to complete his work. Eusebius (who wrote in Greek) became the standard authority on church history in the Middle Ages.

The compilation of Orosius was written at the suggestion of Augustine as a reply to the pagan charge that the disasters of Rome had resulted from the spread of Christianity and the desertion of the old gods. Orosius held the view that the centuries before the Christian Era were also marked by wars, devastations, and illimitable miseries. These pagan epochs were not only worse than his own times, but the farther back you go, he contended, the blacker the saga. Professor Laistner remarks that "a history written deliberately to prove a certain thesis under the most favorable conditions would leave much to be desired as an historical source." Nothing could better show the uncritical nature of the medieval mind than the fact that Orosius' polemic was taken for gospel truth for almost a thousand years. It is mentioned as a standard history as late as Chaucer's *Canterbury Tales* (c. 1387).

With few exceptions Latin Christian poetry is less poetic than propagandistic. The classical models did not seem to fit Christian needs; and few masterpieces were produced. The story of Genesis or the Gospels dressed in the Vergilian or Horatian language and meter often became ludicrous. Moreover, if the material were taken from Scripture, especially the New Testament, the Christian poet was bound to use the exact biblical words, which, while excellent as prose, scarcely served the high needs of poetry.

Gaius Vettius Juvencus in the fourth century versified the four Gospels in dactylic hexameters, which are as close as possible to the language of the Bible. His work bears echoes of Vergil, but he is far from wielding Vergil's mighty line. Nevertheless, Juvencus was widely read in the Middle Ages and set the fashion in the subject matter of poetry.

Prudentius (348-c. 405) was the most accomplished of early Christian poets. He succeeded in converting Latin meters into good Christian verse. His *Apotheosis* defended the orthodox faith against the heretics; his *Hamartigenia* refuted the Gnostics; his *Psychomachia* was the first allegory composed in the West. Besides these explicit pieces of propaganda Prudentius wrote two volumes of lyric verse, the *Cathemerinon* (twelve long hymns) and the *Peristephanon* (fourteen eulogies of martyrs), a verse analogue to St. Jerome's saints' lives.

Professor Rand calls the *Hamartigenia* a "Paradise Lost" and *Apotheosis* a "Paradise Regained." These two theological essays cover a variety of topics—the nature of the soul, immortality, creation of the universe, freedom of the will, origin of evil, and the corruption of nature. For the first time, Christians had the innermost mysteries of their faith presented in verse which might compare with the great classical models. Horace, Lucretius, and Vergil were echoed in Prudentius, and not unworthily.

Professor Rand has excellently summarized the importance of Prudentius:

> Prudentius brushes aside all gorgeousness and lets the story of a sainted life and martyr's death shine in its own light. At the end of the poem on St. Lawrence, he calls himself a rustic poet, and so he is, in deep sincerity, at the moment. But there is only one mood in Prudentius, whom the great Bentley well called the Horace and the Vergil of the Christians. In illustrating so clearly the two opposite styles, Prudentius provided models for them both in medieval Latin literature, where the two courses, high and low, run on in both prose and verse.[37]

Minor Christian poets of the early medieval period were Commodianus, who flourished around 250, Ausonius (c. 310-395), Paulinus of Nola (353-431) and Sidonius Apollinaris (c. 430-c. 487).

Commodianus composed two volumes of verse, *Instructiones* and *Carmen apologeticum*. The first part of the former satirizes the gods of classical mythology; the second part deals with such theological topics as antichrist, resurrection, and the end of the world. The *Apologeticum* is an exhortation to repentance. Commodianus is of interest as a metrist since he was one of the first to abandon quantity in favor of accent. In general his Latin is corrupt; cases and forms of nouns and verbs regularly depart from classical usage.

Decimus Magnus Ausonius was more of a pagan than a Christian poet. He wrote considerable verse and prose, including prose résumés of the *Iliad* and *Odyssey*. He made some translations of the Greek Anthology in his *Epigrammata;* his *Epitaphia* are about the Trojan warriors; and the *Caesares* are memorials to the Roman emperors. The *Idyllia,* with its charming poem about the river Moselle, is his best-known work.

Paulinus of Nola was the pupil of Ausonius and the disciple of the great bishop Martin of Tours. His poetic output includes an interesting epistle to Ausonius; a panegyric on John the Baptist; paraphrases of the Psalms; the usual tirade against the heathen gods; and a really moving homage to Felix of Nola. Sidonius Apollinaris wrote some panegyrics on divers emperors, and nine books of letters and poems remarkable mainly for their data about literary and political history. Sidonius tortured the Latin language in his attempt to obtain an elaborate and affected style. He is the most complete example of the rhetorical school of poets to which most writers in the late Roman Empire belong.

If Christian literature was to make progress it had to take a more natural road and this it slowly did, so that by the time of Charlemagne we find Latin poets writing excellent verse and, even earlier, the Venerable Bede wrote good Latin prose. By the twelfth century medieval Latin became one of the greatest of literary languages, a not unworthy rival to classical Latin.

SELECTED READINGS

Adeney, W. F., *The Greek and Eastern Churches*, Scribner, 1908.

Ayer, J. C., *Source Book for Ancient Church History*, Scribner, 1913.

Browne, Lewis, *Since Calvary: An Interpretation of Christian History*, Macmillan, 1931.

——— *This Believing World*, Macmillan, 1926.

Burrows, Millar, *The Dead Sea Scrolls*, Viking, 1955.

——— *More Light on the Dead Sea Scrolls*, Viking, 1958.

Butterfield, Herbert, *Christianity in European History*, Macmillan, 1953.

Carrington, Philip, *The Early Christian Church*, 2 Vols., Cambridge University Press, 1957.

Case, S. J., *Makers of Christianity*, Holt, 1934.

——— *The Social Origins of Christianity*, University of Chicago Press, 1923.

——— *The Social Triumph of the Ancient Church*, Harper, 1933.

Conybeare, F. C., *Myth, Magic and Morals*, Beacon Press, 1910.

Coulton, G. G., *Five Centuries of Religion*, Macmillan, 1926.

Duchesne, L. M. O., *Christian Worship*, Seabury, 1954.

Edman, Irwin, *The Mind of Paul*, Holt, 1935.

Flick, A. C., *The Rise of the Medieval Church*, Burt Franklin, 1959.

Foakes-Jackson, F. J., *Studies in the Life of the Early Church*, Doran, 1924.

Gaster, T. H., *The Dead Sea Scriptures*, Doubleday, 1956.

Goodspeed, E. J., *History of Early Christian Literature*, Univ. of Chicago Press, 1942.

Guignebert, C. A. H., *Christianity, Past and Present*, Macmillan, 1927.

——— *Jesus*, Knopf, 1935.

Kershner, F. D., *Pioneers of Christian Thought*, Bobbs-Merrill, 1930.

Krüger, Gustav, *History of Early Christian Literature*, Macmillan, 1897.

Lake, Kirsopp, *Landmarks in the History of Early Christianity*, Macmillan, 1920.

Larson, M. A., *The Religion of the Occident*, Philosophical Library, 1959.

Lowrie, Walter, *Monuments of the Early Church*, Macmillan, 1923.

McGiffert, A. C., *History of Christianity in the Apostolic Age*, Scribner, 1897.

——— *History of Christian Thought*, 2 Vols., Scribner, 1932, Vol. I.

Parker, Pierson, *The Gospel before Mark*, University of Chicago Press, 1953.

Shotwell, *Introduction to the History of History*, Section V.

Spencer, F. A., *Beyond Damascus*, Harper, 1934.

Strzygowski, Josef, *Origin of Christian Church Art*, Oxford Press, 1923.

Taylor, *Classical Heritage of the Middle Ages*.

Thompson, J. W., *Economic and Social History of the Middle Ages*, Ungar, 1959, chaps. ii, v.

——— *History of Historical Writing*, Vol. I, chap. viii.

Werner, Martin, *The Foundation of Christian Dogma*, A. & C. Black, 1957.

Wilson, Edmund, *The Scrolls from the Dead Sea*, Oxford University Press, 1955.

Zeller, Hubert von, *The Benedictine Idea*, Templegate, 1959.

VIII

The Thought
and Culture
of the Dark Ages

I. THE NATURE OF THE DARK AGES

One of the chief causes of confusion and misinterpretation in dealing with the Middle Ages has been the tendency to lump together the culture of a millennium, from Augustine to Petrarch, and to attempt to describe it as a unified whole. Any such effort is bound to lead to distorted historical perspective and to the confusion of the student. There are at least three distinct periods between the decline of the Latin culture of Rome and its supreme appreciation during the so-called Renaissance after the middle of the fifteenth century.

First, we have what have come to be known as the Dark Ages from Augustine to Abelard, roughly from A.D. 500 to 1100. This was the era when pagan learning gradually faded out and neither Byzantines nor Muslims had yet reintroduced classical scholarship into western Europe. Then we have the periods of high scholasticism which lasted from Abelard to William of Ockham and Duns Scotus at the close of the thirteenth century. In this age, Aristotle became supreme, the universities arose, and Christianity was fused with Greek logic. Then we come to the fourteenth and fifteenth centuries, when the revived classical knowledge and the Muslim scholarship bore fruit in western Christendom. Scientific interest grew apace and the intellectual results were truly impressive. Classical scholarship broadened and improved. New literary currents were in evidence. The medieval synthesis was undermined and European culture set out on the high road to the modern age.

Even with respect to the Dark Ages, there was no uniformity of intellectual tempo or of scholarly activity. From the sixth to the eighth centuries, the cultural regression was rather marked. Paganism was disappearing and Christian culture had produced few worthy works to compensate for the loss of the pagan classics.

Arid compilations of pagan learning were gathered so that their possible services to Christian instruction might be exploited. Then, in the eighth and ninth centuries, the impulse given to scholarship by English ecclesiastics and by Charlemagne led to the works of men like Bede, and Alcuin and his followers—the first truly creditable Christian scholarship. There was a considerable relapse in the tenth and eleventh centuries. But the combined influence of a number of original thinkers from Erigena to Abelard and the infiltration of classical and Muslim learning, coming from the Greeks of the East and southern Italy and from the Muslims of Spain, served to turn the tables and to head Western scholarship towards the remarkable intellectual achievements of the thirteenth century.

Moreover, the term Dark Ages should be used mainly to describe cultural conditions in western Europe. The period from the sixth to the ninth century witnessed some of the most active phases of Byzantine thought and culture, and they were also the centuries when the Muslims were creating the fund of learning which later amazed western Europe and helped bring the Dark Ages to a close. Even in western Europe, culture did not advance with equal strides in all countries. The regression of the sixth and seventh centuries was far more marked in Gaul and Germany than in Italy, Ireland, and England. Especially in Ireland and England was the classical learning preserved, ultimately to be brought out of hiding and made available to the more benighted areas.

These considerations have led some scholars to recommend dropping altogether the use of the term "Dark Ages" from historical writing. There is little justification for this, if we are to retain any of the conventional historical captions and terminology. For instance, the conception of "Dark Ages" is far more valid, precise and illuminating than that of any "Middle Ages." It would, probably, be better to drop all these antiquated chronological terms, but if we are to retain the use of "Middle Ages," there is far more justification for continuing to utilize the caption of "Dark Ages."

To give a broadly accurate characterization of the Dark Ages we may say that they began with the gradual obliteration of true classical thought and scholarship. Recognizing that pagan Latin culture was doomed, certain persons attempted to perpetuate and transmit it. This attempt began with Boëthius, who had a sincere regard for classical learning on its own merits and for itself, even though he himself had apparently embraced the Christian faith. A little later, Cassiodorus moved closer to the Dark Ages by applying the suggestions of Tertullian and Augustine, who had recommended the cultivation of the classics for the sole purpose of exploiting such learning in promoting the Christian religion.[1] Cassiodorus industriously brought together manuals and compendiums designed primarily to place a modicum of pagan learning in the hands of literate Christians.

He set the pace for the next five centuries. There were greater scholars and more original minds, but most thinkers of the Dark Ages followed Cassiodorus' example in promoting Christian zeal and erudition through the aid of the pagan learning which Christians were logically supposed to despise and eschew. There was little originality. The compiling habit dominated. The imitative tendencies of

[1] See below, p. 333.

the Germanic peoples furnished an added impetus to the compiling tendency which had long before set in with the decadent Latins. The great majority of pagan learning was at least temporarily lost sight of, and the new Muslim culture had as yet little regenerating influence upon the West. The Dark Ages were intermediate between a declining paganism and the intellectual revival of the twelfth and thirteenth centuries which was built upon sharpened philosophical acumen, the revival of Aristotle and the initial stages of the introduction of Muslim science and scholarship.

Even this dull and unoriginal learning of the Dark Ages was the heritage of only a few. Towns declined in population or disappeared altogether. Culture reverted to an agricultural and pastoral type. Semibarbaric Teutonic kings replaced the Roman emperors. Central government weakened, and it became difficult to preserve order in outlying districts of the several realms. Political conditions moved towards the decentralized localism associated with the feudal system.[2] The masses lost all semblance of literacy, and many of them lived in a state of servility. The colonate of the later Roman Empire was gradually transformed into the serfdom of the medieval period.

In the Dark Ages western Europe thus reverted to a condition not unlike that of Greece in the time of Homer, or of Rome in the days of the mythical kings. The main difference lay in the fact that the Dark Ages had a glorious, if all but forgotten, culture behind them. This accounts for the rapid recovery of medieval culture from the near barbarism of the Dark Ages. From various sources antique culture slowly streamed back into western Europe and laid the basis for an impressive intellectual and cultural revival.

Though political history, as such, has no place in this book, it may be well briefly to indicate the political framework of the Dark Ages in order to give a better orientation and to make more intelligible certain historical allusions throughout the chapter.

The political history of this era was characterized mainly by two traits—the continuance of the Roman Empire in fact and fiction, and the rise of new monarchies which gradually moved ahead from a relatively barbarous basis to the feudal structure which characterized western Europe in the Middle Ages.

The Roman Empire was continued in fact in the East, where the real center had been moved long before the fabled fall of Rome in 476. Constantinople became the capital of the Eastern or Byzantine Empire which lasted on until the Turkish conquest in 1453. It was the most powerful and prosperous Christian state in the Middle Ages and was dominated by a centralized bureaucratic government, though feudalism developed in the outlying districts.

The Roman Empire was continued in fiction in the West as the Holy Roman Empire. When Charlemagne was crowned emperor on Christmas day, 800, he regarded himself as actually continuing the Roman Empire, viewing himself as literally a successor of Augustus. The notion of a distinct medieval empire—the Holy Roman Empire—began with the coronation of Otto the Great of the Saxon line in Germany, in 962. The term "Holy" (sacrum) was first introduced by

2 For a description of feudalism, see below, pp. 387-88.

Frederick Barbarossa of the Hohenstaufen line in 1155—shortly after the Dark Ages came to an end.

The first medieval kingdoms in the West were all dominated by Teutonic rulers. The Goths and then the Lombards set themselves up in Italy. The Anglo-Saxons ruled England until the death of Edward the Confessor in 1066, when the Norman dynasty entered. Their most famous king was Alfred (849-901). The first great German dynasty was that of the Merovingians, founded by the Salian Frank, Clovis, who ruled from 486 to 511. The Merovingians were displaced by the Carolingians under Pepin the Short (741-68) during the eighth century. The great monarch of this line was Charlemagne. Conquering the Saxons, Lombards, and others, he ruled over much of what is now France, Germany, Austria, and Italy. In due time the later and weaker Carolingians were succeeded in France by the Capetian line, which came into power with Hugh Capet in 987. In the Germanies they were supplanted by the Saxon kings, beginning with Henry I, who was crowned in 919. The Salians replaced the Saxons in 1024, when Conrad II came to the throne.

These Western monarchies did not become what could be called national monarchies until the height of the Middle Ages. They were half-civilized and were loosely, if barbarously, governed. Charlemagne did much to promote centralized rule, but even he unwittingly stimulated feudal tendencies. As we shall describe feudalism in the next chapter, it will suffice here to point out that it was characterized by decentralization and localism rather than strongly centralized government.

Surrounding the Christian states on almost every side save the north were the powerful Muslim caliphates, with their centers at Baghdad, Cairo, and Cordova. The Muslims contested the control of the Mediterranean with the Byzantines. They actively clashed with Western states in the eighth century and again during the crusades. Ultimately, they overthrew the Byzantine Empire and all but engulfed the Christian states of western Europe.

II. THE FUSION OF PAGAN AND CHRISTIAN LEARNING

While a knowledge of the Greek language and of the Greek classics in philosophy and literature survived in the Byzantine Empire during the Middle Ages, there was little intellectual contact between Constantinople and the West until well along in the Middle Ages. Consequently, what was known of Greek learning in the Latin West before the twelfth century consisted mainly of commentaries, compendiums and translations. Latin literature, of course, was not cherished or preserved in the East. Hence, what remains we have of pagan Roman learning we owe mainly to the early medieval scholars and monks. They condensed or copied it, and preserved much of it in monastic libraries until it was recovered by the humanists of the so-called Renaissance in their enthusiastic search for ancient manuscripts. Some of the more popular works, of course, remained in circulation in the schools.

The first important writer to whom we owe the transmission of pagan thought

to the Latin West was a Greek Neoplatonist, Porphyry (c. 233-c. 304), who was
born in western Asia (presumably at Tyre). He became a devoted disciple and
expositor of Plotinus, the leading Neoplatonic philosopher. Porphyry's significance
as a transmitter of antique thought rests chiefly upon his Introduction to the
Categories of Aristotle, which deals with the important metaphysical question
raised by Plato as to whether reality exists in the type (universals) or in the individual example of the type. Boëthius translated this Greek work into Latin and
most of the early medieval discussion of Aristotle's theories revolved about the
Latin version. Later in the Middle Ages it gave rise to the prolonged and animated controversy between the realists and the nominalists. Porphyry also wrote
a long commentary on Ptolemy in verse, but this was of less significance for medieval thought. Porphyry's *Sentences* constituted a good popular summary of the
influential Neoplatonic philosophy.

One of the most influential aspects of the classical heritage of the Dark Ages
was the school curriculum, which came to be known under the title of the seven
liberal arts. They were, as we have noted, divided into the trivium, or grammar,
rhetoric and logic, and the quadrivium, or arithmetic, geometry, astronomy, and
music.[3]

Aristotle had isolated most of these subjects and had written treatises on some
of them. But the Roman encyclopedist, Varro (116-27 B.C.), was the first to divide
them clearly and to comment on their content in his *Disciplinarum libri novem*.
Varro conceived of nine liberal arts, adding to the seven listed above medicine
and architecture. But, as we have noted, it was a Neoplatonic writer, Martianus
Capella, who produced the particular exposition of the seven liberal arts which
had enough prestige and influence to stereotype the curriculum of the Dark Ages
and to provide the basic educational perspective of the Middle Ages as well. This
important exposition was embodied in Capella's *Satyricon,* or *The Marriage of
Philology and Mercury,* devoted to a mystical and allegorical description of the
marriage of the god, Mercury, to the nymph, Philology. Mercury had been sowing his wild oats and the gods thought that it was about time that he settled
down. Mercury acquiesced, so they sought, contrary to Mercury's preference for
a more vivacious bride, a stable and dignified spouse for him. They found her
in Philology. The seven liberal arts appear in the allegory as presents to the
bride in the form of seven maidservants. Each comes forward, expounds the
content of her art, or branch of learning, and retires. Though the seven liberal arts
were thus separated and described, the specific term, "seven liberal arts," was
not used in Martianus' book. Taylor has given us the classic description of this
fantastic but extremely influential educational work:

> Perhaps the most widely used school book of the Middle Ages was the *De
> Nuptiis Philologiae et Mercurii* by Martianus Capella, an African Neo-platonist,
> who wrote in the first part of the fifth century. It is a work in nine books. The
> first two are devoted to the allegorical narrative of the marriage of Mercury with
> the polymath virgin Philology. Mercury seeks a bride; he cannot have Sophia or

[3] Boëthius was the first writer, so far as we know, to use the term quadrivium.

Mantice or Psyche; Virtus counsels him to ask Apollo's advice, and Apollo advises him to wed Philology. Under the joyful convoy of the Muses and enzephyred by the music of the spheres, Virtus, Apollo, and the bridegroom fly to Jove's palace to ask his consent. A council of the gods is summoned; a favorable decision is reached; the bride shall be raised to divine rank.

With the second book she appears, desiring the marriage, but fearful at the greatness of the honor. Her mother, Phronesis, adorns her for the wedding; four noble matrons, the cardinal virtues, greet her, and the Graces, with three mystic kisses, give her courage. Athanasia, daughter of Apotheosis, comes to lead her to Heaven, but first commands her to deliver that with which her bosom is seen to swell; at this she vomits forth many rolls of papyrus and of linen, which are gathered up by the Virgin Artes and Disciplinae, Urania and Calliope helping. The bride now drains the goblet of immortality, and rises to heaven, where Juno Pronuba meets her with offerings. Under the guidance of Juno, she traverses the circles of the planets and reaches the Milky Way, where Jove's palace is. There all the gods and beings known to Latin mythology assemble, with here and there a deity from Egypt, besides the guards of the elements (*elementorum praesides*) and a most beauteous company of the angelic folk and souls of blessed ancients.

Now the bride's prudent mother demands a reading of the tables of the dower and the *lex Papia Poppaeaque,* regarding the property rights of married women. Thereupon Phoebus rises and leads forward, to place with the bridal gifts, seven maid-servants from his brother's household; these are the seven Artes—Ars Grammatica; Ars Dialectica, "a little paler"; Rhetorica; Geometria; Arithmetica; Astronomia; Harmonia. Each one, as Phoebus leads her forward, tells her parentage, and then expounds the substance of her art, most dryly, all virginal allegory laid aside. They have a book apiece, and make up the tale of the nine books of Capella.

This work became the "standard" school book of the Middle Ages. Its form and character anticipates mediaeval taste, upon which it was to be so influential. It is written in prose and verse, the *chantefable* form; though the song-element is unimportant in the last seven books. These are strictly instructive, and sapless as the rods of mediaeval schoolmasters. The allegory of the first two books is pleasingly pedantic and the whole work presents the sterile union of fantasy with pedantry, so dear to the closing years of pagan scholarship, when the old straw was threshed, re-tied in queer-shaped bundles, and then threshed again. The process produced *pabulum* for coming generations.[4]

Capella thus gave the Dark Ages its academic curriculum. The first textbooks on the liberal arts were compiled by Boëthius, and by Cassiodorus and his associates. Later, such scholars as Bede and Alcuin wrote widely used manuals on the arts. The standard textbooks on grammar were, however, written by the pagan authors, Priscian and Donatus.

Perhaps the most important of the writers who transmitted a knowledge of Hellenism to the Dark Ages was Ancius Manlius Severinus Boëthius (c. 480-524). He was wealthy, of noble parentage, and well educated. Both a statesman and a scholar, he fell into disfavor with Theodoric and was executed in the forty-fourth year of his life, a great blow to the cultural heritage of the Dark Ages. He seems to have adopted the Christian faith, but was also well versed in pagan philosophy,

[4] H. O. Taylor, *The Classical Heritage of the Middle Ages,* 3d ed., Macmillan, 1911, pp. 49-51.

his enthusiasm for which was so great that he resolved to render Plato and Aristotle into Latin. As he wrote: "I shall not merit ill of my countrymen if I shall have instructed the manners of our State with the arts of Greek wisdom." He was unable to accomplish more than a fragment of his project because of his premature death, his tendency to stop and add commentaries to his translations, and his interest in writing educational tracts of his own.

Boëthius translated little or nothing from Plato's works. He translated most of Aristotle's logical treatises, adding commentaries which were drawn in part from the work of Porphyry. Only the translations of the *Categories* and the *De interpretatione* remained in general circulation among scholars, and of these the *De interpretatione* was best known during the Dark Ages.[5] Boëthius also translated Porphyry's Introduction to the *Categories,* as we have noted, and this had much greater influence on the philosophical thought of the Dark Ages than any of Boëthius' translations of Aristotle's texts or his own commentaries. Boëthius also wrote a commentary on Cicero's *Topics* which was widely read and helped to shape the metaphysical and logical thinking of the Dark Ages.

Boëthius was greatly interested in preparing educational manuals, being particularly concerned with the quadrivium. He wrote standard textbooks on arithmetic,[6] geometry and music—the geometry has been lost—and five essays on logic. A theological work, *The Catholic Faith,* has been attributed to him, but recent students doubt its authenticity. Boëthius' immortality rests on his *Consolations of Philosophy,* written while in prison awaiting execution. It is a touching fusion of Stoicism and Christianity and remained influential as late as the time of Dante.

From Boëthius, then, the Dark Ages received most of what it knew about technical Greek philosophy, particularly logic, and the terminology which went with it.[7] Neoplatonism, however, came into the cultural complex of the Dark Ages independent of Boëthius. Its chief transmitters were Augustine (indirectly), the *Celestial Hierarchy* of the pseudo-Dionysius, a merging of Christian dogmas with Neoplatonic cosmology and intellectual attitudes, and John Scotus Erigena who later translated the *Celestial Hierarchy.* Had Boëthius lived to finish his great enterprise of translating Plato and Aristotle, the intellectual life of the Dark Ages and of the whole Middle Ages might have been vastly different. As Professor Laistner has observed: "It would be fascinating to speculate on the development of medieval thought which might have resulted had Boëthius lived to complete his task of making the entire *corpus* of Aristotelian and Platonic writings available in Latin." [8]

The next important step towards shaping the cultural heritage of the Dark Ages was taken by another Christian statesman and scholar in the service of Theodoric, Flavius Magnus Aurelius Cassiodorus (c. 490-c. 583). Unlike Boëthius,

---

[5] Professor C. H. Haskins believes that all of Boëthius' Latin translation of the *Organon* may have survived in southern Italy and that Boëthius' text furnished the first Latin translation of the *Analytics* and *Sophistic Refutations* known in the twelfth century.
[6] His work on arithmetic was apparently mainly a translation of the famous *Introduction to Arithmetic* by Nicomachus of Gerasa.
[7] Cicero's writings also helped to give the Dark Ages some knowledge of pagan philosophy.
[8] M. L. W. Laistner, *Thought and Letters in Western Europe, A.D. 500 to 900,* Dial Press, 1931 (Cornell University Press, 1957), p. 61.

he remained in Theodoric's favor. About 538 he withdrew from public life in order to devote himself to scholarly pursuits in the service of the Christian faith. He retired to his former home in Bruttium and founded at Scyllacium a community of monks which produced many important works that were influential in the philosophical, educational and literary equipment of the Dark Ages. Some of his monks could read Greek, which was of great value in the translating and compiling activities.

Cassiodorus transferred the task of transmitting pagan learning to a purely Christian intellectual setting and executed it under Christian auspices. Boëthius had been motivated primarily by a lingering pagan appreciation of learning for its own sake, even though he was himself a Christian. But Cassiodorus worked under the spell of the ideals of Tertullian and Augustine who had maintained that pagan culture should be studied only as an aid to a better formulation and a more successful promulgation of Christian doctrine. Tertullian had written:

> We know it may be said that, if it is not permissible to the servants of God to teach letters, neither will it be permissible to learn them. How, then, may anyone be trained to human intelligence or to any understanding of business, since literature is the record of all life? How can we repudiate secular studies, without which divine studies are not possible? Let us, therefore, appreciate the necessity of literary learning in its incompatibility on the one hand and its inevitability on the other.

Augustine, as we have seen, took a similar view. While castigating the pagan City of the Devil, he favored exploiting its scholarly resources, insofar as they were essential to the more effective promotion of Christianity. This attitude utterly dominated the scholarly perspective of Cassiodorus and guided the literary enthusiasm of his monks. Indeed, it constitutes the main intellectual revolution produced by Cassiodorus.

A large and varied literary production flowed from Cassiodorus' scholarly community. His *Letters* give valuable information as to his political life. He wrote or supervised several historical works of great importance for the Dark Ages—a *Chronicle* or sketchy chronological survey of world history, a *History of the Goths,* which has been lost and exists only in a debased paraphrase by Jordanes, and the famous *Tripartite History,* a condensed translation from the Greek ecclesiastical historians, Socrates, Sozomen and Theodoret, who had themselves incorporated much of Eusebius' classic ecclesiastical history. This was the standard work on church history during the whole medieval period. Cassiodorus wrote theological books, including a logical work on *The Soul,* which so faithfully reproduced the Aristotelian topical arrangement as to suggest the later scholastic expositions. He also prepared commentaries on the Psalms and the Pauline Epistles.

By far his most important works, however, were his elaborate syllabi prepared to inspire and guide the scholarly labors of his monks. The first was the *Institutes of Sacred Letters,* devoted to a discussion of the proper study of the Scriptures and of the works of the fathers who had helped to interpret them. In an introductory allegory, he compared the preparation for a competent study of the Scriptures to Jacob's ladder. Advice and guidance were also given for the studying, copying, and editing of sacred writings. In his *Institutes of Secular Letters,* Cassiodorus provided a compendium of the seven liberal arts, in which the trivium, especially logic, was most extensively treated. It is worthy of note that the phrase, "seven liberal arts," was first specifically and formally used in Cassiodorus' manual. Another important educational treatise was his work on orthography, which deeply influenced the spelling-practice and word-usage of the Dark Ages.

Not only did Cassiodorus help to preserve pagan learning by his compilations; he also gathered a large library of both pagan and Christian literature, thus saving many books from the general destructiveness of his troubled times.

In a general way, we may say that Cassiodorus' significance in the intellectual history of Europe consists mainly in the fact that he first established in a large, practical way the strictly utilitarian ideal of Augustine with respect to the Christian exploitation of pagan learning—the notion that it must be thoroughly cultivated, but solely for its potential services in promoting the Christian faith.

Cassiodorus' community created the learned monastic tradition, but the leadership in executing the scholarly responsibilities of monasticism passed to Monte Cassino, founded about 530 by the above-mentioned Benedict of Nursia, author of the famous *Regula,* or *Rule,* for the discipline and administration of monastic communities in the West. He provided for the founding of a library of both sacred and secular books. Although personally not greatly interested in the copying of pagan works, he enabled his monks to do so. Many classical manuscripts were copied and preserved at Monte Cassino. Gregory the Great wrote a eulogy of Benedict and his work and thus gave great prestige to Monte Cassino. Here and at other monastic centers, especially Bobbio, St. Gall, Reichenau, Fulda, Ferrières and Luxeuil, were gathered and copied many of the ancient Latin writings, and to these monastic copyists we owe the preservation of such pagan works of the Latin West as have been saved from oblivion. There are some 772 known Latin writers. The works of 144 have come down in fragments; those of 64 have been preserved in small parts; those of 43 in large part; and the writings of 37 have been saved almost intact. Few of these writings were extensively known during the Middle Ages, but they were recovered from the monasteries by the humanist collectors and made available to later generations.

Pope Gregory the Great (540-604) was an important figure in shaping the theology of the Dark Ages and we shall deal with him later on in this regard. With respect to the transmission of pagan learning, his chief positive contribution was indirect and unintentional, namely, that exerted through his praise of Benedict and Monte Cassino. This gave added prestige to the scholarly labors of monasticism. Gregory's direct influence on learning was narrow and negative, since he was intensely intolerant of any secular learning which did not bear directly upon salvation. He wrote that: "The same mouth cannot sing the praises of Jupiter and the praises of Christ," and he had a complete contempt for the cultivation of secular studies as such.

The final stage in the transmission of pagan learning to the Christian civilization of the Dark Ages was accomplished by Bishop Isidore of Seville (d. 636), a churchman of great wealth and influence who had gathered for his use an extensive library of pagan and Christian writings. In the writings of Isidore, the outstanding Christian compiler of the early Middle Ages, we find the pagan and Christian elements inextricably merged. The composite result was purely Christian in the goals to be attained and the services to be expected of human learning. Isidore's mental attitude and scholarly methods were perfectly suited to the thought and learning of the Dark Ages. As Taylor has put it: "By reason of his own habits of study, by reason of the quality of his mind, which led him to select the palpable, the foolish, and the mechanically correlated, by reason, in fine, of his mental faculties and interests, Isidore gathered and arranged in his treatises a conglomerate of knowledge, secular and sacred, exactly suited to the coming centuries."

Isidore wrote a large number of works, most of them dominated by the allegorical or etymological approach. We cannot take the space even to enumerate them here.[9] He wrote many doctrinal, exegetical, liturgical and administrative treatises. He contributed to history through a conventional Christian *Chronicle* or world history, a scanty history of the Visigoths, and a compilation of Christian biographies. But his most famous and influential works were a treatise on physical science, the *De rerum natura,* and the first great Christian encyclopedia, the *Origines,* or, as it is more usually known, the *Etymologies.* The *De rerum natura* was a crude and often fantastic compilation from Hyginus, Solinus, the *Prata* of Suetonius, and above all, from Ambrose's *Hexaëmeron.* It was devoted chiefly to astronomy and geography.

Scientific subjects were also covered in Isidore's encyclopedic *Etymologies,* which was veritably Aristotelian in its scope, but at the opposite pole from Aristotle in knowledge, attitude, and methods. Indeed, it was far inferior even to Pliny's *Natural History,* from which, along with the works of Solinus and Varro, it borrowed heavily. It covered everything from rhetoric to law, etymology, theology, natural history, geology, the practical arts and manners and customs. Its method of presentation was roughly like our modern dictionary. In spite of its superficial and wooden character, its fantastic errors, and its theological slant, it was invaluable as a compilation of the extant knowledge of the time, and it is extremely illuminating as an exhibit of the character of the better grade of learning during the early Dark Ages. It was the most popular Christian encyclopedia down to the time of the elaborate medieval compilations of Alexander Neckham, Bartholomew the Englishman, and Vincent of Beauvais. Professor Laistner says of the *Etymologies:*

> The *Etymologies* far surpassed all other works of Isidore in popularity in the centuries that followed. The book was a *sine qua non* in every monastic library of any pretensions. . . . It was assuredly no small achievement to put together a compendious encyclopedia of the arts and sciences from many sources, at a time when the larger works of earlier authors on different branches of human knowl-

[9] For a good tabulation and summary, see Taylor, *The Medieval Mind,* I, 108.

edge were accessible in few places, and when few men, in any case, would have been capable of studying them.[10]

Ireland, not so violently disturbed by the confusion attendant upon the barbarian invasions elsewhere, was another transmitter of classical learning. The missionary monks carried to Ireland a knowledge of Greek and Latin, where it was preserved, and disseminated to England and the continent. The greatest of the Irish scholars was John Scotus Erigena (810-877), who came to live on the continent in his mature years, mainly at the court of Charles the Bald.

We have now summarized the manner in which pagan learning was in some degree preserved and transmitted to the early Middle Ages and we have indicated how it came to be infused into Christian dogma and scholarship and bent wholly to the services of the church.

In the preceding chapter we have already characterized the early Christian learning and intellectual attitudes which thus engulfed pagan knowledge. The Christian epic drew a sharp contrast between the secular world and the interests of the true Christian, and supplied a new philosophy of history based upon Old Testament lore, Persian eschatology, and Christian doctrine. A clear, definite, and dogmatic conception of the human past was thus supplied, as well as a hard and fast prediction of the brief human future. We have described the allegorical approach to holy writ and made it clear how this method enabled a Christian scholar to vault over any difficulties imposed by contradictions, seemingly incredible situations, and apparently meaningless passages. The allegorical technique spelled the death of a critical and skeptical attitude in literary scholarship. Augustine had extolled the virtues of vagueness and ambiguity in making Christian doctrine more acceptable and more widely influential. The conception of the deity formulated by such dogmatists as Ambrose, Augustine, and Gregory the Great produced the "God of arbitrariness," to use the phrase of the great church historian, Harnack—a God who seemed to be functioning in most natural and godly fashion when departing from the norms of nature and orderly conduct. Finally, we have made it plain that the learned class, from the age of the church fathers onward, was drawn chiefly from the monks who had the time, inclination and protection essential to a life of study and contemplation. With these points recalled to mind, along with the story of the transmission of paganism, we are now prepared to look more thoroughly into the thought and culture of the Dark Ages.

III. ASPECTS OF THE THOUGHT AND CULTURE OF THE DARK AGES

In examining the development of Christian thought from Augustine to Abelard it is desirable to divide the writers considered rather loosely into groups characterized by major interests. Thus we find men who were primarily compilers of pagan and Christian learning, chiefly of the latter. Such were Cassiodorus, Isidore of Seville, Rhabanus Maurus, Walafrid Strabo and the like. Then there were men who, though they were given to the compiling habit, showed a more critical and original bent. Among these were Bede, Alcuin, Servatus Lupus of Ferrières,

[10] Laistner, *op. cit.*, pp. 93-94.

Gerbert of Aurillac, and Fulbert of Chartres. We may call them the scholars of the Dark Ages. Others were devoted chiefly to philosophical problems, as in the case of Boëthius, John Scotus Erigena, Anselm, Roscellinus, and William of Champeaux. Finally, there were theologians, among them Gregory the Great, Elipand, Felix of Urgel, Claudius of Turin, Radbertus, Ratramnus, Gottschalk, Berengar, Lanfranc, and Anselm.

But any such classification can be regarded only as a mere arbitrary convenience adopted for the sake of clarification and emphasis. There were no sharp lines of demarcation between these groups. All were compilers, philosophy was invariably subordinated to theology, theologians employed philosophic terms and methods, scholars were interested in theological problems, and so on. We may first pay attention to the compilers of the Dark Ages.

Aside from school textbooks, compilations were chiefly an assembling of the opinions of the chuch fathers relative to the Scriptures and theological problems. This was the great age for citing authority as a buttress to faith. Patristic writings were searched with a fine-tooth comb and their interpretations of Scripture were collected for the instruction and edification of monks and priests. Special emphasis was placed upon allegorical and mystical interpretations of holy writ. The spirit in which such work was undertaken was admirably summarized by the famous Carolingian scholar, Alcuin of York:

> Devoutly searching the pantries of the holy Fathers, I let you taste whatever I have been able to find in them. Nor did I deem it fitting to cull the blossoms from any meadow of my own, but with humble heart and head bowed low, to search through the flowering fields of many Fathers, and thus safely satisfy your pious pleasure. First of all I seek the suffrage of Saint Augustine, who laboured with such zeal upon this Gospel; then I draw something from the tracts of the most holy doctor Saint Ambrose; nor have I neglected the homilies of Father Gregory the pope, or those of the blessed Bede, nor, in fact, the works of others of the holy Fathers. I have cited their interpretations, as I found them, preferring to use their meanings and their words, than trust to my own presumption.[11]

We have already described the compiling labors of Cassiodorus and Isidore of Seville. The first important compiler after Isidore was the industrious pupil of Alcuin, Rhabanus Maurus (c. 776-856), abbot of Fulda and archbishop of Mainz. Taylor regards him as even more learned than Alcuin. His compilations, unlike those of Isidore, were almost exclusively from Christian writers. Yet he was broadminded for his time in his appraisal of the value of pagan learning, even if he scorned pagan religious notions: "One should use the treasured experience and accumulated wisdom of the ancients, for that is still the mainstay of human society; but one should shun their vain as well as pernicious idolatries and superstitions." His intellectual attitude is well expressed in his statement that "the foundation, the state, and the perfection of wisdom is knowledge of the Holy Scriptures." His life work consisted in gathering the wisdom of earlier Christian writers in order to extend and clarify this all-important grasp upon scriptural truths.

[11] Taylor, *op. cit.*, p. 221.

Rhabanus fully appreciated the educational value of the seven liberal arts, especially the trivium, as an indispensable aid in understanding holy writ. Nor did he ignore the quadrivium, especially stressing the importance of arithmetic and astronomy in clarifying scriptural problems. Astronomy, he maintained, is capable of filling the heavens with divine love. Few scholars of his age went so far as Rhabanus in eulogizing logic as an invaluable aid to the Christian scholar and philosopher. In this respect, he foreshadowed scholasticism. He especially emphasized the value of logic "in discerning the wiles of heretics and confuting their poisoned sayings." But, throughout, he sharply emphasized that the liberal arts were not to be valued in themselves. They were merely auxiliary sciences to aid the theologian and preacher.

Since preachers have the responsibility for expounding the sacred scriptures, the clergy must be adequately trained, and one of the major compilations of Rhabanus was his work on *The Education of the Clergy*. It covered such topics as the grades of the clergy, their responsibilities, liturgy, churchly ritual, and etiquette, and the proper education of the clergy as to both content and mode of instruction. He drew most heavily on Jerome, Augustine, Gregory the Great, Isidore, Bede, and Alcuin—there was very little original material. This work was supplemented by Rhabanus with numerous scriptural commentaries, drawn from leading writers of the patristic period.

Rhabanus' most pretentious work was his vast encyclopedia, the *De universo*, in twenty-two books. This was derived in large part from Isidore's *Etymologies*, but the change of emphasis and the different allocation of space illustrates how intellectual interests had changed in two centuries. Rhabanus gave much more space than did Isidore to purely religious topics, and he added a large amount of new material from the Christian fathers. Much of the latter pertained to mysticism and allegory. Rhabanus was one of the masters of medieval allegory, which he carried to its furthest extreme in his tract on *The Praise of the Sacred Cross*. Rhabanus thus stands out as one of the major compilers of Christian knowledge and mysticism. His was one of the foremost efforts to organize and arrange the wisdom of Christian writers with respect to scriptural issues. Taylor says of him in this respect:

> Perhaps more than any other man (though here his pupil Walafrid Strabo made a skilful second), he contributed to what necessarily was the first stage in this medieval achievement of appropriating patristic Christianity, to wit, the preliminary task of rearranging the doctrinal expositions of the Fathers conveniently, and for the most part in Commentaries following verse and chapter of the canonical books of Scripture.[12]

The type of work which engaged the attention of Rhabanus was rendered even more useful by his pupil, Walafrid Strabo (806-849), abbot of Reichenau. Walafrid was less learned than Rhabanus, but he was a smoother writer. His *Glossa ordinaria* was the best of all the compilations of patristic learning which interpreted the Bible. Interlinear comments were inserted in the Gospels, and longer comments, indicating the source, were placed in the margin. Walafrid's mind ran

---

[12] Taylor, *op. cit.*, I, 224.

towards the mystical and allegorical, and his authorities were partly assembled in order to provide for the faithful such far-fetched interpretations of biblical passages. Of the work of Rhabanus and Walafrid, Professor Laistner has written:

> Men like Alcuin and Hrabanus and their pupils put succeeding generations eternally in their debt by bringing together what seemed to them the best and most readily assimilated utterances of the Fathers, and making this wisdom accessible to a greater circle of monks and clergy. In thus upholding authority and tradition, and transmitting to others the thoughts of those chiefly responsible for fixing the one and formulating the other, the Carolingian theologians were performing what they regarded with full justice as the highest of missions.[13]

This type of compilation, devoted to assembling authorities to expound and uphold the Scriptures, marked the completion of the first stage of medieval Christian scholarship and theological defense. It worked well until the time of Abelard, when the whole edifice was toppled over by the latter's famous tract, *Sic et non* (*Yea and Nay*). Abelard took up one by one the major theological propositions of the Middle Ages and showed that the leading fathers and later theological authorities differed sharply among themselves in their interpretations of holy writ and its supporting theology. To prove that these discrepancies between the revered authorities were apparent rather than real seemed the only way out. And this could be achieved solely by the use of logic. When logic was systematically called to the aid of authority, the Dark Ages in scholarship and theology came to an end and scholasticism appeared.

While the confusion in Italy, Gaul and England incident to the barbarian invasions had disrupted scholarship, Ireland remained aloof. After its conversion, monks led by Columba (521-597) were then able to devote themselves to scholarly work. A knowledge of both Greek and Latin was preserved. Missionary zeal led to the spread of this Irish learning to Great Britain and the Continent. Columba went to Scotland, taking with him Irish scholarship and Christian doctrine. Two other Irish monks, Columban (c. 530-615) and Gallus (c. 560-c. 640), led a missionary party to France, the Rhineland and Switzerland, carrying Irish learning to these regions. Aldhelm (c. 640-709) and Bede, both influenced by Irish studies, were the outstanding early English scholars. Alcuin of York, Bede's fellow countryman, later carried English scholarship to the Continent under the patronage of the illustrious Charlemagne. Hence, the intellectual tradition of the Dark Ages traveled southward from the British Isles, as well as northward from Italy.

The first important scholar of the Dark Ages after Boëthius, who belongs rather to the late patristic period, was Bede the Venerable (673-735), who, resolutely refusing high ecclesiastical office, devoted his life to learning and became one of the most thoroughly informed men in the whole Dark Ages.

Bede's general reputation in the history of European letters rests upon his famous *Ecclesiastical History of the English People,* for its time a remarkably sensible and scholarly piece of historical writing. It was one of the last examples of historical literature in the Dark Ages that still retained a considerable trace of waning classical scholarship, and remains our best contemporary source for the

---

[13] Laistner, *op. cit.,* p. 252.

history of early Anglo-Saxon England. Another important contribution by Bede to historical writing was his world chronicle, the *De ratione temporum,* one of the most valuable and influential medieval discussions of chronology, which introduced the habit of dating backward and forward from the birth of Christ, instead of from the alleged date of creation.

Bede wrote many other books, most of them didactic compilations of one sort or another, intended for the instruction of monks. He paid much attention to the development of the seven liberal arts, particularly mathematics, which he treated competently. He wrote on orthography and grammar and his treatise on versification became a standard medieval manual. Least scholarly of his works was his *De natura rerum,* a weird work on natural science gathered chiefly from Pliny and Isidore.

In volume, if not in value, the greater part of Bede's efforts was devoted to commentaries on the Scriptures and to exegetical works dealing with holy writ. In this field Bede, if not original in scholarship, possessed rather more than the usual technical equipment. He could read Greek and he had some knowledge of Hebrew. Allegory obsessed him and colored all of his commentaries, which drew mainly on the previous writings of Jerome, Augustine, and Gregory the Great. The credulity of which even a great scholar like Bede was capable is well illustrated by the passage from his *Ecclesiastical History* in which he tells of a Northumbrian Christian by the name of Cunningham who arose from the dead and gave a graphic description of his visits to Purgatory and Hell.[14]

As we noted above, the English scholarship, of which Bede was the preëminent representative in the Dark Ages, was brought to the continent by Alcuin (735-804), educated at York in the school established by the archbishop, Egbert, who had been a pupil of Bede. It was at this school that Alcuin was educated. On a trip to Rome, Alcuin met Charlemagne at Parma in 781. Feeling the need for a well-educated clergy to aid in his administrative reforms, Charlemagne prevailed upon Alcuin to head his proposed Palace School (*Schola Palatina*) at Aix-la-Chapelle. As leader of this remarkable educational enterprise, Alcuin came to be known as Flaccus Albinus. He founded other schools, the most notable at St. Martins in Tours, where he spent the latter part of his life and gathered a remarkable library.

Alcuin was a capable linguist. Like Bede, he knew Latin and Greek and had a smattering of Hebrew. His writings were of an elementary didactic character, cast in the form of dialogues, for the instruction of the Frankish clergy. Alcuin's most important textbook was his treatise on *Grammar,* which provides a fair revelation of the intellectual interests and scholarly methods of the time. It was based upon Donatus, Priscian, and Christian compilers. Alcuin also wrote an influential manual on Latin orthography. His contribution to rhetoric was an imaginary dialogue between himself and Charlemagne, *De rhetorica et virtutibus,* in which Charlemagne requests the proper information to enable him to deal with the questions of state and law which come before him. Alcuin proposes rhetoric as the solution and outlines the subject. The work was a rather crude epitome of rhetorical

---

[14] See J. H. Robinson, *Readings in European History,* Ginn, 2 vols., 1904, I, 93 ff.

ideas, drawn mainly from Cicero's *De inventione*. Far inferior to this, however, was Alcuin's treatise on logic, the *De dialectica*, derived chiefly from Boëthius and Isidore. This work was almost threadbare verbiage.

Alcuin's writings on religious subjects comprised a compendium of Augustine's views on the Trinity, a manual on practical morals, likewise taken from Augustine, and commentaries on the Scriptures culled from the fathers. This last example, as we have seen, inspired the more competent and prolific efforts of Rhabanus Maurus and Walafrid Strabo. On the whole, Alcuin's significance in European intellectual history resides in the impetus he gave to Christian compilation and scholarship in France and Germany.

One of the ablest and most erudite Latin scholars of the Dark Ages was Servatus Lupus (805-862), educated in the seven liberal arts and in religious subjects at the abbey of Ferrières, where the library facilities were limited when Lupus was a student. By good fortune, he was able to complete his studies at Fulda under Rhabanus Maurus, the foremost scholar of the day. In 842, he became abbot of Ferrières and held the office for twenty years, during which time he collected a large library of classical authors. He assembled manuscripts of such writers as Cicero, Vergil, Horace, Caesar, Livy, Sallust, Suetonius, and Aulus Gellius, and went further than most librarians and copyists of the time in seeking as many copies of a manuscript as possible, in order to compare and collate them and arrive more closely at the original text. He thus foreshadowed the external criticism of manuscripts, which was carried further many centuries later by the humanists, the Jesuits, and the Paris Benedictines. Lupus' keen and intelligent interest in Latin scholarship was demonstrated by his many epistles on the subject which have been preserved, some addressed to his friend Einhard, the biographer of Charlemagne and a cultivated Latin scholar.

Lupus' contribution to theology was contained in his *Book of Three Questions*, in which he treated the problems of free will, predestination, and redemption, and showed himself a keen logician. In this book and in his letters Lupus revealed the fact that he was also a deep student of the Bible and of patristic commentaries.

The outstanding scholar of the late tenth century—and of the whole Dark Ages —was Gerbert of Aurillac (c. 950-1003), who was later made Pope Sylvester II. He studied the liberal arts as a youth in the Benedictine monastery of Geraldus at Aurillac in Auvergne. He continued his education at Barcelona and Rome and in Rheims, where for years he was a very popular teacher in the cathedral school. His Spanish studies brought him into some contact with Arabic learning, especially in mathematics and astronomy.

Gerbert possessed a wide knowledge of the Latin poets and satirists, whom he used in teaching rhetoric, and was a master of logic, making a wider use of Boëthius' rendering of Aristotle's logic and his commentaries on Aristotle than any other scholar before the latter part of the twelfth century. His most original work, however, was done in the less cultivated field of the quadrivium, where he gave erudite and advanced instruction in all four subjects. He was especially ingenious in teaching astronomy, and seems to have been familiar with the parallels of latitude and with the use of the astrolabe. Gerbert was not only immensely learned for his day, but had thoroughly digested his information. There was in his work a finish and polish that had been lacking in the scholars of the three previous centuries. Taylor says of his scholarly achievements as a whole:

> Gerbert was the first mind of his time, its greatest teacher, its most eager learner, and most universal scholar. His pregnant letters reflect a finished man who has mastered his acquired knowledge and transformed it into power. They also evince the authorship of one who had uniquely profited from the power and spirit of the great minds of the pagan past, had imbibed their sense of form and pertinency, and with them had become self-contained and self-controlled.[15]

Fulbert of Chartres (c. 960-1028), is important in the scholarship of the closing years of the Dark Ages chiefly because he created a great school of the seven liberal arts and classical learning at Chartres, which had been an ancient seat of learning in Gaul. As bishop of Chartres from 1008-1028 he made the cathedral school there the foremost educational institution, with perhaps the largest enrollment, in northern Europe. Fulbert had studied under Gerbert and took full advantage of the erudition of his master. Complete instruction was given in all branches of the seven arts. The textbooks used at Chartres give a splendid illustration of the authorities who reigned before the rise of universities and the dominion of scholasticism. Not only Christian compilations and manuals were used, but also a large collection of pagan authorities on grammar, rhetoric, and logic. A new and enthusiastic interest in the Latin classics was promoted. Even medicine was taught in the form of debased fragments of Hippocratic writings, rendered into verse by Fulbert. The school at Chartres is historically significant because it exemplified the final fruition of scholarship and pedagogy during the Dark Ages. The work of Fulbert was carried on at Chartres by Bernard of Chartres (c. 1120), Theodore of Chartres (c. 1150), whose *Eptateuchon* was a popular manual of the seven liberal arts, and by the famous John of Salisbury (1110-1180). At the close of the twelfth century a rival to Chartres as the leader in the study of the arts and the pagan classics arose at Orleans.

From the time of Boëthius to the origins of the debate between the realists and nominalists in the late eleventh century there was only one original philosopher of outstanding ability. He was John Scotus Erigena (810-877), an Irishman who drifted to the court of Charles the Bald and entered the palace school there about 847. Erigena, the only eminent lay scholar of the Dark Ages, was one of the few men of his generation in the West who could read Greek easily. His chief excursion into scholarship was the translation of the difficult *Celestial Hierarchy* of the so-called pseudo-Dionysius. This, as we have seen, was the work of a Christian mystic of Syria. Dionysius attempted to fuse Neoplatonism and Christianity and thus check the former's growth as a pagan philosophical rival of Christian theology. Dionysius believed that if doctrines identical with Neoplatonism could be found in a Christian book, Christians would no longer be tempted to read pagan works on Neoplatonism. In addition, this might also help to convert pagan Neoplatonists to Christianity. Partly to make it seem earlier than the works of Plotinus

---

[15] Taylor, *op. cit.*, I, 286.

and the Neoplatonists and partly to give it added authority with Christians, the author represented this fifth-century work as written in the apostolic age. The *Celestial Hierarchy* contained the most complete version of Christian doctrines concerning the heavenly hierarchy or angelology. As such, it exerted a deep influence on medieval art. Erigena completed his Latin translation about 858.

Erigena's claim to fame as one of the major figures in the history of philosophy rests upon his effort to reinterpret the Christian world-philosophy and theology in terms of Neoplatonic mysticism, a feat he accomplished in his *De divisione naturae* (*On the Division of the Universe*), which he issued about 870. This was a closely reasoned product, possessing philosophic unity and intellectual coherence. It differed widely from such loose and lifeless compilations as those of his contemporary, Rhabanus Maurus.

Erigena held that reason might be a more powerful instrument for ascertaining truth than either authority or faith. Indeed, as Reginald Lane Poole points out, he suggested that authority must be derived from reason. In this respect, he stood at one with Abelard. Yet Erigena was not a premature scholastic and he had nothing in common with the scholastics save his emphasis on reason. He was a Christian mystic with Neoplatonic leanings, while the scholastics were adherents of Aristotelianism. Erigena praised logic, while the scholastics reduced theology to a logical system. Professor Laistner pays the following tribute to the genius of Erigena and correctly warns against identifying him with the scholastic tradition:

> It was only John Scotus who, having mastered the dialectic method in a manner quite unapproached by any medieval thinker before the great days of scholasticism, proceeded to build up a philosophical system as impressive as it was unique. . . . Unlike his fellow-theologians, he so mastered the teaching contained in his sources, and so fused and even transmuted it, that the result was a work original in its substance and highly individual in its style. . . . Apart from his skilful use of dialectic, . . . there is no common ground between him and the Schoolmen. In the history of philosophy he is a figure of isolated grandeur.[16]

The philosophy of the Dark Ages came to an end with the revival of a vigorous debate that had originated back in pagan times. The intellectual ferment that stimulated Abelard, the rise of the medieval universities, and the perfection of scholastic philosophy, was brought into being by the struggle between the realists and the nominalists. The former were followers of Plato who believed that reality exists only in the general class or type of objects, that class terms or universals have a real existence apart from particular things. The latter went to the opposite extreme and held that there is no reality except in individual or concrete examples of things—particulars—namely, specific horses, men, chairs, stars, and the like.

These abstract issues fail to stir much interest today, but nearly a thousand years ago they were as vital as discussions of the stock market, world-finance, the rise of totalitarianism, the Supreme Court, relativity, or evolution are in our day. They bore directly upon the interpretation of the power, organization, and doctrines of the church. Realism corresponded with the orthodox theory of the church

[16] Laistner, *op. cit.*, pp. 268, 273.

universal. Hence, the controversy was linked to that most important of all medieval issues, the salvation of the immortal soul. The general principles involved also provided much of the theoretical background for the conciliar movement of the fifteenth century, and the struggles between absolute and limited monarchy in the government of the medieval church. It was a question whether reality existed in the church universal or in the individual members of the church. The revival of nominalism by William of Ockham and others in the fourteenth century helped to promote the intellectual ferment that preceded the Protestant revolt. Indeed, the debate has not lost interest even in our day. The American Civil War was fought over a concrete political expression of the principles involved in the realist-nominalist controversy. The issue was whether political reality existed in the unified federal state or in the several separate commonwealths.

The first important philosopher to espouse the realist position was the Platonist, Erigena, with whom we have just dealt. But the controversy did not gain any headway until two centuries after his time. Then Anselm (1033-1109), archbishop of Canterbury, and a French thinker, William of Champeaux (c. 1070-1121), defended realism with zest. Most of the leading scholastic philosophers, like Albert the Great and Thomas Aquinas, were moderate realists. The first notable nominalist was a French philosopher, Jean Roscellinus (b. c. 1050). In the thirteenth century, the nominalist view became implicit in the writings of Roger Bacon (1214-1294). It was revived with much vigor and important intellectual consequences by William of Ockham (1280-1349).

Among all the possible groupings of the thinkers of the Dark Ages the most arbitrary would be the designation of certain writers as theologians. All the compilers, scholars and philosophers of the era were primarily theologians. Theology was the queen of the sciences and all learning was chiefly devoted to promoting a better knowledge of divine truth. Even the one great lay philosopher of the age, Erigena, wrote his chief work with a theological aim and engaged in many theological controversies. Yet it is possible to select the most important figures who dealt with the leading theological issues during the period we are studying. It is with these that we shall now concern ourselves.

The preëminent Christian theologian before Thomas Aquinas was, of course, Augustine, whose work we have already described. Next in time came Gregory the Great (540-604), who best represented the transition in Christian thought from the patristic age to the Dark Ages. The typical attitude of the period, with its absorption in the miraculous, allegorical and mystical implications of Christianity, became a habitual frame of mind with Gregory. He was deeply interested in demonology and his writings on Christian penance were particularly vivid and precise, but his chief significance lies in the fact that he was the purveyor of patristic Christianity to the Dark Ages. As Taylor expresses it:

> Gregory was a purveyor of theology. He purveyed matter very much to the mediaeval taste. . . . The converging currents—decadence and barbarism—meet and join in Gregory's powerful personality. He embodies the intellectual decadence which has lost all independent wish for knowledge and has dropped the whole round of the mind's mortal interests; which has seized upon the near, the tangible,

and the ominous in theology till it has rooted religion in the fear of hell. All this may be viewed as a decadent abandonment of the more intellectual and spiritual complement to the brute facts of sin, penance, and hell barely escaped. But, on the other hand, it was also barbarization, and held the strength of barbaric narrowing of motives and the restlessness of barbaric fear.[17]

In the eighth century there was a vigorous controversy over the constitution of the Trinity and the relation of Christ to God. The old Adoptionist heresy was revived in the writings of Elipand (c. 775), archbishop of Toledo, and of Felix (c. 800), bishop of Urgel. This interpretation laid special stress on the humanity of Jesus. It was contended that Jesus was not inherently or by nature the son of God—He became the son only through divine grace and adoption into the Godhead. This unorthodox position was vigorously combated by Alcuin in his dogmatic work on the Trinity.

The issue of image worship came to a head in the ninth century, the era of the iconoclastic controversy. The most vigorous and relentless foe of image worship in the West was Claudius, bishop of Turin (d. c. 830). He believed that the element of personal responsibility for salvation should be emphasized. Rites, mediation, formal good works, and the like, were unimportant to him. "The worship of images, of pictures, of the Cross itself," says Reginald Lane Poole, "the belief in the mediation of the saints, the efficacy of pilgrimages, the authority of the holy see, seemed to him but the means of deadening the responsibility of individual men." [18] Claudius offered a *reductio ad absurdum* of the habit of venerating relics and memorials of the life of Jesus: "You worship all wood fashioned after the manner of a cross, because for six hours Christ hung upon a cross. Worship then all virgins, because a virgin bare him. Worship stables, for he was born in one; old rags, for he was swaddled in them; ships, for he often sailed in them; asses, for he rode thereon." Claudius' attitude was defended, though more temperately, by Agobard, archbishop of Lyons.

As we have seen, the very core of Catholic Christianity is the Eucharist or the sacrament of the Mass. It was natural that discussion of this vital issue would figure largely in the theological writings of the Dark Ages.

The first important book ever devoted exclusively to a consideration of the Eucharist was the *Sacrament of the Body and Blood of Our Lord* by Paschasius Radbertus, abbot of Corbie, published in 844. He upheld the literal doctrine of transubstantiation, though he did not use the term. He contended that in the sacrament of the Mass the bread and wine become the literal body and blood of Christ, a miracle worked only for believers who have sufficient faith. This theory of the Eucharist implied the "constant repetition by God of a stupendous miracle" with each celebration of the Eucharist. In the act of communion, Radbertus contended, the faithful partake only of the spiritual body and blood of Jesus, though in the miracle of the Mass itself the bread and wine are transformed into the actual physical body and blood. Though this view ultimately became the accepted

17 Taylor, *op. cit.*, I, 102-3.
18 R. L. Poole, *Illustrations of the History of Medieval Thought and Learning,* Dover Publications, Inc., 1960, p. 27.

doctrine of the church, Radbertus' insistence upon a literal interpretation of the alleged words of Christ at the Last Supper is in sharp contrast to the then prevalent allegorical interpretations of the Scriptures which were frequently of a very farfetched character.

The position taken by Radbertus was attacked by Ratramnus, a monk of the same monastery of Corbie. The latter held that the Eucharist was only a memorial of the real sacrifice of Jesus on the cross. What lies on the altar is not the real historical body of Jesus, but the "mystery" of the body—the spiritual body. The communion is only a symbolic commemoration of the sacrifice of Christ. Ratramnus' contention was stoutly upheld two centuries later by Berengar (d. 1088), head of the cathedral school at Tours and a powerful controversialist. In his day, the interpretation of the Eucharist had become exceedingly crude and materialistic. Even the consecrated communion wafer was looked upon as a literal part of the body of Jesus "broken by the hands of priests and chewed by the teeth of the faithful." Berengar protested that the real presence of Jesus is only "spiritually conceived and received." There is no literal transformation into the actual body and blood of Jesus. Berengar was hotly answered by a famous churchman, Lanfranc (d. 1089), bishop of Bec and later archbishop of Canterbury. He went even beyond Radbertus by declaring that not only did the Eucharist involve the literal miracle of transforming the bread and wine into the body and blood of Jesus, but that even sinners eat it at communion in spite of themselves. No act of faith is required for the miracle. Berengar was compelled to recant upon threat of the death penalty by the Lateran Council of 1059.

A little over a half-century later, the doctrine of transubstantiation, a term first used by Hildebert of Tours in the early twelfth century, became an official dogma of the church. In the fourth Lateran Council (1215) the dogma of transubstantiation was adopted: "The body and blood of Christ are truly contained in the sacrifice of the altar under the appearance of bread and wine, the bread being transubstantiated into the body, and the wine into the blood by divine power." Thus triumphed the views of Radbertus and Lanfranc.

A bitter controversy over the doctrine of predestination was stirred up by Fulgentius Gottschalk (d. 868) in the ninth century. He had been brought up at Fulda but later went to Corbie, where he studied under Ratramnus. In 848 he presented his views before the synod of Mainz, a straightforward and uncompromising doctrine of predestination. God by his grace has predestined some to eternal life, and others by his justice to everlasting punishment. Those predestined to salvation cannot be lost through any earthly conduct, while not even the sacraments can save those predestined to damnation. Christ died only for those predestined to be saved.

It was only natural that this position should be fiercely assailed by ecclesiastical authorities. By direct implication, this doctrine branded them as parasites. As Professor Herbert Workman says:

> If saint and sinner were already predestinated, of what use were the intercessions of saints, or even the Eucharistic sacrifice? For if all is immutable decree, there is

neither need nor logic in prayer, penance, or worship. These things are but idle beatings of the wings against the prison bars. The Eucharist itself becomes powerless, as Gottschalk owned, "for those who perish." Such a doctrine, as its later developments in Geneva show, inevitably struck at the power of the priest.[19]

Little wonder, then, that the ecclesiastical hierarchy discerned in Gottschalk's doctrine a threat to their very existence or that they immediately imprisoned him in the monastery of Hautvilliers, kept him there until he died twenty years later, and cruelly flogged him and otherwise maltreated him while in prison. Rhabanus and Hincmar took the lead in these ecclesiastical brutalities.

The theological reasoning of the Dark Ages culminated in the writings of Anselm, whom we have already referred to as the first important medieval realist. Anselm devoted himself to three major problems of theology: the existence of God, the nature of God and the modes of his expression, and the logic of the redemption through Jesus.

Anselm's first theological treatise was his *Monologium* or *Soliloquy,* in which he attempted to prove the existence of God and to show his manifestations. He relied on the cosmological argument that we must conceive of a supreme good and of a supreme being higher than all others. In a later treatise, the *Proslogion,* Anselm developed his famous ontological argument for the existence of God. Even a fool, said Anselm, recognizes in his mind that there is a being, greater than whom none can be conceived. Indeed, the fool who argues against God's existence implies in his very denial this idea of a supreme and perfect being. The existence of this concept in the mind directly involves its existence in reality. Anselm proceeded to eulogize God as the supreme being and to illustrate his manifestations through his love for man and his utterances in holy writ.

In his doctrine of the atonement, Anselm denied the popular notion of the church fathers that the sacrifice of Christ was a ransom paid to the devil. The debt was not owed to Satan but to God. Only God himself is great enough to render satisfaction for man's sins. But man owed the debt to God because it was man's sins that had impugned the honor of God. Hence, only the God-man, Jesus, could make restitution. In voluntarily laying down His life, and in this way alone, could satisfaction be rendered to God for the sins of man. No punishment of Christ for the sins of man was involved; His sacrifice merely rendered satisfaction to God for human sins.

All of these dogmas Anselm attempted to prove by the use of reason alone, without recourse to revelation. In this sense he anticipated the attitude of the scholastics, though he lacked the refined technique which they possessed as a result of superior logical training and a full possession of the resources of Aristotle.

In addition to these writers on theological doctrine, there were others who made important contributions to the practical problems of church administration, notably Gregory the Great, Agobard (779-840), archbishop of Lyons, and Hincmar (806-882), archbishop of Rheims.

[19] H. B. Workman, *Christian Thought to the Reformation,* Scribner, 1914, p. 149.

In any account of the theological activity of the Dark Ages one must emphasize the influence exerted by the *Celestial Hierarchy,* especially after its translation into Latin by Erigena. Through it Neoplatonism achieved its most potent contact with medieval theological thought. It emphasized especially the saving attitude of credulity in matters religious, the mystical approach to religion, and the reality of communion with divinity through ecstasy and visions. As the main source of knowledge and inspiration relative to the angels, it also deeply affected, as we have noted, medieval art.

IV. EARLY MEDIEVAL EDUCATION

The formal educational system of the Dark Ages, aside from the lay training of future nobles in the responsibilities of chivalry, was entirely in the hands of the church. And education for chivalry barely got under way during the Dark Ages. Aside from such an unusual institution as the palace school of Charlemagne, where there were some lay students, education in this era existed almost solely for the moral and religious instruction of Christians and for the training of those who were to instruct the faithful.

Moral and religious training for the mass of believers was mainly in the hands of parish priests, though they were often aided by monks. Quick to recognize the value of shaping minds while they were still young and pliant, the church began its religious instruction of Catholic children at an early age. In the catechetical schools, it taught the essentials of Christian faith and practice by means of catechisms and other simple pedagogical devices. The teachings of the church were final in all matters of faith and morals.

Instruction in the arts, letters and sciences was equally monopolized by ecclesiastics, who constituted the sole literate class. Only churchmen possessed enough information to enable them to be teachers. Likewise, it was not thought worth while in the Dark Ages to offer academic instruction to anybody save those who expected to enter the service of the church in some direct manner—or who, as learned churchmen, might serve the state. Since most of the textbooks were written or compiled by learned clerics, it was literally true that academic education in the Dark Ages was something of, for and by churchmen. General mass education or special training for the lay professions was unknown at that time in western Europe.

There were no universities —they came into being only in the twelfth century. The main western European educational institutions during the Dark Ages were the catechetical schools, the monastic schools, and the cathedral or episcopal schools. Monastic schools were most important and numerous, but towards the end of the Dark Ages the cathedral schools gained in number and prestige. Even in the schools connected with the cathedrals most of the teachers were monks. The leading monastic and episcopal institutions of education were at Rheims, Chartres, Tours, Ferrières, Cluny, Bec, Laon, Orleans, Lyons, Paris, Luxeuil, Auxerre, and Fleury in France; Fulda, St. Gall, and Reichenau in Germany;

Bobbio and Monte Cassino in Italy; Liége and Tournai in the Netherlands; Jarrow, York and Canterbury in England; and Clonard, Clonmacnois, and Durrow in Ireland. The two most famous were the palace school created by Charlemagne at his capital, over which Alcuin presided, and the great cathedral school which Bishop Fulbert built at Chartres in northern France. The dominance of monastic educational activities in the Dark Ages has been well summarized by Professor Paul Monroe:

> The monasteries were the sole schools for teaching; they offered the only professional training; they were the only universities of research; they alone served as publishing houses for the multiplication of books; they were the only libraries for the preservation of learning; they produced the only scholars; they were the sole educational institutions of this period. In each of these lines their activities were, to be sure, meager; but the opportunities were meager, and however great the needs, the conscious social demands of the times were more meager still.[20]

The content of education in these early medieval monastic schools was slight, dull, and largely tuned to the service of religious instruction. Specifically it was limited to the seven liberal arts, and to religious subjects. For the most part, instruction did not go beyond the first three, the so-called trivium. The textbooks commonly used, about which we shall have more to say later, were crude summary manuals, many of them written by associates of Cassiodorus and by Isidore of Seville. In addition to these, students searched Augustine and Boëthius for references to classical culture, made use of Martianus Capella's famous *Marriage of Philology and Mercury,* and sometimes consulted the standard Roman manuals on grammar by Priscian and Donatus. Most of the work of the great Roman rhetorician, Quintilian, was lost in the Dark Ages, and not recovered until Poggio found a manuscript in the so-called Renaissance. Rhetoric was therefore studied in the works of patristic and medieval compilers and in fragments of Roman literature. The leading scholar of the age of Charlemagne, the English monk Alcuin, described education in a monastic school as follows:

> The learned Albert gave drink to thirsty minds at the fountain of the sciences. To some he communicated the art and the rules of grammar; for others he caused floods of rhetoric to flow; he knew how to exercise these in the battles of jurisprudence, and those in the songs of Adonia; some learned from him to pipe Castilian airs and with lyric foot to strike the summit of Parnassus; to others he made known the harmony of the heavens, the courses of the sun and the moon, the five zones of the pole, the seven planets, the laws of the course of the stars, the motions of the sea, earthquakes, the nature of men, and of beasts, and of birds, and of all that inhabit the forest. He unfolded the different qualities and combinations of numbers; he taught how to calculate with certainty the solemn return of Eastertide, and, above all, he explained the mysteries of the Holy Scriptures.[21]

The scantiness of learning and educational facilities, and the permeating illiteracy even during the Carolingian literary revival, has been described by Taylor:

---

[20] Paul Monroe, *Textbook in the History of Education,* Macmillan, 1911, p. 255.
[21] Cited by Monroe, *op. cit.,* p. 261.

Engaged, as we have been, with the intellectual or scholarly interests of the Carolingian period, we should not forget how slender in numbers were the men who promoted them, and how few were the places where they throve. There was the central group of open-minded laymen and Churchmen about the palace school, or following the Court on its journeyings, which were far and swift. Then there were the monastic or episcopal centers of education as at Tours, or Rheims, or Fulda. The scholars carried from the schools their precious modicum of knowledge, and passed through life as educated men living in the world, or dwelt as learned compilers, reading in the cloister. But scant were the rays of their enlightening influence amidst that period's vast encompassing ignorance.[22]

The curriculum, as already observed, was dull and meager. Instruction in the seven liberal arts usually meant only intensive training in the trivium, with slight attention to the quadrivium. It was only in such institutions as the cathedral school at Rheims, where Gerbert taught, or at Chartres under Fulbert, that systematic and competent instruction was given in the quadrivium.

The content of these seven arts was quite different from what is presented in a textbook of our day. Grammar was the basic study in the curriculum. Since it encompassed both language and literature at the time, it was the foundation of all other studies. As Rhabanus Maurus wrote, "grammar is the knowledge which interprets poets and historians; it is also the method of correct writing and speech. It is both the source and the basis of the liberal arts." The ability to read and write the medieval Latin in which all learned instruction and discussion was carried on, formed a part of grammar, under which was also included the parts of speech, word-usage, and the like, presented drily and formally. In addition, emphasis was placed on the magical and religious (allegorical) significance of certain words. Rhetoric embraced the canons of artificial style and oratorical presentation. Dialectic or logic embodied a summary of logical categories and nomenclature and the elementary laws of argumentation, and was, for the most part, dull and uninspired, but was especially prized for its possible aid to theological disputation.

Arithmetic in the Dark Ages had little resemblance to our subject with its multiplication tables, mensuration, computations of compound interest, and the like. There were no Arabic numbers in those days. To understand what this meant, let the reader set himself a problem in long division using Roman numerals. There were no exercises in practical computation. The latter was a secular art, for which the Roman abacus or counting-board might be used, not unlike the devices employed by Chinese laundrymen today. For the most part, arithmetic meant a study of the properties of numbers, especially the theory of ratio and proportion, and the magical traits and allegorical significance of particular numbers. It was more a branch of "mystics" than of mathematics.

In geometry only insignificant portions of the great work of Euclid were preserved and used. The magical and mystical properties of geometrical figures were emphasized. Astronomy was debased Ptolemaic lore. The geocentric theories were emphasized and much was made of the sacred circular motions of the heavens.

[22] Taylor, *op. cit.*, I, 235-36.

The religious significance of the heavenly bodies was stressed, and the whole subject tended to shade off into astrology. The most practical aspects of astronomy were computations relating to the church calendar. In music there was little practical instruction. The subject was limited mainly to the mathematical study of musical sounds and to a description of musical terms and instruments. In the better schools some work was offered dealing with liturgy and church music. Much mystical and allegorical material was presented. Boëthius, for example, stressed "the music of the spheres."

Secular learning was designed as the doorway to theology, the true queen of the sciences. Until the standard textbook on theology had been prepared by Peter Lombard in the later Middle Ages, theology was first studied in Cassiodorus' *Institutes of Sacred Letters,* in the theological compilations of Isidore of Seville and of Bede, and in certain treatises of Augustine and Gregory. After the extensive compilations of scriptural commentaries became available, much use was made of such manuals as the *Glossa ordinaria* of Walafrid Strabo.

We have already referred incidentally to some of the textbooks of the Dark Ages. The most popular general introductions to all the seven liberal arts were the compendium of Martianus Capella, Cassiodorus' *Institutes of Secular Letters,* and the compilations of Isidore of Seville. For grammatical studies the standard texts were Donatus' (c. 350) Latin grammar, *Ars grammatica minor* and *Ars grammatica major* (especially the section "On the Eight Parts of Speech"), compiled in the fourth century, and the manual by Priscian (c. 500), *The Institutes of Grammar.* Donatus was far the most popular. To guide study in versification, the standard text became Bede's *De arte metrica.* In rhetoric, there was no basic text drawn from the classical period. Quintilian was lost in the Dark Ages. Teachers relied upon compilations of the rules of the rhetoricians prepared by Cassiodorus, Isidore, Bede, and Alcuin. Students were also introduced to a few works of great classical orators and leading Christian preachers. In studying logic, those schools which were least equipped used the compilations of Cassiodorus and Isidore. At the best ones, as at Chartres under Fulbert, Boëthius' translations of Aristotle's *Categories* and *De interpretatione,* and of Porphyry's Introduction to the *Categories,* and Cicero's *Topica,* were available.

With respect to the quadrivium, the standard textbook on arithmetic was Boëthius' *De arithmetica,* based on the Hellenistic work of Nicomachus of Gerasa. Boëthius also provided the only passable manuals on geometry and astronomy. For astronomy students also used the scanty and vulgarized versions of Ptolemy found in such works as Isidore's *De rerum natura,* his *Etymologies,* and Bede's compilations. At the end of the period some students had at hand the remarkable studies of Gerbert. In the field of music, Boëthius had also written the best and most popular treatise. We have already indicated the basic texts in theology. We shall describe the compendiums of natural science which were utilized in the Dark Ages in the next section dealing with the natural science of the time.

History was neglected in the schools. When it was cultivated there were two main textbooks: in secular history, Orosius' *Seven Books of History against the Pagans,* a grossly warped and scanty Christian interpretation of the pagan past;

in church history the *Tripartite History,* translated and adapted from Greek ecclesiastical historians under the supervision of Cassiodorus. The latter was more adequate and competent than Orosius' compilation. Historical chronology was derived from Jerome's Latin version of Eusebius' *Chronicle* or from Bede's manual. The sharp distinction drawn by the fathers between sacred and profane history was faithfully continued. It endured until the time of Bayle (1700).

We have noted the fact that the majority of teachers were monks. In the monastic schools the abbot of the monastery had final control over the education it carried on. The supervision was handed over to a scholarly subordinate, called a *scolasticus.* In the case of the cathedral schools, the chancellor of the cathedral chapter licensed teachers, supervised the schools, decided when a new school was desirable, and conducted the examinations. As an educational director the chancellor was known as an *archiscolus.* His control over examinations lasted well down into the period of the rise of universities.

Several things should stand out clearly from this survey of education in the Dark Ages. It was conducted for the church by church officials. It was designed chiefly to prepare persons for an ecclesiastical career, though churchmen so trained might often serve the state as well. The content of education mirrored the age. It embodied the use of a pagan curriculum and compilations of pagan learning, in order better to understand and promote Christianity. Finally, while we cannot but admire anybody who had any interest in learning in those days, the fact remains that the education of the period was hopelessly inadequate, superficial and dreary, and that it touched only the favored few. The mass of mankind remained starkly illiterate.

V. NATURAL SCIENCE IN THE DARK AGES

The attitude of the scholars of the Dark Ages towards science was perfectly logical. The queen of sciences was theology, that branch of learning which taught man how to save his soul. All other aspects of learning were logically subordinate to it and of real and immediate interest to Christians only insofar as they might indirectly aid theology. We have seen that this was true of literary studies, of history, and of the seven liberal arts. It was equally true of science. The latter was not valued for its own sake or for the light it threw upon the physical universe and organic life. It was significant solely as another handmaiden of theology. Scientific facts were of vital interest only as illustrations or illuminations of the problems of the supernatural world. Matters pertaining to the material world became truly relevant only if they helped to clarify the perplexities presented by the hypothetical spiritual world. We noted in the previous chapter how this attitude towards natural science was established by the church fathers.

In the Dark Ages this debasement of natural science bore its logical fruit in the ignorance and fantasy which passed for scientific information. Much of the natural science known to the church fathers, even though they did not prize it, was now lost. To the Dark Ages were available only inferior patristic compilations of classical lore, and these were exploited mainly for their alleged theological and mystical implications. Had the best of classical scientific compilations been handed down to the Dark Ages the situation might have been much improved, in spite of the secondary rôle assigned to science. As Charles Singer has observed:

> It is a world-misfortune that Boëthius did not see his way to prepare versions of those works of the Peripatetic school that displayed powers of observation. Had a translation of Aristotle's *Historia animalium* or *De generatione animalium* survived, or had a Latin version of the work of Theophrastus on plants reached the earlier Middle Ages, the whole mental history of the race might have been different.[23]

Instead, the Dark Ages depended upon compilations by the less competent classical scientists, or upon compilations of compilations, thus getting doubly debased and distorted versions of pagan scientific knowledge. For example, Isidore would compile from Pliny, and then Bede would prepare a compilation based on Isidore. Sometimes this process went even to a third degree, when some compiler would paraphrase Bede's compilation of Isidore's compilation of Pliny's material, which was itself drawn from earlier Greek and Roman compilers.

The chief pagan sources tapped by the compilers of scientific lore in the Dark Ages were, above all, Pliny's *Natural History,* fragments of Ptolemy, Hyginus' *Astronomica,* Suetonius' *Prata,* Solinus' *Wonders of the World,* and the astronomical vagaries of the leader of Neoplatonism, Plotinus, who had much to say about the mystical and magical aspects of astronomy. Next to Pliny, whose encyclopedia of wonders we have already described, perhaps the most prized pagan author was Solinus, author of a work on geographical marvels to which we made reference earlier. In addition to geographical matters, Solinus had also culled from Pliny some of the latter's material on man, animals, and precious stones. Beginning with Martianus Capella and Isidore, medieval compilers of scientific data made much use of Solinus.

Such medical lore as was known in the Dark Ages emanated from fragmentary translations into Latin of the treatises of Hippocrates, Galen, Dioscorides, Origasius, Alexander of Tralles, and Paul of Aegina, as well as fake manuals attributed to some of them.[24] Medicine was chiefly in the hands of monks, and some of the surgery was done by surgeon-barbers.

We have already dealt with most of the scientific compilers of the Dark Ages in other connections. It will be necessary to recall only a few to mind. Martianus Capella was the first. His treatment of astronomy contained a reference to the heliocentric theory of the universe which had been promulgated by certain Hellenistic astronomers. It was ignored by medieval Christian astronomers, perhaps because it challenged their geocentric theology, but it may have influenced Copernicus, who had read Martianus' work. We have already explained how Boëthius, on the basis of Hellenistic manuals, had provided the standard texts on arithmetic, geometry, and music used during the Dark Ages. He had gathered this

---

[23] In F. J. C. Hearnshaw, ed., *Medieval Contributions to Modern Civilization,* Holt, 1922, pp. 115-16.
[24] Cf. Thorndike, *History of Magic and Experimental Science,* Vol. I, chap. xxvi.

material from pagan scholars. The content of these manuals has already been described.

A characteristic scientific compilation of the Dark Ages, both as to intent and content, was the *De cursibus ecclesiasticis* by the historian of the Franks, Gregory of Tours (538-594). It was a short astronomical treatise written to enable the clergy to tell time at night by studying the constellations. Such information would permit them to perform their sacred nocturnal rites at the proper hour. It was the best astronomical work of the Dark Ages until the time of Gerbert. It included an interesting summary of the seven chief wonders of God and man. The former were the tides, growth of plants, the phoenix, Mount Etna, the hot springs at St. Barthelemy, the course of the sun, and the phases of the moon. The main human wonders were Noah's ark, Babylon, Solomon's temple, the Persian mausoleum, the colossus of Rhodes, the theater at Heraclea, and the lighthouse at Alexandria.

Isidore's *Etymologies* was the first notable Christian encyclopedia of science. To its dreary compiling traits were added the nonscientific etymological interests of the author and his antiscientific concern with allegory. These markedly reduced whatever scientific merit the work might have possessed. Professor Laistner has given a good summary of the diversity of sources upon which Isidore drew: "Patristic literature is represented by Tertullian, Lactantius, Jerome, Augustine, and Gregory the Great; secular literature by Pliny, Solinus, Orosius, Servius' commentary on Vergil and other Vergilian *scholia*, Hyginus' *Astronomica*, and the *scholia* on Germanicus's *Aratea*, Placidus, Donatus, Cassiodorus's *Institutione saecularium lectionum*, and other writers on the trivium, Victorinus and Boëthius' logical or scientific writings, Latin translations of Greek medical authors and Gargilius Martialis, Palladius, and the Agrimensores on agriculture and kindred topics." [25] Isidore encouraged the tendency to regard astrology as a legitimate branch of astronomy—he regarded it as half magic and half sound science. He was the main source for the later Christian compilers of scientific data during the Dark Ages.

The scientific knowledge and acumen of the Venerable Bede have been highly praised by many historians of medieval thought, including the eminent Reginald Lane Poole. But Professor Thorndike ridicules such an appraisal:

> Bede perhaps knew more natural science than anyone else of his time, but if so, the others must have known practically nothing; his knowledge can in no sense be called extensive. As a matter of fact, we have evidence that his extremely brief and elementary treatises in this field were not full enough to satisfy even his contemporaries. [26]

Bede's *De natura rerum* was a brief compilation of astronomy and meteorology, drawn chiefly from Isidore, with some references to Pliny. Bede's *Liber de temporibus* was a school text on the divisions of time and the seasons, taken from Isidore, Pliny, and Macrobius. Bede's most creditable scientific achievement con-

[25] Laistner, *op. cit.,* p. 93.
[26] Thorndike, *op. cit.,* I, 634.

cerned chronology, where his *De ratione temporum* exerted a wide influence. It naturally accepted the sacred chronology of Eusebius and Jerome.

Alcuin's interests tended more toward the trivium than toward science, in which he merely passed on the lore of Isidore and Bede. His pupil Rhabanus Maurus compiled, as we have seen, the next great Christian encyclopedia after Isidore's *Etymologies,* but we also noted that he was mainly concerned with the collection of material on religious subjects. His scientific data were derived chiefly from Isidore and he was mainly interested in astronomy which he felt could be made especially edifying for Christian readers.

With Gerbert, as we have observed, there came a new interest in natural science, at least in the quadrivium. Gerbert mastered the textbook mathematics of the Dark Ages and also gathered some knowledge of classical and Muslim mathematics in the course of his studies in Spain. He was the forerunner of the revival of scientific knowledge in the later Middle Ages when the Muslim influence became more marked and some consideration was given to the direct observation of natural phenomena.

We may now consider briefly the content of the major natural sciences as cultivated in the Dark Ages. Astronomy was fused with astrology, magic, mysticism and allegory. The important scientific aspects of astronomy were its practical applications, such as the computations of the divisions of time essential to church rites and festivals.

Physics was scarcely studied at all. The Hellenistic achievements of Archimedes and others were apparently forgotten. Chemistry was chiefly a debased and allegorical alchemy, a description of stones and minerals with their alleged magical qualities. For example, the *Panarion* of Epiphanius of Cyprus (315-403) dealt with the twelve gems in the breastplate of the Hebrew high priest. The magical virtues of these gems are listed. Epiphanius says that the hyacinth, if placed on live coals, will extinguish them without injury to itself, that it helps women in childbirth, and that it drives away phantasms. Isidore was particularly rich in comparable descriptions of the necromantic qualities of stones and minerals; the dye, cinnabar, he reveals, is derived from the blood shed by the dragon in his death struggle with the elephant.

Such geology as existed was mainly connected with the magical virtues of stones. Miraculous interferences with geological processes were recounted. In his *Dialogues,* Gregory the Great tells us how a devout man saved a "monastery from an impending avalanche by frequently calling upon the name of Christ and use of the sign of the cross. By these means he stopped the landslide in mid-course and the rocks may still be seen looking as though they were sure to fall." [27]

Biology, including zoölogy and botany, was hopelessly perverted for the sake of edifying Christians. Pliny and the *Physiologus* were still widely cited. The behavior—real and imaginary—of plants and animals was examined to discover ways in which it could be utilized to emphasize scriptural lessons. Magic and marvels abounded. Isidore tells us how "the fiercest bulls grow tame, under the Egyptian fig-tree, how swallows restore the sight of their young with the swallow-

[27] Thorndike, *op. cit.,* I, 638.

wort, or of the use of the fennel and rue by the snake and weasel respectively, the former tasting fennel to enable him to shed his old skin, and the latter eating rue to make him immune from venom in fighting the snake." [28] The planets were supposed to exert a dominating influence in the formation of the human foetus. Anthropology was, of course, entirely taken care of in the biblical account of creation, amplified by wonders concerning man derived from Pliny. Professor Preserved Smith gives us an admirable summary of the attitude of the Dark Ages towards zoölogy and natural history:

> The medievals cared not a whit to know anything about animals and plants for the sake of curiosity; they wanted to find in them something useful to the body or something profitable to the soul. They wanted folklore and they abhorred experiment. Besides including a large number of mythical beasts—dragons, griffins, cockatrices, basilisks, mantichoras, and phoenixes—in their menagerie, they had much to tell of the stag whose blood would dissolve pearls, of the lion born dead and coming to life after three days as a symbol of Christ, of the albatross feeding its young on its blood as a symbol of the eucharist, of the pelican that kills its young and then brings them to life with its blood as a symbol of redemption, and of the beaver that bites off its testicles when hard pressed by the hunter in order to give a practical lesson in the value of chastity to the sinner beset by that great hunter, the devil.[29]

Geography was a mixture of inadequate knowledge of the earth and excessive emphasis on the miraculous. The sacred geography of the holy land and the regions traversed by the saints became very important. Marvels were particularly associated with these areas, but even secular regions were invested with miracles. This was owing in part to the wide use of Solinus as an authority on geography. The relative completeness and precision of the geographical knowledge of Strabo and Ptolemy were abandoned, although a debased version of Ptolemy was available. Knowledge of latitude and longitude was unusual. There was only very scanty information about the climatic zones, and none about the southern hemisphere. Myth, magic, and allegory figured largely in explaining the names of rivers, mountains, and the like. Knowledge of relative distances on any large scale was lacking. Physical geography was especially fantastic; magical and miraculous explanations were offered for natural phenomena, particularly meteorology. Thunder and lightning, for example, were widely believed to be caused by the collision of clouds. Their banging together created thunder, their rubbing together, fire, the spark and light of lightning.

Medical knowledge was a compound of the faint knowledge of classical and Byzantine medical writers, cited above, and the magic of Pliny, Isidore, and others. Medicine, as we have noted, was almost entirely in the hands of churchmen. There was little study of symptoms. Everything was taken on authority. Chief interest was shown in remedies, in which magic and charms always played a dominant role. Dioscorides was the chief classical authority on the *materia medica,* but his work reached the Dark Ages only through a series of condensa-

28 Thorndike, *op. cit.,* I, 626.
29 Preserved Smith, *History of Modern Culture,* 2 vols., Holt, 1930-34 (Collier Books reprint), I, 123.

tions and forgeries. Other popular works on remedies were the *Herbarium* of the pseudo-Apuleius, and the *De viribus herbarum,* a medical poem, attributed to Macer Floridus, and written sometime between the middle of the ninth century and the eleventh. The author took from Galen a tale about curing epilepsy by suspending the root of a peony about the neck of the patient. From Pliny was derived the idea of a remedy for toothache. The herb, senecio, is to be dug up without using iron, the aching tooth is to be touched with the root three times, after which the herb is to be replanted in the ground.

It is obvious that the scientific knowledge of the Dark Ages was distorted by its subordination to theology and its docile and credulous acceptance of authority —the authenticity of which was not too carefully examined. The only way for science to progress was to get better authorities and, especially, to break away from authority entirely and look at nature directly. This was achieved in the later Middle Ages.

A knowledge of Aristotle was revived. Better texts of the classical medical authorities were obtained when the scientific study of medicine was begun at Salerno in Italy in the eleventh century. The remarkable scientific work of the Muslims was made available. Above all, men like Albert the Great, Adelard of Bath, Roger Bacon, Witelo, and Peter of Abano began to pay some attention to the direct observation of the processes of nature, thus gradually introducing the true inductive and experimental method and permitting scholars to make unprecedented progress.

VI. POLITICAL PHILOSOPHY: CHURCH VERSUS THE STATE

Political philosophy in the Dark Ages, like philosophy in general, was deeply colored by religious problems. Indeed, political theory in this period turned almost wholly about the relations between church and state. In general the church had the better of the argument, grew rapidly and steadily in power and consolidated its organization. Political authority was relatively weak, save under such unusual monarchs as Charlemagne. In theory, there was a nice division of power between church and state. The former was supposed to be supreme in matters of faith and morals, the latter in temporal affairs. But it was difficult to maintain this balance in actual practice. At the end of the Dark Ages, when the kings sought to invest church officials with the symbols of spiritual as well as temporal power, and when many churchmen became feudal lords, temporal and spiritual matters became interlaced and a definite practical basis was laid for a sharp struggle between ecclesiastical and political authorities.

Writers who supported the church were willing to concede to the state dominion over temporal affairs, but they tended to assert that, in the final analysis, the church had authority over the state, since the priestly class had to deal with the sins even of kings. Such was the reasoning advanced by Agobard, bishop of Lyons, Hincmar, archbishop of Lyons, Manegold of Lautenbach (1060-1103), and Pope Gregory VII (1020-1085). The argument was highly controversial and, as in medieval philosophy in general, the chief authorities appealed to were the Scriptures and the writings of the fathers.

The basis for church dominion over temporal sovereigns had been provided by Augustine with his notion of the vast superiority of the City of God over the City of the Devil, and his dogma that justice is possible only in a Christian state. Gregory the Great argued that the main purpose of government is to render heaven more accessible and assured, and he contended that no one unfitted to deal with spiritual matters should have control over affairs temporal.

The specific argument over the "two powers" is supposed to have originated in a letter of Pope Gelasius to the Emperor Anastasius in 494. Gelasius contended that the spiritual power is primary, since priests would have to answer for the kings on the Day of Judgment, and kings must come to the church to secure forgiveness of sins and achieve salvation. The salvation of souls is the all-important issue before man; therefore, the institution which alone can guarantee salvation is certainly superior to one which merely cares for fleeting temporal problems. Hincmar argued forcibly that kings must come humbly before the church to confess their sins and receive absolution. They are not above the law, but subject to it. The fiery monk, Hildebrand, who became Pope Gregory VII, contended that the injunction of Jesus, "feed my sheep," implied the granting of universal power to the church. In defending Gregory, Manegold of Lautenbach, while conceding the divine origin of kings, held that the title of king, like that of duke or count, simply implies that the king is the servant of society; it does not confer upon him any unique authority. The office of king should be awarded only upon merit, particularly the possession of "piety, knowledge and justice." The king is chosen, not to be a tyrant, but to serve society. If he become a tyrant, he violates his contract with his subjects and the latter are justified in deposing him.

The theory of Gregory and Manegold implied, as Ernest Barker has pointed out, the complete sovereignty of the pope over the church, the freedom of the clergy from temporal interference, and the right of the church to correct even kings if the latter violated "the law of Christ." [30] It involved the conception of theocracy (priestly omnipotence). In the words of Ernst Troeltsch: "The State is subordinated to the church, as an instrument under control of the church for the governance of temporal things, and for the bringing of temporal relations and values under the absolute spiritual purpose of which the hierarchy is guardian. The dogma of universal episcopacy involves for its completion the dogma of theocracy." [31] Scripture was quoted to buttress the papal pretensions. It was pointed out that the prophet Samuel had hacked Agag to death before the Lord. At the close of the Dark Ages, even tyrannicide was recommended by certain ecclesiastical writers.

The upholders of monarchical autonomy countered with the theory of the divine right of kings. Here they had a certain advantage for, as we have seen, both Peter and Paul conceded that kings ruled by divine right. Government was,

---

[30] F. J. C. Hearnshaw, *The Social and Political Ideas of Some Great Medieval Thinkers*, Holt, 1923, chap. i.

[31] *Ibid.*, pp. 13-14.

according to them, born of God. Jesus himself had disclaimed political authority. While the king should rule justly and for the good of his subjects, his failures were answerable to God alone and not to priests. The king's beneficence is a symbol of God's mercy, while royal wrath and cruelty reflect the wrath of God. Kings likewise appealed to Scripture, but there they were under some handicap, since holy writ had been composed mainly by the prophetic or priestly class which was hostile to kings and secular authority. It was not until monarchs became powerful in fact and invoked Roman law in their behalf that they got the better of their churchly opponents. We shall have more to say about this in later chapters.

VII. LITERATURE IN THE DARK AGES

1. Medieval Latin and the Vernacular Languages

The literature of the Dark Ages is almost entirely written in Latin. Except for Old English little literature was produced in the vernacular languages before the eleventh century. Latin, used for scholarship, theology, medicine, law, and belles-lettres, is a kind of universal medium for the written word. The reasons for this are clear enough.

Latin became the chief literary language of Europe because it was the speech of the Roman conquerors whose superior culture was adopted by the conquered tribes. When the Romans gained possession of a region they did not try to suppress the native speech; but they did, directly and indirectly, encourage the use of Latin. Latin was the language of government in the Western Empire; official documents were not translated into a local tongue as, in the East, they had been translated into Greek. Latin was likewise the language of upperclass provincial schools and of both municipal and royal officials. Those natives who aimed at careers in the public service were forced to speak it. The local aristocracy learned it because it was necessary for participation in the culture of the conquerors. The lower classes frequently mastered it because they would have been handicapped in legal matters otherwise. Latin spread over the Empire in many ways: through books, the migration of freemen, the importation of slaves, and the return of provincial soldiers to private life. Finally and chiefly, the adoption of Latin as the official language of the church in the third century guaranteed its prestige for a thousand years to come.

Medieval literary Latin was not the Latin of Cicero. The polished rhetorical periods of classical Latin were displaced by the simpler and more colloquial speech which had begun to appear in writers of the later Roman Empire like Apuleius. By the fifth century many words and constructions which the writers of classical Latin would not have used had entered into the written language. This modification increased as Roman civilization decayed. Boëthius in the sixth century translated the Greek classics into reasonably polished Latin, but in the same century we find Gregory of Tours, who wrote the famous *History of the Franks*, lamenting the decline of classical Latin and stating his determination to write in rustic Latin, a language which could be understood by the educated people of his time. From the sixth century onwards it became fairly common to write in rustic or "corrupt" Latin when attempting to reach that small part of the public which could read at all. In Merovingian times this language was modeled almost entirely on spoken Latin. To call this language "corrupt" is not to condemn it; it is simply to indicate that it is different from classical Latin. It still could be dignified, musical, and precise. It changed because, being a living language, it had to change. Its function was human communication; and if a language is to be serviceable it must develop as the civilization which uses it changes. In medieval Latin the sentences became shorter and more direct. The elaborate system of inflections characteristic of classical Latin was gradually modified, much as the inflections of Old English fell away as the language changed into Middle English.

Medieval Latin, however, was not as different from the language of Cicero, Vergil, and Horace as one might suppose. The written language of the writers of the golden and silver ages was a literary rather than a spoken language. Nobody in Vergil's day would have thought of speaking in the vocabulary and with the full inflections of the *Aeneid*. In many ways medieval Latin was clearer and easier than its parent. It was a more flexible and rapid language, and more natural, for it approximated more closely to the spoken tongue.

In the later Middle Ages, side by side with the literature written in medieval Latin, there flourished a literature written in the vernacular languages of Europe. These may be divided into three families: Romance, Germanic, and Celtic, all of which are members of a larger family, the Indo-European. The Romance languages included the medieval dialects of modern French, Spanish, Italian, Portuguese, and Rumanian. The Germanic languages were the medieval ancestors of modern English, German, the Scandinavian languages, and Dutch. Of the Celtic family we need take notice here only of Welsh and Irish in which much important medieval literature was written.

Each of the modern Romance and Germanic languages is a product of a long struggle for supremacy among competing dialects of the same language. For instance, modern Italian is substantially the dialect of Tuscany; modern French evolved from the *langue d'oïl,* the dialect spoken in northern France in the Middle Ages; modern Spanish derived from the dialect of Castile; modern German from both Old High and Low German; modern English from the Midland English dialect.

French evolved from the Latin introduced into Gaul by the Roman conquerors. As spoken in rural Gaul this Latin rapidly departed from the Latin spoken in Rome and became what is known as a *lingua franca,* or pidgin-Latin. This corrupt Latin departed from the mother tongue by losing inflections, contracting words, and altering pronunciation; the process was much like that which occurs when resident foreigners learn to speak English. When the Germans invaded Gaul the old Celtic speech of the Gauls had been almost superseded, and numerous French dialects were already formed. These dialects were so strongly established that in time they absorbed the language of the new Germanic masters of the territory. It is interesting to notice here that the Germanic tribes which conquered France were racially the same as the Germanic tribes which conquered

England, yet the conquerors of England established their own language in England, and from that language modern English derives; the conquerors of France adopted the language of the people they conquered. It is clear from this that the language a people speaks is a matter, not of blood, but of cultural inheritance. However, the language of the French was not entirely uninfluenced by the Germanic invaders, for many vestiges of Latin in the dialects disappeared. Articles and prepositions took the place of inflectional endings. Unaccented Latin syllables were dropped. The vowel sounds were modified. The language, five centuries after its introduction to Gaul, was far removed from Latin. By the sixth century it became known as Frankish, after the conquering Franks.

Writings in the vulgar tongue (French) are found as early as the ninth century. The main features of the northern dialect, the *langue d'oïl,* were already fixed. By the eleventh century there was a polished literature in this language. The dialect of the southern part of France was called *langue d'oc* ("oïl" was the word for yes in the North, "oc" in the South) and the magnificent poetry of Provence was written in this tongue in the twelfth and thirteenth centuries. This language has not yet died. By the fourteenth century the court dialect spoken in Paris had become the prevailing literary language of the North and the conversational speech of the upper classes. By the end of the Middle Ages the language of the Ile de France was supreme in northern France. As early as the thirteenth century the *langue d'oïl* began to penetrate the South, where it made great headway in the next few centuries. In 1539 Francis I ordered all official documents to be written in Parisian French, which by this time had become the standard literary language.

The races living along the Baltic were least influenced by the Latin language during the Roman Empire and afterward. Modern German, like modern Dutch and English, belongs to the West Germanic branch of the German language tree. The old German ancestor of modern German was divided into two dialects, High German (hochdeutsch) spoken in the mountainous midlands, and Low German (plattdeutsch) spoken along the sea in the lowlands of the North. At the time of Charlemagne Germany had not yet developed a literary language; but by the twelfth century it was producing a remarkable literature.

The history of the language may be divided into three periods: Old (from the beginning to 1100), Middle (1100-1500), and (after 1500) New High and Low German. The first period is characterized by full inflections; in the second period most of the inflections have dropped away, the vocabulary is richer, and the language has an unusual flexibility and variety; and in the third period a common literary language, with elements derived from both High and Low German, evolved. This language can be traced to the middle of the fourteenth century. It originated in the chancery of the German Empire at Prague, which was situated where the region speaking High German and the region speaking Low German met. The royal documents written in this dialect were thus intelligible all over the realm, and were later imitated by the chanceries of the separate German states. It was first used chiefly as an official language; but its use by Luther in his translation of the Bible (completed 1534) gave it an enormous vogue. By the eighteenth century it had become the common language of Germany, although the Catholic South was slower to accept it than the North.

English is the most composite of all the languages of western Europe. Originally the speech of the Germanic tribes which settled in England after the retirement of the Roman legions, it is a Germanic language; but it has from its beginning shown a marked tendency to assimilate foreign words, and this assimilation has changed its character. Historically the English language (and literature) may be divided into three parts: Old English (from the beginnings to 1100), Middle English (1100-1500), and Modern English (1500 to the present). Old English is sometimes called "Anglo-Saxon," a term made up in modern times from two of the Germanic tribes which settled in England, the Angles and the Saxons. But the men who wrote Old English had come to call themselves English before the first surviving work of their literature was composed, and their language may most properly be called Old English. Old English is very different from modern English. Its vocabulary is almost entirely Germanic. It is, like Latin, highly inflected; nouns, adjectives, adverbs, and even the article are declined in five cases, and gender is entirely grammatical. Read aloud it sounds more like modern German than modern English. The character of the language remained entirely Germanic until the Norman invasion (1066), when it was subjected to the influence of French, which became the language of the court and upper classes. After the Norman Conquest, English adopted many French words, lost virtually all its inflections, and became a more flexible language.

We must not think of Old English as a standard tongue spoken throughout England. In different parts of the country different dialects were used, and these dialectal divisions survive in Middle English. In Middle English we can distinguish four main dialects: Northern, Midland, Southern, and Kentish. Of these dialects Midland English became the dominant one, largely because it was the speech of the court and of London, and because a great poet, Chaucer (1340?-1400), wrote in Midland and gave the dialect literary prestige. The increase in the circulation of books, brought about by the development of printing in the fifteenth century, was an important factor in creating a uniform language. Most books were written in the Midland dialect, because it was the dominant one, and the language of these books served as models for other books to come. In time Midland English came to be recognized as "standard" or "literary" English. Modern English words come from many sources, chiefly, Old English, French, Latin, and Greek, although the languages that have not contributed some words to the vocabulary are few. Old English was the original stock; to this were added large numbers of French words between 1066 and 1400; and from the fifteenth century on, a great number of learned words were adopted from Latin and Greek. By the time of the King James translation of the Bible (1611) English had assumed substantially its present form.

2. Carolingian Latin Literature

It is well to bear in mind that generally speaking the literature of the Middle Ages is anonymous, and it is the exception rather than the rule in medieval

European literature to find works signed by their authors. Sometimes we know from their own assertions that certain people wrote certain works; frequently we can determine the authorship through the assertions of others; occasionally modern scholarship has been able to make identifications. Of the writers who have been identified, one of the most important to English-speaking people is Alcuin (735-804). In his day the cultural center of England was in the North, and of all the schools there, the one at York was the most active; it had, indeed, no superior in Europe, and Alcuin was one of its most eminent scholars. He became chief adviser in educational matters to Charlemagne. He wrote poems about history, the cathedral at York, and in the intervals of a busy life wrote many lighter pieces.

At the court of Charlemagne the most brilliant poet was the bishop Theodulfus. His poetry, which is distinguished by its originality, shows a love of nature, household things, art, and a nice sense of humor. When he was deposed from his bishopric and exiled from the court, he seems, like a greater writer of later years, Jonathan Swift, to have written with fiery pessimism against the follies of his age. Einhard (c. 770-840) was, like Alcuin, a scholar at the court of Charlemagne and one of the emperor's most trusted advisers. His biography of Charlemagne is, as literature, the best biography of the Middle Ages. It included much legendary material and became the source of many of the legends which found their way into the medieval romances. There were other writers of excellent Latin during this era, but the literature written in the vulgar tongues is of more importance to the modern reader, for in these writings are the beginnings of the literature of the modern world.

3. *Old English Poetry*

When the student of modern English turns to the study of Old English poetry, he will find himself reading in a strange language of a world different, in all superficial respects, from the world of his own experience. He finds the language almost as difficult to learn as modern German; except for a number of familiar words, it sounds like German. Apart from the unfamiliarity of its language, he finds that Old English poetry differs from modern English poetry in another respect—its metrical structure. Near the middle of each line, a pause, called the caesura, divides the line in two. The line has four stressed syllables, two in each part. The number of unstressed syllables varies from line to line. Usually two or three of the four stressed syllables repeat the same sound; that is, they are alliterative. Thus the rime, in contrast to modern poetry, usually comes at the beginning of the word. The opening lines of *The Wanderer* will serve as an illustration.

> Oft him anhaga   are gebideth,
> Metudes miltse,   theah the he modcearig
> Geond lagulade   longe sceolde
> Hreran mid hondum   hrimcealde sae,
> Wadan wraeclastas: wyrd bith ful araed!

The riming syllables in the second line are the ones beginning with *M;* in the last line, with *W.* In his excellent translation of these lines Professor Kennedy [32] has in part preserved the alliteration:

> Oft to the Wanderer,   weary of exile,
> Cometh God's pity,   compassionate love,
> Though woefully toiling   on wintry seas
> With churning oar   in the icy wave
> Homeless and helpless   he fled from fate.

The modern reader may find the patterns of Old English poetry a bit rigid, but he will be greatly mistaken if he thinks them crude. This poetry is primitive only in the sense that it is old. Its creators were writing in an established tradition whose beginnings are lost; that is, this type of poetry was a highly developed art form before any of the Old English poems which have come down to us were written.

The modern reader will find the subject matter of these poems only a little less strange than the form and language. Old English poetry, written before the days of democracy, is not a democratic literature. It makes no mention of the common people; it was written about the upper classes for the upper classes. The society reflected in it is not the unified society of modern England. The poems were written when England was divided into a group of smaller kingdoms, and within these kingdoms the social unit was the clan. Within the clan there had developed the concept of allegiance to the ruler. The individual was bound to serve his leader loyally and to render military service when the leader needed it. It was the leader's obligation to protect the individual and pay him for his services with gifts. In those centuries of frequent warfare the survival of the leader and the individual depended upon their mutual loyalty. This loyalty is the theme of much Old English poetry.

This was essentially the same social structure as the ancestors of the Old English writers had known on the Continent. But since their arrival in England their social life had been modified by their conversion to Christianity, and this modification is especially evident in their literature. Old English poetry was written to be sung or chanted aloud in the banquet hall by the scops or gleemen, men whose business it was to remember the stories of old battles and heroes, or to make new poems of heroic deeds, and sing them to the thanes. When the Germanic tribes settled in England they brought with them stories of their great men and their pagan gods, and when they were converted to Christianity they continued to tell the old stories. But the stories became colored with the new religion, and in the poems the two religions mingled. We find Christian and pagan virtues and heroes praised, side by side, alike.

The oldest bit of English poetry we have is a hymn by Caedmon (c. 670). In his *Ecclesiastical History of the English People,* the Venerable Bede (673-735) tells how the hymn was written. Caedmon was a workman at the monastery of Whitby, and in the evening when songs were played and sung, he would sneak

---

[32] Charles W. Kennedy, *Old English Elegies,* Princeton University Press, 1936.

away because he could not sing. One night he retired to the stable and fell asleep, and a stranger appeared to him and said, "Caedmon, sing me something." Caedmon answered, "I do not know how to sing, and for that reason I left the banquet and came out here." Then he who was speaking to him said, "But you can sing for *me*." Caedmon asked, "What shall I sing?" And he said, "Sing to me of the creation." And in praise of God the creator, Caedmon began to sing verses he had never heard before, whose sense was, "Now must we praise the Founder of the Kingdom of Heaven." Bede quotes a hymn by Caedmon, and that is the only extant poem known to be by him. However, a group of other poems has been attributed to him, largely because one of them, the *Genesis,* paraphrases and elaborates the biblical account of the Creation. These poems, the *Genesis, Exodus, Daniel,* and *Christ and Satan,* were all written after Caedmon's lifetime. The writers tell their stories in terms of their own culture, and the characters become more like Germanic or Old English lords and warriors than like ancient Jews and Egyptians. In the *Exodus* the men carry medieval arms, and the shields gleam in the sun as the hosts march along. The poem tells of Moses, the plagues of Egypt, and the escape of the Israelites. The main episodes describe the pursuit of the Children of Israel by Pharaoh's army and the destruction of the Egyptians. Although there is no battle in either the biblical story or the poem, the poet has managed to create the atmosphere of war. When the Red Sea threatened the Egyptians, they tried to flee, but

> The dreadful rushing sea swept over them. Nor did any of that army come ever again to their homes, but Fate cut off their retreat and locked them in the sea. . . . Blood dyed the deep. The walls of water were shattered; the greatest of sea deaths lashed the heavens. Brave princes died in throngs.[33]

The greatest of Old English poems is *Beowulf* (c. 725), a stately epic of 3,182 lines. The author, probably a monk in a Northumbrian monastery, tells his story with such skill and epic dignity that many scholars have assumed that he knew the *Aeneid* and perhaps the *Odyssey.* The greater part of *Beowulf* takes place in the land of Hrothgar, King of the Danes, who has erected a great hall, Heorot, where he and his thanes feast and drink and hear the songs of his scop. But one night an evil monster, Grendel, came to the hall and killed thirty warriors. For twelve years he continued his ravaging, and no one could conquer him. Beowulf, a thane of Hygelac, King of the Geats, heard of the trouble, and taking fourteen of his strongest men, he went to Hrothgar's assistance. In the night at Heorot he met Grendel in single combat, tore out his arm, and the monster slunk away to die in his lair. But Grendel's mother, a water-monster, grieves for her son, and plots revenge. She captured one of Beowulf's men in Heorot and carried him away. Beowulf followed her trail to a rocky tarn in the woods, full of strange and horrible monsters, and there he found the head of his warrior. To avenge his death Beowulf plunged into the water, was seized by Grendel's mother and carried to her under-water hall where, in heroic combat, he killed

[33] Charles W. Kennedy, *The Caedmon Poems,* George Routledge and Sons Limited, 1916, p. 113.

her. With her death Hrothgar's kingdom was once more at peace, and Beowulf, richly laden with precious gifts, returned home in honor.

After the death of Hygelac Beowulf became king of the Geats, and reigned for fifty years. Then a fire-breathing dragon began to devastate the country. Beowulf set out to meet it with eleven of his thanes, but all but one of them, Wiglaf, deserted him, and the two warriors fought the dragon alone. Although Beowulf killed it, he was mortally wounded. He thanked God for the victory, and died. The men built a great pyre on the headland, and laid the body of their king and his armor upon it. The warriors mourned the death of their hero,

> Called him the best among kings of the earth,
> Mildest of men, and most beloved,
> Kindest to kinsmen, and keenest for fame.[34]

It is clear that the subject matter of *Beowulf* is the accumulation of centuries. Hygelac, Beowulf's king, is a historical character, and the fights with the monsters are obviously variant forms of old pagan legends which the ancestors of the writer of the poem had brought with them to England. But the author gave the old stories local and contemporary color. The locale of the poem is Denmark and Sweden, but the descriptive details are English, and the manners, the social customs, are those of the society in which he lived. From the courtesy and dignity which marks the behavior of the characters the reader may learn much of the high state of civilization in eighth-century England. From *Beowulf* he may learn too, how Christian England assimilated the old pagan culture. There is continual reference to the old pagan concept of a fate (Wyrd) which ruled men's lives and to the Christian God to whom the dying Beowulf gives praise. The hero, an idealized portrait of a king, embodies the pagan virtues but he is also the mildest, the kindest, the most beloved of men.

The writers of most Old English poems, like the writer of *Beowulf,* are unknown, but Cynewulf (c. 750-800) put his name in runic signatures to four of his poems: *Juliana, Christ, Elene* (St. Helena the mother of Constantine), and the *Fates of the Apostles.* Other poems, though unsigned, are pretty certainly written by him: *Andreas* (St. Andrew), *Guthlac, Phoenix,* and the *Dream of the Rood.* There is not enough known about Cynewulf for even the shortest biography, but the learning and devotional nature of his poetry indicates that he was an ecclesiastic. No one can read his poetry without being impressed with his delight in nature, the beauty of the earth and sea, the rising of the sun, and the coming on of night. The most tender and personal of Old English poets—he suggests the poetry of Herbert—he can, like his fellow poets, describe the fury of war. And, when the greatness of his themes demand it, he can rise to heights of passion unequaled in his age.

Old English elegies have little kinship with the personal elegies of later ages, such as Milton's *Lycidas* or Shelley's *Adonais.* The poet does not mourn the death of a friend. The elegies are not part of the pastoral tradition, and they owe no debt to the idylls of classical antiquity. Written in the eighth and ninth cen-

---

[34] Translated by J. Duncan Spaeth, *Old English Poetry,* Princeton University Press, 1927.

turies, they are completely the product of their time. *The Ruin,* a fragment of a longer poem, is the record of the poet's musings on the ruins of an ancient Roman city, in all probability, Bath. He speculates on the departed glory and mourns the transience of earthly things. The theme of *The Wanderer* is the loyalty of thane to his lord. The Wanderer recalls the days when as a youth he served his lord. But the death of his lord had separated them, and he is forced to wander in exile hunting in vain a leader who can take the place of the lord of his youth. Both these poems are Old English to the core. The subject matter rises immediately from the social background and the personal experience of the poets; their form is the epitome of Old English versification, and the elegiac mood is characteristic of the sobriety of Old English literature. They tell of a civilization long since past and of small immediate concern to the modern reader, but they bring to us, too, the awful awareness of the impermanence of all earthly things. In this respect, and in spite of their more superficial strangeness, they are universal. One quality of Old English poetry which survives in later poetry is the faithful depiction of nature. No poem excels *The Seafarer* in its description of the ocean and the seaman's struggles with the forces of nature. Although Old English poetry is separated from us by a thousand years, its truthful recording of the external world and of human experience brings it nearer to us than many things within our memory.

4. Old English Prose

For much of our knowledge of Old English history we are indebted to the Venerable Bede (673-735), a monk of the monastery of Jarrow. Entering as a boy of seven, he spent a life of indefatigable study there, writing saints' lives, poems, hymns, biblical commentaries, books on rhetoric, and his greatest work of all, the *Ecclesiastical History of the English People.* The *History* recounts the settlement of England, the struggles of the kingdoms, and the advent and growth of Christianity. It is, for its time, a model of industrious investigation, packed with information carefully gathered from men from all over England. And it preserves sketches of men (such as the account of Caedmon) which would otherwise be lost to us. Bede wrote his *History* in Latin; it was not translated into English until the time of Alfred.

Alfred the Great (849-901), king of the West Saxons from 871 until his death, was one of the most distinguished men in all English history. A king, soldier, and scholar, he is important in the history of literature not only for what he wrote but for what he caused to be written. Although a good Latin scholar, he was not interested only in Latin literature. He had loved the Old English poems all his life, and when he became king, he made his subjects learn them. Since the days of Bede, two hundred years before, learning had declined in England. Fewer people read Latin, and it seemed to Alfred that he could best encourage learning by the translation of Latin books into English. To this end he first translated the *Cura Pastoralis* (Pastoral Care) of Pope Gregory the Great for the edification of the clergy, and Bede's *Ecclesiastical History.* He also chose for translation a history of the world by the Spaniard, Orosius, and Boëthius' *On the,*

Consolation of Philosophy. In his translations he allowed himself freedom to insert his own observations when he thought they might be helpful, and in the case of Orosius' *History,* he includes contemporary matters such as the remarkable northern voyages of the navigators Ohthere and Wulfstan. Apart from the educational purposes for which the translations were made, they are important in that they mark the beginning of English prose literature. Alfred's military and political successes were also important for cultural history. They made it possible for England to get a large part of its culture from the Latin south instead of being swung wholly into the Scandinavian circle.

5. Old German

Of Old German heroic poetry nothing survives except a fragment of the alliterative *Lay of Hildebrand,* which is part of a cycle of lost Teutonic sagas dealing with the fifth-century king, Theodoric the Goth. The sixty-eight lines of the dramatic *Hildebrand* is a specimen of pagan epic, narrating the combat between Hildebrand, Theodoric's champion, and Hadubrand, his opponent. The warriors meet, their shields are cut to pieces, and the poem ends. Somewhat later, probably, than *Hildebrand,* are two Old German religious poems, *Heliand* (Savior), written between 820 and 840 in alliterative verse, and the *Gospel Book* of Orfrid, written between 863 and 871. Of the two the *Heliand* is the better literature, and like the Old English poems recasts scriptural characters into epic warriors. Jesus becomes a Germanic ruler, and his disciples are warrior thanes! But there are some Old German poems which are purely Christian. There is, for instance, a fragment of an exemplary religious poem called *Genesis.* A translation of this poem into Old English forms part of the so-called Caedmonian poems.

About a century after the *Heliand,* Saxon literature enjoyed something of a rebirth, though this time the chief works were written in Latin, not in the vernacular. The most important productions of this epoch were Ekkehard's *Waltharius* (c. 930) and the works of Roswitha, a member of the nunnery of Gandersheim. Ekkehard's poem deals with the body of historical material which appeared later in the famous *Nibelungenlied,* the story of Gunther, Hagen, and Walter of Aquitaine. The *Waltharius* is made of the stuff of which all medieval epics were made. It deals with war in a vigorous, masculine way, a manner common to Western heroic poetry whether in the Dark Ages or in recent works like Richard Wagner's *Ring of the Nibelungen.* Roswitha, though important, has been accorded more attention than she deserves. A tenth-century nun in the convent of Gandersheim, she wrote six plays modeled on the Latin plays of Terence. Her themes, unlike those of her model, were the glory of martyrdom and chastity. Her plays are of little literary value, but their existence indicates that even in the tenth century the interest in the literary drama had not completely died.

6. Byzantine Literature

Although the period from 500 to 1100 was, in the opinion of many scholars, a dark age in the West, it was a golden period of cultural development and literary expression in the Byzantine Empire and in Muslim realms. This should be kept clearly in mind. The literature of the Byzantine Empire is mainly written in

Greek. Even in Justinian's time (483-565) the use of Latin was decreasing. His later laws are in Greek. In this area the popular language has been Greek since Hellenic times, and when the government gave up the effort to introduce Latin, Greek held the field with no rivals. In the fourth century, however, the nature of the Greek language changed in an important respect. Difference in quantity (or tone) of syllables disappeared, and *accent* took its place.

Greek competed with several other languages in the Byzantine Empire: Syrian, Coptic, Armenian, Georgian, Gothic, Old Bulgarian, and others. Sacred Christian books were translated into these languages, and church services were also held in them wherever they were the prevalent tongues. However, as a result of the popularity of Greek, a knowledge of the classics never entirely disappeared, and when it came, the revival of Hellenic learning received impetus from laymen, many of whom were well-educated government officials. It may be added that the University of Constantinople was reopened in 863.

Byzantine literature is noted for its erudition. Apparently the existence of a great tradition of classical literature tended to curb the impulse of originality. The Byzantines made huge collections of notes, compendia, and excerpts of the older Greek writers. The great names in Byzantine letters are those of compilers like Photius (ninth century) whose *Myriobiblos* (Library) touches upon all Hellenic literature, pagan and Christian, or Symeon Metaphrastus (tenth century) whose *Lives of the Saints* supplied a hungry, pious reading public with thrilling literature. Around 1100 we find another great compiler, the Byzantine Suidas, author of the famous *Lexicon* or encyclopedia of Hellenic literature. To these may be added Constantine Cephalas, the tenth-century editor of the *Greek Anthology,* and eleventh-century Hellenists like Michael Psellus, John Mauropus, John Italus, and Christopher of Mytilene. These men were the real founders of Greek humanism, which flourished in Italy in the fourteenth and fifteenth centuries and then spread through western Europe.

Almost all the intellectual activity in the Byzantine Empire was devoted to the recovery and discussion of pagan learning, which was in the hands of a few wealthy and cultivated individuals. The masses were illiterate. And since, in the ecclesiastical world, the monks were devoting themselves to theological subtleties, "profane" literature did not develop as it did in the West. Profane literature, however, was written both in the literary Greek and in the vernacular. In the former we find the fine twelfth-century romance, *Rodanthe and Dosicles* by Theodore Prodomus and *Drusilla and Charicles* by Nicetas Eugenianus. In Byzantine literature are found many epigrams, by which was meant anything from a playful trifle to long elegiac and narrative poems.

One of the most original Byzantine contributions was its liturgical verse. Here we may distinguish the *rhythmic poem,* which dates from Gregory Nazianzen (fourth century), and which no longer depends on difference of quantity but on accent. Byzantine *hymns* were lengthy songs, consisting of from twenty to thirty similar strophes, connected like acrostics. The chief Greek hymn writer was Romanos, who brought the genre to perfection. There were also *canones,* invented probably by Andreas (c. 650-720), archbishop of Crete, songs artificially wrought out of eight or nine dissimilar lyrics. The chief writer of canones was John of Damascus (d. c. 750).

Byzantine vernacular poetry had a certain virility and originality. It is interesting to note that vernacular Greek was employed in larger literary works only in the twelfth century. The man most influential in this development was the savant and rhetorician, Theodore Prodomus (d. c. 1150). In this vernacular verse we find erotic poems, such as those known as the Rhodian love songs, and great epics dealing with Troy and Alexander, subjects which in the later Middle Ages were widely used in European vernacular literatures. Apart from lyric and epic poetry, there were many Byzantine verse romances, written in a sort of pseudo-classical Greek. Among them we find such things as *Phlorius and Platziaphlora,* the story which in French forms the delightful romance of Floris and Blancheflor.

Byzantine historical scholarship began with Procopius (c. 500-565), who imitated the historians Herodotus and Thucydides. His *History of His Own Time* was a firsthand account of many of the wars of Justinian. His scandal-mongering *Secret History* was a racy account of the court amours and intrigues at the time of Justinian and Theodora. Other important works of Byzantine historians were the world histories of George Hamartolus (c. 850) and John Zonoras (d. 1130); the history of the Near East during the Fourth Crusade by Nicetas Acominatus (d. 1216); and the history of the restoration of the Greek Empire by George Acropolita (1217-1282).

The general significance of Byzantine literature is not to be underestimated. The Christians of the Eastern Empire guarded the classical heritage for about a thousand years and passed it on to the West just before the empire was engulfed by the barbaric Turks. Byzantine culture created a medieval literature of its own, both in vernacular and classical Greek.

The Byzantines communicated pagan as well as Christian literatures to their neighbors, the Syrians, Copts, Armenians, Georgians, Arabians, Serbs, Bulgarians, and Russians. And through their teachings they created the eastern European culture of the modern Greek and Slav and the Orthodox Eastern Church.

7. Muslim Literature

Remote as Muslim literature may seem to us, it will be apparent even in this brief sketch that while Western literature was struggling toward a rebirth, the literature of the East and Near East was mature and exerting an extensive influence in Europe. This influence has continued to our own time.

Muslim literature was already rich when the Bedouins roamed the desert, before they lived in cities and had settled habitations. This literature was oral, and has not survived. Inspired by the poetic nature of the desert and his lonely wandering existence, the Bedouin, to whom poetry was apparently second nature, made rimes and sang ballads. About the sixth century an alphabet was imported from Syria, and a written literature began. And then Mohammed (c. 570-632) came, and the religion known as Islam, and a great impetus was given to Bedouin civilization. Several anthologies of pre-Islamic poetry, collected centuries later, survive, like the *Hamasa* by Abu Tamman, dealing with the adventures of war; the *Moallakát,* a collection of seven long poems comprising a realistic picture of

Bedouin social life, trials, loves, hates, and homely maxims. The most important book of the Muslims, the Koran (their Bible) is composed from the sayings of Mohammed. The scribes in his following carefully preserved his revelations at Mecca, Medina, and other places; and soon after his death his words were collected and arranged in the form in which we have them. The style of the Koran is rich in the imagery of the wilder aspects of nature as well as of the daily life of the wandering tribes, but it is highly involved and cannot be reproduced in English. It is one of the most difficult of the Eastern religious books to read.

With the rise of the Abbassid caliphs in the eighth century, Persian influence became dominant in Islam, and a new literary epoch began. The nature of Muslim poetry changed, too. The songs were now less about tribal quarrels and war, and more about general cultural interests.

Best known to us of the Muslim poets of the tenth century is al-Firdausi (935-1020), the chief epic poet of Persia, whose famous *Sháhnáma* (*Book of Kings*) tells the story of the Persian national hero Rustam, whose story Matthew Arnold tells in *Sohrab and Rustum*. The chief romantic poet of Persia was as-Nimazi (1141-1203), whose five long erotic poems are collected under the title of *The Five Treasuries*. The Muslim writer most famous in the West is Omar Khayyám (d. 1123). Although he was the leading scientist of his age, his popular reputation rests upon his poems, *The Rubáiyát,* a collection of independent quatrains held together by continuous themes of epicurianism and skepticism. They have been best translated into English by Edward Fitzgerald. Al-Hafiz (died 1389) was the great lyric poet of the Muslims, the peer of Shelley, Catullus, and Sappho. His odes are on themes common to the poetry of all nations: love, wine, song, and the beauties of nature.

There is no substitute for the reading of any poetry, and no account of Muslim poetry will give the reader more than a faint idea of its richness, volume, and versatility. In prose we find a similar if not equal wealth.

The earliest important prose work in Arabic was the *Romance of Antar,* of uncertain authorship, but long ascribed to an eighth-century scholar of the days of Haroun al-Raschid. Antar is the King Arthur of Arabia, one of the traditional authors of *Moallakát*. The *Romance of Antar* is important for its picture of the war-life of the wandering Bedouins.

An important influence in European literature was the *Magamát,* a collection of disconnected stories about a vagabond who gains his livelihood by his wit, his moral philosophy, and his large repertoire of more or less shady tricks. This character in a modified form entered Spanish literature from Muslim or other sources, and became the staple of the so-called picaresque novel which later spread to France and England. Muslim literature also popularized the animal fable which it derived from Sanskrit sources. These stories entered European literature through translation into the Latin and Spanish. Thus the beast fable, as derived from India through Islam, ultimately became one of the sources of the masterpieces of La Fontaine and other writers in this genre.

Best known, however, of all Muslim literature are the so-called *Arabian Nights,* a collection of stories introduced by the following device. The King of India and China, enraged by the infidelity of his wife and the wives of his friends, decides to slay all Muslim brides on the morning after their marriage. The clever daughter of a vizier tries to save them from this cruel fate and starts to tell the King a story, which she suspends every night at an interesting point. She continues for 1001 nights, by which time the king retracts his declaration, forgives the Muslim women, and makes the vizier's daughter his queen. The time of the stories is chiefly the eighth and ninth centuries, the age of Haroun al-Raschid (c. 765-809), Caliph of Baghdad. The *Arabian Nights* is a collection of fables, proverbs, adventures, household anecdotes, and erotic exploits. Their underlying philosophy is primarily Persian, the Muslim element is the realistic description of the erotic life of Baghdad and Cairo.

The translation of the *Arabian Nights* into French by Galland in 1704 began a vogue for Oriental stories in western European literature. *Arabian Nights* were followed by *Persian Tales* and *Turkish Tales*. Both England and France were swept by the craze, and a host of so-called Oriental tales were invented. The pseudo-Oriental romance was killed by the satire of men like Pope and Goldsmith. But it left its mark in eighteenth- and nineteenth-century literature. We see it in Addison's tale, the *Vision of Mirza*, in Dr. Johnson's *Rasselas;* and in Voltaire it took the form of a satiric apologue like *Zadig*. Montesquieu used the Oriental framework for social criticism in his *Persian Letters*. Beckford, combining the Gothic horror novel with a true orientalism, created his noted novel, *Vathek*. Most important of all, however, orientalism in the eighteenth century helped to bring about, as it did in the twelfth, the rebirth of the romantic spirit.

Important Muslim works on history were al-Dinawari's *History of Arabia and Persia* (c. 900); Ibn Abi Tahir's *History of Baghdad* (c. 900); al-Tabari's *Annals of the Apostles and Kings* (c. 925); Miskawaihi's *Experiences of the Nations* (c. 975); and Ibn Khaldun's *Universal History* (c. 1400). Ibn Khaldun was the ablest historian of the Middle Ages, Muslim or Christian.

VIII. ART IN THE DARK AGES

1. *Art in the East: "The New Rome"*

We have already witnessed the political shift from Rome to Byzantium, with its new concentration of wealth and of population. "New Rome," as it has often been called, represented a Near Eastern continuation of the Roman Empire and we find here, as we found in Rome, a distinctly imperial art. With the fourth century, Rome's deterioration had begun and it was not long before the unrelenting pressure of the barbarians of central Europe finished the process, making possible soon afterward the rise of the various kingdoms of the Dark Ages. It is at this point, then, that Byzantium took up the torch of European culture and, with minor interruptions, carried it for almost ten centuries. In the darkest period of the Middle Ages, when most of Europe was sunk in economic misery and political bankruptcy, Byzantium was flourishing and productive.

Of the earliest period of Byzantine history (A.D. 300-500) few edifices survive, although we may be sure that many structures had been created in the new city, if only because of its rapid early growth. Outside Byzantium considerable building was going on—in Jerusalem at the Church of the Holy Sepulcher and in Bethlehem at the Church of the Nativity.

Following the tradition of the Roman Empire, Byzantium carried on an elaborate series of defensive and offensive military campaigns in all parts of the Mediterranean world, a fact important for the spread of their art as well as their commercial products. Its central geographical position made Byzantium the gateway to Europe and a bulwark of European defense at the same time. Oriental silks could and did come into Europe through this gate but, by the same token, the Muslims (from the seventh century on) could not. In that world, as in the twentieth century, culture followed the flag, with the result that we find Byzantine fortresses and city walls not only in northern Africa but Byzantine ecclesiastical

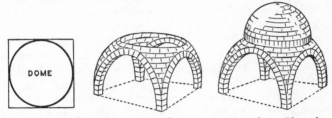

Pendentives making the transition from a square to a dome. Plan of a dome on pendentives (*left*), pendentives set into arches (*center*), pendentives supporting dome (*right*).

architecture, mosaics, and manuscripts in Greece, Armenia, Sicily, Italy and Spain.

Of the sixth-century period in Byzantium proper, the most impressive monument, of course, is the world-famous church of Saint Sophia (Hagia Sophia, or Holy Wisdom), erected under the direction of the Emperor Justinian by two Anatolian architects, Isidor of Miletus and Anthemius of Tralles. Its plan combines the features of a circular, domed structure like the Pantheon with characteristics derived from the basilica, such as atrium, vestibule, nave, and aisles. Because of the length of the nave, half-domes were added to the enormous central dome, which was over 100 feet in diameter.

This great dome is the most arresting element in Saint Sophia. Unlike the dome of the Pantheon, which rests on a circular wall, this dome is supported by four huge piers arranged in a square. The builders solved the problem of setting a hemispherical dome on a square section by means of pendentives. The dome, although rising to a height of about 175 feet from the floor, does not give the impression of great soaring qualities when viewed from the outside. But inside— what marvelous spaciousness, what breath-taking height! The impression of height is emphasized by the way the dome has been set on a drum, a drum pierced all around with windows. This makes the dome appear to be hanging in space. The feeling of verticality is intensified by the superposed arcades and the triple row of windows which break up the walls. Finally, an elaborate decoration of shimmering, colorful mosaics, many ornamented with gold, not only adds to the feeling of insubstantiality but creates a strong contrast to the drabness of the exterior. Intricate color patterns glisten from the veined marble; it is sawn thin and slabs from the same block are placed side by side with veins running in different directions. The whole glows as if covered by a golden sky—the effect of the gold background of the mosaics in the dome. Wonderfully decorative are the basket-like capitals cut with the flat crisp "black and white" carvings.

Some of the most important monuments of early Byzantine culture are found in Ravenna, Italy, among them two fine simple basilican types, Sant' Apollinare in Classe and Sant' Apollinare Nuovo. Both are embellished with splendid examples of Byzantine mosaic. More interesting and important in relation to the later development of European architecture is the church of San Vitale, built in an octagon topped by a dome carried on a drum. The drum in turn is supported by eight sturdy columns. Charlemagne's church at Aix-la-Chapelle, a ninth-century work, was definitely influenced by this building.

Because we lack adequate examples of the mosaics of the sixth century in Byzantium proper, we must turn to an outside center such as Ravenna. Two of the most famous of all Byzantine mosaics embellish the church of San Vitale: the representations of the Emperor Justinian among his soldiers and ecclesiastics, and the Empress Theodora in a group of male and female figures. Both compositions are characterized by the rigid and formal attitudes of the figures, the elaborate costumes, the elongation of the bodies, by the gold backgrounds that tend to shut the figures into a shallow space, and finally by their stereotyped emotional expression.

One seems to have come a good way from the carefully proportioned and graciously dignified art of classical antiquity to find a severe and formalized art in its place. On further examination these figures prove more decorative than solid, the feet frequently overlap each other, sometimes they point downward as though they had no place on which to stand. The floor slopes sharply upward and tends to augment the feeling of two-dimensionality and lack of depth—a sensation intensified by the neutral gold background. One may say, in fact, that these figures begin to exist in a vacuum; just as expression has been drawn out of their faces, the blood has been drained from their bodies. At the same time, their immobility and their distended eyeballs create an impressive fearsomeness in the mind of the observer, perhaps because the subjects seem to be religious fanatics. The soldier in the group carries a shield with the monogram of Christ on it. It might almost be said again, "In this sign, conquer!"

To explain in more rational terms what has just been said, it must be observed that the character of the Byzantine clergy was, for a long time, overwhelmingly Semitic. That the Semitic opposition to image worshiping generously helped to devitalize classical figure art cannot be doubted. But since it could not, with a fundamentally pagan people, destroy images completely, the result was a compromise. A series of images was created, fulfilling the narrative and visual needs of the people, yet so flattened and so removed from reality that they could not any longer fall into the class of idols. Thus a combined classic and Semitic attitude was achieved.

Because of the church's antipathy to images, we cannot expect to find sculptural development as such, but rather a variation of it in the minor plastic art of small ivory plaques. For all practical purposes, these small ivories will be the full extent of sculptural indulgence of Byzantine art. The opposition to image making bore most serious consequences for Byzantine art when the battle between the iconoclasts (or image destroyers) and anti-iconoclasts came out into the open. The former represented the extremely conservative religious group, the latter a more popular element. The suppressed antipathy to images broke loose during the early part of the eighth century (A.D. 726) and lasted for about a hundred and twenty-five years. In addition to the actual destruction of images and the bloodshed incidental to the decrees of Leo the Issaurian, the iconoclastic controversy affected the development of all the arts in the capital.

It was not until the end of the ninth century that this period of relative sterility gave way before a revival. Between the years 726-867 there were practically no buildings erected in Byzantium, though a considerable number arose in other districts. Artistic activity had not stopped completely, for the needs of a predominantly pagan people still had to be gratified by some sort of figure art. The so-called Veroli caskets of this period provided a solution. Their ivory representations of nonreligious scenes, hunters, warriors, etc., satisfied the desire for ornamentation without offending the sensibilities of the iconoclasts. The iconoclastic period, then, marks a transition from the first golden age (527-726).

At the end of the ninth century the second golden age of Byzantine art (867-1204) began. Continuing until the end of the twelfth century, this was the most productive period. Architecturally a new type of church plan came into existence with the Greek cross [35] inscribed within a square. The cross appears only on plan; it is not evident in the exterior until the first story is reached. The main or central dome no longer has the broad sweep of a Saint Sophia, but is much narrower and lighter and is raised farther into the air by a high drum. In fact, the entire accent of the building has changed from squatness (emphasized by the exterior of Saint Sophia) to verticality.

In discussing the other arts of this period we should not insist too much on such a quality of starkness, which we emphasized as characteristic of the mosaics of Ravenna. Very often the long slender figures with the tiny heads are treated with a gentleness and reserve that are almost Hellenic. We find this true of the ivories more often than of the other arts. Various incidental motifs such as planets, personifications, etc., seem to point to a relationship to the art of Hellenistic Greece, which should not be too surprising in view of the classical background of Byzantium itself. Perhaps the very nature of the ivory inspired the calm emotion and quietness of bearing which we find here. But we must always remember that even in the ivories the figure is never treated naturalistically but is distorted, if only gently. When one turns to other arts, particularly to mosaics, manuscript paintings, and enamels, there is a slightly different emotional attitude—one that agrees more with the starkness indicated in the discussion of the Ravenna mosaics. These latter arts are technically as fully advanced as the ivories. The brilliant enamels done in cloisonné style (thin ridges of metal between which enamel paste

[35] *Greek cross:* A cross whose four arms are of identical length.

of different colors is inserted, then fused with the metal) represent the ultimate in stylization and formalization.

The art of mosaic is, after architecture, perhaps of greatest interest, since it has left so many remains and can be so thoroughly studied. Many variations make it difficult to formulate a rule but we can say without too much exaggeration that the general formulae laid down for early Byzantine (and Ravennate) mosaics hold true for those of the second golden age as well. Frequently there is more imagination in the narration of a scene, as well as a more exciting handling of crowds, but the figures are still modeled after the anatomical rules of the earlier period, the backgrounds are still as neutral or the landscape is extremely conventionalized. In the apses of churches the representation of Christ as the Ruler of the Universe frequently takes on an almost terrifying character, both because of the enormous size of the Christ and the evident distortions in the hands and the eyes. Awe-inspiring figures such as these seem to lean out of their backgrounds to judge and punish sinning humanity.

With the sack of Byzantium in 1204 A.D. the second golden age ended. It is indicative of the tremendous vitality of Byzantine culture that, after the invasion, it was able to take up where it had left off and produce so energetically that the period from the middle of the thirteenth century to the final sack of the city in 1453 has merited the name of "the Byzantine Renaissance." In Byzantium itself little building was accomplished because of lack of funds; but the activity took place in the outlying areas of the empire—Asia Minor, Greece, Serbia, and Russia. In these countries the Byzantine style was modified with each new background, showing frequently, as in Russia, considerable originality. The church still seemed to favor the Greek cross plan, but certain older features, such as the domed basilica, frequently revived. There were too many variations at this time to permit broad generalizations as to plan, but verticality unquestionably became even stronger. A good example is the Serbian church at Manassia, in which the ground story was built extremely high and verticality was emphasized by slim pilaster [35a] strips running up the façade. The drum on which the dome rests was alarmingly heightened. For safety's sake the dome itself was made considerably smaller, the general effect approaching closely that of a tower. In later Russian examples (such as St. Basil's in Moscow) the final step occurred and the dome became a twisted and bulbous shape almost completely disengaged from the body of the building.

With the capture of Byzantium by the Turks in 1453, Byzantine culture proper may be said to come to an end, although in Russia its influence was evident in one form or another down to the twentieth century. Christianity had been imported into Russia from Byzantium and its rites together with its plastic art followed in much the same fashion. Indeed, it often is quite difficult to determine whether a work found in Russia was actually created there. Later in its history, Russia developed a more native idiom, though still strongly influenced by the earlier Byzantine style.

[35a] *Pilaster:* a flattened column forming part of a wall.

2. *Art in the West*

The Wandering of the Nations.—We should remember that after the fall of the Roman Empire, Byzantium in the East took up the achievements of Roman culture and carried on for almost ten centuries, while in the West the coalescence of the various barbarian kingdoms resulted in the so-called "Dark Ages." The history of the "Dark Ages" is intertwined with the history of the wanderings of the various barbaric peoples over the face of Europe and of their eventual settlement into Christianized nations. The spread of Christianity into the central and northern parts of the Continent was an extremely slow process. In certain places, as in the Scandinavian countries, the new religion was not adopted until after the year 1000. For the history of art it must be noted that the Christianization of Europe was much more politic a process than had been the Christianization of the Near East. No attempt was made immediately to substitute the new religious culture for the barbaric ones. The missionaries from Rome proceeded with extreme caution. Slowly and firmly they undertook to spread the good word and to show the resemblances between the old religious forms and the new. In establishing the worship of the Virgin they could build upon such feminine deities as Brigitte and Eostre, firmly fixed in the traditions of the Celtic peoples; and in establishing many important intermediary saints they drew on the Teutonic and Scandinavian pantheons. Thus while the Christian religion spread slowly over Europe, Christian art necessarily lagged even farther behind.

Because of the highly unsettled character of this period of the wandering of peoples (about the fifth to the eighth centuries) little could be done in the construction of edifices and just as little could be accomplished in the arts that usually accompany architecture, namely, mosaic, painting, and sculpture. Neither actual buildings nor architectural fragments have survived. Yet we may reasonably suppose that the non-Christianized pagans engaged in very little elaborate building and that the pagan converts, when they did undertake architecture, followed the simplest schemes at their disposal—perhaps some variant of the old-fashioned early Christian basilicas.

Of the period of the fifth to the eighth centuries in northern Europe only jewelry and illuminated manuscripts have survived. Before discussing either art, we may observe that the regions which give forth these remains appear to trace the course of the wandering peoples. The graves have yielded a considerable number of elaborate ornaments in precious and semiprecious metals. Used for personal as well as general decoration, these arms, armor, fine pins, brooches, and buckles worn by men and animals, are almost all marked with the same general artistic qualities. Therefore it is not unreasonable to suppose that the regions where these grave ornaments have been found may indicate the path through Europe of the wandering peoples or imply the various influences on their artistic styles, perhaps both.

In western Siberia an extensive group of jewelry was found, decorated with stylized beast ornamentation. Here a rather sophisticated presentation in goldwork of types of hybrid and imaginary monsters recalls the art of the Far East.

Ornaments in precious metals were found in a group from the shores of the Black Sea. These would seem to be a significant link in the chain. Apparently the nomads in this region learned not only the use of gold but the setting of precious stones in cloisons (metallic settings). Probably the next stopping place of the burial hordes was the section that is today Hungary and Rumania. Here they added to their repertory the interlace motif, one of the most popular of all, and clearly the fruit of their new environment. This new element of ornament goes back to the earliest period in European history, the La Tène era of pre-literary times, when abstract ornament had reached a high level. The graves in this European region reveal the warrior interred in full regalia with his horse similarly attired. Indeed, most of our findings consist of metallic ornaments worn

Left, example of beast ornament; *right,* example of interlace.

by both horse and rider, although other items of ritualistic significance have been found, particularly in Spain.

In examining the typical specimens of this ornamental art used by both men and women, one is struck by its abundant luxuriousness. Various interpretations have sprung from this quality: that it signifies the barbaric nature of the makers, that it is a vulgar sort of display, a desire to overornament one's person, that it betrays the savage love of color for its own sake. All of these observations may be valid to a degree, since the creators of this art by no means worked in a stable and refined culture. But when it is asserted that the plaited and interlaced ornaments indicate a fundamental restlessness, interpretation goes too far. Such an element as the interlace, in common with every other element in this barbarian ornamentation, was borrowed from Eastern and Near Eastern sources. The same may be said of the reduction of animal forms to abstract patterns. The essential contribution of the makers themselves consists in the wonderfully energetic use of the materials borrowed, and in the imaginative approach to the problems of decoration—more imaginative by far than the Near East and Far East might have displayed at a similar stage of evolution.

Of course one is tempted to point to the best examples, to the Petrossa Treasury (in Bucharest) and particularly to the famous Guarrazar Treasury (Cluny Museum, Paris) found near Toledo during the nineteenth century. The Spanish group consists of votive crowns dedicated by a number of early Visigoth kings—the donors' names are indicated in a series of pendant letters—and designed to hang over the altar of their favorite church. The crowns themselves are set with most elaborate cloisons and stones and embellished with fine ornament in low relief. Not only are the crowns significant as examples of the goldsmiths' work of this period; but they help to controvert the layman's persistent notion that the time of the wandering of the nations was literally the age of darkness. Furthermore, they testify to the enthusiastic and almost childlike manner in which the peoples of the early Middle Ages embraced any given cause once they had been convinced of its essential validity.

The arts of writing and book illumination, generally speaking, were poorly developed during this period. The manuscripts of France, Spain, Germany, and Italy are concrete indications of the low state of learning in this era of wandering. There is one brilliant exception—Ireland. Because of its isolated geographical position, Ireland was far less affected by the wandering back and forth of various national groups, the frequent wars, and the general turmoil of this time when Europe was setting its house in order. Perhaps because of its very isolation, Ireland was able to evolve a solid and substantial type of religious culture. Here education was more general than it was fated to be on the Continent for a long time. Compared with the situation on the Continent, the Bible and other religious and secular books existed in Ireland in a relatively uncorrupted state. Naturally, under such conditions, the book as a form of writing and an opportunity for embellishment would flourish. The poor quality of the miniatures in the Merovingian (pre-Carolingian) books of most of western Europe offers a sharp contrast to the extremely skillful and sophisticated decoration produced in Ireland at the same period.

Like the metal art of the same times in the other European countries, Irish art for the most part concerned itself with a series of finely abstracted ornaments derived from both living and purely geometric sources. But the character of Irish manuscript ornament is infinitely more subtle. It begins to partake of the quality of finely made jewelry. The explanation for the evident superiority of Irish motifs may be found both in Ireland's higher degree of general culture and in its evident continuity of the La Tène tradition of stylized ornamentation. Geometrization reached a higher level of refinement and skill in the best examples of Irish manuscripts than ever before in Merovingian times. It is here that the characteristically northern combinations of geometric and animal motifs appear—a feature common to both Celtic and Scandinavian art. Animals pursue and bite each other, as in the previously noted Siberian metal objects, but in a much more complex and fanciful manner until the borders of the page literally writhe.

Even when it is devoted to purely abstract motifs, the page appears to be dominated by a dynamic force nowhere so well expressed as in this Irish art. A typical if slightly exaggerated example is the well-known initial page from the Book of Kells, where the swing from side to side implies a furious energy but one that is well controlled. The typical Irish page, vital as it is, is nevertheless carefully organized. The Irish illuminator is an excellent composer, with a good sense of balance and a fine dash and swing. But the truly amazing part of his creation is the delicacy and complexity of his ornament. Here is evident a relationship to the fine jewelry of these people, as one can see by comparing the scrollwork and the simulated inlays of the books with identical passages in such famous Irish jewels as the Tara Brooch, the Cross of Cong, St. Patrick's Bell Reliquary, etc.

Of Irish architecture during this period nothing remains but the numerous bell towers that were probably originally attached to monasteries since disappeared. These melancholy-looking cylinders usually have a series of elaborate stone crosses near them, embellished either with religious or legendary stories. The figure art of these crosses, like that of the manuscripts, is conspicuously lacking in realism. The crosses are more interesting as probably the last vestige of a pre-Christian veneration of large stones—a pagan idea now transmuted into Christian symbols.

We cannot doubt the tremendous part played by the Irish monks in the culture of the Carolingian and Ottonian periods (ninth and tenth centuries)—not in their immediate vicinity alone (Isle of Man and England) but on the Continent as well. Three of the most famous monastic centers of the Middle Ages appear to have been founded by them: St. Gall in Switzerland, Fulda on the Rhine, and Bobbio in Italy. At the court of Charlemagne (ninth century) they were, in the person of Alcuin and his followers, the initiators of the Carolingian "renaissance."

The Carolingian Period: IX Century.—When he carved out an empire including most of France and Germany as well as northern Italy, Charlemagne considered himself as much a "defender of the faith" as any of the later kings who took to themselves that title. Although not an educated man himself (apparently he never learned to write), he was vitally interested in the spread of culture and in educational reform, particularly in religious learning. To these ends he solicited the aid of the Irish monasteries, where the traditions of the early church had been preserved. The need for reform is evident in even a cursory examination of the manuscripts of the Merovingian period, where both the calligraphy and the text are exceedingly debased. Since learning did not and could not receive any adequate support during the unsettled period of wandering, deterioration and corruption were inevitable. Ireland, of course, was an exception; there the works of the church fathers together with the pagan classics had been preserved in a relatively accurate condition. As for the Continent, it is said that the clergymen of that period were no better than the texts which they used, and that they needed just as much cultural improvement.

Although the term "Carolingian Renaissance" implies a revival of pagan antiquity (particularly since Charlemagne fancied himself a Roman emperor), the art and literature of the period stem from other sources. In architecture the Byzantine influence prevailed; in manuscripts, that of early Christianity as well as Byzantium; and in the minor arts (jewelry, etc.), that of the barbarian period. Since the primary activity involved the reformation of texts and learning in general, it is reasonable to suppose that the early church culture played an important rôle. The important books of the period, the Bible and Psalm books (Psalters) reflect this clearly; and the mere fact that the book itself became such an important object is eloquent testimony to the influence of the Christian past. One may say that the book, during the Carolingian period, acquired a sacred character. Not only was it regarded with religious awe but fittingly embellished with sumptuous decoration.

Almost invariably the books were enclosed within elaborately carved ivory covers which were sometimes worked with precious metals (the Codex Aureus of St. Emmeran is worked with gold). We should not be surprised at the lavishness with which the sacred books were ornamented when we recall that the donors—the Carolingian kings and nobles—had only emerged from the period of barbarism. Indeed, the decorative motifs on the covers and in the pages of the books themselves eloquently emphasize the barbarian residue. Large-size stones are set in cloisons; there are interlaces and other geometric ornaments, all redolent of the not yet forgotten wandering period.

Within the books themselves we may observe certain common features. Frequently we come across dedication pages in which the king or noble for whom the book was produced is represented with his attendants, all of whom are made to appear much smaller than he. Another common element is the evangelist page, inserted before each book of the Gospels representing Matthew, Mark, Luke, or John. Full-page miniatures are often found with a symbol of the Fountain of Life or of the Church drawn in a manner reminiscent of the early Christian period. The books are particularly rich in the so-called "canon tables," which consist of four parallel vertical columns of Roman numbers referring to specific passages in the biblical books. These were used by the medieval priests as a kind of subject index of useful texts. In other books, particularly in the numerous Psalters, other types of illustration appear. Common among these is the large initial letter illustration, such as the letter B used to introduce the first Psalm—"B"lessed is the man . . .

The majority of these manuscripts show an extremely linear style, which varies considerably both in skill and attractiveness. This linear quality does not exclude the fact that many of the figures are extremely sculptural; the three-dimensional nature of the figures frequently exists rather in spite of the emphasis on line. Looking at an example of the most tumultuous of the Carolingian schools, Rheims, one is immediately struck by the intense expression of the eyes, the lively handling of the lines. The groundline billows and heaves, the figures bend forward or backward in an exaggerated manner; even the drapery expresses in its fluttering folds a certain dynamic and emotionalized state of mind. All of these qualities are particularly evident in the Utrecht Psalter whose illustrations are pure line drawings of elongated and nervous figures representing in literal and often naïve fashion the Psalms of David. For the passage in which the rays from the torch of God strike the countenance of the Psalmist, for example, the artist shows God in the upper lefthand corner holding a lighted torch from which rays shoot directly into the face of the singer in the opposite corner.

Of the architecture of the Carolingian era little has survived; but certain facts can be deduced. The resemblance to Byzantine architectural forms becomes close if we judge by such a monument as the octagonally planned Palace Chapel at Aix-la-Chapelle with its covering dome, or the church at Germigny-les-Près (near Loiret), designed on a scheme that might be described as a Greek cross inscribed in a square. In the Aix-la-Chapelle building the derivation from San Vitale at Ravenna is self-evident; in Germigny-les-Près we find a variant of the Eastern type. The few buildings surviving in Germany proper (excepting Aix-la-Chapelle) seem to indicate simple deviations from the buildings of the early Christian period.

One is tempted to make sweeping generalizations about the emotional content of Carolingian art, to attribute it entirely to the barbarian temperament. But we must admit at once that a good many Carolingian ideas have been traced to the culture of Byzantium. The political and social relationships between Charlemagne's court and Constantinople are well enough known to make the implied borrowing plausible. Many figures in early Byzantine or east Christian art can be related to those of the Carolingian period by removing the surface paint from the former and thus exposing the line drawings underneath. Then many figure and landscape motifs emerge clearly. But this Carolingian-Byzantine early Christian relationship does not necessarily tell the whole story. For one thing, the very shift from a mass-painted to a primarily linear art was motivated by something in the minds or in the needs of the Carolingian artists. They borrowed only what was suited either to their temperaments or purposes. Obviously, we know too little of these people to speak with assurance; but we do know the transitional character of the period as well as its highly unsettled religious matrix, and these facts alone would make the extremely emotionalized quality of their art understandable. Following Charlemagne's death, the collapse and subsequent redistribution of his kingdom into numerous small nations contributed generously to the unsettledness of the period. This fact takes on particular significance for the study of art when we realize that much art of the so-called Carolingian period was produced after Charlemagne's death.

With the division of Charlemagne's territory into three major parts (by the Strasbourg Oaths of 843), we begin the transition to the new era. For the history of art, the accession of Otto I of Germany (A.D. 937) is significant. After compelling the nobles of Franconia, Suabia, Bavaria, etc., to pay him homage, Otto journeyed to Rome to be crowned the first chief of the Holy Roman Empire—a loose confederation whose advent may be regarded as the beginning of Germany's Romanesque period in art. Since there appears to have been, under the various Ottos of the tenth century, some sort of important court center, it is not surprising that art should begin to develop. Although this period shows no important architectural or sculptural productions, it did produce an abundance of fine manuscripts—manuscripts related in style to the more nervous and psychotic art of the Carolingians and to the austere, monumental examples of Byzantine art.

When we look at a typical work of this period—such as the Evangelist page from the Gospels of Otto II—we are immediately struck by the intense emotional quality that is no longer a product of the loose, broken style of drawing which it had been under the Carolingians, but a carefully finished painting that is almost soberly mad. The glaring eye of the Evangelist, the agitated character of his drapery, the extremely excited colors of the page, and the circle of figures about his head are intensifications of the Carolingian emotionalism compounded with Byzantine overtones. Most interesting is the fact that these manuscripts anticipate the Romanesque style of the eleventh and twelfth centuries in their elongated bodies and twisted postures. There is no doubting that these Ottonian manuscripts were decisive factors in the evolution of the sculptural style of the succeeding period in Germany.

The agitation and nervousness found in these Ottonian pages is paralleled in the ivories of the same period. Most spectacular is the famous *Doubting Thomas* where in a narrow, vertical space Christ is placed upon a small stool, his arm upraised so that the doubting disciple can put his finger into the wound. Thomas literally climbs up to reach the tiny orifice offered to him, and fits his body into the curve created by Christ's upraised arm. As a tightly knit example of vivid linear composition, this pair has seldom, if ever, been equaled. As an expression of emotional intensity it is one of the finest works of what we may now call the Romanesque period.

IX. MUSIC

The origins of the music performed in Europe in the Middle Ages may be traced back to the music of the Mediterranean civilizations, chiefly the Greek. Only a comparatively small amount of pre-medieval music has come down to us, however, and despite the important part played by music in the life of the Greeks, only a few fragments of it are now extant.

The oldest music that has been adequately preserved in large quantities belongs to the medieval Christian church. In music as well as in letters it was the church alone which served as custodian of older traditions. Unfortunately the church looked upon music solely as an accessory to prayer and was thus indifferent to secular music. Hence, although the common people must have danced and sung, almost all European dance tunes and secular songs of the first eleven Christian centuries have been irretrievably lost.

Deriving in large measure from the music of the Jews and the Greeks, and receiving its important impetus from the musical practices of the early Christians of Syria, the music of the early medieval church developed rapidly and reached its peak as a mature art about A.D. 900. Unlike most of the other arts of its time, this music existed in a highly finished state, and its beauties are just as apparent to modern ears as they were to those of the monks and priests of the Middle Ages.

Today we use various names to designate the ecclesiastical music of this period. Among them are plain song, plain chant, and Gregorian chant.

The music of the church developed concurrently with its liturgy, a body of rites which has undergone no important changes in the last thirteen hundred years. The core of this liturgy is the elaborately dramatized procedure known as the Mass, a symbolic representation of the Last Supper. The various parts of the text of the Mass may be divided into two categories: the Proper (*Proprium Missae*) and the Ordinary (*Ordinarium Missae*). The Proper consists of the Introit, Collect, Epistle, Gradual, Alleluia (or Tract), Gospel, Offertory, Secret, Preface, Communion, and Post-Communion. The parts of the Proper change with each day of the year. Psalm texts find extensive employment in them. The greater part of the collection of plain chants used in the celebration of Mass consists of settings of the Proper and includes about six hundred compositions.

The Ordinary, in contrast to the Proper, has an invariable text which has not been altered since its final formulation in 1014. Non-biblical in origin, the Ordinary consists of five parts—the *Kyrie eleison, Gloria, Credo, Sanctus,* and *Agnus Dei.* As a musical and not a liturgical designation, the term *Mass* later came to denote a setting of the Ordinary. The text of the Ordinary, although prose, possesses splendid musical potentialities and has continually attracted the attention of composers. No other text has been set to music so frequently.

That musical characteristic which differentiates the music of the early medieval church from the music common today is this: it is pure melody, a single vocal line utterly devoid of accompaniment. The materials of the plain-chant melodies are derived from scales unlike those in use in the conventional music of today, that is, the major and minor scales. The scales used for almost all the music written before A.D. 1600 are usually called "modes," and are designated by names used by the Greeks for their scales, though through a curious error in medieval scholarship the ecclesiastical and the Greek modes of the same name are not identical. In their simplest form the ecclesiastical modes are:

It should be observed that all of these modes may be formed by using only the white keys of the piano.

Another feature which differentiates plain chant from more recent music is its rhythmic freedom. Various theories concerning the rhythmic aspects of plain chant have been set forth. In any case, the rhythms of plain chant are not metrical, but derive from the rhetorical implications of the text. This absence of metrical rhythms is responsible for the names *plain* chant or *plain* song.

The plain-chant melodies vary in elaborateness. Some of them are almost monotones. Others are exceedingly florid and abound in flowing figures and complicated melodic lines. But the music is usually subservient to the text.

Two great ecclesiasts, both doctors of the church, stand out prominently in the history of early church music, and both have had collections of music named after them. The first of these ecclesiastical figures is Ambrose (340-397), bishop of Milan from 374. A great scholar, executive, and statesman, Ambrose was responsible for the introduction into the music of the western church of certain features of Eastern music, notably the antiphonal (responsive) singing of psalms, and metrical hymns. The texts of twelve hymns are attributed to Ambrose himself. He also attempted to systematize the music of the church. The type of plain chant fostered by him is known as Ambrosian chant and remains to this day unique to the diocese of the Church of Milan.

The second important figure in the history of ecclesiastical music is Pope Gregory the Great (c. 540-604), after whom the great body of plain chant has been named "Gregorian" chant. Gregory was one of the most famous men of his time and since he took an active hand in the ordering of the liturgy, it was to be expected that his biographers might, in an excess of zeal, erroneously attribute to him the entire collection of chants. Gregory was in reality the editor of the collection of chants bearing his name and played a large part in their dissemination to and their adoption by all the Catholic churches.

The high degree of skill demanded for the performance of plain chant resulted in the formation of a well-organized group of professional singers. A school for the instruction of these singers (*schola cantorum*) was founded in Rome early in the fourth century. The pupils were for the most part orphans, and the school was frequently called an *orphanotrophium*. The *schola cantorum* was thus the forerunner of other famous musical orphanages—the *Conservatorii* of sixteenth-century Naples. The singers, after completing their nine years of training at the *schola cantorum*, served as musical missionaries and were sent all over Europe to promulgate the chants. They also founded branch schools, of which the most famous were located at St. Gall and Metz. Charlemagne formed many schools in various parts of his empire.

The Gregorian melodies have never gone out of active use, although with the advent of polyphony they went into partial eclipse for almost eight hundred years. Many plain-chant melodies were employed by composers of polyphonic music as a framework (*cantus firmus*) around which they wove the complex texture of their works. Other plain chants have come down through the ages and have become a species of sacred folk song. One of the most famous is the hymn *Veni Creator Spiritus*, dating from the ninth century. It may be recognized with its melodic features well preserved in association with Martin Luther's chorale text *Komm, Gott Schöpfer, heiliger Geist* (1524).

Plain chant in all its original splendor was restored by the Benedictine monks of the Abbey of Solesmes, France, in the nineteenth century. Thanks to the tireless activity and the penetrating scholarship of the monks, all of the plain chants are now available, and the Solesmes edition is the Official Edition of the Roman Catholic church.

SELECTED READINGS

Allen, J. R., *Celtic Art in Pagan and Christian Times*, Jacobs, 1908.

Apel, Willi, *Gregorian Chant*, University of Indiana Press, 1958.

Arnold, T. W., and Guillaume, Alfred, eds., *The Legacy of Islam*, Oxford Press, 1931.

Barker, Ernest, ed., *Social and Political Thought in Byzantium*, Oxford University Press, 1957.

Barnes, H. E., *A History of Historical Writing*, Dover Publications, Inc., 1962.

Barrett, H. M., *Boëthius*, Macmillan, 1940.

Byron, Robert, *The Byzantine Achievement*, Knopf, 1929.

Carroll, M. T. A., *The Venerable Bede: His Spiritual Teachings*, Catholic University Press, 1946.

Dalton, O. M., *Byzantine Art and Archaeology*, Dover Publications, Inc., 1961.

Dawson, C. H., *The Making of Europe*, Macmillan, 1932.

Diehl, Charles, *Byzantium: Greatness and Decline*, Rutgers University Press, 1957.

Dopsch, *The Economic and Social Foundations of European Civilization.*

Duckett, E. S., *Alcuin, Friend of Charlemagne*, Macmillan, 1951.

—— *Alfred the Great*, University of Chicago Press, 1956.

—— *Anglo-Saxon Saints and Scholars*, Macmillan, 1947.

—— *The Gateway to the Middle Ages*, Ann Arbor Books, 1961.

—— *The Wandering Saints of the Early Middle Ages*, Norton, 1959.

Eby and Arrowood, *The History and Philosophy of Education*, chap. xv.

Foligno, *Latin Thought during the Middle Ages*, chaps. i-iv.

Hearnshaw, F. J. C., ed., *The Social and Political Ideas of Some Great Medieval Thinkers*, Holt, 1923.

——*Medieval Contributions to Modern Civilization*, Holt, 1922.

Howell, W. S., ed., *The Rhetoric of Alcuin and Charlemagne*, Princeton University Press, 1941.

Hughes, Dom Anselm, ed., *New Oxford History of Music*, Vol. II, Oxford University Press, 1955.

Hussey, J. M., *Church and Learning in the Byzantine Empire*, Oxford Press, 1937.

Ker, W. P., *The Dark Ages*, New American Library.

Kershner, F. D., *Pioneers of Christian Thought*, Bobbs-Merrill, 1930.

Krumbacher, Karl, *Geschichte der byzantinischen Litteratur*, Burt Franklin, 1958.

Laistner, M. L. W., *Thought and Letters in Western Europe, A.D. 500-900*, Cornell University Press, 1957.

Lang, P. H., *Music in Western Civilization*, Norton, 1941.

Lethaby, W. R., *Medieval Art*, new ed., Scribner, 1913.

McGiffert, A. C., *History of Christian Thought*, Vol. II.

McIlwain, C. H., *The Growth of Political Thought in the West*, Macmillan, 1932, chap. v.

MacKinney, L. C., *Early Medieval Medicine*, Johns Hopkins University Press, 1937.

McNeill, J. T., *Makers of Christianity*, Holt, 1935.

Monroe, Paul, *A Textbook in the History of Education*, Macmillan, 1912, chap. v.

Morey, C. R., *Christian Art*, Norton, 1958.

Moss, H. St.L. B., *The Birth of the Middle Ages, 395-814*, Oxford Press, 1935.

Nicholson, R. A., *Literary History of the Arabs*, Macmillan, 1930.

Patch, H. R., *The Tradition of Boëthius*, Oxford Press, 1935.

Pickman, E. M., *The Mind of Latin Christendom*, Oxford Press, 1937.

Poole, R. L., *Illustrations of the History of Medieval Thought and Learning*, Dover, 1960.

Rand, *Founders of the Middle Ages.*

Reese, Gustave, *Music in the Middle Ages*, Norton, 1940.

Rivoira, G. T., *Moslem Architecture*, Oxford Press, 1918.

Runciman, Steven, *Byzantine Civilization*, Meridian.

Singer, *From Magic to Science*, chaps. ii-vii.

Swift, E. H., *Hagia Sophia*, Columbia University Press, 1940.

Taylor, H. O., *The Medieval Mind*, 2 Vols., Macmillan, 1927, Vol. I.

Thompson, A. H., *Bede: His Life, Times and Writings*, Oxford Press, 1935.

Thompson, J. W., *History of Historical Writing*, Books II-III.

Vasiliev, A. A., *History of the Byzantine Empire*, 2 Vols., University of Wisconsin Press, 1928-29.

Wallach, Luitpold, *Alcuin and Charlemagne*, Cornell University Press, 1960.

Workman, H. B., *Christian Thought to the Reformation*, Scribner, 1914.

IX

*Medieval Thought
From Abelard to Dante:
The Medieval Synthesis*

I. THE MATERIAL BACKGROUND

In order to understand medieval civilization at its height one must pay some attention to the material background. This is to be found in the feudal system of politics; the great state church, Roman Catholicism; and the rise of towns and trade, especially after the Crusades. We shall first look at the general nature of the feudal system.

1. *Feudalism*

Feudalism has been a widespread, if not quite universal, stage in the evolution of society and political institutions. Its two fundamental characteristics were: (1) partial protection of the helpless members of society, and (2) their exploitation by the noble classes for economic and military purposes. In return for the protection of his clients against robbery and invasion by outsiders, the feudal lord demanded that his clients work for him, help him in his own raids and brigandage, and follow him into war. The relationship binding together the overlord and his clients under feudalism was primarily a personal one, as distinguished from the real or fictitious blood relationship of primitive society and the financial, territorial and political foundations of later civil society.

Feudalism was a merging of personal, economic, and political elements. On the personal side Rome contributed the *patrocinium* by which an unprotected man allied himself to a powerful patron for protection. Germany added the *comitatus*. This strengthened the personal relationship, which was now based upon enthusiasm and personal devotion as well as upon sheer necessity. The Germanic underlings not only received protection but also willingly took part in the raids and wars of their leaders and received their portion of the spoils. The Muslim invasion transformed a relationship devoted primarily to brigandage into a broader system involving organized military service. The patrocinium and the comitatus were merged through the institution of commendation (*commendatio*) to constitute the vassalage of medieval feudalism, which involved not only protection but military obligations.

On the economic side we start with the Roman *precarium*. This was the land or property handed over by helpless freemen to some local noble as payment for protection. The Germans added nothing comparable to this economic phase of feudalism. But the necessity of raising soldiers to repel the Muslims led the Frankish kings to seize church lands and to confer them upon their followers, in order that the latter might have some material basis for supplying soldiers, horses, and other military equipment. In short, dependents of lords were given what was now called the *beneficium* in return for reciprocal military obligations. The beneficium was the Roman precarium with the military element added. The precarium, moreover, was usually brought to the lord by the dependent, while the beneficium was conferred upon the inferior by the lord.

In due time it became usual to hand down the beneficium from one vassal to his descendants, usually the eldest male descendant, in accordance with the prevailing practice of primogeniture. When the beneficium became definitely hereditary and carried with it the obligation to furnish military equipment and other feudal aids it became the *fief,* the economic core of the feudal system. The vassal owned and transmitted his fief in return for definite and well-recognized obligations of a personal and military character due to his overlord. This gave the vassal his much-needed protection, while it provided the lord with the power and prestige he desired.

The essential political and legal aspects of feudalism appeared in the principles of localism and immunity. The king was not powerful enough fully to assert his authority over the local communities of his realms. Had he been able to do this there would have been no particular need for feudal institutions. As soon as kings became sufficiently strong to govern their realms and to protect their subjects, the feudal system disintegrated. In the meantime, politics and law rested upon the institution of immunity. That is, the feudal lords owed specific feudal obligations to the kings. Once these were met, the lords enjoyed essential sovereignty in their own domains. They were legally, as well as practically, immune to intrusive royal interference, and were empowered to govern and control their own realms in harmony with the prevailing practices of feudal law and administration. Decentralization was supreme, and remained so until the feudal system gave way in the face of the rising tide of nationalism and kingly power.

The political anarchy, which preceded the domination of feudalism and accompanied its earlier stages, was gradually reduced as strong feudal monarchies were shaped by Henry II of England (1154-1189), Philip Augustus of France (1180-1223) and Frederick Barbarossa of Germany (1152-1190). Order was better preserved and conditions became more settled. The towns aided in preserving order and in protecting life and property. Improved political conditions gave medieval thought and culture a more favorable environment for development.

2. *The Church*

Far and away the most important medieval institution was the church, which became thoroughly enmeshed in the feudal system. Some of the most powerful feudal lords were abbots, bishops, and archbishops. The Roman Catholic church has been usually and quite rightly regarded as a spiritual agency designed to procure salvation. But the business of assuring salvation for its millions of communicants necessitated an elaborate administrative and financial organization. At its height, there were over 500,000 clergy in the church. Therefore, incidentally but significantly, the church evolved into the greatest international state that the Western World ever knew down to the rise of the great modern colonial structures after A.D. 1500. Professor Flick has splendidly summarized this basic conception of the church:

> The Church was essentially an organized state, thoroughly centralized, with one supreme head and a complete gradation of officials; with a comprehensive system of law courts for trying cases, with penalties covering all crimes, and with prisons for punishing offenders. It demanded an allegiance from all its members somewhat like that existing today between subjects and a state. It developed one official language, the Latin, which was used to conduct its business everywhere. Thus all western Europe was one great religious association from which it was treason to revolt. Canon law punished such a crime with death, public opinion sanctioned the penalty, and the secular arm executed the sentence.[1]

It is clear, then, that in addition to its spiritual prestige and prerogatives, the Catholic church of the Middle Ages was a vast international state of greater territorial extent and financial resources than any secular power of the period. From parish to provinces, all united under the jurisdiction of the Holy See, it not only embraced much the larger part of Europe but also boasted colonies of converts in Africa and Asia.

The foregoing view of the medieval church helps us to understand the nature of the Protestant revolution. This was not simply an attempt to modify the doctrine of the church. It was far more truly a political and economic secession from the great international ecclesiastical state, based on the desire to be free from its financial exactions.

This picture of the ecclesiastical bureaucracy is likewise essential to an understanding of the church's view of heresy and its ferocious behavior towards heretics. Historians like W. E. H. Lecky and others believed that the church acted with great severity and rapidity against heretics because it felt sorry for the damned who were led astray by them. There is probably some element of truth in this contention. At least, it was an official excuse for the zeal against heretics. Yet the vigor with which heresy was suppressed resulted more from the fact that the church considered it treason or anarchy, a challenge to its political organization. To tolerate heresy would have been to envisage the possibility of rebellion, secession, and the crumbling of its whole administrative structure. Heresy was made

---

[1] Flick, *The Rise of the Medieval Church*, pp. 603-4. Cf. A. C. Krey, "The International State of the Middle Ages," *American Historical Review*, October, 1922.

a crime in European civil law in the twelfth century. Capital punishment for heresy was invariably inflicted by the state, not by the church. As Professor Flick says:

> It must never be forgotten that heresy was the greatest crime of the Middle Ages. God had planted His Church on earth, appointed the Pope as vice-gerent, and prescribed laws and dogmas in the Bible and the canons to govern the Church. Any violation of these laws, or disbelief in the dogmas, was heresy. Consequently, heresy was treason against both the Church and God.[2]

In spite of corruption or laxity the medieval church maintained an inflexible discipline, so that a leading historian of the medieval church, Henry C. Lea, could accurately describe it as a great army protecting spiritual interests against a world of sin:

> The Church Militant was thus an army encamped on the soil of Christendom, with its outposts everywhere, subject to the most efficient discipline, animated with a common purpose, every soldier panoplied with inviolability and armed with the tremendous weapons which slew the soul. There was little that could not be dared or done by the commander of such a force, whose orders were listened to as oracles of God, from Portugal to Palestine and from Sicily to Iceland. . . .
>
> History records no such triumph of intellect over brute strength as that which, in an age of turmoil and battle, was wrested from the fierce warriors of the time by the priests who had no material force at their command, and whose power was based alone on the souls and consciences of men. Over soul and conscience their empire was complete. No Christian could hope for salvation who was not in all things an obedient son of the Church, and who was not ready to take up arms in its defence; and, in a time when faith was a determining factor of conduct, this belief created a spiritual despotism which placed all things within reach of him who could wield it.[3]

As a strong international state, the church checked feudal wars, by means of instruments known as the Truce of God and the Peace of God.

Not only was the church a great international political organization in its administrative control of religious life and beliefs; the pope himself was also a secular prince in his own right. He ruled over a considerable area in and north of Rome known as the States of the church. This territory was gradually enlarged through legacies and annexations, and its ownership was later justified on the basis of an alleged "Donation" of the Emperor Constantine, a forged document of the second half of the eighth century, which alleged that Constantine bestowed these lands upon the pope, who was to reign over them as a king.[4] It was forged to strengthen the claims of the pope to temporal power.

The medieval church devised many ingenious methods for enforcing discipline

---

[2] Flick, *op. cit.*, pp. 557-58.

[3] H. C. Lea, *History of the Inquisition of the Middle Ages*, Harper, 1888, 3 vols. (now Macmillan), I, 1, 4. On the character and extent of the remarkable writings of H. C. Lea on the Medieval Church, see C. H. Haskins, *Studies in Medieval Culture*, Oxford Press, 1929, pp. 256 ff., and E. S. Bradley, *Henry Charles Lea*, University of Pennsylvania Press, 1931.

[4] Cf. Thorndike, *History of Medieval Europe*, pp. 197-98; and C. B. Coleman, *Constantine the Great and Christianity*, Columbia University Press, 1914.

upon all believers from the most impoverished serf to the most powerful emperor. The basis of this discipline was the inexhaustible resources of mental intimidation in a superstitious age. Medieval people feared above all else the activities of the devil in this life and the prospect of damnation in the next. The church was their great bulwark against the devil, both here and in the hereafter. If the church withheld its offices of worship and salvation, the believer felt himself hopelessly lost. No secular ruler ever had any such power over his subjects.

> In the long career of the church [says Henry C. Lea] towards universal dominion, perhaps the most efficient instrument at its command was its control over the sacrifice of the altar (sacrament of the mass). Through this it opened the gates of heaven to the obedient, and plunged the rebellious into the pit of hell; and the generations which implicitly believed in its authority over the world to come were necessarily rendered docile subjects in this world. Armed with a power so vast and vague, it could intervene decisively in the dissensions between sovereign and people, and subdue them both to its designs of highest state-craft, making each the means to humiliate the other; while, at the same time, it could control the life of the obscurest peasant, and bind him helplessly in blind submission to the behests of its humblest minister. This despotism so absolute and so all-pervading, which dictated the action of kings, while it interpenetrated every fibre of society, was based upon the religion of love, and self-sacrifice, and humility. Human history, so fruitful of paradoxes, scarce offers an example more notable of the perversion of good into evil. The divine precepts of charity, forgiveness, and self-abnegation, distorted by the ignorance, the passion, and the selfishness of man, became the warrant by which greed and ambition attained the fruition of their wildest hopes.[5]

This terroristic power was applied specifically in many ways. The authority to absolve from sins that would otherwise lead to damnation was lodged in a priesthood. The ability to withhold absolution permitted churchmen to wield a powerful club over all communicants. To grant absolution was a supreme favor. No material service matched its significance in the eyes of believers. In order to secure complete absolution and forgiveness, the church might compel the sinner to do penance, governing which there were elaborate rules and regulations. Penance might include not only severe personal humiliation but expensive and dangerous pilgrimages to distant holy places. Money payments for penance came to be freely allowed.

An impressive form of psychic terrorism was excommunication from the church. This separated the offender from all ecclesiastical ministrations. He no longer had any access to its saving worship or graces, was at the complete mercy of the devil and was certain to be damned unless he repented and the church was gracious enough to readmit him to membership. Moreover, it was not permissible for good Christians to associate with the excommunicated. Excommunication therefore produced abject terror in the minds of all who really believed in the doctrines of the church, since it made them the legitimate prey of demoniac and human enemies. It was comparable to exile from the gods and the group in primitive society, deemed by early man the most horrible of all punishments.

[5] Lea, *Studies in Church History*, Lea, 1869, p. 235.

Less frequently employed but even more terrible was the interdict, which might be loosed against either a city, a locality, or a nation. It forbade the performance of all acts of public worship. In a country placed under the interdict, the churches were all closed, the church bells remained silent, the administration of the sacraments was refused except in the case of infant baptism and extreme unction (and even these were sometimes denied), no burial rites were performed, and the pallor of death hung over the community.

Today the closing of all churches and the cessation of all religious rites might be taken calmly in skeptical lands. Not so in the Middle Ages. Nothing more terrible than the interdict could be imagined. It denied to the whole population access to those things which protected them from evil spirits and from the awful prospect of damnation. It was particularly effective in bringing a recalcitrant monarch to terms. His subjects might feel that they were innocent of royal sins which had produced the interdict, yet they, as well as the guilty monarch, had to suffer. Terror and resentment united to force the king in most cases to humiliate himself and comply with ecclesiastical commands. One of the most notable examples of the invocation of the interdict was its use by Pope Innocent III against King John of England. The only thing today that would in any way correspond to the terrifying nature of the medieval interdict would be a successful "general strike" in a busy industrial community. And even this would not have the same panicky consequences.

Another effective method of preserving church discipline was the Holy Inquisition. Established in the thirteenth century, this ecclesiastical court was composed of experts in the detection of heresy. Its secret proceedings and incredible tortures made it a powerful terroristic agency. At times the church might order actual warfare upon unbelievers in the form of a holy crusade, like that declared against the Albigenses in southern France by Innocent III in 1208. Thus, it is not difficult to understand why the church exercised and maintained so stupendous an influence over the minds of men for more than a thousand years.

There are plenty of examples illustrating the church's power in humiliating all secular rivals. The disciplining of Henry IV of Germany by Pope Gregory VII in the last quarter of the eleventh century is frequently called to mind. But Pope Innocent III (1198-1216)—in the words of Professor Hulme, "an imperious ruler, handsome, learned in canon law, entirely practical, a master of statecraft, asserting his indomitable will throughout the continent"—humiliated or disciplined every important crowned head of western Europe. He rebuked the powerful King Philip Augustus of France, whose wishes he ignored in regard both to marriage and to succession to the throne of the Holy Roman Empire. He humbled King John of England by placing him under the interdict. Later he released him from the agreements in the Magna Charta and by implication abrogated that document. He brushed aside the Holy Roman emperor, Otto, and excommunicated him. He compelled Frederick II, king of Sicily, when he ascended the throne, to concede all the papal demands and also presided over his election as Holy Roman emperor.

When we think of the great princes of the medieval period we usually call to mind persons like Charlemagne, William the Conqueror, Otto the Great, Philip Augustus, or Frederick Barbarossa. But none of these can be compared for a moment with a powerful pope like Innocent III. Leaving out of consideration his spiritual authority and pretensions, Innocent had far greater political, financial, and judicial power, and even more princely magnificence, than any secular European ruler between Hadrian and Napoleon Bonaparte.

3. *The Rise of Medieval Towns*

One of the most important social developments which stimulated medieval thought and culture was the rise of towns, especially in the eleventh and twelfth centuries. In the towns we find medieval thought and culture sheltered, encouraged, and cherished.

The early Middle Ages had a destructive effect upon urban life. Of the Roman municipality little remained except the tradition. While some of the great Italian and Gallic cities were physically unharmed during the invasions, they were in many ways transformed almost beyond recognition. No longer was there a teeming population actively engaged in commerce and industry. No longer did the municipalities perform the functions of government. In Roman Germany, a few urban communities exhibited signs of commercial life and civic activity. But in the interior of Germany, evidences of town life were very slight before the eleventh century. It is unquestionably true that on the whole the urban civilization of Roman days was undermined during the early Middle Ages.

Between the eleventh and fourteenth centuries, social and economic forces gave birth to a new urban civilization. No other movement throughout the length and breadth of the medieval age bore within it greater significance for the culture of western Europe than the rise of towns. Not only did this produce almost a social revolution, but the towns themselves were pregnant with a new civilization, a new age, which foretold radical changes in the old static agrarian feudal order. If we recognize both a medieval age and a modern age, then the rise of towns, more than any other single movement, signaled the undermining of the first and the initation of the second. But, in the meantime, the towns allowed medieval culture to rise to its highest form of expression.

For moderns, the town is perhaps the outstanding contribution of the later Middle Ages, because the modern city traces its ancestry, in part at least, back to the medieval town. For western European civilization, the urban movement meant the introduction of a progressive element, a vital, dynamic, commercial, and financial force into medieval life. In the towns a new class, the *bourgeoisie,* made its appearance. Novel social and economic organizations developed for the production of commodities, and industry and commerce achieved an unprecedented importance.

However differently from one another the towns might be organized, as self-governing entities they were responsible for the introduction of novel social, economic, political, and legal elements into medieval Europe. Considering the intimate bond between church and state, the medieval municipalities stand out as an early example of government organized upon purely secular lines. It may also be noted, as E. B. Osborn remarks, that "during their struggles for a measure of economic freedom the medieval towns became political laboratories, in which numerous experiments in the use of a reasoned liberty and the methods of democratic government anticipated the later experience of national communities." [6]

Differences in urban institutions were caused by local conditions. Many towns in the Middle Ages succeeded in winning complete independence, but more frequently a compromise was struck between the dominion of a secular or ecclesiastical ruler and communal autonomy. The inner organization of the communes ranged from the very simple to the exceedingly complex. Throughout the diversity, however, Henri Pirenne has been able to find common characteristics:

> Everywhere the governing magistrates were grouped in councils to which members were elected either by the council, by electors following procedures which were usually very complicated, or even by lot. There was great diversity in the duration of office, which might be held for life, or, as was most common, for one year. [7]

These magistrates bore different names throughout Europe. In Italy and southern France the governing officials were consuls; in northern France and the Low Countries they were called *echevins* and *jures;* in England, aldermen; and in Germany, *Rathsherren*. These, as we have seen, formed a town council called *concilium, curia,* or some equivalent; sometimes they also constituted a judicial tribunal, which meant that the members were administrators and judges at the same time. These medieval city councils are of great importance in institutional history, since they probably constitute the first instance of truly representative government in Western civilization:

> This new type of government was distinctly representative; the city council is made up in most cases of representatives of the city parishes. It is here perhaps that representative government, which the ancient world failed to develop, first appeared in Europe, and it is worth while to note that this is first developed in the Latin countries, just as the extension of the representative principle by the appearance of town representatives in the medieval parliaments first appeared in Spain. [8]

The functions of the town council were all-embracing. They included the regulation of commerce and industry, the provisioning of the commune, defense, public works, charity, and the relief of the poor. Legislation passed by the council became the statutes of the commune; few phases of town life escaped regulation through such legislation.

The town became the center of most later medieval manufacturing and commerce. In this way it created a division of labor between town and country. The town was, of course, dependent upon the country for foodstuffs. As a result, towns either sought to increase agricultural settlement in the adjoining countryside, or to gain control over the food supply. Wherever possible, the peasants were sub-

---

[6] Osborn, *The Middle Ages,* Doran, 1928, p. 215.

[7] Pirenne, article "Commune: Medieval," *Encyclopaedia of the Social Sciences,* IV, 62.

[8] Munroe Smith, *The Development of European Law,* Columbia University Press, 1928, pp. 215-16.

jected to town regulation, as a serf was by a feudal lord. Agricultural trade and prices were extensively regulated by the town.

Each metropolis tried to acquire a "sphere of influence" in the adjoining region, and to destroy or control rival municipalities. Every town tried to retain its distinct individuality, and raised around itself not only a physical wall but rigid economic barriers, such as customs duties. When it made treaties or alliances, it usually surrendered few of its privileges, and only under the pressure of special conditions did towns league together. It took the threat of total destruction to force communes to suspend antagonisms and antipathies. Once united, they were sometimes sufficiently strong to dictate to kings and emperors. Apart from such exceptions, the political and economic bonds between medieval towns were slight. A commune was not only self-centered, but to a considerable extent, when taken in connection with the adjacent countryside, it was self-sufficient.

The town was a living force generating new currents in medieval life, as opposed to the inertia of the agrarian order. The rural manor was based on provincialism, tradition, habit, and repetition, which made it insuperably conservative and custom-bound. The town was founded upon trade, intercommunity contacts, novelty, and adventure. All this made for a dynamic and more tolerant outlook on life.

The town culturally emancipated millions of men. It was more than a commercial and industrial center; it was a political, religious, and social unit as well. It was the home of cathedrals and universities. In brief, town life meant the appearance of a new civilization—a civilization unmistakably urban in all its manifestations, in literature, learning, architecture, political thought, and economic organization.

II. THE CULTURAL HERITAGE FROM WEST AND EAST

1. *The Heritage from the Dark Ages*

There were a number of important influences and contributions which combined to produce the well-developed medieval philosophy and science of the age of Thomas Aquinas (1225-1274).

First, we have the progress of thought in the latter part of the Dark Ages. The Christian faith was supported by an appeal to authority—chiefly the authority of the great church fathers. This culminated in the compilations of Rhabanus and Walafrid Strabo. Reasoned defense of Christian doctrine occupied a secondary place, even though the compilers emphasized the importance of logic as an aid to theology.

Beginning with Erigena, however, stress was laid upon logic as a mainstay of the faith. Erigena's cordiality towards Neoplatonism prevented him from rehabilitating the Aristotelian tradition in European thought, but he helped to revive respect for a closely reasoned theology. We have seen that Anselm treated fundamental theological problems on the basis of logic rather than authority or revelation. An even greater impetus to logical reasoning came from the debates between the realists and nominalists which arose near the close of the Dark Ages. Logical disputation was essential in such intellectual exercises. Abelard, the first important intellectual figure in the period covered by this chapter, received his stimulus to keen intellectual analysis from the controversy between realists and nominalists. His teachers were drawn from both camps, a fact which saved him from single-track dogmatism. Finally, Gerbert was not only an able logician, but he also reflected the beginnings of the Muslim influence which was to advance Aristotelian logic and revive interest in natural science for its own sake.

2. *Byzantine Learning*

The learning of the Byzantine or Eastern Empire is worthy of notice, since it was there that classical Greek culture lingered. When logic became indispensable to medieval theology, it was desirable to locate the Greek texts of Aristotle. They were found mainly, as we shall see, in Constantinople and southern Italy.

Although the Byzantine Empire is frequently called the Greek Empire, Latin was introduced and became the official language of both church and state for some time. Indeed, the Eastern Empire was known for a considerable time as the Latin Empire of the East. But Greek was always the language of everyday life in this area, and in the early Middle Ages it began to prevail in government, worship, and scholarship:

> In the course of the fifth and of the following century, the retreat of Latin was rapid. It became headlong even under the reign of Justinian. The commentaries on his collections of laws are in Greek and the authors of these commentaries are partly men like Theophilus and Dorotheus, who were employed to write the manual called the *Institutes*. It is obvious that for the everyday practice of law, it was necessary to use the spoken language, namely, Greek.[9]

The decisive factor in the triumph of Greek over Latin in the East, then, was the official adoption of the Greek language by the government even in Justinian's time. The popular language had always been Greek. When the government gave up the effort to introduce Latin and formally adopted Greek, the latter held the field with no rivals.

As a result of the prevalence of the language, the knowledge of Greek literature, philosophy, and science never entirely disappeared in the East. It was easy therefore to retain in Constantinople a fairly complete command of ancient learning. In the West knowledge was almost exclusively in the hands of the church. Eastern monks were less interested in learning and more exclusively devoted to their original ideal of spiritual contemplation. Some of the secular clergy were noted for their literary and scholarly achievements. But the revival of Hellenic learning in the East was carried out in considerable part by lay scholars. The University of Constantinople, reopened in 863, became the center of classical studies. In this way it was comparable to the "House of Wisdom" that had been opened some thirty years earlier by the Muslims in Baghdad. Those who showed most interest in learning in the East were members of the trained bureaucracy or civil service.

---

[9] Ferdinand Lot, *The End of the Ancient World*, Knopf, 1931 (Harper Torchbooks, 1961), p. 274.

Like their prototypes in the earlier Roman Empire, they were very well educated.

Byzantine learning and scholarship were more notable for their compiling and preserving qualities than for originality or independence. Byzantine literature, says Professor Bayet,

> . . . is especially distinguished for its erudition. In the presence of the treasure of learning and the works which antiquity had bequeathed to them, the Greeks of Byzantium were dazzled, and often lost the feeling for their own individuality. They thought of little else than placing themselves in the midst of all these riches and making an inventory of them; they formed immense collections of extracts, notes, and summaries. Photius, the most illustrious of the Byzantine scholars, was a compiler. He seems to have read everything, pagan or Christian, which the Hellenic literature had produced, in order to compose his *Library* or *Myriobiblos,* a vast collection of analyses and selections. . . . Symeon Metaphrastus, one of the chief officials of Constantine VII, compiled a celebrated collection of *Lives of the Saints.* He preceded the Bollandists, but he was an uncritical Bollandist. In the last half of the tenth century and at the beginning of the eleventh, Suidas, author of the lexicon so well known under this name, was merely a compiler. Many ancient works were lost because of these curious encyclopedias; when the latter were at hand, people too often ceased to read and copy the originals.[10]

We may now consider briefly some of the more important phases of Byzantine scholarship and the leading personalities who carried it on. The outstanding Byzantine classicist was the patriarch of Constantinople, Photius (c. 820-891), an extremely versatile, industrious and erudite scholar. At the request of a circle of learned friends he compiled his famous *Bibliotheca,* a voluminous collection of extracts from Greek literature, accompanied by his own synopses. Since some of Photius' sources have since been lost, we owe what we know of them to his excerpts and summaries. Another important collection of ancient Greek literature was compiled by Constantine Cephalas in the tenth century. He also edited the famous *Greek Anthology.* John Tzetzes (d. c. 1195) was an industrious and enthusiastic, but rather uncritical, collector of classical Greek literature, particularly interested in Homer. Eustathius, archbishop of Thessalonica (d. 1194), ranked next to Psellus in Byzantine scholarship. He encouraged the collection of ancient Greek texts and wrote long commentaries on some of the major works, especially Homer and Pindar. Theodore Prodomus (d. c. 1150), a prolific but uncritical savant, introduced spoken Greek into Byzantine literature, thus occupying a literary position roughly comparable to that of Gregory of Tours in the Latin West.

Since Byzantine scholarship reflected earlier Greek interests, it is not surprising that rhetoric was strongly stressed. Indeed, rhetorical studies are the most characteristic Byzantine contribution to medieval learning. Classicism or philosophy played second fiddle to rhetoric. Probably the outstanding Byzantine authority on rhetoric was Michael Acominatus (d. 1220), archbishop of Athens, an acute theologian and historian as well. Other important rhetoricians were Michael Psellus (1018-c. 1079), professor of philosophy and rhetoric at Constantinople, usually

10 Charles Bayet, in D. C. Munro and G. C. Sellery, *Medieval Civilization,* Century, 1907, pp. 219-20.

regarded as the outstanding savant of the whole Byzantine epoch, Prodomus, and the great authority on Aristotle, Nicephorus Blemmydes (c. 1195-1272). Since nothing is more fatal to intellectual freshness and originality than excessive enthusiasm for rhetoric, this helps to explain the stereotyped, artificial, and unprogressive character of Byzantine culture.

In philosophy, both Aristotle and Plato had their champions and therefore the main philosophical currents in the Greek East and the Latin West were roughly identical. When Justinian closed all Greek schools the followers of Plato in the Academy, and of Aristotle in the Lyceum, were dispersed. The first important Aristotelian and the earliest scholastic theologian of any importance in the East was John of Damascus (d. c. 750).[11] He anticipated by many centuries the effort of Albertus Magnus and Thomas Aquinas to link Christian theology and pagan philosophy. His main work, *An Exact Exposition of the Orthodox Faith,* exerted a direct influence upon Peter Lombard, Alexander of Hales, and Thomas Aquinas, important figures in later Latin scholasticism. The chief Byzantine authority on Aristotle was Blemmydes, who paraphrased many of his works, the most important being an *Abridged Physics* and an *Abridged Logic.* The latter became the most popular Byzantine textbook in logic. Another important Aristotelian was John Italos, a pupil of Psellus, who came from Italy to study in Constantinople. Italos exerted considerable influence in making known to the West the Aristotelian studies of the East. The outstanding Byzantine Platonist was Psellus, who championed Plato in a period of Aristotelian ascendancy. The movement started by Psellus inspired Plethon and Bessarion, who carried their enthusiasm to Italy in the later Middle Ages and helped to launch the Platonic revival of the Florentine Academy. From this brief review we can see how accurate is Professor Theodore Uspensky's observation that: "The circle of ideas in which the European mind was working from the eleventh to the thirteenth century was the same that we find in Byzantium."

We have already noted that Christian theology was based on Greek metaphysics. Therefore, it need occasion no surprise to learn that the Byzantines indulged in theological hairsplitting. In the West this was chiefly limited to erudite theologians, but in the Byzantine Empire even the populace took part in theological disquisition to a degree not matched again until the Protestant revolution. Professor Dawson says that

> . . . to a greater extent than that of any other European society, [Byzantine] culture was a religious one and found its essential expression in religious forms; and even to-day it survives to a great extent in the tradition of the Eastern Church. The modern European is accustomed to look on society as essentially concerned with the present life, and with material needs, and on religion as an influence on the moral life of the individual. But to the Byzantine, and indeed to mediaeval man in general, the primary society was the religious one, and economic and secular affairs were a secondary consideration. The greater part of a man's life, especially a poor man's, was lived in a world of religious hopes and fears, and the supernatural figures of this religious world were just as real to him as the authorities of the

---

[11] Cf. McGiffert, *A History of Christian Thought,* Vol. I, chap. xvii.

Empire. . . . And so, while the people took no share in the politics of the Empire and the affairs of the secular government, they followed with passionate interest the affairs of the Church and the religious controversies of the age. It is difficult for us to understand an age in which the clauses of the Athanasian Creed were matters of passionate debate at street corners, and abstruse theological terms, like "consubstantial" and "unconsubstantial," became the battle-cry of rival monks. No less an authority than St. Gregory Nazianzen has described how, if you went into a shop in Constantinople to buy a loaf, "the baker, instead of telling you the price, will argue that the Father is greater than the Son. The money-changer will talk about the Begotten and the Unbegotten, instead of giving you your money, and if you want a bath the bath-keeper assures you that the Son surely proceeds from nothing." [12]

In science the Byzantines made important contributions in medicine and surgery. Greek medicine was revived and disseminated, particularly by Aëtius of the sixth century, Alexander of Tralles (525-605), and Paul of Aegina (625-690). Byzantine scholars also recovered a considerable part of the mathematical, physical, and biological science of the Greeks, transmitting some of it to the Muslims. But the latter had already obtained much of it from the Christian (Nestorian) scholars in Syria.

The man who best reflected the range and character of Byzantine scholarship and intellectual interests was Theodore Prodomus, though he was not so great a scholar as Psellus. But he popularized the learning of the period and ranged over many fields. The chief Byzantine encyclopedist was Suidas, who lived in the late tenth or early eleventh century. He wrote the only important Byzantine dictionary, which was also a kind of encyclopedia, arranged alphabetically and dealing with both pagan and Christian materials. In addition to the definition of words, there were articles on historical, biographical, geographical, and antiquarian subjects. Many extracts from ancient Greek writers were included, especially Aristophanes. The work is uncritical but full of valuable information about the character of Byzantine learning and culture. As a general résumé of Byzantine philosophy, learning and literature we could probably do no better than reproduce Professor Dawson's cogent summation:

From the ninth to the twelfth centuries a series of great scholars devoted themselves ardently to the study of the classics and the recovery of ancient learning—Photius and Arethas in the ninth century, Suidas, the encyclopaedist, and Constantine Cephalas, the editor of the Greek Anthology, in the tenth, and Michael Psellus, John Mauropus, John Italus, Christopher of Mytilene, and many more, in the eleventh. This was the culminating point of the Byzantine Renaissance, and its greatest representative, Psellus, has all the characteristics of the Italian humanists—their romantic cult of antiquity, above all of ancient Athens, their devotion to Homer and Plato, their sedulous imitation of the classical modes of style, and not least, their literary vanity and quarrelsomeness. But it was not an age of creative genius. Its typical products were the great lexicons and encyclopaedias, such as the "Library" of Photius, the Lexicon of Suidas and the compilations of Con-

[12] Dawson, *The Making of Europe*, pp. 108-9, 110-11.

stantine Porphyrogenitus, works which resemble the literary encyclopaedias of China rather than anything in modern literature. Nevertheless, in spite of its lack of originality, it was an age of refined and sophisticated culture, and it is easy to understand the contempt of a scholar like Photius in the ninth century, or a learned princess like Anna Comnena in the twelfth, for the crudity and barbarism of the contemporary civilization of Western Europe.[13]

Byzantine learning did not go much beyond Greek models for a number of reasons. Secular learning was in the hands of a few wealthy and cultivated individuals. The masses were essentially illiterate. In the ecclesiastical world the monks were preoccupied with spiritual exercises and theological subtleties. Moreover, Byzantine learning was thoroughly concentrated in Constantinople, whereas in the West erudition flourished in so many places that originality and diversity were possible. Again, scholarship, like other aspects of Byzantine civilization, never wholly recovered from the vandalism of the crusaders at the opening of the thirteenth century, and from the unsettling effect of the frequent and determined Turkish attacks upon the last great stronghold of Christian civilization in the East.

More fundamental than anything else, however, was the basic fact that Byzantine learning was stereotyped and retrospective rather than dynamic and progressive. It was dominated by rhetoric and devoted to a rehash of ancient scholarship rather than to experiment and observation. In the western Roman Empire this copying, commenting, and compiling movement, designed to preserve pagan classics, soon became unimportant because of the speedy decline of wealth and the decentralization of political control. In the East, however, the vast wealth of Constantinople and the highly centralized political machinery permitted antique culture to linger for many centuries.

Byzantine activity of the eleventh and twelfth centuries in editing and commenting on Aristotle's philosophical works came to be fairly well known to the more alert Western scholars and helped to develop the impulse to translate Aristotle from the Greek text into Latin. Many Byzantine scholars left for Italy with their books and their large fund of antique knowledge for several generations before the Turks swept down upon Constantinople in the middle of the fifteenth century.

One should, however, be on his guard against the old theory that this migration of Greek scholars to Italy was the sole or major cause for that revival of the classics which we know as humanism. At best it only furnished the Greek elements which played a minor rôle in the origins of Italian humanism. Greek influences served to enrich and stimulate an intellectual movement which the Latin revival had already set in motion in the West.

3. Muslim Scholarship and Philosophy

The great rival of Christian culture in the Middle Ages was Mohammedanism, or, as it is more correctly designated, the faith of Islam. Founded by the prophet

[13] Dawson, op. cit., pp. 173-74.

Mohammed in the early part of the seventh century, it soon spread over western Asia, India, and northern Africa as well as into the Spanish peninsula.[14]

The glories of Islam were not limited to military victories, vast political dominions, or unrivaled material wealth. Muslim learning attained a higher level than any other Western culture before the late medieval period. Not even the Greek civilization of the Eastern Empire matched it for extent or variety.

The Muslim culture is sometimes called Arabic civilization, but this is a misleading term. The Arabs were a rather backward people, and Muslim civilization was created primarily by non-Arab elements. It is more accurate, therefore, to refer to the culture and learning of Islamic peoples as Muslim culture. The Arabic language, however, was everywhere used by cultivated Muslims. This is the reason why Muslim scholarship is so frequently referred to as the Arabic learning of the Middle Ages. In discussions of Muslim learning, it is thus necessary to bear in mind that only a small minority of scholars were Arabs; indeed, a number of the most distinguished were not even of the Muslim faith. In all cases, however, they profited by the intellectual advantages afforded by Muslim surroundings.

It is not difficult to understand the reason for the supremacy of Muslim civilization during the early medieval period. It was based upon a broad tolerance of alien cultures and religions. The Muslims, unlike the Christians, did not hate paganism and pagan learning. For example, the old legend that Omar destroyed the great library of Alexandria has been proved wholly mythical. As a matter of fact, what remained of it was destroyed by Christians more than two centuries before the Muslim conquest of Egypt. Such an unpardonable atrocity as the crusade against the Albigenses, conducted by Western Christians in the thirteenth century, would have been unthinkable in Muslim realms.

While Muslim science and scholarship were the best that the Middle Ages produced before the end of the thirteenth century, they were not so much original or indigenous as a synthesis and exposition of the science and philosophy of Greece, India, and the East. The tolerance of Islam in nonreligious fields made it possible to accept non-Muslim learning with enthusiasm, while the curiosity and industry of Muslim scholars prompted them to develop and elaborate their borrowed knowledge.

The earliest center of any Muslim scholarship was Baghdad and its adjacent cities. The Nestorian monks, a Christian sect, had a school at Ctesiphon near Baghdad. These Syriac scholars and translators were the first to bring Aristotle's logic to the attention of the Muslims. When Baghdad became a great Islamic city, court physicians and scholars gathered there and translated Greek medical, scientific, and philosophical works, particularly Galen, Ptolemy, and Aristotle. At the same time, important Hindu treatises on mathematics were turned into Arabic. The years between 762 and 900 were the great era of translation. In addition to translation the Muslims carried on much independent study in the way of extending this borrowed and translated information.

In 832, a House of Wisdom, consisting of a school and an observatory, was established under the direction of a Nestorian physician. This became a famous center for the transmission of Hellenic and Hindu knowledge throughout Islam, and ultimately to the Jews and Christians of western Europe. The leading scholar of the House of Wisdom in its early years was Hunain ibn Ishaq (809-877), known and revered in medieval Europe as Johannitus.

From the beginning, there were enlightened caliphs who patronized scholarship. Indeed, the very caliph who founded Baghdad in 762, al-Mansur, gathered savants at his court and encouraged the translation of Greek and Hindu books. But the most active of all caliphs in promoting translation and scholarship was his grandson, al-Ma'mun (813-833). The University of Baghdad was the most important of early Muslim schools, but it was rivaled after the tenth century by the large and flourishing University of Cairo and the University of Cordova in Muslim Spain.

As we have seen, much enthusiasm was shown for Greek scientific, medical, and philosophical literature. Plato, Aristotle, Neoplatonic works, Euclid, Archimedes, Ptolemy, Apollonius, Galen, and other Hellenic and Hellenistic writings were paraphrased and translated. With these was merged the scientific lore of India, especially mathematics. The so-called Arabic numerals and medieval algebra appear to have been obtained mainly from India.

In this way Islam took over Hellenic and Indian learning, and passed it on to the Christians, mainly through Muslims in Sicily and Spain. In the tenth century Cordova became large and prosperous, in fact, next to Constantinople, the largest city in all Europe. Muslim learning was dominant there. Christian scholars visited it and took with them some knowledge of the Muslim versions of ancient Greek learning. Jewish scholars passed even more freely back and forth between Spain and Christian Europe and acted as intermediaries between Muslim and Latin culture. Toledo, Muslim in its civilization, was captured by the Christians in 1085, and thereby the Christian assimilation of Muslim learning was still further facilitated. In the twelfth century a Christian ecclesiastic in Toledo established an institute for translators and thus notably promoted the transmission of Muslim knowledge to the scholarly monks of Christendom. Seville also became an important Muslim intellectual center, especially in the later Middle Ages. Muslim philosophy consisted primarily of adaptations and commentaries based on Aristotle and other Greek philosophers, discussions and interpretations of the Koran, and introductions to Oriental mysticism.

Among the commentators on Aristotelian and Greek philosophy the most notable were al-Farabi (d. 950), Avicenna (980-1037), better known as a prominent Muslim physician, Avicebron (1020-1070), a Spanish Jew, and Ibn Rushd, far better known as Averroës (1126-1198).

Al-Farabi, the foremost Muslim logician, was also an encyclopedist and Neoplatonic mystic. Avicenna was the first classic Muslim commentator on Aristotle. He rendered Aristotle into Arabic and devised a system of philosophy based on Aristotle. Avicebron, while influenced by Spanish mystics, was also probably the greatest Muslim commentator on Aristotle before Averroës.

Averroës was the most distinguished of all Aristotelians prior to such Christian scholastics as Albertus Magnus and Thomas Aquinas. He faithfully paraphrased and systematized Aristotle's doctrines. This work he supplemented by elaborate commentaries. And, just as Thomas Aquinas used Aristotelian logic to round out and establish Christian truth, so Averroës utilized it to vindicate the faith of Islam. The legend that Averroës was an antireligious rationalist rests upon a complete misunderstanding of the facts. He was a devout religionist with pantheistic leanings.

The Jewish philosopher Moses Maimonides (1135-1204) was influential in disseminating a knowledge of Averroës among Christian scholars. Michael Scot was the chief translator of Averroës' works into Latin. So popular was the latter with Western scholars that a veritable Averroës cult arose, led by Siger de Brabant, which the church tried to stamp out. Indeed, some of Averroës' books are available only in Latin translations, the Arabic originals having been lost. Another eminent Muslim authority on Aristotle was Ibn Bajja (Avempace, d. 1138).

Probably the most illustrious philosopher who dealt with purely Muslim problems was al-Kindi (c. 875), a mathematician, physicist, and encyclopedist. He was the only great philosopher of the Arab race. His writings indicate wide scientific interests, and show that he was acquainted with Aristotle and with Hellenistic science. Neoplatonic mysticism, which he attributed in part to Aristotle, to the intellectual confusion of later generations, interested him. He was especially esteemed in the Latin West as an authority on astrology. The main philosophic commentator on the Koran was Takhr-ud-Din of the thirteenth century. In interpreting Oriental mysticism to the Muslims, leadership was taken by al-Hujwiri in the middle of the eleventh century.

Muslim theology was closely related to Muslim philosophy, especially to that branch which dealt with purely Muslim problems. Al-Jahiz (d. 869) was the most important early Muslim theologian. In his great encyclopedia, he attempted, like Christian encyclopedists, to show the theological import of natural phenomena. But the outstanding Muslim theologian of the whole Middle Ages was al-Ghazali (1058-1109), who has been fairly called the Muslim Aquinas. Indeed, his theological disquisitions have sometimes been regarded as far more original than those of Aquinas. He exerted a considerable influence on both Jewish and Christian theology. He studied the Aristotelian philosophy carefully, but fell under the influence of the Sufis or Muslim mystics and ended as a mystic. He carried on a considerable controversy with the devotees of Aristotle. One of his notable books, *The Destruction of the Philosophers,* was answered at length by Averroës.

Christian historians have frequently pointed out that the Latin civilization of the West in the thirteenth and fourteenth centuries reached about as high a level as Muslim culture. This may be true, but it must not be overlooked that this remarkable renaissance was owing in large part to Muslim information and stimulation.

While it is readily apparent that Muslim culture and scholarship far outshone anything known in Christian Europe at the time, and, before the end of the thirteenth century, constituted the highest civilization of the medieval world, one should not make the mistake of attributing it entirely to the influence of Islam. The latter was responsible for Muslim interest in science and scholarship only negatively. In no sense did Islam directly encourage learning, except as it might be incidentally involved in the history, jurisprudence, philosophy, or theology of Islam. Like Christianity, Islam was primarily concerned with matters supernatural and religious and was to that degree nonscientific or antiscientific.

The main distinction between Islam and Christianity was Islam's greater tolerance of religious dissent and worldly interests. Islam did not interfere so directly and extensively with scholarly efforts nor so powerfully discourage scientific activity. In this relatively greater tolerance, open-mindedness, and secularism of Islam one must seek the real basis for the superiority of Muslim civilization in the Middle Ages. One must also keep in mind the fact that this superiority was far more marked in comparison with the Latin West than with the Greek East. The learning of both medieval Christians and Muslims was based chiefly on earlier pagan scholarship, particularly that of the Greeks, which Islam made somewhat less difficult to appropriate than did Christianity. Herein, chiefly, is to be found the key to Muslim cultural preëminence. It is a complete mistake to seek it in native Muslim genius, in the inherent superiority of Islam, or in any direct Islamic encouragement of scholarship and art. The assimilative and non-Arabic character of much Muslim culture and learning has been forcefully—perhaps too forcefully—stated by M. André Sevier:

> What is called "Arab civilization," in so far as any manifestation of Arab genius is concerned, has never had any real existence. The civilization that passes under that name is due to the labour of other peoples who, subjected to Islam by force, continued to develop their aptitudes in spite of the persecution of their conquerors. . . .
>
> To give the name "Arab civilization" to the artistic, literary and scientific movement that by a false documentation is made to coincide with the accession of the Abbasside Caliphs, is to fall into error. In the first place, because the Arab element only participated in it to an extent hardly perceptible; and further, because this movement was the result of the intellectual activity of foreign nations only converted to Islam by force; and finally, because the movement was already in existence in the countries conquered by the Arabs long before their arrival. The Syrian, Persian, and Indian works which are the manifestation of this intellectual movement, and which carry on the Greco-Latin work, are anterior to the Musulman conquests. It is, then, in defiance of fact to attribute this artistic and scientific effort to the Arabs, and to give the name of "Arab civilization" to an intellectual movement due to the Syrians, to the Persians, to the Hindus, unwilling converts to Islam, but who, nevertheless, had preserved the qualities of their race. In reality, the movement was nothing more than the continuation, and, as it were, the ultimate flowering of Greco-Latin civilization. It is easy to prove this.[15]

As transmitters of Muslim learning to Western Christians, the Jews, as noted above, took a leading part. They were especially active in Spain, where, under Muslim dominion, Jews were accorded decent treatment. The chief Jewish transmitters were Avicebron and Moses Maimonides. The leading Christian translator of Muslim scientific works was Gerard of Cremona (1114-1187). Others of im-

15 André Sevier, *Islam and the Psychology of the Musulman*, Scribner, 1924, pp. 216-18. See also P. K. Hitti, *History of the Arabs*, Macmillan, 1937 (St. Martin's Press reprint), p. 174.

portance were Constantine the African (d. 1087), Adelard of Bath (d. c. 1150), Robert of Chester (c. 1150), Herman of Carinthia (c. 1150), John of Spain (c. 1150), Daniel of Morley (c. 1175), and Alfred the Englishman (c. 1225). We shall have more to say on this subject presently in dealing with translations of Muslim versions of Aristotle.

4. The Revival of Aristotle

We have made it plain that Aristotelian thought was not without its influence even on the Dark Ages. In the best schools, instruction in logic was based upon Boëthius' translations of Aristotle's *Categories* and *De interpretatione* and Porphyry's Introduction to the *Categories*. Boëthius had translated all of Aristotle's logical works, but the *Topics, Analytics,* and *Sophistic Refutations* had been lost during the Dark Ages.

When Abelard showed by his *Yea and Nay* that the appeal to authority as a definitive defense of the Christian faith was futile, it became imperative to have more of Aristotle, the great logician, at hand. Interest in his logical treatises later led to a demand for his many other writings.

We have already made it clear that the Muslims had taken over Aristotle from the Greeks by way of the Nestorian Christians of Syria. Muslim culture spread to Spain, where many Christian scholars studied. Hence, they were well acquainted with the numerous and elaborate Muslim commentaries on Aristotle, which also embraced a good deal of the actual Aristotelian text. It was only natural, then, that when the works of Aristotle seemed absolutely indispensable Christians would turn to Muslim Spain as the region from which Aristotle might be imported into western Europe in Latin dress. This occurred in the late eleventh and the twelfth centuries.

The processes and stages through which the original Greek version of Aristotle had to pass, in order to reach Christian scholars who went to Spain, are so complicated as to be almost humorous. The Nestorians of western Asia had Aristotle in Greek but they frequently translated the text into Syriac before it reached the Muslims. The latter translated it into Arabic and added elaborate commentaries. But sometimes the Christian scholars of Latin Europe did not get Aristotle from the Arabic text. The commentaries had already been turned from Arabic into Hebrew and were then translated from Hebrew into Latin. Therefore, Ernest Renan could fairly describe the product as a Latin translation of a Hebrew commentary on an Arabic commentary on an Arabic translation of a Syriac translation of a Greek manuscript.

But the process of rendering the Arabic or Hebrew text into Latin was even more complicated than this.[16] If a Christian scholar went to Muslim Spain his only mode of communicating with the average Muslim or Jewish scholar was to learn the vernacular, which was a jargon of mixed Arabic and Latin. The Christian scholar could rarely read Arabic or Hebrew, and the Muslim or Jewish scholar could rarely read Latin. Their only common linguistic meeting ground

---

[16] For an admirable description of the methods of translation, see Charles Singer, in Hearnshaw, *Medieval Contributions to Modern Civilization*, pp. 122-27.

was the vernacular. It was rather more usual for a Christian scholar in search of Aristotle to get the assistance of a scholarly Jew than to seek the aid of a Muslim savant.

The process of translating from Arabic or Hebrew, for the scholarly Jew could read either, was as follows: the Jewish scholar would turn the Arabic or Hebrew text into the vernacular, and then the Christian scholar would translate it from the vernacular into Latin. Since the vernacular had no words for many technical philosophical terms, it was very difficult to get an exact rendition of the Arabic or Hebrew into Latin. Arabic terms were often taken over bodily into the Latin. And we must also remember that the Arabic or Hebrew text itself was never pure and undefiled Aristotle. It was interlarded with Muslim and Hebrew commentaries, which in some cases all but obliterated or superseded the original.[17] Hence, one can well understand the inferior character of early translations of Aristotle and can rightly interpret Roger Bacon's contempt for them when he said that he would like to burn them all, it being a waste of time to study them, since they promoted error and increased ignorance.

While this early translation from the Arabic and Hebrew was proceeding, the first translations of Aristotle from the Greek were beginning to appear. James of Venice seems to have translated *The Topics, Analytics,* and *Sophistic Refutations* from Greek into Latin. He may have obtained the Greek texts from the Byzantines, probably in southern Italy. This work was done by about 1128. More alert scholars could soon have all of Aristotle's logic, the *Organon,* in fairly good translations. Boëthius' translations had provided a Latin version of the two other books in the *Organon.* Professor Haskins believes that James of Venice may have only recovered Boëthius' translations of the three logical treatises mentioned above.

In the twelfth century better Latin translations of Aristotle's nonlogical writings were made from the Arabic. The Christian scholars were then better prepared. The greatest of all these translators, Gerard of Cremona, was assisted by a learned Spaniard Ibn Ghâlib, who knew Arabic, Hebrew, and Latin. Gerard translated many works of Aristotle from Arabic into Latin, including a number of scientific treatises. Others who helped to render Aristotle into Latin by residence in Muslim Spain were Michael Scot (c. 1170-1234), Alfred the Englishman, and Hermann the German (c. 1240). Before the end of the thirteenth century many of Aristotle's philosophical and scientific works found their way into Latin through the translators just mentioned.

Roger Bacon was not the only scholar who recognized the inferiority of an Aristotelian text obtained from the Arabic, no matter how careful the translation. Even before his time there had been a demand for translations from the Greek texts which were available in Constantinople. The scholarly work of Blemmydes, Psellus, and other Byzantines of the eleventh and twelfth centuries became known to Western scholars. We have noted how this may have helped James of Venice to translate parts of the *Organon* from Greek into Latin in 1128. The capture of Constantinople by the crusaders in 1204 also facilitated the process of getting

---

[17] Almost all Hebrew versions were commentaries.

Greek versions of Aristotle. It is also probable that Greek texts of some of Aristotle's works existed in the Greek colonies in southern Italy.

Thomas Aquinas, in particular, demanded a good Latin translation from the Greek. He was aided by Pope Urban IV, at whose command such a translation was executed. The first medieval Latin scholar to attempt to translate the non-logical works of Aristotle from the Greek was Robert Grosseteste (c. 1175-1253), the teacher of Roger Bacon. But the first good translation of Aristotle from the Greek was that ordered by Pope Urban and executed by two Dominican scholars, William of Moerbeke and Henry of Brabant, who started their task in the year 1263. In about a decade the works of Aristotle were available in reputable Latin translations from the Greek. These created an intellectual revolution which we shall describe later on. The pope tried to expurgate some and to ban others, but there was great difficulty in enforcing this papal proscription.

III. ABELARD AND THE ENTHRONEMENT OF LOGIC

While logic had been growing in importance in theological exposition in the tenth and eleventh centuries, the man who was primarily responsible for its enthronement in mature medieval thought was a French monk, Peter Abelard (1079-1142), a personage of revolutionary significance in intellectual history. Important as was Abelard, he was known to moderns down to 1836 chiefly through his touching, if tragic, love affair with Héloïse. In that year the French philosopher, Victor Cousin, published a collection of Abelard's works which first induced modern scholars to read him in the original.

The breadth of Abelard's training doubtless had something to do with his skeptical turn of mind. He studied under Roscellinus, the leading nominalist of the age, and under William of Champeaux, the outstanding realist. He thus understood both sides of the great controversy and took the middle ground of conceptualism, which emphasizes the value of class terms or universals for the clarification and organization of knowledge but holds that reality exists only in individual things. He defeated his master, William, in debate and set himself up as a teacher in Paris, where he enjoyed unprecedented popularity. It was then that he fell afoul of Héloïse's narrow-minded uncle, Fulbert, and the rest of his life was spent in an alternation of pedagogical triumphs and petty persecutions, until finally Bernard of Clairvaux nagged him into the grave. His *History of My Calamities* (*Historia calamitatum*) ranks, along with Augustine's longer *Confessions,* as one of the chief intellectual autobiographies of the Middle Ages.

Abelard possessed some of the faults of his virtues. A brilliant and eager dialectician, he was a little too exultant in his victories and tended to be somewhat overbearing towards his defeated opponents. He carried a logical chip on his shoulder. In his old age, however, he became much more temperate and discreet. But this did not save him from the vindictiveness of Bernard.

Abelard's intellectual temper, which goes far to explain his career, is well expressed in the famous praise of skepticism set forth in the introduction to his epoch-making treatise *Yea and Nay:*

The master key of knowledge is, indeed, a persistent and frequent questioning. Aristotle, the most clear-sighted of all the philosophers, was desirous above all things else to arouse this questioning spirit, for in his *Categories* he exhorts a student as follows: "It may well be difficult to reach a positive conclusion in these matters unless they be frequently discussed. It is by no means fruitless to be doubtful on particular points." By doubting we come to examine, and by examining we reach the truth.[18]

Yet one should not imagine that Abelard's was in any sense a forerunner of such modern skepticism as Montaigne's, Bayle's, or Voltaire's. He was a skilled medieval dialectician who accepted all the important religious dogmas of his age and was primarily interested in using the methods of logical analysis for the purpose of getting closer to religious realities. If he forever impugned the adequacy of uncritical faith, or the piling up of authorities as a satisfactory method of arriving at religious truth, he did no more than launch a quasi-revolution within medieval thought which in no way stands as a precursor of the modern state of mind. He strengthened rather than weakened the medieval attitude by bringing logic to the rescue of faith. In his *Calamities* he asserted that he "preferred the equipment of dialectic to all the teachings of philosophy."

While Abelard was the author of a number of philosophical works, including an ethical treatise, a manual on logic, a commentary on Porphyry, a work on the Trinity and an introduction to theology, his prime importance in the history of European thought and education rests on his *Yea and Nay*.

This was a sweeping attack upon the theological method which had culminated in the *Glossa ordinaria* of Walafrid Strabo, namely, the uncritical collection of patristic opinions as a means of establishing religious truth. He pointed out that the fathers were often contradictory in their comments, and that they tended to use figurative language. He showed that apocryphal books were often given a faked apostolic or saintly authorship. He called attention to the fact that even Peter fell into error and that Augustine confessed numerous fallibilities. If such was the case, it would be foolish to impute infallibility to the lesser fathers. One should reverently, but firmly, question the patristic opinion in order to get at the real truth. This could be done without impugning their good faith.

But Abelard was careful to point out that his method should not be applied to the Scriptures, in which anything seemingly absurd or incredible must be taken as the result of the reader's incompetence, or as figurative speech for which an allegorical meaning must be found.

In this spirit, Abelard listed forty-eight major problems or propositions of Christian theology, of which the following selection is representative:

Should human faith be based upon reason, or no?
Is God one, or no?
Is God a substance, or no?
Does the first Psalm refer to Christ, or no?
Is sin pleasing to God, or no?
Is God the author of evil, or no?

[18] Cited in Robinson, *Readings in European History,* I, 451.

Is God all-powerful, or no?
Can God be resisted, or no?
Has God free will, or no?
Was the first man persuaded to sin by the devil, or no?
Was Adam saved, or no?
Did all the apostles have wives except John, or no?
Are the flesh and blood of Christ in very truth and essence present in the sacrament of the altar, or no?
Do we sometimes sin unwillingly, or no?
Does God punish the same sin both here and in the future, or no?
Is it worse to sin openly than secretly, or no?

Abelard then proceeded to show that regarding all of these crucial propositions the fathers were either contradictory, ambiguous, or both. This sounded the death-knell for the authoritarian method of quoting patristic comments. These conflicting opinions, said Abelard, must be reasoned away or harmonized, a result which only logic could produce. Hence, the logical method was the indispensable tool for vindicating theological dogmas.

Aristotle was the great logician. Therefore, Abelard's intellectual revolution implied the desirability of mastering Aristotle's logical writings. Furthermore, it involved the training of incipient logicians in Aristotelian dialectic. The cathedral schools at Chartres and Orleans were already doing good work in elementary logic but more complete and systematic teaching was required. The answer was the medieval university. The latter was a product of the new passion for logic, of the improved teaching fostered by schools like that of Fulbert at Chartres, and of the need of better-trained teachers, not only in the arts and theology, but also in the revived sciences of law and medicine.

Summarizing Abelard's contributions to medieval thought and culture, Gabriel Compayré says that we owe to his pedagogical gusto and subtlety the promotion of intellectual enthusiasm, the reinstatement of human reason as a technique for ascertaining truth, the eulogy of the intellectual powers of the human mind, the vindication of the skeptical attitude (logical analysis), the impulse to scholasticism and the rise of universities, and the training of many eminent disciples like Peter Lombard and John of Salisbury.[19]

IV. THE RISE OF UNIVERSITIES IN THE MIDDLE AGES

The higher learning in our day is so varied and impressive, and is housed in such vastly expensive physical plants, that it is difficult to realize the humble, practical, and informal character of medieval universities and colleges.

In the late twelfth century there arose, as we have just noted, a new demand for trained logicians, theologians, lawyers, doctors, and secretaries. This placed a heavy responsibility on the existing institutions of learning. The old monastic and cathedral schools could not meet the requirements of the new day. Some guaran-

[19] Gabriel Compayré, *Abelard,* Scribner, 1893. See also Joseph McCabe, *Peter Abelard,* Putnam, 1901, chap. xv.

tee had to be given of the fitness and competence of those who aspired to become teachers, scribes, secretaries, theologians, lawyers, and doctors.

The existing agency for regulating professional training and for guaranteeing excellence of workmanship was the medieval guild or industrial corporation, which supervised industry, trained workers, and vouched for the quality of the finished product.

Exactly the same procedure was quite naturally and informally applied to scholarship (the commodity of learning). The medieval universities and colleges were simply guilds of teachers and students; they constituted a *studium generale*. The very names were derived from Roman and medieval industrial corporations —*universitas* and *collegium*.

The universities and colleges were corporations whose industries were teaching and learning. The bachelor's degree was roughly comparable to the journeyman's certification, the master's to the credentials of a master in industry who was qualified and licensed to teach his trade. (The master's degree in the medieval university carried with it the license to teach a particular branch of learning.) In the early days of the universities there was little or no distinction between the master's and the doctor's degree. They both entitled the holder to give instruction— *jus ubique docendi*.

The homely origin of the medieval university and college is thus readily apparent. While in an educational sense they were mainly a further development of the cathedral schools, their name and organization were directly derived from medieval industrial corporations.

As just indicated, the medieval universities and colleges frequently grew out of preëxisting cathedral schools, but some arose through legal incorporation as guilds of teachers and students. No precise date can be assigned to the origins of the medieval universities, but at the beginning of the thirteenth century the monastic and cathedral schools were generally superseded or supplemented by universities and colleges. The monastic and cathedral schools continued, of course, to exist and to carry on more elementary instruction, particularly in the classics. The University of Paris takes the year 1200 as the date of its origin, though it did not become a corporation until the year 1231; but there was a college in existence at Paris as early as 1180. Throughout western Europe, from the thirteenth century onward, colleges and universities were created. By the close of the Middle Ages there were about eighty in existence.

The organization and administration of the medieval university varied considerably, but there was one common element, namely, they were organized like the guilds under a corporate form of control. We may conveniently take the University of Paris as the basis for a brief description of medieval university organization. This institution had not only an extensive undergraduate department but also embraced graduate schools for the study of theology, law, and medicine.

There were four faculties—arts, canon law, medicine, and theology. The teaching of the civil law was not allowed at the University of Paris after 1219. Over each of the four faculties presided a dean. The students in the faculty of arts, the largest department of the university, were divided into four so-called nations—the French, the Norman, the Picard, and English—broadly interpreted and very inclusive, so that all the major peoples of western Europe were included in one or another of these four nations. An elected proctor presided over each nation. The four nations together periodically elected the head of the university, who was known as a rector—usually he was the bishop of Paris. The close connection between medieval learning and the church is further illustrated by the facts that examinations for degrees were conducted by the chancellor of the collegiate chapter of St. Genevieve in Paris, and only the chancellor of the cathedral chapter of Notre Dame could license university teachers. This point also emphasizes the development of the university out of the earlier cathedral school of Notre Dame.

The customary degrees were Bachelor of Arts, Master of Arts, Doctor of Laws, Doctor of Theology, and Doctor of Medicine. The degrees of Master of Theology, Master of Canon Law, and Master of Medicine were, however, granted in the Middle Ages. The bachelor's degree normally required four years of undergraduate study. The master's degree, a much more serious affair than it is in the United States today, called for several years of graduate work. It always required as much advanced study as our doctor's degree, and had the same standing. A rather extensive period of residence was sometimes required for the Doctor of Theology degree; for example, twelve or thirteen years at the University of Paris.

It is important to note that the Bachelor of Arts degree was not originally connected with demonstrated proficiency in classics and higher mathematics—the so-called humanities, which many today still regard as the only traditional and appropriate basis for the degree.[20] The central feature in the arts curriculum of the medieval university was the trivium—grammar, rhetoric, and logic. Logic completely overshadowed grammar and rhetoric, which were studied mainly as appendages to logic. Neither classical literature nor higher mathematics was included as studies. Even when the quadrivium—arithmetic, astronomy, geometry, and music—was included in the curriculum—a relatively rare event—neither the classics nor higher mathematics, as we understand them today, was involved. Such mathematics as was taught was hardly on the level of modern grammar-school mathematics. Certainly, it did not approach modern high-school mathematics. Rashdall, speaking of the mature medieval university, says:

> From this time onwards Aristotle represents the sum and substance of a medieval education in the Faculty of Arts. A knowledge of Latin, and the rules of Latin grammar are, indeed, presupposed and exacted in the university examinations, and this knowledge was acquired by the reading of a few Latin books, especially Ovid and Vergil. But the teaching of these authors was for the most part left to the grammar school, which the student left at an increasingly early age—often before he was fourteen. There was also some rather perfunctory recognition of the other subjects embraced in the *Trivium* and the *Quadrivium,* and of the authors in which they were learned.[21]

---

[20] See L. J. Paetow, *The Arts Course at the Medieval Universities,* University of Illinois Press, 1910; and E. K. Rand, "The Classics in the Thirteenth Century," *Speculum,* July, 1929, pp. 248 ff.

[21] *Cambridge Medieval History,* VI, 571-72.

Therefore the assertion that we today degrade the bachelor's degree by conferring it upon those not highly versed in the classics and higher mathematics is historically without foundation. It was the influence of the so-called Renaissance and seventeenth-century science which put the classics and higher mathematics into the curriculum.

Indeed, as Professor L. J. Paetow pointed out, the universities were, for a considerable period, the chief obstacle to an appreciative study of the classics. They were an antihumanistic force. Classical studies, which had been gaining headway in good cathedral schools like Chartres and Orleans, were smothered by the universities with their emphasis on logic, law, medicine, and theology. Had it not been for the universities, the humanistic revival of the classics might have occurred in the thirteenth century instead of the late fourteenth and fifteenth.

It may be desirable to indicate here the distinction between the college and the university in the Middle Ages. They had one common element—the corporate form of organization. In the beginning, the college was primarily distinguished by its residential or custodial character. It provided board and lodging for the poorer students who could not meet their own expenses, or it assured custodial supervision of immature students who needed guardianship. The latter accounts for the system of fellows and tutors who lived in the colleges with their intellectual wards. Our present-day tutorial system is a revival of this medieval practice.

While there were colleges at Paris as early as the close of the twelfth century, the earliest characteristic collegiate development occurred at Oxford and Cambridge at the opening of the thirteenth century. The conventual houses of Franciscan and Dominican friars, with their common life, served as a model. Here the colleges became the basic element in these great universities, the university authority being limited to the official corporate supervision of examinations and the legal conferring of degrees. The need for colleges resulted in part from the number of very young men who attended the universities. As Rashdall says:

> Doubtless these crowds of students included thousands whose proper place would have been at a secondary school, but it must be remembered that in these days men went to the universities later as well as earlier than now. High ecclesiastical dignitaries of mature years were found seated on the benches of the schools side by side with mere boys.[22]

Present-day movements for student self-government often invoke medieval experience as a precedent and justification. But medieval universities were by no means governed by their students. The undergraduate departments, as well as entire universities in which the undergraduates predominated in numbers, were usually governed, as they are today, by their faculties.

In a few graduate professional schools, like the law school at Bologna, the students conducted the university, employing and dismissing professors. It may be added that these students were mature adults, interested in specialized instruction and in receiving competent instruction at a minimum cost. Such universities

[22] *Cambridge Medieval History,* VI, 601.

formed by adult students for their own benefit and protection were, thus, often controlled by the students. In the universities founded by the masters, in order to limit the right to teach and to protect teachers, the faculty (that is, the masters) always governed the institution.

Our college and university organization has come down from the Middle Ages with varying modifications. In France and Germany the modern university is primarily a graduate school, there being nothing quite comparable to our undergraduate college. The German *gymnasium* and the French *lycée* resemble our colleges more closely than our high schools. In England, in such characteristic institutions as Oxford and Cambridge, the colleges predominate and the university is nothing more than a unifying legal corporation. In the United States, the university usually implies both the corporate organization and the organic collection of various undergraduate colleges, graduate schools, and professional schools. Moreover, when we think of a modern university, especially in the United States, we usually visualize a large group of impressive buildings, luxurious sleeping quarters, and a giant stadium. In the Middle Ages there was rarely even one permanent university building. The corporations of scholars and students usually rented quarters, often in a not too impressive part of the city, and frequently shifted from one area to another.

While the vast physical plant, some aspects of the curriculum, organized athletics, and certain other characteristics of the modern university differ markedly from its medieval ancestor, the latter has left a large and impressive heritage, including the corporate organization, faculties, tutorial system, departments of learning, official titles, such as professors, deans, and rectors, periodic examinations, the conferring of degrees, the degrees themselves, academic regalia and ritual, and severe, solemn, and stereotyped conceptions of academic dignity and good taste. In recent years, as just noted, there has been a very considerable reversion to medievalism in the form of revived emphasis on the tutorial system of instruction and the provision of special residential halls designed to house small and coherent groups of students.

The Bachelor of Arts curriculum was at first regarded as little more than an academic apprenticeship. Instruction in the trivium was paramount; the quadrivium tended to be ignored or slighted. Conspicuous for their absence from the medieval college curriculum were such universal present-day subjects as classics, modern languages, experimental science, history, and the social sciences.

Logic was the most important medieval study. It prepared the student for advanced work in law and medicine as well as theology. Based primarily upon Aristotle's *Organon*, it became the dominant technique of medieval scholasticism, and its enthusiastic pursuit rested upon the assumption that reality exists in the world of abstract ideas, generally independent of the external sensual world. It was assumed that truth could be surprised and captured if pursued according to the laws of sound argumentation. Avoidance of logical fallacies, rather than observation of commonplace nature, was the path to wisdom.

Undergraduate textbooks were Aristotle's logic (*Organon*), works on grammar by Roman authorities like Donatus and Priscian, and adaptations of classical writers on rhetoric by Boëthius, by the associates of Cassiodorus and by Alcuin. Much the same books were used in the better cathedral schools. The general character and objectives of medieval university instruction were well expressed in the famous formula: "The sword of God's word is forged by grammar, sharpened by logic, and burnished by rhetoric, but only theology can use it."

The overwhelming domination of Aristotle in the medieval arts course is revealed by the following list of books, which were the required textbooks for the degrees of bachelor of arts and master of arts in the University of Paris in 1254 (listed by Professor E. P. Cubberley in his *Readings in the History of Education*):

I. The "Old" Logic.

    1. *Introduction to the Categories of Aristotle*, Porphyry.
    2. *Categories*, and *On Interpretation*, Aristotle.
    3. *Divisions*, and *Topics* except Book IV, Boëthius.

II. The "New" Logic.

    1. *Prior and Posterior Analytics*, Aristotle.
    2. *Sophistical Refutations*, Aristotle.
    3. *Topics*, Aristotle.

III. Moral Philosophy.

    1. *Ethics*, 4 Books, Aristotle.

IV. Natural Philosophy.

    1. *Physics*, Aristotle.
    2. *On the Heavens and the Earth*, Aristotle.
    3. *Meteorics*, Aristotle.
    4. *On Animals*, Aristotle.
    5. *The Soul*, Aristotle.
    6. *Generation*, Aristotle.
    7. *Sense and Sensible Things*, Aristotle.
    8. *Sleep and Waking*, Aristotle.
    9. *Memory and Recollection*, Aristotle.
    10. *On Life and Death*, Aristotle.
    11. *Plants*, Aristotle.

V. Metaphysics.

    1. *Metaphysics*, Aristotle.

VI. Other Books.

    1. *On the Six Principles*, Gilbert de la Porrée.
    2. *Barbarismus* (Bk. 3, Larger Grammar), Donatus.
    3. *Grammar* (Major and Minor), Priscian.
    4. *On Causes*, Costa ben Luca.
    5. *On the Differences of Spirit and Soul* (another translation of *On Causes*).

The textbooks on rhetoric are omitted from the list. Those used were Aristotle's *Rhetoric*, Cicero's *Nova rhetorica* and Boëthius' *Topics*.

While the universities offered graduate instruction in "secretarial science," law, and medicine, theology still remained "the queen of the sciences," though theological students were not as numerous in the Middle Ages as after the Counter Reformation.

The chief graduate schools taught theology, law, and medicine. Theological instruction was based chiefly on *The Book of Sentences* (c. 1150), written by a learned monk, Peter Lombard (c. 1100-1164), who, after teaching in the cathedral school of Notre Dame, became bishop of Paris. This was the first great theological treatise composed after Abelard's revolution, and followed the "yea and nay" method, listing major propositions and citing authorites pro and con. Yet it tried to harmonize conflicting opinions and to arrive at a definite conclusion through logical processes—thus having the opposite aim from Abelard's disturbing treatise. *The Book of Sentences* was divided into four parts: (1) the nature of the Trinity; (2) creation, paradise, and the fall of man; (3) the incarnation, redemption, major virtues, and sin; and (4) the sacraments of the church.

> Lombard had a remarkable gift [says Professor McGiffert] for gathering up and presenting in clear and systematic form the thoughts of others freed from irrelevant and unimportant details. While containing little or nothing that was new, the compend, for all its limitations, was an extraordinarily convenient summary of the Catholic faith of that day, all the more useful because of its very lack of originality. It was no accident that it became very soon and remained for centuries thereafter the great theological handbook of the west. It was, indeed, one of the most successful textbooks the world has ever seen.[23]

Incidentally, this work was the standard medieval authority on the sacramental theory of the medieval church. If one wishes to gain some elementary grasp of the vast gulf between solemn anthropological fact and the amazing rationalizations of medieval theology, he could not do better than to compare the section on the sacraments in Peter's book with Professor R. R. Marett's summary of the realities in his charming book, *The Sacraments of Simple Folk.*

The study of Roman law had been promoted by an industrious legalist, Irnerius, who, about 1088, began lecturing on Justinian at Bologna. Law in the Middle Ages usually meant both civil law and canon or church law. The most widely used textbook in civil law was Justinian's *Institutes,* a concise summary of the principles of Roman law. Justinian's *Digest* was also used extensively for advanced work in civil law. In canon law the popular textbook was Gratian's *Decretum (Concordance of Discordant Canons),* a systematic compilation of church law and cases published in the middle of the twelfth century. Mastery of both types of law led to the degree of LL.D. (doctor of laws). Today, the LL.D. has lost its technical significance and is given chiefly as an honorary degree to public figures who seldom have any knowledge of either canon or civil law.

The earliest important center of medical studies was Salerno, in southern Italy.

[23] McGiffert, *A History of Christian Thought,* II, 251-52.

Muslim scholars had preserved a knowledge of Greek, Roman, and Muslim medicine and passed it on to western Europe. The leading early figure at Salerno was Constantine the African, who began his teaching about the middle of the eleventh century. The chief textbooks were Hippocrates, Galen, Dioscorides, and various Muslim medical writings, especially the *Canon* of Avicenna. Galen was the most widely used of the lot. Other very popular texts were the books on fevers, dietetics and urology of Isaac Judaeus, perhaps the leading Jewish physician of the Middle Ages, and the *Book of Antidotes* of Nicholas of Salerno. Authority and logical analysis, rather than an empirical study of actual cases, dominated the teaching of medicine as well as of theology and law.

Because of the scarcity and high cost of books before the invention of printing, lecturing to large classes was a favorite method of instruction. These lectures usually took the form of dictation. A welcome break in the monotony of such performances were the disputations which grew out of teaching by dialogue, conversation, and questions and answers. The famous medieval teacher, Robert de Sorbon (d. 1274), said of disputation: "This exercise is more advantageous than reading, because it results in clearing up doubts. Nothing is known perfectly which has not been masticated by the teeth of disputation."

An important and often overlooked element in the higher medieval learning was the "business course," or what in our phraseology might be called a course in secretarial science—the *ars dictaminis* and the *ars notaria*. There was a great need for men trained in the art of writing letters, executing legal forms, drawing up proclamations, and the like. Since rhetoric was the indispensable basis for such training, the business course became a practical branch of medieval rhetoric, particularly in universities specializing in law. From the twelfth century to the fourteenth this course flourished, but it gradually declined in the latter part of the fourteenth century. In Italy and Germany strictly commercial institutions, the so-called abacus schools, were established in the fourteenth century. Here students were taught the vernacular language and given instruction in elementary commercial practice—making out bills and the like.

Lay education for the nobility, that is, instruction in the rules of chivalry and courtesy, essential for the polite life of the feudal world, was given at home, in the feudal castle, or royal court. It was not a part of formal academic education.

The University of Paris was the leading undergraduate institution for the training of bachelors of arts, and also the best-known graduate school of theology. Bologna was the most famous law school. Salerno, Bologna, and Padua in Italy and Montpellier in France were the leading medical universities.

While the older students, especially those working for an advanced or professional degree, were usually serious-minded, we should guard ourselves against the overidealized notion that all medieval university students were solemn, industrious, and ascetic. As Professors Munro and Haskins have clearly indicated, medieval students, like their modern counterparts, represented all types. They ran the gamut from the desperately earnest young man who starved and slaved his way through college, oblivious to all charms of the world, the flesh, and the devil, to the frank loafers, rich and poor, who regarded the university as a delightful place in which to waste almost a decade of life. There was plenty of dissipation, vice, marauding, rioting, and the like. Bloody town-and-gown riots were common. Hazing was harsher than today. If, among older professional students, there was often such a determination to learn that an ineffective or careless teacher was fined or discharged, among the younger arts student we find evidence of a sentiment not unknown among modern undergraduates, namely, that a university without any professors would be an idyllic spot. The problems of discipline were often serious.

One of the most conspicuous differences between medieval and modern student life was the absence of sumptuous living quarters. Next to this one might put the nonexistence in medieval times of organized intercollegiate athletics, which occupy so prominent a part in the thoughts, activities, and prestige of modern institutions of higher learning. Again, there was no mass enrollment. Finally, there was neither coeducation nor separate colleges for women. Higher academic education was an exclusively masculine privilege for centuries. Chivalric education for ladies was provided in the feudal castle and royal courts.

There does not seem to have been a great amount of direct and overt interference with the freedom of teaching in medieval universities. At least, we find few records of actual repression. The intellectual radical courted trouble mainly when he tried to popularize heresies. Considerable tolerance for unorthodox views prevailed when expressed semiconfidentially in the solemn and esoteric setting of the university classroom. In this respect, the situation was not greatly different from what it is today.

Yet one should not deduce from the absence of frequently recorded instances of gagging or discharging teachers the assurance that medieval universities were hotbeds of radicalism. The medieval attitude admirably discouraged intellectual dissent and promoted docility. Personal disinclination to heterodoxy probably had more to do with the absence of raids on academic freedom than any other single factor.[24]

In summary, one may justly say that medieval universities aroused a permanent professional interest in teaching; trained teachers to give competent instruction according to existing pedagogical principles; outlined and systematized the essentials of information; encouraged research in subjects then regarded as significant; and perfected the technique for carrying on such research, which was hardly experimental, or scientific. In short, the universities produced the type of instruction and instructors which made possible the intellectual dominion of scholasticism from the thirteenth to the fifteenth centuries.

V. THE ASCENDANCY OF ARISTOTLE IN MEDIEVAL THOUGHT: SCHOLASTICISM

When Abelard introduced logic to buttress faith the resort to Aristotle was inevitable. Aristotle was the greatest logician who had lived down to that time and

24 Cf. G. G. Coulton, in Hammerton, *Universal History of the World*, V, 3016-17.

his methods were well adapted to Christian needs. Soon all his philosophic and scientific treatises were introduced and there developed that remarkable union of Augustinian theology and Aristotelian logic which is known as scholasticism, the preëminent philosophy of the height of the Middle Ages.

Aristotle was peculiarly suited to Christian uses. He held that God was the creator and "prime mover" of the universe. He contended that the heavens were perfect because of their circular motion and of their composition out of a mysterious fifth element. By his fourth "cause" he implied purpose in the universe. His systematic presentation made his works relatively easy to use. Finally, the scholastics toned down or hushed up Aristotle's least palatable doctrines.

If a violently antireligious ancient writer, such as Epicurus or Lucretius, had been the greatest logician of antiquity, it would have been hard for the Christians to swallow the nonlogical writings of such an antireligious writer. But as it was, after a few years of suspicion and hesitation, which we shall note in a moment, the intellectuals of the later Middle Ages embraced Aristotle with respect and enthusiasm. As James Harvey Robinson said:

> He was called "The Philosopher"; and so fully were scholars convinced that it had pleased God to permit Aristotle to say the last word upon each and every branch of knowledge that they humbly accepted him, along with the Bible, the Church Fathers, and the canon and the Roman law, as one of the unquestioned authorities which together formed a complete guide for humanity in conduct and in every branch of science.[25]

While even the most devout churchmen were not averse to using Aristotle's logical treatises as an aid to theology, many long hesitated to adopt the general philosophical and scientific works of a pagan author. Aristotle's treatises in natural philosophy were forbidden at the University of Paris in 1210, and five years later a ban was also placed on his metaphysics. But this censorship was hard to enforce, since Aristotle was permeating other universities. Pope Gregory IX decided that it would be sensible to edit Aristotle, thus preserving material valuable to a Christian scholar and eliminating passages which might be dangerous to the faith. Therefore, in 1231, Gregory appointed a committee of three to examine and expurgate Aristotle. This task proved very difficult and was never fully carried out. But individual scholars attempted to expound Aristotle and to harmonize his logic and philosophy with patristic, especially Augustinian, theology. Their achievement produced what we call the scholastic system of philosophy and theology.

The first important scholastic philosopher was Alexander of Hales, who went to France, became a Franciscan friar, and died there (1245) after establishing a reputation as a teacher at Paris. He still relied primarily on Scripture as the source of truth, but he elucidated and defended Scripture with the assistance of logic. He dealt elaborately with realism and nominalism and showed their relation to theology. His pupil John of Fidanza (1221-1274), better known as Bona-

[25] J. H. Robinson, *A History of Western Europe*, 2 vols., Ginn, 1924, I, 304-5.

ventura, helped to buttress theology with logic, even though he had a fondness for Plato and ultimately lapsed into mysticism.

The first outstanding medieval student of Aristotle was a prodigiously industrious German Dominican friar, Albertus Magnus (Albert the Great, 1206-1280). He labored under the disadvantage of not having for his early work the excellent texts of later days, but in the course of a long life he made many Latin paraphrases of Aristotle and laid the foundations for the accomplishments of Thomas Aquinas.

As Rhabanus Maurus had been the great compiler of authoritative Christian writings in the Dark Ages, so Albert was the outstanding compiler of the scholastic age. He assembled Christian and Aristotelian knowledge (and a good deal of Muslim and Hebrew, as well) and arranged them in systematic form in terms of the categories and methods of Aristotle. Medieval scientific lore was better catalogued in the great encyclopedia of Vincent of Beauvais. But no other writer approached Albert for the thoroughness with which he collected and expounded the formal learning of the height of the Middle Ages. Taylor has clearly appraised the magnitude of his accomplishment:

> Albert the Great was prodigious in the mass of his accomplishment, therein lay his importance for the age he lived in; therein lies his interest for us. . . . Perhaps the world has had no greater purveyor of a knowledge not his own. He is comparable with Boëthius, who gave the Latin world the Aristotelian *Organon,* a gift but half availed of for many centuries. Albert gave his Latin world the rest of Aristotle, the *philosophia realis.* His world was as ready to receive this great donation, as the time of Boëthius was unready to profit by any intellectual gift demanding mental energies for its assimilation. . . . The writings of Albertus Magnus represent, perhaps more fully than those of any other man, the round of knowledge, and intellectual interest attracting the attention of western Europe in the thirteenth century. . . . Albert's labors finally put within the reach of his contemporaries the sum of philosophy and science, contained in the works of Aristotle, and his ancient, as well as Arabian, commentators.[26]

Albert's writings amounted to twenty-one large volumes, constituting a vast encyclopedia of not only Aristotelian science and philosophy but of Christian theology and pietism as well. He also introduced material from Ambrose, Galen, and Avicenna. He adopted Aristotle's classification of knowledge, squared Aristotle's ideas with Christian "truth," added his own notes and digressions, and then supplemented both Aristotle and himself by the commentaries of the more notable Muslim and Hebrew authorities on Aristotle. He thus made available not only Aristotle's text but also the important commentaries on Aristotle. His was a voluminous repertory of medieval knowledge and interests in Aristotelian dress. Or, it might be regarded, with almost equal truth, as Aristotelian wisdom in medieval trappings.

In his first four volumes Albert dealt most directly with the exposition and Christian revision of Aristotle's philosophy and science. Next came extended commentaries on the Prophets, Psalms, the *Celestial Hierarchy,* and Peter Lom-

26 Taylor, *The Medieval Mind,* II, 450-54.

bard's *Book of Sentences,* and a volume of sermons. In the seventeenth and eighteenth volumes we find the most original and constructive of Albert's works, his theology (*Summa theologiae*), the earliest elaborately reasoned statement of Christian faith in terms of Aristotelian logic, thereby fulfilling the requirements of the theological revolution wrought by Abelard. Finally, Albert added volumes on Christian cosmology, Virgin lore, and miscellaneous pietistic essays.

Albert thus performed the first important task of scholasticism, namely, assembling Aristotle and Christian authorities in a real effort to assimilate and harmonize them. But in Albert the collecting and organizing tendencies were predominant. It remained for his student, another Dominican, Thomas Aquinas (1225-1274), "the angelic doctor," to complete the edifice by analyzing Albert's vast materials and presenting clearly all the major religious and secular tents of the time.

While Aquinas made some collections, his genius resided in organization, analysis, and exposition. He had the use of excellent Aristotelian texts translated into Latin directly from the Greek. Though he lived but forty-nine years, his work was so brilliant, so closely reasoned and voluminous that he, beyond any of his predecessors and successors, became the great Catholic theologian of the scholastic period.[27]

Aquinas attempted to justify faith by reason, and the weapon of reason was Aristotelian dialectic. Faith is the basis of his thinking. In his attitude he joined hands with patristic writers and with Plotinus, the great Neoplatonist. In turning to reason to justify faith he trod in the footsteps of Abelard. The following passage illustrates his approach to knowledge:

> This science [theology] does not argue to prove its principles, which are articles of Faith. . . . But if the adversary will give credence to nothing which is divinely revealed, sacred science has no arguments by which to prove to him the articles of Faith, but has only arguments to refute his reasonings against the Faith, should he adduce any. For since Faith rests on infallible truth, its contrary cannot be demonstrated; manifestly the proofs which are brought against it are not proofs, but controvertible arguments. . . . To argue from authority is most appropriate in this science; for its principles rest in revelation, and it is proper to credit the authority of those to whom the revelation is made. Nor does this derogate from the dignity of this science; for although proof from authority based on human reason may be weak, yet proof from authority based on divine revelation is most effective.

Aquinas' purpose, therefore, was to construct a logical system that would vindicate a world-outlook already revealed and determined. In so doing he was perforce obliged, among other things, to define and determine the relation of man and the universe, the position of man, the angels, and God, the relative rôle of the intellect, the will and the passions, and their relation to the will of God and the scheme of the universe.

It was an ambitious and, within its limits, a successful attempt to bring into a

---

[27] For a convenient listing of the almost incredible volume of the writings of Aquinas, see Martin Grabmann, *Thomas Aquinas,* Longmans, 1928, chap. ii.

polished and consistent whole a complete system of Christian knowledge. Aquinas' voluminous efforts to define the relation of the intellect and the will, to distinguish between knowledge derived through the senses and revealed truth, to disentangle the divine and the natural elements in man, constitute a monument to the deductive method. It especially appealed to minds, whether weak or powerful, that demanded precision and definiteness in their beliefs, and preferred truth once and for all delivered unto them. To minds committed to the inductive method and the skeptical outlook, Aquinas' system is a colossal monument to intellectual futility. The virtues and weaknesses of Aquinas' achievement are admirably elucidated by Dr. Hastings Rashdall:

> The contents of whole treatises of the pagan Philosopher—including even his great treatise on Ethics—are embodied in the *Summa theologiae* of Aquinas, still the greatest classic of the Seminaries. To that marvellous structure—strangely compounded of solid thought, massive reasoning, baseless subtlety, childish credulity, lightest fancy—Aristotle has contributed assuredly not less than St. Augustine.[28]

Like Albert, Aquinas encompassed the sum total of Aristotelian knowledge and Christian wisdom. He wrote commentaries on most of the logical, philosophical, and scientific works of Aristotle. Because he had good translations, a penetrating intellect, and remarkable organizing powers, "his work," says Taylor, "shows such a close understanding of Aristotle as the world had not known since the days of the ancient Peripatetics." He also prepared commentaries on the books of the Old and New Testament and several on Peter Lombard's *Sentences*. The latter became a classic textbook in Catholic theological faculties. He also wrote many political and economic tracts, to which we shall revert later. But his great theological expositions were his *Summa contra gentiles* and his *Summa theologiae*. The latter was the unrivaled masterpiece of scholastic philosophy and theology. Indeed, it became the most famous of Catholic treatises on theology, with the sole exception of Augustine's *City of God*, and more important than the latter in subsequent Catholic education.

We may note the essentials of Aquinas' method as an illustration of scholastic exposition.[29] The passage cited above shows that he had no doubt of the impregnability of Christian faith. But he felt that even a semblance of fallibility could be effectively dissipated if all the objections were fully stated and then devastatingly refuted. Hence he listed the authorities and arguments, pro and con, and demolished those contrary to the faith or to Aristotle, in case the latter was in harmony with the faith. Dr. Rashdall gives us an admirable summary of these scholastic acrobatics:

> The Dominican theologians made peace between the contending factions by placing Aristotle and the fathers side by side, and deferring as reverently to the one as to the other, except on the few fundamental points upon which the former could not be interpreted into harmony with the latter. The scholastic form of argu-

[28] Robinson, *Readings in European History*, I, 459.
[29] Those who wish the clearest reliable exposition of the *content* of Aquinas' theology will do well to consult Taylor, *op. cit.*, II, chap. xli.

ment, which attained its full development in Aquinas,—a chain of authorities and syllogisms in defence of one thesis, another series for the opposite view, a conclusion in harmony with Augustine or Aristotle, as the case might be, and a reply to the opposing arguments by means of ingenious distinction or reconciliation,—afforded exceptional facilities for the harmonious combination of orthodoxy and intellectuality.

The Dominicans showed the Latin churchman how to be ingenious, startling, brilliant, even destructive, without suspicion of heresy. [St.] Bernard would have been shocked at the idea of inventing or even of fairly stating objections to the Catholic Faith. By the time of Aquinas it was felt that the better the imaginary opponent's case could be stated, the more credit there was in refuting it.

The scholar's intellectual enjoyment of thirty ingenious arguments against the Immortality of the Soul was not diminished by the thirty-six equally ingenious arguments with which the attack would immediately be met. In scholastic disputation restless intellectual activity found an innocent outlet; love of controversy and speculation, the real ardour for truth and knowledge which distinguished the age of Berengar and the age of Abelard, had for the most part degenerated. . . .[30]

Aquinas' supremacy among scholastics was the result not only of his better knowledge of Aristotle's actual statements, but also of his unparalleled capacity for coherent organization, cogent reasoning and lucid expression:

The consummate fashioning faculty, the devout and intellectual temperament of Thomas, are writ large in his treatises. His work has unity; it is a system; it corresponds to the scholastically creative personality, from the efficient concord of whose faculties it proceeded. . . .

Thomas's intellectual powers work together in order to set his thought of man's *summum bonum* on its surest foundations, and make clear its scope: his faculty of arrangement, and serious and lucid presentation; his careful reasoning, which never trips, never overlooks, and never either hurries or is taken unprepared; his marvellous unforgetfulness of everything which might remotely bear on the subject; his intellectual poise, and his just weighing of every matter that should be taken into the scales of his determination. Observing these, we may realize how he seemed to his time a new intellectual manifestation of God's illuminating grace. There was in him something unknown before; his argument, his exposition, was new in power, in interest, in lucidity. . . .

Thomas's ideal is intellectual, and yet ends in faith. His intellectual interests, by faith emboldened, strengthened, and pointed heavenward, make on toward the realisation of that intellectual beatitude which is to be consummate hereafter, when the saved soul's grace-illumined eye shall reawaken where it may see face to face.[31]

The general import, success, and influence of Aquinas' synthesis has been cogently summarized by McGiffert:

In spite of the criticism showered upon it, and in spite of the party differences that long divided Thomists and Scotists, Thomas' great enterprise, the synthesis of Aristotelian philosophy and Christian theology, proved increasingly popular. Its

[30] Robinson, *Readings in European History*, I, 458-59.
[31] Taylor, *The Medieval Mind*, II, 466-67, 481.

lasting success was due above all to the fact that it offered a new and from the point of view of that age scientific support to the Christian system.[32]

Scholasticism began to be undermined by critics in its own ranks, particularly by two keen Franciscan logicians, Duns Scotus (1270-1308) and William of Ockham (1280-1349). Scotus was born in Scotland and Ockham in England. Both were educated at Oxford. Their fame led to teaching posts in Paris.

Duns Scotus, "the subtle doctor," was the most astute of scholastic logicians. He has been called the "most penetrating critic produced by scholasticism," and "the Kant of scholasticism." Such characterizations are not unmerited, even though he died at the age of thirty-eight. As McGiffert says: "Duns was an adept at discovering logical fallacies and exposing the inconclusiveness of other demonstrations." He refused to accept any scholastic conclusion, no matter if it had been formulated by Thomas Aquinas himself, until he had subjected it to acute and thorough investigation. There were few examples of previous medieval reasoning in which he could not find serious flaws.

Though a realist, and the finest flower of refined scholastic logic, Duns Scotus nevertheless accentuated the decline of scholasticism. This he did, in the first place, by exposing the errors of eminent schoolmen and revealing the limitations and fallibility of the logical method, even in the best hands, when employed in the service of theology. In the second place, so voluminous, tortuous, and long-drawn-out were his dialectical treatises that they repelled later thinkers by their very bulk and complexity. His work was, in a way, the *reductio ad absurdum* of theological dialectic. In the third place, his insistence upon renewed and constant examination of all problems suggested a departure from logical investigation and a step in the direction of observation and experiment.

William of Ockham espoused extreme nominalism in his philosophy. He was impressed by the way in which Duns Scotus had exposed the errors of the scholastics and the limitations of the scholastic method. Therefore, he abandoned Duns's efforts at reconciliation and reconsideration and recommended that religion once more be based on faith and revelation—divine authority—rather than upon reason. This meant, as McGiffert has made clear, the abandonment of the whole scholastic conception of natural theology and of all hope of a rational demonstration of faith:

> A consistent and clear-sighted nominalist like Ockham was faced with one of two alternatives: either he must abandon certain doctrines of the Christian faith, or he must recognize the independence of philosophy and theology and give up altogether the effort to show the rational character of the Christian system. Though a nominalist in his philosophy Ockham was a devout and orthodox believer and he chose the latter alternative. The Christian system is to be accepted in its entirety on the basis of divine revelation, but the claim that it is rational is to be abandoned once and for all. Ockham went still further than this and denied that the divine unit, or infinity, or even the divine existence, could be proved. This meant, of course, the rejection of the category of natural theology.[33]

[32] McGiffert, *op. cit.*, II, 294.
[33] *Ibid.*, pp. 308-9.

Scholasticism had now run its logical course and Christian apologetics had completed its cycle. Paul had preached salvation by faith. From Augustine to Abelard theologians had relied upon authority. Abelard showed that this would not suffice. So logic was tried by the schoolmen for a century or more, but Duns Scotus then made it clear that logic was only slightly less fallible than authority in matters of final truth. Ockham accepted this conclusion and reverted to faith, revelation, and authority. His philosophy was marked by the discarding not only of reverence for logic but also of many of the popular conclusions of the logicians and formal theologians.

Ockham was, however, highly talented in the astute use of the dialectical method, when he chose to rely upon it. Though willing to base religion on authority and revelation, he demanded the most rigorous substantiation of secular knowledge. He laid great stress upon the sole existence of reality in concrete things and turned philosophy in the empiricist direction of Locke and his associates, who, more than three centuries later, endeavored to base knowledge on experience. This Ockham did by turning intellectual attention from universals to particulars. With Ockham and his school realism was utterly routed.

Duns Scotus and William of Ockham weakened scholasticism from within. It remained for Francis Bacon and his forerunners to assault it vigorously from without. Bacon once caustically appraised the methodology and achievements of the scholastic philosophers:

> Having sharp and strong wits, and abundance of leisure, and small variety of reading, but their wits being shut up in the cells of a few authors (chiefly Aristotle, their dictator), as their persons were shut up in the cells of monasteries and colleges, and knowing little history, either of nature or time, [they] did out of no great quantity of matter and infinite agitation of wit spin out unto us those laborious webs of learning which are extant in their books.[34]

Equally severe is a contemporary specialist on the history of Christian thought, Professor H. B. Workman:

> Thus the labours of the later schoolmen are mere mental gymnastics without bearing on life; researches which result in no discovery; the worship of logic for logic's own sake; elaborations of distinctions without difference; endless conflicts in which the foes lose sight of each other in a more than Egyptian darkness and in labyrinths without issue.[35]

Another major intellectual liability in scholasticism was the deep veneration it created for the works of Aristotle. So great was the medieval respect for him that it caused his writings to become a dangerous obstacle to the growth of knowledge. He was really an amazingly encyclopedic writer, whose works epitomized the learning and philosophy of the golden age of Attic culture. But medieval scholars did not see him in this sane and historical perspective. His methods and his materials seemed to them the last word of secular wisdom on all earthly topics. Moreover, they were only interested in his deductive logic. The destruction of

---

[34] Cited in Robinson, *The Mind in the Making*, p. 122.
[35] Workman, *Christian Thought to the Reformation*, p. 242.

Aristotle-worship became a necessary task for the iconoclasts of the early modern period. It was only by doubting the adequacy of deductive logic that intellectual progress was made possible. The discrediting of Aristotle, as used by the scholastics, faintly suggested by Roger Bacon, was the intellectual lifework of Francis Bacon.

Yet it is easy to be overcritical in condemning the attainments of the schoolmen. Considering the intellectual setting of the time, they were a credit to scholarship and to the teaching profession. They aroused a permanent professional interest in teaching, outlined and systematized the corpus of requisite knowledge, perfected the technique of research, as it was then understood, and created real intellectual enthusiasm among multitudes of students who were compelled to study under far less advantageous conditions than now exist in institutions of higher learning. For the greater part of the intellectual activity that existed in the later medieval period the scholastic philosophers and pedagogues were responsible. The superiorities of modern university instruction and scholarly achievement must be assigned primarily to the vast advances in general culture and techniques. Finally, as a present-day historian of science has pointed out, the scholastics indirectly promoted the subsequent development of science and critical philosophy through their assumption that man might presume to examine critically the nature of God and the cosmos.

VI. MEDIEVAL MYSTICISM

While the popular theology of the mature medieval era exalted philosophy and logic, there was another school which had received a great impetus in the Dark Ages from the translation of the *Celestial Hierarchy* by Erigena and from Erigena's own mystical synthesis of Christian theology.

The earliest mystic of this period was Bernard of Clairvaux, the relentless and vindictive foe of Abelard. Bernard was an eloquent and fiery preacher, not a systematic theologian. He was less influenced by works on mysticism than by his own temperament. He held that faith is superior to reason, and that mystical union with Christ and the divine word is superior to faith as an assurance of religious reality. This was the Neoplatonic attitude stated in Christian terms, except that Bernard emphasized union with Christ rather than with the god of the Neoplatonists. The road to God, he asserted, must be found in the affections and not in the intellect. Divine indwelling is the ultimate religious experience. In practical life, the chief task is to imitate the human Christ. Bernard's views were notably practiced by Francis of Assisi (1182-1226), founder of the famous order of mendicant friars.

In Hugo of St. Victor (c. 1097-1141), mysticism found its first systematic theologian after Erigena. He was a versatile writer, covering many fields, but his most notable work was the *Sacraments of the Christian Faith*, in which he combined mysticism and rational theology. In this, as McGiffert observes, he found a place for mysticism in theology and for theology in mysticism. There is much in religious experience, he said, which cannot be rationally demonstrated. Hence we must have recourse to faith. Mystical contemplation, in which the Christian comes into a perfect union with God, is the highest manifestation of faith, but it can be fully realized only in the life beyond the grave.

The most extreme of the medieval mystics was Johannes (Meister) Eckhart (1260-1327). He insisted upon the reality of an indwelling spirit, through which we may rise into a union with the Godhead and "be transformed totally into God, even as in the sacrament the bread is converted into the body of Christ." Eckhart distinguished between a personal revealed God, namely, the triune God of the Christians, and the unknown, unknowable, and unrevealed Godhead or Deity. Union with the Christian God is only the first step in the religious triumph of the Christian. He must press on until he has achieved complete fusion with the unknowable Godhead. Around this unbounded mystical flight Eckhart built a whole system of theology. Among Eckhart's followers was Johann Tauler (1290-1361), one of the greatest of mystical preachers, and Jan van Ruysbroeck (1293-1381), who was even more successful than Eckhart in reducing mysticism to a system of metaphysics.

Mysticism was transformed into an active and impelling creed by Thomas à Kempis, a disciple of Ruysbroeck, who composed his famous *Imitation of Christ* somewhere between 1400 and 1425. In this he repudiated the quietism, negativism, and resignation of earlier mysticism and urged with great conviction an active and realistic imitation of Christ, of whom he drew a moving picture.

Mysticism was especially popular with pious nuns, perhaps as a result of the greater proneness of women to hysteria. Among the more notable female mystics were Catherine of Siena (1347-1380), Catharine of Genoa (1447-1510), and Theresa of Avila (1515-1582).

While mysticism may not be very impressive as a system of thought, it occupies an important place in the religious history of the Middle Ages. And it is almost as important in the history of art as in the history of religion. Mysticism exerted a far deeper influence on medieval art than scholastic theology. Mystical religion and mystical science, the latter taking the form of the analogy between the macrocosm and the microcosm,[36] very definitely shaped the artistic conceptions and creations of western Europe during the Middle Ages.

VII. MEDIEVAL NATURAL SCIENCE TO ROGER BACON

In this section we shall deal with the developments in natural science in western Europe from the Dark Ages to Roger Bacon (1214-1294). The choice of Bacon as a stopping point is not the result of an arbitrary dating of the period or of an acceptance of the old legends about Bacon's uniqueness as a medieval scientist. From Gerbert to Bacon one finds typical medieval science. After Bacon there were set in progress forces which ultimately led to the remarkable scientific achievements of modern times. The full impact of Muslim natural science, the adoption of the inductive method and the experimental technique, and the attacks upon

[36] See below, p. 430.

scholasticism ushered in a new era in natural science with which we shall deal in the following chapter.

In the period from Gerbert to Bacon there was an increased interest in natural science, as a result of Aristotelian and Muslim inspiration. We noted that the great encyclopedia of the Dark Ages, Rhabanus Maurus' *De universo,* was occupied mainly with religious topics. The major encyclopedias of the period we are now discussing were in part devoted to scientific lore. Such were the laborious compilations of Alexander Neckham, Bartholomew the Englishman, and Vincent of Beauvais.

Medieval universities and the schoolmen promoted natural science only incidentally, through their commentaries based on Aristotle's scientific works, which, however, were far less important to them than his logical and philosophical cogitations. In the medical universities, naturally, greater attention was paid to science than elsewhere. At the university of Oxford, for instance, a movement was started by Franciscan teachers, led by Robert Grosseteste (1175-1253), bishop of Lincoln and the master of Roger Bacon, to give more time and attention to the quadrivium, particularly science. The most impressive body of scientific data brought forth in this age emanated from Muslim sources. The true influence of this Muslim science, however, was felt during the age of Bacon, and later.

Astrology, alchemy and magic, the legacy of ancient times, played a prominent rôle in medieval science. The ignorant and the credulous, as well as the learned, upheld their validity.[37]

Astrology had a long history before the medieval period. The ancient Babylonians believed that there is a definite relationship between the destinies of the state and the position and movements of the heavenly bodies. Astrology was introduced among the Greeks during the Hellenistic period. The theory then evolved that there is an intimate connection between the position and movements of the astral bodies and the character and destiny of individuals. The Romans added little to Hellenistic astrology, which they adopted with unprecedented enthusiasm. During the later years of the republic and in imperial times almost every rich Roman family had its personal astrologer. There was some opposition to astrology in early Christianity, which, however, soon came to terms with it, and we find Isidore of Seville declaring that while some astrological notions are mythical, most are sound. In the Middle Ages even men like Roger Bacon were earnest devotees of astrology.

Astrology, in the Middle Ages, was divided into two branches. Natural astrology represented the direct observation of the heavens. At a later date this became astronomy. Judicial astrology determined the influence of the heavenly bodies upon the destiny and fortune of both nations and individuals. In harmony with Greek astrology, it assumed that there is a definite relationship between the position and movements of heavenly bodies, especially the planets, and the fate of individuals. Even wholly imaginary astral concepts, such as the signs of the Zodiac and the planetary houses, were supposed to exert a potent influence on man's

[37] See Thorndike, *History of Magic and Experimental Science,* Vol. II, *passim.*

behavior. Astrology provided portents in the choice of a career, in treating diseases, and in the general perplexities of life.

The core of astrological technique was known as "casting the horoscope." The horoscope revealed the outcome of the occult astral influences which affect the individual and his problems. In order to construct the horoscope it was necessary to know the date and hour of birth, the latitude and longitude of the place of birth, the sex of the individual, the configuration of the planets and stars at the time of birth, the position of the so-called planetary houses, and the prevailing zodiacal signs. The horoscope revealed not only the talents and the destiny of the individual but also solved business and personal problems. "One could locate a ship at sea, decide whether one absent was dead or alive, find out whether a debt was likely to be paid, and clear up pressing problems of health, friendship, love, fidelity and the like." Astrology also had political significance, since astral influences were believed to determine racial traits and national characteristics.

This fantastic "science" still has its grip on the minds of the credulous. The astrological column of a leading American newspaper was recently voted by readers to be the most valuable single item published in the paper. A leading contemporary American astrologer, Evangeline Adams, used to receive more letters each week than President Hoover received in the first week after his great victory in November, 1928. Among her patrons during the great "bull market" of 1929 were some of the leading brokers of the day.

Alchemy, the forerunner of modern chemistry, had two principal aims. It aspired both to lengthen human life and to transmute the baser metals into gold. It was hoped that both of these objectives might be realized by the discovery of the mysterious fifth element or the "philosopher's stone":

> The medieval alchemist believed, following the tradition of the great Aristotle, that man's body, like all other material things, was composed of four elements, earth, air, fire and water. Each individual had his own particular mixture of these—his *temperamentum,* as they called it. This was determined at conception and birth by the influence of the constellations and planets. The aptitudes, weaknesses and chances of success or failure of each human being sprang from his elemental composition. Since no one had been properly mixed since Adam, the problem emerged of discovering some sovereign remedy—*secretum maximum*—which would cleanse and rectify man's composition and so produce a superman, full of physical and mental vigor and enjoying a life prolonged through many joyous centuries. Hence the persistent search for the Elixir, or philosopher's stone, which should produce these marvelous results, as well as transform the baser metals into gold.[38]

While the ancient orientals, and the Greeks and Romans, did preliminary work in alchemy, the most notable achievements were those of Muslims like Gerber, Rhazes, and al-Kathi. But there were numerous Christian alchemists in this period, including Albertus Magnus and Roger Bacon. It was long believed that the most eminent Christian alchemist was Raymond Lull (1225-1315), about whom there were many legends, such as that he transformed 50,000 pounds of quicksilver into

[38] J. H. Robinson, "The Philosopher's Stone," *Atlantic Monthly,* April, 1919, p. 474.

gold for King Edward III of England. Today the works on alchemy attributed to him are held to be spurious. But whoever was their author, they constitute a large body of alchemistic lore. Other important alchemists were Adelard of Bath (d. c. 1150), Nicholas of Poland (c. 1300), and Basil Valentine (c. 1475).

Though the Muslim and Christian alchemists did not find the philosopher's stone, achieve their hoped-for transmutation of the baser metals into gold, or discover the secret of human rejuvenation, they acquired practical knowledge of such chemicals as antimony, saltpeter, arsenic, zinc, bismuth, manganese, ether, and the metallic salts. These researches stimulated chemistry. The ultimate outcome of the work of the alchemists thus justified Francis Bacon's famous characterization: "Alchemy may be compared to the man who told his sons that he had left them gold, buried in his vineyard; while they by digging found no gold, yet by turning up the mould about the roots of vines procured a plentiful vintage. So the search and endeavor to make gold have brought many useful inventions to light."

Medieval thinkers believed in magic. But medieval magic differed materially from primitive magic, in that it was a strange mosaic compounded of primitive beliefs and superstitious Oriental and classical lore. While belief in magic was popular among medieval scholars, it never became quite respectable to Christianity, which regarded it as a sort of "black art." Medieval magic involved words and numbers, and the occult nature and potency of certain plants, animals, and acts. For example, it was believed that figs brought from Egypt could remove wrinkles, and that a bull induced by any method to come under a fig tree would become docile. A stone taken from the crop of a rooster and carried in one's mouth would bring victory in battle. Another stone (magnetite), if put on the head of a wife while she was asleep, would reveal any infidelity that had taken place during the absence of her husband. The mugwort, a wild plant, was believed to ward off fatigue. Magic pervaded medieval medicine, and popular medical remedies were based as much on magic as on the learned treatise of Galen, which was itself compounded in part of magical lore. Medieval magic, says Professor Lynn Thorndike,

> . . . constitutes a varied and formidable class of convictions. There was a notion that from such things as the marks upon one's body, or from one's dream, or from peals of thunder, flight of birds, entrails of sacrificial victims and the movements of the stars, we can foretell the future. There was the assumption that certain precious stones, certain plants and trees and fountains, certain animals or parts of animals have strange and wonderful virtues. There was the idea that man, too, possesses marvelous powers to the extent that he can fascinate and bewitch his fellows. Nor should we forget the attribution to the heavenly bodies of an enormous influence over the minerals and vegetation, over human health and character, over national constitutions and customs, even over religious movements. We find this notion of occult virtue extended to things without physical reality; to words, to numbers, to written characters and formulae. It is applied to certain actions and ways of doing things: to "ligatures and suspensions," for instance. Then there was the belief that wonders may be wrought by the aid of demons, and that incanta-

tions, suffumigations, and the like are of great value in invoking spirits. Finally, there was a vague general notion that not only are the ethereal and elementary worlds joined by occult sympathy, but that all parts of the universe are somehow mystically connected, and that perhaps a single magic key may be discovered by which we may become masters of the entire universe.[39]

Another popular phase of medieval pseudo science was the assumed affinity between the nature of God, the cosmos or macrocosm, and man, the microcosm. The idea originated with the Pythagoreans and was expounded in Plato's mystical *Timaeus,* whence it was adopted and elaborated by the Neoplatonists.

> The medieval mind was fascinated by a supposed analogy between the nature of the Godhead, the astronomical constitution of the Cosmos, or macrocosm, and the anatomical, physiological and psychological structure of man, the microcosm. . . . The conception of the essential similarity of macrocosm and microcosm held throughout the middle ages. It survived the Renaissance, and persisted in literature into almost modern days.[40]

Each element in the macrocosm, earth, air, fire, and water, was supposed to correspond with one of the four humors of the microcosm, man. Earth corresponded to black bile, water to phlegm, air to yellow bile, and fire to blood. "The whole Cosmos is usually imagined as permeated and bound together by a living spirit, which in its turn is pervaded and controlled by the Godhead." This scientific fantasy fitted well the medieval desire of fusing science, religion, and morals. As Dr. Singer remarks: "For such an attitude of mind there could be no distinction between physical events, moral truths, and spiritual existences. In their fusion of the internal and external universe these mystics have much in common with the mystics of all ages." [41] The major medieval expositors of the macrocosm-microcosm fantasy were Hermann the Cripple (1013-1054), Hugo of St. Victor (1095-1141), Bernard Sylvestris (c. 1150), and Hildegard, abbess of Bingen (c. 1170).

We may now examine briefly some of the leading influences on medieval scientific thought. For rendering Muslim science·into Latin the Middle Ages were indebted to translators like Gerard of Cremona, to whom we have already referred. Muslim scientists and philosophers disseminated a knowledge of the scientific works of Aristotle, introduced Arabic numerals and the subject of algebra, which was almost a Hindu and Muslim product, restored Euclid, and contributed to geometry, trigonometry, and medicine. That most impressive of all medieval medical treatises, Avicenna's *Canon,* was a Muslim product. Moreover, most of the medieval knowledge of Greek and Roman medicine first came in through Arabic versions. And medieval Christian alchemy was founded on the Muslim works. Along with fairly sound Muslim science there came, of course, a vast mass of magical and astrological lore.

While on this subject we must not overlook the other source of scientific stimulus from the East, namely, Byzantine science. Among the foremost early medieval

---

[39] Thorndike, *The Place of Magic in the Intellectual History of Europe,* Columbia University Press, 1905, pp. 23-24.
[40] W. C. Dampier-Whetham, *A History of Science,* Macmillan, 1930, pp. 88-89.
[41] In Hearnshaw, *Medieval Contributions to Modern Civilization,* p. 138.

Byzantine physicians and surgeons were Aëtius of Amida (early 6th century), Alexander of Tralles (525-605), and Paul of Aegina (625-690). Alexander was the most original physician since Galen, and Paul was the leading Byzantine surgeon. Their works stimulated the medical revival of the Middle Ages.

The introduction of Aristotle's works on the sciences produced innumerable commentators. Outstanding was Albertus Magnus, "who interwove Aristotelian, Arabian, Jewish and Neoplatonic elements into a whole which included all the contemporary knowledge of astronomy, geography, botany, zoölogy, and medicine." Even more slavish in reproducing Aristotle were the leading medieval encyclopedists. In his *Man and His Universe,* John Langdon-Davies gives some representative examples of the way in which Aristotle was closely followed by medieval scientific writers. He first quotes characteristic descriptions from Aristotle's *History of Animals* and then cites the corresponding comments in medieval scientific lore, particularly from the popular encyclopedia of Bartholomew the Englishman:

1. The chameleon resembles the lizard in the general configuration of its body, but the ribs stretch downwards and meet together under the belly as is the case with fishes, and the spine sticks up as with the fish. Its face resembles that of the baboon. The change in its colour takes place when it is inflated with air; it is then black, not unlike the crocodile, or green like the lizard but black-spotted like the pard. (Aristotle, H. A., II, 11.)

Chameleon is a little beast and his sides be even long to the nether parts of his womb as it were a fish; his face is as it were a beast compounded of a swine and of an ape. And changeth his colour when his skin is blown, and his colour is somewhat black with black speckles therein. (Berthelet's trans. of Bartholomew the Englishman, XVIII. 21, 1535.)

2. Of all animals the newly born cub of the she-bear is the smallest in proportion to the size of the mother: that is to say, it is larger than a mouse but smaller than a weasel. It is also smooth and blind and its legs and most of its organs are as yet inarticulate (*i.e.,* shapeless). (Aristotle, H. A., VI, 30.)

For the whelp is a piece of flesh little more than a mouse, having neither eyes nor hair, and so this lump she licketh, and shapeth a whelp with licking. (Berthelet, XVIII, 112.)

This is the origin of our phrase "licking into shape" and Aristotle says that foxes do the same with their cubs, while Pliny is responsible for the theory as far as bear cubs are concerned.

3. The weasel, when it fights with a snake, first eats wild rue, the smell of which is noxious to the snake. (Aristotle, H. A., IX, 6.)

The Weasel eateth rue, and balmeth herself with the juice thereof, and rages then on the cockatrice, and assaileth, and slayeth him without any dread bodily. (Berthelet, XVIII, 7.)

4. Now the Salamander is a clear case in point, to show us that animals do actually exist that fire cannot destroy; for this creature, so the story goes, not only walks through the fire but puts it out in doing so. (Aristotle, H. A., V, 19.)

The Salamander quencheth the fire that he toucheth as ice does, and water frozen. (Berthelet, XVIII, 92.)

5. The Syrian lion bears cubs five times: five cubs at the first litter, then four,

then three, then two and a lastly one; after this the lioness ceases to bear for the rest of her days. . . . If a hunter hit him, without hurting him, then if with a bound he gets hold of him, he will do him no harm, not even with his claws, but after shaking him and giving him a fright will let him go again. . . . The cubs of the lioness when newly born are exceedingly small, and can scarcely walk when two months old. (Aristotle, H. A., *passim*.)

The lioness whelpeth first five whelps, and afterwards four, and so each year less by one, and waxeth barren when she whelpeth one at last. And she whelpeth whelps evil shapen and small, in size of a weasel in the beginning. And whelps of two months may hardly move. If a man shoot at him the Lion chaseth him and throweth him down, and woundeth him not, nor hurteth him. (Berthelet, XVIII, 65.) [42]

It might contribute to clarity and to our understanding of the character of medieval science to characterize briefly the nature of each of the present-day branches of science in the medieval period.

In mathematics, there was no knowledge of higher mathematics, such as calculus and analytical geometry, or even any complete trigonometry. Nor was there any algebra until it was introduced by the Muslims. Arithmetic and geometry formed the core of mathematical studies. They bore little resemblance to anything we now know by those names. Until the Muslims brought them to western Europe, there were no Arabic numerals, and no complicated arithmetical computations could be carried out in Roman numerals. Practical arithmetic was limited to the abacus or Roman counting board. Academic arithmetic was, for the most part, a combination of magic and superstition. The properties and magic qualities of numbers, for instance, were assiduously studied. Isidore of Seville worked out, for example, a manual on the occult nature of all numbers up to sixty-four. Geometry was represented primarily by fragments of Euclid, with considerable embellishment as to the magic nature of certain angles and geometric figures. Mathematics made little progress in the Middle Ages until the introduction of algebra and the Arabic notation by the Muslims. Yet some, like Gerbert, ingeniously expounded such mathematical knowledge as existed. Both arithmetic and geometry were taught mainly from Boëthius' textbooks, which were based on Hellenistic works.

Astronomy, as we have seen, was primarily astrology, and not of so high a character as in the Greek and Roman period. The theory of the heavens was Ptolemaic, elaborated somewhat by Christian eschatology (theories of the Last Judgment). The Ptolemaic world-picture and pagan astrology thus constituted medieval astrophysics. Until Aristotle was revived in the twelfth and thirteenth centuries, physics was all but ignored. Yet Aristotle's physics benefited science but little, since most of his doctrines were flagrantly erroneous. His theories of the four elements, of dynamics, of light and heavy, and the like, misled men for centuries. Until the later Middle Ages few medieval scholars in the West knew anything about the brilliant physical researches of Archimedes, Hero, and other Hellenistic scientists. The sole exception to medieval ignorance in science was the

42 *Op. cit.*, Harper, 1930, pp. 74-76.

ancient work done in optics by Euclid, Ptolemy, and others, which the Christians recovered through al-Hazen and other Muslim scientists. Chemistry was a weird combination of alchemy, Aristotle's theory of the four elements, astrological doctrine, and magic. Its only promise lay in the practical alchemical experiments which led to the discovery of certain basic metals, acids, and salts before the close of the medieval period.

Biology was based only slightly on practical observation. In the early medieval period the bestiaries were used as illustrations to drive home Christian truths.[43] In the later Middle Ages Aristotle's biological lore was accepted as gospel. His descriptive biology was often remarkably sound and astute, but his theoretical biology was usually erroneous. For instance, he even denied sexuality in plants. Only a few, like Albertus Magnus, departed from Aristotle far enough to check up on nature by direct observation.

Psychology was nonexistent. What passed for it were mainly the dogmas of human conduct drawn from Scripture and theology—a condition which existed, for that matter, until the time of Thomas Hobbes in the middle of the seventeenth century. Aristotle's psychology was studied to some extent, but his views were as wide of the truth as the theological psychology. Aristotle believed that the heart was the center of thought and that the function of the brain was to pump phlegm to the heart to keep it from overheating in periods of intense thinking.

The medieval knowledge of geography was very limited. Little was known of Strabo, Ptolemy, and other eminent classical geographers. Until the time of Marco Polo few traveled widely. The oceans and distant continents were places of mystery and terror—to the average man, the edge of the abyss of hell or the habitat of monsters. The known earth was a small area about the Mediterranean. Fantastic ideas often existed about this. Classical knowledge of latitude and longitude had all but disappeared; so had the science of cartography, which was not revived until the later Middle Ages, after contact with Muslim cartographers. Astrology deeply colored the science of geography. Geology was based on the book of Genesis. There was no comprehension of the age of the earth, the structural history of the planet, the nature of fossils, or anything else of the kind. The theory of a special creation, some thousands of years before Christ, was universally accepted.

Medicine was chiefly a combination of magic and superstition until the coming of Muslim medicine, and the revival of Galen and other Greeks. Surgery was handled in part by the surgeon-barbers. With such men as Roger of Salerno, Roland of Parma, and Guy de Chauliac of Montpellier, surgery, however, became an independent science applied by trained medical men. The nature of medieval medical prescriptions may be gleaned from the following remedy of Bernard Gordon, a late-thirteenth-century physician, for failing eyesight:

. . . "God even to these times has never vouchsafed to reveal a better remedy" than a combination in varying amounts of mountain willow, majoram, eufragia, celidonia, fennel, ginger, spikenard, pepper, gariofil, thucia, Persian gum, ass's

43 See above, pp. 310, 313.

milk, aloes wood, the gall of an eagle, a hawk and a mountain goat, balsam and honey. Of these ingredients "those that need pulverizing are to be pulverized; those that ought to be shaken are well shaken; those which should be reduced to liquid form are to be liquified. Then, if it is summer time, they should for forty days be mixed in the hot sun, and stirred daily. If it be winter, let the mixture be prepared with cinders, where the heat is about that of a sitting hen; and let it be stirred and kept in a glass vessel, and dropped into the eyes; and it is of so great virtue that it enables decrepitude to read small letters without eye-glasses." [44]

We shall treat later medieval progress in medicine in the next chapter.

We may conclude our brief survey of medieval science before Roger Bacon by characterizing a few of the more prominent medieval scientists. This list will, incidentally, show the progress in our knowledge of medieval science within the last generation. For example, it was not so long ago that historians were wont to look upon Roger Bacon as the only important scientist in the Middle Ages.

First and foremost, we must recall the leading translators of Muslim scientific works, the dean of whom was Gerard of Cremona, who is said to have translated no less than seventy-one Muslim treatises and tracts. Some put the number as high as ninety.

Next come the systematizers and commentators on Aristotelian science, led by Albertus Magnus. But Albert's importance in the history of science goes beyond his commentaries on Aristotle. Professor Thorndike, a recent and critical student of Albert, concludes that "he does show unmistakable signs of the scientific spirit." This attitude Albert promulgated in a characteristic passage: "It is not enough to know in terms of universals, but we must seek to know each object's own peculiar characteristics, for this is the best and most perfect kind of science." Hence, he departed from Aristotle to observe the actual behavior patterns of plants and animals, and even performed elementary experiments on the latter.

A versatile scientist was Adelard of Bath (d. c. 1150), one of the early English visitors to Muslim Spain. His most important work was the *Natural Questions,* reminiscent of Seneca. He had some acquaintance with Muslim mathematics and more with Muslim alchemy. He made some progress in optics, revealed originality in geodesy and in studying the center of the earth's gravity. But he also reflected the current magical symbolism, as, for instance, in the statement that the mountains of the moon are spots put there by God as a perpetual reminder of the transgression of Adam and the fall of man.

Another prominent English scientist was Robert Grosseteste, a skilled mathematician and astronomer, one of the first Christian scientists to use lenses for the study of light. Like his contemporaries, however, he was greatly obsessed with astrology and magic. We shall mention his medical work in a later chapter.

The foremost Christian authority on astrology of this era was Michael Scot (c. 1170-1234), the scientific luminary of the court of Frederick II. He made extensive translations of Aristotle's biological works in Arabic, and turned many Muslim astrological tracts into Latin. He was the chief systematizer of Christian

44 Lynn Thorndike, "Natural Science in the Middle Ages," *Popular Science Monthly,* September, 1915, p. 289.

astrological knowledge in the Middle Ages, although John of Spain seems to have exceeded him in the volume of translations of Muslim astrological treatises. Michael also wrote on medical topics.

The scholar chiefly influential in introducing Arabic numerals into Europe was Leonardo of Pisa who wrote his *Book of the Abacus* in 1202. Of special importance was his employment of the cipher or zero.

On geography and geology, the most notable work was accomplished by Ristoro d'Arezzo (c. 1280) in a vast treatise on the composition of the world.[44a] It was a mixture of Muslim learning, scholastic compilations, and Aristotelian science. Its character is shown by his theory that dry land results from the fact that the pull of the stars has uncovered land in certain parts of the earth, while at the same time holding back and piling up the waters elsewhere.

Peter of Abano (1250-1320), an admirer of Averroës, experimented with physics, astronomy, and physiology. He believed that the air has weight, and that the brain is the source of the nerves, and the heart of the blood vessels. He made the closest estimate which had yet been offered of the exact length of the year. His magnum opus, the *Conciliator*, lists over 200 major scientific problems. Lynn Thorndike believes that Peter may be regarded as bringing to a close this period of medieval science. Peter seems to have felt this himself, for he devoted much time to supplementing and correcting his predecessors. But even Peter assigned a great deal of space to astrology and magic.

The most extended treatment of natural science was, of course, contained in the encyclopedias, in which we get the best impression of the general scope and character of medieval science. The leading compilations were *On the Natures of Things*, by Alexander Neckham (1157-1217); *On the Nature of Things*, by Thomas of Cantimpré (c. 1205-1276); *On the Properties of Things*, by Bartholomew de Glanvil (the Englishman), written about 1230; and *The Speculum Majus* (*Mirror of Nature, Doctrine and History*) by Vincent of Beauvais (1190-1264). The latter was the most voluminous, containing about 80 books divided into 9,885 chapters. This would make about 60 volumes of ordinary book size. A little over a third of it was devoted to natural science.

VIII. POLITICAL, SOCIAL, AND ECONOMIC THEORY IN THE MIDDLE AGES

An important aspect of the medieval synthesis was the effort to bring political theory under the domination of Christian doctrine and scholastic philosophy, an achievement credited to Albertus Magnus and Thomas Aquinas. The claims of the church fathers and the writers of the Dark Ages regarding the supremacy of the church over the state were blended with Aristotelian political theory to constitute the systematic political philosophy of this age.

The ecclesiastical arm was so powerful that those who dealt with political theory no longer felt it necessary to defend the hegemony of the church. They merely proceeded to explain the fact. In formal medieval political theory the church was supreme in spiritual and the state in secular matters. But this theory of a nice distribution of powers, as we have seen, did not work well in practice.

[44a] See Lynn Thorndike, *Science and Thought in the Fifteenth Century*, Columbia University Press, 1929, chap. xii.

The church entered actively into the feudal system and thus became inseparably involved in secular administration. The secular rulers, on the other hand, aspired to appoint church officers and to invest these churchmen with the symbols of their spiritual authority. The churchmen undertook to scrutinize and control the moral life and outlook of secular governors. The fine theory of separation thus crumbled in the face of medieval realities.

The church based its supremacy over the state on the fact that it controlled spiritual and moral problems, whereas the state dealt with material issues. Moreover, the church was founded by God for the advancement of his glory. The state, on the contrary, was only tolerated by God as a necessary evil. The state had its beginning in the sinful nature of man, which must be held in check by physical force. The schoolmen tended to place the church over the state, although Dante supported the theory of a universal church and state, coördinate in power and function.

The theocratic doctrine of the state (that is, religious control of politics) received its fullest exposition at this time in the *Polycraticus* of John of Salisbury (1120-1182), a learned English churchman who had studied under Abelard.[45] The inferiority of the prince to the priest was emphasized at great length, tyranny was defined, and tyrannicide was justified in the case of oppressive rulers.

In addition, John outlined the most detailed analogy between the individual organism and the state that had yet been produced. He suggested that in society as well as in the human body there are groups or classes corresponding to the soul, mind, and heart. The prince is the head of the body politic, the priesthood the soul, the senate the heart, the judges and administrators the sense organs, the soldiers and functionaries the hands, the financial officers the stomach and intestines, and the peasantry the feet. This notion had been anticipated by Plato. Aquinas elaborated the concept and it received an even more thorough exposition by Marsiglio of Padua and Nicholas of Cues. It was highly compatible with the medieval system of estates—the ruling princes, the higher clergy, nobility, burghers, peasants, and so on. Professor Randall observes:

> The fundamental note in mediaeval civilization is the complete harmony between the individual and the social. Society is a great hierarchy of ascending orders, in which every man has his God-appointed function and recognized obligations, and at the same time his rights and privileges. Each man is a member of some estate or group, and each estate is an essential organ of the whole, discharging a function at once peculiar to itself and necessary to the full life of Christendom. Only through his participation in this group life can the individual attain his own ends, and conversely, only with the aid of every individual and every group can society afford the appropriate setting for the fullest life of its individual members. All men exist in and for each other, and are bound to each other by an intricate network of mutual obligations.[46]

This functional view of society has been popularized in our day by certain liberal economists like R. H. Tawney, and by the guild socialists. This functional theory

---

45 The "classical" pronouncement was, of course, the papal bull *Unam Sanctam* of Pope Boniface VIII (1302), which summarized previous ecclesiastical doctrine.

46 J. H. Randall, Jr., *The Making of the Modern Mind*, Houghton Mifflin, 1926 (rev. ed., 1940), pp. 58-59.

and the analogy between the social and the individual organism were probably the two most important medieval contributions to social theory.

True scholastic political philosophy originated in the thirteenth century with the work of Albertus Magnus, already mentioned. It stemmed from the desire to give systematic philosophical expression to the Christian view of politics, for which purpose the logic and philosophy of Aristotle were admirably adapted. Albertus incorporated the *Politics* of Aristotle in his political discourse and prepared the way for the better work of his pupil, Thomas Aquinas. The latter's *The Rule of Princes (De regimine principum)*[47] was, probably, the most suggestive and systematic treatment of social and political philosophy which appeared during medieval times.

Aquinas was noted for his reconstruction of the theory of law and justice. He blended the legal doctrines of Aristotle, the Stoics, Cicero, the Roman lawyers, and Augustine into a coherent whole. He preserved much that was sound in pagan legal theory and adapted it to Christian dogmas. He displaced the impersonal forces of nature, and substituted the power and will of the Christian God.

As a scholastic philosopher, Aquinas naturally accepted the dictum of Aristotle regarding the inherent sociability of man. Adopting Aristotle's analysis of political origins, he held that civil society comprehends three ideas: first, that man is by nature social; second, that in society there is a community of purpose and interests, since only through social relations can man best realize his own interests; and third, that a superior power is necessary to direct society for the common good and to enable the ruler to apply his greater talents to the benefit of the community. Law must have for its object the promotion of the "common good." The state had its origin primarily in the patriarchal rule of the heads of families. But in order to create extensive and efficient political organizations it was necessary to delegate power to a common superior through a governmental compact.

Aquinas revealed his scholastic spirit by blending with Aristotelian theory the dogma of the church that political authority comes ultimately from God alone, though he may delegate it with the consent of the people. With this goes the corollary that political power is inferior to the spiritual. Aquinas used Aristotle as well as the church fathers to sustain this contention. He cited the saying of Aristotle that the true end of government is to bring man to his proper destination. The goal of man being eternal salvation, only the church can enable him to realize it. Therefore, the church is superior to all temporal power.

Departing from Aristotle, Aquinas denied that the city-state is the ideal political organization and took a step in the direction of Machiavelli by declaring his preference for a province consisting of several cities. He held, with Polybius, that the ideal form of government is a mixture of monarchy, aristocracy, and democracy. He followed John of Salisbury in outlining the organic analogy of the state. Aquinas' theories regarding the influences of climate upon society and culture embodied with some original comments the tradition common to classical times,

---

[47] Completed according to some authorities by Aedigius Romanus, and according to others, by Ptolemy of Lucca.

as handed down in the works of Aristotle and Vegetius, namely, that the inhabitants of the "middle zones," or temperate climate, are the superior ones. But Aquinas interpreted the zone of superiority to flatter the Italians and the French.

Dante (1265-1321) was both an admirer of the Holy Roman Empire and a devout Catholic. Therefore, his political philosophy was more balanced than that of his predecessors. He was a prophet of Italian unity. He belonged to the Ghibelline faction and believed that Italy could only be united as part of the medieval empire. Hence, he had good things to say for both church and state.

Dante's political doctrines appear in his *Divine Comedy,* but they are developed at length in his *De monarchia,* where he pleaded for a universal monarchy and a universal church, each supreme in its field. This was designed to put an end to international strife, so "that society might realize its function of unhampered exercise of the intellectual faculties of man in speculation and action."

As a coördinator of state and church, Dante stood midway between the theocratic John of Salisbury on the one hand, and those champions of the state, Pierre Dubois and Marsiglio of Padua, on the other. As James Bryce once remarked, Dante's *De monarchia* was an epitaph of the political past rather than a prophecy of the future. Protestantism broke up the universal church, while nationalism disrupted imperial power and destroyed the ideals of international unity.

Of all the ideas of the Middle Ages, perhaps ecclesiastical and scholastic theories of economics are most entitled to respect and permanence. Economic conduct was measured by religious standards; it was "one among other kinds of moral conduct." The Bible, the early church fathers, the later schoolmen, church law, and Aristotle were the chief sources and precedents for the economic concepts and doctrines of the Middle Ages.

As Professor Tawney suggests, religious opinion may assume three clear positions on economic activities and relationships. Conscious of the destructive effects of wealth-getting on men's souls, it may endeavor to escape from the economic realm. It may, having accepted the inevitability of economic activities, regard them with indifference as beyond the sphere of religion. It may adopt a reformist attitude, and demand the eradication of particular economic evils. At one time or another in the Middle Ages all three of these attitudes found expression, but the most characteristic attitude was a fourth, which, in Tawney's words,

> . . . may at once accept and criticize, tolerate, and amend, welcome the gross world of human appetites, as the squalid scaffolding from amid which the life of the spirit must rise, and insist that this also is the material of the Kingdom of God. To such a temper, all activities divorced from religion are brutal or dead, but none are too mean to be beneath or too great to be above it, since all, in their different degrees, are touched with the spirit which permeates the whole.[48]

All things, all phases of life, fall within the all-embracing orbit of religion. In pursuance of this point of view, the church held that society was a "spiritual organ-

---

48 R. H. Tawney, *Religion and the Rise of Capitalism,* Harcourt, Brace, 1926 (New American Library reprint), p. 17. The first chapter of this outstanding volume is a remarkably lucid and competent treatment of medieval economic thought.

ism" and not an "economic machine." Likewise, man's economic activity was regarded as "one subordinate element within a vast complex unity," which must be "controlled and repressed by reference to the moral ends for which it supplies the material means." The church thus made an earnest effort to "moralize" economic life. Medieval principles of ethics, economics and politics should be taken in the light of this and of the functional theory of society—that is, that society should be organized in relation to the functions performed by social groups.

The whole body of medieval economic thought as enunciated by Aquinas and the schoolmen rested upon two assumptions: (1) That the final purpose of man's life is salvation, compared to which economic considerations are insignificant; and (2) that economic pursuits constitute but one phase of personal conduct, to which the rules of morality fully apply. Labor is necessary, honorable, and just, for men must live. Trade, by virtue of its necessity, is also legitimate. But it is excessively dangerous. It must be carried on for the public benefit, and the trader must draw no more from it than a just reward for the labor, skill, and risk involved. Trade certainly imperils the soul. Speculative finance is utterly immoral.

All business, apart from labor, had to be justified in one way or another. The man who bought simply to sell at a higher price was condemned, for he was motivated by selfish interests and lacked social spirit. To strive to acquire riches for the sake of riches was damnable. To profit by speculation at the expense of others—"private gain by the exploitation of public necessities"—was unforgivable.

It was this attitude which led to an ecclesiastic taboo on business practices which are current and respected in our day: forestalling, engrossing, and regrating. Forestalling meant getting to a market before it was open to the public and buying goods before free competition could exist. Engrossing meant cornering the market. Regrating was selling something for more than was paid for it, without in any way changing the nature or value of the commodity.

Nothing illustrates better the medieval injection of ethics into economics than the "just-price" idea. In brief, this principle maintained that prices were to be determined and fixed in such a manner as would enable a man to enjoy those necessities of life which his position called for. The price a craftsman could justly ask for an article would thus be determined by his labor and by his needs—more specifically by the cost of raw material and labor, to which was added an item for "management." Prices were to be fixed by public authorities or, if that were impossible, by the individual, in the light of the above considerations. According to Thomas Aquinas the determining factor should be the costs of raw materials and the labor of the producer. Aquinas held that, according to natural law, surplus goods and income should be given to the needy.

The views of the church on interest and usury are also enlightening.[49] Characteristically enough, interest as we understand it today—payment at a fixed rate for the use of money—was always condemned. What was permitted was indemnification or compensation to the lender if the principal was not repaid when specified, or if the lender suffered loss because the loan had been made; likewise pay-

---

[49] In the Middle Ages the contemporary distinction between interest and usury was generally absent. The two words meant essentially the same thing. See H. C. Lea, "The Ecclesiastical Treatment of Usury," *Yale Review*, February, 1894.

ment was permissible on money invested in a partnership. But simply to charge money for a loan when no risk was run was unpardonable. In the Middle Ages money was borrowed mainly to tide one over a period of special distress. Hence, it was un-Christian to charge interest, namely, to make money out of another's woes. Later, when money was loaned so as to make more money, the attitude towards interest-taking naturally changed. The typical medieval conception of interest and usury is set forth by Tawney:

> To take usury is contrary to Scripture; it is contrary to Aristotle; it is contrary to nature, for it is to live without labor; it is to sell time, which belongs to God, for the advantage of wicked men; it is to rob those who use the money lent, and to whom, since they make it profitable, the profits should belong; it is unjust in itself, for the benefit of the loan to the borrower cannot exceed the value of the principal sum lent him; it is in defiance of sound juristic principles, for when a loan of money is made, the property in the thing lent passes to the borrower, and why should the creditor demand payment from a man who is merely using what is now his own? [50]

These principles of business and finance were reflected not only in ecclesiastical law but in secular law as well. We have records of many cases of punishment of usurers and speculative financiers. That these economic concepts and doctrines were ignored time and again, and that ugly business practices were present during the Middle Ages, there is no doubt. It is likewise true that the church, as the most important financial institution in Christendom, aided in the creation of a class of men—bankers and moneylenders—whose very mode of life was reprehensible according to its ideals. Yet we must not for these reasons unfairly criticize medieval economic thought. The measure of its practical effectiveness is not the sole measure of its value. There was in it far greater appreciation of social service and responsibility than is to be found in modern "price economics" and the "theory of business enterprise." By and large, the effort to moralize man's economic life was earnest and honest. That effort was doomed to failure by the very changes in economic conditions in western Europe which accompanied the rise of trade and the growth of capital.

SELECTED READINGS

Afnan, S. M., *Avicenna: His Life and Works*, Macmillan, 1958.

Artz, F. B., *The Mind of the Middle Ages*, Knopf, 1953.

Baron, S. W., ed., *Essays on Maimonides*, Columbia University Press, 1941.

Compayré, Gabriel, *Abelard*, Scribner, 1901.

Coulton, G. G., *Medieval Panorama*, Meridian, 1955.

Crump, C. G., and Jacob, E. F., *The Legacy of the Middle Ages*, Oxford Press, 1926.

Durant, Will, *The Age of Faith*, Simon and Schuster, 1950.

Eby and Arrowood, *The History and Philosophy of Education*, chaps. xvii-xviii.

Garrison, *Introduction to the History of Medicine*, chaps. vi-vii.

Gewirth, Alan, *Marsilius of Padua: The Defender of the Peace*, Columbia University Press, 1956.

Grabmann, Martin, *Thomas Aquinas*, Longmans, 1928.

Graubard, Mark, *Astrology and Alchemy*, Philosophical Library, 1953.

[50] Tawney, *op. cit.*, pp. 43-44.

Grunebaum, G. E. von, *Medieval Islam*, University of Chicago Press, 1946.

Haskins, C. H., *The Renaissance of the Twelfth Century*, Meridian.

——— *The Rise of Universities*, Cornell University Press, 1957.

——— *Studies in the History of Medieval Science*, Ungar, 1960.

——— *Studies in Medieval Culture*, Ungar, 1958.

Hitti, P. K., *History of the Arabs*, St. Martin's Press.

Hussey, *Church and Learning in the Byzantine Empire.*

Kimble, G. H. T., *Geography in the Middle Ages*, Methuen, 1938.

Klibansky, Raymond, *The Continuity of the Platonic Tradition during the Middle Ages*, Warburg Institute, 1939.

Leff, Gordon, *Medieval Thought from St. Augustine to Ockham*, Penguin Books, 1956.

Lewis, Ewart, *Medieval Political Ideas*, 2 Vols., Knopf, 1954.

Massé, Henri, *Islam*, Putnam, 1938.

McCabe, Joseph, *Peter Abelard*, Putnam, 1901.

McGiffert, *History of Christian Thought*, Vol. II.

McIlwain, *The Growth of Political Thought in the West*, chap. vi.

McKeon, R. P., *Selections from Medieval Philosophers*, 2 Vols., Scribner, 1959.

McKinney, L. C., *Bishop Fulbert of Chartres*, Medieval Institute, 1957.

Norton, A. O., ed., *Readings in the History of Education: Medieval Universities*, Harvard University Press, 1909.

O'Leary, DeL. E., *Arabic Thought and Its Place in History*, Humanities Press.

Poole, *Illustrations of the History of Medieval Thought and Learning.*

Randall, J. H., Jr., *The Making of the Modern Mind*, Houghton Mifflin, 1940, Book I.

Rashdall, Hastings, *The Universities of Europe in the Middle Ages*, 2 Vols., Macmillan, 1895. New edition by Powicke and Emden, 3 Vols., Oxford Press, 1936.

Riesman, David, *The Story of Medicine in the Middle Ages*, Hoeber, 1935.

Rogers, E. F., *Peter Lombard and the Sacramental System*, privately printed, 1917.

Sarton, George, *Introduction to the History of Science*, 3 Vols., Williams and Wilkins, 1927-1948, Vols. II-III.

Singer, *et al.*, eds., *A History of Technology: The Mediterranean Civilizations and the Middle Ages*, Oxford University Press, 1956.

Slaughter, Gertrude, *The Amazing Frederic*, Macmillan, 1937.

Steele, R. R., *Medieval Lore*, Oxford Press, 1924.

Taylor, F. S., *The Alchemists*, Schuman, 1949.

Taylor, *The Medieval Mind*, Vol. II.

Thompson, J. W., *A History of Historical Writing*, Vol. I, Book III.

——— *The Literacy of the Laity in the Middle Ages*, Burt Franklin, 1960.

——— *The Medieval Library*, University of Chicago Press, 1939.

——— *The Middle Ages*, 2 Vols., Knopf, 1931.

Thorndike, *History of Magic and Experimental Science*, Vol. II.

Vasiliev, *History of the Byzantine Empire.*

Vinogradoff, P. G., *Roman Law in Medieval Europe*, Harper, 1910.

Vittorini, Domenico, *The Age of Dante*, Syracuse University Press, 1957.

Walsh, G. G., *Dante Alighieri, Citizen of Christendom*, Bruce Publishing Co., 1946.

Williams, Watkins, *Saint Bernard of Clairvaux*, Manchester University Press, 1935.

Workman, *Christian Thought to the Reformation.*

Wright, J. K., *The Geographical Lore of the Time of the Crusades*, American Geographical Society, 1925.

Wulf, Maurice de, *History of Medieval Philosophy*, 2 Vols., Macmillan, 1926, Vol. I.

——— *Philosophy and Civilization in the Middle Ages*, Dover, 1953.

X

Literature, Art, and Music
1100-1300

I. LITERATURE OF RELIGION AND ROMANCE

1. *Latin Poetry and Prose*

The Carolingians wrote Latin poetry mainly for amusement. The twelfth and thirteenth centuries wrote it for edification. As typical an example as one can find is Alanus of Lille (c. 1105-1202), the theme of whose *De planctu naturae* is Nature's complaint of man's disobedience to her laws, while his *Anticlaudianus* explains the part played in the shaping of man by God, Nature, Fortune, Vice, and Virtue. The *Anticlaudianus* (the meaning of the title is not clear) is an allegory which in Alanus' hands became a fresh and lovely expression of the Christian view of the world, though the poets of the later Middle Ages, with whom he was very popular, wore it thin. Alanus' description of the Perfect Soul is an excellent epitome of medieval ideals: "Chastity and guardian Modesty endow him with their gifts; Reason adds his, and Honesty. These Logic follows, with her gift of skill in argument; Rhetoric brings her stores, then Arithmetic, next Music, next Geometry, next Astronomy; while Theology and Piety are not behind with theirs; and to these Faith joins her gifts of fidelity and truth. Last of all comes Nobility, Fortune's daughter."

The Latin hymns of this period were another form of poetic edification. They might almost be regarded as the sonnets of the era, expressing as they do intense and exalted emotion in little space. There is St. Francis of Assisi's *Canticle of Brother Sun:*

Praised be thou, my Lord, with all thy creatures, especially milord Brother Sun that dawns and lightens us;
And he, beautiful and radiant with great splendor, signifies thee, Most High.

442

Be praised, my Lord, for Sister Moon and the stars that thou hast made bright and precious and beautiful.

Be praised, my Lord, for Brother Wind, and for the air and cloud and the clear sky and for all weathers through which thou givest sustenance to thy creatures.

Be praised, my Lord, for Sister Water, that is very useful and humble and chaste.[1]

The *Stabat Mater dolorosa* of Jacopone da Todi, the *Dies Irae* of Thomas of Celano, the biographer of St. Francis, the *Jerusalem luminosa* of Thomas à Kempis, are still sung today all over the world. Abelard composed a series of hymns for Héloïse's convent at Paraclete. He loved complicated verse forms and in his hands Latin became almost as flexible and lyric as modern English. Perhaps the foremost writer of all was Adam of St. Victor (d. 1192) whose highly symbolic hymns were clothed in stately and melodious Latin.

Latin poetry had its profane uses in the songs of the wandering clerks or scholars who used the universal language and often sang for their living from door to door. The goliardic verse, so called after a certain Golias who is said to have originated it, is almost all extant in a precious manuscript found in the monastery of Benedictbeurn in upper Bavaria. There are complaints about fortune and attacks on simony; there are love songs, drinking songs, begging songs, and songs that celebrate the wandering life; there is even a clever gambler's mass. All are frankly merry and sensuous, full of high spirits.

The most important technical development in the poetry of this period was the change from quantitative to accentual verse. Classical Latin verse was based on the quantity or length of syllables. Medieval Latin begins to make its rhythm depend on the number of syllables and accents in a line. Accentual verse lent itself readily to assonance and it was assonance probably that led to rhyme.

Medieval Latin prose, like medieval Latin poetry, had its merry uses. The *Gesta romanorum* and *The History of the Seven Sages* were collections of entertaining stories from all the ends of the earth, from the Arabic, Roman Greek, Persian, and Hindu, a fount from which storytellers like Chaucer, Boccaccio, and Shakespeare were to draw for centuries to come. There were *exempla,* too, or moral anecdotes very convenient for preachers, but the most popular collection of all was the *Legenda aurea,* or Golden Legend, of Jacopo da Voragine. These lives of the saints gathered together in the thirteenth century are a curious amalgam of Christian propaganda, incredible supernaturalism, and fascinating narrative. Translated into all the important vernacular languages, their effect on art and literature proved incalculable.

Secular history was written in Latin. The chronicle had made its appearance during the Dark Ages. The Middle Ages carried it to maturity, making it more comprehensive and more polished, though only rarely do medieval historians make any mention of social or cultural conditions; they are concerned almost exclusively with political and religious affairs. Since most of them were monks, their work took on a strongly religious coloring, but they were less ready than their predecessors to set down marvels as fact.

[1] Translated by Henry Osborn Taylor in *The Mediaeval Mind,* New York, Macmillan, 1919, I, 455.

The first important English medieval historian was William of Malmesbury (c. 1096-c. 1148), whose *Deeds of the English Kings* surveyed English history from the Saxon invasion to 1128 in clear and dramatic fashion. Consulting many sources, he showed much shrewdness in his historical judgments. So did Henry of Huntingdon (c. 1084-1157) who carried his *History of the English* down to 1154. He rigorously excluded marvels and legends and stressed the value of past events in helping us to understand the present. The Norman Ordericus Vitalis (1075-c. 1143) was discursive and uncritical in his *Ecclesiastical History,* though no other writer of the period took so broad a view of his subject or brought so many matters within his view. Geoffrey of Monmouth's (c. 1100-1154) history of the *Kings of Britain* is a great source book of Arthurian romance and around it endless controversy has raged, for it is more like a historical novel than a history and it is difficult to determine what is fact and what is fiction. The preëminent historical writer of medieval England was Matthew Paris (c. 1200-1259), a monk of St. Albans. He traced the political and constitutional history of the country after Magna Charta and showed a real grasp of foreign affairs as well.

The first important French historian in the Middle Ages, Sigebert of Gembloux (c. 1030-1112), produced a general world chronicle which came down to 1101 and was very popular with later writers who used it as a chronological guide. One of the best histories of the crusades was written by William of Tyre (1130-c.1193). Other important French historians were Robert of Torigni, Robert of Auxerre, Guibert of Nogent, and Vincent of Beauvais.

Italian medieval historical writing began with Liutprand of Cremona (c. 920-972) whose works give us the best account of German, Italian, and Mediterranean historical developments during the tenth century. Of the long struggle between Guelphs and Ghibellines the foremost historian was Albertinus Mussatus (1261-1330), an impartial narrator and an excellent Latin stylist.

German historical writing is distinguished for the *Annals* of Lambert of Hersfeld (d. c. 1080), one of our more important sources for the history of the relations of Germany with the papacy, and the voluminous *Chronicle of the World* by Ekkehard of Aurach (d. c. 1110), an indispensable source of information for the history of medieval Germany. But most notable of all was Bishop Otto of Freising (c. 1114-1158), the uncle of Frederick Barbarossa. His *Book of the Two Cities* constituted the first medieval philosophy of history, illustrating from actual events the allegorical struggle between the City of God and the City of the Devil.

2. *Vernacular Literature*

Most of the great nations of modern Europe can trace the first upwelling of their literature to about the twelfth century, though the Teutonic vernacular created a literature before the Romance languages, perhaps because it did not have to compete with Latin literature. Old English, Old German, and Old Norse literature appeared first, then French literature, followed by Spanish with Italian last of all.

Not well known except to specialists is the existence of a remarkable body of Welsh and Irish literature in which one may study in its infancy that much discussed phenomenon, the Celtic spirit. The Irish is the more copious of the two and exists in more than a thousand manuscripts belonging to the period of about 1100-1550. The bulk of it consists of romances developed orally as far back as the beginning of the Christian Era when, though the Celts were still virtually savages, storytelling was an essential part of their lives. They had a corporate class of poets, the *fili*. Comparable to the Anglo-Saxon *scop*, originally a diviner or magician, the *fili* exercised great influence by means of satiric and narrative powers.

The two important groups of Irish stories are the Leinster-Munster cycle, revolving about Finn and Ossian, and the Ulster cycle, Ireland's most important contribution to world literature. It centers on Conchobar and Cuchulain, the great folk hero of Ireland as Arthur is of Wales. The Cuchulain cycle contains tales of courtships, raiding expeditions, elopements, cattle stealings (indicating that the race was in a pastoral stage of culture), and continual tribal warfare. The chief and longest tale is the *Táin Bó Cuailgne* (Cattle Raid of County Cooley). Nothing quite like its mixture of epic glory and farfetched improbabilities can be found in any other European literature. Here is the story of the death of Cuchulain:

> Then Lewy hurls the spear, and this time pierces Cuchulain through the body, and Cuchulain's other steed burst the yoke and rushed off and never ceased till he, too, had plunged into the lake from which Cuchulain had taken him in far-off Munster. Cuchulain remained behind, dying in his chariot. With difficulty and holding in his entrails with one hand, he advanced to a little lake hard by, and drank from it, and washed off his blood. Then he propped himself against a high stone a few yards from the lake, and tied himself to it with his girdle. "He did not wish to die either sitting or lying, it was standing," says the saga, "that he wished to meet death." [2]

Next to the Cuchulain saga the best known of Irish stories is that of Deirdre, the lady of sorrows, the cause of the death of her husband and his two brothers and who, like Helen of Troy, brings much woe to her countrymen. In recent years William Butler Yeats and James Stephens have retold in modern English the haunting story of Deirdre.

The chief remains of Welsh literature lie in four volumes: *Book of Aneirin* (collected about 1250), *Black Book of Carmarthen* (collected between 1170-1230), *Book of Taliessin* (collected about 1275) and *Red Book of Hergest* (collected between 1375-1425). The volumes associated with the names of the two national bards Taliessin and Aneirin—in Wales also the bards were a corporate class—contains poetic cycles about folk heroes who lived in northern Wales in the sixth century, contemporaries of the bards who sang their deeds. The peculiarity of this epic is its sorrowful mood. There are no victories to recount. The heroes who fought have lost. They quaff their drinks in the mead-hall and go out to battle. There the poet leaves them.

In western Wales where the Celtic civilization died grew up the legends of the Mabinogion, some of them embodied in the *Red Book of Hergest*. Here finally in the twelfth century the Welsh wrote down their marvelous tales after the Normans had fashioned from them a rich Arthurian literature.

[2] Douglas Hyde, *A Literary History of Ireland*, Scribner, 1899, p. 351.

Our chief sources for Scandinavian mythology are two books in the Icelandic language (Old Norse), known as the *Poetic Edda* and the *Prose Edda*. The *Poetic Edda,* a compilation of poems about gods and heroes by different anonymous authors, dating from the ninth to the twelfth centuries, was collected by an unknown Icelander in the early thirteenth century, the golden age of Old Norse literature. The *Prose Edda,* a handbook for poets, giving instruction in the writing of verse, with illustrations taken mainly from mythology, was composed by the Icelander Snorri Sturlason (1178-1241). The *Poetic Edda*—the word *edda* comes from Oddi, a place where Snorri lived—is divided into two parts. The first is a series of lays about the Teutonic myth of the creation, the stealing of Thor's hammer, the death of Balder, the god who prevents evil from ruling the world, and so on. The second part is concerned mainly with the Volsung epic, involving the characters of Sigurd (Siegfried), Sigrdrifa (Brunhild), Gudrun, the dragon Fafnir and the final tragedy at the court of Atli (Attila), material connected on the one hand with the *Waltharilied* of Ekkehard and on the other with the German *Nibelungenlied*.

It was not till the age of chivalry and feudalism that an Austrian poet, not an especially great one, welded the Volsung-Nibelung material into an epic. In the *Nibelungenlied* Siegfried loses his supernaturalism and becomes a twelfth-century knight. Brunhild is transformed from a Valkyrie into an Amazonian maiden and a tenth-century bishop appears as the heroine's uncle.

In the Icelandic saga the ancient Viking temper finally created a great literary genre and built itself a worthy monument. Iceland was settled in the last quarter of the ninth century by the families of Norway who left the country when King Harold Fairhair attempted to establish a strong monarchy. The Germanic love of independence and hatred of vassalage drove thousands of them to the bleak island where, by 930, they had established a thriving colony politically self-governing and under vague allegiance to the homeland.

The century between 930-1030 is regarded as the Heroic or Saga Age, the time of the actual lives of heroes about whom legend clustered. The sagas appeared first in oral form; between 1200-1230 they were put into written prose. Veracity is their distinctive feature. They are a kind of unembroidered biographical fiction. In the sagas the heroes of Old English and Norse epic are scaled down to human proportions. The atmosphere is still predominantly tragic but the canvas is smaller, the action is circumscribed yet intense. Based on themes of personal feuds, of love, hatred, and vengeance, the narrative nearly always centers on an individual or his family. Christian sentiment and homily are woven in as secondary strands. In the following excerpt from the Njals Saga, one of the great prose stories of the world, most of the effects and moods of the saga art may be seen, the brevity of speech, simplicity of action, the courage of the actors, the appalling tragedy. The scene is the death of Njal and his family who are incarcerated in their home, which is being set afire by their enemies:

Then Flosi went to the door and called out to Njal, and said he would speak with him and Bergthora.

Now Njal does so, and Flosi said: "I will offer thee, master Njal, leave to go out, for it is unworthy that thou shouldst burn indoors."

"I will not go out," said Njal, "for I am an old man, and little fitted to avenge my sons, but I will not live in shame."

Then Flosi said to Bergthora: "Come thou out, housewife, for I will for no sake burn thee indoors."

"I was given away to Njal young," said Bergthora, "and I have promised him this, that we should both share the same fate."

After that they both went back into the house.

"What counsel shall we now take?" said Bergthora.

"We will go to our bed," says Njal, "and lay us down; I have long been eager for rest."

Then she said to the boy Thord, Kari's son: "Thee will I take out, and thou shalt not burn in here."

"Thou hast promised me this, grandmother," says the boy, "that we should never part so long as I wished to be with thee; but methinks it is much better to die with thee and Njal than to live after you."

Then she bore the boy to her bed, and Njal spoke to his steward and said:

"Now shalt thou see where we lay us down, and how I lay us out, for I mean not to stir an inch hence, whether reek or burning smart me, and so thou wilt be able to guess where to look for our bones."

He said he would do so.

There had been an ox slaughtered, and the hide lay there. Njal told the steward to spread the hide over them, and he did so.

So there they lay down both of them in their bed, and put the boy between them. Then they signed themselves and the boy with the cross, and gave over their souls into God's hand, and that was the last word that men heard them utter.[3]

The Icelandic sagas, although they are the chief literary masterpieces of the Middle Ages, had no influence. They lay outside the consciousness of Europe and their language was remote from the main stream. The feudal epic of France, on the other hand, spread beyond her borders into Italy and Spain and sounded across the Channel to England.

Most important of the French epics were the *chansons de geste,* or songs of mighty deeds—narrative poems based on real events but embroidered with legend. They delighted the eleventh and twelfth centuries and lived on into the thirteenth. Composed orally for the pleasure of a feudal court, they recite the valor of mighty heroes like Roland, Guillaume d'Orange (William of Orange), Raoul de Cambrai, or the Spanish Cid Rodrigo Diaz, "el Compeador." The fealty of these heroes is twofold, to their overlord and to God who is regarded as the supreme feudal lord. Unlike Germanic epic the *chansons* do little character drawing. Women play a minor part. Exaggerations, particularly as to the number of warriors and their heroic deeds, are common, but their vitality and movement, their humor and high courage, entitle them to be regarded as the beginning of modern European romance.

3 W. P. Ker, *Epic and Romance,* Dover Publications, Inc., 1957, pp. 220-21.

The *Chanson de Roland,* in all respects the finest of the type, tells the tale of the battle of Roncevaux, a minor episode in one of Charlemagne's campaigns, in which his rear guard was wiped out by the Basques in a mountain gorge in the Pyrenees. In the poem Roncevaux assumes major proportions, the Basques become Saracens, and the Christians lose the encounter because of the treachery of Ganelon. The peers of France fall one by one, Roland, the leader, refusing to blow his horn and call Charlemagne to his aid. When finally only Oliver, Archbishop Turpin, and Roland are left Roland blows his horn—but too late. Oliver and Turpin fall; Roland, dying, breaks his magic sword against a rock so that the infidels may not have it and offers his glove in feudal homage to God. Angels descend and carry his soul to heaven and Charlemagne rides up and exterminates the Saracens.

For a long time conflicting theories were held about the origin of the *chansons de geste.* Some decades ago the French scholar Joseph Bédier projected the most acceptable explanation. The monks of churches and monasteries situated on the great highways wished to attract visitors to their relics and shrines. They ordered the wandering *jongleurs,* or minstrels, to work up into oral poems the deeds of heroes particularly associated with the locality, and those poems were eventually written down. This theory explains the curious fact that many of the epic heroes like Roland are minor personages in history. Sober history in the French vernacular first appeared in the famous *Conquest of Constantinople* by Geoffrey de Ville-hardouin (1167-1213).

3. Chivalric Literature

By the end of the twelfth century the vogue for the *chansons de geste* had passed. The aristocracy for whom literature existed had grown tired of the high-wrought epic strain. A wave of emotionalism swept over European literature. Manners softened as society became more stable. The romantic influence of Muslim poetry seeped in through Provence. The influence of women began to be felt. The change can be summarized in one word—chivalry, that code of triple fealty to God, king, and lady. A French rhyme of the period puts it thus:

> A Dieu mon âme,   (To God my soul,
> Mon cœur aux dames,   My heart to the ladies,
> Ma vie au roi,   My life to the king,
> L'honneur pour moi.   Honor for myself.)

The feudal romance that grew up as the literary expression of chivalry was not a product of nationalism. Its themes knew no boundary lines. They are freely and fruitfully transplanted from France to England, Germany, Switzerland, Norway, Italy, and Spain. They may be divided into three classes: those dealing with Greek or Roman subjects (the romances about Alexander, Troy or Thebes); those dealing with a wide miscellany of subjects, many of Eastern origin (*Amis and Amiloun, Floris and Blancheflor, Aucassin and Nicolette*); and the Arthurian romances.

We first hear of a man like Arthur in the melancholy history of the sixth-century Welsh monk Gildas who wrote a Latin sketch of the decline and conquest of the Britons. Gildas does not mention Arthur but describes the battles associated with him. Two centuries later another Welsh monk called Nennius in the *Historia Britonum* speaks of a *dux bellorum* (chieftain) named Arthur who defeated the Teutons at Mount Badon where he killed nine hundred and sixty men in one day.

From the ninth to the twelfth centuries Arthur's stature grew in folk imagination until when we meet him again in Geoffrey of Monmouth's *History of the Britons* (c. 1136) he is a resplendent king who, after a Napoleonic sort of life, dies while defeating the usurper Modred, his nephew, and is carried away to the mystic region of Avalon to be healed of his wound.

In his next appearance in literature, in the Norman French redaction of Geoffrey, the work of an ecclesiastic named Wace (c. 1155), the full panoply of Arthurian romance is present; there are Lancelot, the Round Table (a device probably used in Wales), the Holy Grail, the cup out of which Christ drank at the Last Supper. Feudal, Christian, and heathen elements in the story are fused. In the hands of the poets who next took over the material Arthur was often relegated to a secondary or invisible rôle, like Charlemagne in the *chansons de geste,* and now Lancelot, now Gawain, Perceval, or Galahad became the chivalric hero.

The first important poet to treat the Arthurian stories was Chrétien de Troyes (c. 1130-c. 1180) about whom we know almost nothing except that he lived at the court of Marie de Champagne, where there was a strong chivalric cult and a great enthusiasm for Ovid's *Ars Amatoria* (Art of Love), the textbook of medieval chivalry. Chrétien wrote five Arthurian romances, *Cligés, Erec* (Tennyson's *Geraint and Enid*), *Lancelot, or the Knight of the Cart, Ivain, the Knight of the Lion,* and an unfinished *Perceval* or Grail story. Other noteworthy French versifiers of the "matter of Britain," as this body of material is called, were the two Anglo-Norman poets Béroul (fl. c. 1150) and Thomas (fl. c. 1170), both of whom wrote of Tristan and Iseult, a legend which although probably of Welsh origin was only vaguely connected with King Arthur. The finest treatment of the Tristan-Iseult romance, one of the world's great love stories, is the one by the German poet Gottfried von Strassburg, who lived in the last part of the twelfth century and it is through its musical retelling by the nineteenth-century German, Richard Wagner, that most of us are familiar with it today. Of all the Arthurian stories that of Tristan and Iseult has been most often retold by modern poets.

Another Arthurian romance which lives in the music of Wagner is the *Parzival* of Wolfram von Eschenbach. In Wolfram's poem the story of Parsifal, who after many trials and adventures is granted a vision of the mystic Grail, is a profound commentary on the chivalric life in the full meaning of its trinity, loyalty to God, king, and lady. In *Gawain and the Green Knight* an unknown English writer added Celtic magic and a love of nature to the chivalric theme in another Arthurian legend.

4. Lyric Poetry

France in the Middle Ages was so rich in human values that all the people of Europe borrowed from her. Her epics and romances set the vogue for vernacular literature as did her lyric poetry, in both the *langue d'oïl* of the North and the *langue d'oc* of the South.

Northern France had had a tradition of lyric poetry probably even in pagan times. The earliest written lyrics, however, date from the twelfth century. There were *chansons à toile* sung by the women as they sat weaving or spinning, popular in treatment with assonance instead of rhyme and a refrain repeated after each stanza; *chansons de mal-mariée* (songs of unhappy wedlock), dialogues or monologues in which a young wife laments her luckless state; *pastourelles,* which describe a knight's wooing of a shepherdess; and *chansons de croisade* (songs of the crusade) sung either by a lady whose lover has taken the cross or by a knight torn by the conflict between honor which bids him fight the heathen and love which bids him stay at home.

Because of its accessibility to Eastern and Muslim influence southern France achieved a high state of culture long before the North, and at the end of the eleventh century troubadour poetry made its appearance in Provence where it flourished for two hundred years. This poetry was always sung and its essential factor, as in feudal romance, was chivalry and what is called *"l'art de bien aimer"* (the art of love-making), which became a sort of elaborately stylized game.

Troubadour lyrics may be divided into two groups: *chansons à personnages,* objective in manner and conforming generally to a strict convention; and *poésie courtoise,* wholly subjective and directly addressed by the troubadour to his lady. The latter are more elaborate and subtle and less stenciled than the former.

The *chansons à personnages* comprise six important types: (1) *chansons à toile,* spinning songs, tales of unhappy love; (2) *chansons de mal-mariée* like those of the North; (3) *pastourelles;* (4) *chansons de danse,* dance tunes with incidental lyrics; (5) *reverdies,* or spring songs; (6) *chansons d'aube,* or dawn songs, dialogues between lovers and the watchman who warns of the approaching dawn which means their separation. The parting scene in Shakespeare's *Romeo and Juliet* is a *chanson d'aube.* We know the names of more than four hundred makers of these French songs, among them King Richard the Lion-hearted of England.

In Germany the troubadours were called minnesingers (*minne* means love). Most important of them was Walther von der Vogelweide who flourished between 1190 and 1230. In time poetry ceased to be a knightly virtue and was practiced for pay by journeymen versemakers of less than gentle birth. Then came the formation of local organizations which trained "mastersingers," like Hans Sachs of Wagner's *Meistersinger von Nürnberg,* and gave public exhibition of their compositions.

In Spain, too, poetry, once practiced by the king himself, became the business of a professional class and when Simon Monfort and his fanatic Catholics crushed the Albigensian heresy in southern France (1209-1220) and Provençal literature died, many troubadours fled to Spain. At the courts of James I and Pedro III of Aragon and Alfonso X of Castile, they found ample welcome. The rules of this complicated poetry were published by Raimón Vidal (first half of the thirteenth century) and by Jaufré de Foxa in 1290 as *Regles de Trobar.*

In Italy troubadour poetry touched with its influence the poets of the *dolce stil nuovo* ("sweet new style"), Guido Guinizelli, Guido Cavalcanti, Cino da Pistoia, and Dante himself.

5. Popular Literature

With the rise of the towns and the growing importance of the middle class, the bourgeoisie, European literature entered a new phase. Humor, satire, realism are the characteristics of the *fabliaux,* the allegorical satires and beast fables which delighted the new audiences.

The fabliau, a coarse and humorous poetical skit, seldom more than four hundred lines in length, flourished from about the middle of the twelfth to the fifteenth century and particularly influenced the tone and treatment of low comedy and farce when the secular drama was revived in Europe. Two examples of the fabliau illustrate the whole genre:

A curate, eating mulberries by standing on his saddle and reaching them from the tree, soliloquizes aloud, "What if a passer-by, seeing me thus, were to startle my horse by crying 'Hue!' " His horse is startled by hearing the curate say "Hue!" and that worthy gentleman is thrown to the ground.

In another fabliau a nobleman has taken a poor old woman's cow. Told by a friend that the way to get it back is to "grease the agent's paw," she goes to the nobleman's castle armed with a piece of lard. She finds the agent strolling with his hands behind his back and stealing up applies the lard to his hand, literally carrying out her friend's advice.

The most representative writer of the century is the Frenchman Rutebeuf (d. c. 1230), *jongleur* and *trouvère* (composer and minstrel), an earlier and lesser Villon. He dabbled in every genre, dramatic, didactic, lyric, but his forte was satire on the social problems of his time. In the *Chanson des ordres* he discusses the growing power and number of begging friars. In the *Dit de l'université de Paris* he describes the conflict between the friars and the university. In the *Dispute du Croisé et du Décroisé* (Dispute between crusader and non-crusader) he touches upon the problem of conscripting soldiers for the last crusade. In the *Chanson des ribauds de la Grève* he paints a vigorous portrait of the literary man of the period, the free-lance rhymester always on the verge of destitution.

The thirteenth century also witnessed the establishment in France and Germany of poet-corporations, like the famous *Puy d'Arras* and *Puy d'Amiens,* whose members adapted courtly lyrics for bourgeois audiences. These French poetry schools, however, were chiefly famous for their plays.

The writers of satire took particular delight in ridiculing chivalry, a process which reached perfection some centuries later in *Don Quixote.* There is, for instance, a thirteenth-century German novelette, written in verse, called *Farmer Helmbrecht,* in which a young peasant rides away to become a knight as Perceval did—but a robber-knight. Even that most hallowed of literary forms, allegory, was finally converted to satiric uses. About 1230 Guillaume de Lorris wrote an exquisite long poem, *Le Roman de la Rose,* in which the lover wandering in a garden one May morning longs to pick a bud from a goodly rose tree but is prevented by Shame, Fear, Jealousy, and other symbolic personages. Guillaume de Lorris left the poem unfinished. About forty years later Jean de Meun added a sequel four times as long as the original and utterly different in tone, for the chivalric ideal to him was nonsense and he turned upon it the shafts of a keen and critical intellect. This double tone of the poem made it, curiously enough, enormously popular, for it epitomized perfectly the two schools of thought: the medieval and the modern, which flourished side by side in that period just before the dawn of the modern world.

Most famous of the beast fables is the *Roman de Renart,* known in the German version as *Reinecke Fuchs* and in the English version as *Reynard the Fox,* in which the fable of Aesop and Phaedrus becomes a vehicle for anti-feudal, anti-chivalrous, and anti-clerical sentiments.

6. *Dante: The Medieval Synthesis*

At Easter-time in the year 1300 Dante, then thirty-five and, as he tells us, in the middle of life's road, began the imagined journey through Hell, Purgatory, and Paradise recounted in his *Divine Comedy.* The century just ended had seen the fullest blossoming of medieval culture, and in the work of Dante that culture is most perfectly summed up. However remote to us may seem the view of life and death set forth in his noble poem, no man of his own time would have questioned its philosophy, which was that of Aquinas, its science, which was that of Aristotle, its picture of the universe, its admiration of Vergil, its use of allegory and symbols, its conception of real sin and real punishment for sin. That it was Italian, in temperament as well as in language and in most of its characters, would have made no difference.

The details of the life of Dante Alighieri (1265-1321) are little known. The Florence into which he was born was torn by struggles between Guelphs and Ghibellines, the two factions of German origin which racked Italy in the Middle Ages. In Dante's Florence the Guelph faction, which supported the temporal power of the pope, was represented by the Neri, or Blacks; the Ghibelline, which urged strong rule by the emperor, by the Bianchi, or Whites. Dante, though himself of a Guelph family, joined the White party, and was exiled from Florence in 1301 when its power was lost. For the rest of his life he was a wanderer.

The most important influence in Dante's life, however, was Beatrice, probably Beatrice Portinari, whom he saw first when both were children, and very few times more before she died in 1290, but who became the inspiration of his poetry and the angelic spirit which guided him through Paradise. He first commemorated her in the *Vita nuova* (*New Life*), a prose work interspersed with poems which reflect, despite their spiritualization of love, the conventions of medieval love-poetry, but at their best reach unmatched brilliance. Here Dante hints at that future exaltation of his lady which was to find its place in the *Divine Comedy.*

In the *Convivio* (*Banquet*) Dante again mingled prose and poetry. The work, which set out to be a feast of learning, was not finished, but Beatrice again appears, now as divine philosophy. The *Convivio* contains a defense of the Italian language which was elaborated in the *De vulgari eloquentia* (*Of the Vulgar Tongue*), a treatise composed in Latin to reach learned readers, and devoted, after a curious theological disquisition on the origins of speech, to an examination of various Italian dialects. Its conclusion is that the illustrious and courtly language which the author is seeking must be one common to all Italy and peculiar to no single region, one worthy of treating only the highest subjects: Arms, Love, and Virtue.

In the *De monarchia* (*Of Monarchy*) Dante discusses the nature of government and the proper division of temporal and spiritual power between emperor and pope. To Dante universal rule was divinely ordained, and a monarch or emperor was therefore necessary; the Roman Empire had been appointed by God to rule the earth; the Holy Roman Emperor inherited this power. Thus the emperor's authority did not derive from the church, and the pope's power was to be limited to the spiritual sphere. This conception of universal empire, so soon to be made meaningless by the development of nationalism, was to go into the structure of the *Divine Comedy*.

There went also into the poem the scholastic philosophy, chiefly the synthesis of Aquinas, who had aspired in his *Summa* to bring all experience into a logical framework in which faith and reason were harmonized. His theology is given poetic form in the *Commedia*, where occasionally it obscures the poetry, although it cannot be slighted by a reader who desires a complete understanding of the poem.

Aristotle, whom medieval philosophers admired as the supreme secular authority, is praised near the beginning of the work as "master of those who know," whom all other philosophers regard and honor.

Although, because it passes from realms of damnation to realms of blessedness, and because it is written in a style different from that he thought appropriate to the "high tragedy" which he called the *Aeneid,* Dante named his poem a comedy, the word as he uses it has none of the usual connotations. It is a serious survey of human experience, in terms which may have little meaning to most enlightened persons of today, but which were of tremendous significance to men of Dante's time. Heaven and Hell were real to them, and sin and its consequences were real. Man's struggle for salvation was therefore no figure of speech, but a genuine struggle against sin within him and evil without. And Dante's poem is an allegory of this struggle. If we cannot accept his theology, or his belief in retributive justice, or penetrate the allegorical and symbolical nature of his work, we can accept the pictures of life which he has given us, his visions of unutterable suffering and intensest joy, of aspiration to the source of all good. For he expresses them in concrete, vivid speech which gains strength without loss of dignity through his use of familiar words and comparisons. The colors are fast, the lines still sharp in such descriptions from the *Inferno* as those of the ill-fated lovers, Paolo and Francesca, of Farinata degli Uberti, who looked "as if he entertained great scorn of Hell," of the traitor Ugolino, frozen in eternal ice.

The *Divine Comedy* is carefully constructed, on an elaborate and logical moral plan, which conducts the reader naturally, through various degrees and sub-degrees of damnation, purgation, and blessedness, to the final moments when the poet glimpses the supreme light of the Godhead. The whole poem comprises one hundred cantos, of which there are thirty-four in the *Inferno,* and thirty-three each in the *Purgatorio* and *Paradiso.* Since the first canto is introductory, ninety-nine are devoted to the action of the poem, or to discussion of various problems which it brings up, and this number is a multiple of both nine and three, symbolic numbers (as are seven and ten) of which Dante makes much use in the course of the poem.

The framework of the journey assumes a cosmology very different from our complicated picture of the universe. In Dante's conception the earth is a center about which all things move. Imagine it as a ball suspended in space, around which revolve, one arranged within another in concentric fashion, nine spheres or heavens, the speeds of which increase in proportion to their distance from the earth. The heaven nearest the earth is that of the moon; then in order come those of Mercury, Venus, the sun, Mars, Jupiter, Saturn, and the fixed stars. The ninth is the crystalline sphere, or *Primum Mobile,* from which all the rest take time, space, and movement. Encircling all is the Empyrean, motionless, timeless, and spaceless, the seat of God.

The fall of Satan, or Lucifer, and his followers caused the earth to gape with fear, so that a cavity, roughly cone-shaped, was created, with its apex at the center of the earth. In this place—which is also the center of the universe—is Lucifer, "emperor of the dolorous realm," fixed in ice. From its rim to this center, Hell has nine circles, each receiving certain types of sinners, who are nearer Satan in proportion to the gravity of their sins.

The mass displaced by the formation of Hell rose into a mountain, on top of which is the Earthly Paradise, inhabited until their fall by Adam and Eve. This mountain is now Purgatory; it is arranged in seven circles where penitent souls are cleansed of their sins.

At the opening of the poem Dante, wandering in a dark wood (a moral allegory for sin and error, a political allegory for the troubled state of Italy) is rescued by Vergil, whom Beatrice has sent to be his guide through regions of evil and purgation. Vergil stands for human, as Beatrice does for divine, wisdom. She dominates the poem by her spirit and finally in her own person, and Dante in one of his loveliest images describes his joy on learning that it is she who has sent Vergil:

> Quali i fioretti dal notturno gelo
>   chinati e chiusi, poi che il sol gl'imbianca,
>   si drizzan tutti aperti in loro stelo:
> tal mi fec'io, di mia virtute stanca. . . .

(As flowerets, by the nightly chilliness bended down and closed, erect themselves all open on their stems when the sun whitens them: thus I did, with my fainting courage. . . .) [4]

Guided by Vergil, who rouses his courage in moments of fear, Dante passes through the circles of Hell to the lowest pit, where Lucifer lies, meeting those suffering for acts of Incontinence, Brutishness, and Malice (each category of sin

---

[4] *Inferno,* II, 127-30. Translations from the Temple Dante. J. M. Dent & Sons, London, 1929.

further subdivided) and, in addition, Heathen and Heretics, and the Trimmers whom both Hell and Heaven deny. Lowest in Hell and nearest to Lucifer are the traitors Judas, Brutus, and Cassius. The scenes, the sounds, and the stenches of Hell are concretely described, but the sense of profoundest horror arises from the fact that the torments of the damned are not applied from without, but, arising from within, express their own corruption. Finally, Dante and Vergil emerge to see once more the stars—on the word "stars" each of the three books of the *Comedy* closes; it expresses the aspiration of the human soul upwards towards God.

The little bark of his wit, Dante says, now sails over better waters, and he and his guide come to Purgatory, where souls willingly submit themselves to torment that they may become worthy to ascend to Heaven, purged of sin. On each of the seven circles one of the seven deadly sins is purged—pride, envy, anger, sloth, avarice, gluttony, carnality. Man, who through Adam's fall has lost the Earthly Paradise, must recover it again, and it is here that Beatrice supersedes Vergil as Dante's guide, for she will be the proper guide to Heaven. On seeing her he feels "the ancient flame," but she is stern at first and reproaches him for his errors.

Instructing him in truth as they go, Beatrice conducts Dante in the final book through the various heavens into the pure and living light of the Empyrean, where the redeemed are and the angels who pass between God and them. The language of the *Paradiso* (and in a different fashion that of the *Purgatorio*) is more difficult to comprehend than that of the *Inferno,* for it must render conceptions and treat of states less easily described or appreciated than the torments of the damned. But, however difficult of apprehension, it is suffused with light and warmth. Though we may ourselves not believe in such states of blessedness, we can accept Dante's vision for the beauty with which it realizes the harmony of that existence, the absorption of all degrees of the blessed in God, the fact expressed in a very famous line that *la sua voluntade è nostra pace,* his will is our peace.

Beatrice leaves Dante to ascend the throne assigned her by her merits, and as he prays, she smiles and looks upon him. Then he sees the glory of the Virgin Mary—"a beauty which was gladness in the eyes of all the other saints"—and prays her for power to raise his eyes toward ultimate bliss. Finally looking at the supreme light of God he comprehends all mysteries, and though the vision disappears, the poet realizes the power of God's love, to which all things tend:

> gia volgeva il mio disiro e il *velle*
> si come rota ch'egualmente e mossa,
> l'amor che move il sole e l'altre stelle.

(already my desire and will were rolled—even as a wheel that moveth equally— by the Love that moves the sun and the other stars.)

Such a brief summary as this can give no notion of the extent of Dante's imagination, his powers of construction, his control over the Italian tongue. To understand him is to go far toward understanding the Middle Ages, but even an incomplete comprehension of scholastic philosophy or medieval astronomy, even a lack of sympathy with certain of his ideas, with his austerity and his occasional harshness, should not turn us aside from following him in his poem, although, as he himself warns us near the beginning of the *Paradiso,* "l'acqua ch'io prendo giammai non si corse . . ."—the water which I take was never coursed before.

II. ROMANESQUE AND GOTHIC ART

Before discussing Romanesque art proper, we must consider the absence of two important art expressions in western Europe during the period from the end of the Roman Empire to the eleventh century (the beginning of the Romanesque period): a developed architecture and an art of monumental sculpture. These lacks can be only partially explained by the extremely unsettled conditions in the so-called "Dark Ages." During the Carolingian and Ottonian periods (ninth and tenth centuries) a number of ecclesiastical and secular buildings had been erected, but they contributed little to the development of original forms. Furthermore, in the few examples that have persisted from that period, sculpture played no part. Another reason frequently advanced to explain the backwardness of architecture before the Romanesque period is the almost universal superstition that the world would end at the year 1000, but this theory has been generally discredited.

The absence of an art of monumental sculpture may be the corollary of the absence of an important school of architecture. In addition, a definite fear and abhorrence of image worship prevailed at this time. Not only are sculptures absent from the Carolingian and Ottonian buildings but paintings as well. Figure art was confined to the pages of manuscripts and to the ivory covers in which they were bound. During the pre-Romanesque era there was a considerable influence on Europe from Byzantium, the then cultural center of the Continent. The violent antipathy to sculpture during the Carolingian and Ottonian empires coincides chronologically with the iconoclastic controversy raging in Byzantium.

During the Romanesque period, however, the differences between the church of Rome and Constantinople became more intense. With the growth of a strong and native monastic culture in western Europe, there developed an increasing divergence between the religious points of view of the two groups. To this same growth of Western monasticism during the eleventh to thirteenth centuries must be credited the impetus to the increased building activity of that time. Since the church and the state were too busy with their various political problems to foster much building and decoration, the members of the monastic establishments came to be both builders and decorators. This may help to explain the predominantly monastic character of the art of the Romanesque period.

An important factor in this growth of architecture lies in the character of certain forms of religious enthusiasm deliberately fostered by the church. The belief in the efficacy of intercession by personal and local patron saints naturally led to the dedication of monuments to them. Wealthy nobles frequently endowed monasteries and nunneries with buildings, land, and costly vessels for the patron saint to assure the welfare of their souls. It would appear from this that a direct approach to God was not exactly in keeping with the Romanesque point of view, and that this spiritual contact was only to be secured through the intermediary action of a given saint. This veneration of saints led to the worship of everything connected with the saints and their lives. The place of their martyrdom, an obviously holy spot, was usually honored with an important church. If a saint had not had the good fortune to die for his faith, his burial place was nevertheless similarly dignified.

The graves of the martyrs and saints, heroes of the Christian faith—like their prototypes, the local pagan deities—now became places of regular pilgrimage. It was not unusual for an individual to undertake a journey to Canterbury, Jerusalem, Santiago da Compostela, or Rome as an act of penance or for the general good of his soul. Because of the unsafe conditions of travel, groups of pilgrims bound for the same place would join forces and proceed, like Chaucer's pilgrims, "The holy blisful martir for to seke." En route to their destination, they lodged at the various monasteries and nunneries (few inns existed) and in return for this hospitality many pilgrims left gifts. The steady stream of visitors who crowded to the burial place of a saint, particularly on the anniversary of the beatified one, made a large pilgrimage church essential. This accounts, to a great extent, for the tremendous size of a building like Santiago da Compostela in Spain in an otherwise small settlement.

These pilgrimage churches were not the only type of saint's dwelling built in this so-called "Age of Faith." They were, in fact, but a small part of a vast number of churches that sprang up. The other edifices, although also dedicated to a particular saint, did not enjoy the distinction of housing the mortal remains of that individual; instead they were built around a relic or fragment of that saint's body. This relic was frequently the only religious excuse for the construction of the building. It must be kept in mind that the religious mania engendered by the crusades fostered the quest for and the appreciation of these relics. Many a knight brought back with him from the Holy Land a fragment of the true Cross or of the crown of thorns, and the traffic in relics became as common a practice as the selling of indulgences. When a church already existing in a given community was presented by a local benefactor with some precious object from his crusades, some alteration had to be made in the building to accommodate it. This frequently took the shape of an added chapel. As a result added chapels became one of the recognizable architectural features of the Romanesque cathedral.

The Romanesque church cannot be regarded as the artistic expression of the great bulk of the population. It was the creative responsibility of the nobility and the monastic clergy. The former provided economic support, the latter contributed the construction. In the Gothic period, however, we shall see a radical change in this relationship of the masses of the population to the church.

1. *The Romanesque Cathedral*

Broadly speaking, the architecture of this period was produced in the eleventh and twelfth centuries in many different localities in practically all European countries. As a result there are as many local styles of Romanesque architecture and sculpture as there are large sub-national divisions—Lombardy, Burgundy, Catalonia, etc. The term "Romanesque" is usually interpreted as indicating a derivation from "Roman" in the same sense that the development of the various Romance languages—all based on Latin—evolved in a purely local manner in each of the major divisions of the Roman Empire. This explanation at best is rather vague. One may say that the Romanesque architect faced certain definite problems in the creation of large stone edifices, and that these problems could not be solved entirely on the basis of the architecture then in vogue. The small, centrally planned churches of the Carolingian and Ottonian era in France and Germany, and the pre-Romanesque buildings of Spain, showed definite traces of Byzantine and other Eastern influences. Side by side with this orientalized point of view, can be traced the important influence of the early-Christian period with its simple basilicas.

Romanesque architecture proper is nothing more than the higher development of the basilica idea. The early basilica was small, wood-roofed, and relatively light-walled. The large pilgrimage centers and the important shrines, where a great deal of tangible property and wealth were now centered, created a need for larger buildings. It was impossible to build on a grand scale with any degree of safety or permanence without substituting stone for wood. A tradition of large stone architecture had not existed to an appreciable extent during the period from the end of the Roman Empire to the tenth century except in Syria. Therefore it was logical for the monastic architects to turn back to their Roman predecessors for ideas on the subject. In all the former Roman colonies a number of important examples of large vaulted buildings, such as amphitheaters, aqueducts, and city gates, still existed that could and did serve as prototypes for the now very elaborate vaulting system of the new architecture. In this sense, of course, one can speak of the eleventh and twelfth centuries as "Romanish" or "Romanesque."

On the basis of the old basilica plan (shorn of its atrium) the Romanesque architect erected a building which was both wider and higher than its prototype. Both the nave and aisles were vaulted with stone. This double enlargement meant that a tremendous amount of weight would have to be carried by the high walls and the broad and consequently heavy vaults. Two devices were adopted to keep the walls and the vaults from collapsing. (1) The walls were considerably thickened at their base to help support the tremendous weight. (2) On each side, where the semi-circular vault of the nave touched the nave walls, a second vault over each aisle helped to carry some of the weight to the outermost wall of the building. These latter vaults are really the ancestors of the later "flying buttresses" of the Gothic era. (See drawing on page 467.)

Neither the impinging aisle-vaults nor the thickness of the nave-walls gave the Romanesque builder sufficient confidence in what he had put up to enable him to cut very many windows in the clerestory. The result is a relatively dark building. Although the architect of this period is fully aware of the problem of lighting, there is little he can do about it under the circumstances. A conspicuous lighting device in the tower above the crossing (or transept) gave considerable dignity and impressiveness to the outside of the church. It also allowed a fair amount of light to enter at the point where it would do the most good: directly in front of the apse and altar.

The presence of a transept, creating a cruciform plan, in the Romanesque church represents a marked difference from the early Christian basilica. Other differences in the design of the building are: the greater number of chapels placed around the apse, and the pair of towers on the corners of the main façade. These towers are not merely decorative but serve the practical purpose of reinforcing the walls of the façade.

One of the charms of Romanesque architecture is the element of surprise which it provides through its many variations in each locality. France, for example, shows at least six different styles during the Romanesque era corresponding to the major feudal divisions of the country. Italy shows three outstanding types, Germany two, and Spain two. Many times one feels that the Romanesque architect willfully set out to create an impression of irregularity. He frequently varied the height of columns in the same building, changed the shape of capitals, and in the same district created many versions of such a fundamental form as the triforium.[5] It is in France that one finds the closest relationship to the style of Roman antiquity, particularly in the school of Provence in the south. At Saint Trophime a narrow band of sculptured figures runs across the entire portal much in the same fashion as in the triumphal arches of the Romans. One must remember that this part of France had been more thoroughly Romanized than any other. Important examples of Roman architecture, therefore, were in abundant evidence: the Pont du Gard, the Arles amphitheater, the baths of Diana at Nîmes, the Maison Carrée of the same city, and the well-known Arch of Triumph in Orange. Surely these must have inspired the Romanesque architect in the matter of decorative details and in the character of masonry and vaulting. The predilection of the Romans for the barrel vault was now reflected in the churches of Provence.

The region of Languedoc (southern France) contains one of the most impressive of the several French Romanesque styles. Its cultural center, Toulouse, was the most highly developed in France at that time; one could not wish for more imposing evidence of this than the magnificent church of St. Sernin. Size is the outstanding feature of the Toulouse type. St. Sernin has double aisles and considerable height. Similar buildings, dotting a wide area, were found on all four French roads leading to the shrine of Santiago da Compostela.

The character of the architecture of Aquitaine (southwestern France) during this period shows a twofold division. First, St. Front at Périgueux bears a distinct relationship to Byzantine architecture in the Greek-cross plan, the large central dome placed on pendentives, and the four subordinate domes built over each of the arms of the church. The second form appears as the more original Notre Dame la Grande in Poitiers and the cathedral of Angoulème. These buildings embody the characteristic Romanesque bulkiness, small entrance portals, cone-shaped towers on the façade (decorated with tiles arranged like scales), and a decoration in sculpture that reminds one of the early Christian sarcophagi figures set in round niches. Nothing could be more striking than the contrast between the

---

[5] The story between the ground-story and the clerestory.

Aquitaine Romanesque and a Gothic church of the thirteenth century. The impression of sheer massive bulk made by such a building as Notre Dame la Grande as it crouches close to the ground and sits firmly immovable, is exactly contrary to that created by the average Gothic cathedral, its diffused rhythms moving off into space. Tight solidity seems to be the keynote of the Romanesque edifice and loose dynamism that of its Gothic counterpart. Even in the entrances to the respective buildings, contrasts are clearly seen in the low, single, and un-inviting opening in the façade of Notre Dame la Grande and in the multiple, tall, and beckoning portals of the typical Gothic church. These powerful Roman-esque buildings are overwhelming in an almost Egyptian sense, with their tre-mendous dimensions and dark interiors; but in them we cannot experience the upward thrust and luminosity that is conveyed by the later (Gothic) buildings.

In northern France, especially Normandy, variations of the Romanesque exist that do anticipate the verticality of the Gothic style (example: Abbaye-aux-Hommes, Abbaye-aux-Dames, at Caen). In the Ile de France proper (region around Paris) it is rather hard to evaluate the contribution of the Romanesque style to the Gothic system. So many of the buildings here were remodeled and added to during the latter period that one can cross from the aisle of the Morienval parish church to the nave, and walk out of one period and into the other.

In general the architecture of Spain during this period showed decorative fea-tures derived from its own pre-Romanesque style as well as small details traceable to Moorish influence. Direct French influence, however, is apparent in the pil-grimage church of Santiago da Compostela inspired by St. Sernin of Toulouse.

In Italy three distinct architectural schools may be traced: the Northern or Lombard, the Central or Tuscan, and the Southern. From the structural and organic point of view, the most important is the Lombard. In the church of Sant' Ambrogio the Lombards, instead of roofing the nave with a long unbroken barrel vault, divided it into sections (or bays). Each bay was covered by a groin vault. Four supporting ribs were built along the lines of the groins. This rib-vaulting is of inestimable importance as the forerunner of Gothic construction. Very frequently these Lombard buildings, in spite of the organic nature of their interiors, viewed from the outside, impress one as only enlargements of the old early Christian basilicas. Occasionally this exterior simplicity is varied by a char-acteristic Italian device, a false façade masking the difference between the heights of the nave and the aisles which would otherwise be visible.

Tuscan architecture possesses none of the organic qualities of the Lombard, but is distinguished for its simplicity of construction and the elaboration of its ornamental detail. Architecturally, these buildings are direct descendants of the early Christian basilica, inasmuch as they are not vaulted but roofed with wood. Thus the builders could do away with the massive walls and concentrate on interior and exterior embellishments.

The most celebrated Tuscan example is the cathedral group at Pisa. Here the church and Leaning Tower present a perfect example of the use of ornate decora-tion typical of the time. In elevation, the cathedral appears a simple variant on the early Christian theme, differing only in the fine low tower which rises above the crossing. The ground plan of the cathedral is an ordinary Latin cross arrangement, with nave and double aisles. All this simplicity disappeared, however, when the builder turned to decoration. In the interior he embellished his triforium gallery with alternating colored stone, and on the outside of the building, over a low section of multi-colored marble, tier on tier of varied, gracefully modeled columns and arches rise to the top of the edifice. What better combination than jewel-like brilliance on simple outline!

Southern Italian Romanesque reflects the curiously mixed social and political conditions of the section, particularly Sicily, which had always been the melting pot of the nations: Greeks, Phoenicians, Romans, Byzantines, Mohammedans, Normans, etc. During the Romanesque period the Normans had conquered, and in Sicily the cathedrals of Cefalù and Monreale show a fine mixture of Norman and other forms. Cefalù, for example, combines Norman towers and interlacing arches with Moslem domes, while Monreale is an even more intricate combination of Norman towers, Moslem decorations, and Byzantine figure subjects.

The last style we shall consider is the German Romanesque. Here there are fewer local differentiations than in France or Italy, making a much more homogeneous manifestation. The most typical examples lie in the Rhineland: Mainz, Speyer, Worms, etc. They all show a multiplication of parts that is picturesque, but sometimes rather boring as well. By this we mean that the German architect, following the tradition of the older Carolingian forms, built two apses in his church, which later led him to double all the other elements as well. It is a little startling to see a building with two apses, four corner towers, two crossings (transepts), two crossing towers, etc. To be sure, this is the *reductio ad absurdum* of the process, but it really does exist and cannot be ignored (example: Cathedral of Mainz).

2. *Romanesque Sculpture*

We have observed before that Romanesque art was a primarily monastic manifestation and as such removed from the workaday realities of the period. This may explain the unreal character of the sculpture and its preoccupation with those things which best express the artificial though sincere monastic ideal. We have previously noted the distance separating the individual and his God, reflected in the necessity for intercessors. This can account, to some extent, for the markedly abstract nature of Romanesque sculpture. The manner of expressing this unreal, abstract, and frequently psychotic art varies with the locality in which it is found.

It has been frequently pointed out that the Romanesque sculptor chose his subject matter as well as his technique from the manuscripts of the time; but this does not necessarily explain his source. It merely states it in different terms, since Romanesque manuscripts betray the same psychological character as the sculpture or any other art manifestation of the period. This connection between the art of illumination and that of the three-dimensional plastic (i.e., sculpture) is significant because it emphasizes the lack of immediate sculptural precedents for the large, expressive sculpture of the eleventh to twelfth centuries. Since the sculptors of this period had nothing as large to inspire them, as the work they now conceived, they apparently turned to the only art they knew for artistic prototypes and appropriate subject matter—the manuscripts.

From the purely plastic viewpoint, this borrowing from the primarily linear and flat technique of the manuscript figures, is hardly appropriate for expression in stone or wood; and from a rational viewpoint, some of the swirling and twisting sculptured figures of this period seem a bit absurd. But should one approach so extremely spiritual and excited a period logically? If on the other hand one tries to approach these highly emotional and disturbed sculptures and manuscripts in relation to the times that gave them birth, greater understanding and enjoyment will result.

The local divisions of Romanesque sculpture do not correspond to the schools of architecture in relative importance. In the case of France, for example, Normandy, a very important and precocious architectural center, has almost no sculptural significance. Provence, which commanded our interest for showing the connection between Roman antiquity and the Romanesque, is perhaps the least important of the sculpture schools. Only the schools of Languedoc and Burgundy manage to express to the full the flavor of Romanesque sculpture.

The abbey church of Souillac in Languedoc is famous for its figure of Isaiah. Agitation and movement are expressed in every detail of the typical bent and cross-legged posture, the swirling drapery, the wildly flowing beard, and the toss of the head. Like so many sculptures of this period, the elongated figure of Isaiah has been made to fit within the confines of a niche. But the figure does not occupy all the space at its disposal. It bends and twists and tells the observer it is attempting to escape from the bonds that have been imposed on it. This sense of restriction—whether physical, emotional, or both—indicates one of the psychological bases of the entire art of this period—a basis which today would be called "repression."

In the sculptured groups at Moissac, the same bent, haggard, restricted, and generally unhappy humans appear. In the representation of the various evils, on the tympanum (half-round top of the doorway), one is introduced for the first time to the conception of sin and punishment in a powerful and ugly manner. Apparently the men and women of the early Middle Ages were more worried about evil than about good; and the devil to them was a more tangible force than ever God could be. This preoccupation with the forces of evil is vividly rendered in the tortured forms of the capitals on cloister columns. In addition to biblical subject matter, the Romanesque cloister capitals yield a wealth of demoniac subjects in which men are engaged in desperate nightmarelike struggles with various unreal monsters or with one another. Some interesting and significant subjects are the Psychomachia (conflict of souls) or the Fall of the Devil. The abundance of such material is tangible evidence of the mental climate of Romanesque sculptors.

The sculptures of the Toulouse school betray a greater degree of elegance and are not nearly as wildly emotional as the figures from either Moissac or Souillac. The Toulouse type of nervous elegance is vivid in the well-known capital from Saint-Étienne (now in the Toulouse museum). Herod and Salome are represented in attitudes stylized but exciting, as the massive, lecherous king holds the delicate, little dancer by the chin. The broad shoulders and narrow hips as well as the double-parallel bands of drapery are characteristic. Designs like this inevitably raise the question whether the artist was technically limited in his portrayal of anatomical and photographic truth or whether he deliberately chose to distort in order to achieve a higher emotional effect. Although it is impossible to answer such a question, it seems more than likely that even if the artist had been technically equipped to render forms in a realistic fashion (which he probably was not) the desire to do so was far from his mental processes and purpose.

The last important school of French Rómanesque sculpture flourished in Burgundy, the important northeastern monastic center. In such buildings as Vezelay and Autun the most characteristic examples are the well-balanced main portal tympanum with their apocalyptic representations. The figures are even longer and more tortuous than any others of this period, and certain details, as those portraying devils and tortures, are intensely vivid. In these scenes the punishment of sin and the sufferings of the damned are more than academic lessons. They are made horrible and convincing by the singling out of a significant detail or gesture, as in the pair of gigantic hands seizing upon a little soul in the lowest register of the group at Autun. No more instructive comparison can be found than a representation of the Last Judgment as treated by the Romanesque artist compared with the same in the Gothic period. If the Gothic is more attractive in its rendering of simple, everyday scenes, it never achieves as intense a representation of the true conception of hell-fire.

In no other school of the Romanesque is the dematerialization of form carried to the extreme seen in the school of Burgundy. Germany, for example, shows in the most abstract representation an adherence to certain elements of solidity in the delineation of the body. Solidity is not at all inconsistent with an abstract rendering of the human form—a fact that is as true of twentieth-century sculpture as of the German Romanesque. Such a work as the wooden crucifixion group of the Innichen church is probably one of the most monumental conceptions in sculpture of the Middle Ages, squarely composed and physically reduced to the bare essentials. The simplicity in the rendering of the body of Christ is akin to the most abstract and stylized Negro primitive sculpture or to some of the adaptations of this style done in our own times.

The German school lasted unusually long. Such a work as the Hildesheim font of the thirteenth century still preserves most of the features of early Romanesque art. Similarly in the choir figures in the Cathedral of Bamberg, groups of Old and New Testament prophets and apostles confront one another argumentatively, posed on rolling ground lines, hands frequently waving, bodies twisted, and draperies flying in true Romanesque fashion.

It is to the south of Italy that we must turn for the most interesting manifestations of the Romanesque style. A convenient division into two types readily presents itself: Byzantine and antique. We find examples of the first in the bronze doors of Barisano da Trani in the cathedrals of Ravelo, Trani, and Palermo.

The antique style centered about the court of the great Frederick II of Italy. Early in the thirteenth century a castle was erected at Capua in the form of an ancient triumphal arch. Only a few fragments remain such as the headless figure of the emperor, the bust of one of his ministers, and, most important of all, a marble head of a tutelary goddess of the city of Capua. The remarkable thing about these works is that as early as the twelfth and thirteenth centuries, sculptures and architecture were produced which showed so strong a derivation from classic sources. This can be traced to the cultural interests of the court of Frederick II. It is more important than their intrinsic beauty, in the evolutionary sense, that they apparently furnished the prototypes and inspiration for some of the earliest sculpture of the so-called Italian Renaissance. Niccola Pisano, customarily reckoned as the starting point of that artistically significant period, came from Apulia in the south of Italy at the end of the thirteenth century and settled in Pisa where the great Romanesque cathedral was still being embellished with sculpture. In this manner the first tangible contact between the Middle Ages and the so-called Renaissance was established.

In Spain two outstanding sculpture centers were Santo Domingo de Silos and the abbey church of Santa Maria at Ripoll. Like most Spanish Romanesque, these can be quickly related to antecedent manuscript types, interesting more to the specialist than to the general student.

England has suffered the misfortune of losing most of her Romanesque sculpture through one accident or another. The destruction of the monasteries during Cromwell's reign was more responsible for the disappearance of English Romanesque and Gothic than anything else. One of the interesting features of the few remaining English monuments of this time is the infiltration of stylistic elements and subject matter from Scandinavia. The frequent use of elongated and twisted dragon forms in connection with human beings (example: Church of Kilpeck in Herefordshire) recalls the wooden doors from Hylestad (Norway) now in the Oslo museum. These motifs may be entirely decorative in character or may relate to such stories as Siegfried and the Dragon which appeared in their first written versions during the twelfth centuries. As a matter of fact the various northern countries were in close contact with one another as a result of commerce and war. The spread of "romance" material was only one phase of the cultural interpenetration.

3. Gothic Architecture

While Romanesque art had been founded on a feudal and decentralized social system revolving about the castle and the monastery, the most conspicuous feature of the Gothic period was the development of urban life and the rise of a middle class. It is first to France that we must turn for a survey of what is known as Gothic style and culture. The Ile de France region originated and perfected the Gothic cathedral—the most significant production of the period from both the communal and religious points of view.

The Gothic cathedral was the result of concerted effort on the part of the entire community. All the groups of handicraftsmen worked together, contributing their time and energy to the construction of the house of God. It is frequently argued, therefore, that the Gothic cathedral represents an anonymous community effort from which it is impossible to disengage the names or personalities of the individual builders. It cannot be denied that architects' names such as Robert de Luzarches, Jean le Loup, Villard de Honnecourt, etc., are seldom encountered, but that they did exist as personalities is also true. Recognition of the various guilds of workmen very frequently took tangible form, sometimes in the guilds' portrayal in a stained-glass window, sometimes in the dedication of a large chapel for its private use. In fact, one often learns from these representations in glass and stone not only the names of the guilds and individuals but also certain techniques of production. This clearly indicates the degree of and the respect for lay participation in the construction of the church that sharply differentiates the Gothic from the Romanesque period.

The character of that rather intangible element known as the personality of a community is hard to determine. It has been maintained that cathedrals such as Paris, Rheims, Chartres, and Amiens reflect the "individuality" of those cities to the extent that they were respectively "intellectual," "classical," "mystic," and "bourgeois." One might maintain, with perhaps greater plausibility, that whatever distinguishing features are found in the so-called "character" of these buildings result from the individuality of the "schools" of workmen responsible for their production. The layman's participation in the building of his cathedral is significant of the shift of the religious center from the insulated monastery to the open and enthusiastic town. One cannot account for the tremendous speed with which some of the Gothic cathedrals went up except by the spur of the rare religious fervor that followed this change. The Gothic period not only created a social revolution in the rise of a new class of society, but a shift from the relatively impersonal relic worship of the Romanesque period to a more direct relationship with God, maintained through the very tangible agency of the Mother of God. It is a revealing fact that a great number of the Gothic cathedrals are dedicated to "Our Lady."

Since the cathedral was the most important creation of the Gothic period, every other type of art then produced was colored to some extent by the "architectural ideal." In spite of the fact that the Gothic church has an infinitely greater amount of sculpture on its façade than any Romanesque building, these ornaments are never as obtrusive as the sculpture on the Romanesque surface. All the sculpture of the Gothic cathedral was designed as part of a larger entity and was created to fit a particular niche on the building. It will follow from this that very little sculpture during this period was designed to be freestanding or independent of a particular environment or background. The first impression gained from the Gothic cathedral, then, is a sense of unity and organization, a carefully planned relationship between the building and its decorations.

Whereas the Romanesque building has been described as heavy, static, and crouching, the Gothic building is light, dynamic, and soaring. It will be recalled that the problem facing the Romanesque architect was the creation of a large edifice in stone with stable vaults and walls, fireproofing, and sufficient light and air. Size, stabilization, and fireproofing (through the stone roof), the Romanesque builders achieved; but at what a cost in elegance, dynamism, light, and air! The architects of the eleventh and twelfth centuries could not avoid a somberly massive and dark building because they did not dare tamper with the uniformly semicircular vaulting or with the almost cyclopean character of their walls. Only when a system of creating light vaults and walls was devised did the character of medieval architecture change. This was accomplished by the Gothic builders. They made two major changes: first, they substituted for the Romanesque rounded arch a pointed arch; second, they substituted for the mas-

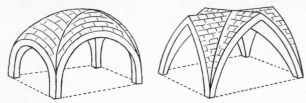

Left, Romanesque groin vault, showing uneven height of crowns; *right,* Gothic ribbed vault, showing how pointed arches result in an identical height of all the crowns.

sive supporting walls of the Romanesque style an exterior support in the form of flying buttresses.

By substituting the pointed arch for the rounded Romanesque arch, the Gothic builder was able to work toward verticality with greater freedom. He could change the shape of the bay (the section supporting the vault) from a square to a rectangle, since a pointed arch can be erected with any radius and the various sides of the bay do not have to be the same length. The consequences of this change were: first, the shorter sides of the now rectangular bay were supported by columns closer together and therefore more vertical in effect. Second, this verticality was emphasized by the pointed arches connecting the various pairs of columns as well as by the steep pitch of arches on the two short sides of the bay, since these were cast from shorter radii than those on the long sides. Third, of equal importance structurally, the pointed arch enabled the architect to raise the crowns of each vault to the same height.

Suppose we were to remove the roofs from typical Romanesque and Gothic buildings and compare the tops of their vaulting systems. What should we see? In the Romanesque the crowns of the vaults are at different levels. In the Gothic (as disclosed by the shooting away of part of the cathedral during the World War bombardment of Rheims) all of the vault crowns are on the identical level. Hence it was possible to tie these crowns together with a stone "spine" that ran the length of the building.

The pointing and narrowing of the Gothic arches brought about a further important change in the character of the vault, for, once the shape of the vault could be altered and controlled, the possibilities became almost limitless. The builder was able to shape the vault so that its chief strain concentrated at the point where it rested on the wall. This point in the structure would require additional support.

The pitched vaults and the pointed arches joining the nave columns all helped create a tremendous verticality. Further, the wall of the Gothic nave was pierced not only by the immensely high arches just mentioned but by a triforium gallery immediately above them; and then, finally, by an elaborate clerestory filled with

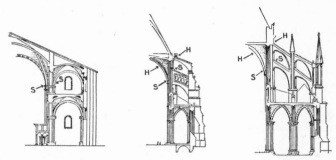

The evolution of the flying buttress. *Left,* section of Sant' Ambrogio, a Romanesque example, showing barrel vault used as buttress and concealed under triforium roof; *center,* section of Chartres Cathedral, showing buttress outside of building; *right,* Rheims Cathedral, showing double buttress. The buttress supports the vault at the point of *S* spring from the walls and at *H* haunch of the vault.

as unsupporting a material as stained glass. For all practical purposes, the wall has disappeared. It is essential, then, for the builder to substitute for his wall some other means to support this high, pierced shell. The incredible invention of the Gothic builder produced the solution—the flying buttress, a device which had no architectural precedent.

The flying buttress is a long, thin, stone support propping the outside of the building at those points where it is most needed: first, where the vault rests on the walls; second, where the vault begins to roll inward to roof the building. One speaks of the buttress as "flying" because, unlike the Romanesque buttress which was a thick mass of stone affixed to the surface of the building, the Gothic flying buttress is a skeletal form diagonally fixed to the two points mentioned and joined at its lower end to a vertical mass of masonry which carries the thrust down to the ground. This is the most important individual contribution of the Gothic builder to architecture.

Obviously a complicated system such as the one just described did not spring full grown overnight. It was the result of a long series of experiments and mistakes. The germs of Gothic had already been present in the Romanesque period. The pointed arch, for example, had been used in a rudimentary form. In the case of the flying buttress one deals with a device whose function had previously been performed by the half-barrel aisle vaults of the Romanesque era. These Romanesque half-barrel vaults were covered by a roof and were hidden participants in the support of the building. From this beginning the gradual emergence of the form and function of the flying buttress can be traced.

We might think at first that the elaborate web of buttressing around the typical Gothic church would detract from its effectiveness. But since the design of the buttresses is either vertical or diagonal, it really adds to the cumulative upward movement of the building as a whole. A series of vital relationships has been built up between those parts of the building which exert downward and outward thrusts (for example, the vaults) and those that resist these thrusts (the columns and buttresses). These thrusts and resistances are invariably functional in the best modern sense, and convey to us a strong relationship between the exterior and interior of the church.

This relationship is prolonged in the careful design of the façade; first, by breaking the façade in correspondence with the width and height of the interior, and second, in piercing the stone surface with lacy sculpture, emphasizing again the unimportance of wall space as such. In effect the entire building has become a gigantic skeleton consisting of a spine, ribs, and arms (buttresses). Over this framework a fabric of stone has been drawn, leaving large openings to provide a maximum of height and illumination—and withal at no sacrifice to stability.

The Gothic designers were possessed by an almost fanatical interest in space-composition and movement. It found expression in the height of the vaults and in the apparent annihilation of walls. Since the tops of the vaults are always shrouded in deep shadow, vaguely limned by the multicolor lights filtering through the stained-glass windows of the clerestory, there grows up an illusion of endless height. The tangible limitations of wall and roof seem to have disappeared. Can one doubt that this impression contributed overwhelmingly to the religious effect of the Gothic cathedral?

The floor plan of the Gothic church shows some changes from the Romanesque. The Gothic building is much broader and frequently wider. Even more side chapels have been added along the aisles and around the apse. Because of the elaboration of church ritual, an ambulatory (walking space for the celebrants of the Mass) around the apse became indispensable. From the crossing of the cathedral to the apse end, an exceedingly fine and elaborate choir was worked out, with sumptuous wooden choirstalls. Their elegantly carved backs are considered among the outstanding achievements of the Gothic wood sculptors.

Let us remember that the foregoing is strictly applicable only to the French Gothic cathedral of the thirteenth century, to its most typical development in the Ile de France in such churches as Chartres, Paris, Amiens, and Rheims. Even the designs of these vary, as the districts vary, since the Gothic system in all parts of Europe grew out of an extremely individualized and localized Romanesque. The fourteenth century in France contributed very little that is new but continued to refine the old. With the advent of the Hundred Years' War, the great productivity of the French Gothic as a source of inspiration was exhausted.

The English Gothic was even more closely related to English Romanesque than the French Gothic to its antecedent style, and to the very end of its development, relied more upon the sturdiness of the old system than upon the inventions of the French. The English cathedral was most usually located in the country—differing, in this respect, from the French Gothic cathedrals, whose background was preponderantly urban. The continued importance of the monasteries in the English ecclesiastical system provided one reason for this phenomenon. The other reason lay in the power of the lords which persisted longer in England than in France. Their strength delayed the emergence of the town and perpetuated the feudal organization of society. The years 1200-1500 may be borne in mind as the period of English Gothic architecture.

From the viewpoint of physical appearance, the English cathedral is narrower than the French and consequently impresses one as being longer and higher,

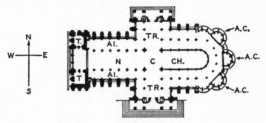

Floor plan of a Gothic cathedral (Chartres): *TR.* transept, *C* crossing, *CH.* choir, *N* nave, *Al.* aisles, *T* towers, *A.C.* apse chapels.

though it is not necessarily either. (Actually the English is usually much less tall than the French.) In addition to these apparent features, the English Gothic presents differences in plan, such as double transepts and square terminations of the apses. One of the original features of the English system is the rather large tower placed over the transept which dominates the design.

The vaulting as well as the supporting ribs in the English cathedral became much too complicated to be functional or organically sound. As the architecture developed, the ribbing became more an opportunity for decoration than for reinforcement, culminating in the famous "fan vaulting" of the fifteenth century. Façades, as well, developed a false but decorative front that had little to do with the character and plan of the interior. The functional French Gothic became reduced in the English style to merely ornamental inspiration. Sculpture used as an integral part of the building became more and more infrequent.

The complete acceptance by the Germans of the French system was impeded, to a great extent, by the strong hold of their native Romanesque, so that Gothic made a slow start in this country. Once the Germans accepted the French system, however, a number of very close imitations arose. The Cathedral of Cologne, evidently inspired by Amiens, is one of the finest examples of Gothic in Germany. The close imitation seems to point to an inability on the part of the Germans to evolve a characteristic and native style of their own. The sole exception is the building called by the Germans the *Hallenkirche,* or hall church, in which the aisle vaults were as high as those of the nave, thus producing the effect of a hall.

Since there are no original contributions made by Spanish Gothic, it can be briefly summarized as a local adaptation of the French Gothic style. The extremely sunny climate of Spain made the problem of lighting nonexistent, which led to the frequent disappearance of either the clerestory or the triforium gallery. The Spanish architects of this period, moreover, showed a decided disinclination to accept the extreme verticality of the French Gothic style. Perhaps this tendency towards horizontality is explained by the fact that Spain was rich in architectural remains of classical antiquity, whose horizontal lines created a calmness and repose. These qualities were more congenial to the Spanish temperament; hence, Spanish Gothic architecture is moderated by a comparative horizontality and calmness of feeling.

Italy, more than any other European country, persisted in refusing to adopt the French Gothic style. This can be better understood when we recall that the continuity of the Roman basilica tradition had never been interrupted in Italy. The French Gothic style entered Italy through the agency of the Cistercian monks and became popular as a style of pointed, nonorganic decoration. Superficially Italian buildings do recall the style of France, but in verticality and in organic unity, which the French themselves deemed important, they are sadly lacking. We must admit, on the other hand, that the Italian Gothic did produce a number of flamboyantly beautiful works, particularly in central Italy and in such cathedrals as those at Siena, Orvieto, and Florence. These are unusual, in the main, for their use of elaborately colored marble, a screen façade masking the interior divisions, and a general horizontality of appearance. Of purely Gothic style Italy has to offer only the Cathedral of Milan, built during the fifteenth century with the aid of German architects representing a combination of German, French, and Italian inspiration.

In Italian buildings as in the Spanish, the need for light is relatively unimportant, causing again the suppression of the clerestory and a minimizing of the triforium gallery. Curiously this moves the style back historically in the direction of the Romanesque, with its broad wall spaces suitable for paintings and mosaics. This indeed occurred in Italy. Some of the most famous examples of fourteenth-century painting and mosaic occur on the walls of Italian Gothic buildings, such as Saint Francis at Assisi, etc.

The cathedral is undoubtedly the most significant art manifestation of the period, but we must not forget that the changes of society gradually brought about new needs for other buildings. In the early Gothic period the most significant nonecclesiastical architectural production is the fortified town or its corollary, the castle. The most important and best-preserved examples of the completely fortified town are Villeneuve-les-Avignon, Aigues-Mortes, and Carcassonne. Where the terrain was irregular the builder took advantage of this feature and constructed a bizarre-shaped unit offering many difficulties to attackers (example: Carcassonne). But where the land was regular, the structure was even and well-planned (example. Aigues-Mortes). To what extent the fortified architecture of the Middle Ages in Europe was original has always been a question. One can merely point to the examples of fortified architecture among the Byzantines and the Muslims both of whom may have furnished some inspiration to the crusaders.

When the nobles moved into the new towns in the fourteenth century the ideal of defense was tempered somewhat by aesthetic necessity, but never enough for the primarily utilitarian character of the building to be completely lost. This combination of the newer, lighter style with the defensive function marks an interesting transition in France from the Gothic to the so-called Renaissance style, particularly in the country residences (examples: Chambord and Chenonceaux). Since the late Gothic period marks the emergence of a new and urban figure, the merchant prince, the occasion arose for the construction of a town house with no particular function of defense (example: the house of Jacques Cœur at Bourges).

As a symbol of the new and more democratic community that grew up during the Gothic period, the town hall is significant. The functions of the town hall and the trade hall were usually combined as in the famous Cloth Hall at Ypres. The style naturally varied from country to country. Other well-known examples are found in Italy—the Palazzo Pubblico of Siena and the Palazzo Vecchio of Florence. There were, to be sure, other secular works such as bridges, fountains, hospitals, boundary monuments, etc.

4. *Gothic Sculpture*

In the same sense that the development of Gothic architecture presented the solution of problems that had existed during the Romanesque period, the sculpture of the Gothic period expressed the same fundamental ideas as the Romanesque from a newer point of view. Thus Gothic sculpture from the very outset assumes a rather dual character. It retains the subject matter of the Romanesque and expresses it in the style of the thirteenth century. The relationship between the Romanesque and the Gothic styles can, perhaps, best be expressed by a comparison with the Greek styles of the archaic and classical periods. In both the Greek and medieval cultures, the earlier style shows a definite starkness and crudeness, where photographic realism plays a secondary rôle and emotional power is expressed through the almost willful distortion of the human figure. This exaggeration in the archaic Greek and in the Romanesque is considerably tempered during the respective periods that follow them, when the proportions of the human figure are, in a sense, codified, and the emotional expression becomes serene, dignified, and restrained. The famous *Beau Dieu* of Amiens and the scene of the *Visitation* at Rheims vividly express this aspect of thirteenth-century Gothic. Immediately apparent in these two typical examples is the perfect majesty and serenity of the mood as well as the regular proportions of the bodies.

Literacy in the Gothic period was a rare possession. Even the nobility itself, more often than not, was ignorant of even the rudiments of reading and writing. There remained then two simple methods of spreading religious information: first, through preaching and, second, through a pictorial or plastic representation. To provide the latter the cathedral was embellished with much figure sculpture and stained glass. If the building itself produced a generalized religious experience, the decorations managed to transmit a body of specific factual stimuli. Although these decorations are frequently referred to as the Poor Man's Bible, they are really Every Man's Bible, one of the greatest achievements of the church. Every type of information was conveyed in these decorations, religious and secular history, the sciences and the arts as they were known at the time, scenes of general interest. The sculptures and stained glass of the cathedral contain a résumé of all of the information possessed at the time, a reflection, we might say, of the "Great Mirror" of Vincent of Beauvais.

As the various parts of the church structure itself were well ordered and regular, so the decorations adhered to a specific plan. Relatively little emerged accidentally. The west side (front) of the building was usually reserved for a representation of the *Last Judgment* in the central portal, with the left- and right-hand portals dedicated respectively to the *Ascension of Christ* and the *Coronation of the Virgin*. Less important scenes were used to embellish the north and south portals (transepts), perhaps the story of a locally important saint.

Symbolism played an important part in the arrangement of the scenes, so that the *Last Judgment* was always portrayed on that side of the church which faced the setting sun, whereas the east end was reserved for a representation of either the Christ or His Mother in heaven. If, for example, Christ was shown with other holy personages, the question of position became important; that person considered the most important was placed at His right hand. A vivid example of this type of symbolism is found in the portrayal of the prophets of the New Testament who are frequently represented as standing on the shoulders of the Old Testament prophets.

In the first half of the thirteenth century four important schools of sculpture developed in France. Chartres was a fairly conservative school which developed slowly and showed a tendency toward mysticism and pious devotion. This may be observed in the austerity of its sculpture as well as in the almost ecstatically religious quality of its stained glass. The great university center, Paris, produced a school of sculpture more intellectual than mystical. The *Coronation of the Virgin* portal of Notre Dame Cathedral is typical. It shows a studied anatomical knowledge, the various parts well integrated. The importance of the university is reflected in the fact that the actual student life of the time became subject matter for the decoration of the cathedral. Amiens may be termed the typical bourgeois town of the period, consciously interested in realism, portraiture, even in prettification. No better example of this style could be found than the famous *Vierge dorée* whom the French themselves have dubbed "La Soubrette de Picardie." Rheims, the fourth of the important schools of the thirteenth century in France, may be called academic, since its style is most classical of all. The *Visitation* group at Rheims cathedral is an almost conscious reproduction of a classical scene of greeting or leave-taking, with the figure and drapery of one of the figures reminiscent of a Roman matron's.

The most striking feature of thirteenth-century Gothic sculpture consisted in its ability successfully to relate small details of realism to the composition of which they were a part. These details were always subordinated to the work as a whole and the work, in turn, was subordinated to the design of the building itself. It has been said that a piece of Gothic sculpture cannot stand alone as a work of art. In a measure this is true, since it was designed as part of a totality, and when the spectator observes, as in museum examples, a single figure isolated from this totality, he is bound to have a feeling of incompleteness.

The end of the thirteenth century in France brought "mannerism" in sculpture —what might be termed the "Hellenistic phase" of the Gothic style. *La Vierge dorée* at Amiens, with its sweet sentimentality, its exaggeration of the relationship between mother and child, is as good an example as the Saint Stephen portal at Paris, where the drapery became a bit baggy because of the sculptor's attempt to represent violent movement before he had acquired the necessary technique. In the Virgin portal of the north transept in Paris the figures begin to squint a bit, a characteristic of mannered Gothic (the squint together with the bagginess of the drapery will appear shortly in the early fourteenth-century art of Italy).

In fourteenth-century French sculpture a marked aristocratic element reappeared with the attenuation of the forms, the elaboration of costumes, and the curiously mannered postures which the figures frequently assumed. The famous *Virgin of Paris*, in the odd concave curve of her posture, in the long sweeping line of drapery from one shoulder to the opposite foot, and in her squinting and diffident expression, sums up this phase of fourteenth-century French Gothic effectively.

The figure of the *Virgin of Paris* demonstrates how the architectonic quality of the high Gothic (thirteenth-century) sculpture was destroyed in the mannerism of the fourteenth century. The swaying posture of the *Virgin of Paris* is not an organic part of the column on which is stands. With the figure's relationship to the column weakened, its relationship to the entire building becomes superficial. The organic interrelationship of details to all other elements characteristic of a thirteenth-century Gothic cathedral was later sacrificed to an interest in detail alone.

The outstanding physical elements of the fourteenth-century style, the attenuated forms, the aristocratic and affected postures, the swing of line, the elegant curve of the body, and the frequently mincing expression, are found in great profusion not only in the cathedral sculptures but in the minor arts as well. Ivory carvings offer clear examples, particularly in their rendering of the currently popular romances such as the Arthurian cycle. Here we find a fine combination of upper-class subject matter and elegant style.

The so-called idealism of the French high Gothic of the thirteenth century gave way in the first half of the fourteenth to elegance and later to stark realism. No stronger contrast to the prettified manner of the *Virgin of Paris* could be imagined than the monumental *Well of Moses* by Claus Sluter, originally constructed as the base for an imposing calvary in the Monastery of Champmol, near Dijon. Although the figures here retained all the solidity of the French High Gothic style, there was a complete and deliberate disregard for the architectural consciousness of that period. Instead a greater individuality was substituted. This applies not only to the relationship of the figure to the larger unit in which it was placed but to the interpretation of the personality of the various figures as well.

We might say that for the first time in the Middle Ages historical characters were represented with historical faithfulness. The Moses looked like the Moses of his time and not a late fourteenth-century personage. We may further note that the drapery had by now reached a fullness never before attained in the Middle Ages. This amplitude together with the infinitely more varied and complicated convolutions of the fabric not only added to the figure's impressiveness but to its emotional quality as well.

The rise of Gothic sculpture in Germany came late because of the strong hold of the Romanesque style. When it did appear, however, it bore a close relationship to France. The schools of Rheims and Bamberg maintained intimate contact over a long period; indeed, the cathedrals of the two cities show that Rheims influenced Bamberg, only to be influenced by it toward the end of the century; then Rheims influenced Germany once again, at Strassburg. German Gothic as a whole is characterized by intense sentiment, fine portraiture, and heavy draperies. A tendency toward the bizarre and picturesque may account for the appeal of German Gothic to the masses of the people—and hence for the careful preservation of most of the German Gothic buildings which survive in an infinitely better condition than most French Gothic examples.

In England, as we have observed above, monumental sculpture played a small part in cathedral design. Wells produced one of the few important groups. Except for these and for the fine recumbent royal bronze tomb figures in Westminster Abbey, there was remarkably little.

Spain offers a close parallel to the French Gothic style, at least for the beginnings of its sculpture. The cathedrals of Burgos and León, in particular, are replete with elaborate French sculpture. Later there was a marked falling off in quality as the Spanish sculptors freed themselves of French influence. Native sculpture took on a vulgarization and provincialism.

Italian Gothic sculpture is the most interesting of the styles outside of France for it carries within it the germs of some of the most important developments of the Italian tradition. The leading Italian master of the thirteenth century is Niccola Pisano (c. 1215-c. 1280) who came from the south of Italy (Apulia) to Pisa where he did some of his most important work. His contribution to the development of Italian art is crucial, for he is the first medieval artist (sculptor or painter) in whom we find a highly developed consciousness of the art of antiquity. In such works as the pulpit in the Baptistery of the Cathedral of Pisa (1259), he shows an interesting combination of medieval subject matter and of forms influenced by the art of Rome. His figures are monumental like those of the Roman sarcophagi and he gave much attention to attain a quality of substantiality in drapery. We shall see the influence of his work upon painting in the last quarter of the thirteenth and the first quarter of the fourteenth century in Italy.

The work of his son, Giovanni Pisano (c. 1249-c. 1328), a much more tempestuous artist, is more specifically Gothic in character, and closer to the already mannered efforts of the later thirteenth century in France. The dramatic quality of his sculpture will be mirrored in the works of contemporary Italian painters such as

Giotto. He also produced a pulpit for the Cathedral of Pisa (1301-1311) now in the Museo Civico in that city, as well as other works in Pistoja, Siena, and elsewhere.

5. Gothic Painting

The stained glass windows in the Gothic cathedral served as substitutes for the wall paintings of the Romanesque period. Stained glass, as a developed art, dates from the second half of the twelfth century and retains its Gothic character through the thirteenth and fourteenth centuries. The technical innovations made at the beginning of the fifteenth century in painting, the evolution of perspective, foreshortening, and other devices, spelled the doom of this art which was fundamentally flat and coloristic.

Undoubtedly the most famous example of medieval stained glass is found in the late twelfth-century cathedral of Chartres. Here the character of the figures is still Romanesque but portrayed with all the vivid blues and reds associated with Gothic color. When the color was applied simply, it retained its Gothic integrity; when, in the late thirteenth century, it became more elaborate and detailed (like its sister arts, sculpture and manuscript painting), the result was to the same degree "mannered."

Such a window as the famous *Notre Dame de la Belle Verrière* at Chartres contains the dazzling cobalt blues and the vivid reds that set the standard for all subsequent productions. At this stage in the development of the art, the colors were rendered in wide patches and cut across by heavy leads that bound the component pieces of glass together. All factors combined to create a certain irregularity: the uneven and sometimes arbitrary placing of the strips of lead, the relatively unnatural drawing of the figure, and finally the imperfections and bubbles in the glass itself. These irregularities tend to refract the light rays as they enter from the outside, and they create a shimmering effect of color on the cathedral interior. Whether or not the Gothic artist was completely conscious of the possibilities of stained glass is scarcely important, judging by the effect achieved. The red glow in the morning hours and the vivid and pulsating blue predominant in the afternoon are possibly not accidental at all. The morning sun intensifies the reds of the glass; in the afternoon, when the violet tones prevail in the sun's rays, the blues of the stained glass become more jewel-like and varied. To the problem of lighting a church effectively, the stained glass of the Gothic cathedral is a harmonious and inspiring solution.

Italy, during the Gothic period, produced the only noteworthy school of painting in Europe for the period of c. 1275-1350. Real wall paintings developed here because Gothic construction with its many windows never won the full acceptance of the Italians. Italy, as we have already seen, preserved the early Christian basilica forms relatively intact; thus, instead of open window spaces to fill with stained glass, the Italian artist had large wall spaces to cover.

The two most prominent names of this period are Cimabue and Giotto. Giovanni Cimabue (c. 1240-c. 1302), active in Florence and Rome, is known to us through a number of fragments in the Church of St. Francis at Assisi and a small number of panel paintings. His art made a sharp break with the ordinarily lifeless and Byzantine-influenced painting of the Italian peninsula during the twelfth and thirteenth centuries. He was one of the first to insist upon a degree of naturalness in both the faces and figures of his characters. In one or two examples he even rises to a high emotional level.

Giotto di Bondone (1267-1337) was the most influential master of the fourteenth century. Following the tradition laid down by the sculptor Niccola Pisano, he concerned himself with the problem of monumentality in the human figure expressed through its voluminous draperies. A contemporary of the poet Dante, he based the psychological content of his art upon human passions and suffering, which he expressed with restraint and power. In the Church of St. Francis at Assisi we find a number of Giotto's frescos, painted with the aid of assistants, which tell the story of the patron saint. Giotto's most individualized interpretations of holy legend may be seen in the Arena Chapel in Padua and the Franciscan Church of the Holy Cross (S. Croce) in Florence. In his powerful draughtsmanship, his emotional content, his gift for pictorial narrative and economy in composition, he laid the foundations for the later painters of Italy.

III. THE BEGINNINGS OF MULTIVOICED MUSIC

The two most important features of the music of the later Middle Ages are the development of polyphony and the rise of secular one-line music, the latter analogous in some respects to the one-line music which had been employed in the churches.

1. Early Polyphony

Polyphony results from the simultaneous sounding (i.e., the combination) of two or more melodies possessing a degree of independence. Polyphonic music is thus multivoiced. The history of European music from 900 to 1600 is largely the history of the development of the polyphonic style.

The earliest technical account of polyphonic music is the *Musica enchiriadis,* a manual of uncertain authorship written in the tenth century. Polyphonic singing, however, is known to have existed before this time. The *Musica enchiriadis* describes a type of part singing in which the plain chants were sung by voice groups which remained substantially parallel in their motion, singing the same melody, but at pitch levels removed from one another by an interval of a fourth or a fifth. This rudimentary species of polyphony was known as *organum.*

The polyphonic procedure immediately raises the question: Under what circumstances may melodies be combined? Melodies, we have already pointed out, consist of successions of tones and may thus be said to proceed in a horizontal fashion. The combination of melodies, in the simultaneous sounding of tones of different pitches, introduces a vertical concept, namely *harmony.* For melodies to be sung or played in combination it is necessary that those tones which are heard simultaneously possess certain relationships, relationships which may be classified either as *consonances* or *dissonances.* Consonances are restful satisfying combinations. Dissonances, while not unpleasant, are neither restful nor satisfying but produce a tension which demands progression to an ultimate consonance.

A significant part of the history of music since A.D. 900 might conceivably be written in terms of changing standards of consonance and dissonance. Organum flourished from 900 to 1200 and its standards of consonance were built around the intervals of the fourth and the fifth. To Victorian ears organum seems to have sounded "atrocious," and a distinguished French teacher of the early twentieth century maintained that its parallel voice progressions were "agglomerations of sound entirely inacceptable to our modern hearing." Modern listeners, however, are no longer outraged by the parallel fourths and fifths of organum, probably because they have become accustomed to them through the extensive use of identical procedures in the works of recent composers, notably Claude Debussy. When two or more melodies are sung simultaneously there is the need for some synchronizing agency—a system for indicating the relative duration of tones. Such a system was first compiled by Franco of Cologne, a distinguished theoretician of the thirteenth century. He codified the relative time values of notes in a somewhat involved series of "rhythmic modes." All of the rhythms of the music written between 1150 and 1350 were governed by a ternary principle (similar, for example, to our "three-quarter" time) and for some unknown reason triple rhythms were the only ones employed.

Organum experienced rapid development in standards of both consonance and dissonance, and in independence of motion of the voices. It reached its climax (about the middle of the thirteenth century) in what is probably the first great school of composition, the group of composers active in the service of the Cathedral of Notre Dame in Paris. Two of its most celebrated members were Leonin and Perotin, both of whom achieved a high degree of fame. Their works were approvingly cited by contemporary theorists and commentators. Perotin enjoys the distinction of having been the first composer of a polyphonic work with four real parts.

The musical form par excellence of the period was the *motet,* of French origin. A polyphonic composition usually in two or three parts, its characteristic feature was the use of a different text for each part. The lowest of the voices, the *tenor,* consisted of some well-known melody, often a plain chant, and the two upper parts, the *motetus* and the *triplum,* were the original creations of the composer. The use of secular texts and melodies was not disdained by the medieval musician. Tenors of a decidedly worldly nature served as the basis (*cantus firmus*) for sacred motets; plain chants were combined with amorous or ribald songs. Again, apparent incongruities of this sort must not be judged by contemporary standards. The sacred and the secular did not represent mutually exclusive viewpoints during the Gothic period. Indeed, Gothic architecture, with its naturalistic carvings and grotesques, presents many features analogous to those found in Gothic music.

In England as well as in France music was being actively cultivated. Partsinging seems to have been native to that country, and its abundance was observed and noted down by early visitors there. The English used a system of singing in thirds and sixths known as *faux-bourdon,* a method which later found its way to the Continent. The degree of perfection achieved by English composers is demonstrated by a famous piece of secular music, the *rota Sumer Is Icumen In,*

dating from about 1240. *Sumer Is Icumen In* is a canon for four voices over a
ground bass which is also a canon. (A canon is an imitative device in which there
is literal repetition—imitation—of one voice by a succeeding voice or voices.) The
celebrated work, while an unusually fine example of thirteenth-century polyphony,
is not untypical of its methods.

During the period now under discussion music was regarded more as a branch
of knowledge than as an art. It had a close relationship to mathematics. Many
of the great musical theorists of the period were excellent mathematicians as
well, and their learned treatises set forth the various elements entering into the
composition of musical works with almost scientific precision. Lectures on music
were a regular part of the curricula of the medieval universities. The subjects
with which music was grouped indicate the medieval scholar's concept of its
nature and function as one of the seven liberal arts. As we have had occasion to
point out before, music was linked with arithmetic, geometry, and astronomy to
form the mathematical group—the *Quadrivium Academicum*.

Up to this point we have been chiefly concerned with music as an accessory
art in the ritual of the church. Commencing at about 1150 secular music came
into its own, notably in France. The curious feature about this secular music,
however, is the fact that in many respects it was an offshoot of plain chant, and
unlike the sacred music of its time was predominantly single-line music.

2. *The Troubadours and Trouvères*

Secular music of the period is best discussed in terms of the *troubadours* as they
were called in the north of France and the *trouvères* as they were called in the
south. Both names imply "inventing" or "finding." The troubadours and
trouvères were courtly poet-musicians whose creations were conceived under the
influence of the Age of Chivalry. The names of 460 troubadours and about 200
trouvères have come down to us.

The earlier troubadours were members of the upper classes and included a few
kings in their number. They did not perform their works, but entrusted them
to assistants of a much lower social status, called *jongleurs*. The jongleurs were
skilled musicians who through their wide travels were important factors in the
dissemination of the troubadour music.

Many troubadour and trouvère melodies have been preserved. Inasmuch as the
notation employed is somewhat unspecific, transcribing them into modern notation raises important rhythmic questions. Various pictorial representations furnish
conclusive proof that the troubadour and trouvère songs were performed to some
sort of instrumental accompaniment. None of this instrumental accompaniment,
however, was written down, so we may assume it was extemporized by the singer.

An important aspect of troubadour and trouvère music is its emphasis on
formal balance in a musical composition. Many of the songs consist of orderly
sequences of couplets and refrains, the audience often joining in singing the
refrain. Some of the patterns are exact forecasts of vocal and instrumental forms
of eighteenth- and nineteenth-century music. Dance rhythms are prominent and
impart a new freshness to the music. The melodies, while not entirely abandoning

the modes of plain chant, exhibit a decided preference for the major and minor scales of modern music.

Adam de la Hale (c. 1220-1287), a trouvère active at Arras, was the composer of the best-known musical work of the school—*Le jeu de Robin et de Marion,* a pastoral drama written· for the French court at Naples and presented for the first time in 1285. The music consists of fifteen dance songs of considerable charm.

The *Minnesinger* (German: *Minne,* love) were the German counterpart of the troubadours and trouvères. Richard Wagner based a romantic opera on incidents˙in the life of a well-known minnesinger, Tannhäuser (1205-1270). Two famous minnesingers, Walther von der Vogelweide (c. 1170-1230) and Wolfram von Eschenbach (fl. c. 1200-1220), also appear in this work. The minnesingers used no jongleurs and always sang their own compositions. Their music lacked the freshness and spontaneity present in the work of their French contemporaries.

SELECTED READINGS

Adams, Henry, *Mont-Saint-Michel and Chartres,* Anchor Books, 1959.

Baldwin, C. S., *Medieval Rhetoric and Poetic,* Peter Smith, 1959.

———*Three Medieval Centuries of Literature in England,* Little, Brown, 1932.

Chambers, E. K., *Arthur of Britain,* Sidgwick, 1927.

———*The Medieval Stage,* Oxford Press, 1903.

Dent, E. J., "Social Aspects of Music in the Middle Ages," *Oxford History of Music,* Oxford University Press, 1929, Introductory Vol.

Duncan, Edmonstoune, *The Story of Minstrelsy,* Scribner, 1907.

Gardner, Arthur, *French Sculpture of the Thirteenth Century,* Stokes, 1915.

Guerber, H. A., *Myths and Legends of the Middle Ages,* Harrap, 1926.

——— *The Book of the Epic,* Lippincott, 1913.

Hammett, R. W., *Romanesque Architecture of Western Europe,* Architectural Book Publishing Co., 1927.

Harrison, F. L., *Music in Medieval Britain,* Dover Publications, Inc., 1958.

Hauser, Arnold, *The Social History of Art,* Knopf, 1951.

Hughes, *New Oxford History of Music.*

Jackson, Sir T. G., *Gothic Architecture in France, England and Italy,* University of Chicago Press, 1915.

Ker, W. P., *Epic and Romance,* Dover Publications, Inc., 1957.

——— *English Literature: Medieval,* Oxford University Press.

Lang, *Music in Western Civilization.*

Lewis, C. S., *The Allegory of Love,* Oxford Press, 1936.

Mâle, Emile, *Religious Art in France, XIII Century,* Peter Smith, 1958.

Myers, B. S., *Art and Civilization,* McGraw-Hill, 1957.

Rindge, A. M., *Sculpture,* Harcourt, Brace, 1929.

Rosenberg, M. V., *Eleanor of Aquitaine,* Houghton Mifflin, 1937.

Schlauch, M., *Romance in Iceland,* Princeton University Press, 1934.

Thompson, *The Medieval Library.*

Toynbee, Paget, *Dante Alighieri, His Life and Work,* Macmillan, 1910.

Waddell, Helen, *The Wandering Scholars,* Anchor Books.

Wagner, A. R., *Heralds and Heraldry in the Middle Ages,* Oxford Press, 1956.

Williams, Michael, *The Book of Christian Classics,* Liveright, 1933.

XI

*The Decline
of Medievalism
from Roger Bacon
to Petrarch*

I. THE HISTORICAL BACKGROUND

In this chapter we shall deal with developments in European thought and culture from the height of scholasticism to the rising classical enthusiasms of the fifteenth century. Since Roger Bacon may well be taken as the sort of figure logically to introduce this era, it may be fitting to terminate the chapter with the movement to which Petrarch (1304-1374) gave so much added stimulus, namely, an increased interest in the literary and social values of classical antiquity. This so-called revival, which was more an impetus to the already increasing cultivation of the classics than a sudden reawakening, is generally known in the historical writing of our day as humanism.

Since Petrarch was an early member of the neoclassical school, we shall naturally mention historical figures and historical developments somewhat later than his specific lifetime. Yet, if one were to select two outstanding personalities whose interests may be said to characterize the earlier and the later stages of the trends discussed in this chapter, it is doubtful that a better selection could be made than Bacon and Petrarch.

The period which carried Europe from scholasticism to humanism, once regarded as arid and sterile, is now looked upon as one of the great turning-points in intellectual history. It marked the actual transition from medievalism to the modern age. Many of the intellectual and cultural developments once associated exclusively with early modern times had their roots in this transitional period. The older conception of a sudden classical "renaissance" in the fifteenth century, and of an almost precipitate development of natural science between 1550 and 1700, has been supplanted by a more truly historical perspective which stresses the continuity of cultural development between the late twelfth and the fifteenth centuries.

The most important single factor in the institutional background of the decline of the medieval system was the growth of towns, of trade, and of an urban middle class.

In the preceding chapter we have shown how the rise of towns promoted medieval culture, and fostered an intellectual revival. Later developments in town life played a leading rôle in bringing medievalism to an end.

A potent factor in urban growth and prosperity was commerce. The crusades brought the West into closer relations with the Near East. New trading possibilities were recognized and exploited. In the thirteenth and fourteenth centuries Europeans traveled in China, Japan, and India and brought back reports of the great riches there to be tapped. Commercial relations developed and not only fostered the growth of towns but led straight to the discovery of America and the origins of the modern age.

Well-known travelers to the far Orient were John of Piano Carpini, William of Rubruquis, John of Monte Corvino, Jordanus, and Oderic of Pordenone. Most famous of all was Marco Polo (1254-1324), whose *Travels* enjoyed a wide popularity and enormously increased European interest in the Far East. As Eileen Power says: "It is almost impossible to speak too highly either of the extent of his observation or of its accuracy."

First to profit from the revival of trade were the Italian coastal cities, Venice, Genoa, Amalfi, and Pisa. But even inland cities, such as Milan and Verona, also gained therefrom. While Florence did not garner much Eastern trade, except as a retailer, other factors made the city on the Arno wealthy and influential. Her wool-manufacturing was famous, and after the great commercial revival, Florence became the banker of Italy, enjoying the actual financial preëminence sometimes assigned to the Lombards. On the whole, the period from Marco Polo to Columbus was the commercial golden age of Italian cities. They retained this commerce to a large extent for some years after the great Genoese explorer had crossed the Atlantic.

Northern cities leagued together in mercantile associations known as *hanses,* most important of which were the Flemish or London *hanse* and the Hanseatic League of north-German cities founded in the thirteenth century. The latter gained control of German trade in Baltic, Russian, and English regions, maintained an army and navy, and waged successful wars against secular states. Jealousy of Italian monopoly of Eastern trade on the part of the national states on the Atlantic seaboard of western Europe supplied the dynamic impulse to discover an all-water route to the East, eventuating in the maritime exploits of Columbus, Vasco da Gama, and Magellan.

The increasing number, size and prestige of commercial cities naturally enlarged the urban middle class and extended its influence in all phases of late medieval life. Merchant princes and bankers demanded representation not only in cities but also in the national government. This necessitated the establishment of a branch of the legislature which would represent the middle class. The third estate thus made its way into politics.

The bourgeoisie promoted the growth of nationalism. This class had a deep and abiding grievance against the feudal lords who laid heavy burdens on merchants in medieval trading operations. Therefore it lined up, for the most part, with sovereigns who endeavored to suppress feudal anarchy and centralize government. From the middle class came most of the lawyers who defended the royal prerogative and the officials who served as royal administrators. This urban aristocracy patronized the revival of letters and art which accompanied the passing of the medieval age. The increasing secularism and worldliness of urban business life helped on this tendency.

At the close of the Middle Ages the peasantry also became restless, partly because of the decay of the manorial system. Bad economic conditions and an attempt to curtail their freedom to work for wages fomented revolutions. The revolt in France, the *Jacquerie* of 1358, was brutally suppressed. The peasant revolt of 1381 in England was also unsuccessful. In Germany, owing to retarded agrarian development, peasant revolts did not occur until 1524-1525. All these uprisings attest to the disruption of the medieval agrarian economy.

The emergence of strong national monarchies may be ranked next to the expansion of town life among the institutional factors hastening the decay of medievalism. Feudalism was doomed. The ablest of Plantagenet kings, Henry II (1154-1189), strengthened the English monarchy, including royal control over the courts and the army. Edward I (1274-1307) solidified this control and permitted middle-class representation in the Model Parliament of 1295. In France, Philip Augustus (1180-1223) curbed the feudal lords, centralized the administration, and increased the authority of the king's court. St. Louis (1235-1270) not only greatly extended the scope of royal justice but also brought the French towns under royal control. Finally, Philip the Fair (1285-1314) became the first European monarch who successfully defied the Roman Catholic church. After Philip's victory over Pope Boniface VIII (1294-1303) the papacy could never again safely challenge the power of a French king.

Specially difficult local conditions in Germany, together with the intervention of German emperors in Italian politics, retarded the solidification of the monarchy. Not until the rise of Prussia in the seventeenth century was there created a power which ultimately was able to unify the German states.

Finally, we may notice the decline of the most impressive political organization of the Middle Ages, the Roman Catholic church. In the first quarter of the thirteenth century Pope Innocent III dramatically demonstrated his preëminence over the kings of England, France, and Sicily, and over the Holy Roman emperor. His representative openly insulted King John of England by absolving his subjects from obedience in the very presence of the king. Just about one hundred years later, Nogaret, an agent of the French king, Philip IV, arrogantly defied Pope Boniface, and may even have assaulted him. This act symbolized the declining power of the papacy. What undermined the most powerful international state in human history down to that time?

No one, perhaps, has better summarized this process than A. C. Flick in his *The Decline of the Medieval Church*. He divides the causes into two types, negative and positive. The negative causes were: (1) The revolt against the temporal pretensions of the pope; (2) the insistence of the pope upon the exclusive right of ecclesiastical appointment; (3) the exemption of the clergy from secular courts and laws; (4) the papal determination to exempt church property from taxation; (5) the political applications of papal power and papal intrusion into secular politics; (6) the venality and corruption of papal administration; (7) the immorality and degradation of the clergy; (8) the purely formal nature of much religious ritual; and (9) the failure of the church to keep pace with cultural and intellectual changes.

The positive causes of ecclesiastical decline were: (1) The rise of intellectual independence and a spirit of skeptical inquiry; (2) the triumph of nationalism and of nationalistic political theory over medieval theocratic unity; (3) the popularity of Roman law and the resulting theory of secular absolutism, and the omnipotence of the civil state; (4) the intellectual effects of printing, which, after some delay, disseminated a knowledge of ancient philosophy and modern science; and (5) economic and social transformations, such as the rise of towns and trade, the expansion of Europe, the growth of capitalism, the development of the middle class, the decline of the manor, and the restlessness of the peasantry.

We may look into some of these causes a little more thoroughly. There was a remarkable multiplication of heresies. In the earlier Middle Ages, the church had been able to suppress these heresies, but the later struggle with heterodoxy was fatal to its prestige and unity.

The first important medieval heresy was that of the Cathari and Albigenses of northern Italy and southern France. The latter were a cultivated and inoffensive group, who followed in a general way the Manichaean heresy of the early church. They were protected by the counts of Toulouse and created the finest culture in western Europe outside of Muslim Spain. Innocent III preached a crusade against them and a Christian army led by Simon de Montfort wiped them out.

More serious was the Waldensian revolt led by Peter Waldo after 1170. The Waldensians desired to return to primitive Christianity and to take the Bible as their guide. They were excommunicated in 1184. Many were killed in the crusade against the Albigenses.

The next uprising was led by John Wycliffe (1320-1384), an English scholar who attacked not only the abuses of the church but the whole system of priestly mediation. He was condemned by the pope but was protected by a powerful patron and died before he could be harmed. At the Council of Constance in 1414 his body was ordered burned, and his ashes scattered. An even more ominous heretic was John Huss (1369-1415), who attacked the church in terms almost identical with the assault of Martin Luther in the sixteenth century. Huss was brought before the Council of Constance, condemned, and, in spite of a promise of safe-conduct, burned at the stake. Down through the age of Huss, the church thus successfully coped with heretics. When the Hussite doctrines were later revived by Martin Luther, the church split wide open.

Mysticism, which we have already briefly mentioned, also challenged ecclesiastical power. Mysticism, through its emphasis on the individual and personal elements in religious experience, denied the need of an elaborate hierarchy of priestly mediators to assure salvation. It was harder for the church to suppress mysticism than heresy, for the mystics did not challenge the church power directly. They, as it were, bored from within. Moreover, most mystics were notable for their devout and pious lives and their profound religious experience. Nevertheless, mysticism was a powerful theological forerunner of the Protestant revolt. It suggested the Protestant doctrine that the believer could worship God directly without clerical agency.

Belief in the superfluity of priestly mediation was also emphasized by a leading political theorist of the period, Marsiglio of Padua (1270-1342). He challenged the assumption of ecclesiastics that they held in their hands the keys to heaven and hell. We shall have more to say about Marsiglio later.

In the late fourteenth and fifteenth centuries an active schism rent the church in twain. In 1305, Philip the Fair induced the pope to move from Rome to Avignon, which remained the seat of the papacy until 1377 —the period of the so-called Babylonian captivity. After the return to Rome in 1377, confusion ensued and soon the great schism developed. There were two colleges of cardinals and two men who claimed the office of pope (the vicegerent of God on earth)—a highly disconcerting situation for one supposed to be chosen through the direct guidance of the Holy Ghost. Indeed, at the Council of Pisa in 1409, there were three contenders for the papacy.

In due time, the schism was healed, but the church never regained its prestige after this undignified squabble. The period embraced by the schism is generally known as the age of church councils—the conciliar movement of the fifteenth century. The major councils met between 1409 and 1439 at Pisa, Constance, Ferrara, and Florence.

The great riches of the church invited venality, corruption, and greed. There was graft in financial administration. Lavish expenditures forced the church to levy heavy taxes, which were resented by kings, feudal lords, and the middle class alike. Among all the causes of the Protestant revolt, probably the most potent was the desire to escape from financial exploitation. Hence, the Protestant revolt was, in one sense, primarily a nationalistic secession from the great international ecclesiastical state. Only in this way could exemption from papal levies be secured.

Finally, at the close of the Middle Ages, the papal hierarchy frequently became very worldly. Its devotion to art, letters, and mundane pleasures may have been a boon to secular culture, but was unbecoming to an organization designed to uphold and advance the City of God and hold in subjection the City of the Devil.

Many churchmen were not unaware of these dangers and several reform movements arose. The Cluniacs of the eleventh century, among whom was Hildebrand (later Pope Gregory VII), attempted to free the church from secular interference, increase papal power and eliminate financial corruption. The simple clerical life eagerly recommended by the Carthusian and Cistercian monks in the eleventh and twelfth centuries met with indifferent success.

Next in time were the reforms sponsored by the new mendicant orders, the Franciscans and the Dominicans, founded respectively by the great mystic, Francis of Assisi (1182-1226), and by Dominic of Guzman (1170-1221). The friars traveled about, in contradistinction to monks who resided in monasteries. The Franciscans advocated the alleviation of human suffering through social service and the preaching of personal regeneration. The Dominicans were devoted to scholarship, pedagogy, and preaching the orthodox faith. The two great scholastics, Albertus Magnus and Thomas Aquinas, were Dominicans.

These reform movements doubtless lessened abuses, and to some extent rehabilitated the church. But they failed to go deeply enough or to last long enough to prevent the coming of Protestantism and the bifurcation of the church.

The institutional basis of medievalism, namely, a dominant agricultural economy, feudal politics, and an omnipotent church, was thus sharply and effectively challenged in the period between Roger Bacon and the rise of Italian humanism.

II. DEVELOPMENTS IN THOUGHT AND PHILOSOPHY DURING THE LATER MIDDLE AGES

1. *The Eclipse of Scholasticism*

We have seen that well-rounded scholasticism, as represented by the *Summa* of Thomas Aquinas, was the characteristic philosophy of the mature Middle Ages. In an intellectual sense, it was, indeed, the "medieval synthesis"—a synthesis of Aristotle and the church fathers, with some admixture of Muslim and Hebrew learning. In the three centuries following Aquinas certain developments in European thought helped to undermine scholasticism, in spite of the fact that it was tenaciously cherished in orthodox intellectual circles.

In the first place, scholasticism wore itself out. With Aquinas, it was a fresh and daring effort to demonstrate fundamental truths. In the later Middle Ages it became an end in itself, disputation for the sake of disputation. The passage we quoted above from Professor Workman illustrates the artificial, involved and ingrown methods of later scholasticism.[1]

The debilitating process began with Duns Scotus. While his acute exposure of scholastic errors was helpful, his tortuous reasoning initiated a revulsion against scholasticism. Erasmus expressed this attitude when he said that reading Duns only made him angry and annoyed, while Cicero soothed his mind. As scholasticism degenerated, it lost Duns's astuteness and became even more involved and repulsive, terminating in arid mental gymnastics. The tough-minded turned to the nominalism of Ockham or the naturalism and experimentalism of Roger Bacon. The tender-minded gravitated toward mysticism, which became more popular as the Middle Ages drifted into modern times.

Nominalism, as revived in the later Middle Ages by William Durand of Saint-Pourçain, William of Ockham, Bacon, Jean Buridan, Pierre d'Ailly and Albert

[1] See above, p. 424.

of Saxony, strengthened critical and scientific thinking by directing men's minds away from universals in the direction of particulars. This movement was encouraged by the experimental method of Roger Bacon and his followers.

Less in line with modern tendencies was mysticism, which, nevertheless, was inimical to natural theology and scholasticism. The mystics cared less for Aristotle than for Plato and Neoplatonism, and while they wandered in an abysmal mental fog, they lessened Aristotle's hold on the human mind, something which was necessary if natural science was to progress. This does not mean that Aristotle could not encourage science and rationalism. His logic, scientific observations and eulogy of reason were the very breath of the modern spirit. But Aristotle in the hands of the medieval theologian was quite different from the original Hellenic Aristotle—a fact later emphasized by George of Trebizond, Theodore Gaza and Pietro Pomponazzi. This medievalized Aristotle had to be destroyed, and mysticism helped to weaken his influence.

2. Roger Bacon and Experimentalism

If Aquinas was the major figure in medieval thought, Roger Bacon (1214-1294) was the oustanding personality in the transition from medieval to modern thinking. Few persons so completely embodied the old and the new in the philosophy of any era. He was at once a scholastic theologian and the prophet of a scientific age.

Bacon assailed the attempt to arrive at religious truth by disputations on Peter Lombard's *Book of Sentences;* bitterly criticized the existing texts of Aristotle; pronounced magic a delusion; denounced reliance on authority and clearly stated and eloquently extolled experimentation and induction; and was himself a mathematician, a scientist, and a pioneer in philology and textual criticism. Such were his foreshadowings of modernism.

On the other hand, Bacon was a clergyman writing for clergymen, whose main desire was to elevate religion and the church. His criticism of Aristotle was designed chiefly to procure better texts so that a more fool-proof scholastic dogmatism could be constructed. He was a firm believer in astrology, and astrological medicine, and desired to promote science and the experimental method in order to solve religious problems, such as biblical science, history, and geography. He enthusiastically proclaimed theology queen of the sciences and was far more interested in salvation than in the future of airplanes. His linguistic scholarship was devoted to seeking a more accurate biblical text so that its authority over the mind of man might be the more complete. In these ways he was a man of his time, a pure medievalist.

We have already referred to the intellectual background of Bacon, an Oxford Franciscan inspired by the eminent mathematician and classicist, Robert of Grosseteste, chancellor of Oxford and bishop of Lincoln. Robert had protested against the neglect of natural science. Bacon carried his protest further.

It is only by a lucky accident that we know much of Bacon's philosophical system. Guy de Foulques, a jurist and statesman, became interested in Bacon's work while in Paris, and asked him to compose a statement of his doctrines. In

1265 Guy was made Pope Clement IV, and in June, 1266, he again requested of Bacon an exposition of his system of thought. Bacon's reply consisted of three books, the *Opus majus,* an introductory statement of his views, the *Opus minus,* a supplementary work, and the *Opus tertium,* a loosely written compendium, sent in hope of sustaining Clement's interest. From these and lesser works our knowledge of Bacon's views is derived.

Bacon's chief significance in the history of philosophy is that he was the first man in western Europe clearly to understand and expound the method which lies at the basis of modern science, namely, induction and experimentation. Aristotle had elucidated the inductive method in his day. But in Bacon's time Aristotle had become identified with scholastic deduction.

Many predecessors of Bacon, as we have seen, practiced the experimental method in at least a crude way. Some of the most touching passages in Bacon's writings embody his praise of contemporaries he regarded as admirable exponents of the experimental method. But Bacon was the first to deal with induction in the abstract, and to discourse upon its incalculable consequences. A vast gulf separated his *Opus majus* from the casual declaration of Albertus Magnus that, in order to promote science, attention should be diverted from universals to particulars. As Dr. Bridges, one of Bacon's editors, says:

> No one before Bacon had abstracted the method of experiment from the concrete problem, and had seen its bearing and importance as a universal method of research. Implicitly men of science had begun to recognize the value of experiment. What Bacon did was to make the recognition explicit. Experiment took its place as a distinct department of philosophy.

Charles Singer drives home the same point: "He attempted to set forth a system of natural knowledge far in advance of his time. The basis of that system was observation and experiment. He was clearly the first man in modern Europe of whom this can be said." It may be true, of course, that if some of Bacon's contemporaries had been similarly commanded to write out their theoretical views their position in intellectual history might have rivaled Bacon's.

Bacon was well aware of the opposition to the inductive method. His reasons for intellectual stagnation and the persistence of erroneous beliefs are very significant, and the four fundamental causes of error and ignorance he enumerates may be compared with Francis Bacon's four idols [2]—of the cave, the tribe, the market place, and the theater:

> There are four principal stumbling blocks . . . to comprehending truth, which hinder well-nigh every scholar: the example of frail and unworthy authority, long-established custom, the sense of the ignorant crowd . . . and the hiding of one's own ignorance under the pretense of wisdom. In these, every man is involved and every state beset. For in every act of life, or business, or study, these three worst arguments are used for the same conclusion: this was the way of our ancestors, this is the custom, this is the common view: therefore it should be held. But the

[2] See below, pp. 718-20.

opposite of this conclusion follows much better from the premises, as I will prove through authority, experience and reason.

If these three are sometimes refuted by the glorious power of reason, the fourth is already ready, as a gloss for foolishness; so that, though a man know nothing of any value, he will impudently magnify it, and thus, soothing his wretched folly, defeat truth. From these deadly pests come all the evils of the human race; for the noblest and most useful documents of wisdom are ignored, and the secrets of the arts and sciences. Worse than this, men blinded by the darkness of these four do not see their ignorance, but take every care to palliate that for which they do not find the remedy; and what is the worst, when they are in the densest shades of error, they deem themselves in the full light of truth.

But Bacon's faith in the efficacy of experimentation was unshaken: "Of the three ways in which men think that they acquire a knowledge of things, authority, reasoning and experiment, only the last is effective and able to bring peace to the intellect." In the following passage he eloquently proclaimed the superiority of scientific experimentation to scholastic argumentation:

> There are two modes in which we acquire knowledge, argument and experiment. Argument shuts up the question, and makes us shut it up too; but it gives no proof, nor does it remove doubt, and cause the mind to rest in the conscious possession of truth, unless the truth is discovered by way of experience; for example, if any man who had never seen fire were to prove by satisfactory argument that fire burns and destroys things, the hearer's mind would not rest satisfied, nor would he avoid fire; until by putting his hand or some combustible thing into it, he proved the fact. But after actual experiment had been made, his mind receives certainty and rests in the possession of truth that could not be given by argument but only by experience.

In estimating Baconian thought one must set over against his eulogy of induction the fact that he hoped to apply its results to buttress the supernatural. The improvements he called for in science and scholarship were to be used primarily for holy purposes—to clarify scriptural geography, locate heaven and hell more exactly, get the measurements of the ark, the tabernacle, and the temple, and help combat the Antichrist.

Nevertheless, Bacon's modernism influenced later ages. Propagators of the scientific attitude overlooked the antique elements in Bacon's thought and proclaimed him the unique scientific genius of the Middle Ages—a man who turned his back resolutely on the old theological system. We now know, partly as a result of the work of Professor Lynn Thorndike, that Bacon also clung strenuously to supernaturalism. But we also know that he encouraged an intellectual movement which revolutionized civilization.

Bacon not only wrote eloquently about experimental science, he became one of the epochal figures in medieval research. In this way he differed from his namesake, Francis Bacon, three centuries later, who wrote even more charmingly on behalf of the inductive method, but was a pitiful failure as an experimentalist. Indeed, he ignored or ridiculed most of the notable scientific work of his day.

The old legend that Roger Bacon was long imprisoned by the church because he eulogized experimentalism has passed into limbo along with the idea of his solitary grandeur as a medieval scientist. However, that Bacon may have been condemned and briefly imprisoned for some reason is not improbable.

3. The Revival of Nominalism

The rehabilitation and development of nominalism in the later Middle Ages, as we have noted, helped to destroy scholasticism. Even with a devout Christian like William of Ockham, nominalism was antagonistic to scholasticism. Ockham showed that religion cannot be substantiated by logical demonstration. It must be accepted on faith, authority, and revelation. In other words, nominalism challenged the scholastic effort to bolster theology with reason and logic. This was the position of men like Ockham. If a nominalist were not so devout he might go farther and admit that nominalism meant the abandonment of many basic and crucial religious dogmas.

Although Ockham denied the efficacy of logic in religious thought, he insisted upon the fullest support of secular knowledge by clear thinking and careful reasoning. He was interested in particulars and in sense perceptions through which alone particulars can be recognized. This eventually led to the empiricism of John Locke, the philosophy of the modern scientific revival. Indeed, Ockham directly stimulated scientific research. Disciples like Albert of Saxony, who made experiments in physics and astronomy, and Jean Buridan and the Paris Ockhamites, heralded the scientific spirit. The challenge to the medieval system offered by nominalism is expressed as follows by Professor Cushman:

> Nominalism, as the church fathers say, would be absolutely fatal to Church authority. It was the antithesis of realism. It turned man away from the affairs of the spirit. It incited him to modify the realism of dogma. It pointed out the importance of practical experience. It emphasized individual opinion, neglected tradition, and placed its hope on the possibilities of science rather than in the spiritual actualities of religion.[3]

If nominalism regarded science as a vital phase of intellectual activity, it also paved the way for the German idealism of the eighteenth and nineteenth centuries, which took God and religion on faith.[4]

Nominalism, in many antipapal writers of the conciliar movement of the fifteenth century, also influenced political theory. It fitted well with the doctrine that the legal reality in Christendom resides in the communicants and in their representatives assembled in the council.

4. Mysticism and Heresy

Mysticism also challenged medievalism in its tendency to depreciate the potency of logic and reason in demonstrating religious realities, which mystics believed a matter of emotional experience rather than reason. Mysticism also threatened the ecclesiastical hierarchy by emphasizing the personal and intimate character of religious experience, requiring no priestly intervention.

---

[3] Cushman, *A Beginner's History of Philosophy*, II, 6.   [4] See below, pp. 845 ff.

In addition to the mystics mentioned in the preceding chapter, we might call attention to the Brethren of the Common Life founded at Deventer in the Netherlands by Geert van Groot (1340-1384), under whose auspices Thomas à Kempis wrote his *Imitation of Christ*. Mysticism, as taught by Johann Staupitz, exerted a strong influence on Martin Luther's early religious development.

Mysticism, which was mainly Neoplatonism in devout Western garb, also paved the way for the revival of Plato and Neoplatonism by such men as Marsilius Ficinus and Cardinal Bessarion. With similar gusto the humanists of the fifteenth and sixteenth centuries welcomed the weird and fantastic mysticism of the Jewish cabala which was shot through with Platonism and Neoplatonism.[5] Christian and Neoplatonic mysticism tended to undermine Aristotle, even if it all too often replaced him with far less dignified and substantial intellectual baggage.

An important thinker who combined Christian and pagan mysticism was the diplomat, jurist and churchman, Nicholas of Cues (1401-1464), frequently known as Cusanus. His most important philosophical work was *Learned Ignorance* (*Docta ignorantia*), a masterpiece of mystical skepticism, elaborating the theme of the basic ignorance of even the most learned and stressing the doctrine that nothing is fixed or centered save in God. He emphasized the limitations of human knowledge and showed that we cannot expect to attain absolute truth. At best, we can only entertain assumptions and conjectures. We cannot know God through reason, for God is infinite and our minds are finite. Nicholas solved the problem of bringing man into contact with God by advancing the mystical theory of the union of all contrarieties in God and by a revival of the medieval analogy of the macrocosm and microcosm: "The microcosm, man, is constituted as the macrocosm. The union between matter and the World-soul is reproduced in the union between the human body and the human soul. The life of man on earth hangs on the mutual drawing together and realization of the two in this union."[6] Cusanus' mystical pantheism considerably influenced the philosophy of Giordano Bruno. Cusanus also contributed to the political theory of the conciliar movement. However, the exaggerated claims often made for his knowledge of physics and astronomy are largely unfounded, as we shall see later on.

The religious heresies of the period also combated scholasticism and ecclesiastical absolutism. The efforts to go directly to the Bible as the source of religious inspiration and guidance tended to discredit Thomism and the great body of scholastic commentaries, to say nothing of commentaries on the commentaries. Emphasis on the personal and individual character of worship struck a blow, as we have seen, at the ecclesiastical hierarchy and at priestly mediation.

III. EDUCATION IN THE LATER MIDDLE AGES

Medieval universities gave instruction in scholasticism, which employed Aristotle and other secular learning to buttress theology. In the professional and graduate schools, theology, law and medicine were also taught by the scholastic method of

---

[5] See below, p. 553.
[6] H. O. Taylor, *Thought and Expression in the Sixteenth Century*, 2 vols., Macmillan, 1920, II, 288.

lectures, commentaries and disputations. Little attention was paid to the natural or social sciences, or to history and literature.

At the height of the Middle Ages the Dominican order came into being and took a leading part in developing scholasticism in the universities. We have noted that Albert and Thomas were members of that order. The universities were only slightly affected by the classical revival of the later Middle Ages. The historian, then, has little new to report regarding university education in the fourteenth and fifteenth centuries, save for the more thorough study of medicine and surgery, especially at Italian universities.

There was, however, an educational revolution in the secondary schools, namely, the introduction of the humanities. At first, this meant an interest in the educational philosophy and curriculum of the Greeks and Romans. Later generations, unfortunately, stereotyped it into sterile instruction in classical grammar and literary texts.

The humanistic revival in education is associated chiefly with Paulus Vergerius (1349-1420), Vittorino da Feltre (1378-1446), Guarino da Verona (1370-1460), his son Battista Guarino, and the scholars and teachers of the Brethren of the Common Life.

It was in the work of such teachers that education switched from a primary absorption with theology and with the incidental exploitation of the seven liberal arts to a deep interest in the so-called *humanities*. The latter, in the beginning, were understood to be the intellectual equipment of a civilized man, as viewed by the most cultivated minds of Greece and Rome. The term had been used by Aulus Gellius in his *Attic Nights* to describe Cicero's conception of a civilized education.[7] The humanities embodied the literature, philosophy, culture and rhetoric of classical civilization. Christianity was not lost sight of, but education was designed to prepare man for social and political life as well as for salvation in the world to come. In short, the ideal was the training of a perfect Christian citizen.

> We call those studies liberal [says Paulus Vergerius] which are worthy of a free man; those studies by which we attain and practice virtue and wisdom; that education which calls forth, trains, and develops those highest gifts of body and of mind which ennoble men and which are rightly judged to rank next in dignity to virtue only. . . . For the vulgar temper, gain and pleasure are the one aim of existence; to a lofty nature, moral worth and fame.[8]

The new educational program not only took into account social responsibilities but also the development of individuality. Commenting on its well-rounded objectives, Professor Monroe says: "This education aimed at the development of the *free* man possessing individuality of his own, and power of efficient participation in everyday life, based on a wide knowledge of life in the past and an appreciation of opportunities of life in the present."[9]

This new curriculum made some use of the seven liberal arts, but put more

[7] *Op. cit.*, XIII, 17.
[8] Monroe, *Textbook in the History of Education*, pp. 365-66.
[9] *Ibid.*, pp. 369-70.

emphasis on physical education and especially on aesthetic subjects, which were virtually ignored in the universities. Rhetoric was restored to its classical position as a guide to, and appraisal of, the best in literary and oratorical styles. The study of literature for its aesthetic values was warmly recommended.

In his famous treatise, *De ordine docendi et studendi* (*A Program of Teaching and Study*), written in 1459, Battista Guarino wrote as follows of the breadth of the new curricular ideal: "Learning and training in virtue are peculiar to man: therefore, our forefathers called them 'Humanitas,' the pursuits, the activities, proper to mankind. And no branch of knowledge embraces so wide a range of subjects as that learning I have now attempted to describe." [10]

The foremost exemplar of this new humanistic education was Vittorino da Feltre, who was summoned by the Prince of Mantua to set up a school at his court in 1428, which came to be known as "The House Joyous," and represented, as Professor Monroe says, "the first thorough organization of the new learning for school purposes, as distinct from university lectures. The master here gave the Greek idea of a liberal education its first modern embodiment, and taught to the youth for the first time the literature, history, and civilization of the Romans instead of the mere form of their language." [11] Even physical training and personal hygiene, which had received due attention in classical education, were included. Vittorino was not only a curriculum innovator, he was a pioneer in pedagogy. As Professor W. H. Burnham remarks, his "main point was to appeal to the interest of the pupil and to adapt instruction to his individual talent." [12]

The classics or humanities, still the basis of our so-called liberal education, were in their origins, then, worthy of the name of liberal, an aim they soon lost. From the use of classical literature and philosophy as a preparation for life, the classical tradition degenerated into a stereotyped and dull cultivation of syntax and linguistics. In its first stages, this degeneration took the form of an obsession for mastering Ciceronian style. For instance, in the school (gymnasium) of Johannes Sturm (1507-1589) at Strassburg, according to Professor J. W. Adamson, a show was made of teaching the seven liberal arts, "but its lengthy course of study was very obviously devoted to one aim, the mastery of Ciceronian prose, and the Strasbourg Gymnasium became the model of Protestant Germany and of Northern Europe." [13]

The revival of the classics affected the education of the nobility. Mere courtesy and chivalry were no longer enough. To training in the use of arms was added instruction in classical literature. Vergerius wrote to a Paduan noble in 1392 concerning the education of his son: "So soon as he is able to use his limbs let him be trained to arms; so soon as he can rightly speak let him be trained to letters." This view of knightly education was embodied somewhat later in the great manuals on the training of nobility, Castiglione's *The Courtier* (1528), Elyot's *The Boke of the Governour* (1531), Peacham's *The Compleat Gentleman* (1622), and Brathwaite's *The English Gentleman* (1630).

[10] Cited in Monroe, *op. cit.*, p. 370.
[11] *Ibid.*, p. 376.
[12] W. H. Burnham, *Great Teachers and Mental Hygiene*, Appleton, 1926, p. 110.
[13] In C. G. Crump and E. F. Jacob, *The Legacy of the Middle Ages*, Clarendon Press, 1932, p. 284.

The growth of secondary education, especially in the towns, neglected for the most part in the earlier Middle Ages, made this period remarkable in educational history. Emphasis was laid on rudimentary education and on the practical or commercial subjects. There also arose the so-called chantry schools, well endowed by the church, and providing elementary instruction for children of the parish. The merchant and craft guilds often established schools in the towns devoted to the "3 R's," and to industrial and commercial subjects, but not providing, of course, craft training, which was handled through the apprenticeship system. Sometimes the guild schools became regular public town schools. Finally, there were the commercial or "abacus schools," providing the rudiments of instruction for a business career. In these town schools some see the origins of our elementary school. Professor Adamson writes:

> The origin of the elementary school as such is to be found in the demands made by commerce and industry for junior clerks and workmen who could read and write the *vernacular* and, in fewer instances, make out or at least understand a bill. Such schools, quite distinct from the grammar or song schools, grew up in the great industrial and commercial centers during the fourteenth century in Italy and Germany; they appeared in England in the following century, when the country was passing from an agricultural to an industrial and commercial status.[14]

The breach in the medieval system of education, then, consisted of a revolt against scholasticism and formal university instruction, and an abandonment of the seven liberal arts in favor of the humanities. Education for the masses improved, especially in towns, and training in vernacular languages and practical commercial subjects was stressed.

IV. MEDIEVAL SCIENCE FROM ROGER BACON TO COPERNICUS

1. *The True Origins of Modern Science*

In this section we shall deal with the most epochal progress in human thought since the origins of free-thinking among the Greeks. That movement which revolutionized human civilization in the last few centuries surely stemmed from the mathematical and scientific achievements between Bacon and Copernicus.

It was long customary to regard Roger Bacon as the only notable scientist between Archimedes and Galileo, and to discover the rise of modern science in the so-called Renaissance from Petrarch to Francis Bacon, that cultural "springtime" which produced the humanist revival of classical literature and a remarkable efflorescence of art. We have since discovered that there was no Renaissance, as formerly understood, and, hence, that natural science could not have been one of its by-products.[15]

In our day scholars, chiefly natural scientists interested in the history of their subject, imagined a great scientific revival in the late sixteenth and seventeenth centuries, most of it sudden and associated with events in England.

---

[14] Cited in Hearnshaw, *Medieval Contributions to Modern Civilization*, p. 207.
[15] See below, pp. 549-51, 557.

We know now that both conceptions of the rise of modern science are unhistorical. There was a steady development of mathematical and scientific knowledge from the days of Roger Bacon, and even earlier, to our own. If particularly impressive discoveries were made between 1550 and 1700, scientists from Roger Bacon to Copernicus had laid the basis for them.

Even historians have repeated the boasts of sixteenth- and seventeenth-century scientists about their own originality, in spite of the fact that all the discoveries of those centuries were continuous developments of earlier achievements. For instance, in the fourteenth and fifteenth centuries the law of falling bodies, the rotation and revolution of the earth, the principles of analytical geometry, and the basic ideas of calculus were anticipated. Modern anatomy and physiology were also created. In short, Copernicus, Galileo, and Descartes are directly connected with their predecessors, whose books, widely taught at the time, they had read.

These facts force the abandonment of the old over-simplified theory that centuries of "medieval superstition" were suddenly superseded by the discovery of "scientific truth." The late Middle Ages contained four major intellectual currents: the scholastic heritage, mysticism, humanism, and the impulse towards experimentalism and natural science. We have already had something to say of the first three. We shall now turn to the scientists.

2. *Muslim Science Gives European Science a New Impulse*

The science of the Muslims, who had preserved many Hellenic and Hellenistic discoveries and added a great deal of their own, was the most important single cause of the scientific revival. This Muslim science began to trickle into western Europe in the late twelfth century through the work of translators like Gerard of Cremona. Its effect was not completely felt until the thirteenth and following centuries, an effect which had repercussions in every branch of science. The chief points of contact between Latin Christendom and Muslim science were Spain and Sicily.

We have space here for a characterization of only a few representative Muslim scientists and scholars. The following is no mere pedantic listing of obscure names. These men are among the world's foremost scientists, and anyone who pretends to understand the history of Western civilization should be as familiar with al-Khwarizmi as with Napier, with al-Biruni as with Leibnitz, with al-Battani as with Copernicus, with al-Hazen as with Newton, with Gerber as with Paracelsus, with Idrisi as with Alexander von Humboldt, with Rhazes as with Hippocrates, and with Averroës as with Roger Bacon.

The Muslims derived their mathematics and astronomy chiefly from the Greeks, Hindus, and Chinese. This information they assimilated and transmitted to Christian Europe with revolutionary results. The Greeks had contributed to the Western World arithmetic, geometry, and some elementary trigonometry. The Muslims added Arabic numerals, algebra, and more advanced trigonometry. Thus, medieval Muslim mathematics was the basis of European mathematics, which in turn was essential to the remarkable scientific discoveries of the fourteenth century.

Arithmetic, the advances in which consisted chiefly in the introduction of

Hindu, or so-called Arabic, numerals, was cultivated by al-Khwarizmi (d. c. 850), who is believed to have invented the concept of zero, and is regarded as one of the ablest of Muslim mathematicians, and by al-Kindi, an eminent Muslim scientist and philosopher. The foremost Muslim students of algebra were al-Khwarizmi and the well-known Persian poet and philosopher, Omar Khayyám (d. 1124). The latter carried algebra beyond anything previously known of it. Progress in geometry was promoted by Thabit ibn Qurra (d. 901), who not only used Euclid but also copied Apollonius' work on conic sections. Nazir al-Din (d. 1274), an able student of geometry, was perhaps the greatest mathematical genius of the Muslims. The chief Muslim trigonometricians—we owe much of our trigonometry to the Muslims—were al-Battani (d. 929), Abu-l-wafa (d. 998), Ibn Yunus (d. 1009), and Nazir al-Din. The latter created spherical trigonometry. The whole range of Muslim mathematics was systematized and collected by al-Biruni (d. 1048).

The Muslims accepted the Ptolemaic system, amplifying it with some of Aristotle's theories. Perhaps the most important of their astronomical contributions were the construction of good observatories at Meraga, Baghdad, Damascus, and Cordova, and the manufacture of the best astronomical instruments—the astrolabe and quadrant—known before Tycho Brahe.[16] The Muslims calculated the precise latitude and longitude of their cities, an achievement almost unheard of in western Europe until the later Middle Ages. They also widened our knowledge of chronology and the calendar.

We may single out a few astronomers of outstanding significance. Al-Farghani (Alfraganus, d. 865) investigated celestial motions and the diameter and distances of the planets. Al-Battani, usually regarded as the greatest Muslim astronomer, was an indefatigable and accurate observer. His star catalogues were famous. Abu-l-Husian (d. 986) collected Muslim astronomical discoveries and systematized them in his *Book of the Fixed Stars*. Al-Biruni and Omar improved the calendar and historical chronology. The most comprehensive synthesis of Muslim astronomy was prepared and translated into Latin by the Jewish savant, Levi-ben-Gerson (1288-1344).

Accompanying their astronomical knowledge was a vast body of astrological beliefs. Indeed, the Muslims were the most prolific and indefatigable of astrologers. Heading the list were al-Kindi, Albumasar (d. 886), and Messahala (d. 815). The first Christian scholar to transmit this Muslim astrology was, apparently, Gerbert of Aurillac; the most prolific translator of Muslim astrology into Latin was John of Spain. Michael Scot wrote the standard Latin manual on the subject, the *Introduction to Astrology*.

In physics, the Muslims elaborated Greek achievements. Muslim translators preserved considerable Hellenistic mechanics. Thebit ben Corat (836-901) translated Archimedes, and Costa ben Luca translated the work of Hero about 865. Al-Biruni and Omar made original studies of the lever, pulley, the triangle of

---

[16] Al-Fazari is reputed to have constructed the first excellent astrolabe about 775. It was later improved by al-Zarkali (1029-1087) in Spain. The latter also edited the famous Toledo planetary tables, later widely used in Latin Europe.

forces, and specific gravity. In optics the chief figure was al-Hazen (Ibn al-Haitham, 965-1039), who, according to George Sarton, was "the greatest of Muslim physicists and one of the greatest students of optics of all times." Starting with the optical researches of Euclid and Ptolemy, al-Hazen left the Greek masters far behind. He worked with prisms, spherical and parabolic mirrors, and even studied atmospheric refraction. He greatly extended knowledge of lenses, the anatomy of the eye, and the character of vision. His work was translated into Latin and aided Roger Bacon and Witelo (Vitello), founders of the science of optics in the West. A later Persian physicist, Kamal ad-Din (d. 1320), went farther than al-Hazen in certain ways, especially in his use of the camera obscura and in studying the primary and secondary rainbows.

The Muslims systematized alchemy, that rudimentary chemistry which attempted to transmute the baser metals into gold and to discover the mysterious elixir which would prolong life. They started with the Hellenistic alchemy of the pseudo-Democritus and then carried the subject to the borders of scientific chemistry. The most renowned of Muslim alchemists was Jabir ibn Haiyan (Gerber, c. 775), greatly admired by the Christian alchemists of the Middle Ages. He tried to explain the geological formation of metals; suggested the sulphur-mercury theory, namely, that the six basic metals differ primarily because of a varying mixture of mercury and sulphur; prepared lead carbonate, arsenic, antimony, and certain acids; and devised preparations like dyes, varnishes, and chemicals to aid in glassmaking. A great advance appears in the work of Abu Bakr ar-Razi (Rhazes, d. 924), who was more of a rudimentary chemist than an alchemist. He devised elaborate chemical apparatus, worked out an extensive classification of chemical substances, especially minerals, and applied his chemical knowledge to medicine. Muslim alchemy was systematized by al-Kathi in his *Essence of the Art and Aid to Workers* (1034).

Muslim alchemy was thus by no means merely fanciful dreaming. Besides the drugs and chemicals already mentioned, the Muslims produced carbonate of soda, sal ammoniac, alum, copperas, borax, nitrate of silver, cream of tartar, and corrosive sublimate. In short, the work of Muslim alchemists was borrowed by Christian scientists and it permitted them to progress rapidly towards modern chemistry.

Few or no original contributions to zoölogy, biology, or botany were made by the Muslims, who rested content, for the most part, with debased Hellenistic and Hindu knowledge. They also fell into the habit, shared by medieval Christian writers, of compiling bestiaries and other books of wonders. For instance, al-Asmai of Basra (d. 828) produced a number of curious and interesting works, *On the Horse, On the Camel, On Wild Animals,* and *On Plants and Trees.* The Muslim historian, al-Tabari (838-923), wrote an encyclopedic *Paradise of Wisdom* which contained many anecdotes and observations dealing with zoölogy and embryology. Al-Jahiz (d. 869) compiled a discursive *Book of Animals,* full of theological interpretations. The *Book of Plants* by the encyclopedist and historian, al-Dinawari (d. 895), was more philological than biological, but contained, nevertheless, striking botanical generalizations. Far the most extensive of Muslim compilations of natural history was the *Zoölogical Lexicon* of al-Damiri (d. 1405), a work comparable to that of Bartholomew the Englishman.

In connection with biology, it is worth noting that much of the anatomical nomenclature of the late Middle Ages was of Muslim origin. When Mondino de Luzzi (1276-1326), the first great Western anatomist, groped for anatomical terms, he turned to the Arabic language to find them.

Muslim geographers made many original contributions to human knowledge. They were wide travelers, faithful observers, and relatively accurate reporters. Moreover, the large number of distinguished Muslim mathematicians and astronomers linked astronomy and geography and encouraged the scientific study of theoretical geography. Under the auspices of Caliph al-Ma'mun the mathematician al-Khwarizmi prepared a *Description of the World,* following, in general, the notions of Ptolemy. The first important descriptive geographer was al-Musudi (d. 957), who put down the scientific results of his wide travels in his *Meadows of Gold and Mines of Precious Stones.* The memoirs of the early Muslims who visited the Far East were edited by Abu Zaid about 920 in a book called *Information about India and China,* the most important work of its kind before Marco Polo. Accurate cartographers were al-Balkhi (d. 934), al-Istakhi (c. 950), and Ibn Hawqal (c. 975). In the latter part of the tenth century, al-Maqdisi visited nearly all the Muslim realms and wrote up his extensive observations in the *Best of Divisions for a Knowledge of the Climates* (986).

Al-Biruni was the first medieval scholar to measure latitude and longitude accurately and to explain geographical phenomena according to the laws of physics and mathematics. Al-Bakri of Cordova (d. 1094) was the leading Muslim geographer of the eleventh century. He wrote a voluminous descriptive work on Muslim realms, presented in the form of an itinerary, the *Book of Roads and Provinces.*

Probably the foremost of medieval geographers were Abu Abdullah Muhammed (Idrisi, 1099-1154) and Yakut (1175-1229). They made a real effort to systematize geographical knowledge and to deduce general principles. Idrisi seems to have been one of the first to show the significance of the fact that the earth is a sphere. On a globe representing the earth he located the chief climatic zones. Yakut compiled a voluminous and informative geographical dictionary. The most complete and precise description of the Muslim world was given by Abu-l-Fida (d. 1331). The most intrepid of explorers was Ibn Battuta (1304-1378), who covered more ground than Marco Polo.

Muslim achievements in medicine were considerable, if less original than in geography. They borrowed from Greek and Greco-Roman medicine, Hippocrates, Galen, and Dioscorides, and from the Persians and the Hindus. The leading translators and adapters of Greek medical books were Hunain ibn Ishaq (Johannitus) and Thabit ibn Qurra, already mentioned.

There were many important Muslim physicians. Ali-al-Tabari synthesized Greek and Hindu medicine in his *Paradise of Wisdom* (850). Rhazes, the greatest clinical physician of the Middle Ages, drew heavily on Galen but made many original observations. His encyclopedia, *The Comprehensive Book,* gave the first important description of treatment for smallpox, added to our knowledge of gynecology and obstetrics, discussed the surgery of the eye, and suggested many ways in which chemistry might aid medicine. Ali ibn Abbas (d. 994), who wrote the standard Muslim treatise on medicine before Avicenna's *Canon,* added important clinical observations, especially on the mechanics of childbirth.

The most influential Muslim physician and, next to Averroës, the most widely known of all Muslim scientists and philosophers, was Ibn Sina (Avicenna, 980-1037), who wrote a million-word encyclopedia, *The Canon,* summarizing all existing medical knowledge. His book was supreme among the Muslims, and competed with Galen in Western medical instruction.

The Spanish savant, Ibn Zuhr (Avenzoar, 1113-62), a great clinician, diagnosed cancer of the stomach, and prescribed antidotes for poisons. Ibn Khatima (d. 1369), also a Spaniard, discussed the ravages of the Black Death in one of the first important treatises on contagious diseases. Abu Mansur Muwaffak (c. 975) and Masawaih al-Mardini (d. 1015) extended existing knowledge of drugs and materia medica. Al-Mardini wrote a complete encyclopedia of pharmacy which, in Latin translation, was for centuries a standard textbook in the West.

The outstanding Muslim surgeon was Abu-l-Qasim (Abulcasis, d. 1013) of Cordova, who, among other things, described major operations and the chief surgical instruments of his time. He is regarded by many as the first surgeon to pay special attention to antisepsis. The diseases and surgery of the eye were carefully studied by Ali ibn-Isa (c. 1030).

In summarizing Muslim science we may say that it collected Greek and Hindu mathematics, and supplied the West with virtually all its knowledge of higher mathematics as then understood, namely, algebra, geometry, and trigonometry. This laid the foundation for European progress not only in mathematics but in physics and astronomy as well. At the same time, the Muslims enormously simplified elementary computation by the introduction of Arabic numerals.

They added considerably to Hellenistic astronomy, especially in mathematical calculations, compiled astronomical tables, widened stellar observation, created good observatories, and devised the first significant astronomical instruments.

In physics, they transmitted Hellenistic mechanics and optics, with some additions of their own. This work inspired European researches in optics which ultimately produced the lens, microscope, and telescope.

The Muslims carried alchemy to the very borders of chemistry, and hastened the creation of that science. Their geographical achievements, both descriptive and theoretical, particularly their knowledge of latitude and longitude and of climatic zones, surpassed all other medieval geography. The Muslims synthesized Hindu, Persian, and Byzantine medicine and surgery, made revolutionary discoveries of their own, and thus helped to launch European medicine at Salerno and elsewhere. On the whole, if modern science got its start in the period from 1250 to 1500, it received its fundamental impetus from the Muslims.

Perhaps no better conclusion to this section on Muslim science could be found than the observations of the Baron Carra de Vaux on the rôle of the Muslims in the history of culture:

The Arabs kept alive the higher intellectual life and the study of science in a period when the Christian West was fighting desperately with barbarism. The zenith of their activity may be placed in the ninth and tenth centuries, but it was continued down to the fifteenth. From the twelfth century everyone in the West who had any taste for science, some desire for light, turned to the East or to the Moorish West. At this period the works of the Arabs began to be translated as those of the Greeks had previously been by them. The Arabs thus formed a bond of union, a connecting link between ancient culture and modern civilization. When at the Renaissance the spirit of man was once again filled with the zeal for knowledge and stimulated by the spark of genius, if it was able to set promptly to work, to produce and to invent, it was because the Arabs had preserved and perfected various branches of knowledge, kept the spirit of research alive and eager and maintained it pliant and ready for future discoveries.[17]

3. Western European Science in the Later Middle Ages

In an earlier section, we noted that Roger Bacon not only advocated the experimental method but practiced it himself. Nevertheless, as Professor Thorndike has clearly shown, Bacon was a better expositor of the scientific method than an experimentalist. He made few if any discoveries of importance.

Bacon laid great stress upon mathematics as the foundation of natural science, but it seems that he was only echoing his teacher, Robert Grosseteste. He added little to our mathematical knowledge. His best work was pursued in optics, where he was able to make use of earlier Muslim achievements. He studied the reflection and refraction of light, particularly the rainbow. He used mirrors, lenses, and burning glasses. It is doubtful, however, if he added much to what had already been achieved by al-Hazen and Kamal ad-Din.

Bacon systematized existing optical knowledge and his work was used as a textbook for many years. There seems to be no basis for the theory current a few years ago that he wrote a manuscript in cipher describing the compound microscope. He compiled many astronomical tables and is said to have proposed a correction of the calendar. Here again, however, he seems to have followed Grosseteste. Bacon coördinated existing knowledge of alchemy, but did not, as some believed, invent gunpowder. In a famous letter on applied science he predicted the steamboat, automobile, submarine, airplane, mechanical crane, and the like.

Even more important than Bacon as a transmitter and elaborator of Muslim optics was the Polish scientist, Witelo (c. 1270). He was in fact more than a mere transmitter. He strongly recommended experimentation: "Experience more than books will teach the varied possibilities of images." His comments on experimental technique and the use of instruments are superior to Bacon's. Witelo was familiar with the usual mirrors, lenses, and burning glasses and attempted to place the science of optics on a definite geometrical basis. His work, *Perspective*, became a more popular text in optics than Bacon's. Professor Thorndike concludes that: "In general, he is believed by collecting the tradition of the past and filling in the gaps therein to have made the whole subject clearer to the Latin world and to have produced a work which served for several centuries as an excellent textbook

[17] In T. W. Arnold and Alfred Guillaume, ed., *The Legacy of Islam*, Oxford Press, 1931, p. 377.

in the field of optical science." [18] Along with Witelo we should mention the work on perspective and other optical problems by the Englishman, John Peckham (d. 1292), and by John of Paris (d. 1306) and Dietrich of Freiberg (c. 1250-c. 1310).

We may now consider some of the European scientific achievements of the fourteenth and fifteenth centuries, achievements which led to the scientific efflorescence of the seventeenth century and the industrial revolution of the eighteenth.

In arithmetic, most notable were the introduction of Arabic numerals, the use of decimals, the development of numeration, and the systematic organization of mathematics in general. The *Arithmetic* of Jehan Adams, composed in 1475, divided the subject into nine parts: numeration, addition, subtraction, halving, duplication, multiplication, division, progression, and extraction of roots. In numeration Jehan went as far as ten trillions, being the first writer we know who mentioned the terms billions and trillions. Other treatises on arithmetic in the later Middle Ages were the *Arithmetic* of Jordanes Nemorarius (c. 1200) and the *Triparty* of Nicholas Chuquet (1484). Luca Pacioli (c. 1440-c. 1515) collected all the arithmetical knowledge of his time in his *Summa*. The *Grounde of Artes* (1540) of Robert Recorde (1510-1558), another arithmetical compendium, went through thirty editions.

In algebra (the word itself is Muslim) the remarkable achievements of Muslims like al-Khwarizmi and Omar Khayyám and of the Hindu, Bhaskara (b. 1114), were assimilated by Europeans. There was not much progress in algebra until the sixteenth century when the Italian, Nicola Tartaglia, and the Frenchman, François Viète, founded modern algebra. We may note that Jordanus Nemorarius seems to have designated algebraic quantities by using the letters of the alphabet, probably the first mathematician to do so.

In geometry, John Campano of Novaro had already extended Euclid's *Elements* in the thirteenth century. Blasius of Parma (d. 1416) is thought to have worked out many of the principles of spherical geometry. Nicolas Oresme (d. 1382) anticipated Cartesian analytical geometry. In his *De configuratione qualitatum,* he clearly established the use of coördinates.

The most notable mathematical progress, perhaps, was made in trigonometry, based, of course, on earlier Muslim achievements.

Richard of Wallingford (d. 1336), bishop of St. Albans, wrote the first important Latin treatise on trigonometry. Jean Fusoris (d. 1436) compiled a table of sines and chords. Georg von Peuerbach (1423-1461) reconstructed Muslim and Ptolemaic trigonometry. The work of his pupil, Johann Müller (1435-1476), better known as Regiomontanus, summarized existing mathematical knowledge in trigonometry for a generation which had forgotten many of the sources of its information. He was one of the first to apply algebraic methods to the solution of special triangles.

The best general fifteenth-century summaries of mathematical knowledge were produced by Prosdocimo de' Beldomandi (c. 1425), and especially Luca Pacioli, whose *Summa de arithmetica, geometrica, proportioni et proportionalita* (1494), was the ablest mathematical synthesis of the period, and the first mathematical

[18] *History of Magic and Experimental Science,* II, 456.

work to be printed, except for the Latin edition of Euclid's *Elements* (1482), which incidentally gave the latter a revived vogue.

An attack on astrology paved the way for the growth of astronomy. Among the leaders in this assault were Henry of Hesse (1325-1397) and Nicolas of Oresme. The latter vigorously and completely exposed this pseudo science. Nicolas assailed it on both religious and scientific grounds. Nevertheless, most astronomers remained mainly astrologers. Levi ben-Gerson provided Europe with the best summary of Muslim astronomy (ordered translated into Latin by the pope) in his *Wars of God,* a criticism of Maimonides' synthesis of Aristotle and Jewish theology.

Geoffrey of Meaux (c. 1340) contended that comets are a natural product of the interaction of planets and stars. Paolo Toscanelli (d. 1482) made unusually thorough observations of comets in the fifteenth century. Jean de Meurs (c. 1350) anticipated Tycho Brahe by providing a large quadrant for observing heavenly bodies, corrected the prevailing ideas of astral positions and existing astronomical tables, and described accurately the conjunction of three planets in the year 1345. Prosdocimo de' Beldomandi also produced relatively accurate astronomical tables. Giovanni Bianchini (c. 1450) worked out elaborate astronomical tables and calculated with remarkable accuracy (for the time) the movements of the planets.

Peuerbach popularized existing astronomical knowledge and produced a treatise on planets and planetary motion. His translation and digest of Ptolemy's *Almagest* was finished by Regiomontanus. The latter studied Halley's comet in 1472,[19] and recorded interesting observations. This was made possible by the establishment of the first good astronomical observatory in western Europe, built for Regiomontanus by his patron, Bernhard Walther, in Nuremberg. It is said that the former computed lunar distances in order to determine longitude at sea. He died at Rome while working on an improvement of the calendar. Although an important popularizer, the old idea that Regiomontanus revolutionized astronomy has been abandoned. Indeed, it is now believed that Walther's own observations, praised by Copernicus and Tycho Brahe, were superior to those of Regiomontanus. Walther seems to have been the first to take atmospheric refraction into account.

The theory that the earth is in motion and may turn on an axis was suggested in the fourteenth century by Franciscus de Mayronis, Albert of Saxony, and Nicolas Oresme, and in the fifteenth century by Nicholas of Cues. The notion that the Ptolemaic system was shattered by Nicholas of Cues has been thoroughly exploded by Lynn Thorndike, who has shown that his idea of triple planetary motion was mystical rather than astronomical. John of Brescia's translation of al-Zarkali's great work on the astrolabe provided an impetus for the construction of better astronomical instruments. This revival of astronomy culminated in the work of Maria de Novara, the teacher of Copernicus.

Calendar reform was urged by Jean de Meurs, Pierre d'Ailly (c. 1350-c. 1420), Nicholas of Cues, Regiomontanus, and Paul of Middleburg (c. 1490). But the reform was not actually accomplished until the Gregorian calendar was adopted

19 So named later, see below, p. 683 in Volume II.

in 1582. More accurate astronomical measurements were made possible, however, by the new mechanical clocks, about which we shall have more to say later.

Perhaps the foremost achievement in physics was the attack on Aristotle which began with William of Ockham and was carried on by the Paris Ockhamites like Jean Buridan (c. 1360). It persisted into the sixteenth century in the writings of such men as Peter Ramus (1515-1572).

The Ockhamites of the fourteenth century made the chief physical discoveries of their time. Buridan believed that the same mechanical principles govern the heavens and the earth. His discussion of mass anticipated Newton's. Albert of Saxony definitely foreshadowed Galileo's law of falling bodies by maintaining that the fall of a heavy body is uniformly accelerated as it drops through space. Nicholas of Cues suggested dropping weights from towers and thought that air resistance should be taken into account. The mystical aura surrounding these important physical innovations can, however, be detected in the theory of James the Carthusian (1381-1465), who believed that bodies fall faster as they approach the earth because of their desire to reach their natural destination and to come to rest.

The invention of a better mechanical clock by James de Dondis (d. 1359) and his son John (c. 1318-c. 1390), who described it in his *Planetarium*, and the division of the clockface into hours, minutes, and seconds, facilitated research in physics.

Perhaps the most important physicist of the fourteenth century was Richard Suiseth, author of a work called *Calculationes*, from which Suiseth came to be known as "the Calculator." He laid the theoretical basis for mathematical physics. Suiseth dealt profoundly with such problems as rarefaction, density, velocity, luminous bodies and their media. Blasius of Parma, in the early years of the fifteenth century, gave especial attention to mechanics, attempting to combine Aristotle and Archimedes. He executed novel researches in the theory of weights and specific gravity. We have already called attention to the important work on optics done by Bacon, Witelo, and Peckham.

Chemistry seems to have stood still in this period. Numerous alchemistic treatises, attributed erroneously to Raymond Lull [20] and Arnald de Villanova, were mainly, as Professor Thorndike [21] has shown, Christian appropriations and assimilations of Muslim alchemy. These systematizations, however, made it possible at a later date for Paracelsus and the iatrochemists gradually to divorce chemistry from mysticism, magic, and alchemy.

In the latter part of the fifteenth century, after printing became a practical art, illustrated natural histories began to appear in which the representations of plants and animals were quite faithful to nature. Such were the *Book of Nature* (1475) of Conrad von Megenburg; *The Garden of Health* (1485), evidently prepared by a physician; and the *Hortus sanitatis* (1491).[22] At the close of this period modern botany was launched by the Germans, Otto Brunfels (1489-1534), Jerome Bock (1498-1554), and Leonard Fuchs (1501-1566), thus preparing the way for the sys-

---

[20] Lull appears to have written none of them. Arnald may have composed some.
[21] Lynn Thorndike, *History of Magic and Experimental Science in the Fourteenth and Fifteenth Centuries*, 2 vols. Columbia University Press, 1934, Vol. I, chap. iv; Vol. II, chap. xxxviii.
[22] See W. A. Locy, *The Growth of Biology*, Holt, 1925, chap. vii.

tematic biological works of Conrad Gesner (1516-1565), and Andreas Cesalpinus (1519-1563).

Travelers to the Far East, whom we shall note more extensively in a later chapter, greatly widened European knowledge of the world. Lynn Thorndike, while admitting that the western and southern hemispheres were unknown, indignantly repudiates the traditional view of the geographical ignorance of the time:

> "The thirteenth century knew China better than we knew it in the middle of the nineteenth century." Jordan, the Catalan, writing about 1324, gave the best account of India by any medieval Christian writer. Caravans crossed the Sahara to the interior of Africa, and Genoese vessels made an attempt to circumnavigate that continent. In 1316 Dominican missionaries went far up the Nile, and William Adam began a cruise of twenty months duration in the Indian Ocean. Architects from Granada constructed a royal palace on the Niger.[23]

This geographical knowledge, together with studies of latitude and longitude, produced more accurate maps. World maps, like the *mappimondi,* might still be a little fantastic, especially around the fringes, but the *portolani* or nautical maps, particularly those which dealt with the Mediterranean, became quite accurate by the close of the thirteenth and the beginning of the fourteenth century. It is especially desirable to explode the myth that the spherical conception of the earth was wholly novel, even in the days of Columbus. As Thorndike says: "This utterance represents one of the worst slanders current against the fair name of the middle ages, when every astronomical textbook or lecturer taught that the earth was a sphere, and this was known to any educated layman such as Dante." [24]

Late medieval European medicine was substantially a compound of Greek, Roman, Byzantine, and Muslim knowledge. Some original research was conducted. The Muslims were familiar with the ideas of Galen, Hippocrates, and Celsus,[25] and with the work of Byzantine physicians like Aëtius, Alexander of Tralles, and Paul of Aegina. In addition, they borrowed the medical lore of the Hindus and Persians and synthesized all the disparate elements in such works as the *Canon* of Avicenna. Muslim medicine first made its way into western Europe through the health resort of Salerno, on the Bay of Naples, where physicians and aristocratic patients gathered and the first medieval medical university was ultimately established.

The first medical writers whom we can definitely connect with Salerno are Petrocellus and Gariopontus in the middle of the eleventh century. The latter's *Passionarius* was an encyclopedia of Greek, Roman, and Byzantine medicine. He seems to have known nothing of Muslim medicine, but had an elementary knowledge of the Muslim pharmacopoeia. Constantine the African (d. 1087), the earliest important translator of Muslim medical works into Latin, lived for a time at Salerno and acquainted the doctors there with Muslim medicine. Eventually

---

[23] Thorndike, *Science and Thought in the Fifteenth Century,* Columbia University Press, 1929, pp. 20-21.

[24] Thorndike, *op. cit.,* p. 20.

[25] The writings of Celsus were lost to Europe during the Middle Ages and were not recovered until the humanistic period.

the medical universities of Padua, Bologna, and Montpellier came to rival Salerno.

It must be remembered that this medieval medicine was unscientific. To the fanciful Hippocratic theory of the four humors was added Galenic and Muslim magic and astrology. Furthermore, this medical knowledge was taught by scholastic methods, by citing, analyzing, and refuting authorities, rather than by carefully studying symptoms, diseases, and remedies.

At this time medical practice was gradually passing into the hands of laymen. From the twelfth century onward the church tended to discourage medical practice by monks, who had virtually monopolized it in the Dark Ages. The Council of Rheims in 1131 forbade the monks and regular clergy to practice. Soon after, even the secular clergy was barred from medicine by Pope Honorius III. The new mendicant orders looked askance at clerical doctors. Hence, the custom of lay practice, which had been established at Salerno, gradually came to prevail in western Europe.

Gilbert the Englishman (c. 1180-1250) was one of the first practitioners of the new medicine, compounded of the Muslim synthesis of Greco-Roman medicine and medieval astrology and magic. From his *Compendium of Medicine* some indication of the character of medieval remedies can be gleaned. His treatment for apoplexy, for example, was the application of the flesh of a lion, the oil of a scorpion, and the eggs of an ant. Even more edifying is his remedy for human sterility:

Let a man, twenty years of age or more, before the third hour of the vigil of St. John the Baptist, pull up by the roots a specimen of *Consolida major* (comfrey) and another of *Consolida minor* (healall), repeating thrice the Lord's prayer (oratio dominica). Let him speak to no one while either going or returning, say nothing whatever, but in deep silence let him extract the juice from the herbs and with this juice write on as many cards as may be required the following charm:

Dixit dominus crescite.   Uthihoth.   multiplicamini.
thahechay.   et replete terram.   amath.

If a man wears about his neck a card inscribed with these identical words written in this juice, he will beget a male. Conversely, if a woman, she will conceive a female.[26]

Leading physicians of the next century were Bernard Gordon (c. 1300), a professor in the medical school at Montpellier, and Thaddeus Florentinus (1223-1303) of Bologna. We cited Gordon's extraordinary comprehensive remedy for failing eyesight in the preceding chapter.[27] He is thought to have been one of the first to recommend the truss for rupture, though the device had been invented by Salvino da Armati a generation earlier. Thaddeus wrote commentaries on Avicenna and Hippocrates, and had a tremendous following among students and patients. He exploited his fame by charging high fees, even refusing to attend the pope for less than a hundred ducats a day.

[26] Cited by David Riesman, *The Story of Medicine in the Middle Ages*, Hoeber, 1935, pp. 87-88.
[27] See above, pp. 433-34.

We have already referred to Peter of Abano, who was also a doctor with a large reputation. He was one of the first—if not the very first since the Greeks—to suggest that the brain is the center of the nervous system and the heart of the blood vessels. The following quotation from his *Conciliator* indicates the range of his medical curiosity:

Is the number of elements four or otherwise; has air weight in its own sphere; does blood alone nourish; does the marrow nourish the bones; is there a mean between health and sickness; is a smaller head a better sign than a large one; are the arteries dilated when the heart is, and contracted also when it is; can a worm be generated in the belly; should one take exercise before or after meals; should heavy food be taken before light; should one eat once, twice, or several times a day; should dinner be at noon or at night; should one drink on top of fruit; should one sleep on the right or left side; does confidence of the patient in the doctor assist the cure; is every cure by contrary; does sleep help the cure; should treatment begin with strong or weak medicine; is cold water good in fevers; can fever coincide with apoplexy; is paralysis of the right side harder to cure than that of the left; can consumption be cured; does milk agree with consumptives; is a narcotic good for colic; is bloodletting from the left a proper treatment for gout in the right foot? [28]

The most famous of medieval physicians was Arnald de Villanova (c. 1235- c. 1311), professor at Montpellier, author of the comprehensive *Breviarium*. Some of his medical injunctions show real enlightenment: "He who in his chosen branch educates himself not for science but for gain, becomes an 'abortion.' A knowledge of names is essential to science but no cure is achieved by a mere formula. That mode of treatment is best which achieves the desired end with the fewest means. An intelligent and pious physician makes every effort to cure disease with proper foods rather than with drugs." [29] Yet, Arnald could, as Professor Thorndike observes, combine modern insight with the practice of astrology and magic. The medical science of southern Europe was introduced into England by Thomas Linacre (1460-1524), who, more than any other single physician, organized British medical practice.

All in all, medicine made less progress than surgery between the scholastic age and the fifteenth century. It rested more on authority and tradition and was less cordial to experimentation and observation. True empirical medicine did not get under way until the seventeenth and eighteenth centuries.

The materia medica of the time was a combination of what was known of Dioscorides, the great Muslim manual of pharmacy by al-Mardini, and the current magical practices of the doctors of western Christendom.

Surgery offered more scope for observation than medicine. It was more difficult to perpetuate magic, superstition, and traditional errors in surgery. The body could be opened up and looked at and the eye could register what was seen.

Truly scientific surgery depends upon a knowledge of anatomy as well as of disease. The surgeon must know the location of the nerves, the blood vessels and

[28] Cited by Riesman, *op. cit.,* p. 93.
[29] *Ibid.,* pp. 84-85.

the internal organs. The practice of dissection made slow headway, due, some believe, to the opposition of the church. At any rate, dissections did not become common, even in the great medical schools, until the fourteenth century. Charles Singer believes that autopsies which were conducted to learn the cause of death first led to dissection. The earliest autopsy in Bologna was made in 1281. Padua did not practice dissection until 1341, and Montpellier not until 1376:

> Now it is recognized that "anatomies" or systematic dissections of human bodies for purposes of instruction were held regularly in the schools of medicine of the fourteenth and fifteenth centuries, and the skill of the practicing surgeons of the same period is becoming better known. The bodies used in the university dissections were commonly those of executed criminals or other outcasts; the surgeons would usually treat only those cases where they thought that recovery was likely.[80]

Thorndike further shows that autopsies by reputable physicians, with the consent of the family of the deceased, to discover the nature of the fatal disease, were by no means uncommon.[81]

First of the eminent medieval anatomists was William of Saliceto (1201-1280) whose investigations influenced Mondino da Luzzi (1276-1328), a teacher in the medical school at Bologna where dissection got its first real start. Mondino's *Anothamia* was a standard treatise on anatomy until the protracted study of dissection rendered it obsolete. Mondino illustrates the combination of tradition and experiment, since his researches were attempted as much to vindicate Muslim authorities as to make new discoveries. It should be obvious, from what has just been said, that, however great a genius Vesalius [32] may have been, he did not suddenly create the science of anatomy. He utilized the methods of two previous centuries, which the appearance of printed books helped to disseminate.

The simpler surgical services, such as blood-letting and the like, were performed in large part by the surgeon-barbers, *rasators* or *sanguinators,* who became prominent in such activities from the eleventh century onward. This is the source of our red and white barber-poles of today. But the more complicated operations were taken care of by professional surgeons, and even the surgeon-barbers often sought technical instruction in the schools of surgery.

The first eminent medieval surgeon was Roger of Salerno (c. 1180), an authority on the surgery of the head. His surgical wisdom was edited and preserved by Roland of Parma (c. 1250), himself the first to perform a successful operation on a ruptured lung. Hugh of Lucca (c. 1170-c. 1240) and Theodoric of Bologna (c. 1205-1288) established the famous surgical school of Bologna. They were succeeded by Henri de Mondeville (d. c. 1320), a colleague of Bernard Gordon at Montpellier and surgeon to Philip the Fair. He emphasized the anatomical basis of surgery, gave a good account of the ligature of arteries, and was a pioneer in antisepsis through removing pus from wounds.

The foremost surgeon of the fourteenth century was Guy de Chauliac (1300-1370), who studied at all the leading medical schools and became the papal physician at Avignon. He wrote at length about surgical methods and surgical instru-

[80] Thorndike, *Science and Thought in the Fifteenth Century,* p. 125.
[31] *Ibid.,* pp. 124-26.
[32] See below, p. 572.

ments. In the latter he made many improvements. His treatise, *The Great Surgery*, was the standard authority until the days of Ambrose Paré. Guy was a reactionary, however, in failing to follow Mondeville in antisepsis and the pusless treatment of wounds. Like most medieval surgeons, he believed that healing was promoted by leaving pus in the wounds—the so-called wet treatment (suppuration). Other eminent fourteenth-century surgeons were Lanfranc of Paris (c. 1300) and Jean Yperman (1295-1351). Lanfranc wrote a comprehensive manual, *The Complete Surgical Art*, while Yperman promoted antisepsis and advocated the use of styptic powders to arrest bleeding.

By the fifteenth century medicine, anatomy, and surgery had made considerable progress:

> Summing up the recent researches of various investigators, Paul Diepgen shows the practice of systematic dissection of the human body in the fourteenth century for purposes of instruction; the advance made in measures against infection as the source of disease, so that far more diseases were recognized as contagious than in antiquity, while leprosy largely disappeared in the fourteenth and fifteenth centuries; the use of mercury salve against syphilis long before the close of the fifteenth century, when it used to be thought that that disease first appeared in Europe (its American origin is still maintained by Barduzzi and others); the invention in southern France in the fourteenth century of the dental instrument of extraction known as the pelican; the employment of inhaled narcotics or *Spongia somnifera;* the fact that medieval surgery did not slavishly follow tradition but went its own way; the development of hospitals; the progress in legal regulation of the medical profession; and the inclusion in university instruction of seminar exercises, clinics, and bedside instruction.[33]

In this era applied science was for the first time accorded equal rank with pure science. In the Hellenic age applied science never kept pace with, or stimulated the growth of, natural science. In the closing centuries of the Middle Ages Roger Bacon's dreams of the potentialities of applied science gradually began to be realized.

A number of inventions or discoveries have already been mentioned. Such were the mirrors, lenses, and chemical substances devised by the Muslims. Lenses made possible not only human spectacles, invented apparently by Salvino da Armati in the thirteenth century,[34] but also the telescope and microscope which were indispensable to astronomy and biology. By the time of Roger Bacon reading glasses were coming into use, and in the early seventeenth century practicable telescopes and microscopes were provided.

The most important immediate outgrowth of alchemistic chemistry was the discovery of gunpowder, made from charcoal, saltpeter, and other substances. Roger Bacon did not invent it but he gives us one of the best early descriptions of it. Gunpowder and firearms provided the instruments for the destruction of feudal strongholds and inaugurated a revolution in the science of warfare on land and sea alike.

[33] Thorndike, *Science and Thought in the Fifteenth Century*, p. 5.
[34] Perhaps by Alexander da Spina.

One of the major obstacles to the progress of physics and astronomy had been the lack of good timepieces. In the fourteenth century accurate mechanical or balance clocks were devised by James de Dondis and his son John, based perhaps upon earlier Muslim inventions. At any rate, they were the forerunner of the pendulum clock invented by Huygens in the seventeenth century. The crude clocks of the early thirteenth century had no divisions into minutes and seconds. By the middle of the fourteenth century, clock faces with hour, minute and second divisions were common, at least in scientific laboratories. Professor Thorndike emphasizes the fact that clockmaking stimulated other inventions. Many of our later inventions, down through the first practicable mechanical loom, were devised by clockmakers.

The most important single factor in bringing mankind out of medievalism and into the modern age was the conquest of the oceans and the expansion of Europe overseas. Late medieval inventions such as the mariner's compass revolutionized navigation. Tradition connects the magnetic compass with the Chinese early in the Christian Era. Its first authentic mention is by Shen Kua who died in 1093. A decade later Chinese writers refer to its use in navigation, implying that it had been known at least a generation before. The Muslims were probably the source through which western Europe obtained a knowledge of the compass, though it is barely possible that Christian traders may have brought it from China. The Muslim geographer Idrisi speaks of the compass half a century before the first Christian reference to it in Alexander Neckham's *De naturis rerum*, written about 1195. Neckham comments on the compass as follows:

> The sailors, moreover, as they sail over the sea, when in cloudy weather they can no longer profit by the light of the sun, or when the world is wrapped in the darkness of the shades of night, and they are ignorant to what point of the compass their ship's course is directed, they touch the magnet with a needle, which is whirled around in a circle until, when its motion ceases, its point looks direct to the north.

The compass steadily improved after this date. The compass card, divided into 32 points or rhumbs, had been worked out by 1391, for Chaucer makes reference to it in that year in his *Treatise on the Astrolabe*. The needle was, in the beginning, mounted on a card and floated on water. It was first mounted on a pivot by Flavio Gioja of Amalfi in the fourteenth century. The compass, more than any single improvement in shipbuilding, enabled Columbus to accomplish his momentous transatlantic voyage, inaugurating European expansion overseas.

Very important also for navigation were certain astronomical instruments like the astrolabe, constructed by al-Farazi at Baghdad as early as 775 and greatly improved by al-Zarkali in Spain in the eleventh century. Knowledge of the Muslim astrolabe was imparted to western Europe by translators and commentators, particularly Hermann the Cripple (1013-1054), Henry Bate (c. 1274) and John of Brescia (14th century). Towards the middle of the fourteenth century Levi ben-Gerson and Giovanni Bianchini had mastered the principle of the quadrant which was destined to replace the astrolabe. Through the quadrant one could measure the height of celestial bodies. There were also important inventions in boatbuilding. The rudder, devised about 1300, was followed by masts, spars, and rigging. These became vital to the expansion of Europe and the dawn of the modern age.

The blast furnace introduced a new era in iron and steel manufacture. Unfortunately, it was operated chiefly with charcoal, which helped, by the way, to strip England of her forests. There was some use of coal, however, as early as 1300 in England.

An epochal invention, momentous in its cultural consequences, was the introduction of papermaking by the Muslims. The Chinese, utilizing the pulp of the mulberry tree, had probably been the first to manufacture it early in the Christian Era. The Muslims introduced paper made of cotton fiber into Spain, where it was being widely manufactured before 1150. The Europeans made paper of flax and rags. Papermaking became relatively common in western Europe by the close of the thirteenth century. Paper, plus the invention of printing by means of movable type in the middle of the fifteenth century, revolutionized man's intellectual life. On the invention of printing we shall have more to say later.

A nonmechanical invention of the greatest importance was double-entry bookkeeping, which may be credited to Luca Pacioli. This was not only of epochmaking significance for commercial practices but indirectly produced a great intellectual and moral revolution. The ledger probably did more than anything else to give a special slant and stereotype to economic morality. It helped to produce the profit system and the theory of business enterprise. It prevented even mentally superior men from seeing further into economics than the ledger sheet. Today, it is potent in holding mankind back from appropriating and enjoying the economy of abundance. It indirectly accounts in large degree for the so-called "stupidity" of business and financial leaders. Werner Sombart's comment on the origins and implications of double-entry bookkeeping is to the point:

> Ideas of profit seeking and economic rationalism first became possible with the invention of double-entry bookkeeping. Through this system can be grasped but one thing—the increase in amount of values considered purely quantitatively. Whoever becomes immersed in double-entry bookkeeping must forget all qualities of goods, and services, abandon the limitations of the need-covering principle, and be filled with the single idea of profit; he may not think of boots and cargoes, meal and cotton, but only of amounts of values, increasing or diminishing.

V. POLITICAL AND SOCIAL THEORY DURING THE DECLINE OF THE MEDIEVAL SYSTEM

The political and social philosophy of the age following Aquinas reflected the institutional and intellectual changes which we summarized in the preceding pages. The decline in the power of the medieval church, the conciliar movement, the heresies, the increased strength of monarchies, and the growth of commerce and the middle class, were all involved in the political doctrines of the age.

The struggle between church and state was continued. The arguments in behalf of the church and the papacy illustrate the attitude which modern psychologists call "overcompensation." The church was actually declining in authority and prestige. Yet its supporters set forth more fantastic claims for its supremacy than were ever advanced at the height of its power. Relations between church and state came to a head in the famous struggle between Philip the Fair of France and Pope Boniface VIII. The dispute centered mainly around questions of church property, taxation, and papal exactions.

The classic pronouncement of the papal doctrine was set forth by Pope Boniface VIII in his bull *Unam sanctam* in 1302. Boniface, in his quarrel with Philip the Fair, asserted that the king was subject to the pope in all matters pertaining to sin and salvation, and implied the supremacy of the church in temporal affairs as well. Boniface's supporter, Aegidus Romanus, went even further in his *De ecclesiastica potestate* (1301). He contended that power and proprietorship can only be bestowed through God's grace, and that God bestows it in direct proportion to the hierarchy of earthly rank, at the head of which stands the pope. He held, accordingly, that the ultimate ownership of temporal goods resides in the church. Hence, even temporal affairs are subject to the final control of the church. Nobody outside the church has any just title to property. As Professor C. H. McIlwain asserts:

> We have in this book the completest and most thoroughgoing of all the theological and philosophical defences of the furthest doctrines of the canonists, that the Pope is the supreme lord in his own right over all the world and in all matters temporal as well as spiritual, and that all princes are his mere subordinates even in the secular administration of their own realms. This position is here explained and defended from every point of view and for the first time completely and exhaustively.[85]

The most arrogant version of the papal theory was embodied in the *Summa de potestate ecclesiastica* of Augustinus Triumphatus (1243-1328). He contended that the jurisdiction of the pope is greater than that of any angel. Even pagans must obey him. He has the power to depose a ruler for reasonable cause. As the vicar of God, the pope has ultimate power over all property and no property can be legitimately placed beyond his control. Comparable views were also held by James of Viterbo and Henry of Cremona. As Professor Dunning observed, such exaggerations of papal pretensions were in direct ratio to the decline of the real power of the papacy.

Opponents of papal views returned to the charge, armed with new ammunition. The revival of Roman law by Irnerius at Bologna (beginning about 1088) renewed and encouraged the doctrine of the supremacy of the state over the church and all other social institutions. Roman law had declared that the power of the state was absolute and could override the opposition of any group within the state. It thus upheld the doctrine which we call secular absolutism, a conception utterly at variance with the churchly dogma of the final superiority of ecclesiastical power. In Roman theory even religion must be, in the last analysis, a creature of the state. Experts in Roman law, therefore, tended to support the secular monarchs, who were only too glad to exploit and reward this timely

---

[85] C. H. McIlwain, *The Growth of Political Thought in the West*, Macmillan, 1932, p. 249.

theoretical vindication. Among the most notable proponents of royal prestige in this age were John Quidart of Paris, Pierre Dubois, and Marsiglio of Padua.

John Quidart (d. 1306) contended in his *Tractatus de potestate regia et papali* that the church cannot justly claim any coercive power. It can only use persuasion. Though the pope may be superior in spiritual matters, the king is superior in temporal affairs, and only the king can punish offenses against the church. John held that the pope may err, and specifically asserted that Boniface had erred in his claims against Philip. The property of laymen is their own. Church property belongs to the whole church, of which the pope is only steward. The general council is the supreme authority in matters of faith.

Pierre Dubois (1255-1321), in his *De recuperatione terre sancte,* warmly defended Philip the Fair in his struggle with Pope Boniface. He warned the pope not to meddle with temporal affairs, since such interference in the past had cost the Christians the possession of the Holy Land. He outlined a comprehensive program of social reform in which, among other enlightened suggestions, he advocated a reconstruction of the French government, the reform and codification of law and the expediting of justice, more practical and efficient education— including education for selected classes of women—the confiscation of church property, the reconstruction of the French army, and international arbitration to settle disputes between nations. He has been hailed by many modern scholars as the chief social reformer of the Middle Ages. Recently, Professor W. I. Brandt has reduced this estimate and considers him primarily a man who echoed the novel political and social ideas of his age.

Marsiglio of Padua (1270-1342), in his *Defensor pacis* (perhaps written in part by John of Jandun), one of the most important political treatises of the late medieval period, attacked the Catholic church with something of the spirit and modernity of the deists and Voltaire. As Pierre Dubois had defended the French monarchy against the church, so Marsiglio came to the aid of the Holy Roman emperor. He offered a powerful criticism of the doctrine of the primacy of Peter. He declared that the priests were merely the ministers of salvation, and denied that they possessed the power of forgiving sins or the right to interfere in temporal matters.

In his strictly social and political philosophy, Marsiglio was somewhat less original. He accounted for the origin of society on a purely utilitarian basis, following the argument of Aristotle. Society is essential to mankind in order to carry on those coöperative activities necessary to group existence and human comfort. But unregulated society is likely to degenerate into disorder. Hence civil government is indispensable. Ultimate political authority is merely delegated by the people, in whose hands reposes sovereign power. Marsiglio was the first notable medieval exponent of the classical notion of popular sovereignty and representative government—two of the leading dogmas of modern politics. These views he derived in part from Aristotle and in part from Roman law. In harmony with his general conceptions, Marsiglio expressed preference for an elective monarch.

Marsiglio carried his political theories into an analysis of church government, anticipating, as had John Quidart of Paris, the conciliar movement. He declared that the ultimate authority in the church resides in the whole body of believers. They merely delegate this authority to a church council. Papal decrees are not real ecclesiastical law, which can be made only by church councils. Even a church council cannot enforce its rulings, which must be executed by secular rulers. The pope has no authority to employ the interdict or excommunication without the consent of the lay ruler. The pope is no more than the president of the clergy. The rule of the pope is merely an administrative convenience. It has no divine sanction. All this was in harmony with the political theory of the later conciliar movement.

Marsiglio also emphasized the organic unity and functional character of society by outlining the organic analogy in an original way. The six estates or professions were made to correspond to the organs in the individual organism. Further, by his separation of politics from theology, Marsiglio took a step towards Machiavelli's separation of politics from ethics.

Wycliffe and Huss assailed the papal pretensions, but their political philosophy was less important than that developed during the conciliar movement of the first half of the fifteenth century. John Gerson (1363-1429), chancellor of the University of Paris, held that the church council is superior to the pope. The latter is merely the administrative agent of the council which cannot conveniently remain in perpetual session. The council is the only legitimate organ for expressing the ultimate will of the church. The pope is not above the edicts of the council or above church law thus promulgated. Yet Gerson conceded that the council should never depose a pope except under direst necessity. Essentially the same views were expressed by Pierre d'Ailly (1350-1420), chancellor of Notre Dame, who likewise believed that only a general church council could heal the schism.

Nicholas of Cues (1401-1464), in his *De concordantia catholica,* tried to apply the doctrine of popular consent to both church and secular government. A council must be the ultimate basis of authority in both church and state. Nicholas reconciled this dogma of popular consent with the Apostolic declaration that all power comes from God by holding that God works in and through the people. He joined Marsiglio as a leading exponent of representative government.

Nicholas presented, as well, the most elaborate development of the analogy between the individual organism and the state that had yet appeared. He introduced in this the conception of political pathology and, reviving the Platonic phrase, designated the ruler as physician-in-chief to the sick state. He must prescribe for its ills according to the best advice of political doctors (philosophers), past and present.

The final culmination of conciliar theory was the statement of the controversy in terms of the Roman law of the corporation. The whole body of Christians were likened to the stockholders in a corporation. The council appeared in the guise of the elective board of directors. The pope was the presiding officer, chairman as it were, of the board. The council did not depend upon the pope's convocation. If the pope did not summon it, the council could assemble on its own authority and responsibility, and it could stay in session as long as it wished.

It may be noted here also that papal pretensions suffered a severe blow when, in 1438, the humanist critic, Lorenzo Valla, proved the Donation of Constantine to be a church forgery. On this alleged donation had rested in part the papal claims to temporal power.

The conciliar theory of representative government in the church was quickly carried over into secular political theory. The precedent for this was found not only in the conciliar theory but in that of Marsiglio of Padua. The authority of the lay ruler was represented as subject not only to popular consent but also to the dictates of natural law as well. The utility of the state was regarded as its major justification. When it ceased to be useful its power was placed in jeopardy. Much was said about the right of private property, which was held to be exempt from the power of the king or emperor. In these later phases of medieval political theory one may discern the influence of the middle class and its growing solicitude about property rights.

Aeneas Sylvius (1405-1464), in his *De ortu et auctoritate Imperii Romani,* discussed historically, as well as theoretically, just how the element of popular consent became established in human society. He advanced the clearest distinction between the social and governmental contracts to be found in late medieval authors. According to Aeneas, people originally lived in a state of nature. This proved warlike and unsatisfactory; so they agreed to establish orderly social relations (the social contract). Afterwards they found it necessary to institute government and set forth its powers and limitations (the governmental contract). Aeneas here clearly anticipated the doctrine of the social contract which was so popular in the seventeenth and eighteenth centuries, upon the foundations of which our own Declaration of Independence was issued.[36]

VI. A NEW AGE ARRIVES

Developments in European civilization from 1250 to 1450, briefly summarized in this chapter and certain sections of the preceding chapters, should make it clear that Europe was moving towards a new cultural era quite different from that which was given its immortal portrayal and synthesis in Dante's *Divine Comedy.* These changes were preparing Europe for the so-called Renaissance, the Protestant revolt, and the far more momentous shake-up of medievalism produced by overseas expansion.

Feudalism was being supplanted by nationalistic monarchies, in which at least the middle classes enjoyed more privileges and prestige. In Italy feudalism had never made great headway except in Naples, where Norman feudalism had been introduced. The Italian communes asserted their independent spirit even in the earlier Middle Ages. In the later Middle Ages democracy made some progress in the Italian city-states, thus promoting political individualism. This was tempered at times by tyranny, but even the tyrants were resourceful, valiant, colorful, and often benevolent rulers.

Economic conditions even more potently made for a new order of things. The increasing wealth of the mercantile classes brought in its train greater leisure,

[36] See below, p. 661 in Volume II.

culture, curiosity, and urbanity. Ascetic supernaturalism could not thrive in an atmosphere of prosperity, which definitely favored secularism and mundane pleasures. The travels, explorations, and discoveries associated with the revived Mediterranean and Oriental trade increased curiosity and interest in the facts of this world, particularly in the riches of the East. With the decline of guilds and manors, social classes became less rigid, and rigorously controlled community life weakened. Both journeymen and peasants became self-assertive. The latter frequently broke into rebellion against medieval restraints. Italian cities were the commercial leaders of the later Middle Ages and hence felt these new influences more keenly than other areas.

Social life was also changing. Travel became more feasible and popular. The middle class became more self-conscious, aggressive, and ambitious. The unsettling of guilds and manorial groups introduced social flexibility and individual expression on the part of even the lower classes. Medieval modes of social control and community cohesion were breaking down.

The major instrument of moral and intellectual control during the Middle Ages was the Roman Catholic church. We have already seen how it declined. The political power of the popes faded, and, outside the papal states, amounted to little, even in Italy. All this increased the free play of individual and social interests. Even the great pietistic developments of the later Middle Ages, those of the Franciscans and mystics, were individualistic in character.

With the rise of vernacular literature, culture lost its uniformity and became increasingly nationalistic. Even Dante, the great synthesizer of medieval culture, was more Italian than Latin and Christian in his linguistic and literary affiliations. His "Italianism" was thoroughly akin to the spirit of the early humanists.

To these Western influences, which sapped the medieval social, cultural, and intellectual order, must be added the interaction of Muslim culture and the revival of Greek and Roman literature and ideas. Byzantine culture, which was Greek in nature, also made its impact on the West after the crusades.

There was a distinct revival of interest in the classics in the twelfth century, particularly in the Norman kingdom of southern Italy and Sicily, where Latin Christian, Byzantine, and Muslim elements freely intermingled, and in the cathedral schools of France. As western Europe became more urban and secularized, it became, quite naturally, more receptive to the literature and culture of pagan antiquity.

These unsettling influences in later medievalism were most active in Italy, which was the center of the new commercialism and urbanism and least affected by the characteristic features of medieval politics and social life. Moreover, contact between Italy and pagan antiquity was closer than between the rest of western Europe and the pagan past. Roman civilization to some extent lingered in Italy, while commercial activities brought her into intimate relationship with the Greek culture of the Byzantine East. Many Byzantine people settled in southern Italy. Urban life, secularism, individualism, humanism, and mysticism, were all more highly developed in Italy than elsewhere as the Middle Ages drew to a close.

SELECTED READINGS

Becker and Barnes, *Social Thought from Lore to Science*, Vol. I, chap. vii.

Burnham, W. H., *The Great Teachers and Mental Health*, Appleton, 1926, chaps. iv-v.

Chabod, Frederico, *Machiavelli and the Renaissance*, Harvard University Press, 1958.

Cheyney, E. P., *The Dawn of a New Era, 1250-1453*, Harper Torchbooks.

Clagett, Marshall, *The Science of Mechanics in the Middle Ages*, University of Wisconsin Press, 1959.

Dunning, W. A., *History of Political Theories: Ancient and Medieval*, Macmillan, 1902, chaps. vi-x.

Easton, S. C., *Roger Bacon and His Search for a Universal Science*, Columbia University Press, 1952.

Eby and Arrowood, *The History and Philosophy of Education*, chap. xviii.

Flick, A. C., *The Decline of the Medieval Church*, 2 Vols., Knopf, 1930.

Gewirth, *Marsilius of Padua*.

Graves, F. P., *History of Education during the Middle Ages and the Transition to Modern Times*, Macmillan, 1910.

Hearnshaw, *Medieval Contributions to Modern Civilization*.

———*The Social and Political Ideas of Some Great Medieval Thinkers*.

Hyma, Albert, *The Christian Renaissance*, Century, 1924.

Jarrett, Bede, *Social Theories of the Middle Ages*, Newman Bookshop, 1942.

Kristeller, P. O., *The Classics and Renaissance Thought*, Harvard University Press, 1955.

Locy, W. A., *The Growth of Biology*, Holt, 1925, chaps. vi-ix.

McGiffert, *History of Christian Thought*, Vol. II.

Monroe, *Textbook in the History of Education*, chap. vi.

Newton, A. P., ed., *Travel and Travellers in the Middle Ages*, Knopf, 1926.

Pachter, H. M., *Paracelsus: Magic into Science*, Schuman, 1951.

Riesman, *The Story of Medicine in the Middle Ages*.

Robinson, J. H., and Rolfe, H. W., *Petrarch*, Putnam, 1914.

Salter, H. E., *Medieval Oxford*, Oxford University Press, 1936.

Sarton, *Introduction to the History of Science*, Vols. I-III.

Sedgwick and Tyler, *A Short History of Science*, chaps. viii-ix.

Singer, Charles, *The Story of Living Things*, Harper, 1931, chaps. ii-iii.

———*et al.*, eds., *A History of Technology: From the Renaissance to the Industrial Revolution*, Oxford University Press, 1957.

Taylor, H. O., *Thought and Expression in the Sixteenth Century*, 2 Vols., Macmillan, 1920.

Thompson, *History of Historical Writing*, Vol. I, Book IV.

Thorndike, Lynn, *History of Magic and Experimental Science in the Fourteenth and Fifteenth Centuries*, 2 Vols., Columbia University Press, 1934.

———*Science and Thought in the Fifteenth Century*, Columbia Univ. Press, 1929.

Woodward, W. H., *Vittorina da Feltre and Other Humanist Educators*, Cambridge University Press, 1921.

Workman, H. B., *Christian Thought to the Reformation*.

——— *The Dawn of the Reformation*, 2 Vols., London, 1900.

Wulf, *History of Medieval Philosophy*, Vol. II.

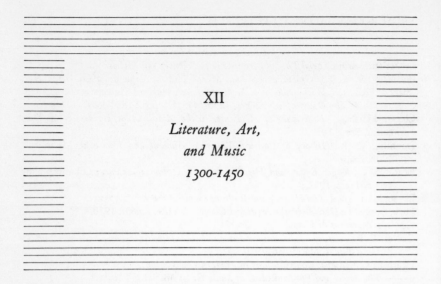

XII

Literature, Art,
and Music
1300-1450

I. THE TRIUMPH OF THE VERNACULAR IN LITERATURE

This period was one of change from the medieval to the modern world. Feudalism weakened as the mercantile middle class rose to power and a new economic order emerged. The Peasants' Revolt in England, the Jacquerie in France, peasant disorders in Germany, were birth-pangs of the new world. The universal church had declined from its supreme position of the thirteenth century, and serious and satirical criticism of ecclesiastical privilege and corruption foreshadowed the Reformation. A new secular spirit developed in literature, a humanistic concern with this life and with the individual man, an interest in the pagan authors for their own sakes, and not for possible Christian values. Folk literature flourished and the drama, itself an offspring of the church, moved gradually toward non-religious themes and forms. In general, men wrote more of this world as it is, and in their own tongues rather than in Latin.

Such changes were not brought about at once, or easily, and feudal forms and trappings persisted as feudalism itself decayed. Literary modes of earlier days—the saint's legend, the allegory, the dream vision—were employed by authors in whom the fresh spirit was strong. Other-worldliness, the medieval contempt for earthly life, asserts itself—and not merely as a conventional tag—in one of the most "modern" of fourteenth-century poems, Chaucer's *Troilus and Criseyde*.

The great names in fourteenth-century literature are Italian and English, those of Petrarch, Boccaccio, and Chaucer. War and internal struggle discouraged literary production in France, which lapsed from her former splendor, though not into total darkness.

1. Religious Literature

The church declined in power and respect, but it was still the one church, and within its fold all men lived, all authors wrote. Religious literature itself was not obliterated by the increasing secular spirit.

Certain Englishmen of the time uttered, though in very different ways, religious thought and emotion. Robert Manning of Bourne, whose dates are not known, in the twelve thousand lines of *Handlyng Synne,* concerned himself with the ten commandments, the seven deadly sins, and other theological subjects, but in no long-faced fashion. He wrote familiarly, for all men, and his admonitions and rebukes he adorned with illustrative anecdotes which still have the freshness of life. His homely, good-natured tone is far removed from the ecstatic mysticism of Richard Rolle of Hampole (c. 1300-1349), a hermit and wandering preacher, who exhorted men to a good life, attacked unworthy churchmen, and in Latin and English uttered his own passionate yearning toward Christ, in intense and even erotic images. His fame was great in his own time, and spread after his death.

The unknown poet who wrote *Sir Gawain and the Green Knight* has also been regarded as the author of three religious poems, *Patience* and *Purity,* homilies enlivened with biblical stories, and *The Pearl,* an elaborate, structurally strict, dream vision and allegory, the theological interpretation of which does not obscure its human feelings of loss, grief, and final resignation.

In Germany there was an escape both from the troubled world of strife and plague and the cold reasoning of scholastic philosophy in the mystical prose of Johannes Eckhart, best known as Meister Eckhart (c. 1260-c. 1327), who urged renunciation of the world and complete absorption in God, the union of the soul's essence with God's. The church could not accept Eckhart's teachings, and he partially recanted his doctrines before the Inquisition.

A century later than Meister Eckhart another German wrote a mystical work which was to become one of the most widely read of Christian writings. Thomas à Kempis (Thomas Hämmerlein or Hämmerken, 1380-1471) described in the four books of his *De imitatione Christi* (*The Imitation of Christ*) the progress of the soul from the world toward perfect union with God. His style is simple and intensely eloquent. The book has been translated into many languages.

Manning and Rolle were aware of and mentioned the abuses of the church in their time; the *Gawain* poet and the German mystics did not concern themselves with them. But two English writers of the fourteenth century not only aware but actively opposed to such abuses have left a record of their feelings. These were the poet commonly known as William Langland (c. 1330-c. 1400) and the reformer John Wycliffe (c. 1320-1384).

Who Langland was and if that was indeed his name no one knows, and there is disagreement about whether he was the author of all the versions of the great work, *The Vision of Piers Plowman,* which traditionally bears his name. But there is no doubt of the quality of the poem. It is allegorical, a series of dreams, in which the poet, falling asleep on a May morning in the Malvern hills, sees a great castle (Truth) and a deep dungeon (Falsehood), and between a "fair field full of folk"—men and women in all walks of life going about their work. Personified abstractions appear—Holy Church as a lady; Lady Meed (bribery), False, Flattery, Reason, and Conscience—but the author gives them and their actions life and individuality. The poem shows the corruption in high places of state and church and the debased condition of the masses, in vivid and living pictures, with homely, muscular speech and realistic detail. The figure of Piers Plowman, the honest laborer, who had learned not from books but from abstinence and conscience, who urged hard work upon all men as the way to truth, took the fancy of the oppressed peasants whose language and life he knew so well; and his name was on the mouths of men in the Peasants' Revolt of 1381.

The poem is written in the alliterative verse inherited from Old English times, with each line divided into two half-lines and two main stresses in each half line, as the following passage from the beginning of the poem will illustrate:

> In a somer sesun,   whon softe was the sonne,
> I schop me into a shroud,   as I a scheep were;
> In habite as an hermite   unholy of werkes,
> Wente I wyde in this world   wondres to here;
> Bote in a Mayes morwnynge,   on Malverne hulles,
> Me bifel a ferly,   of fairie, me-thoughte.
>
> (In a summer season   when soft was the sunshine,
> I got me into a garment   that grew on a sheep's back;
> In habit like a hermit   unholy in living,
> I went wide in this world   wonders to seek out.
> But on a May morning,   on Malvern hillside,
> I met with a marvel,   of magic I thought it.) [1]

Wycliffe was the greatest reformer of his time, a fighter against corruption, degenerate priesthood, and the misery and wretched state of the great masses of Englishmen. He urged poverty for the clergy instead of the wealth in which priests and prelates grew soft, attacked the authority of the pope, and denied the doctrine of transubstantiation. His questioning and courageous work naturally led to personal danger; he was banned by Pope Gregory XI and condemned by an ecclesiastical court, and it is difficult to understand how he escaped death at the stake for his heresy. Indeed, forty years after his death, the bishop of Lincoln ordered that his body be disinterred and burned and his ashes scattered. This did not prevent the underground spread and persistence of Wycliffe's doctrines, nor did the cruel persecutions of his followers, the Lollards.

Wycliffe wrote much in Latin and in a strong, simple, and moving English, but more important than his sermons and treatises was the translation of the Bible which he made with two assistants. He believed strongly in the right of every man to know the Bible for himself. His version was a landmark in English prose as well as an anticipation of future translations.

[1] Trans. from J. M. Manly, *English Prose and Poetry*, Ginn, 1926.

2. Early Humanism

Dante summed up the Middle Ages but left no successors. Petrarch (Francesco Petrarca, 1304-1374) was the first humanist, the first modern man of letters, the real founder of modern Italian literature. It was in Italy, and in the work of Petrarch, that literature began turning away from the medieval view of life and art to one in which the individual man and the world this side the grave acquired dignity and importance, in which general truth and pleasure as well as religious instruction were sought in literature.

Petrarch's father was expelled from Florence by the Guelphs in the same year as Dante, and the poet and humanist knew the world beyond Italy from his early years. He became a man of affairs, achieved ecclesiastical preferment and office but without taking orders, went on diplomatic missions for the pope and various Italian rulers, was an ardent patriot, and found time for a vast amount of writing in Latin and Italian. In 1341 he was crowned poet laureate at Rome, declining the same honor, offered in the same year, from Paris.

It was his curiosity, his desire for enlightenment beyond the traditional bounds, which caused Petrarch to ransack libraries for Greek and Latin manuscripts, and to copy or have copied all that he could find. His discovery of some of Cicero's letters to Atticus was an important event in modern literary history.

Although there had been growing appreciation of Latin literature and culture for centuries—indeed, it had never really died—Petrarch was one of the first to give proper recognition to the fact that Greek underlay Roman culture. Hence, although he was himself unable to read Greek, he was of great significance in the history of Greek studies. And he urged the reading of classical literature for its own sake, not for the possible Christian interpretations which might be read into such authors as Vergil, Ovid, and Cicero. The style, the ideas, the wide intellectual horizons of the ancient writers, attracted him. His love of pagan culture and his distaste for scholastic philosophy did not, however, conflict with his Christianity, which he regarded as a means of salvation, while he regarded the classical writers as guides in the world.

Enthusiasm for ancient Rome led Petrarch to celebrate the brief rise to power in 1347 of the tribune Cola di Rienzi as a sign of the resurrection of Rome from its sad state; he mistook the rabble which supported Rienzi for the citizenry of the ancient republic. The same enthusiasm inspired his own Latin writings, especially the epic *Africa,* which he thought his most important work, although he himself recognized that his Latin lacked the excellence of his Italian poems.

Petrarch inspired his friend Boccaccio with ardor for the classics, and encouraged him to have made a Latin translation of Homer. He performed another valuable service in dissuading Boccaccio from a plan to renounce the world. Others besides Boccaccio were inspired or encouraged by Petrarch in humanistic studies and the search for ancient manuscripts, coins, and mementoes. He achieved much in this direction through his friendship with powerful Italian princes and nobles.

3. *Narrative Poetry and Prose*

In Chaucer and Boccaccio the fourteenth century had two of the finest story-tellers of all time, and two in whose works there is a movement away from instructive and didactic literature to a free, secular spirit in both the selection and handling of themes. Spain in the same century possessed excellent tellers of tales in the Infante Don Juan Manuel (1282-1348), author of the *Conde Lucanor* (*Count Lucanor*), a collection of narratives with an apparently moral purpose, drawn from folk and Arabic sources, and Juan Ruiz (c. 1283-c. 1350), whose *Libro de Buen Amor* has been compared with Chaucer's *Canterbury Tales*. Ruiz, a priest, was no ascetic, and regarded life with a strong comic sense. He drew his various people—Moorish dancers, nuns, patrician ladies, peasant girls, sentimental lovers—with vivacity and humor, but he was also capable of a canticle in praise of the Virgin, and of exquisite fables.

Giovanni Boccaccio (c. 1313-1375) has been mentioned as a friend of Petrarch and a humanist; he was also a student of Dante, on whose work he lectured, a diplomat, author of learned treatises, and a poet, but his greatest fame is as the author of the prose *Decameron*, as a master of narrative, often considered the first modern novelist.

In the confused and dull (though historically important) *Filocopo* and the simpler *Fiammetta* (a forerunner of the psychological novel), Boccaccio had tried his hand at prose fiction, before he attained in the *Decameron* a style adapted to all tastes, neither affected as aristocratic literature tended to be nor crude in the manner of popular literature, but combining the refinement of one with the strength of the other. Boccaccio made use of the "framework" device in telling these stories, as Chaucer was to do in the *Canterbury Tales*—that is, he did not tell them directly, but through the mouths of imagined narrators. These narrators are a company of well-born Florentines, seven ladies and three gentlemen who fled the plague in the year 1348 to a pleasant retreat near Florence—"a little eminence, remote from any great road, covered with trees and plants of an agreeable verdure, on the top of which was a stately palace, with a grand and beautiful court in the middle. . . ." To while away the time in this delightful spot, they agree to tell stories, each member of the company one a day for ten days (whence the title, which means "ten days"). Thus there are a hundred stories altogether.

Few of the stories were original with Boccaccio. He drew most of them from the vast store of fables and legends which floated about the world, accessible to any who cared to use them. But Boccaccio made them his own through his perfect handling of the language, his skill in constructing an easy, graceful narrative. Certain of his subjects have resulted in giving the *Decameron* a reputation for licentiousness, but only a small number of stories are devoted to so-called "objectionable" themes, and these themes themselves are treated with wit and honest frankness to be found in no work deliberately pornographic.

Boccaccio's mastery of narrative technique was not confined to prose; his poems, *Teseide* and *Il Filostrato* reflect it, and both were used by Chaucer, the first in the

Knight's Tale, the second in *Troilus and Criseyde.* Later English writers, and writers of other nations, were to feel his influence.

The first great name in English poetry is that of Geoffrey Chaucer (c. 1340-1400), and he has not ceased to be for us what he was for Edmund Spenser in the sixteenth century,

> Dan Chaucer, well of English undefiled,
> On Fame's eternal beadroll worthy to be filed.

A son of that middle class (his father was a wine-merchant) which during his own century and the following would rise to power and help alter the face of the world, he was himself a man of action all his life. He was early in the service of Lionel, who became Duke of Clarence, and later under the patronage of John of Gaunt; he saw military service in France, and was taken prisoner; served at court, went on diplomatic missions to Italy and elsewhere on the Continent, was controller of the customs and clerk of the king's works. But he found time for reading, as he tells himself ("Of bokes rede I ofte, as I yow tolde"), both in the Latin authors known to his time, and in Italian and French (if he had desired, he could have written in French). There are echoes in his work of these old and new authors, of the astronomy-astrology so important to men of his day, and of medical and other lore.

Thus both in the active world and in books Chaucer came to know the curious ways of men, and no saner or more tolerant observer has ever written down his thoughts. Neither a scholar, for all his medieval display of learning, nor a philosopher despite his translation of Boëthius, nor capable of seeing men from within with the intense awareness of Shakespeare, he comprehended his world with shrewdness and calm good sense, with a humor which even Shakespeare did not surpass.

In Chaucer the age that was passing and the new age meet; if that ambiguous adjective "modern" may be applied to him, it must not be forgotten how much a man of the Middle Ages he was. If he poked fun at corrupt church officials, he was no radical like Wycliffe, no satirical reformer like Langland. The final stanzas of *Troilus and Criseyde* mentioned earlier in this chapter, contain an abjuration of worldly vanity, an admonition to love God, too moving to be merely a conventional reflection of the medieval contempt for "This litel spot of erthe, that with the se enbraced is."

In form as well as in his orthodox faith he made no violent break with tradition, although as he grew older he moved from the French conventions which influenced his early work to the fresh spirit of his great Italian contemporaries, and to a sturdy independence in his maturity. The dream-vision, the allegory, the exemplum, the saint's legend are to be found in his work, with other medieval forms.

But withal, he is a man of the changing world; if he loves God, he loves the individual man, and describes him with no immediate concern for his fate after death. He treats life without moralizing, though not without a high moral sense;

he savors its gross earthiness, its absurdities, its beauty and pathos, and (though much less often) its grimness, as in these tense lean lines describing

> The crueel Ire, reed as any glede,
> The pykepurs, and eek the pale Drede;
> The smylere with the knyf under the cloke;
> The shepne brennynge with the blake smoke;
> The tresoun of the mordrynge in the bedde;
> The open werre, with woundes al bibledde. . . .[2]

Among Chaucer's lesser works may be mentioned *The Book of the Duchess,* an elegy upon the death of Blanche, Duchess of Lancaster, wife of John of Gaunt; *The Parliament of Fowls,* a possible allegory on a royal betrothal, with birds for actors; *The House of Fame,* a long unfinished dream-allegory, with echoes of Dante and Vergil, which contains among many things a delightful conversation between Chaucer and a heavily pedantic eagle.

The greatest completed poem of Chaucer's was *Troilus and Criseyde* (the *Canterbury Tales* were not finished). Chaucer used the *Filostrato* of Boccaccio, altering and adding to the Italian poem, giving the story both the coloring of his own wit and style, and a deeper moral significance. The legend had come to Boccaccio through the spurious accounts of the Trojan War popular in the Middle Ages. It tells the love of Troilus, son of King Priam, for the lovely Trojan widow, Criseyde; their union (though not in marriage) through the instrumentality of Pandarus, Troilus' friend and Criseyde's uncle; Criseyde's departure for the Greek camp to join her father, a Trojan priest who knows that Troy will fall; her forsaking Troilus for Diomede, a Greek, and Troilus' despair and death. Chaucer made his account one of the finest narratives in English; the five books of his poem are carefully constructed and move not with rapid action but in dramatic scenes, to the crisis of the story and the final stanzas mentioned above. In mood the work ranges from the gayest wit, the most worldly irony, to serious consideration of fate and fortune, and moments of tragic grief. And although the conventions of courtly love are used, the characterization is true, especially that of Pandarus, the gay ironist and man of the world, and that of Criseyde, whose shifting emotions Chaucer analyzes with the care and detachment of a great psychological novelist. And as the poem itself treats ancient Troy in terms of fourteenth-century dress and manners, so it treats human experience (with reservations for the sentimentality of Troilus) in terms still meaningful to men and women.

The *Troilus* is Chaucer's most finished, the *Canterbury Tales* his most famous and most varied, work. Like the stories of the *Decameron* (though Chaucer did not know that work) these are set in a framework—a pilgrimage from London to the shrine of St. Thomas à Becket at Canterbury. There are thirty pilgrims, including Chaucer himself, and in addition Harry Bailey, the host of the Tabard Inn in Southwark where the pilgrimage began. The original plan called for four stories from each pilgrim—one hundred and twenty in all—but only twenty were

---

[2] The *Canterbury Tales:* Knight's Tale, ll. 1997-2002. From the description of the Temple of Mars. "Cruel Anger, red as any ember | the pickpurse and also pale Fear | the smiler with the knife under the cloak | the shed burning with the black smoke | the treason of the murdering in the bed | the open war with wounds all gory | . . ."

completed, and the order in which they were intended to appear has not been finally determined.

No work shows better Chaucer's wide knowledge of the world and understanding of men, for the pilgrims come from all walks of life, from knight to plowman, and possess the familiar virtues and vices. Chaucer treats them, even the most villainous, with good humor; his satire is robust, but with nothing in it of the whiplash.

The pilgrims themselves are described in the general Prologue to the tales, and elaborated upon in the "links" between tales, or (like the Wife of Bath and the Pardoner) in prologues to individual tales. Sometimes Chaucer's description is sharply detailed, sometimes the picture is more generalized, and the character becomes a type of a profession or trade. But whatever his method, he created people as living now in his familiar, humorous speech as they were on that April morning nearly six centuries ago. The fourteenth century passes before us in the gentle knight and the love-hot squire, in the lean Oxford student and the self-satisfied, not always honest, business and professional men—lawyer, physician, shipman, merchant. Closer to earth are the red-bearded miller who loves to jest of "sin and harlotries," and the Wife of Bath, whose experience has taught her to regard marriage with much sense and no illusions.

Most memorable is the group connected with the church: the too dainty prioress, the monk who prefers hunting and a fat roast swan to study and lean living, the wanton and merry friar, the summoner (who brought offenders before ecclesiastical courts) hideous to look at, lecherous, a master bribe-taker. There is, too, the Pardoner who passes off stones and pigs' bones as holy relics. In contrast with these worldly or corrupt churchmen and hangers-on of the church Chaucer places the poor parson, a true preacher of Christ's gospel, "a shepherd not a mercenary." And his brother, the plowman, is an honest laborer very different from the more pretentious members of the group.

As the pilgrims are of all sorts, so are the stories they tell, which range from vulgar comedy with the miller to pathos with the clerk, from witty accounts of deceived husbands to the knight's chivalric tale of Palamon and Arcite, from the prioress's tender story of a little martyred boy to the hypocritical Pardoner's vivid sermon on the evils of avarice and other sins. There is meat for every taste in the tales, and though Chaucer, like Homer, nodded now and then, the best of them remain in the poet's own words "evere ilyke faire and fressh of hewe"—ever fair and fresh of hue.

Chaucer's accomplishment was not only the writing of great poetry. As an earlier chapter has pointed out, English in his day was broken up into dialects, and it was largely his genius which gave one of them, the Midland dialect spoken in London and at the court, a dignity and importance sufficient to make it the foundation of a national language.

The century after Chaucer's death witnessed a sharp decline in the quality of English poetry, except for the popular ballad and the work of certain poets north of the river Humber who wrote in the dialect now known as Scotch. In the poems of King James I of Scotland (1406-1437) and William Dunbar (c. 1465-c. 1530) there is a charm and freshness entirely lacking in the enormous mass of verse ground out in England by Thomas Occleve (c. 1370-c. 1450) and John Lyd-gate (c. 1370-c. 1451).

During this period there was produced the most brilliant piece of historical lit-erature of the whole medieval age, the *Chronicles* of Jean Froissart (1337-1410) on the Hundred Years' War. Masson has observed that "in point of style and bril-liant coloring, Shakespeare alone can be placed on the same line with Froissart."

4. Folk Poetry

Chaucer and Boccaccio were sophisticated artists, learned in past literature, writing for an upper-class audience. But from deep in time there had been a poetry of the people, songs composed orally and orally transmitted through the centuries, and written down comparatively late in history. Such a poetry of the people are the English and Scottish ballads and the German folk songs.

It was once held that a ballad was the product of community authorship—the spontaneous result of group effort, with each member of the group contributing to its growth into a story. This theory is now generally abandoned for one which assumes that ballads were first composed by individual singers, but even so, gen-erations of oral transmission brought additions and changes which made such poems community possessions in a very real sense.

Though ballads vary one from another in detail, in general they possess certain distinguishing characteristics. A ballad is, to begin with, a song, and possesses the strong rhythms, the refrains, and the repetitions of poetry meant to be sung. It tells a story, and tells it without delay for exposition or explanation, or for the intrusion of the author's own feelings—it is impersonal and unreflective. The subject of the story may be any event striking to the popular imagination: a love affair or a domestic tragedy, a historical action, the supernatural, the exploits of a folk hero like Robin Hood, a humorous occurrence. The form is simple—the most popular is a four-line stanza rhyming a-b-c-b, the first and third lines con-taining four accents each, the second and fourth three each. The language is simple, direct, and concrete, unadorned with figures of speech, and distinguished by the use of conventional epithets. The device of "incremental repetition" is very characteristic of the ballad—that is, repetition of lines or stanzas with change in a word or phrase. The story may be told directly, or through a dialogue.

The following famous ballad (of which there are many variants) will illustrate some of the qualities mentioned above. There is no information concerning the identity of the speakers; there is no preliminary explanation of events leading up to the episode with which the ballad deals: the story explains itself.

> "O where hae ye been, Lord Randal, my son?
>   O where hae ye been, my handsome young man?"
> "I hae been to the wild wood; mother, make my bed soon,
>   For I'm weary wi hunting, and fain wald lie down."
>
> "Where gat ye your dinner, Lord Randal, my son?
>   Where gat ye your dinner, my handsome young man?"
> "I din'd wi my true-love; mother, make my bed soon,
>   For I'm weary wi hunting, and fain wald lie down."

"What gat ye to your dinner, Lord Randal, my son?
What gat ye to your dinner, my handsome young man?"
"I gat eels boiled in broo; mother, make my bed soon,
For I'm weary wi hunting, and fain wald lie down."

"What became of your bloodhounds, Lord Randal, my son?
What became of your bloodhounds, my handsome young man?"
"O they swelld and they died; mother, make my bed soon,
For I'm weary wi hunting, and fain wald lie down."

"O I fear ye are poisond, Lord Randal, my son!
O I fear ye are poisond, my handsome young man!"
"O yes! I am poisond; mother, make my bed soon,
For I'm sick at the heart and I fain wald lie down."

Among other famous English and Scottish ballads, with numerous variations in different versions, are *The Twa Brothers, Sir Patrick Spens, The Hunting of the Cheviot, The Douglas Tragedy, Edward, The Twa Sisters, The Wife of Usher's Well,* and many on Robin Hood and his followers.

The popular ballad is not yet dead, though the conditions of modern life are not conducive to its production. Many of the old English ballads came to America in early days, and are still sung in remote regions like the Tennessee and Virginia mountains. Native ballads have grown up in this country too, some based on traditional stories, others on the exploits of such heroes as Jesse James or John Henry, the legendary Negro steel-driver, others on the lives of cowboys and pioneers, or of southern Negroes, true lovers of song and storytelling.

In the eighteenth and nineteenth centuries the new romantic interest in the past led to the first important collection and study of ballads, and to the creation of the so-called "literary" ballad, imitative of old forms, but written in a spirit and with a purpose foreign to the popular songs. Sir Walter Scott was both a collector and writer of ballads, and other English poets who tried their hands at the form were Coleridge, Byron, Keats, Rossetti, William Morris, and Swinburne.

The German folk song, like the English and Scottish ballad, is of unknown authorship, and for many centuries had a similar oral transmission. In every dialect, the German people made its songs, singing in simple but deeply moving verses the joys and sorrows of love, the pleasures of drinking and student life, the beauties of nature, the love of fatherland. The great age of the folk song was the fifteenth and sixteenth centuries. In the eighteenth and nineteenth a new interest in the simple melodies of the past developed, and the lyrics of Goethe, Heine, and other later poets owe much to them. No nation has had a richer or more enduring folk poetry than Germany.

5. Lyric Poetry

The lyric, as a cultivated form, did not reach in general so high a level in this period as narrative poetry. England's golden age of the lyric would begin in the sixteenth century, largely under the influence of the greatest of fourteenth-century lyrists, Petrarch. In fifteenth-century France Charles d'Orléans and François

Villon enlivened sterile conventional forms, and in Spain the Marquis de Santillana (1398-1458) wrote sonnets in the Italian style.

Petrarch has been mentioned as a humanist, and in his total work his labors as a humanist bulk much larger than his composition of poetry. His scholarly work, however, was absorbed in the general stream of the cultural revival to which he gave the impetus; his lyrics maintain an independent life.

As Dante's name is linked for all time with that of Beatrice, so Petrarch's is with that of Laura, his one abiding subject and inspiration. Who this shadowy lady really was cannot be said, though tradition makes her an older woman, married, and a mother. But whoever she was, she was the guiding star of Petrarch's life and poetry while she lived, and the memory of her fills the poems written after her death in 1348. "What little I am, such as it is," the poet said, "I am through her."

It was into his *canzoniere* [3] (songs) that Petrarch poured his feelings for Laura, his longings for her while she lived, his dejection after she was dead, or his feeling of consolation in thinking of her in heaven. She remains always ethereal and ideal; the odes and sonnets describe as a rule the poet's feelings rather than the lady herself; he is submissive, rebellious, adoring, by turns; reproaches her for her cruelty, or is ennobled by love's power, by the unyielding chastity which elsewhere he regrets. In the *Trionfi* (*Triumphs*), an allegory in *terza rima,* written after Laura was long dead, Petrarch presents the conquests of Love, Death, Fame, and Time, and here too his persisting love for her is celebrated.

Petrarch was not the first Italian poet to write sonnets, but he was the greatest master of the form, and most influential on later sonneteers. The Petrarchan sonnet is divided into an octave and a sestet, the former invariably rhyming a-b-b-a-a-b-b-a, the latter most often c-d-e-c-d-e. The theme is set forth in the octave (first eight lines), the conclusion drawn in the sestet (last six lines).

In France there developed in the fourteenth century a fashion for strict, highly artificial lyrical forms, of which the ballade [4] and the rondeau [5] were most popular. Into their narrow limits any subject could be squeezed, and though they have a certain charm at times, they are largely sterile. Guillaume de Machault (1300-1377) and Eustache Deschamps (1340-1410) led in the writing of these forms in the fourteenth century; echoes and even translations of their lines are to be found in Chaucer, to whom Deschamps addressed a poem of praise.

These limited genres were given life and color by Charles d'Orléans (1391-1465) and François Villon (1431-?). D'Orléans, a nephew of Charles VII, was a prisoner in England for twenty-five years after the battle of Agincourt; his poems on love or homesickness are graceful and often expressive of genuine feeling.

Villon, whose real name was probably Montcorbier, was a scholar, a thief, and

---

[3] The full title is *Rime in vita e morte di Madonna Laura—Rhymes in Life and Death of My Lady Laura.*

[4] The ballade (very different from the ballad) consists of three stanzas of eight (or ten) lines, and a final stanza, called the *envoy,* of four lines. The same rhymes, in the same order, are repeated in the long stanzas, and the last four rhymes in the envoy. The scheme is a-b-a-b-b-c-b-c, and in the envoy b-c-b-c. The same line is repeated at the end of each stanza to make the *refrain.*

[5] The rondeau is a thirteen line poem, with two rhymes throughout, and a refrain made from the first part of the first line of the poem.

a murderer, condemned to the gallows but pardoned, to disappear into the unknown. He infused blood and passion into the stale ballade and rondeau. In his poems there is a sense of the hardness and bitterness of life in the murky streets of Paris at the very end of the Middle Ages, and mingled with irony and wit, an ever-present sense of man's mortality and the horrors of death. His language is strong and muscular, the language of men, of the street, and tender or brutal as he writes a ballade for his old mother in prayer to the Virgin, or describes the depravity of life with fat Margot "en ce bourdel ou tenons nostre estat"—"in this brothel where we keep our state."

In his Testaments Villon made mock bequests to enemies and friends; most of the poems for which he is famous are interpolated in the *Grand testament* written in the thirtieth year of his age. Here are the poignant regrets of the belle Heaulmière, recalling in her aged misery the beauty and joy of youth, and the ballade of good counsel to those of evil life. Here is the lovely *Ballade des dames du temps jadis (Ballade of Dead Ladies)*, whose refrain sums up the poet's haunting sense of life's shortness: "Mais ou sont les neiges d'antan?"—"Where are the snows of yesteryear?" Elsewhere he imagined himself on the gallows with the companions with whom he expected to be hanged, and the rotting and drying of death is in the ballade which he made for them—his plea for pity and prayer is set against a picture of bodies swinging ceaselessly in the wind, corrupt, decaying, pecked by birds.

6. The Rise of the Drama

The Christian churches have often in history been hostile to plays and players, but it was in the church itself in the Middle Ages that modern drama was born. Centuries before the period under discussion words were interpolated in the service of the Mass on Easter Sunday, and members of the choir sang a little dialogue representing the questions and answers at the sepulcher of Jesus between the three Marys who came seeking His body and the angels who told them of the Resurrection. These interpolations, or "tropes," were the foundation of the liturgical dramas, acted by churchmen in the precincts of the church, which grew up throughout Europe. They gradually lost their place in the Mass proper, acquired rudimentary dramatic elements—augmented dialogue, a certain amount of gesture and action, even suggestions of suspense and climax. The liturgical plays were long given in Latin; the introduction into them of the vernacular was an important step toward a drama acted by laymen and away from the church building, in the street or market place.

The vernacular drama which grew up in the later Middle Ages continued to make use of religious themes, though a secular drama ultimately began to emerge. In general this drama is classed under the heading of "miracle plays," though a further distinction has been made between miracle plays proper, on the lives of saints, and "mystery plays," on episodes from the Old and New Testaments. Morality plays, dramatized allegories on the conflict of good and evil, developed somewhat later. The mysteries were acted on feast days, most often on Corpus Christi day (the Thursday after Trinity Sunday), by townspeople, members of trades and guilds, or in France by such a special organization as the Confrérie de la Passion, which had a monopoly in Paris for the presentation of plays from 1402-1548. The presentation of the biblical story in the market place or on stages which moved about the streets sometimes required several days. The influence of the German Passion plays, which showed the significant events in the life of Christ, endures in the famous Passion play at Oberammergau, and elsewhere in Germany.

The plays on biblical episodes from the Creation to the Last Judgment were gathered in cycles, and many of these cycle plays are extant in English, French, German, and Spanish. In England the texts of four such cycles have survived. They are known by the names of the towns where they were performed—York, Coventry, Chester, and Wakefield (these last better known as the Towneley plays, from the long possession by the Towneley family of the sole manuscript in which they exist). A few non-cycle mystery plays have also survived.

In English towns each guild was responsible for one scene of the cycle—thus the glovers of Wakefield acted the killing of Abel, the dyers of Chester the story of Pharaoh. Records of towns and guilds list expenses incurred in presenting the plays—the purchase of gowns (God wore a white coat, for instance), the upkeep of the "pageant" or stage on wheels, food and fees for the actors. In 1490 the smiths of Chester itemized the cost of exhibiting the trial and passion of Christ; so much for purchases of ale, bread, and ribs of beef; two shillings each to God and Pilate's wife, four shillings each to Pilate and his son, eighteen shillings to the devil and Judas.

Crude in form and language as they were, these plays were not entirely without merit. Most important in foreshadowing the eventual secularization of drama was the introduction at an early date of a comic element, either in certain actual biblical people, or in characters and actions added to the Bible stories. The comedy was often slapstick or horseplay, the language vulgar and abusive, but it had in a large degree the force of life. An earthy realism is found in such added or altered characters as Cain's insolent servant, Noah's wife, who would rather stay with her gossips than enter the ark, the bullying and rascally torturers of Jesus. The ranting and raving of those popular villains, Herod, Pilate, and Pharaoh, was more stereotyped than the familiar speech and action of characters of less degree, who like most of their auditors came straight out of the fields and towns of contemporary Europe. In the later moralities this realistic strain continued in the Vice, who is far more alive than his virtuous opponents.

It was not entirely in low comedy that the medieval drama came closest to actuality. The most moving of all these early plays is the non-cycle mystery called the Brome *Abraham and Isaac* (from the preservation of the manuscript at Brome Manor). The unassuming story, simply told, expresses human emotions as truly as many a more elaborate and more profound work of art. Abraham's humble rejoicing and thanks to God for the child of his old age ("I love no thing so much, ywis"), his heartbreak when the command comes to sacrifice this child, the innocent trust and fear of Isaac, who asks that his mother not be told—these are handled with true pathos, with no touch of sentimentalizing.

Most perfect of English mysteries is the *Second Shepherds Play,* one of the Towneley cycle. Though it treats ostensibly of the shepherds' visit to the stable where the infant Jesus is lying, for most of its length it is pure farce, a skillfully handled representation of the comic conflict between the shepherds and a sheep-stealer. The language is vigorous and colloquial, the shepherds true English peasants, complaining of the winter weather and ill-treatment by "these gentler men," and of the woes of marriage.

The best-known of morality plays is *Everyman,* which, despite its allegorical nature, the fact that its characters are personified abstractions, is concrete and true in its treatment of life and death. The chief character is indeed "every man," but he is also an individual faced with death, for which, as Villon also knew, no child or brother or friend will be his pledge. In *Mankind* the comic predominates; the work lives in the rugged and riotous language of the villainous Mischief, Newgyse, Now-a-days, and Nought.

The secular drama of the late Middle Ages was the final steppingstone to the drama of modern times. In France as early as the thirteenth century Adam de la Halle (1230-1287) had written satirical and pastoral plays with skill and wit. In the fifteenth century there appeared "soties," clownish satires which did not spare church and state, and farces which dealt realistically with the life of everyday. Chief among farces is *Master Pathelin,* which ridicules lawyers and their trickery. In Germany the traditions of minstrelsy and the comic elements of religious drama developed into the secular *Fastnachtspiel,* or Shrovetide play, performed just before the beginning of the lean days of Lent, and concerned, like the French farce, with common life—marital squabbles, drinking, the gulling of rustics.

The English "interludes" (the origin of the name is unsettled) did not all shake off the characteristics of the morality, but the best are secular and strongly farcical. Those of John Heywood (c. 1497-c. 1580) belong to the sixteenth century. With the interludes the break with the religious tradition in the drama was definite; their comedy is comedy for its own sake, not merely relief from sometimes tedious piety, and with them the theater as theater comes into its own.

II. ART IN ITALY AND NORTHERN EUROPE

In this chapter we shall deal with the material customarily referred to as "early Renaissance" art, whose relationship to the tradition of the Middle Ages we have already pointed out. We must look for a continuous development from the period of Giotto (early 14th century) to Fra Lippo (Filippo) Lippi (middle of the 15th century) during which the specific elements of medievalism gave way before the new cultural forces and attitudes already abundantly described in this volume.

One of the most conspicuous aspects of the new mode of thought was the growth of individualism. Most of the art manifestations of the Middle Ages had been anonymous. Such great creations as the French cathedrals are more significant as expressions of the spirit of their locale than as the work of any individual. The sculptures decorating these buildings were similarly the product of "schools" rather than of individuals. Art was a phenomenon inextricably bound up with the corporate nature of politics and religion and the artist belonged to a guild or union. At the end of the thirteenth century this fog of anonymity lifted. Particularly in Italy a great many artists began to sign their works and the spirit of free competition in art was born.

At this time we notice a change in the status of the artist. He gains in social position because of the increased culture and enlightenment of the new merchant class and the powerful princes of the age. The demand for works of art became greater and by the early fifteenth century every petty noble and despot, every well-to-do merchant wished to have his home decorated with pictures, fine furniture, tapestries, etc. To maintain his prestige, his family must be well dressed, his dishes of a superior quality, and the painting which he donates to his local church must have sufficient excellence. So, too, the growth of individual expression and fame, whether military or commercial, inevitably led to the rise of an art of portraiture, an unfailing manifestation of the rise of a middle class with money and leisure. The artist who had heretofore worked almost exclusively for the church (and to a lesser degree for the aristocracy) now found a new patron, the merchant class, in Flanders as well as Italy.

The prevailing mode of expression reflected the growth of curiosity in the world. The more abstract spiritual ideas of the Middle Ages (Romanesque period) had already begun to relax with the birth and formation of the guilds in the Gothic period. During the transition (from about 1300-1475) this process was crystallized into the practical, worldly attitude of fifteenth-century Italy and Flanders.

The fifteenth century produced a type of person with whom we, as moderns, have much in common. He was rationally educated, interested in the world about him, and responsive to material beauty. For him the things of the flesh were desirable and since he no longer believed that his body was his worst enemy, the nude acquired an important place in art. How natural, therefore, for the artists and others of this time to study nature and portray it as they thought it really was. They gave their attention to perspective, foreshortening, color, drapery, anatomy, and a host of other phenomena, among them chemistry, engineering, mathematics, aeronautics, physics, and philosophy—truly universal interests. As a result, even religious art became affected by naturalism. The abstract architectural art of the Middle Ages became supplanted by religious paintings in which Madonnas, prophets, and others were given the appearance of everyday people; so much so, that in many cases we are able to tell from which part of Italy the peasant girl who posed for a Madonna had come.

The fourteenth and fifteenth centuries in Italy bear a strong relationship to the period of classical antiquity. Both periods fostered the growth of the individual and an interest in nature. In Italy this feeling for classicism had never completely died. What more rational than for Italian fourteenth- and fifteenth-century artists to turn wholeheartedly to the study of ancient Greek and Roman remains! The result was not merely a superficial imitation of classical ornaments in painting, sculpture, and architecture, but a complete absorption of the "humanistic" ideal revealed there. Hence the artist of the new period approached the problem of interpreting his age conditioned by the noble and impressive manner in which the Roman artist had dealt with a similar task. This conditioning resulted in an art which was undoubtedly dedicated to the depiction of man and his environment, but was more interested, humanistically, in man and, furthermore, inclined to express itself in a more idealized manner than in the countries of northern Europe. This shift from the mass point of view of the Christian Middle Ages, wherein the individual counted for little, to a point where the individual man was the measure of all things, was one of the significant marks of the emergence of modern times.

1. *Architecture*

Before we proceed to a study of painting and sculpture, we may consider the architecture of the fourteenth and fifteenth centuries in Italy, for it is in this medium that the dual nature of the period is most evident. Italian architecture of this time most clearly shows a dependence on the Middle Ages for most of its plans and on classical Rome for the outer layer of ornament to embellish façades. Older types of building such as the basilican church were continued and these, too, added classical ornament, showing with what freedom the new artist mingled the old with the new to achieve greater individuality and freshness in design and ornament. The simpler arches and columns of the Italian Romanesque period were now continued with even closer classical derivatives which quickly overcame the never too firmly acclimatized Gothic vaults and piers. Romanism, the basis of Italian ornamentation of this period, was the logical continuation of the native classical architecture whose Roman remains dotted the Italian peninsula.

This period of transition is important for the development of secular architecture such as the civic building and the palace (palazzo) of the early fifteenth century. Italian palaces were built with a simple, and often austere, exterior around a hollow square plan with the rooms all interconnected in the modern "railroad flat" fashion. The inside of the square, the courtyard, was surrounded by an open colonnade behind which one could proceed from one part of the building to another. The civic buildings of the transition period adapted the earlier medieval town hall or guild hall plans by the addition of Roman ornament.

The most important architect of the early fifteenth century in Italy was Brunelleschi (1377-1466), who greatly influenced the direction of architecture in this period toward the antique. His first great enterprise was the dome of the Cathedral of Florence, a building begun in the early fourteenth century in the typical native basilican style of the Italian peninsula, which he attempted to complete with the steeply pitched dome that now covers it. Although this dome has been compared with the dome of the Pantheon in Rome as an example of classical influence, such is far from valid. Perhaps Brunelleschi was inspired by the size of the earlier Roman example, but we must remember that Roman architecture, for the most part, depended on poured concrete which was admitted into brick cells to form a static unified whole. In the dome of the Florentine cathedral, however, the sharply pitched dome consists of two concentric shells bound together by stone ribs, with the inner shell held together by stout logs connected with iron chains

—the entire arrangement was a combination of the dynamic system of the Middle Ages and the static system of classical architecture brought into being by the originality of the architect. In his typical treatment of a church building, Brunelleschi was not as imaginative as in this cathedral. He used the conservative plan of the early Christian basilica, applying to it the columns and entablature of Roman times.

One of the most important characteristics of the architecture of the fifteenth century is the curious unfunctional manner in which classical ornaments were used. Like their Roman predecessors, who had taken over a series of motifs from the Greeks to apply them superficially, the Italians of this period used Roman ideas as forms of pure decoration, completely forgetting the fact that these forms had originally served some practical purpose.

2. Sculpture

The adaptation of Roman architectural material to the buildings of this transitional period strikingly influenced the sculptors of the time who combined architectural backgrounds with their work and, like the painters, absorbed from antiquity its approach to the interpretation of nature.

In the same manner that the sculpture of the Pisano family at the end of the thirteenth century had exerted a powerful influence upon the development of painting during the early fourteenth century (school of Giotto), the sculpture produced at the end of the fourteenth and beginning of the fifteenth centuries was the motivating background for the painting of its time. It is always easier for the artist to work out ideas of form in a plastic medium such as clay or wood, since he does not have to simulate the appearance of a third dimension which is already there, and if it is the aim of a given group of men to interpret realistically the appearance of nature, it will more probably be successful if they approach the matter in three dimensions. For this reason, we take up the development of sculpture before we attempt to study painting during this period.

Between the work of the painter Giotto in the first quarter of the fourteenth century and that of the sculptor Ghiberti in the first quarter of the fifteenth, the two important names in sculpture are Andrea Pisano and Orcagna. Pisano was responsible for the first large pair of bronze doors on the baptistery of the Cathedral of Florence (done between 1330-1336). They are still medieval in composition, spirit, and message, but, influenced by the painting of Giotto, they are unusual examples of solid form, betraying a tremendous interest in the natural world. Orcagna, a many-sided artist, carved the famous shrine in the church of Or San Michele, one of the important guild churches in Florence in the middle of the fourteenth century. Although basically still Gothic, this shrine shows the influence of the realistic art of Giotto and Andrea Pisano.

The fifteenth century was ushered in by two great personalities: Lorenzo Ghiberti (1378-1452) and Donatello (1386-1466). At the very beginning of the century Ghiberti won a competition for the execution of a massive pair of bronze doors to be attached to the baptistery of the Cathedral of Florence. Together with his assistants he worked on these doors for more than twenty years, turning out twenty-eight panels dealing with the life of the Savior, the four Evangelists, and the four church fathers. In the individual panels there is still discernible any number of Gothic overtones, particularly in the swaying, elegant bodies of the figures as well as the shape of their frame. The doors form a remarkable parallel to the earlier set done by Andrea Pisano and mark an improvement over the latter in being more richly filled. Ghiberti's most important work, however, is the second pair of doors which he created for the same building (1425-1452), the doors which Michelangelo later said were fit to be the Gates of Paradise. Ten large reliefs dealing with Old Testament subjects from the Creation of Adam down to Solomon's Visit to the Queen of Sheba show a distinct departure from the earlier style. What is particularly amazing about these relief sculptures is the fact that in these square spaces he has rendered so clearly and vividly the effect of the most developed painting with all of its technical tricks and devices. Rich architectural backgrounds vie with deep landscape perspectives to furnish a naturalistic setting for the dramatic scenes portrayed here. The entire depth of the relief is not more than one and a half to two inches and yet in this shallow space he has given us the impression of vast distances, the city of Jericho with its encircling walls, the palace of the Queen of Sheba, the mountain of Sinai, etc. "In the ten subjects treated," he said, "I have represented the buildings in such proportions as they appear to the eye, and in such a manner that from a distance they seem to be detached from the background. They have little relief, and, as in nature, the nearer figures are larger and the remoter smaller." In these narrow box-like spaces, the figures, all arranged with taste and compositional foresight, appear to move back and forth as though in and out of a landscape or architectural setting. Some are almost completely separated from the background and remain attached only by the slimmest threads, a great tribute to the sheer technical skill in bronze casting shown by this great artist. The classical derivation of Ghiberti's work on these doors is most clearly seen in the forms decorating the framework in which they are set. For these he used a series of full-length draped and undraped figures some of which were copied directly from antique statues, as were the small medallion heads with which they alternate. As an imaginative and individualistic *tour de force*, nothing in the modern world could make the same startling artistic impression until the time of the great Sistine Chapel ceiling of Michelangelo.

The second great sculptor of the first half of the fifteenth century was Donatello, a friend and pupil of Brunelleschi with whom he made a journey to Rome to study the monuments of classical antiquity. He is one of the greatest realists of the entire Italian tradition. If his realism reminds us of the direct and practical approach of the ancient Romans, it is not only because he studied and imitated them but also because the conditions of the period in which he lived made this form of expression almost mandatory. We may say, in general, that his art represents a combination of the past and the present in the typical Italian fashion of the time. His first great work, the *St. George*, is still reminiscent of the Gothic Middle Ages and may be compared with the St. Theodore of Chartres in spiritual character. This work possesses the inherent qualities of balance and rhythm, which are so characteristic of the semi-classical production of the transitional period.

During the second stage of his career (1416-1432) Donatello rose to amazing heights of realism, as in the portrait figure of *Niccolo da Uzzano* where he appears to reproduce the incisive characterizations and unflattering veracity of the Romans. In spite of the unclassical features of the subject portrayed here, the result is in every way noble and even impressive with beautiful color added to the clay. The third period of Donatello's artistic life (1432-1444) included his trip to Rome which resulted in a more direct influence of the antique upon his style. Such an example as the famous *Singing-Gallery* for the Cathedral of Florence, a work in marble representing a group of wildly dancing children who are supposed to be singing the praises of the Lord, is interesting for its almost Bacchic, pagan spirit, while the youthful figure of *David,* a beautiful nude with a torn shepherd's hat, is unquestionably in the spirit of the best Hellenistic art and one of his most finished pieces.

The greatest work of his last period (1444-1466) is the celebrated equestrian portrait of *Gattamelata,* the great mercenary general. Here he has revived the ancient Roman conception of the conqueror on horseback but in an individual manner characteristic of only Donatello himself. Not only is this work distinguished for the unusually fine knowledge of anatomy which the artist has indicated, but in the remarkable restraint of the portrait which is both classical and dramatic at the same time. The *Gattamelata* is one of the most interesting evidences that art reveals and interprets the civilization of its age, since it represents one of the most characteristic and important types in Italian society of that day, the *condottiere* or mercenary. Instead of portraying him as a bravo, Donatello has given to this quiet figure an almost menacing quality which is much more impressive than any degree of blustering ever could be.

One final figure must be added to our list of sculptors during the first half of the fifteenth century in Italy, Luca della Robbia (1399-1482), important as the founder of a technique in glazed terra cotta (baked clay) which was charmingly colored and much cheaper, hence available to larger numbers of people than marble or bronze. The mild beauty and gentle naturalism of this artist's creations parallels the more sentimental type of painting which flourished during the first half of the fifteenth century in Florence (as Fra Lippo Lippi). The lovely blues, yellows, and greens of these terra-cotta sculptures were repeated by his descendants to become one of the most popular products of the Italian school. Even today tourists in Italy are charmed by these pieces and buy the various crude imitations of them which are still being sold.

3. *Italian Painting*

At the end of the Gothic period with the advent of Giotto in Italy, we find the predominantly architectural ideal of the Middle Ages relaxing to allow the development of painting and sculpture as independent arts, although architecture, painting, and sculpture exerted a mutually beneficial influence. Painting reached the highest development and interest, first, because of its inherent fluidity, and secondly, because the growth of commerce and travel encouraged the exchange of aesthetic influences among the various countries of Europe. The latter fact was further stimulated by the development of the easel picture,[6] for while it is almost impossible to transport a fresco,[7] an easel picture is readily portable.

In the North of Europe during the Gothic period stained glass had been the important pictorial art (together with manuscript illumination). Italy, however, never deeply affected by the northern Gothic style, limited itself to simple basilican buildings whose broad walls lent themselves admirably to wall painting. This accounts for the early appearance of the art of fresco in the South, as in the work of Giotto in the first quarter of the fourteenth century.

In Italian painting we may divide the tremendous number of artists into two general groups: realists and lyricists, both of which had their analogies in the sculpture of the time. Of the realists, the earliest and perhaps most important member was Masaccio (1401-1428), one of the most individual geniuses produced during the period of transition. Although most Florentine artists were interested in the processes of draughtsmanship as they had been first laid down by Giotto, this precocious painter achieved his effects primarily through color and tone. In the Brancacci chapel of the Carmine church in Florence, Masaccio executed a number of frescoes for a private patron, dealing with the important incidents in the life of St. Peter. Although our first impression of these works is not overwhelming we can feel in the landscape in which the figures are set a conception of space and roominess which will not recur until the time of Raphael. By pouring air into the spaces between his characters, Masaccio has not only related them to one another but has convinced us for the first time that they actually move in a tangible space. The characters of Giotto had been monumental but static; those of Masaccio hold the same impressiveness for us, but they are less abstract in the sense that their environment is more convincing. The celebrated *Tribute Money*, the largest of the frescoes in the chapel, adds a fine sense of linear perspective in the architecture at the right (again a great advance over Giotto) and a very subtle light and shade used in the modeling of the figures which succeeds in making them three-dimensional, sculptural entities. The compositional relationships of the various figures, although casual at first glance, soon reveals a fine understanding of the mechanism of arranging figures in depth (what is known as space composition) which will be the envy of every artist down to the time of Raphael. What we think of Masaccio today is relatively unimportant compared with the attitude of his contemporaries who not only mourned his untimely death as a serious blow to art, but who used the Brancacci chapel as an informal academy where for the next century painters came to learn the rudiments. Leonardo, Michelangelo, and Raphael, three of the outstanding artists of the first part of the sixteenth century, were among the many who learned from the painter of the *Tribute Money*. What made Masaccio so important to the subsequent generations of realists was not only his masterly handling of the

---

[6] Easel picture: painting on an unattached wood or canvas panel, not produced for any specific wall.

[7] Painting with water color on a wet plaster wall; as the plaster dries the pigment becomes permanently part of the wall.

draped and nude figure (as in his *Expulsion from Paradise*), but the fact that he was the most important dramatic interpreter who had appeared in art up to that time. In this he anticipated the keynote of much later Italian art, for, although he used as his subject an apparently simple emotion such as sorrow or shame, in his hands it became transmuted into a higher form of realism containing an almost universal significance which could include all sorrow or all shame. Universality is the essence of all great classical art and it is this quality which separates the art of the Italians during this period from that of the Flemings in the North whose interpretations were much more specific. The Adam and Eve of Masaccio wend their shamefaced way out of Paradise, bearing on their shoulders the burden of sin of all mankind, and the magisterial gesture of the Christ who gives Peter his orders in the *Tribute Money* is a monument for all time. His drama, like that of his great contemporary, Donatello, is restrained and dignified in the manner of Greek tragedy, and it is the same search for universal values that makes the kinship clear.

After Masaccio the search for scientific effects could not fail to progress, although hardly with the same brilliant pioneering genius he had shown. One of these scientists was Paolo Uccello (1397-1457) whose chief artistic preoccupation was the problem of perspective and foreshortening. A good many of his paintings may be regarded as merely exercises to demonstrate his peculiar proclivities which made him an eccentric even in his own day. Battle pictures strewn with bits of broken lances, fragments of corpses, and curiously shaped horses which look as though they had been borrowed from a merry-go-round indicate this phase of his work which, added to its most unusual coloring, makes him an extraordinary personality. The interest in perspective was, of course, bound up with a desire to master the problem of representing distance in a picture space, a problem which had been brilliantly mastered in the light and dark effects of Masaccio but which Uccello tried to solve in a linear fashion.

Since painting is the art of representation upon a two-dimensional surface, it is the function of the artist to supply the third dimension—depth. This he can do by lowering the color intensity of objects which are supposed to be farther back in the picture. This is called aerial perspective and accords with the visual phenomenon which actually takes place because the intervening layers of air between the object and the spectator make distant objects appear blurred. A second method of achieving the effect of distance or depth in a picture (and this was the one followed by most of the painters of the first half of the fifteenth century) was the trick of making lines converge as they move away from the spectator, just as parallel railroad tracks appear to meet at a distant point. This device of converging lines is called linear perspective. This last was practiced by Uccello who became so wrapped up in technical experiments that he tended to forget such things as natural coloring and careful anatomical delineation.

We find the work of Uccello (like that of almost all the contemporary so-called scientific painters) related to the progress of sculpture during this period. Just as he had ignored the true color of landscape in his battle pictures (with their unusual greens, oranges, etc.) he worked out in his tomb-portrait of *Sir*

John Hawkwood a type of monochrome painting which was a direct imitation of tomb sculpture, with the mounted figure of the English soldier of fortune placed upon an elaborately carved stone sarcophagus. We learn from this painting that Uccello had an incomparable knowledge of horses (when he wished to apply it) and that he must have furnished some of the inspiration for the later sculptured equestrian monuments of Donatello, Verrocchio, and Leonardo da Vinci. In this instance a painter who had originally learned a good deal from sculptors, exerted in his turn an influence upon them.

The painter Andrea del Castagno (1370-1451) produced a fine companion piece to Uccello's *John Hawkwood* in the equestrian protrait of *Nicola da Tolentino*. This artist too reflects an association with works of the sculptor Donatello and the painter Masaccio, in his preoccupation with sculptural effects in painting and his frequent concentration on the substructure of the human body with the sinews, muscles, and veins which overlay it.

Both Castagno and Uccello (and most of the Florentine realists who came after them) expressed themselves primarily through precise and careful draughtsmanship. Their paintings represent a summary of countless elaborate drawings prepared before the painting was even begun. The figure was studied from various angles and in various possible poses, with the final painting not so much what the artist had seen in direct visualization as what he *knew* to be there. We may say that the basis of the Florentine method was knowledge and that although the Italians of that early period were very much interested in the world about them and in the character of man particularly, the fact remains that the artist did not paint what he saw (the modern method) but gave us, rather, the result of his investigations. Nothing could be more indicative of the mental processes of the period than this approach.

Domenico Veneziano (1400-1461) should be mentioned for the fact that he is reputed to have introduced into Florence the technique of oil painting, which was destined to have so much influence in changing the direction of Italian art from the sharp lines of the tempera panel [8] to the more subtle and softer possibilities of the newer and more transparent medium. Oil lends itself to correction, tempera (drying quickly) does not. This will ultimately mean the artist's ability to work in a free and more casual style, since he will not have to move as carefully as before. Greater fluidity was already visible in Veneziano's *Madonna with Four Saints.*

Piero della Francesca (1416-1492) not only synthesizes all of the scientific advances of this early fifteenth century period but adds his own most significant contribution. Naturally he was interested in all formal problems, in the modeling of sculptural and monumental figures in painting, in landscape, in architectural backgrounds, etc. A pupil of Veneziano, he developed the technique of aerial perspective in a very striking manner. His most important group of paintings is in the church of St. Francesco at Arezzo where he executed ten monumental episodes from the *Legend of the True Cross*. In these, a series of impressive

---

[8] Tempera panel—painting with water-color, mixed with egg as a binder, on a specially prepared wood panel.

figures moves majestically against an out-of-doors background which (for the first time in the history of Western art since the period of ancient Rome) begins to take into account the effect of real rather than artificial light. *The Dream of Constantine* is represented under the light of the moon. In the *Adoration of the Child* and the *Baptism of Christ* we see out-of-doors effects of sunlight and shadows handled in a manner astoundingly new and unexplained for the fifteenth century. Although Piero della Francesca was not completely understood in his own day, his work is of tremendous importance in the development of art.

So much for the technical and scientific artists of the Florentine tradition. Parallel with their development rose a group of men who may conveniently be labeled "lyricists." These artists painted in a relatively flat and decorative manner reminiscent of the technique of the late Middle Ages and displayed sentimental proclivities which were similarly derivative. This type of painter emphasizes the linear at the expense of the plastic (sculptural), and is more interested in the musical rhythms which move back and forth across the flat of the picture than in the three-dimensional devices of such painters as Uccello, Castagno, and della Francesca.

The first of the important figures in this group was Fra Angelico (1387-1455), a painter of tremendous religious sincerity and of a delicate emotional appeal which will be characteristic of the lyricists who follow him. In his early work, he appears to be a purely medieval book illustrator and for a long time he remained behind the more scientific painters of his epoch in his grasp of the technical advances of the time. His most important group of works exists today in the monastery of San Marco in Florence, a series of frescoes done for the cells of the monks and other parts of the building. The flat composition of one example, *The Annunciation,* and its delicate and tender emotional appeal are typical of his style. It is only natural that the almost feminine quality of his art should be unsuitable to the depiction of such tragic and intense themes as the Crucifixion.

In this delicate vein we also find the paintings of Fra Lippo Lippi (c. 1406-1469) who, perhaps because of his own intensely worldly career (see Browning's poem on him), imparted to his religious works a curiously unspiritual character. He used his wife as the model for many of his paintings of madonnas, and was generally interested in a kind of gracious beauty. His painting of the *Adoration* shows a typical Fra Lippo Lippi madonna, revealing the artist's intense preoccupation with the delicate, introspective type. He may be called a feminine psychologist, for no one else in the early fifteenth century has given us such interesting representations of women. The logical consequences of this method of analysis will be seen later in the paintings of Botticelli and Leonardo da Vinci.

4. Flemish Painting

Flemish painting of the early fifteenth century, like Italian painting, derived from a previous school of sculpture. Political relations with Burgundy naturally brought the northern artists into contact with examples of the school of Claus Sluter, the Burgundian sculptor, whose great works fill the Carthusian monastery of Dijon (among them the *Well of Moses* discussed in our chapter on Gothic art). Flemish painting was the logical outgrowth of an intensely worldly civilization, whose materialism, like Italy's, soon reflected itself in demands for the embellishment of their homes and persons. Portraiture grew here very rapidly as well as a highly developed landscape art which was not to appear in Italy for some time. The Flemings are credited, in the person of Jan van Eyck, with the invention of oil painting, a medium essential in the damp climate of the North, where fresco could not flourish because it demands dryness. By virtue of their oil technique they were able to indicate the subtle changes in light generations earlier than the Florentines. Their colors were brighter and since they had not been affected by the classical and humanistic ideas of the South, their religious attitude remained firmer. Their realism lacked that quality of an essence abstracted from a body of knowledge present in such Italians as Castagno and Piero della Francesca, but is simply a record of what they actually saw. Religion to them was still a potent force, but materialism was just as real, and the distinction between the spiritual and the physical became less and less important.

Many qualities of the Flemish school can be summed up in the celebrated *Altarpiece of the Lamb* by the two brothers, Hubert and Jan van Eyck. In this work the brilliant luster of the oil colors is immediately apparent, and the draperies are distinguished by a wide sculptural sweep which reveals one of the derivatives of this art. Adam and Eve in this composition are painted in a harsh light, revealing all of their nakedness in a detailed manner—an interesting contrast to the tragic and universal Adam and Eve in Masaccio's *Expulsion*. In the contrasting representation of this same subject we see the essential differences between Flemish and Italian art.

The *Worship of the Lamb* section of this altarpiece depicts a beautiful green meadow gay with flowers from whose corners various religious groups advance to offer homage. This lucid representation of the out-of-doors is ample proof of the highly developed landscape art in Flanders at this early period of the fifteenth century (the altar was finished in 1432). When we close the altar we find an interesting scene of the *Annunciation* on its outside, showing a room filled with small details of everyday housekeeping which, upon analysis, reveal an allegorical significance. The washstand in the background, for example, with its shiny clean bowl and the untouched towel hanging at its side, is a fine example of the symbolism of this art, for these details represent the purity of the Virgin.

The portraits of Jan van Eyck and his school are small, in the fashion of miniature art, and much more finished in realistic detail than the Italian works of that time. Small details such as hairs, eyelashes, grains of skin, are multiplied until the painter has built up his figure in a complex, sculptural fashion.

The religious intensity of the Flemings is best typified in the work of Rogier van der Weiden (c. 1400-1469) whose technique is based upon a nervous and elegant line conveying high emotional intensity. Such a painting as the *Descent from the Cross* shows a group of figures rhythmically arranged about the cross from which the body of Christ is being lowered. Powerful and unrestrained grief is the keynote of this and other works by Rogier. In his portraits he shows the typical fine characterization of the Flemish school with the same sharp linear technique used in his religious works.

The art of Flanders during this period is characterized by an intense religiosity, a love of everyday (genre) detail, a splendid ability to seize the essential character of people in portraits, brilliant oil colors, and the development of an interest in landscape which will become the basis of the later evolution of landscape art in the North.

III. THE FIRST SCHOOLS OF COMPOSITION

1. *The Fourteenth Century*

The opening of the fourteenth century marked the beginning of an important epoch in the history of music. Like later creative artists in equally exciting periods of innovation, the composers active in this century possessed a strong self-consciousness of their break with tradition and an infectious enthusiasm for the new powers of expression which had been made available to them.

French Ars Nova.—The term *ars nova* (new art) describes both the outlook and the creations of the composers of the period with which we are concerned. The expression is indissolubly bound up with the name of its originator—the poet, court official, diplomat, bishop, composer, and theorist—Philippe de Vitry (c. 1291-1361). De Vitry had used the term *ars nova* as a title for a theoretical work which was published about 1320 and exerted a strong influence on many contemporaries and successors.

Ars nova, like other artistic movements, did not spring into life spontaneously. Many of its features existed, even if none too prominently, in earlier music. The chief innovation of *ars nova* is a rhythmic one: triple rhythm was demoted from its former monopoly and duple rhythm (similar, for example, to our "two-quarter" time) was given an equal place beside it. This introduction of a new rhythmic system brought in its wake not only a tremendous enrichment of the expressive possibilities of music, but also a significant advance in musical notation.

De Vitry's work also espoused the cause of *musica falsa,* later called *musica ficta,* a practice in which the alteration by a half tone of the pitch of certain notes was left to the discretion of the performers. With the introduction of these half tone deviations from the pitches of the established modes, the way was paved for our modern major and minor scales as well as for the development of chromaticism, the use of semitonal (half step) progressions within the framework of the conventional scales.

While de Vitry was the theorist of the *ars nova* movement, its great creative talent was Guillaume de Machaut (c. 1300-1377). Universally regarded as the outstanding French composer of the fourteenth century, de Machaut had a colorful career. For over twenty years he was secretary to King John of Bohemia and accompanied that restless monarch on his expeditions to Poland, Lithuania, Austria, and Italy. After John's death in 1346 de Machaut entered the service of French royalty. He was made a canon of Rheims Cathedral in 1333. An important poet as well as a musician, he was one of the most prominent artistic figures of his time and his writings were frequently reproduced in contemporary manuscripts all over Europe.

Although de Machaut has been credited with the authorship of one of the first complete settings of the Ordinary of the Mass, his fame rests on his secular compositions. It may be observed in this regard that secular music was in the ascendancy during the fourteenth century, and that the two great masters of the period, the Frenchman de Machaut and the Italian Landini, devoted their talents primarily to creating music for the delectation of the aristocracy. Music had now become one of the amenities of gracious living, and its entertainment value was coming to the fore. Thus the *ars nova* movement was in many respects a continuation of the traditions of the troubadours and trouvères.

Of the numerous forms cultivated by de Machaut, the most important is the *ballade*. The de Machaut ballade (not to be identified with later literary or musical forms of the same name) was in reality an accompanied song, the melody of which appeared in the topmost voice. Two lower parts were performed by instruments. The prominence thus given to the top part was a definite anticipation of the harmonic style of later music. De Machaut also cultivated the motet, and with considerable craftsmanship. His art is a perfect reflection of the aristocratic society for which it was created.

Italian Ars Nova.—Italian music first came into its own in the fourteenth century, probably in the wake of the French *ars nova*. Its representative composer was the blind Florentine organist, Francesco Landini (1325-1397). Like de Machaut, Landini was a poet as well as a musician and in 1364 received the laurel crown of Venice. He was among the characters included by Giovanni da Prato in his *Il Paradiso degli Alberti*, a work which like Boccaccio's *Decameron* described the life of a group of cultured individuals residing in a lovely villa.

The three forms which predominated in the Italian music of the period are the *ballata*, the *caccia*, and the *madrigal*. The ballata, akin to the French ballade, was meant for singing, playing, and dancing (Italian—*ballare*, to dance). The *caccia*, derived from the French form, the *chace*, was an early type of descriptive music. As the name implies, its text originally dealt with hunting episodes, but almost any sort of animated happening might be described in it. Musically the most important characteristic of these witty and entertaining pieces was the use of *canon*, which, as we observed in a previous chapter, is an imitative device in which there is literal repetition (i.e., imitation) of one voice by a succeeding voice or voices. These canons were usually sung to some sort of instrumental accompaniment.

The Italian *madrigal* is of especial importance, for it was later revived in Flanders and England and became one of the most prominent manifestations of Elizabethan music. Compared to the *ballata* or the *caccia*, the madrigal was a highly refined form, much more aristocratic in style. Originally pastoral in its interests (Italian—*mandra*, herd), its text often introduced some philosophical thought or some commentary on events of the day. All of the parts of the madrigal were designed for performance by voices.

In this Italian music we find stylistic features that have recurred continually in the musical history of the country: spontaneously conceived melody of great expressiveness, and florid vocalism. The spirit and the technique of Italian *ars nova,* however, were continued not so much by the composers of Italy as by those of Burgundy, and it is to this land that we shall soon turn our attention.

Medieval Musical Instruments.—A host of pictorial and sculptural representations supply us with much information about European musical instruments. The rôle assigned to instrumental accompaniments in the performance of troubadour and trouvère music, in the music of the Notre Dame school, and in the French and Italian *ars nova* has already been mentioned. The question now arises: what instruments were used?

It is interesting to know that all of our European musical instruments are of Asiatic origin, although, to be sure, Europeans have been largely responsible for their perfection. The Byzantine Empire, in close contact with the Orient, served as a port of entry for Asiatic instruments; and the Saracens, who at one time occupied Spain and Italy, introduced many Arabian and Persian instruments into Europe.

In this volume we cannot go into a detailed study of the enormous number of musical instruments in use between A.D. 500 and 1500. Instruments, however, fall into well-defined categories, and the more important ones in each of these categories may be briefly mentioned and described here.[9]

Plucked Stringed Instruments

(1) The harp
(2) The lyre
(3) The dulcimer or psaltery—a flat trapezoidal instrument, a prototype of the harpsichord
(4) The lute—a pear-shaped instrument with a fretted fingerboard
(5) The mandola—a small lute
(6) The guitar

Bowed Stringed Instruments

(1) The fiedel—a prototype of the violin
(2) The monochord—a large one-stringed instrument, also known as the marine trumpet or nun's fiddle
(3) The hurdy-gurdy—fitted with a keyboard and sounded by a revolving wheel which pressed against the strings. Also known as the organistrum.

Keyboard Instruments

(1) The clavichord } Forerunners of the piano. First came into use about 1400,
(2) The clavicymbel } but were of little importance before 1530.

Keyboard Wind Instruments

(1) The organ
(2) Smaller, portable organs:
   The regal
   The portative

[9] Twelve players of these instruments are shown in sculptural relief on the triforium of Exeter Cathedral. The frontispiece and Plate LXIV of Volume IV of *Grove's Dictionary of Music and Musicians* are valuable reproductions of medieval representations of musical instruments.

Wood-Wind Instruments

(1) The flute—held both horizontally and vertically.
(2) The syrinx (Panpipes)
(3) The oboe (schalmei, or shawm)

Brass Instruments

(1) The trumpet
(2) The horn
(3) The trombone (sackbut)

Percussion Instruments

(1) Castanets
(2) Cymbals
(3) Triangle
(4) Bells
(5) Tambourine

2. The Fifteenth Century

While the art and literature of the fifteenth century are almost universally known and esteemed, the music of the period has not yet received its full measure of appreciation. Precisely as the kindred arts were being assiduously cultivated, much music was being performed; and while many artists were in the employ of the wealthy rulers, ecclesiastical and secular, a great number of musicians also found service in large establishments. It is during the fifteenth century that the catalogue of great composers was considerably enlarged. All in all, music as an independent art came into its ascendancy during this period.

The significant advances were the result chiefly of the mastery by composers of the language of polyphony, a technique which had been evolving for five hundred years. An additional impetus came from the widespread formation at the courts of sovereigns, wealthy noblemen, and bishops, of regularly functioning groups of performers, the so-called chapel choirs (Italian: *cappella,* German: *Kapelle*). Musicians vied for the honor of belonging to these chapel choirs, and the composers attached to them shared in their fame.

The composer who set the pace for fifteenth-century music was an Englishman, John Dunstable (c. 1370-1453). Widely praised as a master of composition, Dunstable devoted himself largely to sacred music. The distinctive features of his style were its striking melodic power, its polyphony with its rich consonances, its combination of imagination and technique.

The Burgundian School.—The English innovations in technique were soon transmitted to a land politically allied with England at the time, the Duchy of Burgundy. Philip the Good, ruler of Burgundy from 1419 to 1467, besides being the founder of the order of the Golden Fleece, was an enthusiastic patron of arts and letters. The nerve centers of Burgundy were its rich and populous cities of the Low Countries, and it was in the Low Countries—Brabant, Flanders, and Hainault—that a long line of celebrated Burgundian musicians originated.

The attainments of the Burgundian school of composition are amply demonstrated in the works of its two masters, Guillaume Dufay (c. 1400-1474) and

Gilles Binchois (c. 1400-1460). The Burgundian school made full use of the technique of *ars nova,* adopted the melodic symmetries and the pleasing consonances of the English composers, and made a significant contribution of its own. Thus it not only summed up the past but anticipated the future.

The Burgundian composers cultivated all the forms of their day. To one form, however, they gave a supremacy which it retained till the end of the sixteenth century. That form was the Mass, and it achieved its position of eminence through being made the first of the world's store of extended musical forms.

Music as a physical phenomenon exists only in time. Form is imparted to a musical composition through a unified system of identities and diversities, arranged in some temporal succession. The creation of extensive structures of sound presents a difficult problem, one that has found varying solutions through the ages. The polyphonic Mass was one of the first of these solutions.

The Mass as a musical form, it will be recalled, is a setting of the five parts of the Ordinary. The Burgundian composer, Dufay, while anticipated by de Machaut in the composition of an entire Mass, was responsible for the introduction of a unifying feature of signal importance: the use of one melody as a framework around which to weave the polyphonic texture of each of the Mass sections. This melody, known as the *cantus firmus* (fixed melody), was usually assigned to the tenor. It might be either liturgical or secular in origin. Masses were usually named after the melodies around which they were built. One of the most celebrated tunes employed as a *cantus firmus* was the secular song *L'homme armé* (*The Armed Man*). There is hardly a master of the fifteenth and sixteenth centuries who did not compose a Mass on this melody. Sacred *canti firmi* were preponderantly fragments of plain chant.

The polyphonic Mass carefully constructed around a *cantus firmus* is thus seen to be a highly organized work in several quasi-independent sections (movements). These sections, in being built around the same melody, thus have a musical as well as a liturgical affinity. Dufay's innovation may be regarded, therefore, as the first step on the road leading to the sonata and the symphony of more recent times.

Dufay's style represents an admixture of English, French, and Italian influences. Like a number of his fellow countrymen he spent many years of his life in Italy, serving for a time in the papal choir. The celebrated dome of the Cathedral at Florence was dedicated in 1436 to the majestic tones of a Dufay motet. Dufay's maturity as a composer dates from the beginning of his residence at Cambrai in 1450 where he was canon of the cathedral until the day of his death.

SELECTED READINGS

Abbott, E. R., *The Great Painters,* Harcourt, Brace, 1927.
Barnes, M. F., *Renaissance Vistas,* Payson, 1931.
Bates, K. L., *The English Religious Drama,* Macmillan, 1893.
Biagi, Guido, *Men and Manners of Old Florence,* McClurg, 1909.
Bode, Wilhelm von, *Florentine Sculptors of the Renaissance,* Scribner, 1909.

Burckhardt, J. C., *The Civilization of the Renaissance in Italy*, trans. by S. G. C. Middlemore, Harper Torchbooks, 1958.

Cheyney, *The Dawn of a New Era.*

Chubb, T. C., *The Life of Giovanni Boccaccio*, Boni, 1930.

Clark, Kenneth, *Leon Battista Alberta on Painting*, Cumberledge, 1946.

—— *Leonardo da Vinci*, rev. ed. Cambridge University Press, 1952.

—— *Piero della Francesca*, Phaidon, 1951.

Gerould, G. H., *The Ballad of Tradition*, Clarendon Press, 1932.

Grout, D. J., *A History of Western Music*, Norton, 1959.

Hauser, *The Social History of Art.*

History of Christianity in the Light of Modern Knowledge, A Collective Work, Harcourt, Brace, 1929.

Hughes, Dom Anselm, and Abraham, Gerald, eds., *New Oxford History of Music*, Vol. III, Oxford University Press, 1960.

Hutton, E., *Giovanni Boccaccio, a Biographical Study*, London, 1910.

Jameson, A. B., *Sacred and Legendary Art*, 2 Vols., Houghton Mifflin, 1911.

Janson, Horst W., *Sculpture of Donatello*, 2 Vols., Princeton University Press, 1957.

Krautheimer, R., *Lorenzo Ghiberti*, Princeton University Press, 1956.

Labriolle, Pierre de, *History and Literature of Christianity*, Knopf, 1925.

Lambotte, Paul, *Flemish Painting before the Eighteenth Century*, Studio, 1927.

Latourette, K. S., *A History of Christianity*, Harper, 1953.

Lowes, J. L., *Geoffrey Chaucer and the Development of His Genius*, Houghton Mifflin, 1934.

Mather, F. J., *A History of Italian Painting*, Holt, 1923.

Meiss, Millard, *Painting in Florence and Siena after the Black Death*, Princeton, 1951.

Myers, *Art and Civilization.*

Pope-Hennessy, John, *The Complete Works of Paolo Uccello*, Phaidon, 1952.

Reese, Gustave, *Music in the Middle Ages*, Norton, 1941.

Robinson, J. H., and Rolfe, H. W., *Petrarch, the First Modern Scholar and Man of Letters*, Putnam, 1914.

Roeder, Ralph, *The Man of the Renaissance*, Meridian.

Sachs, C., *History of Musical Instruments*, Norton, 1940.

—— *The Commonwealth of Art*, Norton, 1946.

Schevill, Ferdinand, *A History of Florence*, Harcourt, Brace, 1936.

Snell, F. J., *The Fourteenth Century*, Edinburgh, 1923.

Spingarn, J. E., *History of Literary Criticism in the Renaissance*, Columbia University Press, 1938.

Stainer, John, *Dufay and His Contemporaries*, Novello, Ewer, and Co., 1898.

Tatham, E. H. R., *Francesco Petrarca*, Macmillan, 1925-1926.

Tilley, Arthur, *The Dawn of the French Renaissance*, Cambridge University Press, 1918.

Ward, A. W., and Waller, A. R., *Cambridge History of English Literature*, Cambridge University Press, 1908, Vol. II.

A CATALOGUE OF SELECTED DOVER BOOKS
IN ALL FIELDS OF INTEREST

A CATALOGUE OF SELECTED DOVER BOOKS
IN ALL FIELDS OF INTEREST

AMERICA'S OLD MASTERS, James T. Flexner. Four men emerged unexpectedly from provincial 18th century America to leadership in European art: Benjamin West, J. S. Copley, C. R. Peale, Gilbert Stuart. Brilliant coverage of lives and contributions. Revised, 1967 edition. 69 plates. 365pp. of text.

21806-6 Paperbound $3.00

FIRST FLOWERS OF OUR WILDERNESS: AMERICAN PAINTING, THE COLONIAL PERIOD, James T. Flexner. Painters, and regional painting traditions from earliest Colonial times up to the emergence of Copley, West and Peale Sr., Foster, Gustavus Hesselius, Feke, John Smibert and many anonymous painters in the primitive manner. Engaging presentation, with 162 illustrations. xxii + 368pp.

22180-6 Paperbound $3.50

THE LIGHT OF DISTANT SKIES: AMERICAN PAINTING, 1760-1835, James T. Flexner. The great generation of early American painters goes to Europe to learn and to teach: West, Copley, Gilbert Stuart and others. Allston, Trumbull, Morse; also contemporary American painters—primitives, derivatives, academics—who remained in America. 102 illustrations. xiii + 306pp. 22179-2 Paperbound $3.00

A HISTORY OF THE RISE AND PROGRESS OF THE ARTS OF DESIGN IN THE UNITED STATES, William Dunlap. Much the richest mine of information on early American painters, sculptors, architects, engravers, miniaturists, etc. The only source of information for scores of artists, the major primary source for many others. Unabridged reprint of rare original 1834 edition, with new introduction by James T. Flexner, and 394 new illustrations. Edited by Rita Weiss. 6⅝ x 9⅝.

21695-0, 21696-9, 21697-7 Three volumes, Paperbound $13.50

EPOCHS OF CHINESE AND JAPANESE ART, Ernest F. Fenollosa. From primitive Chinese art to the 20th century, thorough history, explanation of every important art period and form, including Japanese woodcuts; main stress on China and Japan, but Tibet, Korea also included. Still unexcelled for its detailed, rich coverage of cultural background, aesthetic elements, diffusion studies, particularly of the historical period. 2nd, 1913 edition. 242 illustrations. lii + 439pp. of text.

20364-6, 20365-4 Two volumes, Paperbound $6.00

THE GENTLE ART OF MAKING ENEMIES, James A. M. Whistler. Greatest wit of his day deflates Oscar Wilde, Ruskin, Swinburne; strikes back at inane critics, exhibitions, art journalism; aesthetics of impressionist revolution in most striking form. Highly readable classic by great painter. Reproduction of edition designed by Whistler. Introduction by Alfred Werner. xxxvi + 334pp.

21875-9 Paperbound $2.50

VISUAL ILLUSIONS: THEIR CAUSES, CHARACTERISTICS, AND APPLICATIONS, Matthew Luckiesh. Thorough description and discussion of optical illusion, geometric and perspective, particularly; size and shape distortions, illusions of color, of motion; natural illusions; use of illusion in art and magic, industry, etc. Most useful today with op art, also for classical art. Scores of effects illustrated. Introduction by William H. Ittleson. 100 illustrations. xxi + 252pp.
21530-X Paperbound $2.00

A HANDBOOK OF ANATOMY FOR ART STUDENTS, Arthur Thomson. Thorough, virtually exhaustive coverage of skeletal structure, musculature, etc. Full text, supplemented by anatomical diagrams and drawings and by photographs of undraped figures. Unique in its comparison of male and female forms, pointing out differences of contour, texture, form. 211 figures, 40 drawings, 86 photographs. xx + 459pp. 5⅜ x 8⅜.
21163-0 Paperbound $3.50

150 MASTERPIECES OF DRAWING, Selected by Anthony Toney. Full page reproductions of drawings from the early 16th to the end of the 18th century, all beautifully reproduced: Rembrandt, Michelangelo, Dürer, Fragonard, Urs, Graf, Wouwerman, many others. First-rate browsing book, model book for artists. xviii + 150pp. 8⅜ x 11¼.
21032-4 Paperbound $2.50

THE LATER WORK OF AUBREY BEARDSLEY, Aubrey Beardsley. Exotic, erotic, ironic masterpieces in full maturity: Comedy Ballet, Venus and Tannhauser, Pierrot, Lysistrata, Rape of the Lock, Savoy material, Ali Baba, Volpone, etc. This material revolutionized the art world, and is still powerful, fresh, brilliant. With *The Early Work,* all Beardsley's finest work. 174 plates, 2 in color. xiv + 176pp. 8⅛ x 11.
21817-1 Paperbound $3.00

DRAWINGS OF REMBRANDT, Rembrandt van Rijn. Complete reproduction of fabulously rare edition by Lippmann and Hofstede de Groot, completely reedited, updated, improved by Prof. Seymour Slive, Fogg Museum. Portraits, Biblical sketches, landscapes, Oriental types, nudes, episodes from classical mythology—All Rembrandt's fertile genius. Also selection of drawings by his pupils and followers. "Stunning volumes," *Saturday Review.* 550 illustrations. lxxviii + 552pp. 9⅛ x 12¼.
21485-0, 21486-9 Two volumes, Paperbound $7.00

THE DISASTERS OF WAR, Francisco Goya. One of the masterpieces of Western civilization—83 etchings that record Goya's shattering, bitter reaction to the Napoleonic war that swept through Spain after the insurrection of 1808 and to war in general. Reprint of the first edition, with three additional plates from Boston's Museum of Fine Arts. All plates facsimile size. Introduction by Philip Hofer, Fogg Museum. v + 97pp. 9⅜ x 8¼.
21872-4 Paperbound $2.00

GRAPHIC WORKS OF ODILON REDON. Largest collection of Redon's graphic works ever assembled: 172 lithographs, 28 etchings and engravings, 9 drawings. These include some of his most famous works. All the plates from *Odilon Redon: oeuvre graphique complet,* plus additional plates. New introduction and caption translations by Alfred Werner. 209 illustrations. xxvii + 209pp. 9⅛ x 12¼.
21966-8 Paperbound $4.00

THE ARCHITECTURE OF COUNTRY HOUSES, Andrew J. Downing. Together with Vaux's *Villas and Cottages* this is the basic book for Hudson River Gothic architecture of the middle Victorian period. Full, sound discussions of general aspects of housing, architecture, style, decoration, furnishing, together with scores of detailed house plans, illustrations of specific buildings, accompanied by full text. Perhaps the most influential single American architectural book. 1850 edition. Introduction by J. Stewart Johnson. 321 figures, 34 architectural designs. xvi + 560pp.

22003-6 Paperbound $4.00

LOST EXAMPLES OF COLONIAL ARCHITECTURE, John Mead Howells. Full-page photographs of buildings that have disappeared or been so altered as to be denatured, including many designed by major early American architects. 245 plates. xvii + 248pp. 7⅞ x 10¾. 21143-6 Paperbound $3.00

DOMESTIC ARCHITECTURE OF THE AMERICAN COLONIES AND OF THE EARLY REPUBLIC, Fiske Kimball. Foremost architect and restorer of Williamsburg and Monticello covers nearly 200 homes between 1620-1825. Architectural details, construction, style features, special fixtures, floor plans, etc. Generally considered finest work in its area. 219 illustrations of houses, doorways, windows, capital mantels. xx + 314pp. 7⅞ x 10¾. 21743-4 Paperbound $3.50

EARLY AMERICAN ROOMS: 1650-1858, edited by Russell Hawes Kettell. Tour of 12 rooms, each representative of a different era in American history and each furnished, decorated, designed and occupied in the style of the era. 72 plans and elevations, 8-page color section, etc., show fabrics, wall papers, arrangements, etc. Full descriptive text. xvii + 200pp. of text. 8⅜ x 11¼.

21633-0 Paperbound $5.00

THE FITZWILLIAM VIRGINAL BOOK, edited by J. Fuller Maitland and W. B. Squire. Full modern printing of famous early 17th-century ms. volume of 300 works by Morley, Byrd, Bull, Gibbons, etc. For piano or other modern keyboard instrument; easy to read format. xxxvi + 938pp. 8⅜ x 11.

21068-5, 21069-3 Two volumes, Paperbound $8.00

HARPSICHORD MUSIC, Johann Sebastian Bach. Bach Gesellschaft edition. A rich selection of Bach's masterpieces for the harpsichord: the six English Suites, six French Suites, the six Partitas (Clavierübung part I), the Goldberg Variations (Clavierübung part IV), the fifteen Two-Part Inventions and the fifteen Three-Part Sinfonias. Clearly reproduced on large sheets with ample margins; eminently playable. vi + 312pp. 8⅛ x 11. 22360-4 Paperbound $5.00

THE MUSIC OF BACH: AN INTRODUCTION, Charles Sanford Terry. A fine, nontechnical introduction to Bach's music, both instrumental and vocal. Covers organ music, chamber music, passion music, other types. Analyzes themes, developments, innovations. x + 114pp. 21075-8 Paperbound $1.25

BEETHOVEN AND HIS NINE SYMPHONIES, Sir George Grove. Noted British musicologist provides best history, analysis, commentary on symphonies. Very thorough, rigorously accurate; necessary to both advanced student and amateur music lover. 436 musical passages. vii + 407 pp. 20334-4 Paperbound $2.25

ALPHABETS AND ORNAMENTS, Ernst Lehner. Well-known pictorial source for decorative alphabets, script examples, cartouches, frames, decorative title pages, calligraphic initials, borders, similar material. 14th to 19th century, mostly European. Useful in almost any graphic arts designing, varied styles. 750 illustrations. 256pp. 7 x 10.   21905-4 Paperbound $4.00

PAINTING: A CREATIVE APPROACH, Norman Colquhoun. For the beginner simple guide provides an instructive approach to painting: major stumbling blocks for beginner; overcoming them, technical points; paints and pigments; oil painting; watercolor and other media and color. New section on "plastic" paints. Glossary. Formerly *Paint Your Own Pictures*. 221pp.   22000-1 Paperbound $1.75

THE ENJOYMENT AND USE OF COLOR, Walter Sargent. Explanation of the relations between colors themselves and between colors in nature and art, including hundreds of little-known facts about color values, intensities, effects of high and low illumination, complementary colors. Many practical hints for painters, references to great masters. 7 color plates, 29 illustrations. x + 274pp.
20944-X Paperbound $2.50

THE NOTEBOOKS OF LEONARDO DA VINCI, compiled and edited by Jean Paul Richter. 1566 extracts from original manuscripts reveal the full range of Leonardo's versatile genius: all his writings on painting, sculpture, architecture, anatomy, astronomy, geography, topography, physiology, mining, music, etc., in both Italian and English, with 186 plates of manuscript pages and more than 500 additional drawings. Includes studies for the Last Supper, the lost Sforza monument, and other works. Total of xlvii + 866pp. 7⅞ x 10¾.
22572-0, 22573-9 Two volumes, Paperbound $10.00

MONTGOMERY WARD CATALOGUE OF 1895. Tea gowns, yards of flannel and pillow-case lace, stereoscopes, books of gospel hymns, the New Improved Singer Sewing Machine, side saddles, milk skimmers, straight-edged razors, high-button shoes, spittoons, and on and on . . . listing some 25,000 items, practically all illustrated. Essential to the shoppers of the 1890's, it is our truest record of the spirit of the period. Unaltered reprint of Issue No. 57, Spring and Summer 1895. Introduction by Boris Emmet. Innumerable illustrations. xiii + 624pp. 8½ x 11⅝.
22377-9 Paperbound $6.95

THE CRYSTAL PALACE EXHIBITION ILLUSTRATED CATALOGUE (LONDON, 1851). One of the wonders of the modern world—the Crystal Palace Exhibition in which all the nations of the civilized world exhibited their achievements in the arts and sciences—presented in an equally important illustrated catalogue. More than 1700 items pictured with accompanying text—ceramics, textiles, cast-iron work, carpets, pianos, sleds, razors, wall-papers, billiard tables, beehives, silverware and hundreds of other artifacts—represent the focal point of Victorian culture in the Western World. Probably the largest collection of Victorian decorative art ever assembled— indispensable for antiquarians and designers. Unabridged republication of the Art-Journal Catalogue of the Great Exhibition of 1851, with all terminal essays. New introduction by John Gloag, F.S.A. xxxiv + 426pp. 9 x 12.
22503-8 Paperbound $4.50

A HISTORY OF COSTUME, Carl Köhler. Definitive history, based on surviving pieces of clothing primarily, and paintings, statues, etc. secondarily. Highly readable text, supplemented by 594 illustrations of costumes of the ancient Mediterranean peoples, Greece and Rome, the Teutonic prehistoric period; costumes of the Middle Ages, Renaissance, Baroque, 18th and 19th centuries. Clear, measured patterns are provided for many clothing articles. Approach is practical throughout. Enlarged by Emma von Sichart. 464pp. 21030-8 Paperbound $3.50

ORIENTAL RUGS, ANTIQUE AND MODERN, Walter A. Hawley. A complete and authoritative treatise on the Oriental rug—where they are made, by whom and how, designs and symbols, characteristics in detail of the six major groups, how to distinguish them and how to buy them. Detailed technical data is provided on periods, weaves, warps, wefts, textures, sides, ends and knots, although no technical background is required for an understanding. 11 color plates, 80 halftones, 4 maps. vi + 320pp. 6⅛ x 9⅛. 22366-3 Paperbound $5.00

TEN BOOKS ON ARCHITECTURE, Vitruvius. By any standards the most important book on architecture ever written. Early Roman discussion of aesthetics of building, construction methods, orders, sites, and every other aspect of architecture has inspired, instructed architecture for about 2,000 years. Stands behind Palladio, Michelangelo, Bramante, Wren, countless others. Definitive Morris H. Morgan translation. 68 illustrations. xii + 331pp. 20645-9 Paperbound $2.50

THE FOUR BOOKS OF ARCHITECTURE, Andrea Palladio. Translated into every major Western European language in the two centuries following its publication in 1570, this has been one of the most influential books in the history of architecture. Complete reprint of the 1738 Isaac Ware edition. New introduction by Adolf Placzek, Columbia Univ. 216 plates. xxii + 110pp. of text. 9½ x 12¾. 21308-0 Clothbound $10.00

STICKS AND STONES: A STUDY OF AMERICAN ARCHITECTURE AND CIVILIZATION, Lewis Mumford.One of the great classics of American cultural history. American architecture from the medieval-inspired earliest forms to the early 20th century; evolution of structure and style, and reciprocal influences on environment. 21 photographic illustrations. 238pp. 20202-X Paperbound $2.00

THE AMERICAN BUILDER'S COMPANION, Asher Benjamin. The most widely used early 19th century architectural style and source book, for colonial up into Greek Revival periods. Extensive development of geometry of carpentering, construction of sashes, frames, doors, stairs; plans and elevations of domestic and other buildings. Hundreds of thousands of houses were built according to this book, now invaluable to historians, architects, restorers, etc. 1827 edition. 59 plates. 114pp. 7⅞ x 10¾. 22236-5 Paperbound $3.00

DUTCH HOUSES IN THE HUDSON VALLEY BEFORE 1776, Helen Wilkinson Reynolds. The standard survey of the Dutch colonial house and outbuildings, with constructional features, decoration, and local history associated with individual homesteads. Introduction by Franklin D. Roosevelt. Map. 150 illustrations. 469pp. 6⅝ x 9¼. 21469-9 Paperbound $4.00

DESIGN BY ACCIDENT; A BOOK OF "ACCIDENTAL EFFECTS" FOR ARTISTS AND DESIGNERS, James F. O'Brien. Create your own unique, striking, imaginative effects by "controlled accident" interaction of materials: paints and lacquers, oil and water based paints, splatter, crackling materials, shatter, similar items. Everything you do will be different; first book on this limitless art, so useful to both fine artist and commercial artist. Full instructions. 192 plates showing "accidents," 8 in color. viii + 215pp. 8⅜ x 11¼.   21942-9 Paperbound $3.50

THE BOOK OF SIGNS, Rudolf Koch. Famed German type designer draws 493 beautiful symbols: religious, mystical, alchemical, imperial, property marks, runes, etc. Remarkable fusion of traditional and modern. Good for suggestions of timelessness, smartness, modernity. Text. vi + 104pp. 6⅛ x 9¼.
                                                                20162-7 Paperbound $1.25

HISTORY OF INDIAN AND INDONESIAN ART, Ananda K. Coomaraswamy. An unabridged republication of one of the finest books by a great scholar in Eastern art. Rich in descriptive material, history, social backgrounds; Sunga reliefs, Rajput paintings, Gupta temples, Burmese frescoes, textiles, jewelry, sculpture, etc. 400 photos. viii + 423pp. 6⅜ x 9¾.   21436-2 Paperbound $4.00

PRIMITIVE ART, Franz Boas. America's foremost anthropologist surveys textiles, ceramics, woodcarving, basketry, metalwork, etc.; patterns, technology, creation of symbols, style origins. All areas of world, but very full on Northwest Coast Indians. More than 350 illustrations of baskets, boxes, totem poles, weapons, etc. 378 pp.
                                                                20025-6 Paperbound $3.00

THE GENTLEMAN AND CABINET MAKER'S DIRECTOR, Thomas Chippendale. Full reprint (third edition, 1762) of most influential furniture book of all time, by master cabinetmaker. 200 plates, illustrating chairs, sofas, mirrors, tables, cabinets, plus 24 photographs of surviving pieces. Biographical introduction by N. Bienenstock. vi + 249pp. 9⅞ x 12¾.   21601-2 Paperbound $4.00

AMERICAN ANTIQUE FURNITURE, Edgar G. Miller, Jr. The basic coverage of all American furniture before 1840. Individual chapters cover type of furniture—clocks, tables, sideboards, etc.—chronologically, with inexhaustible wealth of data. More than 2100 photographs, all identified, commented on. Essential to all early American collectors. Introduction by H. E. Keyes. vi + 1106pp. 7⅞ x 10¾.
                        21599-7, 21600-4 Two volumes, Paperbound $11.00

PENNSYLVANIA DUTCH AMERICAN FOLK ART, Henry J. Kauffman. 279 photos, 28 drawings of tulipware, Fraktur script, painted tinware, toys, flowered furniture, quilts, samplers, hex signs, house interiors, etc. Full descriptive text. Excellent for tourist, rewarding for designer, collector. Map. 146pp. 7⅞ x 10¾.
                                                                21205-X Paperbound $2.50

EARLY NEW ENGLAND GRAVESTONE RUBBINGS, Edmund V. Gillon, Jr. 43 photographs, 226 carefully reproduced rubbings show heavily symbolic, sometimes macabre early gravestones, up to early 19th century. Remarkable early American primitive art, occasionally strikingly beautiful; always powerful. Text. xxvi + 207pp. 8⅜ x 11¼.   21380-3 Paperbound $3.50

JOHANN SEBASTIAN BACH, Philipp Spitta. One of the great classics of musicology, this definitive analysis of Bach's music (and life) has never been surpassed. Lucid, nontechnical analyses of hundreds of pieces (30 pages devoted to St. Matthew Passion, 26 to B Minor Mass). Also includes major analysis of 18th-century music. 450 musical examples. 40-page musical supplement. Total of xx + 1799pp.
(EUK) 22278-0, 22279-9 Two volumes, Clothbound $15.00

MOZART AND HIS PIANO CONCERTOS, Cuthbert Girdlestone. The only full-length study of an important area of Mozart's creativity. Provides detailed analyses of all 23 concertos, traces inspirational sources. 417 musical examples. Second edition. 509pp.
(USO) 21271-8 Paperbound $3.50

THE PERFECT WAGNERITE: A COMMENTARY ON THE NIBLUNG'S RING, George Bernard Shaw. Brilliant and still relevant criticism in remarkable essays on Wagner's Ring cycle, Shaw's ideas on political and social ideology behind the plots, role of Leitmotifs, vocal requisites, etc. Prefaces. xxi + 136pp.
21707-8 Paperbound $1.50

DON GIOVANNI, W. A. Mozart. Complete libretto, modern English translation; biographies of composer and librettist; accounts of early performances and critical reaction. Lavishly illustrated. All the material you need to understand and appreciate this great work. Dover Opera Guide and Libretto Series; translated and introduced by Ellen Bleiler. 92 illustrations. 209pp.
21134-7 Paperbound $1.50

HIGH FIDELITY SYSTEMS: A LAYMAN'S GUIDE, Roy F. Allison. All the basic information you need for setting up your own audio system: high fidelity and stereo record players, tape records, F.M. Connections, adjusting tone arm, cartridge, checking needle alignment, positioning speakers, phasing speakers, adjusting hums, trouble-shooting, maintenance, and similar topics. Enlarged 1965 edition. More than 50 charts, diagrams, photos. iv + 91pp.
21514-8 Paperbound $1.25

REPRODUCTION OF SOUND, Edgar Villchur. Thorough coverage for laymen of high fidelity systems, reproducing systems in general, needles, amplifiers, preamps, loudspeakers, feedback, explaining physical background. "A rare talent for making technicalities vividly comprehensible," R. Darrell, *High Fidelity*. 69 figures. iv + 92pp.
21515-6 Paperbound $1.00

HEAR ME TALKIN' TO YA: THE STORY OF JAZZ AS TOLD BY THE MEN WHO MADE IT, Nat Shapiro and Nat Hentoff. Louis Armstrong, Fats Waller, Jo Jones, Clarence Williams, Billy Holiday, Duke Ellington, Jelly Roll Morton and dozens of other jazz greats tell how it was in Chicago's South Side, New Orleans, depression Harlem and the modern West Coast as jazz was born and grew. xvi + 429pp.
21726-4 Paperbound $2.50

FABLES OF AESOP, translated by Sir Roger L'Estrange. A reproduction of the very rare 1931 Paris edition; a selection of the most interesting fables, together with 50 imaginative drawings by Alexander Calder. v + 128pp. 6½x9¼.
21780-9 Paperbound $1.25

POEMS OF ANNE BRADSTREET, edited with an introduction by Robert Hutchinson. A new selection of poems by America's first poet and perhaps the first significant woman poet in the English language. 48 poems display her development in works of considerable variety—love poems, domestic poems, religious meditations, formal elegies, "quaternions," etc. Notes, bibliography. viii + 222pp.
22160-1 Paperbound $2.00

THREE GOTHIC NOVELS: THE CASTLE OF OTRANTO BY HORACE WALPOLE; VATHEK BY WILLIAM BECKFORD; THE VAMPYRE BY JOHN POLIDORI, WITH FRAGMENT OF A NOVEL BY LORD BYRON, edited by E. F. Bleiler. The first Gothic novel, by Walpole; the finest Oriental tale in English, by Beckford; powerful Romantic supernatural story in versions by Polidori and Byron. All extremely important in history of literature; all still exciting, packed with supernatural thrills, ghosts, haunted castles, magic, etc. xl + 291pp.
21232-7 Paperbound $2.00

THE BEST TALES OF HOFFMANN, E. T. A. Hoffmann. 10 of Hoffmann's most important stories, in modern re-editings of standard translations: Nutcracker and the King of Mice, Signor Formica, Automata, The Sandman, Rath Krespel, The Golden Flowerpot, Master Martin the Cooper, The Mines of Falun, The King's Betrothed, A New Year's Eve Adventure. 7 illustrations by Hoffmann. Edited by E. F. Bleiler. xxxix + 419pp.
21793-0 Paperbound $2.50

GHOST AND HORROR STORIES OF AMBROSE BIERCE, Ambrose Bierce. 23 strikingly modern stories of the horrors latent in the human mind: The Eyes of the Panther, The Damned Thing, An Occurrence at Owl Creek Bridge, An Inhabitant of Carcosa, etc., plus the dream-essay, Visions of the Night. Edited by E. F. Bleiler. xxii + 199pp.
20767-6 Paperbound $1.50

BEST GHOST STORIES OF J. S. LeFANU, J. Sheridan LeFanu. Finest stories by Victorian master often considered greatest supernatural writer of all. Carmilla, Green Tea, The Haunted Baronet, The Familiar, and 12 others. Most never before available in the U. S. A. Edited by E. F. Bleiler. 8 illustrations from Victorian publications. xvii + 467pp.
20415-4 Paperbound $2.50

THE TIME STREAM, THE GREATEST ADVENTURE, AND THE PURPLE SAPPHIRE— THREE SCIENCE FICTION NOVELS, John Taine (Eric Temple Bell). Great American mathematician was also foremost science fiction novelist of the 1920's. *The Time Stream,* one of all-time classics, uses concepts of circular time; *The Greatest Adventure,* incredibly ancient biological experiments from Antarctica threaten to escape; The *Purple Sapphire,* superscience, lost races in Central Tibet, survivors of the Great Race. 4 illustrations by Frank R. Paul. v + 532pp.
21180-0 Paperbound $3.00

SEVEN SCIENCE FICTION NOVELS, H. G. Wells. The standard collection of the great novels. Complete, unabridged. *First Men in the Moon, Island of Dr. Moreau, War of the Worlds, Food of the Gods, Invisible Man, Time Machine, In the Days of the Comet.* Not only science fiction fans, but every educated person owes it to himself to read these novels. 1015pp.
20264-X Clothbound $5.00

THE RED FAIRY BOOK, Andrew Lang. Lang's color fairy books have long been children's favorites. This volume includes Rapunzel, Jack and the Bean-stalk and 35 other stories, familiar and unfamiliar. 4 plates, 93 illustrations x + 367pp.
21673-X Paperbound $2.50

THE BLUE FAIRY BOOK, Andrew Lang. Lang's tales come from all countries and all times. Here are 37 tales from Grimm, the Arabian Nights, Greek Mythology, and other fascinating sources. 8 plates, 130 illustrations. xi + 390pp.
21437-0 Paperbound $2.50

HOUSEHOLD STORIES BY THE BROTHERS GRIMM. Classic English-language edition of the well-known tales — Rumpelstiltskin, Snow White, Hansel and Gretel, The Twelve Brothers, Faithful John, Rapunzel, Tom Thumb (52 stories in all). Translated into simple, straightforward English by Lucy Crane. Ornamented with headpieces, vignettes, elaborate decorative initials and a dozen full-page illustrations by Walter Crane. x + 269pp. 21080-4 Paperbound $2.50

THE MERRY ADVENTURES OF ROBIN HOOD, Howard Pyle. The finest modern versions of the traditional ballads and tales about the great English outlaw. Howard Pyle's complete prose version, with every word, every illustration of the first edition. Do not confuse this facsimile of the original (1883) with modern editions that change text or illustrations. 23 plates plus many page decorations. xxii + 296pp.
22043-5 Paperbound $2.50

THE STORY OF KING ARTHUR AND HIS KNIGHTS, Howard Pyle. The finest children's version of the life of King Arthur; brilliantly retold by Pyle, with 48 of his most imaginative illustrations. xviii + 313pp. 6⅛ x 9¼.
21445-1 Paperbound $2.50

THE WONDERFUL WIZARD OF OZ, L. Frank Baum. America's finest children's book in facsimile of first edition with all Denslow illustrations in full color. The edition a child should have. Introduction by Martin Gardner. 23 color plates, scores of drawings. iv + 267pp. 20691-2 Paperbound $2.25

THE MARVELOUS LAND OF OZ, L. Frank Baum. The second Oz book, every bit as imaginative as the Wizard. The hero is a boy named Tip, but the Scarecrow and the Tin Woodman are back, as is the Oz magic. 16 color plates, 120 drawings by John R. Neill. 287pp. 20692-0 Paperbound $2.50

THE MAGICAL MONARCH OF MO, L. Frank Baum. Remarkable adventures in a land even stranger than Oz. The best of Baum's books not in the Oz series. 15 color plates and dozens of drawings by Frank Verbeck. xviii + 237pp.
21892-9 Paperbound $2.00

THE BAD CHILD'S BOOK OF BEASTS, MORE BEASTS FOR WORSE CHILDREN, A MORAL ALPHABET, Hilaire Belloc. Three complete humor classics in one volume. Be kind to the frog, and do not call him names . . . and 28 other whimsical animals. Familiar favorites and some not so well known. Illustrated by Basil Blackwell. 156pp. (USO) 20749-8 Paperbound $1.25

MATHEMATICAL PUZZLES FOR BEGINNERS AND ENTHUSIASTS, Geoffrey Mott-Smith. 189 puzzles from easy to difficult—involving arithmetic, logic, algebra, properties of digits, probability, etc.—for enjoyment and mental stimulus. Explanation of mathematical principles behind the puzzles. 135 illustrations. viii + 248pp.
20198-8 Paperbound $1.25

PAPER FOLDING FOR BEGINNERS, William D. Murray and Francis J. Rigney. Easiest book on the market, clearest instructions on making interesting, beautiful origami. Sail boats, cups, roosters, frogs that move legs, bonbon boxes, standing birds, etc. 40 projects; more than 275 diagrams and photographs. 94pp.
20713-7 Paperbound $1.00

TRICKS AND GAMES ON THE POOL TABLE, Fred Herrmann. 79 tricks and games— some solitaires, some for two or more players, some competitive games—to entertain you between formal games. Mystifying shots and throws, unusual caroms, tricks involving such props as cork, coins, a hat, etc. Formerly *Fun on the Pool Table.* 77 figures. 95pp.
21814-7 Paperbound $1.00

HAND SHADOWS TO BE THROWN UPON THE WALL: A SERIES OF NOVEL AND AMUSING FIGURES FORMED BY THE HAND, Henry Bursill. Delightful picturebook from great-grandfather's day shows how to make 18 different hand shadows: a bird that flies, duck that quacks, dog that wags his tail, camel, goose, deer, boy, turtle, etc. Only book of its sort. vi + 33pp. 6½ x 9¼.
21779-5 Paperbound $1.00

WHITTLING AND WOODCARVING, E. J. Tangerman. 18th printing of best book on market. "If you can cut a potato you can carve" toys and puzzles, chains, chessmen, caricatures, masks, frames, woodcut blocks, surface patterns, much more. Information on tools, woods, techniques. Also goes into serious wood sculpture from Middle Ages to present, East and West. 464 photos, figures. x + 293pp.
20965-2 Paperbound $2.00

HISTORY OF PHILOSOPHY, Julián Marías. Possibly the clearest, most easily followed, best planned, most useful one-volume history of philosophy on the market; neither skimpy nor overfull. Full details on system of every major philosopher and dozens of less important thinkers from pre-Socratics up to Existentialism and later. Strong on many European figures usually omitted. Has gone through dozens of editions in Europe. 1966 edition, translated by Stanley Appelbaum and Clarence Strowbridge. xviii + 505pp.
21739-6 Paperbound $3.00

YOGA: A SCIENTIFIC EVALUATION, Kovoor T. Behanan. Scientific but non-technical study of physiological results of yoga exercises; done under auspices of Yale U. Relations to Indian thought, to psychoanalysis, etc. 16 photos. xxiii + 270pp.
20505-3 Paperbound $2.50

Prices subject to change without notice.
Available at your book dealer or write for free catalogue to Dept. GI, Dover Publications, Inc., 180 Varick St., N. Y., N. Y. 10014. Dover publishes more than 150 books each year on science, elementary and advanced mathematics, biology, music, art, literary history, social sciences and other areas.